W9-BYV-157

M[r] Secretary
WALSINGHAM
and the policy of
QUEEN ELIZABETH

Sir Francis Walsingham
1587
From the portrait belonging to King's College, Cambridge
Photographed by leave of the Provost & Fellows

Emery Walker ph.sc.

Mr Secretary WALSINGHAM

and the policy of QUEEN ELIZABETH

by

CONYERS READ

VOL. III

ARCHON BOOKS, 1967

WINGATE COLLEGE LIBRARY
WINGATE, N. C.

First published 1925 THE CLARENDON PRESS

Reprinted 1967 by permission of
OXFORD UNIVERSITY PRESS
HARVARD UNIVERSITY PRESS
in an unaltered and unabridged edition

Library of Congress Catalog Card Number: 67-19513
Printed in the United States of America

CONTENTS

LIST OF ILLUSTRATIONS

40924

XII

THE BABINGTON PLOT

Walsingham's intrigues with the English Catholics in France were not directly designed to entangle Mary Stuart, although he probably hoped that damaging evidence might be secured against her by that channel. At any rate it was through these English Catholics, or rather through one renegade among them, that he was finally enabled, after some eighteen years of ceaseless effort, to bring her to the reckoning.

It will be recalled that in the year 1585 Walsingham was trying his best to widen the breach between the two factions which divided the English Catholics in France, the Jesuits and the Seculars. To that end he was negotiating secretly with Dr. William Gifford, one of the leaders of the Secular Party. It was in connexion with these negotiations that Gilbert Gifford, the *agent provocateur* in the events which follow, appeared on the scene.

This Gilbert was the cousin of Dr. William Gifford, and like William identified himself with the Seculars. Although he came of a good Staffordshire family he was a good deal of a reprobate from the beginning, and his influence over his cousin William appears to have been as malignant as it was potent. Gilbert had left England in 1577 and had entered the English College at Rome two years later, where he managed to stir up a lot of trouble. In March 1582 he had returned north again and had gone to England, but he was back in Rome again a little later. In October 1583 he finally turned up at the English College at Rheims, penniless, and, for the moment at least, penitent. At Rheims he remained for about two years and presumably mended his ways not a little, for he was admitted to the diaconate there in April 1585, but he left Rheims in October of the same year and repaired to Paris. There he got in touch at once with Thomas Morgan and Charles Paget, both of them violent Seculars, and plunged deep again into the wranglings of the English Catholic refugees. In December he went over to England.[1] According to his own account he was sent over by Morgan to oppose the Jesuits there and to make arrangements for the coming over of his cousin, Dr. Gifford.[2] This was certainly no more than partly true, but is worth noting because it was Gilbert's connexion with this factional quarrel which enabled him later to cover his tracks and to explain away his dealings with Walsingham. Morgan's chief reason for sending Gilbert to England was to re-establish a channel of correspondence with his mistress, the Scottish Queen.

Gilbert accordingly carried with him a letter of recommendation from Morgan to Mary. In that letter Morgan told her that Gilbert Gifford was a Catholic gentleman of good faith and honesty, with many connexions in the country and many opportunities for doing her service. He said he had given Gifford particular instructions as to the steps he ought to take in order to establish correspondence with her. 'This', Morgan added, 'he promised to put in execution with care and I hope he will show his good will and diligence in the cause. He required my letters to your Majesty, thereby to give him credit and a mean to enter into intelligence with your Majesty.' [3]

When Gifford landed in England he was apprehended at Rye by the searcher at the port, who conducted him straightway to Walsingham.[4] It is impossible to say what passed between the two at their conference, but at that time, if not before, Gilbert Gifford entered Walsingham's service as a spy and agreed to betray his friends for a consideration. From this conference, in all probability, dates the inception of those arrangements which

[1] Cf. Butler and Pollen, *Doctor Gifford in 1586, passim.*

[2] Cf. Gifford's confession, 14 Aug. 1588, *Cal. Salisbury MSS.*, iii. 346. This confession contains so many manifest falsehoods that it is difficult to attach credibility to any part of it, but Gilbert's earlier dealings with Dr. Gifford lend some support to his statement here. In the life of Gilbert Gifford in *D. N. B.* it is stated that he first entered Walsingham's service in 1583. This is evidently a misprint for 1585, for the evidence given in support of the statement in *D. N. B.* (Adam Blackwood, *Martyre de Marie Stuart* (Paris, 1587), reprinted in Jebb, *Vita de Maria Scotorum Regina*, etc. (1725), ii. 279) states: 'Concerning Gilbert Gifford, two years before [Mary's death] he was won over by Walsingham.' This of course would indicate 1585, not 1583. Berden in a letter to Walsingham, dated 18/28 Dec. 1585, indicates that Gifford left for England early in December 1585 (*Cal. Domestic*, Adda., 1580–1625, p. 162).

[3] Morris, *Sir Amias Paulet*, p. 112.

[4] Pollen, 'The Babington Plot', *The Month*, Oct. 1907.

were fraught with such dire consequences for the Scottish Queen.

Ever since the discovery of the Throgmorton Plot, with its revelation of the methods by which the Scottish Queen had maintained a secret correspondence with her friends, Walsingham had exerted every effort to prevent her from further communication of a like sort. No doubt he was largely instrumental in having her transferred from the corrupt household of the Earl of Shrewsbury to safer quarters. During the interval when Sir Ralph Sadler and John Somers had temporary charge of her, he constantly impressed upon them the necessity of unceasing vigilance,[1] and it is evident from Sadler's and Somers's letters that they exerted themselves to the utmost to satisfy him upon this point. At Wingfield their task was not easy because of the nature of the place, but when Mary was removed to Tutbury in January 1585 they were able to keep a stricter guard. It is quite evident that Mary was treated with greater rigour from the moment she entered Tutbury gates, and was made to feel little by little that she was no longer even in form a royal guest, but a royal prisoner. She complained bitterly of the change both to the French ambassador and to Elizabeth herself. Indeed she wrote to Mauvissière on the 9th of April that she feared her enemies would make away with her without Elizabeth's knowledge.[2] Her fears were certainly exaggerated, but no doubt her protests against the increasing rigour used towards her had some foundation in fact.

The situation, from Mary's point of view, was made more unbearable when Sir Amias Paulet replaced Sadler and Somers as her keeper in April 1585. Paulet was a stern Puritan, a close friend of Walsingham, and a declared enemy of all the political and religious ideas that Mary cherished. He was indeed a man well calculated to enforce a rigorous régime against her. 'I

[1] In September 1584 Walsingham had discovered that letters in cipher were passing between Curle, one of Mary's secretaries, and Baldwin, a servant of the Earl of Shrewsbury's, and had promptly put a stop to it. Curle's intercepted letter revealed something like a plot to convey Mary out of the realm (Curle to Baldwin, 20 Sept. 1584, *Sadler Papers* (ed. Clifford), ii. 403), and Walsingham in consequence sent special orders to Sir Ralph Sadler to have a special care to his charge (Ibid., 409). Not long after this discovery and possibly to some extent because of it, Mary was transferred from Wingfield to stronger quarters at Tutbury.

[2] Mary to Mauvissière, 9 Apr. 1585, Labanoff, vi. 157.

will never ask pardon ', he wrote to Walsingham, ' if she depart out of my hands by any treacherous slight or cunning device, because I must confess that the same cannot come to pass without some gross negligence or rather traitorous carelessness ; and if I shall be assaulted with force at home or abroad, as I will not be beholden to traitors for my life, whereof I make little account in respect of my allegiance to the Queen my sovereign, so I will be assured by the grace of God that she shall die before me.' [1]

When Paulet went to Tutbury to assume charge there he took with him very strict instructions for preventing the Scottish Queen from any secret correspondence with her friends. These instructions had been drawn up by Walsingham himself, and though of course he had acted at the Queen's command, he was probably himself responsible for the details. He directed Paulet to forbid all conference between his servants and the servants of the Scottish Queen except in his presence, to allow none of her servants to leave the castle without a guard, to admit no stranger on any pretext whatsoever, and to have a special watch over ' laundresses, coachmen and the like ' as they had formerly afforded an easy means for the conveyance of letters. He even went so far as to add to these restrictions : ' You shall order that she shall not, in taking the air, pass through any towns nor suffer the people to be in the way where she shall pass, appointing some always to go before to make them to withdraw themselves, for that heretofore, under colour of giving alms and other extraordinary courses used by her, she hath won the hearts of the people that habit about those places where she hath heretofore lain.' [2] Plainly Walsingham's intention was to shut off Mary from communication with the outside world altogether, except through channels which he could carefully scrutinize.

The only way, indeed, which was left to Mary for corresponding with her friends abroad, even upon the most indifferent matters, was through the medium of the French ambassador. She was still permitted to send and receive letters by the means of Mauvissière, although her packets, both coming and going, were carefully examined by the Secretary. It appears that for a long time Walsingham, who knew how to get at the inside of

[1] Morris, *Sir A. Paulet*, p. 49.
[2] S. P. Mary, Queen of Scots, xv, no. 50 ; Morris, *op. cit.*, p. 6.

a letter without disturbing the seal, opened these packets without Mary's knowledge,[1] but in May 1585 he finally abandoned this underhand method of procedure and directed Paulet to open the packets himself, to read them through carefully, and to deliver them open to his prisoner. Walsingham wrote to Paulet that the reason why he took this course was because ' my own leisure is very scarce ', [2] but the fact has a far greater significance than that. It shows that Walsingham and his mistress both felt that there was no use maintaining a feeble pretence any longer, and wasting valuable time in playing a part which deceived nobody.

It was hardly more than three months after this that Mary was cut off even from the poor consolation of such correspondence with the French ambassador as was left her. Walsingham wrote to Paulet on the 13th of September directing him to inform Mary ' that all packets that she doth hereafter send into France must be directed unto me, and not unto the new French Ambassador, for that her Majesty's meaning is that he shall not have anything to do with the conveyance of her letters into France, having also given orders unto the Bishop of Glasgow that such letters as he shall send from thence shall be delivered to Mr. Stafford '.[3] Probably the reason for this was that Châteauneuf, Mauvissière's successor, who arrived in England in September 1585, was known to be friendly to Mary's cause. What was more, Walsingham probably felt that he could no longer count upon maintaining in Châteauneuf's household the spies who had kept him in such close touch with Mauvissière's doings. At any rate, in September 1585, Mary's last legitimate channel with the outside world, save through the medium of enemies, was closed.

It is curious to observe that all the time while Walsingham was carefully devising measures to defeat the purposes of the Scottish Queen, he was still posing before the French ambassador as her friend. In one of Mauvissière's letters to Mary, Paulet had come upon a passage in regard to this which evoked from him a sardonic smile. ' He [Mauvissière] telleth this Queen,'

[1] Somers wrote to Walsingham, 6 Apr. 1585, that Nau, one of Mary's secretaries, had displayed great curiosity about the seals of their letters (*Sadler Papers*, ii. 54) ; cf. also Paulet to Walsingham, 2 May 1585, Morris, p. 17.

[2] 28 May 1585, S. P. Mary, Queen of Scots, xv, no. 96.

[3] S. P. Mary, Queen of Scots, xvi, no. 40.

so Paulet wrote to Walsingham, 'that he will visit you at Barn Elms and that you are a friendly furtherer of all her causes, affirming no less for Mr. Somer, wherein I think you are more beholden unto him than you deserve.'[1] As late as the 8th of September Paulet reported that Mauvissière had written to assure Mary that the Secretary would not fail to do all good offices for her as he had promised.[2] Too much reliance must not, of course, be placed upon this testimony of Mauvissière, which was doubtless written with the knowledge that it would come before Walsingham's eyes. It may indicate no more than that the French ambassador hoped to win something from the Secretary by a show of confidence, but it shows at least that Mary's friends did not yet altogether despair of Walsingham, although he was giving them very little more than fair words to build upon.

In December the Queen of Scots was removed from Tutbury to Chartley. This change of residence was made at her own urgent request. Sixteenth-century houses with sixteenth-century sanitary arrangements had a way of growing foul when one lived in them too long, especially when one lived in them as a prisoner. There is no reason whatever to assume any darker reason for the change. Tutbury would have been as good a place as any to carry out designs against Mary if designs at the moment had been intended.[3] On the 13th of September Walsingham directed Paulet to examine Chartley and see if it were well adapted to his purposes. He wrote to Paulet that the Queen, 'doubting that the coldness of Tutbury Castle may increase her [Mary's] sickness, thinketh meet that she should be removed to some other place, and hearing that Chartley, the Earl of Essex's house, is both large and strong, in respect that it is environed with water, she would have him to see it and certify how he liketh it.'[4]

Paulet reported favourably on Chartley, but the Earl of Essex objected, and his objections were sustained by no less a person than Leicester himself, who seems to have remonstrated with Walsingham on the subject. 'Sir Amias Paulet', Walsing-

[1] Morris, p. 34. [2] S. P. Mary, Q. of Scots, xvi, no. 39.

[3] Morris, p. 127 n., has effectually disposed of Froude's statement that Mary was transferred to Chartley in order to facilitate Walsingham's intrigues against her. [4] Morris, p. 93.

ham wrote to Leicester on the 27th of September, 'proceeded further in the preparations for Chartley than I looked for. I will do what I can to stay the intended remove thither, but I fear neither Sir Walter Aston's house nor Gifford's will be found so apt.' [1]

Sir Walter Aston's house and the house of Mr. John Gifford, none other than Gilbert Gifford's father, were the alternatives. Paulet examined each one of them in turn, but found neither of them, as Walsingham had feared, so apt. Walsingham was clearly in favour of using Gifford's house, and he said as much to Paulet, but Paulet argued eloquently against it and finally, in spite of the Earl of Essex's objections, Chartley was decided upon and Mary, who greatly welcomed the change, was conveyed thither on the 24th of December.[2]

It is pretty clear that from the time of Mary's removal to Tutbury in January 1585, she was effectually shut off from all secret correspondence with her friends.[3] In May 1585 Walsingham heard from Berden, the spy, that letters were being carried to the Scottish Queen by a man named Ralph Elwes, who was servant to Mr. Fenton of Derbyshire.[4] Walsingham instructed Paulet to have an eye to this Elwes. 'The party whose name I send you in the enclosed note', he wrote to Paulet on the 28th of May, 'hath heretofore been used as an instrument for the conveyance of that Queen's letters and there is a plot new laid to continue his service that way in the place where she remaineth at this present. You shall therefore do well, upon conference with Sir John Zouche in the matter, an honest, well affected gentleman whose advice and assistance may perhaps stead you much therein, either to lay wait how the said party may be apprehended, not coming to the castle, but after he hath been there and shall be seen going back, for then is it likely that he carrieth somewhat with him; or else to find means how some fit man may become so well acquainted with him as to discover when he hath either

[1] Harleian MSS. 285, f. 133.

[2] Morris, pp. 100 ff.

[3] Cf. Archbp. of Glasgow to Mary, 8/18 July 1585. Glasgow apologizes for not having written sooner, explaining that he had been informed that his letter to her of 20 January still remained in Mauvissière's hands, 'sans qu'il y eût moyen aucun de les vous envoyer.' Glasgow added that he had not heard from Mary since 4 January (S. P. Mary, Queen of Scots, xvi, no. 19. This letter appears to have been omitted in Boyd's *Scottish Calendar*).

[4] Cf. Berden to Walsingham, 11 May 1585, S. P. Domestic, clxxviii, no. 52.

letters or messages with him worthy the discovery, to the end he may then be suddenly apprehended.' [1] These instructions are interesting because of the light they throw upon Walsingham's methods of work. He plainly wanted to take Elwes red-handed in his carrying and if possible to intercept important letters of the Scottish Queen at the same time. Paulet wrote to Walsingham on the 26th of July that he had communicated with Sir John 'who hath travailed faithfully and carefully in seeking to discover the practices of Ralph Elwes according to your instructions in that behalf, but no good effect hath followed as yet'.[2] No effect indeed, either good or bad, seems to have followed at all. Either Berden had been misinformed or else Elwes was warned in time.

Another attempt by Mary's friends to establish a correspondence with her, which was made not long after this, Walsingham dealt with in a different way. Some time in the spring of 1585 Thomas Morgan wrote from Paris a letter to Christopher Blunt, a gentleman in Leicester's retinue. Some way or other Morgan had at one time saved Blunt's life, and he counted now on turning this fact to the advantage of his mistress. He asked Blunt to do nothing less than to assist him in conveying letters to the Scottish Queen. Blunt replied by sending over to Morgan a special messenger named Robert Poley. It seems very likely, although it cannot be proved, that Blunt did this with the connivance of his master, and that Poley went over to France with the fixed intention of playing a double game. Morgan spoke with Poley early in July, and on the 10th wrote to Mary a letter commending him to her in most cordial terms. Morgan advised her, however, to make some test of his fidelity before employing him in any delicate business.[3] Poley seems to have returned to England about five days later. Morgan, who saw some reason to distrust him, did not confide to his care any matters of importance and does not appear to have made great use of his services in England. Nevertheless, the credit which Poley gained with Mary's friends by his passage abroad served Walsingham later to very good purpose.

The next effort Morgan made to communicate with his

[1] S. P. Mary, Queen of Scots, xv, no. 96.
[2] Morris, p. 70.
[3] *Cal. Scottish*, 1585–6, pp. 11 ff.

mistress was through the means of Gilbert Gifford, who had left Paris for England in December 1585.

It must be borne in mind that the problem which Gifford had to solve in order to convey letters to Mary was simply the problem of getting those letters from London to Mary's hands. They were easily sent from Paris as far as the French Embassy at London in the official packets of the French ambassador. Gifford, as has appeared already, was apprehended upon his arrival in England and sent to Walsingham. The outcome of their conference was an arrangement by which Mary should have a means given her to carry on a secret correspondence with her friends in such wise that all the letters she sent and all that she received should pass through Walsingham's hands. It is not easy to say whether Walsingham had conceived of such an arrangement before he talked with Gifford in December or not. There is practically no evidence to prove that he did. The probabilities seem to be that the opportunity suggested the expedient. Gilbert, by his dealings with his cousin William and the Seculars, had already established himself in a position in which he could play a double game without much danger of discovery. The letter which he brought from Morgan to his mistress gave him an excellent means of winning her confidence and at the same time the confidence of the French ambassador. Gifford was in fact in every way prepared to serve as a medium for secret correspondence between Mary and her friends and to betray this correspondence to Walsingham under cover of his dealings in the interests of the Seculars, which he had begun with Morgan's connivance more than a year before. Probably this fortunate concurrence of favourable circumstances suggested to Walsingham the design which he was presently to carry into effect.

Having pitched upon a plan Walsingham proceeded at once to arrange for its execution. He had in his service and deep in his confidence a man named Thomas Phelippes who had been of great use to him in the past because of his extraordinary skill in the deciphering of letters. Phelippes was certainly not an upright man, but he was a very shrewd one, and shrewdness rather than uprightness was the quality which the situation demanded. About Christmas time Walsingham sent Phelippes to Chartley to arrange a means by which letters could be secretly conveyed to

Mary without arousing her suspicion that they came with the connivance of her keeper.

It happened that at Chartley there was no private brewing establishment, and in consequence the beer which Mary's household consumed had to be procured from a brewer in the neighbouring town of Burton. This beer was brought to Chartley once a week in kegs. Now it occurred either to Walsingham or to Gifford or to Phelippes—it is impossible to say which of the three was the originator of the scheme—that these same beer kegs might serve as post boxes, and that letters might be sent in them when they were delivered full and returned in them when they were taken away empty. This in fact was the plan agreed upon. The merely mechanical part of it was simple enough. All that was necessary was to construct a watertight casket large enough to contain letters and small enough to slip through the bung hole of a beer keg. But it was also necessary to take the brewer into confidence and to arrange with him that letters which were to be conveyed in this way should be received and delivered to the proper person. These arrangements Walsingham entrusted to Phelippes when he went to Chartley late in December, and with the assistance of Sir Amias Paulet he completed them to the Secretary's satisfaction. On the 10th of January he left Chartley for London.[1]

Meantime Gilbert Gifford remained in London, practising with the Catholics and establishing himself in the confidence of the French ambassador.[2] About the 12th of January Gifford learned that Phelippes had made all necessary arrangements. He accordingly went to Châteauneuf, said he had devised a plan for the conveyance of letters, described it to him, and asked him for a letter to the Scottish Queen. Châteauneuf, with some hesitation, gave Gifford the letter from which he carefully omitted any matters of moment. Doubtless Gifford had done all this in accordance with Walsingham's instructions, or rather in accordance with the instructions of Thomas Phelippes, to whom Walsingham had given the handling of the matter. Immediately after the interview with the French ambassador

[1] Morris, pp. 146 ff.

[2] Compare the memoir of Châteauneuf on the whole affair printed in Labanoff, vi. 275 ff.

Gifford set out for Chartley. Apparently he carried nothing with him except his letters of recommendation from Morgan and from Châteauneuf. He delivered them to the brewer, and they came safely to Mary's hands on the 16th of January.[1]

It is not clear in what manner Mary was informed in the first place of the plan of communication which had been devised for her, but at all events she did learn of it and she grasped at it with avidity. No wonder. She had practically been isolated from the whole world for over a year. The hope of receiving letters from her friends must have been to her like the shadow of a great rock in a thirsty land. In the next week she and her secretaries were busy preparing letters to send back by Gifford, who waited in lodgings not far off.

Early in February Mary's letters were ready to be dispatched. She sent them out through the kindly offices of the beer keg. Gifford got them from the brewer and handed them over to Paulet on the 5th of the month. Paulet forwarded them to Walsingham at once. 'He [Gifford] desired', Paulet wrote, 'that these packets might be sent unto you with speed, and that his father might be advised by Mr. Phelippes to call him to London as soon as were possible, to the end he might deliver these letters to the French ambassador in convenient time for the better conservation of his credit that way.'[2]

It is evident from this letter of Paulet's that Gifford himself did not carry the letters to London, nor did he employ the services of Catholic gentlemen as he told Châteauneuf. After all, it made little difference to the success of the scheme how the letters got to London so long as they were delivered to Châteauneuf in such a way as not to arouse his suspicions.

As soon as Walsingham received Mary's letters from Paulet, he handed them over to Phelippes to be deciphered. There was a letter to Morgan, a letter to Glasgow, a letter to the Duke of Guise, and a letter to Châteauneuf among them. Walsingham cannot have expected to learn anything of importance from these first packets. Nevertheless he must have read them over with great interest and have perceived with considerable satisfaction that Mary was delighted with the arrangement. Particularly he must have been gratified to read in her letter to Châteauneuf her

[1] Châteauneuf's Memoir, Morris, p. 151.
[2] Ibid., p. 153.

instructions to him to send Gifford all the packets which he held for her, *les enfermant en une petite boîte ou sac de cuir fort.*[1]

Gifford came to London about the middle of February, received from Walsingham the letters Paulet had sent, and on the 19th of February delivered them to Châteauneuf.[2] In accordance with Mary's instructions the French ambassador delivered to Gifford all the letters which for the past two years had been accumulating for her at the embassy. Gifford carried them straightway to Phelippes. 'The party', Phelippes wrote to Walsingham on the 28th of February, 'hath brought one and twenty packets great and small, but not so soon as I looked for and himself thought. It seemeth they are those that were required in the letters from the place to be sent in a bag together, and I find them of very old dates, which I impute, considering the number also, to the stay of intelligence since the change of officers.'[3]

Phelippes was right. Walsingham now had in his hands almost every letter which had been written to Mary from her friends since the discovery of the Throgmorton Plot. There were letters from Morgan and Paget and Glasgow in Paris, letters from Owens and Liggons in the Low Countries, letters from Parsons and Sir Francis Englefield in Spain, letters from the Duke of Guise and the Prince of Parma. Walsingham was able to read at a sitting all about the plans and purposes of Mary's friends abroad; of how they had pinned their hopes at first to the large promises of the Duke of Guise; of how Guise, becoming more and more distracted by the course of affairs in France, had disappointed their hopes; of how they had turned then to the King of Spain and had built up new projects about the person of the Prince of Parma; of how they had plotted for her escape; of how their plots had fallen through; of how they had quarelled among themselves; in a word, of practically everything they had done in her behalf one way or another for the past two years. He must have found the solution of many mysteries in that bundle of letters and gathered from them much information of use in time to come.

[1] Morris, p. 165.

[2] Châteauneuf says that Gifford returned to him, 1 Mar., which in the English style of dating would be 19 February (Châteauneuf's Memoir).

[3] S. P. Domestic, clxxxvi, no. 78.

As soon as Phelippes had deciphered these letters Walsingham sent them, or at least some part of them, to Paulet. Gifford did not apparently go to Chartley on this occasion. Walsingham was contemplating sending him to France, so it was arranged that a substitute should be found to take his place as carrier. Who the substitute was does not appear. Gifford spoke of him as a cousin. Paulet describes him as a man 'of honest credit, good wealth, good understanding, and servant to the Earl of Leicester'.[1] Gifford himself commended the man to Mary, and she in turn commended him to the French ambassador.[2] This done there was no need of Gifford's longer stay in England, and he seems to have left for France some time in April or May.

The 'substitute' was the man entrusted with the delivery of the twenty-one packets which had come to Walsingham's hands from the French ambassador late in February. During the month of March these were handed over in instalments to the brewer, whom Paulet liked to call 'the honest man'. Altogether they were too bulky to be sent through the narrow passage of a bung hole. Consequently they had to be divided. This circumstance gave a plausible excuse for breaking the seals, and saved Phelippes a lot of unnecessary trouble in opening them as they came into his hands.[3]

It is not necessary to follow out in further detail the steps in this secret correspondence. Mary was cautious about the use she made of it at first, but as time went on she opened her mind more freely to her friends. Charles Paget and others had written to her about the intentions of Philip of Spain to invade England on her behalf. On the 20th of May she replied to Paget upon the subject.[4] She showed herself to be strongly in favour of the invasion; she promised to induce her son, if possible, to join in the enterprise; she charged Paget to take counsel with Mendoza, and she suggested certain preliminary steps which she thought ought to be taken in Scotland. In another letter of the same date to Mendoza himself she spoke in similar terms.[5] These two letters identified Mary completely with the purposes of Elizabeth's enemies and were sufficient in themselves to prove

[1] Morris, pp. 149, 154.
[2] Mary to Châteauneuf, 24 Mar. 1586, Labanoff, vi. 261.
[3] Morris, p. 165. [4] *Cal. Scottish*, 1585–6, p. 390. [5] Ibid., p. 389.

WINGATE COLLEGE LIBRARY
WINGATE, N. C.

that the Scottish Queen was conspiring against the welfare of England. Both of them of course came into Walsingham's hands. He might have produced them at once, shut the door on Mary's further correspondence, and exposed her to Elizabeth. But whatever his ultimate purposes were, there was little to be gained that way. It was evident that no plot for invasion had yet been matured. Walsingham knew well enough that Elizabeth would never proceed to extremities against her prisoner merely upon the grounds that she had been caught plotting against the State. As Walsingham looked at it, it would be better every way to let matters go on a little farther. By so doing he might gain further information as to the precise intentions of Philip of Spain. He might also learn something of a more damaging character against Mary herself.

There can be very little doubt that Walsingham hoped that Mary would write down things which would expose her to the extreme penalties of the law. From the very first he had regarded her as the 'bosom serpent' and had been convinced that the proper way to solve her problem was the way of the block and the axe. During the whole course of her secret correspondence he was plainly on the look-out for evidence enough against her to make such a solution possible. So much may be said against him—so much and no more. It is dangerous to assume a priori, as some of his enemies have assumed, that he would go so far as to fabricate evidence. There are two sides to the question. The Scottish Queen had certainly done enough in the past to warrant the assumption that she would not balk at any plot devised to remove her enemies and establish her friends. If we are to argue from intentions, as strong a case can probably be made out against her as can be made out against Walsingham. Mary was probably more interested in removing Elizabeth than Walsingham was in removing Mary. It is well to realize this fact at the outset. It is well to realize another fact also. Most writers upon this subject have proceeded either with an intention of defending Mary's conduct or of defending Walsingham's. There is a defence at hand for either of them. Looking at the question from Mary's point of view, few can blame her for any measures she took to obtain her liberty. Elizabeth had been her great enemy practically ever since she was born. For eighteen years Elizabeth had kept her a prisoner on no sufficient grounds except those of political expediency. No wonder if one of Mary's lively temperament and active mind found her fetters galling. No wonder if she was willing to use any instrument which came into her hands to strike them off. The picture of her, a woman in distress, and a singularly charming woman at that, has aroused the chivalry of many a dull historian and taught him to write better than he knew. Mary's cause appeals to the sympathies and to the imagination. It is a theme for poets and dramatists, and it must always arouse the poetic and dramatic instinct of every one who approaches it. Yet there is another side to the question as well, a less romantic side perhaps, but a side which it was highly important for Elizabethan statesmen to consider and which it will not do for historians to neglect. Mary was Elizabeth's declared rival for the throne of England. From the time when, as Queen of France, she had quartered the English leopards with the French lilies upon her escutcheon she never in her heart relinquished her purpose of unseating Elizabeth if she could. On these grounds alone Elizabeth's loyal servants were bound to regard her as a dangerous enemy. But more than the rights of two women were staked upon the issue. Mary was the candidate of Catholic Europe for the English throne. Every blow which she aimed at Elizabeth was aimed at the same time against the Protestant cause. To a man of Walsingham's religious convictions this was a matter even graver than the life or death of Elizabeth herself. In characteristic sixteenth-century fashion he came to regard Mary not only as the enemy of his sovereign but also as the enemy of his God. From the sixteenth-century point of view he was probably right. Now by a curious combination of circumstances over which Walsingham had no control this enemy was introduced into England itself. She came as a guest; she remained as a prisoner. Walsingham called her the 'bosom serpent' and Mary justified the title. During the whole course of her life in England there was hardly a plot directed against the State or the Queen in which Mary was not some way concerned. If she did not actually conspire with the plotters, her cause at least was the mark at which they shot. The problem of disposing of her was an awkward one, but Walsingham and many in England with him saw very clearly that she must be disposed of for the safety of the State. The Duke of Norfolk had failed, Don John had failed, Throgmorton and the Duke of Guise had failed, Somerfield had failed, Dr. Parry had failed, but who could tell at what moment a man more resolute than all the rest might appear who would not fail? Certainly Walsingham could not tell. He had lived long enough to see more than one champion of the Protestant cause die at the hands of a Catholic assassin. Mary's own friends, he knew, had disposed of two Protestant regents in Scotland. Upon Elizabeth's life hung not only her own life but also, as he firmly believed, the life of every principle for which he fought. In Mary Stuart he justly recognized an enemy who lacked only the means to destroy himself, his sovereign, and his faith. No wonder if he thought she ought to be put out of the way. No wonder if he was diligent in his search for means to put her out of the way. Mary, in conspiring against Elizabeth, was fighting for her liberty and her creed; Walsingham, in conspiring, if you like, against Mary was fighting for his life, his sovereign, and his creed. Those who believe with Mary will support her cause; those who believe with Walsingham will support his cause. There are plainly two sides to the question and one thing is clear, that the truth will never be got at by approaching the solution of it with a preconceived animus one way or the other. The only safe course is to state the facts and to leave all questions of justification to the moralists.

After the middle of May evidence began to accumulate thick and fast against Mary and her friends. She had written to Paget on the 20th urging him to push forward the invasion of England. Her letter crossed on the road one which Paget had written to her the day before on this very subject. A priest named Ballard, Paget wrote, had just arrived out of England bringing with him assurances from the English Catholics that they were ready to take up arms in Mary's cause if they had help from abroad.[1]

This man Ballard introduced a new element into the situation. He was a Cambridge man who had fled from England in 1579. After two years' residence at the seminary at Rheims he was ordained priest on the 4th of March 1581.[2] Less than a month afterwards he set out for England. His career after he landed in

[1] *Cal. Scottish*, 1585–6, p. 386. [2] Cf. *Douay Diaries*, pp. 158, 177–8.

England is not easy to trace, because he travelled about under many false names and never stayed for very long in one place.[1] It is said that at one time he served the Government as a spy upon his fellows.[2] Whether this be true or not, it is certain that he had abandoned this disreputable business several years before he crossed the thread of Mary Stuart's destiny. There is some reason for believing that he left England early in the year 1584, and went on a pilgrimage to Rome. He seems to have returned at Christmastide of the same year and to have resumed his roving life.[3] In May 1585 Berden, the spy, reported that he was lodged in London at one of the 'common inns'.[4] During the next year he evidently continued his wanderings up and down England. At Whitsuntide he was in Leicestershire, at Bartholomew's tide in London, and some ten or fourteen days before Christmas in Kent. After Christmas he went north once more, but was back again in London on the 23rd of April 1586.[5] Not long after this he crossed to France and early in May, as has appeared already, presented himself to Charles Paget at Paris.

Ballard told Paget that he was well acquainted with the leading Catholics in England and Scotland and that he had been sent to declare their readiness to take up arms if they might be assured of foreign help. Paget thereupon conducted Ballard to the Spanish Embassy at Paris and there Ballard repeated his statement to Mendoza, adding that the time was ripe for an invasion of England because all the best Protestant soldiery were away with Leicester in the Low Countries. Ballard made large statements about the strength of the Catholic party in England, but he was

[1] From the confession of James Hambly, *alias* Tregewether, it is plain that a priest named Fortesque (Ballard's usual *alias*) was in London in May 1583 (S. P. Domestic, cxcii, no. 46). In a letter which James Hill, a renegade Catholic, wrote to Walsingham in Aug. 1584 (Harleian MSS. 286, f. 52) he confessed having met 'Ballard *alias* Fortesque' in London and that Ballard lived chiefly in Hampshire 'at the Lady West's'.

[2] Labanoff, vi. 288.

[3] This, on the authority of the notorious Antony Tyrell, *Cal. Scottish*, 1585–6, pp. 641 ff. Tyrell is thoroughly unreliable, but it is hard to believe that he invented the whole story of his journey to Rome in 1584 with Ballard; cf. Pollen, *Mary Stuart and the Babington Plot*, pp. lxvi ff.

[4] S. P. Domestic, clxxviii, no. 72.

[5] Cf. Tyrell's confession, n. 3 above; Christopher Dunne confessed (10 Aug. 1586) that his son brought one called Mr. Brown (another *alias* of Ballard's) to Addington in Kent ten or fourteen days before Christmas (S. P. Domestic, cxcii, no. 21); Abingdon's indictment in Cobbett's *State Trials*, i. 1143; Berden to Walsingham, 23 April 1586 (S. P. Domestic, clxxxviii, no. 37).

not prepared to name any names and Mendoza justly suspected that the priest was speaking on slight warrant. He accordingly replied in general terms and with vague promises, declaring that his master could take no definite steps until he had more precise information and more particular assurance from the recognized leaders of the Catholic party. He bade Ballard return to England and gave him minute directions how to proceed there in order to prepare the way for the accomplishment of his designs.[1]

Ballard returned to England on the 22nd of May. It is difficult to say how far his movements were known to Walsingham up to this time. Walsingham had certainly been aware of his presence in England for something like two years. From the reports of Berden he must have guessed that the priest was a dangerous fellow. Berden had written from France in August 1585 that Ballard was one of the principal agitators among the discontented Catholic nobility and had found him in April ' much conversant with the Lord Windsor ', a nobleman of some importance who was vehemently suspected of Catholic sympathies.[2] Camden says that one of Walsingham's spies, a shrewd fellow named Maude, accompanied Ballard on his voyage to France and wrung from him all his secrets.[3] It would be hard to

[1] Pollen, *The Month*, July 1902; Paget to Mary, 19 May 1586, *Cal. Scottish*, 1585–6, p. 385; Mendoza to Philip II, 11 May 1586, *Cal. Span.* 1580–6, p. 576. There are almost no grounds for believing that the Catholics at large in England were cognizant of Ballard's plans or any way assistant to them. He was a man prone to rash statements. When he got back to England, for instance, he told both Babington and Savage that he had promise of an army of 60,000 men (cf. Babington's Confession, Yelverton MSS. xxxi, f. 218; Savage's Confession, *Cal. Scottish*, 1585–6, p. 611).

[2] Berden to Walsingham, 11 Aug. 1585, *Cal. Foreign*, 1584–5, p. 716; same to same, 23 April 1586, S. P. Domestic, clxxxviii, no. 37, not signed, but in Berden's hand.

[3] Camden, *Annales* (Eng. trans. 1635), p. 302. This man Maude is an elusive fellow and probably if more could be found out about him more light could be thrown upon the whole matter. Robert Poley in his confession (Aug. 1586, S. P. Mary, Queen of Scots, xix, no. 26) says that Babington told him that Ballard and Maude went to France together. It appears from the confession of one Tipping (*Cal. Scottish*, 1585–6, pp. 695–6) that Maude accompanied Ballard when he went north in June 1586. John Charnock confessed (ibid., p. 690) that Babington told him that Maude knew all Ballard's secrets and would tell Mr. Secretary [Walsingham] (ibid.). The chances are that Walsingham, who had heard from Berden on two separate occasions of Ballard's practising with Catholic noblemen in England, set some sort of watch upon his movements. Furthermore the strange silence in regard to Maude, when the conspiracy was exposed, is significant. Although he was mentioned more than once in the confessions of other people implicated he was never called into question. What is more,

prove this absolutely, but the probabilities are that Camden was right. In that case Walsingham was informed of Ballard's purposes from the moment he set foot in England in May 1586, and it is not to be doubted kept a careful watch upon his movements thenceforward.

Ballard was known among his fellow Catholics as a man naturally lofty of condition, seemingly ambitious of putting himself into great company, loath to be contradicted, and one 'who followed the company of young gentlemen in England without attending to his function '.[1] This judgement is borne

none of the conspirators was questioned about him. What information came out about him seems to have come out incidentally. This curious neglect of Maude by the authorities struck at least one man in England, to wit Edward Windsor, brother of Lord Windsor. Windsor was more or less implicated in the Babington Plot. He escaped death but was imprisoned in the Tower. At his examination at Westminster Hall he accused Barnard, Maude, and Captain Jakhous 'to be the chief workers of the conspiracy, and to be wholly employed by Ballard to be ready in anything they could do for the assistance of the invasion—the one in the north, the other in Ireland. And Maude a chief persuader with me [Windsor] for going forward in those causes.'

'I know', Windsor added in writing to Sir Christopher Hatton, 30 May 1587, 'that by means of Jakhaus and Maude these treasons hath been wrought and one other who shall at this time be nameless. Then, considering they have been the chief cause of the loss of many young gentlemen's blood and those two the chief persuaders of myself to frequent Ballard's company and not to leave the cause, as I have accused Maude first in Candlemas term of all his conspiracy and treason, and never brought to any question, and Jakhaus, before the Queen's commissioners, I have in like manner accused of high treason. If it be justice that these men shall live, offending so monstrously as by the laws they have, and be chief workers of such disturbation in the realm and the chiefest cause of the shedding of so much blood, I must say, as I did in Westminster Hall, that the King's Bench should be a place where justice should be executed' (S. P. Domestic, cci, no. 50, dated at the Tower).

Windsor's sentence structure eludes punctuation, but his meaning is clear enough. Whether Maude and the mysterious Captain Jacques were guilty of all Windsor accused them of or not, it certainly was strange that they were never brought to question. Therefore I say the presumption is that Camden was right.

This view of the matter is supported by Pollen, *op. cit.*, pp. lxxxiv–lxxxvii. Pollen points out also that Maude had formerly been a gentleman in the household of the Archbishop of York and had been put in jail for three years in 1583 for attempting to blackmail his master (cf. S. P. Domestic, clv, no. 102).

Captain Jakhous or Jacques is mentioned by Tyrell in his confession, already cited. He calls him the Vice-Chamberlain's (Hatton's) man and declares he was a fellow conspirator with Ballard and had received him when he first landed in England. Burghley, in a marginal note written with his own hand, speaks of Jacques as the Italian (S. P. Mary, Queen of Scots, xix, 66). Pollen gives some further details about him, without citing his sources, in *Mary Stuart and the Babington Plot*, p. lxxxvi, n. 1.

[1] Cf. Morris, *Troubles of our Catholic Forefathers*, ii. 340; cited by Pollen, *The Month*, July 1902.

out by Ballard's conduct after he landed in England. He went to London at once and began to associate with a group of ardent young Catholics who were gathered about the Court. The most prominent man among them was Antony Babington, who was only twenty-five years old at the time. He came of a good Derbyshire family and had a respectable fortune. In 1579 he had come into contact with Mary Stuart as a page in the service of the Earl of Shrewsbury. About the same time he definitely identified himself with Roman Catholicism. He went to Paris in 1580, where he met Thomas Morgan and the Archbishop of Glasgow, Mary's ambassador to France. They treated him with great courtesy and when he returned to England commended him by letters to their mistress. Babington himself said that Mary had written him a courteous letter in reply. He confessed that he had been a means of conveying several letters to her during the time when she was in the charge of the Earl of Shrewsbury.[1] From these facts it is evident that Babington was regarded by Mary Stuart's friends as one of her staunchest supporters in England at least two years before the final catastrophe. This is a point worth observing, for it explains why it was that Morgan advised his mistress to re-establish her relations with him, and why Babington, rather than any of his fellow conspirators, was the one to whose lot it fell to communicate the conspiracy to the Scottish Queen.

Ballard found Babington at his lodgings in London late in May.[2] They were already well acquainted and probably had

[1] Babington's Confession, Yelverton MSS. xxxi, ff. 218 ff. This valuable paper forms part of the collection of Lord Calthorpe. I was unable to secure sight of the original, but Father Pollen very kindly placed his copy of it at my disposal. If one may trust the statements made at the trial of Mary Stuart, Babington made his confession quite freely and without any torture. This ought to give it greater credence, especially upon minor points. Upon this matter of the convoy of letters to Mary Stuart, Babington's confession is confirmed by a letter of M. Fontenay to Mary, written sometime in 1585 or 1586 (*Cal. Scottish*, 1585–6, p. 210). Fontenay asks if she has received some letters which have been left for her at Babington's house. 'These letters', he wrote, 'were sent by Antony Rolston, Babington being then in London. Rolston left the letters with a servant of Babington's who promised they would be delivered.' Since this note was written Father Pollen has printed the confessions of Babington, *op. cit.*, pp. 49 ff.

[2] Babington's Confession, Yelverton MSS. xxxi, f. 218. Tyrell in his confession (S. P. Mary, Queen of Scots, xix, no. 68) says that Ballard had spent some time with Babington at his home in Derbyshire in the summer of 1585, and that they had later dined together in London. Tyrell says further

discussed on former occasions plans and purposes for alleviating the condition of the English Catholics. It was quite natural, therefore, that Ballard should have taken Babington into his confidence at once, should have told him all about his interview with Mendoza, and should have invoked his aid to prepare the way for the invader. From Babington's report of the interview it appears that Ballard gave him a very exaggerated idea of the preparations on foot, speaking of a great Catholic league under the Pope and of an invading army of sixty thousand men. Babington professed himself to be somewhat sceptical, but Ballard had an answer ready for all his objections. So the fire was started and Babington himself proceeded to spread it among his friends, a group of young, hare-brained Catholic enthusiasts like himself.

According to Babington's story, after he had discussed the plan of invasion with his friends, he came to the conclusion that the best thing to do was to fly the realm. It is not very easy to keep the order of events straight in his confession, but it appears that he determined to fly some weeks before he wrote his fatal letter to the Queen of Scots. Accordingly he applied to the Court for a licence to travel and to this end sought the acquaintance of Robert Poley, a man in the household of Secretary Walsingham.

We have met this Poley already. He had gone to Paris in the midsummer of 1585 and had tendered his services to Thomas Morgan. Without much doubt he was acting even then as a spy of Walsingham's. Morgan found some cause to suspect his sincerity at first and Charles Paget had warned Mary to beware of him, but after Poley returned to England he seems to have won his way completely into Morgan's confidence. He commended Poley to Mary in a letter of the 8/18th of January 1586 [1] and on March 11/21st he informed her that after a year's trial he was satisfied as to Poley's sincerity. ' I am of the opinion ', he added, ' that you entertain Poley who, by Blunt's labours and my advice, is placed with the Lady Sidney, the daughter of Secretary Walsingham, and by that means ordinarily in his house and

that in the autumn of 1585, at a dinner at which Ballard was present, Babington had proposed a plan to kill all the Councillors at once in Star Chamber.

[1] *Cal. Scottish*, 1585–6, p. 197.

thereby able to pick out many things to the information of your Majesty.' [1]

Meanwhile it appears that Poley was in reality doing Walsingham good service. Immediately after his return from France he seems to have established relations, doubtless at Morgan's recommendation, with Châteauneuf, the new French ambassador at London, and to have made regular reports of Châteauneuf's doings to Walsingham.[2] At the same time he maintained a correspondence with Morgan and Paget with which Walsingham was also made acquainted,[3] so it is clear that Morgan's confidence was misplaced and that when Poley entered the household of the Principal Secretary he entered it not as Morgan's secret friend but as his secret enemy.

But to return to Babington. It appears from his confessions and from the confessions of Poley himself that the arch-conspirator made overtures to Walsingham for a licence to travel abroad. Babington implies that he made these overtures some time before he wrote his fatal letter to Mary Stuart. Poley confirms the statement, declaring that they were made in June.[4] Their bearing upon the plot itself will be discussed presently. Here the important point to note is that they served as a means for one of Walsingham's agents to ingratiate himself with Babington and to become partaker of his secrets some time before the conspirators had arranged their plans for the murder of the Queen.

Walsingham then, not long after Ballard and Babington had begun their plottings, was in a fair way to discover their secrets. He had spies upon Ballard ; he had a spy upon Babington. He probably knew from Maude all about Ballard's dealings with the Spanish ambassador. He saw every letter that passed to and fro between the Scottish Queen and her friends. Poley was

[1] S. P. Mary, Queen of Scots, xvii, no. 31.

[2] Cf. Poley to Walsingham, *Cal. Scottish*, 1585–6, p. 20. The original of this letter (S. P. Mary, Queen of Scots, xvi, no. 9) is signed P., but it is indubitably in Poley's hand. It is not dated or addressed, but the form of the letter makes it almost certain that it was sent to Walsingham. Although Châteauneuf is not expressly mentioned in it, the context again reveals the fact that Poley was in his household.

[3] Cf. S. P. Mary, Queen of Scots ,xvii, no. 2. A paper in Poley's hand which contains ' Principal Particulars of letters from Morgan and Paget of 6 January '. Endorsed, in hand of Phelippes, ' Poley.'

[4] Cf. Poley's Confession, *Cal. Scottish*, 1586–6, p. 595.

watching the French ambassador. Gilbert Gifford, who went to France late in April or early in May, was watching Paget and Morgan in Paris.[1] With all these sources of information at Walsingham's command there was very small chance that the conspirators could make any important move without his knowledge.

So far the conspiracy has appeared to follow the course which conspiracies against the realm of England had followed in the past. There was to be an invasion by Catholic armies from without and simultaneously a rebellion of Catholic subjects from within. But very early in the so-called Babington Plot another consideration arose which differentiates it from its predecessors. According to Babington's confession, when Ballard had first proposed to him the fine scheme of a concerted attack against the Government, Babington had declared that he saw very little chance of success, 'so long as her Majesty doth live.' Ballard had answered that that difficulty 'would be taken away by means already laid'. In a word Ballard had revealed to Babington that his plans included not only invasion and rebellion but also the assassination of the Queen.[2]

It will be worth while to investigate the murder plot with some care, and to find out if possible where and how it originated. It has appeared already that in 1583 George Gifford, the brother of Gilbert, the spy, had undertaken to assassinate Elizabeth, and had gained the support of the Duke of Guise to his nefarious project and something like the assent of the Pope himself.[3] George Gifford's plans came to nothing. Another zealous young Catholic, however, stimulated probably by the successful murder of the Prince of Orange in 1584, undertook to succeed where Gifford had failed. This man was John Savage, an Englishman, a Catholic, and by way of being a soldier. Early in January 1581 he had fled from England to the English College at Rheims, where he had remained until December of the same year and then had returned to England again. In March 1583 he was back in Rheims a second time.[4] He went thence to the Low Countries,

[1] Gifford wrote to Walsingham from Paris on June 1, 'I doubt nothing of obtaining everything of Morgan and Paget' (Harleian MSS. 288, f. 161).

[2] Babington's Confession, Yelverton MSS. xxxi, f. 219.

[3] Pollen, *The Month*, Sept. 1907.

[4] *Douay Diaries*, pp. 174, 183, 195.

where he took service under the Prince of Parma.[1] But Savage had a short military career. He lacked the vigour indispensable to a soldier who followed the banners of Alexander Farnese. Before midsummer 1585 he had turned up at Rheims a third time.[2] Savage confessed that while at Rheims in the late summer of 1585 he had resolved, after some conference with three of his friends, to undertake the murder of Elizabeth. Indeed he said he had sworn an oath to do it. He named the three friends: Christopher Hodgson, a priest, Dr. William Gifford, and Gilbert Gifford. As far as can be judged from Savage's own confession, Dr. Gifford was the chief instigator in the matter, but it is abundantly clear that Gilbert Gifford had a great deal to do with it.[3] Savage left Rheims in August 1585, and probably came straight to England with intent to carry out his project at the first opportunity. But he lacked the cool courage for so bold a stroke. After eight months spent in London and about the Court he somehow had not found his chance. When Ballard landed in England in May, Savage had as yet done practically nothing.

It appears from Babington's confession that Ballard, at their first conference together, had known all about the oath John Savage had sworn, and had revealed his purpose to Babington at that time. From this statement it might be concluded that Savage was the real father of the assassination plot of 1586, and that one should date its commencement from the conversation between Savage and the two Giffords and Hodgson at Rheims in the preceding summer.[4]

[1] Father Pollen (*The Month*, Sept. 1907) thinks that Savage did his soldiering between December 1581 and March 1583. I am inclined to place it between March 1583 and August 1585. The *Douay Diaries* plainly say that Savage returned to England in December 1581, and the confession of Savage as printed in Cobbett's *State Trials*, i. 1129 ff., suggests, if it does not definitely state, that Savage went from the Low Countries to Rheims, swore his oath there, and proceeded at once to England to fulfil it. It does not necessarily follow that because the *Diaries* speak of his arrival at Rheims in March 1583 and of his departure thence in August 1585 that he was present there during the intervening period. The *Diaries* are not always precise in this respect.

[2] *Douay Diaries*, p. 207.

[3] Cobbett, *State Trials*, i. 1129 ff. Cf. Father Pollen, *The Month*, Sept. 1907. Father Pollen's vindication of Dr. Gifford is not altogether justified by the other confession of Savage, to which presumably he refers, in S. P. Mary, Queen of Scots, xix, no. 38 (*Cal. Scottish*, 1585–6, p. 611).

[4] Antony Tyrell, the renegade priest who turned Queen's evidence against his fellows in order to save his life, told a different story. He maintains that

It has been intimated that perhaps if one traced the matter far enough the originator of the murder plot would be found to be no less person than Walsingham himself, not of course because he wished the death of Elizabeth, but because he wished, by implicating Mary Stuart, in such wise to compass her destruction. This charge rests fundamentally on the assumption that Walsingham wished Elizabeth to execute Mary and that he would not scruple to use any means in order to bring his wish to pass. That Walsingham favoured Mary's execution no one will doubt. That he was capable of fabricating a murder plot in order to attain it is a matter which demands proof. Walsingham's enemies base this charge upon the behaviour of his secret agents, Gilbert Gifford, Robert Poley, Captain Jacques, and Barnard Maude.

The case against Poley, so far as it concerns this particular point, is a slight one. It cannot be proved that Poley knew anything at all about the murder plot until it was well under way. Both from his confessions and from the confessions of Babington it is evident that at some stage or other in the development of the plot Babington asked Poley whether he thought it lawful to kill the Queen. Poley appears to have given a non-committal answer. He reported the conversation to Walsingham and Walsingham instructed him to learn more. This Poley laboured

Ballard himself had murder in his mind at least a year before Savage took his oath. According to Tyrell's account the pilgrimage of Ballard to Rome in 1584 was chiefly devoted to the purpose of obtaining from important members of the Church their endorsement to a plan for removing Elizabeth by violence. Tyrell represents Ballard as conferring on separate occasions with Dr. Lewis at Milan, with Agazarri the Rector of the English College at Rome, and with Pope Gregory XIII himself upon the subject; all of whom, Tyrell said, declared the deed to be necessary and every way commendable (S. P. Mary, Queen of Scots, xix, no. 68). If, then, we are to believe Tyrell, Ballard himself was the father of the murder plot, and Savage nothing more than an instrument conveniently offered, to carry that plot into execution. This view of the matter finds some support from Savage himself, who confessed that there were two separate plots to kill the Queen, his own and the Ballard-Babington Plot (S. P. Mary, Queen of Scots, xix, no. 38). Probably Tyrell exaggerated the case against Ballard considerably, but it seems not unlikely that Ballard was the prime mover in the assassination scheme and that at first he contemplated using Savage because Savage offered himself, but that afterwards, at Babington's suggestion, he placed the matter in the hands of Babington and his friends, Savage being admitted to the group because of his vow (Yelverton MSS. xxxi, f. 220). This was the point of view taken by the Government at the trial of the conspirators and there seems to be no good reason for believing that it was the wrong one.

to do, but it was not apparently until after Babington's fatal letter to Mary and only a few days before the warrants were out for his arrest that he took Poley into his confidence, so that Poley, although he did many other disreputable things, cannot be fairly regarded as the instigator of the plot.[1]

Of Maude and his mysterious fellow Captain Jacques there is not enough known to trace any connexion between them and the murder plot. They were agents of Walsingham and probably conversant with the plans of the conspirators. Edward Windsor, one of Babington's company, made the gravest charges against them, but not even Windsor accused them of originating the murder plot.

Gilbert Gifford's skirts are by no means so clear. He was undoubtedly acquainted with the purposes of John Savage in 1585 and very likely had a great deal to do with provoking him to it. Savage said that he had been ' moved ' at Rheims to undertake the killing of the Queen by the persuasion of Dr. Gifford and ' by the solicitation of Gilbert Gifford '. He said further that since his repair into England Gilbert Gifford had written him letters urging him to carry out his intentions.[2] Babington in his confession added that Gilbert Gifford ' was come over to Savage [December 1585] much discontented that he could not be discharged in conscience '.[3]

No doubt Savage and Babington alike were anxious to throw as large a share of responsibility for their misdoings as they could upon the shoulders of others. Nevertheless their separate charges against Gifford bear every evidence of probability, especially in view of the fact that Walsingham was plainly interested in concealing as far as possible the part which his agent had played in the matter.[4] Gilbert Gifford, we may fairly assume, helped Savage to take his resolution and more than once urged him to carry it out. He did this urging, moreover, after he had definitely entered Walsingham's service. So much may be said, and, having been said, the strongest case against Walsing-

[1] Cf. Confessions of Poley and Babington, cited above.

[2] Cf. Summary of Savage confessions, 14, 17 Aug. 1586, S. P. Mary, Queen of Scots, xix, no. 91, p. 2.

[3] Yelverton MSS. xxxi, f. 221.

[4] Cf. the garbled account of Savage's confession in the official account of the trial (Cobbett, *State Trials*, i. 1129 ff.), with Savage's confession in S. P. Mary, Queen of Scots, xix, no. 38.

ham as the originator of the murder plot has been stated. Of course the one thing essential to convict Walsingham on this charge is lacking. There is no evidence to prove that Walsingham was at all aware of Gifford's dealings with Savage. There is some slight evidence to prove the contrary. After Gifford fled to France to escape the consequences of the Babington Plot he wrote Thomas Phelippes a letter in defence of his conduct. In this letter he took occasion to mention his dealings with Savage. 'I know', he wrote, 'Savage thought I had detected him, with whom I kept company in truth only for that he was one of the best companions.'[1] Now Gifford was a liar and a rascal no doubt, but there would have been no point in his writing that he kept company with Savage 'only for that he was one of the best companions' if Walsingham had known the real reason for his association with Savage. There is other evidence to prove that Gifford was playing fast and loose not only with his Catholic friends but also with Walsingham himself. Possibly, for all his treachery, he was not altogether out of sympathy with the plot to murder Elizabeth. He may have hoped to reveal Mary Stuart's correspondence on the one hand and to accomplish by Savage's means the death of her rival on the other. It is useless to try to sound the full depth of his evil heart. The one thing certain about him is that he was a thoroughly bad man and quite incapable of honesty, fidelity, or truthfulness to any person or cause except to the person and the cause of Gilbert Gifford. Walsingham is perhaps to be censured for employing such a fellow in his service but he is not to be held responsible for all the evil that fellow did.

At the worst, it is fair to say that the charges made against Walsingham by Catholics, at the time and since, of being the instigator of the murder plot in order to compass Mary Stuart's destruction[2] remain absolutely unproved. Even if it be

[1] Gifford to Phelippes, undated, S. P. Mary, Queen of Scots, xx, no. 45, in Morris, *Sir A. Paulet*, p. 380.

[2] Cf. Stonyhurst MSS. printed by J. Morris, *op. cit.*, p. 386, which states the extreme Catholic view, but which can hardly be taken as serious evidence upon the case. It would be quite easy, but it is hardly worth while, to point out numerous mistakes in this document. Father Pollen in his scholarly study of the plot holds that Walsingham was early conversant with the plot and that his agents had much to do with prompting the rather reluctant conspirators to proceed. He points to Maude and Gilbert Gifford as the

assumed that he was morally capable of such an act there is good reason to believe that his adversaries were not themselves so scrupulous as to oblige him to tax his ingenuity so far. In the sixteenth century the attitude of Catholic prelates and Catholic Princes towards the murder of heretics was plainly one of approval. There was money and apostolic benediction waiting for the man who would be bold enough to attempt the life of the Queen. When that weakling George Gifford had proposed to do it in 1583 the Duke of Guise had promised him large rewards and the Pope of Rome had commended him. When Dr. Parry proposed to do it in 1584 the Papal Secretary had urged him 'to execute his holy purpose'. Dr. Gifford encouraged Savage to swear his oath. One has but to read the pamphlet which Dr. Allen wrote and circulated against Elizabeth just before the defeat of the Armada to understand how he would have felt had she been conveniently removed. Elizabeth's enemies may have lacked the means to murder her but they clearly did not lack the goodwill. In the persons of hare-brained enthusiasts like Savage and Ballard and Babington the means was presented to them. Is it likely that in such a condition of affairs Elizabeth's minister had to take the trouble to create murder plots? If one gets to trading in assumptions Walsingham will not be the chief sufferer. On the facts alone he has yet to be proved guilty.

Although Walsingham was probably not an accessory before the fact to the murder plot, he very likely got word of it through some one of his secret channels of information before Babington's fatal letter fell into his hands. At least he had very shrewd suspicions that some such matter was in the air. Poley in his dealings with Babington heard hints to that effect. The consequence was that Walsingham kept close watch upon Mary's correspondence, hoping that in that way Babington would reveal his mind and furnish a handle by which to catch him, and perhaps his mistress as well.

two great provokers, but he does not establish his case against Maude, and he assumes rather too lightly that Gilbert Gifford in everything he did was acting under Walsingham's instructions, though it is quite evident that Gifford was at times disloyal to Walsingham as he was disloyal to every other cause he ever embraced. In general, Father Pollen, who is otherwise scrupulously careful in his weighing of evidence, seems to throw care to the winds whenever any evidence, however flimsy, derogatory to Walsingham appears.

It will be remembered that after Gilbert Gifford had opened the secret way for the conveyance of Mary's letters and had made sure it was in good working order, he had returned to France.[1] Some time before he left he made arrangements by which the correspondence should be conveyed without him. Early in March a substitute had been appointed who received letters from the brewer and forwarded them at times when Gifford himself was not at Chartley.[2] The course which the letters took

[1] It is not easy to trace G. Gifford's movements exactly at this time. The last trace of him in England is a letter he wrote from London, 24 April 1586 (*Cal. Scottish*, 1585–6, p. 333). Walsingham, writing to Thos. Phelippes, 3 May 1586 (Morris, *Paulet*, p. 189), says, 'Some warning is to be given to G. and Foxley looketh for an answer.' This G. was Gilbert G.; Foxley was Grately the priest who was involved in Walsingham's intrigues with Dr. Wm. Gifford and had contracted to write a book in defence of Elizabeth's policy towards the Catholics. Early in April Dr. Wm. Gifford had gone to Paris to confer with Sir E. Stafford, the English ambassador. In reporting this interview Stafford wrote Walsingham, 'For particular advertisements he [Dr. Gifford] doth judge it necessary that Jacques Colderin [G. Gifford] come speedily to Rouen where with him he may at large discourse, and according to Mr. Secretary's direction proceed in particular action here on this side, which is convenient for his better credit in England' (Butler and Pollen, *Doctor Gifford in 1586*, p. 330). This doubtless was the reason for Gilbert Gifford's departure for Paris late in April or early in May. Gilbert wrote to Walsingham from Paris, 22 May (o. s.), saying that he had reached there the day before. Probably he had spent the intervening time at Rouen conferring with his cousin Dr. Gifford, also, it appears, collaborating with Grately in preparing his defence of Elizabeth. Gifford wrote to Walsingham, 22 May 1586, 'The book is in hand and I doubt not will be of great importance, only my fear is lest Dr. Gifford for want or fear of discovery faint not' (Harleian MSS. 288, f. 161).

Gifford remained in Paris until about the middle of June (*Cal. Domestic*, Adda., 1580–1625, p. 179). According to his letter to Walsingham of 22 May/1 June, Morgan had received him with open arms but had expressed regret that he had left England and had pressed him urgently to return. 'Your honour may consider,' he wrote, 'whether it be convenient I promise him to return, which willingly I would not truly, except it be thought necessary, for that he will not be so free with me unless I were there present. I can pretend thousand excuses to deal with your honour, for he liketh that course exceedingly, but unless very urgent reason urge me I would not willingly depart from my study. . . . I doubt nothing in obtaining everything of Morgan and Paget with time being settled. Nevertheless I think by going into Italy I could do great service, where not only I shall be acquainted with their actions here, as I will order matters, but also I have great familiarity with Dr. Lewis' (Harleian MSS. 288, f. 161). I quote from this letter at length because it tends to show that Gilbert Gifford was not quite so important a factor in the Babington Plot as has sometimes been supposed. It is to be observed that he was in France at the time the conspirators were maturing their plans for the murder of Elizabeth, and it is evident that so far as the convoy of letters to Mary was concerned, he regarded his job as finished. He did, however, return to England late in June, ostensibly for the purpose of carrying over Grately's 'mad book' (*Cal. Scottish*, 1585–6, p. 514), and had something to do, as will appear presently, in the last stages of the Babington Plot.

[2] Paulet to Walsingham, 10 March 1586, Morris, *op. cit.*, p. 154.

at Chartley was an intricate one. The brewer received the letters from Mary and handed them over to Paulet. Paulet dispatched them at once to Walsingham, who had them opened, deciphered, and then returned them to Paulet. Paulet thereupon returned them to the brewer and he delivered them to the substitute, who returned them to Paulet again to be forwarded to their destination. This was obviously a very slow and a very cumbersome system. The reason for it was of course that Walsingham wished to have a check upon his secret agents. He pretended to the 'brewer' that he was the only corrupt party to the transaction, and persuaded him that when he received the letters back again from Paulet and delivered them to the substitute they went straight forward to their destination by bona fide agents of the Scottish Queen. The substitute, on the other hand, probably thought that he was the only corrupt party and that the brewer was a bona fide agent of the Scottish Queen. In this wise Walsingham prevented collusion between his two agents to defraud him, and by getting a double view of the letters, first as they came from the brewer and second as they came from the substitute, checked one agent by the other.[1]

After Walsingham received the letters a second time he probably conveyed them to the French ambassador through the medium of Gilbert Gifford himself, so long as Gifford remained in London. When Gifford left London for France it seems likely, although this point is not quite clear, that a second substitute was appointed to take his place at the London end of the correspondence.[2] Walsingham's and Paulet's own messengers saw

[1] Morris, *op. cit.*, p. 211.

[2] Paulet to Walsingham, 29 June 1586: 'It may please you to signify unto me what course I shall take with the substitute hereafter. . . .'. And whereas you require me to reward him, I purpose to give him £5 if I hear not from you to the contrary by your next letters; but I would think that your friend's substitute at London should procure his reward from this Queen' (Morris, p. 212). Paulet here distinguishes between two substitutes, one near himself and the other at London. Gilbert Curle, Mary's secretary, wrote to one Barnaby, 19/29 June 1586: 'Yours dated the 28th of April, with your cousin's and the whole mentioned therein, came safely to her Majesty's [Mary's] hands. . . . Her Majesty thinketh herself not a little beholden to your said cousin for the finding out of you and your brother to pleasure her Majesty in this intercourse' (Morris, p. 376). That the cousin referred to was Gilbert Gifford appears from Barnaby's letter to Curle (Morris, p. 378). 'I have received your last of the 12th of July by my cousin Gilbert.' It is evident from this that Gilbert Gifford before he left London for France commended two men to Mary as reliable servants, whom Gilbert said were his cousins. Whether they

to the conveyance of the letters between Chartley and London. The only essential point was to prevent suspicion at the places of receipt and delivery.

With this system of convoy at his disposal and under his control Walsingham now proceeded to apply it to the entanglement of Antony Babington. Thomas Morgan, Mary Stuart's agent in Paris, had written to her of Babington as early as July 1585. Morgan wrote another letter to Mary on the same subject on the 29th of April 1586.[1] He informed her that he had been dealing with Babington in her behalf, that Babington was somewhat jealous at not having heard from her in such a long while, and that it would be advisable for her to write him a friendly letter to show that she had not forgotten him. Morgan indeed went so far as to enclose a draft of the letter which he thought his mistress ought to write. Both these letters remained in Walsingham's hands. For some reason or other he had not seen fit to send them through to her. Possibly, as his enemies suggest, he was retaining them to await developments. At all events, when he heard from Poley in June that Babington was discussing the lawfulness of murdering the Queen, Walsingham found them very apt to his purpose. He proceeded to forward Morgan's letters in commendation of Babington to Mary Stuart. It is not quite clear just when these letters went through, but Mary had certainly received them before the 25th of June, because on that day she dispatched a letter to Babington in accordance with Morgan's advice.[2] With this letter Curle sent a note to Barnaby directing him to have it delivered to Babington as soon as possible.[3] The brewer brought the letter the same day to Paulet, who observed that it was small and judged that it was unimportant, so he did not forward it to Walsingham but after keeping it in his own hands for two days returned it to the brewer, who delivered it to Barnaby. He in turn handed it back to Paulet on the 29th of June. On that day Paulet sent it to

were his cousins in truth is a hard point to determine. Anyway there were two men employed about the business, one of whom Curle called Barnaby and the other whom Barnaby called his brother. The identification of Barnaby with Thomas Barnes (cf. *Cal. Scottish*, 1585–6, *passim*) is without justification, as will appear later (p. 65), and simply serves to confuse the situation.

[1] *Cal. Scottish*, 1585–6, p. 344.

[2] Labanoff, vi. 345.

[3] Morris, p. 378.

Walsingham.[1] Barnaby saw to its delivery to Babington and received in reply a letter from Babington to Mary which was none other than the fatal letter.[2]

This letter was conveyed from London to Chartley by Thomas Phelippes himself, who left London on the evening of the 7th of July.[3] For some time Walsingham had contemplated sending Phelippes to Chartley, in order doubtless to expedite the conveyance of the letters.[4] Phelippes arrived at Chartley on Saturday, the 9th of July, and Babington's letter was probably sent in to Mary the same day, Saturday being the day on which the brewer generally delivered his beer. After some nine days' waiting Mary sent her reply. 'You have now', Phelippes wrote to Walsingham on the 19th of July, 'this Queen's answer to Babington which I received yesternight.'[5]

Doubts have been expressed in some quarters as to whether any letter over Babington's name went to Mary at all, it being suggested that the so-called letter of Babington was really a later fabrication made by Walsingham to prove his case against the Scottish Queen. This view can hardly be entertained, and is not entertained by the saner writers on either side of the controversy. It has indeed no more solid ground to stand on than the marked animus of Walsingham's enemies. Other doubts have been expressed as to whether the letter which did go to Mary over Babington's name was not a forgery made at the time to draw her into a plot against Elizabeth's life. This view likewise has grown up out of the prejudice of those who set out with the idea that Walsingham would stop at nothing which would serve to bring Mary to the block. It is disproved by Babington's own confession, by the letter of Barnaby to Curle, by the testimony of Curle and Nau, Mary's secretaries, and by the general circumstances of the case itself. Babington had in the past corresponded with Mary; he was the acknowledged leader of the conspirators. The co-operation of Mary was essential to the success of their plans. A way, apparently sure, was offered to communicate these

[1] Paulet to Walsingham, 29 June 1586, Morris, p. 211.

[2] Cf. Barnaby to Curle, 10/20 July 1586 (S. P. Mary, Q. of Scots, xviii, no. 63). This letter is printed by Morris, p. 378, but contains some pardonable errors in transcription. The original should be consulted.

[3] Morris, pp. 218, 224.

[4] Paulet to Phelippes, 3 June 1586, Morris, p. 198.

[5] Morris, p. 234.

plans to her. It would indeed have been surprising had he not written to her. In order to prove the contrary, Walsingham's opponents have to assume the subornation of half a dozen witnesses and the forgery of at least half a dozen letters, both of which facts, though easy to assume, would be very hard to establish.

In like manner Walsingham's enemies have questioned whether Mary Stuart really wrote a reply to Babington's letter. Upon this point the evidence overwhelmingly favours the belief that she did. In the first place there is the letter from Phelippes at Chartley describing the conveyance of the letter by means of the brewer, and its receipt. This evidence is worth considering. It is hard to believe that Phelippes, writing to Walsingham in confidence, would have taken the trouble to pretend that he had 'received the letter yesternight' if he had simply fabricated the letter. Furthermore there is the letter from Curle to Barnaby giving instructions for the delivery of the letter. There are the confessions of Nau and Curle, Mary's secretaries, that the letter was sent; there are Mary's letters to prove that she wrote some letter of instructions to the Catholics; there is her own tacit admission that she wrote *a* letter to Babington, though she denied having written *the* letter which was offered in testimony against her.[1] What the latter contained is another matter. Upon the point in question there can be little doubt, namely, that on the 18th of July 1586 Phelippes received from the brewer a letter written by Mary Stuart to Antony Babington.

It is not easy to trace the course of this letter after it reached Phelippes's hands. It appears that he himself contemplated sending the original to Babington without delay.[2] He probably did not do so, however. Walsingham wrote to him on the 22nd of July instructing him to return to Court, adding in a postscript: 'Babington shall not be dealt withal until your return. . . . The original letter unto him you must bring with you.'[3] Acting upon these instructions, Phelippes left Chartley on the 27th of July[4] and probably carried the original letter to Babington with him. Two days later the letter, in some form or

[1] Labanoff, vi, *passim*; *Hardwicke Papers*, i. 235 ff.

[2] Phelippes to Walsingham, 19 July 1586, *Cal. Scottish*, 1585–6, p. 531.

[3] Morris, p. 245. [4] Paulet to Walsingham, 29 July 1586, Morris, p. 246.

other, was delivered to Babington 'by a homely serving man in a blue coat'.[1]

Now the gravest question connected with the whole affair arises. On the basis of this letter to Babington, and practically on the basis of this letter alone, Mary Stuart was charged with having conspired against the life of Elizabeth. In what we may call the 'official' version of this letter produced at Mary's trial her implication in Babington's plot to murder Elizabeth is set forth clearly enough.[2] But Mary's defenders maintain that the official version of the letter was not identical with the letter as it passed from Mary's hands. They admit that Mary wrote a letter to Babington and that her letter contained much of what the official version attributed to it. They admit that Mary, in the letter she actually wrote, ratified Babington's plans for invasion and rebellion and for the liberating of her from captivity. But they deny that she actually wrote the passages in the official version which implicated her in the plot to murder the Queen.[3] They insist that this passage was interpolated between the time when the letter left Mary's hands and the time it reached the hands of Babington. If this is so Mary was, on the evidence, unjustly condemned, and either Walsingham or his agents are guilty of having conspired against her life.

Probably this is the gravest charge which has ever been seriously urged by reputable historians against Walsingham's character. On that account it deserves to be investigated with some care.

Now there were four people living at the time of Mary's trial who very likely knew exactly what her letter to Babington contained. These four people were Mary herself, Nau and Curle, her two secretaries, and Thomas Phelippes, who received her letter from the brewer's hands at Chartley. There is a possibility, which Mary herself suggested at her trial, that either Nau or Curle, who actually penned the letter, may have inserted passages in it without her knowledge, but it is hardly likely that

[1] Yelverton MSS. xxxi, f. 222; for the date, cf. Sepp, *Maria Stuart's Briefwechsel mit A. Babington*, p. 51.

[2] The French version of this letter is given in Labanoff, vi, p. 383, the English version in *The Bardon Papers*, p. 33; cf. also *Cal. Scottish*, 1585–6, pp. 525 ff.

[3] Lingard (ed. 1854), vi, pp. 214 ff., has made the best statement of this view of the case, in which he is supported by Labanoff, Tytler, Morris, Hosack, and Sepp, among many others.

either of them would have taken such a grave responsibility upon his own shoulders. At any rate there is no proof whatever that they did. It is fair to assume that the letter which passed into Phelippes's hands at Chartley was the letter which Mary herself had dictated and to hold her answerable for every word it contained. Mary, Nau, Curle, and Thomas Phelippes knew what it contained. Their testimony on the subject is therefore of great importance.

Mary at her trial tacitly admitted that she had written a letter to Babington and that her letter contained a complete ratification of his plans for rebellion and for her own liberation. She could not very well deny this much. In letters to Thomas Morgan, to Charles Paget, to Sir Francis Englefield, and to Mendoza, the Spanish ambassador at Paris, of which the drafts were found among her papers at Chartley, she had practically confessed it. But she did deny vehemently that she had ever mentioned or in any way ratified a plot for the murder of Elizabeth. It is worth while to consider how much reliance is to be placed upon her mere denial. At the beginning of her trial she had denied that she ever had had any dealings with Babington at all. It was not until she was faced with the overwhelming evidence against her upon that point that she changed her pleading. This ought to be sufficient to show that Mary meant to admit no more than was actually proved against her. She was fighting for her life and she knew it. She knew also that her fate practically hung upon the question of her implication in the murder plot. Of course she denied it. To have admitted it would have been for her little short of suicide. Her pleading in itself is worth nothing, and will prove nothing either as to her guilt or her innocence. Mary did what every person accused of crime who had the shadow of a case would do. She pleaded innocent and challenged proof.

The proofs which the prosecution produced were: (1) the official version of the letter, (2) Babington's confession, (3) the confessions of Nau and Curle. The 'official' version of the letter must, for the time being at least, be ruled out of court. It would be begging the whole question to accept it as evidence. Nevertheless this much ought to be said. It has been pointed out by Mary's defenders that the original letter was never produced and that the official version was not nor ever pretended to be more than a copy. It has even been asserted that Walsingham had in his own possession the original minute of the letter and the letter itself as it had come to his hands from Chartley. This last point cannot be proved. As to the original minute of the letter, Walsingham certainly did not have it. He evidently wanted it badly. ' I would to God ', he wrote to Phelippes on the 3rd of September, ' those minutes were found.' [1] The very next day he wrote again : ' I took upon me to put him [Curle] in comfort of favour in case he would deal plainly, being moved thereto for that the minute of her answer is not extant.' [2] Probably, as Curle said, it had been destroyed. As to the letter itself, it may very well have been sent through to Babington.[3] At all events there is no proof whatever that Walsingham had it in his possession at the time of the trial, so the reason why a copy and not the original was produced may have been because the prosecution did not possess the original to produce. As for Babington's confession, since Mary's defenders maintain that the interpolations were made in Mary's letter to him before it reached his hands, his confession must also be ruled out of court.

The confessions of Nau and Curle would appear at first sight to be of first-class importance. Both of these men testified under oath that the official version of the letter contained in all essentials the substance of the letter written by Mary to Babington.[4] They could hardly have been expected to testify that it was the exact letter because they could not have

[1] Morris, p. 284.

[2] Ibid.

[3] In any case, it must be recalled that the original letter was in cipher, written in the hand of one of Mary's secretaries. The production of it would not have strengthened the case much for the prosecution. If, however, the original minute for the letter, particularly had they been in Mary's own hand, could have been produced they would have greatly strengthened it ; Walsingham realized that. Morris argues (p. 233) that Elizabeth's ministers possessed either the original cipher letter or Phelippes's copy of it, basing his case upon a note of Burghley's. In Burghley's ' A Brief Plot for the course of proceedings against the Scottish Queen ' he has inserted in the margin against a reference to Mary's letter to Babington the words ' Note that the cipher be carried with us '. This, however, may mean any one of a score of things. It may mean the cipher key, it may mean a copy of the letter in cipher which was evidently used in the examination of the Secretaries because they both testified as to the authenticity of the cipher key which Phelippes had used (*Hardwicke Papers*, i. 225 ff.). It certainly cannot be taken to prove that the ministers had the original cipher letter, or even Phelippes's original copy of it.

[4] Morris, p. 283.

remembered the letter word for word. They later confirmed their testimony viva voce before the commissioners appointed to try the Scottish Queen.[1] This seems conclusive, but as a matter of fact it is not so. Curle and Nau were evidently under constraint when they made their testimony. Their own lives were at stake as well as the life of their mistress, and it is pretty clear that they only escaped severe treatment by making a full confession.[2] The value of a 'full confession' made under these circumstances is certainly questionable. Moreover both Curle and Nau seem to have changed their minds upon the point more than once. It was only four days after Nau had endorsed the official letter that he wrote a private letter to Elizabeth in which he denied absolutely that his mistress had ever 'any way desired, invented, proposed or practised' the death of the Queen.[3] Little over a month after that he changed his tune and declared before the Commissioners a second time that the official copy of Mary's letter was accurate. Curle seems to have wavered less than his fellow. Six months after Mary's execution he wrote a letter in which he declared that the facts were so patent against his mistress that he could not choose but confess.[4] Yet even this letter is open to some question. The fact is that Nau and Curle were moved to deviate from the truth by so many considerations, by fear of punishment, by promises of reward, by devotion to their mistress; and they wavered so much one way and another, that it is impossible to draw any sound conclusions from their testimony.

The last witness from among those who pretty certainly knew the truth is Mr. Thomas Phelippes, servant to Secretary Walsingham, an expert in deciphering documents, an expert also, as it appeared later, in the gentle art of forgery. Phelippes

[1] *Hardwicke Papers*, i. 225; Walsingham to Stafford, 27 Oct. 1586, Galba E vi, f. 326.

[2] Cf. Burghley to Hatton, 4 Sept. 1586, 'I think Nau and Curle will yield in their writing somewhat to confirm their mistress' crimes, but if they were persuaded that they themselves might escape and the blow fall upon their mistress, betwixt her head and her shoulders, surely we would have the whole from her [them ?]. If you shall bring any more writings with you from thence to touch both Nau, Curle, and Pasquier, it will serve us the better and spare our threatenings to them.' (*Bardon Papers*, Royal Hist. Soc., p. 43).

[3] 10 Sept. 1586, S. P. Mary, Queen of Scots, xix, no. 98, endorsed in Burghley's hand, 'Nau's long declaration of things of no importance sent privately to her Majesty.

[4] Cotton MSS. Caligula D i, f. 90 b.

was the man who had in charge the deciphering of all Mary's secret correspondence which passed through Walsingham's hands. He was the man who received Mary's letter to Babington from the brewer at Chartley and who prepared the official version used at her trial. No doubt Phelippes was quite clever enough and quite unscrupulous enough to have tampered with this letter. That, however, is a long way from saying that he did tamper with it. He was not produced by the prosecution at Mary's trial. Perhaps, as Mary's defenders maintain, he should have been. But Phelippes was a man of low estate and Mary Stuart a Queen. At the best it would have been his word against hers, and Mary might very well have complained that she was being condemned upon the testimony of mere servants. At all events, though he was not produced at the bar of justice then, he may properly be produced now, for Phelippes has something to say upon the point in question and his testimony has been neglected too long.

It will be remembered that he received Mary's letter to Babington on the evening of the 18th of July. The next day he wrote to Walsingham to inform him of its receipt.

> 'You have now this Queen's answer to Babington', he wrote, 'which I received yesternight. If he be in the country, the original will be conveyed unto his hands and like enough an answer returned. I look for your honour's speedy resolution touching his apprehension or otherwise, that I may dispose of myself accordingly. I think under correction you have enough of him, unless you would discover more particularities of the confederates, which may be [done] even in his imprisonment. If your honour mean to take him, ample commission and charge would be given to choice persons for search of his house. It is like enough for all her commandment, her letter will not so soon be defaced.[1] I wish it for evidence against her, if it please God to inspire her Majesty with that heroical courage that were meet for avenge of God's cause and the security of herself and this State. At least I hope she will hang Nau and Curle, who justly make Sir Amias Paulet take upon him the name she imputes to him of a gaoler of criminals.' [2]

Phelippes wrote these words less than twenty-four hours after Mary's letter to Babington had come into his hands. He had

[1] Referring to Mary's instructions to Babington to burn her letter, Labanoff, vi. 394.

[2] Morris, p. 234.

already deciphered it. So much is evident from the allusion which he makes to its contents. Consequently the attitude he takes towards it is based upon a knowledge of what it contained. There is no reason to believe that this attitude is a feigned one. Phelippes was not writing for the public ; he was writing a confidential letter to his master. Mark now what his attitude was. In the first place he contemplated sending the original letter to Babington. There was no hint at emendation or interpolation. He spoke of sending forward the original to Babington as though that were the obvious course to pursue. Surely if he had contemplated interpolations at this time he would have spoken in other terms. In the second place he clearly favoured the immediate apprehension of Babington. 'I think under correction', he wrote, 'you have enough of him.' In a word Phelippes, in view of Mary's letter, believed that Walsingham now had all the evidence he needed. Finally he believed that the original letter might be recovered when Babington was apprehended, in spite of the fact that Mary had expressly commanded it to be burned. He said he wanted the original to use as evidence against Mary, in case Elizabeth should find courage 'that were meet for avenge of God's cause and the security of herself and this State'. Plainly Phelippes saw in Mary's letter matters which concerned the 'security' of Elizabeth. He also saw in it evidence which would prove Nau and Curle to be criminals. It would perhaps be pushing the point a little far to argue from this letter alone that Mary's 'original' letter to Babington did contain express reference to the murder plot. Nevertheless Phelippes's testimony, so far as it goes, clearly does favour that point of view.

After an examination of the four witnesses who knew most about the case, it is hard to decide which way the judgement should be given. Mary's testimony was clearly of no value. Nau and Curle at the bar of justice testified for the prosecution, but Nau at least weakened his testimony by retracting privately what he had admitted under oath in public, and both of them were plainly under some constraint. Their evidence is not therefore of first-class value. Such value as it has is for the prosecution. Phelippes has little to say. That little favours the case for the Crown, so that the testimony of the witnesses as a whole inclines rather against Mary than for her.

But Mary's defenders base their chief argument not upon the testimony of the witnesses but upon the testimony of the papers produced by the prosecution against her, or, to be more exact, upon the nature of the so-called 'official' version of Mary's letter to Babington. Prince Labanoff has maintained that there are inconsistencies in this official version which can be explained only upon the assumption that certain interpolations were made in Mary's original letter during the eleven days in which it remained with Thomas Phelippes. Certainly there does appear to be an inconsistency, but this inconsistency is not perhaps so great as Morris and others would have us believe. Mary, in the first place, according to the official version, advised Babington to make full preparations for invasion from abroad and for rebellion at home before he attempted anything further. 'When your preparations both in England and abroad are complete,' she continued, 'let the six gentlemen who have undertaken to assassinate Elizabeth proceed to their work and when she is dead then come and set me free. . . . But do not take any steps towards my liberation until you are in such force that you may be able to put me in some place of perfect security lest Queen Elizabeth should take me again and shut me up in some inaccessible dungeon, or lest, if she should fail in recapturing me, she should persecute to extremity those who have helped me.' [1] In the first place Mary assumed that Elizabeth would be disposed of before her release was attempted; in the second place she assumed that after her release Elizabeth would be alive and perhaps strong enough to work vengeance. This looks like an inconsistency, certainly, but it is evident that Mary, in these two apparently irreconcilable statements, was looking at the situation from two different aspects. On the one hand, she was pointing out the way to success; on the other, she was considering the possibility of failure. She believed that in order to achieve success Babington must first of all be assured of foreign aid and of domestic uprising. She wished to impress this fact upon his mind. Although she favoured his scheme of assassination she did not wish him to think that a lucky dagger stroke would solve the whole problem. She knew that her enemies were

[1] I quote not Mary's words, but Morris's summary of them (*op. cit.*, p. 228).

strong in England, and she may very well have reasoned that the death of Elizabeth alone would not better her case. For that reason, perhaps, Mary insisted upon the order of proceeding which she had set down. She proceeded then to point out to Babington the dangers involved in deviating from that order. Straightway her viewpoint changed. She was now no longer contemplating success; she was contemplating failure. In her contemplation of failure she may have assumed what she did not expressly state, that Elizabeth would escape her murderers and become an instrument of bloody vengeance. Mary had her own plan in her mind and, woman-like, she saw no virtue in any opposed plan. If her plan was followed, very good; Elizabeth would die. If her plan was not followed,—well, in that case very likely the pistol would miss fire, or the dagger turn on a stay, or some other unforeseen contingency arise to spoil everything. Mary did not write these words or anything like them, but they may possibly express the process of her mind. What she did write was an inconsistency, no doubt; but if we begin to argue that every inconsistent thing a woman has written is *ipso facto* a forgery, we shall soon destroy many interesting records of womankind. At all events an inconsistency alone seems hardly sufficient to establish proof of interpolation.

Mary's defenders think they have other proof. They bring forward a piece of paper written in the cipher used between Mary and Babington and endorsed in the hand of Thomas Phelippes, 'The Postscript of the Scottish Queen's letter to Babington.' The paper is short enough and important enough to be quoted in full. It is as follows: 'I would be glad to know the names and qualities of the six gentlemen which are to accomplish the designment, for that it may be I shall be able, upon knowledge of the parties, to give you some further advice necessary to be followed therein; as also, from time to time particularly how you proceed; and as soon as you may, for the same purpose, who be ready, and how far every one privy hereunto.'[1]

Now Mary's friends point triumphantly to the fact that this postscript does not appear in the official version of Mary's letter to Babington. They quote, moreover, Camden's statement that a postscript had been added to Mary's letter in Walsingham's

[1] *Bardon Papers*, p. 131.

office.[1] On the basis of these facts they proceed to conclude that Phelippes, intending to make an addition to Mary's letter to Babington in order to inculpate her in the murder plot, at first contemplated making this addition in the form of a postscript, but that he afterwards decided to insert the inculpating passage in the body of the letter itself. The paper in cipher which remains they declare to be Phelippes's original draft of this postscript.

Now it must appear that they have made large drafts upon their evidence in order to build up such an elaborate theory. It seems hardly likely on the face of it that Phelippes would have taken the trouble to endorse and to file away among his master's papers a memorandum which was never put to any use. Nevertheless, there the paper is, and there also is Camden's statement. Both of these demand an explanation.

Possibly an explanation may be found. It is to be noticed that the postscript does not contain the same material that appears in the body of Mary's letter. It is simply an inquiry as to who the six gentlemen are who are to undertake the assassination. It was a question, and it demanded an answer. Suppose Babington had answered it? In that case he would have set forth the names of his accomplices. One can readily appreciate the value of such a statement in his own handwriting. It would not have affected Mary's case one way or the other, but it would have affected Babington's case mightily. Mary's defenders seem to think that she was the only offender involved. To Walsingham it must have been a matter of considerable importance to find out exactly who were conspiring against the Queen's life and to be able to produce good evidence to prove their guilt. It is possible that this postscript may have been added to Mary's letter simply for the purpose of getting Babington to reveal his fellows. This would explain Camden's statement; it would explain the paper itself, and it would also explain why the postscript does not appear in the 'official version' of the letter. If Mary did not write it, it would have been a great mistake to have reproduced it in the copy of the letter used as evidence against her. This theory is worth considering, and there is some evidence at hand to support it.

[1] Camden, *Annales* (Eng. trans. 1635), p. 305.

Walsingham to Phelippes, 3 August, 1586, referring to the postscript to Mary's letter to Babington
From the original in the British Museum, Cotton MSS., Appendix L, f. 144

In the first place Babington in his confession set forth in considerable detail the contents of the letter which he had received from Mary. His summary of it corresponds fairly accurately with the official version except at the very last. 'She ended,' Babington declared, 'requiring to know the names of the six gentlemen that she might give her advice thereupon.'[1] From the official version of Mary's letter it is evident that she ended in no such fashion, but assuming that the postscript had been added, she would have ended just so. Babington's final statement is nothing more, obviously, than a concise summary of the contents of the postscript which is under discussion. It seems fair to assume from this that though the postscript was not in Mary's letter when it came to Walsingham's hands, it was in Mary's letter before it reached Babington's hands. In a word it had been added at the Secretary's office. There is a passage in one of Walsingham's letters to Phelippes which practically confirms this statement. The letter was written on the 3rd of August. The burden of it was that Walsingham feared Babington would escape after all. 'You will not believe', he writes, 'how much I am grieved with the event of this cause and fear the addition of the postscript hath bred the jealousy.'[2] If we take jealousy in its ordinary sixteenth-century sense of 'suspicion' it is apparent that Walsingham meant to say that he was afraid the addition of the postscript would have aroused Babington's suspicions. Here, then, Walsingham practically confessed that a postscript had been added to Mary's letter to Babington. Babington himself has shown that such a postscript was contained in his letter. Thomas Phelippes has providentially preserved the very draft of the postscript itself. It was directed not against Mary but against Babington and his confederates. For that reason it naturally did not appear in the copy of the letter produced against her at her trial.

In view of these facts it is clear that the existence of Phelippes's draft of the postscript can hardly be used to support the theory that the original letter which Mary wrote to Babington was interpolated with matter to implicate her in the murder plot. In fact the theory of interpolation has no other substantial ground

[1] Babington's Confession in Yelverton MSS. xxxi, f. 223.
[2] Cotton MSS., Appendix L, f. 144.

to stand upon except the apparent inconsistency of the letter itself. This alone does not appear to be sufficient to establish the case for the defence. On the other side stands the sworn testimony of Nau and Curle, the letter of Thomas Phelippes, and the apparent conviction of Walsingham himself that if the original minute of the letter could have been found it would have established the genuineness of the official version. The legal assumption is that a man is innocent until he be proved guilty. Walsingham has been accused of compounding a felony. He has not been proved to have compounded a felony. The positive evidence on the whole points to the fact that he did not compound a felony. On these grounds one is justified in concluding that unless further evidence can be produced to the contrary, the official version of Mary's letter to Babington is in all essential respects the correct version, and that Mary stands guilty of being implicated in Babington's conspiracy to murder Queen Elizabeth.

When Thomas Phelippes received Mary's letter from the hands of the brewer at Chartley on the 18th of July he advised Walsingham to proceed at once to the arrest of the conspirators. The apprehension of Ballard had already been determined upon some weeks previously. Phelippes asked for warrants to arrest him as early as the 7th of July,[1] but for some reason or other the arrest was deferred, probably because Walsingham did not wish to arouse the suspicions of the other conspirators at that time. Gilbert Gifford, who was in London in July, wrote to Walsingham on the 11th that he had met Ballard and talked with him.[2] This seems to have suggested to Walsingham that he might get further information about the conspiracy by deferring Ballard's arrest a little longer and by setting Gifford to spy upon him. Gifford reported a second interview with the priest on the 12th of July.[3] The substance of this interview must have alarmed Walsingham, for Gifford wrote that Ballard knew all about Phelippes's movements and was aware of his tampering with the packets sent to the Scottish Queen. In consequence Walsingham made up his mind to delay no longer.

[1] *Cal. Scottish*, 1585–6, p. 509.
[2] Morris, p. 221.
[3] Gifford to Walsingham, 12 July 1586, Harleian MSS. 286, f. 136.

'I hope Ballard will be taken before your return,' he wrote to Phelippes on the 22nd of July.[1] The worst of it was that Ballard had somehow or other got hold of an official warrant to leave England which assured him of a passage at any port of the realm.[2] It would, therefore, be no easy matter to stop him if he once reached the coasts. Walsingham handed over the matter to Gilbert Gifford with instructions to find out where Ballard was and to report to Francis Milles, Walsingham's secretary, who was to make the arrest.[3] But Gifford played his part badly, so badly that Milles began to distrust his good faith and set Nicholas Berden, another one of Walsingham's spies, to hunt the priest down. Berden could not find him, but heard that he was expected by his friends in London.[4] The truth of it was that Gilbert Gifford, as soon as he saw that Walsingham was beginning to make arrests, thought it well to get out of the country. He had been playing a double game with Walsingham, and the chances were that this would appear when matters came to a trial. He accordingly obtained passage from the French ambassador and slipped over to France in disguise.[5] Certainly he went without Walsingham's knowledge or consent.[6] Fortunately, however, Ballard did not escape. Berden found him in London on the 4th of August and Francis Milles arrested him there the same day.[7]

It was not until some days later that Babington was taken. Phelippes, as soon as he had received Mary's incriminating letter at Chartley, had written to Walsingham urging that Babington be apprehended at once, but Walsingham thought differently. He hoped to get more out of Babington. For that reason he

[1] Morris, p. 245.

[2] Milles to Walsingham, 22 July 1586, S. P. Mary, Queen of Scots, xviii, no. 66.

[3] Ibid.

[4] Milles to Walsingham, 29 July 1586, S. P. Mary, Queen of Scots, xviii, no. 90.

[5] Châteauneuf's Memoirs, Labanoff, vi. 275 ff.

[6] Walsingham to Phelippes, 2 Aug. 1586, 'Sorry I am that G. G. is absent. I marvail greatly how this humor of estranging of himself cometh upon him' (Cotton MSS., Appendix l, f. 140). When Walsingham wrote this G. G. was on his way to France. He wrote a long apology for his flight to Phelippes from Paris (Morris, p. 380). Walsingham evidently contemplated the arrest of G. Gifford. His name is included in a list prepared by Walsingham early in August of persons to be apprehended (S. P. Domestic, cxcii, no. 17).

[7] Milles to Walsingham, 4 Aug. 1586, S. P. Mary, Queen of Scots, xix, no. 14.

instructed Phelippes to add the postscript to Mary's letter, expecting in this wise to learn from Babington the names of his confederates.

Meantime he was keeping in touch with Babington through the medium of Robert Poley. Ever since June Babington had been seeking through Poley's means to obtain a licence to travel abroad.[1] It is not quite clear why he wanted to go. In his several confessions he contradicted himself upon this point. At first he said that he simply wished to go for the sake of religion. Later he confessed that he sought this means of conferring with Mendoza about plans for invasion.[2] In order to win Walsingham's consent he offered to do spy service in foreign parts.[3] Walsingham had one or two conferences with him on the subject early in July, promising to further his suit if Babington would set forth in precise terms the service which he meant to do. But Babington could not be brought to make a more explicit statement. While the negotiations hung in air Walsingham got wind of his treacherous projects and learned from his letters to Mary about his plots against the Queen's life. Nevertheless Walsingham still kept up a show of soliciting his services. Of course Babington at this time was not aware that his letters had been intercepted. Judging from his confession, and from the confession of Robert Poley, he did not regard these negotiations as a mere blind to cover his real purposes. He seems to have been a half-hearted conspirator at best and more than half inclined to throw the whole matter over more than once. But our sources of information upon this point are so untrustworthy that it is hard to tell what he really intended. At all events he continued his dealings with Walsingham, and went so far as to offer his services to spy upon two priests lately come to England. Walsingham continued to encourage him, hoping in this way to inspire him with confidence to continue his correspondence with the Scottish Queen. On Monday, the 31st of July, Babington told Poley that he was aware of a conspiracy against the State. He even went so far as to betray Ballard's name. He offered to reveal all the circumstances to Walsingham. Poley reported this to

[1] Cf. Poley's Confession, *Cal. Scottish*, 1585–6, p. 595.
[2] Yelverton MSS. xxxi, ff. 219v, 233v.
[3] Cf. Poley's Confession, cited above.

Walsingham, who arranged to meet Babington on the following Thursday and to hear the whole tale from him.[1]

Meantime Walsingham and his servant Phelippes were anxiously awaiting Babington's answer to Mary's letter. Phelippes gave up hoping for it on the 2nd of August. 'We are all cozened', he wrote to Walsingham that day, 'in attending Babington's answer, for having appointed this day for to deliver his answer I find that he rid out of town yesternight.'[2] Phelippes was mistaken upon the point of Babington's departure, as he discovered the day following. Babington was still in town, dining with his friends, and to all appearance quite unaware of the sword that hung over his head. Nevertheless Walsingham began to think he had played the game long enough. 'I think', he wrote to Phelippes on the 3rd of August, 'if the messenger receive not answer this day at Babington's hands, then were it not good to defer the apprehension of him, lest he should escape. If you hope, by giving of time, that an answer will be drawn from him, then wish I the stay. It may be that the deferring of the answer proceedeth upon conference [between Babington and his friends] which, if it be so, then were it a great hindrance of the service to proceed overhastily to the arrest. These causes are subject to so many difficulties as it is a hard matter to resolve. Only this I conclude, it were better to lack the answer than to lack the man.'

Walsingham went on to speak of his appointment to confer with Babington on the same day. 'I do not mean to speak with him,' he added, 'for many causes. And therefore if Poley repair hither I will put off the meeting until Saturday [5 August] to the end he may in the meantime be apprehended.'[3] Later the same day Walsingham wrote to Phelippes that Poley had been with him and had brought news from Babington about

[1] Ibid. Father Pollen (*op. cit.*, pp. cxx–cxxix) takes the position that Walsingham in his interviews with Babington tried to win him to confess in order to ruin Mary. The only evidence he adduces in support of his position is Father Weston's narrative, which is too inaccurate in many particulars to be relied upon. Even Weston does not go so far as to maintain that Walsingham's efforts to get Babington to confess were designed to ruin Mary. If Walsingham did want Babington to confess it is rather curious to observe that he avoided a final interview in which it seems likely that Babington might have confessed.

[2] S. P. Mary, Queen of Scots, xix, no. 3.

[3] Cotton MSS., Appendix l, f. 141.

Ballard's invasion projects. 'I willed him [Poley] to give him [Babington] great thanks for his advertisements and to require him in my name to draw from Ballard what he [Babington] could touching such parties as he [Ballard] hath dealt withal, and to meet me at my house on Saturday next. Though I do not find but that Poley hath dealt honestly with me yet am I loath [to] lay myself any way open unto him, but have only delivered such speeches to him as might work [assurance] in Babington. I do not think good, notwithstanding, to defer the apprehension of Babington longer than Friday.' [1]

The events of the next four days are difficult to trace, but it appears that Walsingham played his game with Babington just one day too long. His suspicions were aroused and upon the news of Ballard's arrest he fled. Camden tells the story that Babington wrote a letter of complaint to Walsingham as soon as he heard of Ballard's arrest, and that Walsingham in reply informed him that Ballard had been arrested as a seminary priest and that he [Babington] would be in danger of arrest as a harbourer of priests unless he took refuge in Walsingham's house. Camden says that Babington followed the advice, but finding himself in reality a prisoner in the hands of Walsingham's servants he invited them to supper, left them upon pretence of paying his bill, and so made his escape.[2] There is no good reason for doubting Camden's accuracy in these details. At all events the important fact is beyond doubt. Babington fled out of London to St. John's Wood. There he and some of his confederates concealed themselves until he was driven by hunger to seek sustenance at the house of a friend named Bellamy. At Bellamy's house in Harrow they were finally captured and led away under a strong guard to the Tower. The rest of the conspirators were picked up one by one in various places. Even before Babington's apprehension the news of his plots and purposes had spread abroad. On the lips of the London populace these purposes quickly grew to the dimensions of a second St. Bartholomew's. Popular excitement rose high, and when the conspirators were finally taken and led through the streets of

[1] Cotton MSS., Appendix l, f. 143.

[2] This story receives some slight support from Poley's Confession and Babington's. It is not at all unlikely to be true (cf. Lingard, vi. 207).

London, the Londoners rang their bells and lighted bonfires to show their joy at the escape of their beloved Queen.[1]

It will not be necessary to follow the fate of these young men further. Walsingham naturally had a great deal to do with their examination because he more than any one else was in possession of the evidence against them. The account of their trial is fine reading. Babington himself played the meanest part of all. The others revealed themselves to be brave gentlemen and true friends, high traitors though they were. It is hard to resist the conclusion that they were misguided youths rather than deep-dyed villains. In September 1586 they were executed at Tyburn after the barbarous manner of the times.

And now the grave question arose as to what should be done with the Scottish Queen. The first thing to be done of course was to get hold of her papers before she had a chance to destroy them. This step had been decided upon even before Ballard, the first of the conspirators to be arrested, was taken. Very early in August Walsingham sent William Waad, Clerk of the Privy Council, to consult with Paulet as to ways and means. Waad's mission was very secret; probably no one but Walsingham and the Queen herself were aware of it. Paulet took the precaution to speak with him in the open fields so as to avoid all possible eavesdroppers. On the 3rd of August Waad returned to London, bringing with him a memorandum from Paulet in which he suggested that Mary might be invited to go hunting and while she was away her rooms might be entered, her secretaries arrested, and all her papers seized.[2] Walsingham and Elizabeth agreed that Paulet's plan was a good one, and they sent instructions to him, on the 9th of August, to carry them out at once.[3] They were carried out. Mary was asked to hunt the deer in Sir Walter Aston's estate near by. She accepted with alacrity, as a prisoner would, but after she had ridden as far as Sir Walter's house at Tixall and would have returned, Paulet detained her. In spite of tears and protestations and threats she was shut up with a few body-servants at Tixall. Meantime William Waad, with three gentlemen of the neighbourhood, entered her apartments at Chartley, arrested her secretaries, and

[1] Lingard, vi. 207–8.

[2] *Cal. Scottish*, 1585–6, p. 585.

[3] Ibid., pp. 606–7.

seized all her papers which they could lay their hands on. Secretaries and papers together were sent up to London. Mary, after a fortnight of strict confinement at Tixall, was led back to Chartley towards the end of August.

This preliminary step having been taken, the question still remained as to what was to be done with the Scottish Queen. During August Babington and his conspirators had been examined and their confessions convinced both Elizabeth and her principal councillors that Mary was deeply implicated in the murder plot. The papers seized at Chartley served on the whole to strengthen this conviction. This being so, what further?

Elizabeth herself found it hard to answer the question. As usual, when the time came to take a definite step forward, she hesitated. Among her councillors it is not easy to pick out the individual opinions. Camden says that Leicester, who was in the Netherlands at the time, thought that Mary might be conveniently removed by poison, and that he went so far as to send a clergyman to Walsingham to justify that course.[1] But Walsingham, though he was convinced of Mary's guilt and desired that she should suffer the extreme penalty of high treason, was no advocate of poison. He favoured a speedy and public trial.

His attitude seems to have been shared by Burghley and the Conservatives in the Privy Council. Burghley appeared throughout Mary's trial as her chief prosecutor. It is doubtful, however, whether or not this represented his real attitude towards her. Mary herself always regarded Burghley as her friend and advocate beside Elizabeth. Even as late as July 1586 Mary was constantly urging the French ambassador at London and her own ambassador, the Archbishop of Glasgow, at Paris to intercede with Burghley on her behalf. 'I have heard', Mary wrote to Châteauneuf on the 17th of July, 'that it has been proposed to hand me over to the Earl of Shrewsbury, and that Walsingham, to prevent this, has suggested Lord St. John. . . . I pray you send me what you hear about this, and if such a change is to be made, remind the Lord Treasurer of the assurances he has always given

[1] Camden, *Annales* (Eng. trans. 1635), p. 309. His story is unsupported. In general Camden shows himself to have been singularly well informed about matters connected with the trial and death of Mary Stuart, but Camden probably drew his information from Burghley, and Burghley of course was never one of Leicester's defenders.

me that he would have a care for my safety in such an event so far as was compatible with his duty to his mistress.' [1] It is clear that both Glasgow and Châteauneuf shared Mary's opinion of Burghley. Glasgow had written to Mary as early as January 1585 that he accounted Stafford, the English ambassador at Paris, whom he spoke of as a dependant of Burghley's, as altogether her friend.[2] In March 1586 Glasgow wrote again that Stafford had promised to intercede with Burghley on her behalf.[3] How much ground Mary and her friends had for pinning faith to Burghley it is difficult to say. He himself protested afterwards that they had had no grounds whatever,[4] and certainly no man was more forward in the proceedings against Mary, both at her trial and at her execution, than Burghley himself. It is clear, however, that Walsingham was not altogether sure of his colleague. Walsingham had intercepted Glasgow's letters to his mistress and Mary's letters to Châteauneuf. He thought it wise for the good of the 'cause' not to make these letters public,[5] but they clearly aroused his suspicions. This must have been one of the reasons why he was so careful to conceal his plans for the interception of Mary's letters from his colleagues in the Privy Council. Except Elizabeth herself, Leicester was the only member of the Government whom he took into his confidence [6] before he was ready to make the whole matter public.

Early in September the Privy Council met to discuss the case of the Scottish Queen. It was decided that she should be removed to the Tower, tried before a commission, and that in

[1] Labanoff, vi. 427.

[2] Cf. 'The Fame of Sir E. Stafford', *Amer. Hist. Review*, xx, p. 298.

[3] *Cal. Scottish*, 1585–6, p. 256.

[4] Cf. Burghley to Stafford, 2 Oct. 1586, Murdin, *Burghley Papers*, p. 569. Stafford in reply to this letter wrote an elaborate defence of his own bearing towards Mary, 6 Nov. 1586, S. P. France, xvi, 139.

[5] It must be these letters to which Walsingham referred when he wrote to Phelippes, 3 May 1586, 'I have solved the point that toucheth the great person as neither he nor the cause shall take lack' (S. P. Mary, Queen of Scots, xvii, no. 60). Morris, p. 189, reads for 'solved' 'saved', and for 'point' 'packet'. After a careful examination of the original I am confident that my reading is the correct one.

[6] Cf. Walsingham to Leicester, 9 July 1586, Bruce, *Leicester Correspondence* (Camden Society), p. 340. In the printed version of this letter there is one serious mistake. According to the printed copy Walsingham wrote: 'I dare make none of my servants here privy thereunto.' In the original (Cotton MSS., Galba C ix, f. 290) Walsingham uses the word 'fellows' not 'servants'.

case she was found guilty her condemnation should be ratified by Parliament.[1] Elizabeth consented to her trial, and after some hesitation she was brought to consent to parliamentary action. She would not hear of Mary's imprisonment in the Tower, and it was only after rejecting in turn two or three other suggestions that she finally consented to the removal of Mary to Fotheringay. Burghley himself had managed this part of the business, Walsingham being confined to his house by a severe boil on his leg.[2] 'I wish your health and presence here,' Burghley wrote to him on the 9th of September, 'where your ability to attend on her Majesty at all times might greatly further causes through by importunity, that now, for lack of following, which I cannot do by [reason of] my lameness, remain unperfected.' [3]

Elizabeth was clearly still far from 'resolution'. All her council urged her to follow the course they had recommended. Walsingham laid all the evidence before her eyes. But she still delayed and seized upon every straw of difficulty to delay further. Finally she was induced, at the end of September, to name commissioners for the trial of the Scottish Queen. They were forty-six in all, peers, privy councillors, and judges, constituted by special warrant to inquire into and determine all offences committed against the statute for the security of her Majesty's person either by Mary or by any other person whatsoever.[4]

Walsingham was named one of the commissioners. September had been a busy month for him. He had had the examination and trial of the Babington conspirators on his hands. After they were disposed of he had had to set straight to work gathering together the evidence against Mary. To make matters harder

[1] Lingard, vi. 211.

[2] Walsingham to Paulet, 5 Sept. 1586, Morris, p. 286.

[3] S. P. Domestic, cxciii, no. 28.

[4] The commission is printed in full in Camden, *op. cit.*, p. 310. Even after the commission was prepared Elizabeth cavilled at the form of it. 'I find by Mr. Secretary Davison', Walsingham wrote to Burghley on 6 October, 'that her Majesty does not rest satisfied with the form of the commission drawn by her learned counsel, with the advice of the judges, in the point of the Scottish Queen's title. I would to God her Majesty could be content to refer these things to them that can best judge of them as other princes do' (S. P. Domestic, cxciv, no. 14).

for him he was very unwell. He recovered his health, however, towards the end of the month. The good news that the ' bosom serpent ' was at last to be called to account seems to have set him on his feet again.[1]

Of the forty-two commissioners appointed to take part in Mary's trial, thirty-six proceeded to Fotheringay Castle to undertake that trial early in October. They arrived at Fotheringay on the 11th of the month,[2] Walsingham among them. It will not be necessary to follow here the details of their proceedings. Walsingham appears to have played only a formal part. Burghley voiced the sentiments of the Privy Council. Elizabeth's attorneys based their case upon the testimony of Mary's secretaries and upon her own correspondence. The famous letter to Babington was, of course, the most important document produced. When Mary had heard it read she denounced it as a forgery. It was easy, she said, to counterfeit the ciphers and characters of others. She added that she was afraid this was Walsingham's work, who sought by this means to bring her to her death ; that she had heard of former practices of his against her life. At that Walsingham rose to his feet. ' I call God to witness ', he said, ' that as a private person I have done nothing unbeseeming an honest man, nor, as I bear the place of a public man, have I done anything unworthy of my place. I confess that being very careful for the safety of the Queen and the realm, I have curiously searched out all the practices against the same. If Ballard had offered me his help I should not have refused it ; yea, I would have recompensed the pains he had taken. If I have practised anything with him, why did he not utter it to save his life ? '

Mary protested that she was satisfied with his avowal. She said she had spoken only what she had heard, and she begged him not to credit her slanderers any more than she credited his.[3] The incident is a small one in itself, yet interesting because it reveals that Mary, at the last as well as at the first, looked upon Walsingham as her great enemy. Her instinct did not betray her. No doubt of all the persons gathered to try her, none had

[1] Cf. Paulet to Walsingham, 29 Sept. 1586, Morris, p. 294.
[2] Lingard, vi. 213.
[3] *State Trials*, i. 1182 ; in which the account of this incident is a direct translation of Camden's account.

done so much to bring her to the bar of judgement as had Walsingham himself.

The trial of Mary took place on the 14th and the 15th of October. It was apparently the original intention of the Queen that at the completion of the trial the commissioners should pronounce their verdict and the judges proceed to give sentence at once. But Elizabeth had a change of heart once more. On the 13th of October she summoned Davison at the dead of night and ordered him to write 'a few hasty and scribbled lines for the stay of the sentence', commanding the commissioners to return to London and make their report to her. 'I know not,' Davison added, 'neither do I think the letter will come time enough to hinder the sentence, which by our calculation here should be given yesterday or this morning, which error I could be content might happen for the shortening of your business.'[1] Davison, however, had miscalculated. His letter did arrive in time and caused the adjournment of the Commission on the 15th of October. On the same day Walsingham wrote to Leicester:

'She [the Scottish Queen] hath been publicly charged not only to have been privy and assenting to the murder of her Majesty, but also in encouraging of those that should have been executioners. The matter was so sufficiently proved, especially by the testimony of her two secretaries under their hands and delivered upon their oaths, as she had no other defence but a plain denial; so as in the opinion of her best friends that were appointed Commissioners she is held guilty.

'We had proceeded presently to sentence but that we had a secret countermand and were forced under some other colour to adjourn our meeting until the twenty-fifth of this month at Westminster. I see this wicked creature ordained of God to punish us for our sins and unthankfulness, for her Majesty hath no power to proceed against her as her own safety requireth.'[2]

The Commission adjourned to meet again, as Walsingham had told Leicester, on the 25th of October at Westminster. Two days before this reassembly the French ambassador wrote a letter to Elizabeth urging her to stay proceedings against the Scottish Queen, but Elizabeth, her purposes strengthened once

[1] Davison to Walsingham, 14 Oct. 1586, S. P. Domestic, cxciv, no. 43.

[2] Cotton MSS. Caligula C ix, f. 502 (not printed in *Leicester Correspondence*). Walsingham gives another account of the trial in a letter to Stafford of 27 Oct. 1586, Cotton MSS. Galba E vi, f. 326.

more by the presence of her Council, replied that she did not find it convenient to stay proceedings. She said further that she would take very unkindly any intercession on the part of the French King in Mary's behalf.[1] Consequently, on the 25th of October, the commissioners reassembled in the Star Chamber at Westminster. There is a brief account of the proceedings on that day from Walsingham's pen.[2]

'At which day', he wrote to Stafford on the 27th of October, 'the commissioners met again in the Star Chamber and there, after a repetition made by the Queen's learned counsel of that which had passed before in this matter, the Scottish Queen's two Secretaries were brought forth before the Lords and openly affirmed as much *viva voce* as they had before deposed in writing, which brought a great satisfaction to all the commissioners, in so much as that, albeit some of them, as you know, stood well affected to her, yet considering the plainness and evidence of the proofs, every one of them after other gave their sentence against her, finding her not only accessory and privy to the conspiracy but also an imaginer and compasser of her Majesty's destruction.'[3]

So much, then, had been done. Mary had been charged, tried, found guilty of plotting against Elizabeth's life, and sentenced to die a traitor's death. There was nothing more to be done than to proceed to her execution. All that was needed was Elizabeth's signature to the death warrant, but no one knew better than Walsingham that that signature was not going to be an easy matter to get. He and his colleagues accordingly, during the next few months, devoted themselves to wringing from Elizabeth a reluctant consent that the sentence pronounced upon her enemy should be carried into effect.

The first step was taken in Parliament. When the question of

[1] Cf. Walsingham to Stafford, just cited.

[2] A more complete account is in *Hardwicke Papers*, i. 225.

[3] Cf. n. 1, above. In an apology which Claude Nau, Mary's secretary, wrote some twenty years later he declared that he had done all he could before the commissioners in Star Chamber to maintain Mary's innocence, and had openly declared the accusations against her to be altogether false and calumnious. He said that Walsingham had been greatly angered at this avowal, had risen to his feet, sworn at Nau, and shaken a fist in his face. This story is accepted by Lingard (vi. 217), but as K. de Lettenhove, who was certainly no friend of Walsingham's, has pointed out, it has little or no foundation in fact. Lettenhove shows that the subsequent relations of Walsingham and Nau effectually give the lie to it (K. de Lettenhove, *Marie Stuart*, ii. 50 ff.).

dealing with the Scottish Queen in consequence of the Babington conspiracy arose, the Privy Council had advised Elizabeth to call her Parliament. She had done so and Parliament accordingly assembled on the 29th day of October. In Parliament the question of the Scottish Queen was taken up at once. Burghley stated the case before the Lords and Hatton before the commons. It was voted that a joint committee should be appointed from the two houses to present a petition to the Queen 'for the speedy execution of Mary, late Queen of Scots, according to the just sentence which had been pronounced against her'. This petition was presented on the 12th of November. Elizabeth received it and thanked her subjects for their care of her. The answer, however, which she made, was hardly calculated to satisfy them. 'If', she said, 'I should say unto you that I mean not to grant your petition, by my faith I should say unto you more than perhaps I mean. And if I should say unto you that I mean to grant your petition, I should then tell you more than is fit for you to know. And thus I must deliver you an answer, answerless.'[1]

Nevertheless there can be no doubt that the parliamentary petition had had its effect. It practically decided Elizabeth to make public the sentence pronounced against Mary, which so far had been kept an official secret. Châteauneuf, the French ambassador, did his best to stay this publication, and Elizabeth postponed it for ten days at his request, but she wished to prorogue Parliament and she thought it unwise to do so without some better acknowledgement than mere thanks for their efforts. Burghley pressed this argument home upon her. 'The thanks', he wrote to Davison, 'will be of small weight to carry into the countries; and then the realm may call this Parliament a vain Parliament or otherwise nickname it a Parliament of words. For there is no law made for the realm, and if also there be no publication presently of so solemn a sentence, the sentence against the Scottish Queen will be termed a dumb sentence, whereof the nobility that have given it and all the Parliament that have affirmed it, may repent themselves of their time spent.'[2]

[1] Cf. D'Ewes *Journals* (ed. 1682), pp. 375 ff.; the correction of some mistakes in Camden's account should be noted. [2] Morris, p. 306.

Elizabeth saw the weight of this reasoning, and on the 1st of December she finally consented to the proclaiming of the sentence. It was formally proclaimed two days later.

This was a step forward, certainly, but it was by no means the final step. Bernardino de Mendoza, the Spanish ambassador at Paris, who knew something about Elizabeth's character, was pretty sure that she would go no farther.[1] To shake her resolution, special embassies arrived both from France and from Scotland to plead for Mary's life. She heard them with impatience and answered them with a bold defence of her conduct, but they had their effect upon her.[2] As for Walsingham, he was in despair. At the moment he was urging a private suit to the Queen which she received with every show of disfavour. In consequence he left Court for a time. 'I humbly beseech your Lordship,' he wrote to Burghley on the 16th of December, 'to pardon me in that I did not take my leave of you before my departure from the court. Her Majesty's unkind dealing towards me hath so wounded me as I could take no comfort to stay there. And yet if I saw any hope that my continuance there might either breed any good to the church or furtherance to the service of her Majesty or of the realm, the regard of my particular should not cause me to withdraw myself. But seeing the declining state we are running into, and that men of best desert are least esteemed, I hold them happiest in this government that may be rather lookers-on than actors.'[3] Eight days later, from his house at Barn Elms, he wrote to Leicester: 'The delay of the intended and necessary execution doth more trouble me, considering the danger her Majesty runneth, than any particular grief.'[4] He informed Burghley early in January that his grief of mind had thrown him into a dangerous disease. In fact, for some months after this, Walsingham, by reason of his malady, was practically *hors de combat.*

It must have been some time before he left Court that he drew up, probably for the benefit of Elizabeth, 'A Project of a Discourse touching the Scottish Queen', which was nothing more than a draft for an argument in favour of Mary's speedy execu-

[1] *Cal. Spanish,* 1580–6, p. 669.

[2] A good account of these embassies will be found in K. de Lettenhove, *Marie Stuart,* ii, *passim.*

[3] S. P. Domestic, cxcv, 64.

[4] Cotton MSS., Titus B vii, f. 24.

tion. The paper is rather long and it is incomplete, but it is practically the only statement on the subject from Walsingham's pen and is worth giving in full because it sets forth his own views :

' The Dangerous Alteration likely to ensue both in England and Scotland in case the Execution of the Scott. Q. be stayed.

' The Alteration in England

'Such as are worldly affected that have been used as instruments as well in the late proceeding against the said Queen as at other times, will seek to make their own peace to her Majesty's danger. The best affected that have heretofore showed themselves careful of her Majesty's safety, seeing their care frustrate will give over and provide for their own safety by retiring themselves out of the realm.

' The number of Papists, Atheists and Malcontents will marvellously increase in respect of the hope they will conceive that the said Scottish Queen shall come to the crown as a thing fatal.

' The Jesuits and Seminaries and their confederates that build only the hope of alteration of religion upon her person, doubting that in respect of the infirmity of her body that a more strait keeping of her will hasten her death, will use the greater expedition for the prevention thereof in putting in execution such practices as may shorten her Majesty's days.

' The Alteration in Scotland.

' The number of the evil affected both to the religion and amity of this crown will increase. Such as do now stand well affected both in religion and in the amity will be enforced for their own particular safety to change their course.

' The King himself, when the well affected shall be removed from him and that he shall see the number of the ill affected increased in his realm, whereby he need not to doubt any English party, it is to be looked for he will be carried, what through the persuasions of the ill affected at home and the encouragement he shall receive from the Catholic princes abroad, to attempt somewhat both for the liberty of his mother as also for the pursuing of his pretended title.

' And lastly, it is also to be looked for that, besides the procuration of his own subjects at home and the Catholic princes abroad, he will be greatly provoked to attempt somewhat by the ill affected of this realm, especially when he shall see the number of them increased.

' A consideration of the perils that may grow by the executing of the said Queen.

' Forasmuch as both the K. of Scots and the K. of Spain and

their fautors pretend to have some present interest to this crown, it may be doubted that somewhat may be by them attempted after her death to the peril of her Majesty's person, it is therefore to be considered whether the perils likely to grow that way are of like danger as those that may ensue by the preservation of the said Q.

'First, the matter being considered in generality, it will appear very manifestly that by the conservation of her, the perils that may grow either by the K. of Spain or the K. of Scots will be redoubled, for the causes ensuing:—

'First, for that she is already a Catholic and so established in the opinion of the Catholics of this realm.

'Secondly, for that she hath already by her practice and long continuance here won a great party within the realm, which number will greatly increase when they shall see her preserved fatally, contrary to all reason.

'Fourthly (*sic*), the Catholic princes in respect of the opinion they have of the zeal of her religion, will according unto their promise concur and join with the king her son, both in the seeking of her liberty and putting him in possession of this crown.

'And whereas it may be objected that they will not attempt anything in respect of the peril that may grow unto her, it may be answered that there is no likelihood that there will fall out no (*sic*) impediment that way, first, for that she herself doth encourage them thereto, praying them to have no regard to her peril but to the advancement of the common cause.

'Secondarily, for that it is to be thought that, being kept more straitly than heretofore she hath been, she cannot long continue and therefore that her friends will rather attempt some desperate remedy than to suffer her to perish without attempting anything.

'Lastly, they will hope, not without cause, that when the wise men of England shall see her party increased within the realm and a general combination without the realm for her delivery, they will make dainty to advise any violence to be attempted against her.

'Now, touching the perils that are to ensue either by the K. of Scots or the K. of Spain by a particular consideration of them, it will appear they are nothing equal to the peril that is likely to grow from her.

'And first, if the perils be considered that may ensue by the K. of Scots, it will appear that there is no cause to doubt of any danger to ensue from him so long as he continueth to be a Protestant, his own weakness being sufficiently known; the danger that is like to grow is by the change of his religion.'[1]

[1] S. P. Mary, Queen of Scots, xxi, no. 8, endorsed in Walsingham's hand and corrected in his hand.

Walsingham did not, however, confine himself to arguments. He managed to get news from foreign parts of plots designed against Elizabeth's life, and he was careful to bring these to her attention. There is, moreover, some reason to believe that he had a hand in the designment of a spurious plot against Elizabeth which, if not designed to hasten her resolution, certainly happened very aptly to that purpose.

It is not easy to get to the bottom of the so-called Stafford plot. Different parties to the action told different stories. William Stafford, around whose person the whole matter turned, was a younger brother of Sir Edward Stafford, English ambassador to France. William seems to have been a rather useless young man who had got himself into trouble by his folly more than once. Some way or other he placed himself deeply in Walsingham's debt. 'I am as ever at your command,' he wrote to Walsingham on the 10th of June 1585, 'and there is no man living to whom I am so beholden. If I should live to see my blood shed in your cause I should think it but some recompense for the great good I have received at your hands.'[1] This is extravagant language to say the least. How much of it is the exaggeration of courtesy to one in a high place it is not easy to say. No doubt, however, William Stafford was under an obligation to Walsingham which he wished some way or other to cancel.

Now, according to his own confession, Stafford, at the instigation of des Trappes, secretary to Châteauneuf, French ambassador at London, had been led into a plot against Elizabeth's life. Stafford said that he had conferred with Châteauneuf upon the subject and had received his approval. Stafford said further that he had been a means of introducing des Trappes to one Michael Moody, a prisoner in Newgate for debt, and that Moody had undertaken to murder the Queen by placing a bag of gunpowder under her bed and touching it off. When matters had reached this point Stafford declared that he had been moved to repentance and had gone to Walsingham's house at Barn Elms and revealed the whole matter to him.[2]

Upon the basis of this confession, which Walsingham placed in

[1] *Cal. Dom.*, Adda., 1580–1625, p. 144.

[2] Cf. Stafford's Confession, 11 Jan. 1586/7, S. P. Domestic, cxcvii, no. 15. Michael Moody had been one of Sir Edward Stafford's servants in France.

Elizabeth's hands, the Queen at once took action. She ordered the arrest of des Trappes, then on his way to Dover, and she appointed four of her councillors, Burghley, Leicester, Hatton, and Davison, to interview the French ambassador. These men, having met together at Burghley's house in London, summoned Châteauneuf to appear before them. After some hesitation he came. Thereupon Burghley, speaking for the rest, laid before him Stafford's confession, pointing out to him that Stafford had directly implicated both himself and his secretary in a plot against the Queen's life. Stafford himself was at hand and was brought forward to confirm his statement. He charged the ambassador to his face. Châteauneuf thereupon accused Stafford of having invented the whole plot himself. Châteauneuf confessed that Stafford had made some such murderous proposals to him, but that he had rejected them altogether and had threatened to expose the young man to Elizabeth. Burghley maintained that he should have done so. Châteauneuf maintained the contrary, citing precedents to establish his point of view. With that the interview closed. No further steps were taken against the French ambassador, but he was denied audience, kept a virtual prisoner in his own house for over a month, and his communication with France stopped.[1]

The English Government based its action entirely upon Stafford's confession. Des Trappes' confession revealed the matter in a somewhat different aspect. He said that Stafford had come to him seeking passage to go over to France with M. de Bellièvre, who was just about to return after his mission on behalf of the Queen of Scots. Des Trappes had offered to secure the passage for him. Upon this business the two men held more than one consultation. At one of these meetings, des Trappes said, Stafford had spoken of a resolute man named Moody, in prison for debt, who was willing to do any desperate act for money. Des Trappes said that Stafford had induced him to go and speak with Moody at Newgate and that Moody had offered to carry a bag of gunpowder into Elizabeth's chamber. This project des Trappes admitted he had told his master, and that his master in great anger had forbidden Stafford to come to his house again.[2]

[1] Cf. Burghley's account of this interview in Cotton MSS., Galba E vi, f. 333.

[2] Des Trappes' Confession, S. P. Domestic, cxcvii, no. 7.

Moody, on the other hand, maintained that Stafford's version of the story was substantially correct and that des Trappes had offered him large rewards if he would undertake the murder of the Queen.[1]

This much is certain. There was a plot against the Queen spoken of. Stafford, Moody, des Trappes, and Châteauneuf were privy to it. The only matter in question is as to who instigated it in the first place. The English Government was, or pretended to be, for some time in doubt. Finally, two months later, when Mary Stuart was safe under ground, Elizabeth sent Walsingham to London to confer with Châteauneuf. They met together, and after some preliminary remarks in explanation of the execution of Mary Stuart, Walsingham said that he was very sorry about the Stafford episode. He said both the Queen and her council believed that des Trappes was entirely innocent and that they saw clearly that the whole matter was no more than mere effrontery on Stafford's part in order to extort money. Walsingham said further that Châteauneuf might have audience with the Queen at any time he desired it.[2] Some time later Elizabeth received Châteauneuf, treated him with great cordiality, and made a handsome apology to him for the treatment to which he had been subjected.[3]

Stafford then was officially recognized by the Government as an impostor. The question remains, whether he was an impostor of his own making, or by special creation from above. Châteauneuf's friends believed that the whole matter had been invented by the Privy Council in order to embitter him with the people and to incite them against the Scottish Queen. He accused no one in particular. In reporting his interview with Walsingham he said that Walsingham had blamed Davison, who was then serving as scapegoat for all the sins of the Government, and had declared that if he had been at the Court des Trappes would never have been detained. Châteauneuf was inclined to credit this story.[4] It receives some support from the fact that Walsingham at the time was certainly ill at Barn Elms and that he had at no

[1] Moody's Confession, S. P. Domestic, cxcvii, 10.

[2] Cf. Châteauneuf to the King of France, March 1587, Teulet, *Relations diplomatiques de la France et l'Espagne avec l'Escosse*, iv. 181.

[3] Cf. Châteauneuf to the King of France, 13 May 1587, Teulet, iv. 94.

[4] Cf. n. 2, above.

time appeared in the affair. And yet suspicion points a finger at Walsingham. His former relations with Stafford, already alluded to, suggest his influence, and the trick itself bears marks of his genius. At any rate, whether Walsingham was himself responsible for it or not, every indication points to the fact that some of the councillors were behind it. It served a double purpose. In the first place it cut off the ambassador from France at a time when he might have exerted considerable influence in arousing his master to intervene for the Scottish Queen. In the second place it frightened Elizabeth into taking the final step against Mary.

Elizabeth indeed finally came to the conclusion that her Parliament and her Privy Council were right, and that if she would live in safety Mary must die. On the 1st of February, after some conference with the Lord Admiral (Howard), she bade him send William Davison, her secretary, to her with the death warrant, which still awaited her signature. Davison came and delivered it into her hands. Without more ado she called for pen and ink and signed it. She thereupon commanded Davison to take it to the Lord Chancellor to receive the Great Seal. On his way she directed him to stop and see Walsingham, who was lying sick at his house in London, and to communicate the matter to him. 'The grief thereof', she added with a flash of wit, 'will go near to kill him outright.' [1]

Yet even after Elizabeth had taken the last legal step necessary in order to execute Mary Stuart according to law, she once more asserted her preference for indirect and underhand methods of proceeding. At the very moment of signing the death warrant she bade Davison join with Walsingham in writing a letter to Sir Amias Paulet, urging him to find 'some way to shorten the life of that Queen'. Davison reasoned with her, telling her that Paulet was a man of too great integrity to listen to such a suggestion, but Elizabeth insisted, so Davison at the same time that he showed Walsingham the death warrant, signed, communicated to him also Elizabeth's wishes in this behalf. Of course to Walsingham, as to Davison, the Queen's wishes were equivalent to commands. Walsingham drafted the letter to

[1] Cf. Nicholas, *Life of Davison*, Appendix A, pp. 231 ff. This is Davison's own account of the affair.

Paulet. He could not well do otherwise. Certainly he never endorsed such a course of proceeding himself. And no doubt, knowing Paulet as well as he did, Walsingham drew up the letter with the full assurance that Paulet would never entertain such a project. The letter went, to the eternal shame of Queen Elizabeth. Paulet answered it in words which reveal at once the kind of man he was. 'My good livings and life', he wrote, 'are at her Majesty's disposition and I am ready to so lose them this next morrow, if it shall so please her, acknowledging that I hold them as of her mere and most gracious favour, and do not desire to enjoy them but with her Highness' good liking. But God forbid that I should make so foul a shipwreck of my conscience, or leave so great a blot to my poor posterity to shed blood without law or warrant.' [1]

Elizabeth was irritated at this answer. She spoke of Paulet as a 'precise and dainty fellow', and when Davison defended him she closed their conference abruptly.

Meantime Davison had carried the death warrant to the Lord Chancellor, who had sealed it with the Great Seal. Nothing now remained but to put it into execution. Burghley and the councillors decided to do this upon their own responsibility, and the final steps in the tragedy of Mary Stuart were taken, if not without Elizabeth's knowledge, at least without her express consent. It is well known how she sought afterwards to shift the whole blame for the execution upon Davison. His proceedings were without doubt quite legal, but he made the mistake of not being precise to a fault upon a matter of such moment. Had he understood the character of Elizabeth better, he would have been. As it was, he conveyed the death warrant, signed and sealed, to Burghley, and Burghley and the Privy Council together resolved to execute it without delay. Walsingham himself had no hand in these proceedings. He was very providentially ill at the time.

The closing scene of Mary Stuart's history is touching in the extreme. She walked to the block like a queen and like a queen she died. Nothing perhaps in her life became her more than the leaving of it. Certainly nothing in her life so completely commends her to the admiration and sympathy of after-generations.

[1] Morris, *op. cit.*, pp. 359, 361.

Yet, in pausing beside the grave of a very charming and a very unfortunate woman, one ought not to forget that she was perhaps, in herself, as great a menace as ever threatened the safety and welfare of England under Elizabeth. The English breathed more freely after she had gone. They felt that a bosom serpent had indeed been removed and they turned with stout hearts to meet the overt enemy at their gates.

APPENDIX TO CHAPTER XII

It has been said and steadily maintained by writers on this subject from Froude until the present that Thomas Barnes was the man employed to carry the letters between Babington and Mary Stuart and that he, like all the rest, was an agent of Walsingham's. I have found some reason for thinking that the traditional story about Barnes is not the correct one and I shall set forth these reasons as briefly as may be. The first appearance of Barnes upon the scene is in a letter which he wrote on the 10th of June to Mary Stuart herself (Morris, *Sir A. Paulet*, p. 375). In this letter he said that he had long wished to do her service and had said as much to his cousin (Gilbert Gifford) who had suggested that he might serve her as a carrier of letters. He accordingly sent her a packet from France and said she would have had it long ago had he not fallen among thieves on the way who had deprived him of his horse and his money. This letter in itself is worth little or nothing. If Barnes was an agent of Walsingham, probably the most of it was false. But this much is clear. The letter was written in Gilbert Gifford's cipher, which shows that Barnes had opened relations with Mary, as he said, through Gilbert Gifford's means. Now G. Gifford was Walsingham's agent. The question therefore comes down to this: Did G. Gifford employ Barnes at Walsingham's instructions or did he employ Barnes for private purposes of his own? The first supposition on the face of it bears greater evidence of probability; the second, when we consider the character of Gilbert Gifford, is not impossible. The positive evidence about Barnes comes from three sources:

1. From the letters of Sir Amias Paulet to Walsingham and Phelippes.
2. From the letters of Gilbert Gifford to Walsingham and Phelippes.
3. From the letters between Curle and one named Barnaby.

Paulet makes his first mention of Barnes (under the name of the 'second messenger') in a letter to Walsingham of the 21st of June (Morris, p. 210). He says that the bearer had brought him that morning a packet from the Scottish Queen directed to Barnes who was waiting for it 'as it seemeth' at Lichfield. This packet Paulet said that he was forwarding to Walsingham and that he had instructed the bearer to tell Barnes that the Scottish Queen's answer to him had been delayed by her illness and that he was to return for it in ten days' time. Paulet at the end of his letter to Walsingham added, 'If you think the time which I now give you to be too short for the perusing of the packet it may please you to signify unto me what time I shall appoint hereafter.'

Taking this letter as it stands, without any reference to preconceived opinions about Barnes, it appears first of all that Paulet found it necessary to make excuses to Barnes, not directly, but through the bearer, for the delay of the letter which he had sent up to Walsingham. It appears in the second place that all the information Paulet supplied to Walsingham about Barnes he had received from the brewer, and all the dealings he referred to as having had with Barnes had taken place through the brewer. There is no sign of any direct relations between Paulet and Barnes, no sign that Paulet knew Barnes or recognized him as being an agent of Walsingham.

The next mention Paulet made of Barnes is in his letter to Walsingham of the 29th of June 1586 (Morris, p. 211). He acknowledged the receipt of the packet he had sent to Walsingham on the 21st and said that he had delivered it to the brewer for Barnes who was waiting for it at Lichfield. 'The honest man [the brewer]', Paulet added, 'believeth verily that this second messenger came by direction from your friend [Gilbert Gifford] because he bringeth a true token. . . . He calleth himself Barnes and saith (untruly I doubt not) that he is nearly allied to Sir Walter Aston and Mr. Richard Bagot.' It appears from this letter that Paulet had been questioning the brewer about Barnes and that the brewer was sure he had come from Gilbert Gifford. Now it is possible to assume that Paulet was sounding the brewer to test his honesty. It is also possible to assume that he was really seeking information about this man Barnes, and this assumption finds some ground in the last statement, 'he calleth himself Barnes, &c.' If Paulet had been aware that Barnes was Walsingham's agent, this information would have been perfectly gratuitous.

These two letters of Paulet's contain all the information about Barnes which is to be got from him. Taken in their most direct and obvious sense they suggest that this second messenger was an outsider who had suddenly thrust himself into the secret correspondence and that Paulet was trying to find out through the brewer who the fellow was, where he came from, and what he was about. Paulet wrote cautiously and with less excitement than one would have expected under the circumstances. But Paulet was probably not quite sure in his own mind whether Barnes was an agent of Walsingham's or not. Moreover, the situation was not so alarming as at first sight it may have appeared. By the end of June the brewer had proved himself reliable, and since he brought all the letters he received from Mary or from her friends to Paulet, it was easy to keep a careful check on this stranger's business.

So much for Paulet's testimony. It seems to point to the fact that Barnes was no agent of Walsingham. At any rate it furnishes no grounds at all for believing that Barnes was an agent of Walsingham.

The next witness in the box is Gilbert Gifford, as rare a rascal and as large a liar as any man in England. For all that, he was a clever knave and was careful not to lie when he was sure of being found out, so that some grains of truth may perhaps be winnowed from his statements. He speaks of Barnes for the first time in a letter to Thomas Phelippes, written evidently from Chartley on the 7th of July (Morris, p. 216). Gifford told Phelippes that he had gone to Chartley for two reasons, first to try the honesty of the brewer, and second to discover the second messenger. Doubtless in this he was telling the truth. Phelippes must have known why Gifford went to Chartley. Walsingham had written to Paulet late in June that he intended to send Gifford down to investigate matters (cf. Morris p. 212). So we may accept Gifford's statement that one of the reasons for his going to Chartley was 'the discovery of the second [messenger]'. He wrote to Phelippes further that the brewer had told him that Barnes had gone up to London over a week before. 'Whereof', Gifford adds, 'this morning I have amply written to Sir Amias declaring the necessity of my return. . . . If he [Barnes] be already in London, as is probable . . . then it is likely that I shall find him there coming up speedily, whence we will dispose of him. . . . I promise and undertake of my credit to cut him clear off from this course and to that end I have written to Z.'

Now whether Gifford was speaking in good faith or not it is evident that he wished to convey to Phelippes the idea that he was doing his best to catch Barnes and to cut him off clear from the course. His reference to a letter to Z is probably explained by a letter which Curle wrote to Barnaby on the 12/22 July 1586 (Morris, p. 379) from which I extract the salient passage: 'I trust you have caused deliver her Majesty's answer to the second messenger, although (to say truly) her Majesty agreeth with your cousin Gilbert his advice not much to employ the man.' From this it appears that Gifford had written to Mary Stuart and had warned her against using Barnes. So that Z in his letter to Phelippes was very likely none other than the Scottish Queen herself.

Gifford's letter to Walsingham of the 11th of July (Morris, p. 220) would seem to indicate that he was still hunting for Barnes. 'Barnes', he wrote, 'hath not yet appeared in any of his frequented places so that I think he came not yet to town. . . . I am assured he shall no sooner come to town but I shall hear of him, and needs he must come for I have his letter with me.'

The last word apparently which Gifford wrote on the subject of Barnes he wrote after he had left England finally for France. (Morris, p. 380). This letter was directed to Phelippes and was by way of being an apology on Gifford's part for his misdeeds. The letter is well larded with oaths and is on the face of it untrustworthy. Nevertheless, although we may rightly distrust the defence which Gifford put up for his various misdeeds, it is safe to assume that the particular misdeeds which he undertook to defend were the ones with which Walsingham charged him. It is significant that first of all he spoke of his dealings with Barnes. 'When Morgan', he wrote, 'examined me secretly touching the parties that conveyed the letters I was forced to name two whereof Barnes was one, and for that purpose I dealt with Barnes, never thinking, as Christ Jesus save me, but to make him a colour for Emilio [otherwise known as Barnaby] and his writing once or twice would cause all blame to be removed from myself when things should be opened, which I knew must needs be shortly, and so in truth it is fallen forth, and otherwise it had been impossible to have continued, but as God is my witness, I thought to have withdrawn him after that Morgan fully perceived that the convoy was sure.'

It requires some twisting to wring anything else out of this passage than a feeble and incoherent excuse on Gifford's part for drawing Barnes into the secret correspondence without Walsingham's knowledge or approval.

Taking Paulet's testimony and augmenting it with Gifford's, there appears to be very little doubt that Barnes was not Walsingham's agent in the convoy of letters to and from Mary Stuart, and that the part he played in that convoy was played without Walsingham's knowledge. It remains to be shown how the mistake in regard to him has arisen. Probably the root of the difficulty lies in the identification of Barnes with a man to whom Curle wrote many letters, called Barnaby (cf. Morris, pp. 376 seq.). This man Barnaby, no doubt, was deeply engaged in the secret correspondence. It is clear from Curle's letter to him of the

24th of June that he was the very man who had charge of Mary's first letter to Babington and from his letter to Curle of the 10/20 July that it was he who conveyed Babington's fatal letter to Mary. But from the same correspondence it is evident that Barnaby and Barnes were two different persons. Barnes, for instance, wrote to Mary on the 10th of June offering his services. He used Gilbert Gifford's cipher and did not sign his name (Morris, p. 376). Curle referred to this letter in writing to Barnaby on the 19/29 June. 'On Monday last this bearer [the brewer] brought hither a letter written to her Majesty in his [Gilbert Gifford's] alphabet without any name or sign who he may be that wrote it, except only that he asserted his kinsman imparted this way to him. The inclosed is for him desiring to know his name.' Curle enclosed a letter for the unknown fellow, who was of course none other than Barnes. Now if Barnes and Barnaby had been the same man, Curle's letter would have been pointless. More than that, Barnes's letter to Mary offering his services would likewise have been pointless, because it is evident that Curle and Barnaby had been corresponding together since the last of April at least (cf. C. to Barnaby, 19/29 June, Morris, p. 376). Furthermore, witness Curle's letter to Barnaby of the 12/22 July already quoted to the effect that the Scottish Queen meant not to employ 'the second messenger', nor any other than 'yourself, your brother and your cousin Gilbert'. Curle here distinguished clearly between Barnaby and the 'second messenger' (Barnes).

Regarding Barnaby, Lingard (*History of England*, vi. 201) identified him with Thomas Throgmorton, citing in support of his view Châteauneuf's account of the whole plot (Labanoff, vi. 284–6). Châteauneuf, however, does not give sufficient ground for Lingard's position. It ought to be said, however, that a brother of Thomas Throgmorton is mentioned as being in Walsingham's service in November 1587 (*Cal. Spanish*, 1587–1603, p. 163).

There can be no doubt that Barnaby and Emilio were the same man. Curle wrote to Barnaby under the name Emilio, 28 July/7 August 1586 (Morris, 243). This will explain Gifford's letter (cited above) when he wrote to say that he had used Barnes as a 'colour for Emilio'.

Possibly Barnaby should be identified with an Irishman named Barnaby Macgeogan who was acting as spy for Wotton in Scotland in 1586 and who apparently won his pardon for some heinous crime or other by undertaking hazardous enterprises for Walsingham (*Cal. Scottish*, 1585–6, pp. 35, 58, 79, 87, 90, 252). Father Pollen (*op. cit.*, pp. 1, 2) maintains that Barnaby was none other than Thomas Phelippes himself. The suggestion is a plausible one, though Father Pollen cannot be said to have proved his point.

There can be no doubt that Gilbert Gifford was directly responsible for Barnes's correspondence with the Scottish Queen. Barnes said as much himself in his letter to Mary. He confirmed this in a confession he made in the Tower a year later. Furthermore, Gilbert Gifford himself admitted it in his letter of apology to Phelippes. Now what object Gifford had in bringing in a 'second messenger' without Walsingham's consent or knowledge is a question to which Gifford himself supplies the only answer. He did it, he said, in order to 'colour Emilio's dealings'. This may be true, it is just as likely to be false. A great many things about this man Gilbert Gifford remain unexplained.

At all events, Barnes had to pay the price of it. He was captured and imprisoned in the Tower and only purchased his release by agreeing to play the spy upon his old friends (Barnes to Walsingham, 17 March 1586/7, Morris, p. 379). There is no reason to assume that his imprisonment was a mere mockery or that his confession to Walsingham was a mere blind. It seems to have been at Gifford's own suggestion that Barnes was brought to enter Walsingham's secret service. 'If you handle the matter cunningly,' Gifford wrote to Phelippes, 'Barnes may be the man to set up the convoy again for Paget' (Morris, p. 380). This was precisely what Barnes undertook to do, and in 1588 and 1589 we find him playing the same double game with the Catholics abroad that Nicholas Berden had played in 1586 and 1587.

XIII

THE BEGINNING OF WAR, 1584-6

WITH a view to clarifying somewhat a very confused period in Elizabethan history it has seemed desirable in the chapters immediately preceding to depart from the strict chronological order in following the course of Walsingham's public career. For that reason the story of Scotland down to the conclusion of the League of 1585 has been singled out for separate treatment, and the plots and counterplots which culminated in the Babington Conspiracy and the execution of Mary Queen of Scots have been unravelled from the tangled skein of domestic and foreign affairs with which they were in fact almost inextricably entangled. The effect of this method of treatment has been, no doubt, to make the problems and difficulties which faced Walsingham appear somewhat simpler than indeed they were, but some such distortion appears to be preferable to the chaos which would inevitably emerge from any attempt to carry forward together the multitude of different affairs in which he was from day to day engaged. With Scotland, Ireland, France, and the Low Countries all at once demanding attention, with foreign plots to be unravelled and incipient domestic rebellion to be checked, with a difficult mistress to be managed and intriguing colleagues to be circumvented, to say nothing of a thousand and one lesser affairs which distracted him, it is difficult enough to conceive how the man kept his feet in the thickets without attempting step by step to follow him.

It has been pointed out more than once that Walsingham's main effort throughout his official life was directed to foreign affairs. Broadly speaking, he hardly interested himself in domestic problems except when, as in the case of the English Catholics, the domestic problem was intimately related to the foreign one. An effort has been made in earlier chapters to trace his connexion with foreign affairs down to about the end of the year 1584. It will now be appropriate to follow that same thread during the remaining five years of his life.

Sir John Seeley in his notable essay on the *Growth of British Policy* has pointed to the year 1585 as the turning-point of the reign of Queen Elizabeth. In that year, after nearly a generation of peace, she finally unsheathed her sword. Among the important reasons which prompted her to this momentous step, not the least of them was the insistent urging of her principal secretary. Walsingham had held from the first that the great issue of his time was the issue between Roman Catholicism and Protestantism. He had maintained that upon this fundamental issue no real compromise was possible. He had singled out Philip II of Spain as the great protagonist of the old faith and had tried his best to make of his reluctant mistress the protagonist of the new. He always believed that bloody war between them was inevitable and his whole effort had been directed to bringing this war to pass under conditions most favourable to England. For fifteen years Elizabeth, supported in the main by Burghley, had resisted his importunities, but in 1585 the die was cast; not consciously to be sure, but inevitably nevertheless. Elizabeth herself would have been the last to admit that the dispatch of English troops under Leicester to the Low Countries in 1585 constituted a definite and final break with her old policy of keeping the peace at all costs. But nevertheless it proved in the end to be so, and it marked the triumph of all that Walsingham had striven for, though he was to find it about as hard to keep Elizabeth at war when she had begun as it had been to induce her to begin.

The immediate occasion of this change of policy, as has been pointed out in a previous chapter, was the murder of the Prince of Orange in July 1584. It would be hard to gather from Elizabeth's relations with Orange during his lifetime that she regarded him as such an important factor in the determination of her foreign policy. As a matter of fact, during the six years preceding his death, she had had surprisingly little to do with him directly. It is of course true that she had interested herself in the cause of which he was the acknowledged leader, but she had expressed that interest through the Duke of Alençon and had contributed what support she had to give through him. It is not easy to discover just what she had expected Alençon to accomplish in the Low Countries. She certainly did not want him to annex them to France. In view of his proximity to the French crown she hardly wanted him to establish his own supremacy over them. In part, no doubt, she supported him there in order to divert him from his rather embarrassing suit for her hand. It appears likely that she hoped he might reveal enough strength to keep the rebellion in the Low Countries alive and that his presence there might serve to stir up strife between France and Spain. At any rate his death in June 1584 had effectually eliminated him as a factor in her calculations. Orange alone had remained, and so long as he remained it still seemed to Elizabeth possible that the rebels might hold their own. For Orange, although he was an indifferent soldier and no match for the Prince of Parma in the field, was a consummate statesman and diplomatist. He was the one leader whom the Dutch were prepared to follow and he was perhaps the only man alive who knew how to operate the complicated machinery of their government and to realize what strength there was in their loose and unstable union. To his contemporaries he appeared in fact to be the very keystone of the Dutch revolt, and they confidently expected its immediate collapse with his death. Elizabeth shared their views and was considerably alarmed by the prospect, since for her it meant that Philip II of Spain, whose hostile purposes towards her were sufficiently apparent, would have a large army at his disposal within short range of her and good ports for his armadas at her very gates.

A very good idea of her state of mind at this juncture may be gathered from the following memorandum of matters to be presented for discussion to the Privy Council drawn up by Walsingham, doubtless at her command, probably not long after the news of Orange's death reached England.

' *Matters to be resolved in Council.*

Whether Holland and Zealand, the Prince of Orange being now taken away, can with any possibility hold out unless they be protected by some potent prince.

Whether it be likely that the King of Spain, being possessed of these countries, will attempt somewhat against her Majesty.

Whether he shall not be provoked thereunto by Scotland and the ill-affected in this realm.

What means he shall have to put her Majesty to peril in case he shall attempt it, being by them provoked thereto.

Whether therefore it be not fit for the prevention of the same to seek to keep him from the possession of the said Countries.

If it be thought fit then to consider what course is to be held for the prevention of the same.

Whether it be not fit that the French King should be moved to concur in the action and if it be fit in that sort he shall be moved to concur therein.

If the French King shall not be disposed to concur therein whether it be fit to her Majesty to proceed therein alone and if it be in what sort.

Whether if her Majesty enter into the matter it will not draw on a war.

What means her Majesty shall have to maintain and continue the war.

What charges *by estimate*, the said war will amount unto.

What charges the protection of the said Countries will amount unto.

By what means it is like the King of Spain, if the war shall fall out, will attempt to annoy her Majesty, and how the same may be prevented.

What way there may be devised to annoy the King of Spain.

How far forth the traffic shall be impeached if any war shall fall out with Spain.

What commodities has this country need of, which are of necessity to be furnished out of Spain.

Whether the King of Navarre may not be set a work to attempt somewhat for the recovery of the Kingdom of Navarre.

What things are to be required at the French King's hands in case there should fall out war between Spain and this Crown and whether it be likely he will assent thereunto.

If it be not meet for her Majesty to take the protection of the said Countries but to suffer them to come into the hands of the King of Spain, then what course is to be taken to withstand his attempts.

What ways it is likely he will attempt anything against her Majesty.

If he be possessed of the Low Countries and stand ill affected towards her Majesty what way there may be devised for the vent of the commodities of the realm.

Whether it be not likely that he will impeach our trade with Germany as well by sea as by procuring an inhibition in Germany for the sale of English commodities.

Whether he will not seek to advance by all means the use of the Spanish wools and what prejudice may grow to this land thereby.' [1]

It is evident from this that Elizabeth hardly believed that the Dutch could maintain themselves against Philip II without outside assistance, and that she was weighing in her mind the alternatives of going to their assistance alone or of proposing joint intervention to the French. What answers the Privy Council as a whole made to the royal questions is not recorded, though Walsingham gives some inkling of them in a letter which he wrote to Sir Edward Stafford, English ambassador to Paris, on the 17th of July:

'Since the death of Orange divers consultations have been held here touching the course to be followed for the relief of the Low Countries. And finding upon thorough debating of the matter that according to man's judgement they should not be able to withstand the potency of the King of Spain, it hath grown to half a resolution that the peril would be so great in case Spain should possess the said countries, as whether France concurs in the action or not, yet doth it behoove her Majesty to enter into some course for their defence.' [2]

Acting upon this half a resolution Elizabeth dispatched almost simultaneously envoys to the Low Countries and to France. John Somers was sent to the Dutch on the 9th of July with orders to inquire what course they meant to pursue in consequence of the Prince's death. He was to make to them general offers of assistance and to 'feel their minds' as to what support they would demand from her if she consented to take them under her protection, how much they would themselves contribute to the wars, and what towns they would surrender to her for her security. At the same time he was to discover if he could how far they had proceeded in treating with the French.[3] All this was absolutely non-committal, though not without promise. Sir Philip Sidney was sent to France.

'I suppose', Walsingham wrote Stafford on the 6th of July, 'he [Sidney] will have direction to discover whether the King

[1] S. P. Domestic, clxxi, no. 80; passages in italics are in Walsingham's own hand. [2] S. P. France, xii, f. 91 (in *Cal. Foreign*, 1583-4, p. 622).
[3] *Cal. Foreign*, 1583-4, p. 598.

is now disposed to enter into some good course for the bridling of the King of Spain's greatness, which it doth so much import both her Majesty and him to agree presently on as I do not see how they can any longer defer the same without manifest danger and peril to grow thereby, first to themselves and next to the whole state of Christendom. You shall therefore do well in my opinion to prepare their minds aforehand, not only to hearken willingly to any motion that her Majesty may make therein, but also, and rather if it might be, to show themselves so forward therein as to make the motion to her themselves and to seek to stir her up to join with them in this action ; which, if it might be brought to pass, I do not doubt but that her Majesty would, for her part, concur in the action with them to their reasonable satisfaction, for upon the news of this late accident of the Prince's death, I find her very resolutely disposed to take that way of counsel, in seeking to stop the course of the greatness of Spain, that her own safety and the necessity of the time doth require.' [1]

It is evident from a letter which Walsingham wrote to his friend William Davison that he was heartily in sympathy with this policy of joint intervention with France.

'Knowing that it will stand you greatly in stead to understand what hath lately ensued in the Low Countries since the late mischievous act done upon the person of the Prince of Orange, I have thought good to send you these enclosed papers . . . by the which you shall see, as we hear also by the report of all that came from thence, that the people of the country have hitherto showed themselves but little amazed with the accident. Rather the wickedness of the deed hath hardened their stomachs to hold out as long as they shall have any means of defence. And if those princes, their neighbours, whom the consequence of the fact doth nearly touch, both in respect of the present and future, would roundly join together to yield them any reasonable assistance, it might be that God would now in their extremity make this accident an occasion to work their relief and safety. Otherwise there is no appearance, in any worldly possibility, but that, being left to themselves, they shall be forced, ere Christmas next, to become Spanish. . . . The best hope we can have is that our good God in the midst of their weakness will show his own strength, to the end he may have the whole glory.' [2]

Walsingham's one thought for the moment was to save the Dutch from imminent peril, and he saw in joint action by

[1] S. P. France, xii, f. 57 (in *Cal. Foreign*, 1583–4, p. 594). Sidney's instructions are in *Cal. Foreign*, 1583–4, p. 601.

[2] S. P. Holland and Flanders, xxii, 42 (in *Cal. Foreign*, 1583–4, p. 607)

France and England the most certain means to that end. But Elizabeth was troubled by many things. She saw danger for herself one way if the Spaniards triumphed in the Low Countries; she saw it another way if Spanish rule was simply replaced by French rule there. It is quite apparent that her willingness to join with the French proceeded in part from the fear that if they did not join with her they would act alone. And she had good grounds for that fear. During the winter and spring of 1584 Orange had been working his hardest to induce the different provinces to come to terms with the Duke of Alençon and to offer him once more the sovereignty of the Low Countries. With much labour and sorrow the Prince had eventually succeeded, and all conditions had virtually been agreed upon when Alençon died. For the moment his death dealt a serious blow to the Prince's plans. But the Estates General, having made up their minds to take the French course, determined to follow it further. They dispatched two deputies to join their agent in Paris with instructions to offer to the French King himself the same measure of sovereignty which they had designed for his brother.

Elizabeth was of course aware that these negotiations were afoot, though she did not know exactly how far they had progressed. Stafford, her ambassador at Paris, although he reported the arrival of the Dutch deputies in France early in July, could not enlighten her as to their instructions.[1] She was therefore very much relieved to learn late in July that though the Dutch had made their offer, the French King had definitely refused it. This refusal for the moment relieved her fears of French ambition and predisposed her to consider even more favourably the project of joint action with France. When the French ambassador proposed some such course late in July she expressed amazement that he had not spoken of it sooner. She was quite prepared, she told him, to do her part, and she even offered to send her navy to the seas to intercept the Spanish plate fleets.[2]

It is evident nevertheless that while both the English and the

[1] Murdin, *Burghley Papers*, pp. 411–12.

[2] Cf. Walsingham to Davison, 29 July 1584, in S. P. Scotland, xxxv, no. 62; *Cal. Foreign*, 1583–4, p. 647; Teulet, *Relations diplomatiques de la France et l'Espagne avec l'Écosse*, iii. 304.

French were willing to endorse a policy of joint intervention in behalf of the Dutch, each of them was working underhand in the Low Countries to counteract the influence of the other. Joachim Ortell, who had been in England during the early summer, returned to Holland in August with instructions from Walsingham himself to urge an English alliance on his masters.[1] Des Pruneaux, a French agent in the Low Countries, was there at the same time, pointing out that the refusal of the French King to accept their offers of sovereignty was not due to his lack of desire to help them, but simply to the fact that they had not made their offers large enough. He therefore urged them to renew their offer with fewer restricting conditions.[2] So it was that for some months the Estates General of the rebellious provinces were pulled this way and that between an English and a French faction. Paul Buys, Advocate of Holland, was the most conspicuous figure in the party which favoured an English alliance. But the preponderance of strength lay with the French group, which included both John of Barneveldt and St. Aldegonde, perhaps the two most influential men in the councils of the Dutch.[3] In some measure the provinces themselves divided on the point. Holland, Zeeland, Utrecht, and Friesland seem on the whole to have preferred the English alliance, while the provinces of the south-west favoured the French. Since each province claimed practically sovereign rights this might have led to a break in their union. As a matter of fact, the four states of Holland, Zeeland, Utrecht, and Friesland dispatched Ortell and de Grise to England late in August with a practical offer of sovereignty. The envoys declared that they did not doubt that if her Majesty accepted the offer, the other provinces also would be agreeable, but they pressed the Queen for a speedy answer, since Brabant, Flanders, and Mechlin were very urgently pressing the acceptance of the French King as sovereign.[4]

Walsingham for his part felt that whatever was to be done should be done quickly. 'The state of things in the Low Countries', he wrote to Sadler on the 16th of September, 'groweth to very hard terms, Ghent and Vilvorde being already yielded

[1] S. P. Holland and Flanders, xxii, 57.
[2] Motley, *United Netherlands* (ed. 1870), i, pp. 58–60.
[3] Ibid., pp. 88 ff.; Meteren (French trans., 1670), i, p. 245.
[4] Clifford, *Sadler Papers*, ii. 395; *Cal. Foreign*, 1584–5, p. 40.

into the enemies hands. And it is likely that Brussels and Mechlin will not long hold out, for that they do already begin to enter into parley. So if we do daily consider how our foreign helps begin to wear away and our inward corruption doth daily increase, we shall then see just cause to fear the continuance of our happy peace that we have so long enjoyed.' [1]

Elizabeth, however, although she had encouraged the Dutch to believe that she would come to their assistance, when the offer of sovereignty was actually laid before her drew back. 'It is thought', Walsingham wrote to Sadler, 'to be a matter of greater charge than her means can well reach unto. Whereupon it is likely that they will run the course of France (being resolved by no means to agree with Spain) which, of what dangerous consequence it may be for this state, I leave to yourself to judge.' [2]

For all that, the most that Elizabeth would consent to do was to allow Colonel Morgan, at the request of the Estates of Brabant, to levy some 1,500 troops and to solicit contributions from the churches.[3] The result was that the French party won the day in the Netherlands, and in September the Estates General decided to make a larger offer of sovereignty to the French King.[4]

Although Elizabeth had herself largely to thank for this issue of the matter, the news of it was naturally not pleasing to her. While matters still hung in the balance in the Low Countries, she had been instructing Stafford, her ambassador at Paris, to urge upon the French King the desirability of joint intervention. But if Henry III was indeed to have the full sovereignty of the Low Countries, joint intervention would mean nothing more than English co-operation in furthering French ambitions. She accordingly ordered Stafford to press the matter no further. A few days later, however, she had more encouraging news from overseas. It now appeared that the plan to offer the absolute sovereignty was 'not so forward as it was at first thought to be', that several of the provincial Estates in fact still opposed it.

[1] Clifford, *Sadler Papers*, ii. 401.
[2] Ibid., ii. 395.
[3] *Cal. Foreign*, 1583–4, p. 625; cf. also Mauvissière to Catherine de Médicis, 18/28 Aug. 1584, in Teulet, *op. cit.* iii. 304. Mauvissière says that 2,000 troops went. He also says that Elizabeth advanced £20,000 for their pay, to be repaid as soon as the promised contributions from the churches were collected, but this lacks confirmation and seems inherently improbable.
[4] Motley, *op. cit.* i. 72–3.

If that were so, she might, by pledging the French King quickly to joint intervention, prevent him from accepting the sovereignty on his sole behalf. She accordingly directed Stafford to secure the King's pledge if he could.

But her letter had scarcely got started towards Paris before fresh news from the Low Countries convinced her that the offer of sovereignty was certain to be made. She sent a second courier post-haste after the first, revoking her last dispatch and ordering Stafford to protest against the King's 'impatronizing' himself in the Low Countries. Yet, before the week was out, she had another change of heart. 'She is so hardy persuaded', Walsingham wrote to Stafford on the 26th of October, 'of the King of Spain's good will toward her, as she preferreth the peril that may grow unto her by his recovery of the possession of these countries, before any inconvenience that may fall out by the interest that France may get in the said countries.'[1]

Under the circumstances the best thing she could think of doing was to call her Privy Councillors together and lay the whole question before them, and this she did early in October. They met and discussed the matter at length. Unfortunately there is no record of their deliberations, but it is not difficult to reconstruct the position which the principal members took. Leicester and his partisans, including Mildmay and Hatton and Walsingham, no doubt argued vigorously in favour of a policy of direct and immediate intervention without waiting on the French.[2] Walsingham certainly preferred that course. 'For mine own particular opinion in this cause of the Low Countries,' he wrote to Stafford late in October, 'I think the French King (as he hath reason so to do) will have no dealing with them unless he may have the absolute sovereignty over them, which they of that country will in no case assent unto, but will rather grow to some composition with Spain. I would the king therefore could be content (without entering into an open war against Spain) to assist his mother in the prosecution of Don Antonio's title and the King of Navarre in the recovery of that part of his kingdom which is now possessed by Spain; which thing, if it could be brought to pass, with a general restraint that no victuals be

[1] *Cal. Foreign*, 1584-5, pp. 49, 54, 86, 119.
[2] Ibid., p. 96, contains Mildmay's opinion.

carried into the Low Countries out of that realm, might greatly comfort the Estates and provoke her Majesty to do somewhat for their relief, if she might be assured that France in some sort, though underhand, would join with her in the action.' [1]

The attitude of Burghley and the more conservative element in the Council is harder to gauge. There is good reason to believe that heretofore Burghley's influence had been exerted pretty steadily in favour of keeping the peace with Spain. Mendoza, while he was Spanish ambassador in England, had regarded him as one of the best friends of his master in the Privy Council.[2] It is to be presumed that he was not very enthusiastic for a vigorous, aggressive policy in behalf of the Dutch at this juncture. His memoranda on the subject, which he evidently drew up in connexion with the deliberations of Council, leave his position in considerable doubt and lay him open to the suspicion that he was badly infected by the same germ of indecision that possessed his mistress. On the one hand, he realized clearly enough the dangers to be feared from Spain; on the other hand, he appreciated the enormous expense involved in open war, the unreliability of the Dutch, the menace to commerce, the uncertainty of the outcome. He mustered arguments to prove that Elizabeth was bound by God's law to defend herself against Philip, and on the basis of them he maintained that it would be better for her to grapple with the Spaniard in the Netherlands than to await his descent on her own coasts. But he was equally apt with other arguments against such a course and developed from them an alternate policy in pursuit of which his mistress was to strengthen her position at home, to raise money to reinforce her navy, to levy troops, to enlist allies, and to abide her enemy at the gates, strong in the consciousness that '*Si Deus nobiscum quis contra nos*'.[3] At all events it is clear that if he did not vigorously

[1] S. P. France, xii, f. 281.

[2] *Cal. Spanish*, 1568–79, pp. 572, 586–7. In this connexion it is worth noting that when the Babington Plot was afoot and it was proposed to murder not only Elizabeth but also Burghley, Walsingham, Hunsdon, Knollys, and Beale as well, Philip II observed: 'It does not matter so much about Cecil although he is a great heretic, but he is very old and it was he who advised the understandings with the Prince of Parma and he has done no harm. It would be advisable to do as he [the conspirator] says with the others', *Cal. Spanish*, 1580–6, p. 607 n.

[3] S. P. Domestic, clxxiii, no. 65; *Cal. Salisbury MSS.* iii. 67–70.

support Walsingham's bellicose policy he did not vigorously oppose it. He himself has left on record the outcome of these deliberations. 'In the end, and upon a comparison made betwixt the perils on the one part and the difficulties of the other, it was concluded to advise her Majesty rather to seek the avoiding and directing of the great perils than, in respect of any difficulties, to suffer the King of Spain to grow to the full height of his designs and conquests, whereby the perils were to follow so evident as, if presently he were not, by succouring the Hollanders and their party impeached, the Queen's Majesty should not hereafter be any wise able to withstand the same.'[1] In a word, the Council advised Elizabeth to assist the Dutch against the Spaniards, though it is to be hoped that they put the matter in rather plainer English than the Lord Treasurer could contrive. The Council then went on to outline the course of policy in detail. A 'wise person' was to be sent to Holland to discover whether France was committed to their assistance, and if not to offer the Queen's aid. This wise person was also to discover what aid the provinces would require, what their resources were, and whether they would be willing to place Flushing, Briel, and Middelburg in the Queen's hands as security for her expenses. Meantime Gebhard Truchsess, the converted Archbishop of Cologne, who was carrying on a losing fight for the possession of his see against a Hapsburg candidate, was to be assisted with money. Duke Casimir was to be solicited to make a diversion in Gelderland. Peace was to be made with Scotland. The King of France was to be reminded that the Treaty of Blois obliged him to assist, upon the rather specious grounds that Spain had actually invaded Ireland and meant to invade England. The King of Navarre and Don Antonio of Portugal were to be launched against Spain itself. Parliament was to be summoned to grant money and to make further provision for the Queen's safety. 'The conclusion of the whole', said Burghley, 'was this. Although her Majesty should thereby enter into a war presently, yet were she better to do it now, while she may make the same out of her realm, having the help of the people of Holland and before the King of Spain shall have consummated his conquests in these countries, whereby he shall be so provoked with pride, solicited

[1] S. P. Holland and Flanders, xxiii, no. 28.

by the Pope and tempted by the Queen's own subjects, and shall be so strong by sea and so free from all other actions and quarrels, yea, shall be so formidable to all the rest of Christendom, as that her Majesty shall no wise be able with her own power, nor with the aid of any other, neither by sea nor land, to withstand his attempts, but shall be forced to give place to his insatiable malice, which is most terrible to be thought of, but most miserable to suffer.'[1]

This decision was substantially in accordance with Walsingham's own views. It conveys the impression, which is borne out by other evidence, that he and Leicester pretty well dominated the Privy Council at this juncture. Indeed, they not only succeeded in imposing their views upon their colleagues, but, what was much more remarkable, they even induced the Queen herself to act upon the Council's advice. She was still, it is true, disposed to pin more faith to the possibility of joint intervention with France than seemed wise,[2] but at least she agreed to send a ' wise person ' to the Dutch, with instructions which accorded in the main with the advice which her Privy Councillors had given her.[3]

The man chosen for the mission was William Davison, and probably no man in England was better equipped for the task than he. On several occasions in the past he had represented the Queen's interests with the rebels in the Low Countries. He was unusually well versed in the intricacies of their government and fully in sympathy with their cause. In religion he was a zealous Puritan and, though discreet in committing himself to any party in the Privy Council, he was in complete agreement with Walsingham's own views. A little later a Spanish agent in London referred to him as Walsingham's creature.[4]

Davison left for Holland in mid-November. He had been instructed to discover first of all what progress the Dutch had made in treating with France and to intimate to them that if

[1] S. P. Holland and Flanders, xxiii, no. 28, quoted by Motley, *op. cit.* i. 96.

[2] Mauvissière, the French ambassador, thought that the Queen favoured French intervention in the Low Countries: 'a ce que j'en puys voir et apprendre des propos que j'ay euz avec ses conseillers, mesme les sieurs grand-trésorier, contes de Lestre et de Walsingham, la dicte royne ne sera pas marye que vous entrepreniez la protection des dits pays, pourveu elle se puisse, pour le présent et l'avenir, asseurer de votre protection et amytié.' Letter of 16/26 Oct. 1584, cited by Hubault, *Ambassade de Castelnau*, p. 123.

[3] *Cal. Foreign*, 1584-5, p. 149.

[4] *Cal. Spanish*, 1580-6, p. 656.

they had not already come to terms they might hope for assistance from her. Otherwise he was to protest that she would take no action in their behalf except at the invitation of the French King. It was clearly intended that he should prevent the offer of sovereignty to France if he could, but without definitely opposing it on the one hand, or definitely committing Elizabeth on the other. Davison got to work on the matter at once and his first impressions were distinctly encouraging. Although he learned that the deputies to France had already received their dispatch, he discovered that there was a good deal of sentiment, in Holland particularly, opposed to the French 'course'. Paul Buys told him that much might yet be done underhand 'to thwart the French designs'. Davison was rather struck by the strength and resources of the Dutch and declared that what they needed most was good government and some supreme authority over them all to unite their efforts.[1]

He was evidently anxious to convince the Queen that if she would take the cause resolutely in hand and place herself at the head of the rebels their chances of success were distinctly good. His report had the effect, very probably designed, of strengthening Walsingham's arguments to the same end. Opportune dispatches from France conveyed the impression that the French King was not disposed to accept the Dutch offers of sovereignty. These also Walsingham used to advantage. Elizabeth's reaction was on the whole encouraging. She refused audience to an envoy from Parma late in December [2] and she consented to a tentative initial investment of £6,000 for the advancement of the cause. It is striking, however, to observe that this money was not designed for the Dutch themselves, but for Truchsess, the elector of Cologne.[3] Walsingham was absent from the Court

[1] *Cal. Foreign*, 1584–5, p. 176.

[2] The purpose of this embassy is not revealed. Parma wrote to Walsingham on 19/29 October that he was sending an envoy on matters of importance (S. P. Holland and Flanders, xxiii, no. 38). Burghley wrote to Walsingham on 4 January 1584/5: 'Her Majesty would gladly know what the Prince of Parma hath to say and is now sending you his [Parma's envoy] safe conduct. She would have you by some means urge him thereto. She would also have it declared that she refuseth to hear him, not only because Don Bernardino [de Mendoza] hath done evil offices, but also because the King of Spain refuseth to admit the ambassador who went to declare to the King Don Bernardino's evil service,' S. P. Mary, Queen of Scots, xv, no. 5.

[3] *Cal. Foreign*, 1584–5, p. 208.

'for the cure of my old disease' when this latter step was decided upon. He attributed it to Burghley's influence. In his own view it was a bad investment and gave no promise of results. He advised Davison to be wary about paying the money over.[1] To Elizabeth it had, however, this great advantage that it did not commit her to a policy hostile to Spain against whom Truchsess of course was not directly engaged. Emanating from Burghley as it did it strengthens the impression that he was still seeking to avoid the main issue. But at any rate it revealed the fact that the Queen's grip upon her purse-strings was loosening a little. So far it was good.

It was singularly unfortunate that Walsingham's illness kept him away from the Queen just at the time when every effort was necessary to hold her to a resolute course. In his absence Burghley sent further instructions to Davison on the 14th of January. 'Her Majesty thinks', Burghley wrote, 'that no policy is more allowable than that the countries might be succoured, protected and defended jointly by the French King and her Majesty proportionately for her part according to the difference of their greatness. And so, by succouring them against the Spanish King, they might be able to win time, wherein many accidents may ensue, and to recover such a peace as might bring surety with it. Or else in time (which were the best of all the rest) to recover the States of the contrary side, being called the Malcontents, that they might relinquish the government of the Spaniards and strangers and like good patriots to reunite themselves altogether again for the maintenance of the liberties of the country and to yield obedience to the King of Spain.' Burghley went on to direct Davison, 'to devise how, by holding fast to their restrictions, the French may be stayed from acquiring to them the absolute dominion of the countries, and to make some assay how the principal heads of the Malcontents might be recovered'. Davison might also make some vague and general promises of English assistance. And he was to do all this in secret, so that the French would not be aware of it. In brief, he was to prevent the Dutch from accepting independent aid from France if he could, but was not authorized to offer them any more alluring alternative than a vague Elizabethan promise.

[1] *Cal. Foreign*, 1584–5, p. 208.

He was, in fact, to mark time while Parma thundered at the gates of Antwerp. It may be urged that Burghley did little more than repeat the original instructions with which Davison had gone to the Low Countries, but the time had come when something more needed to be done and done quickly. Elizabeth had sent him to tell the Dutch that she would either help them herself or stand aside and let the French help them. Davison had reported that they were not committed to the French and were quite ready to welcome her help. And now when the obvious next step was to dispatch troops or money, or both, Burghley dished out counsels, stale promises, and caveats.[1]

Walsingham had sight of this dispatch before it was sent and made a comment on it in a letter to Davison which went in the same packet:

'I was made by my Lord Treasurer acquainted with this dispatch before the sealing up of the letter. Sorry I am to see the course that is taken in this weighty cause, for we will neither help the poor distressed countries ourselves, nor yet suffer others to do it. I am not ignorant that in time to come the annexing of those countries to the crown of France may prove prejudicial to England, but if France refuse to deal with them and the rather for that we shall minister some cause of impediment by a kind of dealing under hand, then shall they be forced to return into the hands of Spain, which is like to breed such a present peril towards her Majesty's self as never a wise man that seeth it and loveth her but lamenteth it from the bottom of his heart. I could wish that the French King were carried with that honourable mind into the defence of these countries that Her Majesty is, but France hath not been used to do things for God's sake, neither do they mean to use either our advice or assistance in the making of the bargain. Besides, as far as I can learn by letters out of France, the King there is not so forward in the matter but the least crossing in the world (especially from hence) may draw him to abandon the action. For they still hold a jealous conceit that when Spain and they are together by the ears, we will seek underhand to work our own peace, and therefore I conclude that her Majesty (with reverence be it spoken) is ill advised to direct you in a course that is like to work so great peril. I know you will do your best endeavour to keep all things upright and yet it is hard, the disease being now come to this state, or as the physicians term it, crisis, to carry yourself in such sort but that it will, I fear, breed a dangerous alteration in the

[1] S. P. Holland, i, no. 8.

cause. For your doings, no doubt of it, are observed by the French faction and therefore you cannot proceed so closely but it will be espied. Howsoever it be, seeing direction groweth from hence, we cannot but blame ourselves if the effects thereof do not fall out to our liking.' [1]

Walsingham also wrote at length to Burghley on the same subject:

'This morning about seven of the clock I received your Lordship's letters, together with one enclosed to be sent to Mr. Davison, upon the perusal whereof as also of the other directed to Mr. Stafford, which I returned yesternight unto your Lordship, I find that her Majesty is loathe that the French King should have any absolute interest in the Low Countries not presently possessed by the Spaniard, in respect of some future peril that might grow thereby to this Crown—a matter worthy of good consideration were it not that time hath wrought a necessity of speedy resolution, considering the perilous state that those countries do presently stand in. For now it groweth to be a question whether it were more perilous to have those countries in the hands of the French or of the Spaniard, which can no other way be prevented but by her Majesty's taking into her hands the protection of the said countries, with a determination to be at the charges of two hundred thousand pounds by the year for two years space, a burden I suppose would be willingly borne by this realm rather than it should come into the hands either of the French or of the Spaniard. To think that the French King will enter into the action with that honourable and conscionable mind that her Majesty is carried withal, experience of their doings in times past showeth what is to be looked for in time to come. For if he had had any such honourable meaning, then had he ere this assented unto her Majesty's motion for the meeting of commissioners at Boulogne; but his delay used therein doth show manifestly that he either seeketh an absolute possession of those countries, or else doth entertain them with the vain hope to make the way easier for a Spanish conquest. Besides, it is to be considered that he is so coldly affected to embrace any cause that carrieth either honour or surety withal (as one given over to a careless security unfit for his calling), as the least impediment that may be ministered may easily stay him from embracing the present offer of the Low Countries, albeit the said offer were accompanied with as large conditions as he in reason could desire. And therefore I conclude (always referring myself to your Lordship's better judgement) that the direction presently given to both her Majesty's ministers

[1] S. P. Holland, i, no. 10.

in France and the Low Countries, tending to impeach that the French King shall have no full footing in those countries, can be but most perilous unto her Majesty unless she shall resolve to take the protection of them herself, which would be most profitable for the cause, the most surest course for herself, and the only and likeliest way to draw the Malcontents to revolt from the Spanish course, which would work more furtherance to the cause than a million of pounds. Thus your Lordship seeth how by the provocation of your letter I am moved to deliver my opinion more resolutely than wisely in this so weighty cause. And so I commit your Lordship to God. From my house, the eleventh of January 1584.'[1]

There can be little doubt from the tone of both these letters that Walsingham entirely disapproved of Burghley's management of the Dutch situation during his enforced absence from Court. He had remarked some months before the Lord Treasurer's fondness for by-courses and his lack of resolution, and he was clearly disposed to attribute the Queen's delays and tergiversations at this juncture to his prompting. In view of the fact that Burghley had joined with the Privy Council at large to advocate a vigorous, aggressive policy in the Low Countries Walsingham was naturally irritated at what looked like underhand opposition on Burghley's part to this course.[2] This irritation was fed further by rumours which reached Walsingham just at this time that Burghley was secretly opposing his petition to the Queen for a farm of the customs of certain English ports. Indeed the Secretary's antagonism to his colleague became so patent towards the end of January 1585 that the Lord Treasurer ventured to remonstrate with him about it in plain terms. Walsingham's reply is a pleasant tribute to his frankness and it reveals the fact that he had been on the very verge of an open declaration of hostilities.

'My very good Lord: Your honourable and plain manner of proceeding towards me giveth me just cause to hold the like course towards your Lordship.

'I cannot deny but as your Lordship hath had heretofore some reports made unto you that might work some doubtful conceipt

[1] S. P. Domestic, clxxvi, no. 5.

[2] Leicester complained a little later that Burghley held one view in Council and urged another upon the Queen privately. Strype, *Annals of the Reformation*, iii, pt. 2, p. 506.

of my good will towards you, so have there *the like been made unto me* that might have bred like conceipt. But when I saw some cause to suspect that the ground thereof grew of faction (that reigneth ordinarily in courts) and that the authors thereof sought by such indirect means to draw me to be a party with them, I gave no way unto them, as one that did greatly affect your Lordship's friendship and good opinion, whom in course of counsel I have always found to proceed most sincerely in the ordinary course of justice. But touching my late conceipt had of your *opposition* in my suit for the farming of the customs (a matter I found did greatly touch me in credit having waded so far therein as I had done) I must needs confess, I saw so many reasons (*confirmed so many ways*) to lead me so to think, as did not only induce me to believe that to be true, but did in a sort work in me a confirmation of the truth of former reports of your Lordship's mislike of me. And thereupon I did plainly resolve with myself that it was a more safe course for me to hold your Lordship rather as an enemy than as a friend; and yet did always determine (as a thing agreeable with justice and christian charity) before I did make any open show unto the world thereof, to have broken with your Lordship therein. Now whiles I was possessed with this discontentment, I confess I sought up such informations as heretofore (unsought for) had been given unto me that might anyway touch your Lordship, and meant (had I not received assurance from Sir Thos. Cecill of your Lordship's friendship towards me) to have proceeded by conference with the parties to have drawn some further light from them therein—a course of proceeding I have ever heretofore rejected, being more careful to discharge my own duty than curiously look into other men's charges.

'And touching the particular matter your Lordship maketh mention of in your letter, that a friend of mine should deal with an Exchequer man by my order for the search of some matter that might touch your Lordship, I do assure your Lordship I do not remember any such matter, and therefore do hold myself wronged therein by the informer.

'Thus my Lord have I plainly let your Lordship understand my grief and the cause thereof, assuring your Lordship that if it shall please you hereafter to make account of the good will of one so far separated in quality from you, you shall find no man by effects more ready to deserve your Lordship's friendship than myself. And so, resting in hope, thereof I commit your Lordship to the protection of the Almighty, most humbly taking my leave.' [1]

[1] S. P. Domestic, clxxvi, no. 19. The passages in italics are underlined in the original, possibly by Burghley.

The effect of this letter was to call forth a friendly reply from Burghley; and Walsingham, writing again, agreed to bury the hatchet.

'I most humbly thank your Lordship for your friendly accepting of my plain manner of writing, assuring your Lordship that you shall find at my hands all due and sincere performance of my promised good will towards your Lordship. And touching the producing of the reporters, if I might do it with the credit of an honest man, I would not fail to satisfy your Lordship therein. Besides it may reach to such persons as are not to be called in question. But this I will assure your Lordship that hereafter I will not fail to acquaint you with the reports before I give credit unto them. And so I most humbly take my leave.'[1]

Even so, both men must have realized that they differed too radically both in temper and in politics to make any cordial co-operation possible. Walsingham was young, in spirit if not in years, fiery and resolute; Burghley was old, cautious and indecisive. Walsingham was an ardent Protestant and eager to devote the resources of his country to the service of his faith. Burghley was fundamentally a *politique* and more disposed to exploit the resources of Protestantism in the service of his country. Walsingham was an idealist—Burghley a confirmed opportunist. There could be no sustained harmony between such opposites. They represented the fundamental discord of crabbed age and youth. Neither could hope to win the other to his point of view; neither perhaps was disposed to try. Their efforts were directed rather to the winning of the Queen. At that point their differences impinge upon the question of the Low Countries. For the better part of the year 1585 Burghley was striving steadily but covertly and indirectly to keep the Queen out of war with Spain, while Walsingham was striving just as steadily but much more frankly and much more vigorously to push the Queen into war. Walsingham had this advantage, that he was sure he was right and went straight ahead to his goal while Burghley was constantly hampered by doubts within himself which made his course vague and his progress in it uncertain. Walsingham, moreover, commanded the support of both Leicester and Hatton, the Queen's dearest favourites, and

[1] Ibid., no. 20.

of the council at large, and he held the reins of the whole diplomatic and secret service in his hands. Burghley, on the other hand, was far more influential with the Queen herself. Had the situation been a shade less critical, he would inevitably have won the day. As it was, he postponed the actual outbreak for a twelvemonth to come.

In January 1585, with Walsingham away taking physic, Burghley commanded the field. In his letter to Davison which had evoked Walsingham's spirited protest, he had intimated that the Queen was disposed to renew once more her approaches to France in the hope of inducing the French King to consent to a policy of joint intervention. With that in mind Elizabeth dispatched Lord Derby to Paris late in the month. The ostensible reason for Derby's mission was to convey the Order of the Garter to Henry III. Probably the main purpose of his going was to make a great show of friendship between France and England. He was instructed to discover if he could the attitude of the King towards the Dutch and to sound him upon the question of concurrent action.

While he was at Paris the deputies of the Estates General made their formal offer of sovereignty to the King and received his final answer. In Derby's presence he definitely refused their offer. The reason he gave them for his refusal was that he was faced with problems within his own kingdom which commanded his whole attention. Later, in private conference with Stafford and Derby, he declared that he dared not undertake a war with Spain without more certain assurance of Elizabeth's co-operation. He protested that he was willing still, as he always had been, to concur with her in assisting the Dutch.[1]

Elizabeth was ready enough to take him at his word. She did in fact dispatch William Waad to Paris in March to arrange for joint intervention.[2] But she realized that the Dutch cause was in too critical a state to attend upon long negotiations. Unless they were to perish some more immediate steps must be taken for their relief. Fortunately Walsingham was back again at Court to impress this view of the matter upon her. Already by the middle of February he was credibly informed that the French

[1] Cf. Walsingham to Davison, 7 March 1584/5, S. P. Holland, i, no. 56; Froude, xii. 93.

[2] *Cal. Foreign*, 1584–5, p. 338.

King would probably refuse the offers of the Dutch, and he induced the Queen to authorize Davison to intimate to them 'secretly as of himself' that she was prepared to come to their assistance if they would hand over certain towns to her for security.[1] Later, on the 7th of March, when the King's refusal was positively known in England, she bade Walsingham to urge Davison a little farther forward on the same road. 'Her Majesty', he wrote, 'hath willed me to dispatch this bearer, my servant, presently unto you with direction that you should do all the good offices and use the best persuasions you can to put them in good comfort that her Majesty will not abandon them . . . if she shall find a like disposition in them to do for themselves.'[2]

Edward Burnham, who carried this letter overseas, took further verbal instructions both to Davison in Holland and also to Gilpin, Walsingham's unofficial agent in Zeeland. In this wise they were both directed to declare the Queen's intention to take the Dutch under her protection upon condition that they would hand over to her the towns of Briel, Flushing, and Enkhuizen as security, to point out that she had greater need of security than had the French King because she was not to have the sovereignty of the country, and to insist that unless they made offer of these towns she would give no ear to them. Davison and Gilpin, however, were instructed to make this proposal 'as proceeding from themselves'. 'For that', Walsingham added, 'it is conceived here that if they might espy that her Majesty were moved to take them into protection in respect of the necessity of her own estate, it would move them to stand upon more harder terms and make their offers unto her Majesty the more base and thereby alienate her devotion from them.'[3]

Walsingham and Leicester both seem to have been considerably encouraged by the Queen's attitude at this juncture. The latter wrote to Davison on the 8th of March that he thought the Dutch had been very shabbily treated by the French. 'And yet', he added, 'I think if they will heartily and earnestly seek it, the Lord hath furnished them a far better defence. But you must

[1] S. P. Holland, i, no. 44, draft of a letter to Davison, corrected in Walsingham's hand, dated 18 February 1584/5. [2] Ibid. 56.

[3] Ibid. 61 (another copy in Harleian MSS. 285, f. 123).

so use the matter as they must earnestly seek their own good, though we shall be partakers thereof.' [1]

Walsingham and Leicester at this time were holding frequent conference with Ortell and his colleague de Grise, the Dutch agents in England, and encouraging them to believe that the Queen would prove friendly to their cause. Even Burghley assured Ortell that his mistress was quite ready to assume the protectorate as soon as it was offered with fitting guaranties. On the 12th of March Ortell and de Grise had an interview with Elizabeth herself, who assured them that if a deputation with full powers and reasonable conditions should be immediately sent to her, she would not delay and dally with them, as had been the case in France, but would dispatch them back again at the speediest and would make her good inclination manifest by deeds as well as words.' [2]

The effect of this interview Walsingham set forth in a letter to Davison written the day following:

'Sir: This gentleman M. de Grise repaireth presently thither to try if he can induce the States to send their deputies hither furnished with other manner of ample instructions than they had to treat with the French King, considering that her Majesty carryeth another manner of princely disposition towards them than the said King. And in the meanwhile, for that her Majesty doubteth lest in this hard estate of their affairs and the distrust they have conceived to be relieved from hence, they should through despair throw themselves into the course of Spain, her pleasure therefore is (though by Burnham I sent you direction to put them in comfort of relief only as of yourself) that you shall now as it were in her name, if you see cause sufficient to lead you thereto, assure some of the aptest instruments that you shall think meet to make choice of for that purpose, that her Majesty, rather than that they should perish, will be content to take them into her protection, so as she may find them for their part as willing to yield her such sufficient cautions and assurances as she may in reason demand. But if you do not see good cause to proceed thus far with them, then doth her Majesty think meet you should forbear the same.' [3]

These instructions reached Davison in the nick of time. A few days later the Dutch envoys returned from France. Their

[1] S. P. Holland, i, no. 59.

[2] Memoir of Ortell and de Grise, dated 14/24 March 1584/5, cited by Motley, i, pp. 289 ff.

[3] S. P. Holland, i, no. 69.

report of their failure left the Estates General no alternative but to appeal to England. They appointed a committee to wait upon Davison and inquire of him what his mistress would be willing to do for them. With Walsingham's letter in his hands he was, happily, in a position to offer them comfort in Elizabeth's own name.

She would help them if they would give her the towns demanded in security. Davison wrote to Walsingham on the 3rd of April that although he had not yet received their answer to this demand, he thought they would make no difficulties. He repeated what he had said formerly that their chief need was for a sovereign Prince to 'guide the stern, for touching their means otherwise, they are no doubt very great notwithstanding all the troubles they have passed, in which respect they do much rather wish her Majesty would embrace their cause as sovereign than as protectress '.[1]

Meanwhile in France events were taking a turn which precluded the possibility of assistance from that quarter. Ever since the death of the Duke of Alençon in June 1584, the question of the succession to the French crown had been becoming more and more serious. It was practically certain that the King would have no children to succeed him. In that case the succession passed by right to Henry de Bourbon, King of Navarre, a shrewd and vigorous gentleman, with most of the virtues and many of the vices of his breed, but a heretic. The King of France had made some effort to get him to change his faith and would no doubt have acknowledged him as heir if he had. But since Navarre refused, Henry III would not officially recognize him.[2] The Duke of Guise and the Ultra-Catholics, on the other hand, were determined to have no heretic on the throne. And at the end of the year 1584 at Joinville they formed a league with Philip II of Spain for the preservation of the Roman Catholic religion, the extirpation of heresy both in France and the Low Countries, and the exclusion of the heretic of Navarre from the throne of France. Philip agreed to pay 50,000 crowns a month in support of the league; the French princes agreed to restore to him Cambrai.

[1] S. P. Holland, i, no. 88 a.
[2] Lavisse, *Hist. de France*, vi, pt. 1, pp. 239 ff.

For some months this league was kept secret. Walsingham got wind of it in March 1585, but knew nothing in detail.[1] On the very day on which the news reached him the Catholic princes launched their formal declaration at Péronne (20/30 March 1585), in which they protested against the King's government, his favourites, and his slackness in dealing with heresy—and declared their intention to take up arms for the rectification of these grievances. It was clear enough that the proclamation was directed against the King of Navarre and against Protestantism. The support of Spain was not expressed but fairly obvious. Presumably the Pope was somewhere in the background. To Protestants at large, who had been scenting for twenty years at least a general league against their faith, it really seemed as though their fears were realized.

Elizabeth herself felt the danger keenly, the more so because the Throgmorton Plot, followed hard by the Parry Plot, had taught her to appreciate the designs which the Leaguers had upon her own throne and her own person. She accordingly set about at once to form a counter-league. Edward Wotton was dispatched to Scotland to invite the co-operation of King James, Sir Thomas Bodley was sent to the continent with instructions to invoke the co-operation of the King of Denmark and the German Protestant Princes, and Arthur Champernown to the King of Navarre to promise him her help if the French King attempted anything against him and to invite his assistance in the formation of a Protestant league.[2]

It was perhaps to be expected of Elizabeth that her advances in behalf of Protestantism in these quarters had the effect of dampening such ardour as Walsingham and his partisans had succeeded in kindling in her for the cause of the Dutch. The Estates General had written her on the 11th of April expressing their intention of sending a deputation to her at once with offers of the sovereignty of their country and requesting her immediate assistance with a force of 4,000 or 5,000 men to relieve Antwerp. Ortell delivered this letter to her on the 21st of April and she received it with every show of graciousness,[3] but Burnham

[1] *Cal. Foreign*, 1584–5, pp. 371–2.
[2] *Cal. Scottish*, 1584–5, p. 611; *Cal. Foreign*, 1584–5, pp. 394, 415.
[3] Motley, *op. cit.* i. 296–7.

wrote to Davison on the same day: 'I find the negotiation something colder than it was at my coming to you.'[1] Leicester informed Davison that the Queen was provoked at him for having prompted the States to offer her the sovereignty,[2] and Walsingham himself was exceedingly doubtful of the outcome. He wrote to Davison on the 22nd of April in a very pessimistic strain: 'I find those in whose judgement her Majesty reposeth greatest trust so coldly affected unto the cause as I have no great hope of the matter, and yet, for that the hearts of princes are in the hands of God who both can and will dispose them at His pleasure, I would be loathe to hinder the repair of the commissioners.'[3]

It is plain that Walsingham attributed the Queen's irresolution to Burghley's influence. Three days later he wrote to Burghley himself: 'I am sorry, knowing both her Majesty's indisposition and others to deal in these causes, that the deputies do come over, whose dismission without relief will hasten their ruin and work an immortal hatred in them against this state.'[4]

The fact of the matter probably was that Elizabeth was considerably frightened by the news from France and more than ever disposed to stand on the defensive. It seemed to her hardly the time to begin an aggressive campaign in the Netherlands and to send her best fighting men out of England when the forces of the Holy League might descend at any moment on her coasts. She would, at any rate, have clearly preferred to postpone action for the present. And she realized that if the Dutch commissioners were allowed to come over she would be unable to avoid the issue any longer. She would either have to reject their offer and run the risk of forcing them into a treaty with Spain, or else agree to take arms in their behalf. Burghley and his partisans were apt enough to encourage this mood in her. They spoke of the expense and the uncertainty of a war; they reminded her that the Dutch were after all rebels in arms against their anointed sovereign. They hinted that although the menace from Spain was great, war was never certain until it came; and that she might even yet avoid it if she did not deliberately

[1] S. P. Holland, i, no. 102.
[2] Leicester to Davison, 24 April 1585, Harleian MSS. 285, f. 127.
[3] S. P. Holland, i, no. 103.
[4] Harleian MSS. 6993, f. 78.

provoke it. Under the circumstances they thought she might do well to conserve her strength and stand on the defensive. She was rich, her subjects were numerous, better armed, and better trained than ever they had been. Let her strengthen her navy, fortify her coasts, and show herself ready for all comers and the enemy would think twice before he attacked her.[1]

Arguments like these were bound to carry weight with the Queen. She never had liked the idea of consorting with rebels and she was passionately eager to avoid war. Walsingham soon discovered that although she had already virtually promised the Dutch her assistance she had to be convinced of the wisdom of that course all over again. He insisted again, as he had insisted many times before, that there could be no manner of doubt as to the hostile intentions of Spain. Burghley himself had admitted it a few months before. To Walsingham the real question at issue was as to whether she would fight Philip in England when Parma had disposed of the Dutch and was flushed with victory, or forestall his attack by facing him in the Low Countries where she could count upon the vigorous co-operation of his rebels. He warned her not to pin too much faith to her own strength. It was true, he admitted, that she had treasure and that treasure was a very serviceable commodity in any protracted war. But he pointed out that treasure was no safeguard against a sudden attack. She had need rather of 'forts and castles to serve as places of retreat', and in these she was almost entirely lacking. He confessed also that her subjects were numerous, but he bade her consider that 'the strength of princes consisteth not in the number but in the soundness of subjects'. 'Nothing', he declared, 'can be more dangerous [than] that when such as should join in the common defence shall unite themselves to the enemy, which breedeth a distrust of unsoundness even of those that shall concur in opposing themselves to the enemy.' He referred of course to the discontented English Catholics, whose disposition to join with her enemies had been manifested both in the Ridolfi and in the Throgmorton plots. He admitted also 'that this realm was never better furnished

[1] Cf. Camden, ed. Kennett, ii. 507-8. Since Camden drew largely upon Burghley for his information, it seems likely that he was setting forth Burghley's views. Cf. *Cal. Salisbury MSS.* iii. 70.

with armour, and so', he added, 'is it also true that never were there fewer that could skill less of the use of their weapons than at this present. It is not enough to be armed unless he know the true use of armour. And therefore it is dangerous that by sudden invasions men shall be drawn to the use of his weapons before he hath skill how to use it.' Walsingham was even willing to concede that on the whole her subjects were better trained to arms than they ever had been. 'But', he added, 'they never saw the face of the enemy and their captains are void of experience; and [in] how to supply that want, in such a scarcity of men of that profession, resteth the difficulty. Besides, if there were sufficient men to have charge of particular bands, where be your generals, lieutenants and marshals to furnish three sundry armies, without the which, howsoever a realm be furnished with particular leaders and trained soldiers, there will be but confusion in an army.' His general position was that Elizabeth was in no condition to withstand invasion, and that it would be better policy for her to prevent invasion by keeping her enemy engaged abroad.[1]

In the end Walsingham's arguments, strongly supported by Leicester and Hatton, seem to have prevailed against the Queen's irresolution and the covert opposition of Burghley and his tribe. Early in May Elizabeth professed a determination to take the rebels under her protection, provided they would accede to her demands. But it now appeared that the Dutch were beginning to make difficulties on their side. Davison wrote to Burghley on the 1st of May that the Zeelanders were reluctant to consent to the delivery of Flushing and of the towns which Elizabeth had demanded for security.[2] Their hesitation was not surprising. Flushing stood sentinel over their main gateway to the sea. It commanded their whole position. Its loss would not only expose their flank to the enemy but would jeopardize their command of the sea, which was the chief source of their strength. Under these circumstances they were naturally somewhat wary of handing it over to England. They knew enough of Elizabeth's shifty ways to fear that once she had the

[1] S. P. Domestic, clxxix, no. 59. This paper is entitled 'Objections with their Answers'. It is in Walsingham's hand, and though it is undated it probably belongs to this time.

[2] *Cal. Foreign*, 1584-5, p. 450.

town in her possession she might use it for the purpose of winning a favourable peace for herself from Spain. Yet Walsingham, who had had hard enough work in all conscience to win Elizabeth over to his way of thinking, was naturally considerably irritated by their attitude. 'I am sorry', he wrote to Gilpin on the 7th of May, 'to understand that the States there are not yet grown to a full resolution for the delivery of the town of Flushing into her Majesty's hands who, finding that people, especially of that island [Zeeland], so wavering and inconstant, besides that they can hardly, after so long enjoying a popular liberty, bear a royal authority, would be loathe to embark herself into so dangerous a war without some sufficient caution received from them. And it is greatly to be doubted that if by practice and corruption that town might be recovered by the Spaniard it would put all the rest of the country in peril. I find her Majesty, in case that town may be gotten, fully resolved to receive them into her protection, so as it may also be made probable unto her that the promised 300,000 gilders the month will be duly paid.' [1]

A day or so later Walsingham had a secret interview with Ortell on the same subject.

'What can we possibly advise her Majesty to do,' Walsingham asked him, 'since you are not willing to put confidence in her intentions. You are trying to bring her into a public war in which she is to risk her treasure and the blood of her subjects against the greatest potentates of the world and you hesitate meantime at giving her such security as is required for the very defence of the provinces themselves. The deputies are coming hither to offer the sovereignty to her Majesty, as was recently done in France, or, if that should not prove acceptable, they are to ask assistance in men and money upon a mere *taliter qualiter* guaranty. That 's not the way. And there are plenty of ill-disposed people here to take advantage of this position of affairs to ruin the interests of the Provinces now placed on so good a footing. Moreover, in this perpetual sending of dispatches back and forth, much precious time is consumed and that is exactly what our enemies most desire.' [2]

At Walsingham's prompting Ortell wrote to his masters imploring them to remedy the matter and not build a wall to

[1] S. P. Holland, ii, no. 4.

[2] Ortell to the Estates General, 13/23 May 1585, as quoted in Motley, i. 302.

knock their own heads against. And they finally decided to leave the question of the cautionary towns to their commissioners.

Meantime Elizabeth had already begun to make her preparations for fighting in a way which showed she meant business after all. On the 12th of May Walsingham wrote to Sir John Norris, then in Ireland :

'Her Majesty, foreseeing how dangerous a matter it would prove to this realm to suffer the King of Spain to recover a full possession of the Low Countries, hath resolved upon good conditions to be offered unto her by the commissioners that are come from thence, to take upon her that protection of the said Countries and is minded to acquaint the Parliament with that resolution, which for that purpose is appointed to be held the 7th of June next, by whom it is hoped the same will be very well liked of, for that no good subject can judge amiss of it that considereth the danger that dependeth toward us upon the King of Spain's greatness. And her Majesty, knowing nobody more fit to be employed in some honourable charge in the enterprise than your Lordship, hath willed me to let you understand that her pleasure is that you make your present repair over hither, not giving it out that it is by commandment for the service of the Low Countries but only upon some special business of your own. And I have written to my lord Deputy signifying so much unto him and how he is to dispose of your government in your absence. And so I bid your Lordship heartily farewell. Her Majesty doth think that the cause of your repair hither should be kept secret and therefore I doubt not but that your Lordship will use it accordingly.' [1]

While Elizabeth during the winter and spring of 1585 was making up her mind to assist the Dutch against Spain in the Netherlands she was at the same time contemplating an attack upon Spain in another quarter. Ever since Sir Francis Drake's triumphant, treasure-laden return in 1580 from his voyage round the world Walsingham had been revolving in his mind various plans for utilizing Drake in further attacks upon Spanish shipping and Spanish colonies. In 1581 he had almost succeeded in inducing the Queen to dispatch Drake under Don Antonio's flag against the Azores and the Indian treasure fleets. But Don Antonio's own weakness, the reluctance of the French to co-operate with her, and probably also the arguments of the

[1] Bodleian Library, MSS. St. Amand, viii, f. 67.

conservative elements in her own Council, had defeated the plan. During the next two years Elizabeth entertained the hope of patching up her differences with Spain and she gave no encouragement to any project for attacking Philip by sea. Walsingham, however, ventured to revive the idea after the discovery of the Throgmorton Plot had convinced his mistress of the hollowness of all Spanish shows of friendship. He found her irresolute, of course, but not altogether hostile. Of all forms of attack this particular one appealed to Elizabeth most. It did considerable damage to the enemy at his weakest point. It did not, according to the loose standards of the time, commit her definitely to war. The initial outlay involved was relatively small, the profits had heretofore proved enormous. She could always disavow Drake at a pinch. As a matter of fact his expeditions had ordinarily taken the form of private company adventures in which the Queen's part had been simply that of the largest of several investors.

Exactly when Elizabeth began to consider seriously the idea of sending Drake forth again is not quite clear. She spoke of it to the French ambassador late in July 1584.[1] She laid it before the Privy Council in October and in mid-November Walsingham bade his step-son, Sir Christopher Carleill, who was operating with a small squadron on the Irish coast, come home and join an expedition which Drake was to command. On the 24th of December Drake received his commission for the organization and command of his fleet. But this by no means settled the matter. In April the Queen was still undecided, although rumours of Drake's preparations had already reached the Spaniards and were causing them some anxiety. There is some reason to believe that she had abandoned the idea altogether, when an event occurred in Spain which virtually forced her into the more resolute course. Late in that month Philip suddenly declared an embargo upon all English shipping in Spanish ports.[2]

The seizure was well timed. A failure of crops in Galicia and Andalusia had led Philip to extend a special offer of protection to English grain shippers. In consequence a large fleet had come

[1] Teulet, *op. cit.* iii. 304.
[2] Corbett, *Drake and the Tudor Navy*, ii. 7–10.

from England to Spain in the spring. They were no sooner in Spanish ports than Philip secretly ordered them to be seized. The action practically precipitated the war. Philip's best friends in England were the merchants of the Spanish trading company which had enjoyed the monopoly of Spanish trade for some eight years. Their influence had been steadily on the side of peace [1] and it is probable that their representations to the Queen had served as a considerable counterpoise to those who were calling for war. By seizing their ships, Philip incurred their hostility and created in them naturally a desire for reprisals.

The effect was immediate. The seizure had taken place the last week in May. In June Drake was authorized to requisition ships for his expedition and on the 1st of July his new commission was signed.[2]

Nor was this the only measure of reprisal to which the Queen agreed. Early in the spring of 1585 Walsingham had drafted a 'Plot for the Annoying of the King of Spain', in which he proposed that three ships of war should be dispatched against the Spanish fishing fleets at the time when they made their spring voyage to the Newfoundland banks. He believed that such an enterprise would do considerable damage to Spanish shipping, would greatly distress Spanish mariners, and would seriously affect the Spanish food supply. From a financial point of view he foresaw that a considerable profit might be made out of this venture by the sale of the captured ships with their cargoes. He considered, however, that it would on the whole be wiser to burn the ships and forgo the profit, on the rather curious grounds that the Spaniards would be less likely to regard such a course as an act of open hostility than if the ships were brought home and sold.[3]

When the news of the seizure of the English ships in Spain reached England Walsingham persuaded Elizabeth to adopt his

[1] Cf. *Cal. Spanish*, 1580–6, pp. 8, 9, 19, 72, 130, 208, 283–4, 385.

[2] Drake did not get away from Plymouth until 14 September, and then he slipped out hastily with his stores tumbled in anyhow, fearing lest the Queen would change her mind before he got clean away. Cf. Carleill to Walsingham, 4–11 Oct. 1585, *The Spanish War, 1585–7* (Navy Records Society), pp. 39 ff.

[3] Froude, xii, p. 143, attributes this 'plot' to Hawkins, but the draft of it in S. P. Domestic, clxxvii, no. 58, is in Walsingham's own hand.

plan, no doubt with modifications to suit the altered circumstances. Elizabeth could now point to Philip's own action in capturing English ships as ample justification for her capture of Spanish ships. There was no longer any need of burning her plunder on the high seas. Accordingly the Queen sent instructions to Sir Walter Raleigh to dispatch a squadron from the western ports and intercept the Spanish fishermen. Probably Raleigh received his orders at about the same time that Drake received his new commission. He seems to have executed them promptly. The enterprise was on the whole successful; a good number of Spanish ships was taken and some 600 mariners.[1]

Meanwhile in France matters were going from bad to worse. It became apparent late in the spring of 1585 that the French King and his mother, who had heretofore rather inclined to support Henry of Navarre against the Guises, were going over to the other side.[2] Early in May Navarre had made a strong appeal for support to England, Scotland, and the Protestant princes in Germany.[3] His agent, Ségur, reached England before the end of May. Ségur addressed himself first of all to Leicester and Walsingham, whose sympathy he was assured he could count upon. Burghley, he was told, would hinder his negotia-

[1] This enterprise seems to have escaped the notice of historians altogether. It is not to be confused with Raleigh's colonizing expedition which set forth earlier in the year and returned later. The only evidence I have been able to find of the expedition is in a letter of the Privy Council to Sir John Gilbert in S. P. Domestic, clxxxiii, no. 13, dated 10 Oct. 1585, but this is conclusive. The following is an abstract of this letter: 'Whereas, upon news received here of a general arrest made in Spain of English ships and goods, it was of late thought good by her Majesty to direct Sir Walter Raleigh to set forth certain ships to the seas out of the west ports of this realm for the intercepting of such Spaniards as should repair to the Newfoundland fishing, which the said ships have accordingly executed, with such good success as to bring into this realm a good number of Spanish vessels taken at the said fishing, wherein there are some six hundred mariners. Since her Majesty's subjects are entertained in Spain in a very hard and insufferable sort, whereas the Spanish prisoners here have an allowance of 3*s.* 4*d.* a week for diet, their diet is to be reduced to 3*d.* a day, the charge thereof to be allowed out of the third part of the fish to be by you allotted to the victuallers of the said ships of war, the other two parts, one to the owners and the other to the mariners of the said ships of war. All the said fish are to be sold either within the realm or in foreign countries in league and good amity with England.'

Probably the fish alluded to here were those captured in the Spanish vessels. Carew Raleigh (Sir Walter Raleigh's older brother) evidently was the commander of the expedition (cf. *Cal. Foreign*, 1584–5, p. 572).

[2] *Lettres de Catherine de Médicis*, viii, introd., pp. xxiv ff.

[3] Cf. particularly Anquez, *Henry IV et l'Allemagne*, *passim*. On Ségur's negotiations in Scotland cf. Teulet, *op. cit.* iii. 331–40.

tions if he could.[1] On the 9th of June Ségur sent to Walsingham a statement of his master's needs. Navarre wished to recruit an army of German and Swiss mercenaries. He needed money. If Elizabeth would advance him 200,000 crowns he would be in a position to do her a service worth a thousand times that amount.[2] At first Walsingham was hopeful of the outcome. On the 1st of June he wrote to his cousin, Wotton, in Scotland: 'M. Ségur is returned hither, sent by the King of Navarre to move her Majesty to have some care of his preservation and safety, wherein I am in good hope that some good will be done.'[3] But after Ségur's interview with the Queen, Walsingham was much less optimistic. He wrote to Wotton again on the 17th of June: 'Monsieur Ségur is come hither . . . to move her Majesty for a loan of money and some contribution besides towards the levying of certain forces in Germany; but the loan is denied him and the contribution offered is so small as it will not work that good that is desired, wherein the gentleman is much grieved and so are as many besides as do see how much it importeth her Majesty's safety to maintain so necessary an instrument against the Duke of Guise.'[4]

On the 22nd of June word reached England that Catherine de Médicis was just about to come to terms with the Leaguers. A few days later the Treaty of Nemours was actually signed. This news was more effective than all of Ségur's and Walsingham's arguments combined in arousing Elizabeth to the necessity of prompt action in Navarre's behalf. On the 23rd of June Walsingham wrote to Sir Thomas Bodley, the English agent in Denmark: 'By letters received yesterday out of France we hear that the King and the Leaguers are now agreed amongst themselves, as I did ever guess they would, to the ruin and overthrow of those of the religion. . . . Her Majesty proposes for her part to send presently a convenient proportion of treasure into Germany by her minister that is to repair thither, who I hope will be ready to embark at the end of this month in company of M. de Ségur.'[5] It appears from Ségur's letter to Walsingham of the 2nd of July that the Queen offered at this juncture to lend

[1] Strype, *op. cit.* iii, pt. 2, p. 384.

[2] *Cal. Foreign*, 1584–5, p. 534; cf. also *Lettres de Henri IV*, viii, p. 289 and note.

[3] *Hamilton Papers*, ii. 647.

[4] Ibid. ii. 654.

[5] S. P. Denmark, i, f. 130.

100,000 crowns. He told Walsingham that he thought it would be sufficient.[1] A day or so later, however, Ségur had a further interview with the Queen in which it appeared that she was beginning to repent of her impulsive generosity. She now declared that she would only lend the money upon condition that Denmark and the German Protestant princes would also consent to assist,[2] and a little later, that in any case she could not lend more than 50,000 crowns for the present. Ségur told Walsingham frankly that he could not accept the loan upon such terms. The result was that he left England in despair, hoping that Walsingham might be able to induce the Queen to be more generous. Walsingham's own reaction appears in a letter which he wrote on the subject to Stafford, the 20th of July : 'M. Ségur is already departed hence, though not well satisfied because Her Majesty had not sent the money into Germany before his going away and that it was not more than 50,000 crowns, which will do little good. And I fear me he shall find no great zeal nor forward disposition in the Princes of Germany to concur in the furtherance of the common cause.' [3]

Walsingham was no doubt right in insisting that Elizabeth could not afford to let the King of Navarre's cause fail. Yet it is easy to see why she hesitated to advance him any large sum of money at this juncture. She was just about to plunge into war with Spain and she had need of every penny she could raise for that enterprise. Her natural thriftiness was prompted for once, at least, by very solid considerations. How far Burghley was instrumental in preventing the success of Ségur's mission it is difficult to say. Although he was charged with the fact, he indignantly denied it and insisted that he had done his best to further the negotiations. Yet it seems not unlikely that his zeal was tempered with many words of caution. He certainly did not reveal in action any exuberant enthusiasm in Navarre's cause. Some time later a Spanish agent in London believed him opposed to it.[4] In any case, however, the chief explanation for Ségur's failure is probably to be found in the Queen herself and in her negotiations, already far advanced, with the Dutch.

The Deputies from the Estates General had arrived in England

[1] *Cal. Foreign*, 1584-5, p. 577. [2] Ibid., p. 584.
[3] S. P. France, xiv, f. 134.
[4] Strype, *op. cit.* iii, pt. 2, p. 384; *Cal. Spanish*, 1587-1603, p. 168.

before Ségur took his departure. They reached London on the 26th of June and had their first audience on the 29th.[1] Stow has preserved the words of their oration to the Queen. The substance of them was to offer her the sovereignty of the Low Countries upon conditions which they submitted in writing. Elizabeth had already decided that she would not accept the sovereignty of the Low Countries though she was prepared to consider taking them under her protection, and the following day the Lord Chancellor expressed her views on the subject at length.[2]

The Dutch, however, were not content to accept the decision, but drew up a memorial in reply in which they urged upon the Queen their need of a sovereign to unite their efforts and command their common obedience. Burghley told them flatly, however, that there was no use in drawing up memorials. The Queen's decision was final. They had better set to work arranging terms on the basis of her simple protection.[3]

This process began at once. It is not necessary to follow the negotiations in detail. As usual, Burghley, Walsingham, and Leicester were the councillors chiefly employed about the business, but it is difficult to separate their work or to get much light upon their individual contributions. Both parties to the treaty were disposed to drive as sharp a bargain as they might. For about a fortnight there was pretty constant haggling over figures and securities. 'Touching the Low Countries cause,' Walsingham wrote to his cousin, Wotton, 'we are busy as well in looking into their offers as in entering into a consideration of their state. . . . What the issue of our counsels will be touching these causes He only knoweth who disposeth of all things according to His pleasure.' [4]

[1] *Stow's Chronicle* (ed. Howes, 1615), pp. 707–8, says that they arrived in London, 26 June, and were lodged in the Clothworkers' Hall in Tower Street at the Queen's charges. A warrant by Privy Seal was issued by the Queen, 30 July 1585, for £400 'for diet and household expenses of the deputies of the states of the Low Countries', Signet Book, Eliz. i.

[2] There is a short diary in Walsingham's hand among the S. P. Holland (*Cal. Foreign*, 1584–5, p. 595) which covers the stages in the negotiations between 29 June and 12 July 1585. The Chancellor's speech is not preserved, but the substance of it is probably embodied in a paper entitled 'Reasons why her Majesty should rather accept the title of Protector than of Sovereign', written by Walsingham himself, which is among S. P. Holland (*Cal. Foreign*, 1584–5, pp. 571–2, which does not, however, note the fact that the original is in Walsingham's hand).

[3] Motley, *op. cit.* i. 321.

[4] *Hamilton Papers*, ii. 659.

It must have been on the 12th of July that the deputies presented a general estimate of their needs. They wished the Queen to pay one-third of the charges. Burghley said it was too much. They estimated that an army of 13,000 foot and 2,000 horse would be necessary for the field and 23,000 foot for garrison duty. Burghley admitted that the first was reasonable, but said the second was excessive. Their other estimates seemed on the whole reasonable.[1]

The next day the Deputies sent to the English councillors the draft of a treaty. They demanded that the Queen should furnish them with 5,000 foot and 1,000 horse and agreed in turn that they would repay all sums which she disbursed in their behalf ten years after the war, one-tenth part every year. They would also hand over to her one or two towns in each province as security, would admit one or two of her representatives to their Council of State, and would sign no treaty with the enemy without her consent. There were other points as well, but these were the main ones.[2]

On the 17th of July Burghley delivered to the Deputies the Queen's answer to these proposals. She could not allow of so great a charge as 5,000 foot and 1,000 horse would put her to, considering her other great charges. But she was content to yield them help to the sum of £5,400 a month, if they would give her Briel and Flushing as security. Meantime, for the relief of Antwerp, she would send 4,000 foot and for assurance of their expenses would require bonds, or else, within certain months after their landing, to have Sluys and Ostend for security.

This was sharp bargaining indeed. The Deputies said that the offer was not sufficient. They inquired to know at whose charges Flushing and Briel should be kept. 'We answered,' says Burghley, 'at theirs.' If that were so, the Deputies replied, they would not have a half of the loan offered them, which they declared to be against all reason.[3]

Two days later Walsingham wrote to Wotton: 'This cause of the Low Countries doth at this present wholly entertain us. Her Majesty's own natural inclination to peace is not unknown, and

[1] Motley, *op. cit.* i. 324–5; *Cal. Foreign*, 1584–5, p. 705.
[2] *Cal. Foreign*, 1584–5, p. 707.
[3] S. P. Holland, ii, f. 123, very imperfectly given in *Cal. Foreign*, 1584–5, p. 708, as 'Further notes by Burghley', &c.

the entering into a war with so puissant a prince as the King of Spain, especially at this time that things in France take such a course, may seem an enterprise of dangerous consequence; and therefore the matter requireth the longer deliberation.' [1]

His letter to Stafford on the 20th reveals the fact that Elizabeth had not yet brought herself to consent to assist the Dutch openly. 'We are here at this present in very earnest consultation with the States Commissioners of the Low Countries, the substance whereof consisteth principally in these two points, the one that they require a provisional support for the prompt relief of the town of Antwerp, to which it is uncertain whether her Majesty will yield, though the letters be already signed by her for the levying of men, so loathe is she to enter into a war; the other that her Majesty refuseth to enter into the action otherwise than underhand, wherein the whole council, howsoever they stand inwardly effected, do nevertheless outwardly concur in opinion that it is a dangerous course for her and that it is impossible she should long stand unless she enter openly and soundly into the action.' [2]

On the 24th of July Walsingham informed the Dutch Commissioners that the Queen was willing to add 400 horse to her offer of 4,000 foot, provided she might have Briel and Flushing as security. They responded that they had no commission to yield the towns unless Elizabeth granted them the 5,000 foot and 1,000 horse they asked for.[3]

But the news from beleaguered Antwerp would admit of no delay, so the question of the general treaty was deferred until a special treaty could be negotiated for the relief of the city. Walsingham wrote optimistically to Wotton on the 30th of July: 'For the present cause of the Low Countries we are now so forward in it that there is a commission already under the great seal directed to certain of my Lords [of the Council] to treat with the deputies, as well touching the present relieving of the town of Antwerp as for a further aid to be yielded by her Majesty to the said States. For which purpose, 2,000 men are already sent over and 4,000 more shall be ready to embark by the 15th of the next month.' [4]

[1] *Hamilton Papers*, ii. 661.
[2] S. P. France, xiv, f. 134 (in *Cal. Foreign*, 1584–5, p. 618).
[3] *Cal. Foreign*, 1584–5, p. 628.
[4] *Hamilton Papers*, ii. 664.

On the 2nd of August the subsidiary treaty for the relief of Antwerp was signed. 'We are now', Walsingham informed Wotton on the 3rd of August, 'grown to a full resolution with the Commissioners of the Low Countries to send under the conduct of Col. Norris 4,000 soldiers for the relief of Antwerp.'[1] The terms of the treaty were, briefly, that the Queen should send over 4,000 foot and should provide money for their levy and pay from month to month, for three months after they had passed muster in the Low Countries. In return she was to have Ostend and Sluys for security and repayment of the expenses entailed within three months after the relief of Antwerp, or failing that within fifteen months from the day of muster.[2]

Three days later Walsingham wrote to Wotton: 'This day we had news of the loss of Antwerp which doth not a little trouble us, but most particularly myself. Her Majesty, notwithstanding, is fully resolved to send over with all speed four thousand men, to comfort the people there, who otherwise are like (forced through despair) to grow to some peace with the enemy.'[3]

This news, however, proved to be premature, though it had the effect of stimulating the negotiations for the general treaty. On the 12th of August an agreement was finally reached between the English Councillors and the Dutch Commissioners, subject to the ratification of the Queen and the Estates General. By it the Queen bound herself to provide 4,000 foot, 400 horse, and 700 men for garrison duty to serve at her cost until the end of the war, the States on their part promising to make over to her the towns of Briel and Flushing with the Rammekins as security until they repaid the money which she should spend in their behalf. These were the essential points of the preliminary

[1] *Hamilton Papers*, ii. 665.

[2] Cotton MSS., Galba C viii, f. 114. It was estimated that the charges of cost and conduct money, transportation, and three months' pay of 4,000 soldiers would amount to £18,680 (*Cal. Foreign*, 1584–5, p. 647).

[3] Cotton MSS., Galba C viii, ff. 116, 130. On the copy of the ratifications of the articles by the States General which Davison sent over to England in September, Burghley has made annotations; opposite the article which provides for the repayment of the Queen's expenses at the end of the war he has jotted, 'ad Cal. Graec.' (S. P. Holland, iii, f. 162).

It is to be noted that Motley has confused his dates somewhat in giving an account of the Dutch embassy in England. He prefers in general the new style of dating in use on the continent, but occasionally, as when he gives the date of signing the preliminary treaty for Antwerp, he reverts to the old style.

treaty, though it contained some thirty articles altogether. Directly after these terms had been agreed upon the Dutch Commissioners took their leave of Elizabeth and she bade them farewell in eloquent terms: 'You see, gentlemen, that I have opened the door, that I am embarking once for all with you in a war against the King of Spain. Very well, I am not anxious about the matter. I hope that God will aid us and that we shall strike a good blow in your cause.' And more in the same spirit. The Dutch remarked that her tongue was wonderfully well hung, and Elizabeth seems indeed to have shared with Henry of Navarre the knack of saying the right thing at the right time—in her public utterances at all events.[1]

The next day Walsingham wrote to Wotton: 'The States of the Low Countries, saving four of them, return to-morrow with reasonable contentment—4,000 foot being sent over for the relief of Antwerp which is able to hold out for three months.' [2]

Two days after that Walsingham wrote to Stafford: 'Her Majesty's forces between voluntary and others I think will rise to the number of 7,000 men, who are already shipped, and we hear creditably that the bridge [closing the river of Antwerp] is so weak as it may easily be broken through, which being brought to pass and the town consequently relieved, the Prince of Parma's credit will so decay as it is likely he shall not be able to do any great matter all this next year.' [3]

It is clear enough, from this letter as well as from the whole tone of Walsingham's correspondence at this juncture, that he did not feel that Antwerp was in any immediate danger. The current view that Elizabeth was well aware that the town was at its last gasp, and that her criminal delay in going to its assistance was largely responsible for its fall, is not borne out by his testimony at least. Furthermore, it is unquestionable that Elizabeth was by no means wholly to blame for such delay in coming to terms with the Dutch as there was. Early in March she had with her own lips definitely promised to assist them, had indicated her terms, and had invited them to send over commissioners to conclude a treaty. Yet, with Parma already tightening his grip on Antwerp, they dallied with her proposal for

[1] Motley, i. 330 ff.
[2] *Hamilton Papers*, ii. 673.
[3] 15 Aug. 1585, in S. P. France, xiv, f. 164.

over two months—so long in fact that even Walsingham got indignant at their delay. It was not until the end of June that their commissioners did finally arrive in London. After that they made unusually good speed. Six weeks was not an excessive allowance for the arrangement of a matter of such importance.

At all events, whoever was to blame, Antwerp capitulated long before Norris could bring his forces to its assistance. The probabilities are that both Walsingham and his mistress were amazed at the news. They were disposed, as were the Dutch themselves, to ascribe it to the treachery of St. Aldegonde, who was in charge of its defence. Its fall was a considerable blow to the cause and a fresh indication of the inability of the Dutch, unaided, to cope with Parma. Walsingham more than ever felt the necessity of prompt measures for their relief, and Elizabeth for once shared his views. It might have been expected that the disaster would frighten her back into her normal mood of indecision. In fact it quickened her resolution. She decided at once to dispatch Davison, who had returned to England late in the spring, back to the Low Countries.

Walsingham wrote to him a hasty note on the 22nd of August: 'I am commanded by her Majesty to send for you to my house at Barn Elms and to confer with you about the state of the Low Countries. I pray you meet me there this night if you can possibly for to-morrow about eight of the clock I have prayed the Deputies with Ortell to be there, for that I have somewhat to say to them from her Majesty, as you shall understand this evening. . . . You shall have the tide with you this evening so as you shall find it but an hour's work.' [1]

What passed between Davison and Walsingham on that occasion is not recorded. A few days later Davison set out for Holland.[2] Walsingham has summarized his instructions in a letter to Wotton of the 26th of August. 'Mr. Davison', he wrote, 'was yesterday dispatched from the court unto them of Holland and Zeeland to assure them that her Majesty will

[1] S. P. Holland, iii, f. 45. Davison of course was to come by boat from London. Barn Elms was at what is now Barnes on the Thames. Part of Walsingham's house is now incorporated in the Ranelagh Club house.

[2] About the same time Elizabeth dispatched Sir John Smith to the Prince of Parma to urge him to come to terms with the Dutch, or at least to agree to an armistice until he could communicate with Philip II on the subject, *Cal. Foreign*, 1584-5, p. 671.

furnish them with 5,000 footmen and 1,000 horse according to their own demand, and that a nobleman shall be sent over unto them—all which is to be performed presently when her Majesty shall understand that they are content to deliver into her hands the towns of Flushing and Briel, whereof it is thought they will make no difficulty if my Lord of Leicester may have the charge of the army and Sir Philip Sidney of Flushing.' [1]

It will be remembered that in the preliminary agreement of the 12th of August Elizabeth had refused to send more than 4,000 foot, 400 horse, and 700 men for garrison duty. The fall of Antwerp convinced her that it was no time to stand on terms, and accordingly she enlarged her offers to the measure of what the Dutch commissioners themselves had demanded.[2] In passing her word to send a nobleman over to them she did not precisely indicate whom she would send. She was in fact undecided about the matter. The commissioners had urged her to appoint Leicester as Governor-General and Sir Philip Sidney as Governor of Flushing, an arrangement which Walsingham himself strongly favoured and was doing his best to further. 'Touching Sir Philip Sidney,' he wrote to Davison on the 26th of August, 'I will move her Majesty to take order both for my Lord of Leicester and him, wherein by letters received lately from Calais I find it is very necessary she should hasten her resolution, which you shall do well to further by writing hither as soon as you are over, that her Majesty must needs send thither with speed lest otherwise there be an accord made before she be aware.' [3]

There are indications here that Walsingham had some grounds for fearing that the Dutch were going about to make their own peace with Spain. At least he wished to impress his mistress with a sense of that danger. His device of bringing pressure to bear upon her by prearrangement with her representatives overseas was one which he resorted to more than once.[4]

[1] *Hamilton Papers*, ii. 685. Davison's instructions are printed in Strype, *Annals*, iii, pt. 2, p. 363.

[2] Cf. on this Burghley's Diary (Murdin, *Burghley Papers*, p. 783), the entry under September 1585. 'Nota, before John Norris could pass out of England Antwerp was won, so as a new treaty was made for another contract, by which was yielded an aid of 5,000 foot and 1,000 horse.'

[3] S. P. Holland, iii, f. 71.

[4] Cf. on this point, *English Historical Review*, Jan. 1913, p. 42, n. 27.

After Davison's departure Walsingham's first concern was to get a new treaty arranged with the Dutch commissioners in accordance with Elizabeth's enlarged offers. This was easy enough. The Dutch were glad to make the necessary changes and by the beginning of September the amended treaty was ready for their signatures. But at this point a new difficulty arose. The majority of the Dutch commissioners had returned home immediately after the negotiations for the original treaty had been completed. Those who had remained were unwilling to sign the new treaty until they could communicate with their colleagues overseas. Walsingham wrote Davison on the 4th of September : 'The act is thought meet by my Lords [the English commissioners] to be interchangeably signed, also by the Deputies [of the Dutch] here who do like very well of the same. But yet I think they will make some difficulty to sign it until they hear from the rest of their colleagues, for that they are now divided from them, unto whom I suppose they will send it or else I mean to do it myself.'[1] Four days later Walsingham did, in fact, send a copy of the treaty signed by the English commissioners. But the document had no sooner been sent off before the Dutch discovered that some words had been omitted. 'The point of reformation', Walsingham wrote to Davison, 'standeth only upon this, that they require that the assistance promised by Her Majesty may be 5,000 foot and 1,000 horsemen, besides the garrisons that are to be placed in the cautionary towns, which clause of reservation or exception was omitted in that sent unto you.'[2]

This would seem to have been a matter of more moment than Walsingham was inclined to regard it, involving probably the supply and the maintenance of at least 700 more men. Elizabeth indeed afterwards censured her commissioners severely for assenting to it. But assent they did, nevertheless, and as soon as they had put their hands to the document Walsingham sent it to the Dutch commissioners in London with the request that they forward it to Davison.[3]

They requested that they might defer sending it until the arrival of a messenger whom the Estates General were about to

[1] S. P. Holland, iii, f. 104.
[2] Ibid., f. 129, 12 Sept. 1585.
[3] *Cal. Foreign*, 1585–6, pp. 28, 113–14.

dispatch to England. But the Queen would not hear of it. She regarded it simply as a subterfuge to delay the delivery of Briel and Flushing until she had got so far forward with her preparations that she could not in honour draw back. 'And on the other side,' Walsingham added, writing of the matter to Davison, 'I fear me that they will make . . . stay in the delivery of the towns, being as they do rightly [conceive] therein the keys of their surety, until they [the commanders] be nominated unto them [the States] that shall receive them [the towns] at your hands; wherein how you may carry yourself I leave to your own discretion, now you know her Majesty's desire and are there an eye witness of their proceedings and of the humours and dispositions of those that are to be dealt withal, not doubting but that you will always have regard, that such as are ill affected may have no advantage given them to breed any doubt or jealousy in the people's heart of the sincerity of her Majesty's dealing toward them.' [1]

This letter found Davison labouring manfully with the Dutch commissioners in Holland to secure their assent to the treaty. He was having a good deal of difficulty in bringing them to terms. 'In how doubtful and uncertain terms I found things at my coming hither,' he wrote to Burghley later, 'how thwarted and delayed since for a resolution and with what conditions and for what reasons I have been finally drawn to conclude with them as I have done, your Lordship may perceive by what I have written to Mr. Secretary. The chiefest difficulty in fine hath rested upon the point of entertaining the garrisons within the towns and places of assurance, over and besides the five thousand footmen and the one thousand horse.' [2]

It seems from the tone of Davison's letter that he had found it necessary to concede this point without further instructions from England. On that basis he secured the Dutch ratification to the treaty on the 24th of September. Fortunately for him Walsingham had already induced the English commissioners to concede the point in England, so that the responsibility for the concession, which angered Elizabeth considerably when she heard of it, did not rest upon Davison's shoulders.

[1] S. P. Holland, iii, f. 137 (in *Cal. Foreign*, 1585–6, p. 28).
[2] *Cal. Foreign*, 1585–6, p. 35.

The day after the treaty was ratified the Dutch commissioners dispatched it to England.[1] But the ship which was to carry it was stayed by contrary winds and it did not in fact reach Elizabeth's hands until the 21st of October. She complained bitterly of the delay and swore she would have no further commerce with them unless they treated her with greater consideration.

Yet now that all was agreed upon and it only remained for her to carry out her promises she herself returned again to her old procrastinating tactics. She had already declared late in August that she intended to send over the Earl of Leicester to represent her interests and command her forces and Leicester himself had expressed his willingness to undertake the charge.[2] But she could not make up her mind to give him his commission. 'I see not her Majesty disposed,' Walsingham wrote to Davison on the 5th of September, 'to use the service of the Earl of Leicester. There is great offence taken in the carrying down of his lady. I suppose the lot of the government will light upon Lord Gray. I would to God the ability of his purse were answerable to his sufficiency otherwise. Here we are but lukewarm, and yet from sundry quarters we hear of great practices against this poor crown.'[3]

A little later the Queen bade Leicester go forward with his preparations. But she changed her mind again. Walsingham wrote to Leicester on the 26th of September: 'Her Majesty sent me word by Mr. D—— that I should signify unto your Lordship that her pleasure is you forbear to proceed in your preparations until you speak with her. How this cometh about I know not. The matter is to be kept secret. These changes here may work some such change in the Low Countries as may prove irreparable. God give her Majesty another mind and

[1] Motley (i. 339) says on 5 October, but fails to point out that this was N.S. He dated Davison's letter just cited 24 September (O.S.). So he makes an interval of eleven days between the letter and the dispatch of the treaty, whereas in fact there was only one.

[2] Cf. Leicester to Walsingham, 28 Aug. 1585, in S. P. Domestic, clxxxi, no. 68.

[3] S. P. Holland, iii, f. 106 (in *Cal. Foreign*, 1585–6, p. 8). Motley (i. 336) quotes this letter, but wrongly renders 'lukewarm' 'book-worms'. On Lettyce, Countess of Leicester and her children, cf. Nichols in *Gentleman's Magazine*, 1846, i. 250.

resolution in proceeding. Otherwise it will work both honest and best affected subjects' ruin.' [1]

The explanation of the delay is to be found no doubt in the inconstant character of the Queen herself. There is, however, some reason for believing that the conservative party in the Privy Council under Burghley's lead was also working underhand to thwart the expedition. A Spanish agent in England wrote home on the 19/29th of September: 'There is great disagreement between the Earl of Leicester and the Lord Treasurer, Cecil persuading the Queen not to break with the House of Burgundy whilst Leicester uses all his great influence to bring her to an opposite course and to weaken the party of the Lord Treasurer.' [2]

'I cannot deny', Walsingham wrote to Davison later, 'but some practices have been used to draw her Majesty to mislike of the present action and of such as advised her to enter into the same.' [3]

There was particular opposition further to the appointment of Sir Philip Sidney to the command of Flushing, presumably upon the grounds that if Leicester commanded, and Sidney, his nephew and Walsingham's son-in-law, held the most important cautionary town, the enterprise would be altogether too completely in the hands of the war faction. Sidney, indeed, was so disgusted with the Queen's tergiversations that he declared his intention of going to the seas with Drake.[4] And Leicester wrote to a friend sometime in September, 'There is never a man here will believe her Majesty will do anything. I will never agree for Flushing to any but to my nephew. If Sluys or Ostend may content Sir Thomas Cecil I would be glad also.' [5]

Just how far Walsingham and his partisans were justified in attributing the Queen's attitude to Burghley's influence it is difficult to say. The testimony of the Spanish agent gives to their views some credence. At all events they chose to regard him as their enemy and set to work, underhand, to discredit him.

[1] Cotton MSS. Galba C viii, f. 150, printed in Bruce, *Correspondence of Robert Dudley, Earl of Leicester, in the Years 1585 and 1586* (Camden Soc., no. xxvii), p. 4.

[2] *Cal. Spanish*, 1580–6, p. 547.

[3] *Cal. Foreign*, 1585–6, p. 146.

[4] Ibid., p. 23.

[5] S. P. Holland, iii, no. 115 (in *Cal. Foreign*, 1585–6, p. 53). Sir Thomas Cecil was Burghley's eldest son. He was finally appointed to command at Briel, and throughout his stay there revealed a scarcely disguised contempt of Leicester.

Their chief instrument for this purpose, apparently, was William Herle, one of Burghley's old secret service men. Herle's share in the business apparently was to pose as Burghley's friend and in that guise to retail to him the various criticisms that were levied against him. Accordingly Herle wrote to Burghley that he was currently spoken of as enemy both to the King of Navarre and the Dutch ; that he was the chief opponent to the King of Scots' pension, that his buildings were too splendid, his revenues too large, that his influence with the Queen was such that none could hope to enjoy her favour save by his mediation—in short that the realm of England was little more than a *regnum Cecilianum.*[1]

Exactly what Walsingham and his partisans expected to accomplish by these tactics is not clear. Perhaps they hoped to impress upon Burghley a sense of his growing unpopularity with a view to frightening him into compliance with their views. If so they seem in part to have succeeded. Burghley at any rate thought it necessary to answer Herle's letters at length, with a long denial of their charges, an elaborate justification of his position, and many appeals to God in support of his innocence. There is some evidence also that Walsingham was attempting through Herle to quicken Burghley's ardour in the cause of the Low Countries by tempting his cupidity. This appears in a letter of Herle's to Walsingham of the 25th of July.

'I have done to the full as much as your instructions imported . . . and this day shall I receive answer to the same, whereof it is necessary that you forthwith direct what I shall say touching the £10,000 a month to be paid Her Majesty and the £1,000 monthly to himself; for I writ that one person of authority (as indeed is true) had broken with me herein under the seal of confession, and that the matter should pass silently beknown then 2 (*sic*) notwithstanding for I would presume to know no further in the same. So as I know that either of policy or

[1] Strype, *Annals*, iii, pt. 2, pp. 379–82. The originals of Burghley's letters to Herle printed by Strype are in S. P. Domestic, clxxx, nos. 23, 34, 46, 50, 53. Other letters of Herle on the same subject are in S. P. Domestic, clxxxi, nos. 33, 42. These were apparently bundled together at one time and no. 42 used as a wrapper for the bundle. It is endorsed '1585. Letters to Wm. Herle from the Lord Burghley, Lord Treasurer of England, found amongst his writings and brought to the Earl of Leicester at the death of Herle.' (This endorsement seems to be, though it is not certainly, in Burghley's hand.)

inclination he will seek to understand the mystery it contains and that her Majesty shall be made acquainted with the whole, wherefore I attend your present answer. For the party, I say of authority, that hath broken with me, shall be whosoever that your honour, either of the deputies or otherwise, shall appoint to deal in the cause, for no doubt the other side will desire to hear him.

'I have been in hand with some friends of mine . . . to have £40 upon your honour's bonds who affirm wisely to me that no man upon the offer of your bond dare lend any for fear of displeasing you, so as the offer of your bond is a secret restraint (as it seems to them all) that they should not be forward on it because for your honour, being most liberal, are indiscriminately pressed by many for money towards whom it is necessary to use some rampart to avoid others also. . . . Hoping to do you some service shortly that shall make me worthy of your favour. . . . relying and trusting only and confidently in your goodness.

'I pray you send me word whether you know one Ringout that is here out of the Low Countries. He is in profession a . . . and financier.'[1]

This letter apparently had reference to a scheme which was broached more than once at this time for exploiting the coinage. The English rose noble and double noble both circulated at a considerable premium in the Low Countries, and it was fancied that if they were minted in the Netherlands to avoid the expense of transfer a considerable profit might accrue to the Crown. In fact a London alderman offered to buy the right of coining them and to pay 30 shillings for every pound weight of gold he coined, which was twenty-six shillings more than had formerly been paid. It was estimated that the Queen would make anything from £5,000 to £40,000 a year by the transaction.[2] Herle was apparently holding out to Burghley an even more glowing prospect—£120,000 a year to the Queen and £12,000 to himself. Burghley's reply to this proposal effectually disposed of any hopes of corrupting him.

'For that which you desire to be answered how I can be tempted with allowance of a device to gain to her Majesty £10,0000 monthly and to myself one other £1,000, so as her Majesty will help the States, I think I know the matter very well, having heard thereof a month past and have within these few

[1] B.M. Harleian MSS. 286, f. 68.

[2] Cf. Bruce, *op. cit.*, pp. 153, 356; S. P. Domestic, Addenda, 1580–1625, p. 145.

days seen and read the project. What I think thereof I cannot but pronounce doubtfully thereof until I shall speak with the party that offereth it. In my opinion if the matter may appear feasible (which I most doubt of) and reasonable as being feasible, I think it allowable with some correction of some points. I were to blame if I would not assent to her Majesty's profit, thereby to enter into defence of the Low Countries, seeing I am persuaded and do maintain it, that Her Majesty for her own surety ought to charge herself with the defence of them against the common enemy, without which attempt her Majesty shall not be able with expense of thousands to defend herself, that now she may with God's assistance do with hundreds. But for any offer to myself, I do utterly refuse either such or a less sum, thinking it more charity to yield of mine own to the common cause than to receive a penny. . . .

'I marvel that any malicious discourses can note me a councillor that do abuse my credit to my private gain.' [1]

There can be little doubt that Burghley suspected that Leicester at least was implicated in these various schemes to discredit him. Indeed he even took occasion to write to Leicester about it, although he was careful not to mention Herle's name. Leicester in reply denied the charge, but not in a way which carried much conviction. He took the occasion to remind Burghley what great benefits he had formerly received at the hand of Leicester's father, the Duke of Northumberland, in the days of Edward VI.[2] But neither the appeals to Burghley's gratitude, nor to his cupidity, nor to his fear of slander, had the effect apparently that Leicester and Walsingham desired. In spite of his protestations to the contrary they still felt that he was the chief obstacle in the way of a resolute forward policy in the Low Countries. Somewhat later in the autumn, when Leicester, having made all his preparations to depart, was quite distracted by the Queen's inability to make up her mind to dispatch him, he complained openly to Burghley of his double dealing.

'I know not', he wrote, 'from whence my hap hath it, but it hath fallen out sundry times, quite contrary to my expectation (and much less by any desert of mine), that I have found your Lordship more ready to thwart and cross my endeavours than any other man's, especially in the presence of her Majesty, and for

[1] S. P. Domestic, clxxx, no. 46.

[2] Strype, *op. cit.* iii, pt. 2, pp. 386–91.

such causes as I have been the more earnest in, when by your Lordship's own allowance and opinion it hath been so resolved on by our conference before, as fit and meet advices to be given her Majesty for the best furtherances of her own services. And these causes have lately been most in question, in which I myself by her appointment, have been furthest employed, and therefore did, both at your Lordship's hands and other Lords, hope to be assisted and comforted, so far as my opinion should tend to the service of her Majesty, and to matters being before, by your Lordship and others, debated and agreed upon. . . . Albeit I know and grant among councillors there may and must rise, by way of argument, divisions in opinion, which is both lawful and very convenient. . . . But, my Lord, in these causes we have been two or three times before her Majesty, we had debated the matter before and the course I took was no other than your Lordship did best like and most advise. And to fall into contrary opinions before her Majesty caused me both to take it ill and to show it plainly to you as I did.' [1]

Leicester's complaint in brief was that Burghley supported one policy before the Council and another one before the Queen. Probably there was some truth in the charge. Walsingham at any rate thought so. Yet it seems on the whole most likely that Burghley's disingenuous behaviour sprang rather from his indecision than from any settled policy of opposition to a resolute, aggressive course.

At all events, in spite of Burghley's deterrent influence, Leicester and his partisans gradually brought the Queen around to a reluctant ratification of the course they were advocating. Towards the end of September, Walsingham, who had been wellnigh desperate, began to write somewhat more hopefully.

'I will not fail', he wrote to Leicester on he 27th, 'to acquaint her Majesty with the great comfort your Lordship took through her gracious dealing towards you, at such time as she did deliver her pleasure unto you, touching the employment of you in the Low Countries.

'My Lords [of the Council] have seemed to be very willing to further anything your Lordship shall require for the advancement of the service. But if your Lordship's requests shall minister matter of charge, though it be for the public service, the impediment will be found in her Majesty with whom I have had very sharp conflicts about the Scottish causes, and all for charges.' [2]

[1] Ibid., iii, pt. 2, pp. 506 ff.

[2] Bruce, *op. cit.*, pp. 8–9.

A few weeks later Elizabeth took a long step forward and published to the world her justification of her intervention in the Low Countries. It is not clear just when the pamphlet *A Declaration of the Causes Moving the Queen of England to give aid to the Defence of the People afflicted and oppressed in the Low Countries* appeared. It is divided into two parts. The first part is an eloquent attempt to justify the Queen's course on the grounds that Spain was trampling upon the ancient privileges of England's ancient ally. The second part, with the sub-title, *An Addition to the Declaration,* is an answer to an Italian pamphlet published in Milan which had charged Elizabeth with ingratitude towards the King of Spain and with an intent to encompass the assassination of the Prince of Parma. There can be no doubt that Walsingham himself composed the second part of the pamphlet, and there is a strong presumption that he wrote the whole of it. If so it gives him a high place among writers of literature of this sort. The *Declaration* is indeed a masterpiece in its way, eloquent and ardent, yet essentially moderate and sane, pregnant with sound reasoning, concise yet elegant. There is no fine writing about it, but the phraseology fits the thought like a glove. The fact that Walsingham was chosen to compose this official utterance, one of the most important perhaps that Elizabeth ever put forth, demonstrates that he was already recognized as past master of the art and encourages the supposition that many of the other official publications of the reign proceeded from his pen.[1]

[1] This pamphlet is printed in full in *Somers Tracts*, i. 410–19, and in Holinshed's *Chronicles* (ed. 1587), iii. 1414. There is a MS. copy of the second part of it in Walsingham's handwriting among the Salisbury MSS. at Hatfield (printed in Murdin, p. 294). The pamphlet is dated 1 October, but it is clear from the following passages out of a letter from Walsingham to Burghley, dated 12 October 1585, that it did not actually appear until somewhat later. 'My very good Lord: Finding her Majesty's conceipt what might best content her in the course of the answer to be made unto the malicious points contained in the Italian's pamphlet, I have performed the same in writing and acquainted her withal, and finding that she does not dislike thereof, I have caused it to be copied out, which your Lordship shall receive to-morrow in the morning, praying your Lordship to yield such necessary correction as to you shall be thought meet. I think it most expedient that the commissioners here should be made acquainted with the declaration before it be printed. It may be that there is somewhat contained therein that happily may more prejudice the cause than yield benefit in point of justification. The perusal thereof can no way hinder her Majesty's intent, and therefore in my poor opinion your Lordship shall do well to acquaint them therewith' (Harleian MSS. 6993, f. 110).

On the 12th of October Walsingham wrote to Burghley: 'I send your Lordship a draught of a warrant dormant for the transporting of victual for the relief of the army in the Low Countries which I pray your Lordship, after you have perused and corrected, to return. I attend here for the dispatch of the Earl of Leicester's commission, wherein he desireth expedition so as I cannot wait upon your Lordship to-morrow at the Star Chamber.' [1] It is apparent from this letter that by this time Elizabeth had finally made up her mind to the dispatch of Leicester. But she had not yet received the Dutch ratification of the treaty and she was getting more and more irritated by what she considered a sharp practice of the Dutch to draw her into the war before they had committed themselves to terms—'a manner of proceeding', Walsingham protested to Davison in a letter of the 23rd of October, 'not to be allowed of, and may well be termed mechanical, considering that her Majesty seeketh no interest in that country. . . . But seeing the government of those countries resteth in the hands of merchants and advocates, the one regarding profits, the other standing upon advantage of quirks and terms of advantage, there is no better fruits to be looked for from them.' Walsingham complained to Davison also that the States were not meeting their current engagements for the pay of the English troops already dispatched—'wherewith', he added, 'her Majesty is not a little offended, seeing how little care they have to yield her satisfaction in such things as they promise unto her, which she imputeth rather to proceed of contempt than of any want or necessity; which if it should fall out to be such as by them is pretended, then doth she conceive her bargain to be very ill made to join her fortune with so weak and broken an estate. And surely, sir, it is a thing greatly to be feared indeed, that the contributions they bear us in hand they will yield will fall out more true in paper than in payment, which if it should so happen, it would turn some to blame, whereof you (amongst others) are to bear your part as not exempt of that number.' [1]

Elizabeth, indeed, was so much provoked at the Dutch that she did not hesitate to say openly that she was sick of her whole

[1] Harleian MSS. 6993, f. 110.
[2] S. P. Holland, iv, f. 201 (in *Cal. Foreign*, 1585-6, pp. 113-15).

bargain. In so doing Walsingham protested that she was going too far. He admitted that she had a just grievance, but he insisted that it was in the highest degree impolitic for her to denounce publicly the allies whom she had but just agreed to support.

'I thought good to let your Lordship understand,' he wrote to Burghley on the 26th of October, 'that I learn by divers that repair unto me at this time of my indisposition, that her Majesty doth deliver unto divers persons the great mislike she hath of her own resolution taken in this cause of the Low Countries—a matter, being once known either by the enemy or those of the Low Countries, cannot but work some dangerous change.

'If her Majesty be disposed to make a peace and compound the differences between her and Spain, she cannot but make it with far greater advantage now than before when she had not Flushing and Briel in her hands. But the way to make it good is not in outward show to seem to mislike of the bargain she hath now made, but rather to put on a good countenance on the matter for a while until there shall be some way devised to compound things both with honour and safety.' [1]

There is no reason to believe that Walsingham favoured such a course. His immediate problem was to urge the Queen forward until she had definitely committed herself. If he could do it by showing that a vigorous war would facilitate an early peace, he was quite prepared to follow that method, though an early peace was probably far from his thoughts.

Early in November Walsingham found the situation at Court more encouraging. He wrote to Davison on the 6th, 'Our stay in sending over the governors of the towns [of Briel and Flushing], a thing so greatly desired by the well-affectioned, cannot but breed some doubt there of our disposition to the cause, or rather that (being now possessed of Flushing and the Briel) we shall seek to serve our own turn at their cost and peril. I cannot deny but some practices have been used to draw her Majesty to mislike of the present action and of such as advised her to enter into the same; but the matter is now salved and I hope free from like practices. The Earl of Leicester with the two governors do mean with the leave of God to embark the 16th of this present for Flushing.' [2]

[1] S. P. Domestic, clxxxiii, no. 56.
[2] S. P. Holland, v, f. 25 (in *Cal. Foreign*, 1585-6, p. 146).

But the 16th came and went and Leicester was still in England. He had his commission signed and sealed, but the Queen was now making difficulties over his supplies. She was very reluctant to advance the money he required. Leicester told Walsingham flatly that he could not and would not go without money, and in desperation he offered to sell his lands to the Queen at a considerable loss for ready cash.[1] Walsingham foresaw trouble ahead on this question of finances. He knew Elizabeth's cheeseparing policy of old and was confident that nothing much could come of the enterprise in so far as it was dependent upon her disbursements.[2]

'I find you grieved,' he wrote to Davison on the 19th of November, 'and not without cause in respect of the overthwart proceedings as well there as here. I hope upon the arrival of the Earl of Leicester you shall be eased of the care of the disorders there, which would be easily redressed if we could take a thorough, resolute course here, a matter that men may rather pray for than hope for. And therefore it is very doubtful that the present action now in hand will be accompanied with very good success, unless they of the country there may be drawn to bear the greatest burden of the charges of the wars and not to attend any greater support from hence than the continuance of the payment of 4,000 footmen and 1,000 horse.'[3]

Nor was money the only difficulty in the way. Elizabeth was determined to restrict Leicester's authority in the Low Countries as much as possible, with a view probably to avoid committing herself too deeply in their behalf. She would not allow him any higher place there than that of general of her forces and refused to consider his taking an oath of fidelity to the Dutch.[4] Leicester himself swore he would resign his commission if she did not give him greater scope in this regard. 'I had as lief be dead,' he wrote to Walsingham on the 3rd of December, 'as be in the case

[1] Bruce, p. 21.

[2] Sometime towards the end of the year 1585 Walsingham made an estimate of the probable cost of the Queen's campaigning in the Netherlands. He placed the annual cost at £125,856 8*s*. (*Cal. Domestic*, Addenda 1580–1625, p. 164). Another estimate made at the same time came to £126,006 14*s*. 8*d*. (ibid.) Elizabeth seems to have taken £126,000 as the maximum amount which she was prepared to spend annually. In June 1586 Walsingham wrote to Leicester to be careful not to exceed £126,000 annual expenditure (S. P. Holland, viii, f. 218).

[3] *Cal. Foreign*, 1585–6, p. 172.

[4] Bruce, p. 100.

I shall be in if this restraint hold for taking the oath there, or if some more authority be not granted than I see her Majesty would I should have. I trust you will all hold hard for this or else banish me England withal.' [1] Leicester said afterwards that the Queen gave him secret assurance that he might accept anything at the hands of the Dutch so long as it did not proceed from herself, intimating that she merely wished to keep her own skirts clear.[2] This may have been so. But she gave him no public warrant to that effect and made him suffer later for the lack of it.

To discourage Leicester still further he heard through Walsingham that there was already a project afoot for making peace with Spain. 'I perceive by your message', he wrote to Walsingham on the 3rd of December, 'that your peace with Spain will go fast on.' [3]

It does not appear from Leicester's letter what peace with Spain he referred to. There were, in fact, no less than three in progress at this juncture. One of them seems to have been set in motion by Walsingham himself. It had its beginnings as far back as April 1582, when Antonio de Castilio, who had been ambassador of Portugal in England, was recalled by Philip II after the union of Portugal with Spain. Just before Castilio left Walsingham had invited him to a private conference, had discussed with him the desirability of a peace between England and Spain, and had urged him to broach the matter to Philip on his return. Castilio had entertained the suggestion cordially but had declined to take it up with his master without some written warrant from Elizabeth. This, however, she had refused to give him, so nothing had come of the matter at that time.[4] In the late autumn of 1585, however, just before Leicester's departure for the Netherlands, Walsingham decided to renew his former suggestion to Castilio. The probabilities are that he took this step at the Queen's prompting, who very likely wished to sound Philip's disposition towards peace before she proceeded to open war. This, however, is mere surmise. At any rate Walsingham directed Dr. Hector Nũnez, a Portuguese physician in London, and one of Castilio's English correspondents,

[1] Motley, i. 347. [2] Bruce, p. 100. [3] Motley, i. 348.
[4] *Cal. Spanish*, 1580–6, p. 345; *Cal. Foreign*, 1585–6, pp. 472–5.

to write to him and recommend that he take up this matter of peace with the Spanish King or some one of his council. Nũnez wrote the letter and it was dispatched to Castilio in November. It had the desired effect. Castilio acquiesced, brought the matter to the attention of the King, and wrote back to inquire upon what terms the Queen would be willing to treat. His reply did not reach London until late in March 1586. Walsingham then directed Nũnez to answer that the Queen would be prepared to negotiate for a peace upon condition that Philip would grant to his Dutch rebels toleration in religion and such other concessions as had been embodied in the Pacification of Ghent. Nũnez was also to suggest that Castilio should come to England for the ostensible purpose of treating about Portuguese affairs and should open direct negotiations for peace with the Queen.[1] This letter did not reach Castilio until July 1586. When he showed it to the King's ministers they directed him to reply that the terms were such that he did not even dare to present them to his master.[2] Notwithstanding this reply Walsingham still thought the matter worth pursuing as late as April 1587.[3]

Exactly what he expected to gain from these negotiations is not clear. He could hardly have hoped that Philip would be willing to concede to his rebels the one point of religion upon which all former attempts at peace had been wrecked. It seems most likely that he promoted the affair, not because he had any hope of its success, but merely to satisfy the inclinations of his mistress towards peace. Possibly he hoped by directing peace negotiations into a channel which he could control to prevent the opening of other negotiations upon terms far less favourable to the Dutch and to the Protestant cause.[4] If so he failed. There were, indeed, other projects of peace already afoot in

[1] *Cal. Foreign*, 1585–6, pp. 472–5, 508. A Spanish account of these negotiations will be found in *Cal. Spanish*, 1580–6, p. 654. The carrier of Dr. Nũnez's letters was Jeronimo Pardo, a Lisbon merchant who was later accused of being one of Walsingham's spies in Spain (ibid., 1587–1603, pp. 221–2).

[2] Castilio to Nũnez, 14 Sept. 1586, S. P. Spain, ii, unnumbered folios; cf. Nũnez to Walsingham, 30 Sept. 1586, ibid.

[3] Cf. 'The heads of a letter to be written by Mr. Doctor Hector to D. Antonio Castilio', corrected in Walsingham's hand, dated April 1587, S. P. Spain, ii, unnumbered folios.

[4] It is worth noting that he, like Burghley, tried to deceive Leicester as to these peace negotiations; cf. Bruce, *op. cit.*, p. 188.

December 1585 in which he had no commerce and in regard to which every effort was made to keep him in the dark.

One of these was instigated by Sir James Crofts, a councillor whose Spanish sympathies were notorious, who had in fact for some years been a pensioner of the King of Spain. Now Crofts had a kinsman named William Bodenham, who lived in the Low Countries and had access to the ear of the Prince of Parma. Sometime late in the year 1585 or early in the year following Crofts sent a servant of his, named Morris, to Dunkirk ostensibly for the purpose of buying horses. But Morris was charged to seek out Bodenham and induce him to go to Parma at Brussels and inform him, in Crofts' name, that if he sent a secret agent to England a peace might be arranged. Morris obeyed orders, Parma eventually got the message, and so another channel for negotiations was opened.[1]

It may have been in consequence of Crofts' advances, it may have been independently, that another channel was opened from Antwerp. On the 14th of December Carlo Lanfranchi, an Italian merchant dwelling in Antwerp, and a close friend of M. de Champagny, Parma's governor in that city, wrote a letter to Andrea de Loo, a Flemish merchant in London, urging him to suggest the possibility of peace to some influential member of the Queen's Privy Council. De Loo showed the letter to Burghley, and he in turn conveyed it to the Queen. As was to be expected she leaped at the suggestion and bade Burghley exploit it for all it was worth. So much had been done by the time Leicester left for the Low Countries.[2] Every effort

[1] Cf. '*A Declaration, &c.*', printed in Appendix i; Bruce, pp. 231, 319; *Cal. Spanish*, 1580–6, pp. 474, 653; Motley, i, pp. 490 ff.; *Cal. Foreign*, 1585–6, Introd., pp. xxxiii ff. Walsingham's connexion with these underhand negotiations for peace was too remote to justify a discussion of the negotiations as a whole, though they need to be studied with more care than has hitherto been given to them. The most complete accounts of them are in Froude, and in Motley, but neither are to be relied upon. Mrs. Lomas in the introduction to the *Cal. Foreign*, 1585–6, has discussed the evidence on the subject down to 1 June 1586, and promises a discussion of later events in the forthcoming volume of the Foreign Calendar. Some important documents on the Spanish side of the story are printed in the Appendix to vol. xii of Paullet et Piot, *Correspondance de Cardinal Granvelle*. The Spanish Calendar does not give these documents, nor 'indeed any other Simancas documents of 1585 or 1586 except those taken to France during the Peninsular War and now in the Paris archives'.

[2] Cf. Appendix i; *Cal. Foreign*, 1585–6, p. 240.

was made to keep the negotiations secret both from him and from Walsingham. There is no certain evidence that Walsingham knew of them until the following April. Burghley's share in the matter is one more indication of the hollowness of his zeal for the militant aggressive course.[1]

All these projects of peace were being launched at just about the time that Leicester was making his final preparations to depart for the Netherlands. They served as so many obstacles

[1] The attitude of Burghley towards these secret manœuvres for peace is not easy to state with certainty. Mrs. Lomas (*Cal. Foreign*, 1585–6, Introd., p. xlvi) takes the view that his attitude was reserved and distinctly critical. It would perhaps be more accurate to say that it was cautious. One cannot read the letters which passed from de Loo to him without reaching the conclusion that de Loo was acting under his advice and was very likely coached by him in his informal correspondence with Lanfranchi. Certainly de Loo kept Burghley in close touch with every step in this correspondence and supplied him with copies of the letters he wrote to Lanfranchi. It is evident also that de Loo was eager to keep the whole matter as secret as possible (*Cal. Foreign*, 1585–6, pp. 546, 616), and that Burghley co-operated with him in this until the news leaked out through other channels. De Loo even asked Burghley's advice as to what he should say to Walsingham in case Walsingham found out about it (ibid. 547).

In the correspondence from Palavicino to Burghley regarding the possibility of making approaches for peace through Prince Doria, it is pretty clear, though nowhere expressly stated, that Palavicino was acting at Burghley's prompting (ibid. 516), and also that he could depend upon Burghley's hostile attitude towards Leicester (ibid.).

Finally the letters from Morris and Bodenham to Burghley (ibid. 544–5) pretty clearly reveal that Burghley was encouraging both these men to proceed.

As to whether Burghley encouraged de Loo and Lanfranchi to believe that Elizabeth would not insist upon religious toleration for the Dutch as a condition of the peace, the letter of Lanfranchi of 28 Jan. 1586 (ibid. 329), and especially the last part of de Loo's letter to Burghley of 11 Feb. 1586 (ibid. 368), in which he wrote that he had been 'greatly comforted by what you said to me yesterday on the matter of religion and that her Majesty seeks nothing but the pacification of the afflicted Netherlands', seem to lend support to the view that he did. Motley (i. 495 ff.) takes the position that Burghley stood out strongly for toleration for the Dutch, but that the Queen behind his back through Buckhurst gave assurances to the contrary. Motley bases his opinion of Burghley's attitude upon copies of Burghley's letters to de Loo in the archives of Simancas. Burghley's draft of the letter upon which Motley chiefly relied is in S. P. Flanders, i, and is dated 7 Mar. 1586/7. Motley assigns it to 1586. In the British Museum, Cotton MSS., Galba C ix, f. 124, is a paper in Burghley's hand, endorsed with the date 9 Mar. 1586/7, which contains a brief account of de Loo's negotiations. In each of these papers Burghley represents himself as having insisted upon the point of toleration in religion, but it is to be observed that they were written a year after the negotiations had been under way. Motley (i. 499) bases his story of Elizabeth's underhand dealing through Buckhurst upon de Loo's own account of the negotiations in the archives of Simancas, which is printed in full in Paullet et Piot, *Correspondance de Cardinal Granvelle*, xii, appendix, pp. 404 ff.

in his way by encouraging Elizabeth to persist in her irresolute course. Walsingham for his part was sick and tired of the whole business. 'He is utterly discouraged', Leicester wrote to Burghley on the 9th of December, 'to deal any more in these causes. I pray God your Lordship grow not so too, for then all will to the ground on my poor side especially.'[1] To Walsingham himself Leicester wrote on the same day: 'I am sorry her Majesty doth deem you so partial. And yet my suits have not of late been so many nor so great, the greatest, I am sure, are for her Majesty's own service. For my part I will discharge my duty as far as my poor ability and capacity shall serve, and if I shall not have her gracious and princely support and supply, the lack will be to us for the present, but the shame and dishonour will be yours there.'[2]

For all that, Leicester left England confident that Walsingham, desperate though he was, would do all in his power to assist the campaign. To Walsingham and Hatton, indeed, Leicester seems to have looked as his principal counsellors and champions.[3] Burghley he distrusted. His farewell letter reveals that clearly:

> 'Your Lordship', Leicester wrote, 'cannot but remember the cause for which it hath pleased her Majesty to send me to the Low Countries. It was not only by your Lordship, but by the whole number of councillors agreed upon. . . . I trust, my good Lord, now that I have taken this voyage upon me, to serve her Majesty as she hath commanded, your Lordship will be mindful of me. . . . Her Majesty, I see, my Lord, often times doth fall into mislike of this cause, and sundry opinions it may breed in her withal, but I trust in the Lord, seeing her Highness hath thus far resolved and grown also to thus far execution as she hath and that mine own and other men's poor lives and substances are adventured for her sake . . . that she will fortify and maintain her own action to the full performance of that she hath agreed upon. . . . And, good my Lord, for my last, have me only thus far in your care, that in these things that her Majesty and you all have agreed and confirmed for me to do, that I be not made a metamorphosis, that I shall not know what to do.'[4]

[1] Motley, i. 352.

[2] *Cal. Foreign*, 1585–6, p. 205.

[3] Cf. Leicester to Walsingham, 3 Dec. 1585: 'Mr. Secretary: I have written a letter to her Majesty which I send you open, and if you think it needful, it may please you to deliver it. You may speak with Mr. Vice-Chamberlain [Hatton] also therein. . . . If you and Mr. Vice-Chamberlain shall think good to deliver the letter, I pray you seal it with a little hard wax and your little seal' (S. P. Holland, v, f. 149).

[4] Bruce, pp. 22–3.

Burghley replied the next day:

'My very good Lord, I have received your courteous letter wherein your Lordship doth commend to me your honourable cause, that your state and service now in hand doth require, whereof truly, my Lord, I do assure you, no less a portion of my care and trouble for many respects to the furtherance of your own honour than if I were a most near kinsman in blood; and for the advancement of the action, if I should not with all the powers of my heart continually both wish and work advancement thereunto, I were to be an accursed person in the sight of God, considering the ends of this action tend to the glory of God, to the safety of the Queen's person, to the preservation of this realm in a perpetual quietness, wherein for my particular interest both for myself and my posterity, I have as much interest as any of my degree. And this I pray you, my Lord, make a perfect account of me and for my doings.' [1]

And yet already Burghley was beginning to turn over in his mind projects of peace, and before the month was out was discussing them secretly with the Queen.

As for Walsingham, he waved his farewell to Leicester with misgivings. 'I wish', he wrote to Davison, 'he may find more comfort in his being there than he hath received in his departure from hence.' [2]

Leicester took ship at Harwich on the 8th of December and arrived in Flushing two days later.[3] His accounts of his reception were optimistic in the extreme, but Walsingham found no answering enthusiasm at the English court.

'As far as I can learn,' he wrote to Leicester late in December, 'by such of my friends as are acquainted with our court proceedings, it worketh not that good effect that were to be wished, so unpleasant are all things that minister matter of charge. . . . I am very glad that the promised contribution of the States carries likelihood of performance, which stoppeth the mouths and practices of those that sought to work another conceit in her Majesty, by bearing her in hand that she was abused and that the burden of the charges would light upon her, or at least that she

[1] Bruce, pp. 24–5. Leicester gathered no little comfort from this letter; cf. his comment on it to Walsingham in *Cal. Foreign*, 1585–6, p. 202.

[2] *Cal. Foreign*, 1585–6, p. 198.

[3] There is a journal of Leicester's movements from 4 Dec. 1585 to 13 Feb. 1586 among the manuscripts of the Royal College of Arms, printed in *Retrospective Review*, 2nd series, i. 277; cf. also Burrough's journal (8–17 Dec.) in Bruce, Appendix i.

should in the end be forced, in respect of charges, to give over the cause. I would to God their means might have been found such as some part of her own charges might have been diminished, whereby she might have been the rather encouraged to have put on a resolution to have proceeded constantly in the maintenance of the cause.' [1]

In another letter to Leicester written about the same time Walsingham intimated clearly that to his thinking nothing but the promise of an early peace and the sparing of all extra charges would hold the Queen long to an aggressive policy.

'Her Majesty,' he wrote, 'as I hear by my friends in Court, hath received very great contentment and satisfaction with the comfortable message you have sent her by Mr. Thomas George that if it pleased her to go roundly to work with that action she should be assured at the year's end of the advantage of a peace accompanied both with honour and safety, besides some special benefit to herself. And indeed so good hope was given her in very good time, for we began already to grow too weary of the charge of the war and to fear too much the long continuance thereof, as it was half doubted lest some over hasty course would have been taken for some dangerous and dishonourable peace. The note sent by your Lordship of the wants at Ostend was not best welcome to her Majesty, who conceiveth thereby that it is meant to procure the supplying of the same out of her own purse, over and above the support agreed upon. . . . Seeing that she is so coldly affected unto the cause as she is, there must be no cause of suspicion or jealousy ministered unto her that she is like to be drawn into any further charge than by the treaty is accorded, lest there follow greater inconvenience thereby than the advantage thereof can do good.' [2]

One of the first problems which faced Leicester upon his arrival in the Netherlands was that of defining his exact position in the government. By title he was merely lieutenant-general of the Queen's forces, but it was clearly intended from the first that he should take cognizance of other than purely military matters. His instructions, for instance, directed him to oversee the collection of the money levied by the Dutch for the maintenance of the wars and to take some steps to reform the disordered state of their government. It is true that before he left England the Queen had expressly charged him not to stretch his authority

[1] Bruce, p. 35.

[2] 22 Dec. 1585, S. P. Holland, v, f. 249.

beyond his warrant, but she had intimated to him as well that he might accept any position which the States were prepared to bestow upon him, so long as the commission came from them and not from her. And she had apparently said as much to the Dutch commissioners. Leicester had clearly conceived of a position for himself similar to that which the Prince of Orange had enjoyed. The Dutch evidently intended from the first that he should take general charge of their affairs. Their government, since the Prince's death, had been very much confused, and they had made no effort to reform it, in expectation of Leicester's coming. They had some reason to believe that although Elizabeth had refused to assume formally the position of either sovereign or protector, she would make no objection to any authority which they might find it necessary to confer upon her favourite.[1]

At all events Leicester had hardly arrived in the Netherlands before they proceeded to remove all the ambiguities attached to his charge by definitely tendering to him the position of absolute governor. The offer was formally made by a deputation of the States General on the 11th of January. Leicester feigned reluctance to accept it, and for some days postponed his definite answer. But his mind was made up from the first, and his hesitation seems to have been occasioned rather by the fact that the Dutch were offering him too little than too much. The interval between the formal tender of the office on the 11th and his formal acceptance of it on the 24th was devoted to negotiations designed to secure for him a more absolute kind of authority than was at first intended. He apparently had no thought of securing the Queen's consent before he made his decision. Although he did write to Walsingham about the offer three days after it was tendered, he wrote in such terms as to indicate that he had already made up his mind to accept it.[2] Very likely he felt that there was a much better chance of getting Elizabeth to accept a *fait accompli* than of winning her approval to the step before it was taken. Convinced as he was of the wisdom of his course, he persuaded himself that his mistress would not be

[1] Bruce, pp. 12, 20, 121.

[2] Ibid., p. 57; cf. also Davison to Walsingham, 16 Jan. 1586, in *Cal. Foreign*, 1585-6, p. 303.

averse from reaping her profit from it if she could at the same time disclaim all responsibility. That he feared her wrath is evident, but his ambition tempted him to risk it. He trusted to his strong influence over her to conciliate it when it came.

Froude has intimated that Leicester acted in this matter at Walsingham's secret advice, and Leicester himself charged Walsingham with having encouraged him to accept it.[1] But Froude was merely guessing, and Leicester made his charge at a time when he was doing his utmost to shift the responsibility for his action upon other shoulders. There is almost no direct evidence on this particular point in question. In general, however, Walsingham's letters at this juncture reveal an unusually cautious attitude and no disposition on his part to counsel any step likely to offend the Queen or to weaken her resolution. This appears, for example, in a letter which he wrote to Leicester on the 22nd of December with reference to the Dutch finances: 'You have, in mine opinion, done very advisedly not to accept of the charge and employment of their treasure until you have acquainted yourself thoroughly with the state of affairs. But if your Lordship do find it such as may answer your expectation then will it be very necessary (*her Majesty being first made acquainted withal*) both for her service and the benefit of the country in every respect that your Lordship take that charge upon you.' [2]

On the other hand there is no doubt that Walsingham appreciated fully the confused state of the government in the Low Countries and the necessity for reforming it. His letter to Gilpin of the 19th of November is clear upon that point.

'I find by sundry reports from thence,' he wrote, 'that there is no form of government held there, pretending for excuse to depend altogether upon the Earl of Leicester's coming. And yet have they, in a matter of very good weight, (by placing the Count Maurice governor of Holland and Zeeland) taken more speedy resolution than in reason were fit. But the merit of the Prince his father was so great as there is good cause why men

[1] Froude, xii, p. 184. Leicester wrote to Walsingham, 8 Feb. 1586: 'And if I be not forgetful, it seemed then to you likewise that her Majesty was willing enough that I should receive such charge and entertainment as of themselves the Estates would lay upon me and give me; but I will not stand greatly hereupon' (Bruce, p. 100).

[2] S. P. Holland, v, f. 249 (the italics are my own).

should forbear to mislike thereof, so as the same were not done to breed some offence or mislike here and so work a division between those whom necessity ought, for common defence, to combine and unite together. I find the Earl's repair thither most necessary for many causes, and yet when I consider the great confusion that he shall find there and how hardly the same will be cured, weighing the sundry practices held in these parts to breed disunion amongst them, I am not a little grieved. I pray you therefore, as one that wisheth well both to the public and to his Lordship, confer with some of the best affected patriots there about some plot to be presented unto him, as well for the removing of the great abuses reigning there as also for the establishing of some well-settled government, wherein especially there would be somewhat thought on for the well-employing and distributing of the contributions, which being, as you know, the sinews of the wars, the body of that policy cannot but grow to utter ruin if the same be not carefully provided for.' [1]

Walsingham clearly thought that the Dutch should reduce their government to some more settled order. He thought also that they should present their 'plot' or plan of reform for Leicester's approval when he came. He was of the opinion that they had gone ahead too fast in appointing Maurice of Nassau Governor of Holland and Zeeland without consulting the interests of England. But these facts can hardly be construed into an intention on his part to have the sovereignty bestowed on Leicester contrary to the expressed purposes of the Queen. He knew too well how half-hearted Elizabeth's zeal for the cause was to run the risk of alienating her altogether by a slip so well calculated to excite her wrath.

Leicester sent word to Walsingham of the offer made to him by the States General on the 14th of January. Apparently Walsingham received the news quickly,[2] because he wrote back to Leicester on the 17th to warn him that the Queen had already taken umbrage at the title of Excellency by which the States had addressed him from the first and was likely to be more incensed at this new addition to his authority and dignity.[3] But Walsingham apparently hesitated for some days before he showed Leicester's letter to the Queen, and it may be that he

[1] Ibid., f. 90.

[2] The wind was steadily favourable to the voyage from Holland to England at this time, and consequently unfavourable to the voyage back; cf. Bruce, p. 76.

[3] *Cal. Foreign*, 1585–6, p. 303.

did not show it to her at all, preferring that some one else should be the herald of the news. At all events Elizabeth heard of it about the 25th of the month, and she immediately ordered her principal councillors to write a joint letter to Leicester commanding him not to accept the offer. Burghley drafted the letter. The effect of it was that the Queen was amazed that he had not rejected the offer forthwith, 'considering as she saith that none knew her determination therein better than yourself, whom at your going from hence she did peremptorily charge not to accept any such title or office upon you.'[1] But long before this letter reached Leicester, before indeed it was written, he had definitely and formally accepted the offer.

When Elizabeth heard of this her wrath knew no bounds. 'Her Majesty will not endure to hear any speech in defence thereof,' Burghley wrote to Leicester on the 7th of February.[2] She decided to send a special envoy to Leicester at once with orders to him to resign the office forthwith. Sir Thomas Heneage was the man chosen for the office, and Walsingham himself was obliged to draft the letters of instructions. He tried his best to induce the Queen to consider the possible effect of such a resignation upon the public sentiment in the Low Countries before she took this step, but to no purpose.[3] Nothing would do but that Leicester must lay down his office at once and in as public a manner as he had assumed it.[4] Since Walsingham could not induce the Queen to mitigate Heneage's instructions he did his best to delay Heneage's departure. Thomas Dudley, one of Leicester's servants, wrote to him on the 11th of February:

[1] S. P. Holland, vi, f. 54. Burghley's draft is in S. P. Holland, vi, f. 53.

[2] Bruce, p. 104.

[3] In Walsingham's original draft of these instructions (S. P. Holland, vi, 110) a passage is inserted instructing Heneage to take council with wise heads in Holland, and if he find them of the opinion that Leicester's resignation was 'likely to breed, by the practice of such as are ill-affected to this state, such an alienation in them as may happily work a revolt unto the Spaniard' he was to advise the Queen before proceeding further. This passage is struck out by Walsingham and marked on the margin 'Not allowed of'. Unfortunately the *Cal. Foreign*, 1585-6, p. 365, does not print this original draft, which with its corrections reveals eloquently Walsingham's efforts to mitigate Elizabeth's severity towards Leicester.

[4] To make matters worse some one of Leicester's enemies told the Queen that Leicester's wife, whom Elizabeth cordially hated, was about to go over to Holland in great state (Bruce, p. 112).

'Her Majesty hath, these ten or twelve days, devised and been in hand with many courses how and in what manner to overthrow that which your honour . . . hath most gravely and politically begun, and hath set down many plots for that purpose, which I hope your Excellency is not ignorant in. And truly the Lord Treasurer hath always besought her Majesty to keep one ear for your answer to her dislikes and to suspend her judgement until Mr. Davison come or that your honour did write unto her Majesty. The Lord Treasurer having been from the court these eight days, her Majesty hath, four days agone, purposed to send Sir Thomas Heneage unto you, with what commission I know not; but Mr. Vice Chamberlain [Hatton] and Mr. Secretary [Walsingham] very honorably both delay his dispatch by all means they can and hope to put it off till Sunday next, at which time the Lord Treasurer will be at the court, and then, by his help, they hope to qualify some part of her Majesty's intentions, looking before that time that Mr. Davison will arrive and satisfy all furies.' [1]

A day or two later Davison arrived in England. He signified his arrival to Walsingham at once and sought his advice as to what course he should take. Walsingham's reply was not encouraging. He said that Davison should have come sooner, that his long delay had 'wounded the whole cause', that he thought the Queen would not even see him; but yet charged him to come to Court forthwith. The same afternoon Davison saw Walsingham and found him 'utterly discomforted at her Majesty's hard opinion and course against the cause'. 'He let me understand', Davison wrote to Leicester, 'how heinously she took your acceptation of the government, how she had resolved to dispatch Sir Thomas Heneage to command you to resign it up, and to protest her disallowance thereof to the States, that she had threatened Sir Philip Sidney and myself as principal actors and persuaders thereof.' [2]

After some discussion of the matter, Walsingham went up to the Queen, and a short while afterwards Davison himself was summoned to the royal presence. His interview was a stormy one, and though he pleaded hard in defence of Leicester, he apparently made but a slight impression upon Elizabeth's wrath. The next morning he saw her again and he succeeded in inducing her to accept a letter from Leicester which she had refused to

[1] Bruce, pp. 112-13. [2] Ibid., pp. 117-18.

receive the day before. She even admitted that she did not mislike the fact of Leicester's authority so much as the form of it. But she swore that Davison was altogether too partial in his views and that she did not feel that she could altogether trust him—a charge which provoked from him the request that he might be allowed to retire from her service and devote the rest of his days in prayer for her, 'whom in all appearance, salvation itself was not able to save, if she continued the course she was in.'[1] Yet on the whole Davison was distinctly encouraged by the result of his second day's conference. Late the same night Elizabeth gave orders that Sir Thomas Heneage should be stayed until he heard her further pleasure.

The next day Davison saw the Queen yet a third time and found the 'heat of her offence' so much abated that he had hope she might in time be brought to reason. Nevertheless she was still determined to send Heneage over, and still insisted that Leicester should resign his office. She did, however, mitigate his instructions to such an extent as to save Leicester from a public and open disgrace.[2]

There can be little doubt that Walsingham was doing his uttermost at this juncture in Leicester's defence. Dudley and Davison both bear testimony to that fact. Davison wrote to Leicester on the 28th of February: 'Mr. Secretary hath been behindhand to no one of the rest in an honest and honourable defence of your doings, but the opinion of his partiality to your Lordship hath somewhat prejudiced his credit with her Majesty.'[3] Hatton likewise was Leicester's staunch advocate.[4] As to Burghley's attitude there was some difference of opinion. According to Dudley, he was dealing 'most honourably and friendly' for Leicester.[5] Davison thought Leicester ought to thank Burghley for his good offices, but does not seem to have been altogether sure of him. 'I do not forget', Davison wrote to Leicester, 'to labour him [Burghley] all that I may.'[6] But the French ambassador in London and Thomas Morgan, Mary Stuart's agent in Paris, held different views. Morgan wrote to Mary in March, 'Leicester, before his departure out of England, laboured to make four new councillors to the state to help to back him

[1] Ibid., p. 124.
[2] Ibid., pp. 124, 142.
[3] Ibid., p. 143.
[4] Ibid., pp. 175–6.
[5] Ibid., p. 112.
[6] Ibid., p. 143.

in all causes. The councillors whom he desired to prefer were the Earls Huntingdon, Pembroke, and Kent, and the Lord Gray. But Burghley, who was weak of friends in the Privy Council, in Leicester's absence hath made the Queen to admit of her Privy Council the Archbishop of Canterbury, Lord Cobham, and the Lord of Buckhurst, being all three for their lives opposite to Leicester and his designments.' [1] The French ambassador wrote to Mary in February that Burghley was making use of these new councillors to oppose Walsingham's efforts in Leicester's behalf. 'The Earl of Leicester', he wrote, 'is in Flanders, where he is establishing himself, and it is said that the Queen of England is angry at his behaviour, fearing lest he make himself over great. Walsingham, his friend, supports him as much as he can, but Lord Burghley opposes him and has joined three councillors to his party, the Archbishop of Canterbury, Lord Cobham, and Lord Buckhurst, which irritates Leicester and his followers not a little.' [2]

It is quite easy to attach too much importance to the testimony of these two men. Like many of Mary's friends they cherished the belief that Burghley was more kindly disposed towards her than he probably was in fact, and were inclined to over-emphasize his opposition to her sworn enemies the Puritans. Yet it is certain that the three councillors were appointed early in the year 1586, and highly probable that they owed their appointment to Burghley's influence and belonged to his party. Their presence in the Privy Council, joined with Leicester's absence, must have had the effect of increasing Burghley's influence in that body considerably.[3] To what extent he was disposed to

[1] S. P. Mary, Queen of Scots, xvii, no. 31.

[2] Ibid., no. 24. The original is, of course, in French; cf. also the extract from Buzanval's (Navarre's agent in London) letter to del Bene in *Cal. Foreign*, 1585–6, p. 672. It is worth noting that the Prince of Parma was also of the opinion that Burghley and his party were doing everything in their power to obstruct Leicester's progress in the Netherlands; cf. Parma to Philip II, 11 June 1586, cited by Motley, i. 508. Apropos of the appointment of the Archbishop of Canterbury to the Council, Roger Manners wrote to the Earl of Rutland, 14 Feb. 1586: 'The Lord Archbishop we say here was only made a councillor by old William [Burghley] to the overthrow of the Puritans, whereat they much malign and yet dare not complain but in secret' (*Rutland Papers*, i. 190).

[3] Sir Walter Raleigh was charged with belonging to the party opposed to Leicester, a charge which he indignantly denied in a letter to Leicester of 29 Mar. 1586 (Bruce, p. 193). Elizabeth expressly charged Walsingham to

exploit his new-found strength to Leicester's detriment it is difficult to say with certainty. The French ambassador, from whom Morgan probably got his cue, held to one view, but men who were even more closely in touch with events at the English court disagreed with him. Not only Dudley and Davison, but even Walsingham himself bore witness to Burghley's friendly offices.[1] And their opinion carries greater weight. Yet it is hard to believe that Burghley cherished any great friendliness for Leicester or any zeal for his cause. It may be he had come to the conclusion that Leicester could do less harm abroad than at home, and that it was better to maintain his cause in the Netherlands than to call him back even in disgrace. Elizabeth certainly contemplated revoking her favourite at this juncture.[2] It may have been Burghley's fear that she would carry out this policy which induced him to come forward as Leicester's champion. Burghley knew, none better, how great an influence Leicester could still exert over the Queen. Though he might return in disgrace, he was pretty certain to win his way to favour again. Sir Edward Stafford, English ambassador to Paris, and one of Burghley's staunchest partisans, may have hit upon Burghley's own view of the situation when he wrote, in November 1586, 'If I had as much credit as your Lordship hath, and he [Leicester] born to do me no more good than he is, I would keep him where he is and he should drink that which he hath brewed. Her Majesty is not for his tarrying there bound to do more than she shall see fit, but I would keep him there to undo himself and sure enough from coming home to undo others.'[3]

Sir Thomas Heneage, delayed by contrary winds, did not reach the Netherlands until the 3rd of March. Before he left England Burghley had succeeded in inducing the Queen to allow him a certain discretion in carrying out his instructions.[4] Davison also had written to Leicester at the time of Heneage's departure:

'Though I dare not take upon me to give advice to your

write to Leicester in her name and assure him that Raleigh had played the friend. Walsingham did so, but did not express any opinion himself as to Raleigh's attitude (Bruce, p. 207). [1] Ibid., p. 161. [2] Ibid., p. 151.

[3] S. P. France, xvi, f. 139. [4] Bruce, p. 124.

Lordship how to proceed with Sir Thomas Heneage, yet would I wish, under your correction, in case he have order to proceed in the delivery of any other letters than to yourself, that they were retained until, upon the information of your Lordship and others, he had signified the danger and inconvenience thereof to her Majesty and received her full pleasure; because, in the meantime, I hope things may be wrought here as you wish them, so your Lordship forget not to amend your noted fault in her Majesty's behalf; for, in particular I find not her Majesty altogether so sharp as some men look, though her favour outwardly cooled in respect both of this action and of our plain proceeding with her here in defence thereof.' [1]

This was the course which Heneage, after consultation with Leicester, elected to follow. He did not present the Queen's letter of remonstrance [2] to the Estates General, but wrote instead to inform her of the danger of such a proceeding, and took no further action until he had received her answer.

Meantime in England Walsingham was doing his best to induce the Queen to send Leicester the money he needed for current expenses. Money, money, money, had been the burden of Leicester's cry ever since his departure. On the 22nd of January he had written to Walsingham, 'Our money goeth very low'; on the 3rd of February, 'I must let you know all our treasure is gone and I have laid out three or four thousand pounds besides my expenses'; on the 24th of February, 'Forget not money, money'. He was demanding also fresh supplies of men to fill the gaps in his ranks.[3] But Elizabeth turned a deaf ear to all these pleas. For months on end neither Burghley nor Hatton could wring a penny or a soldier from her. As for Walsingham, she would hardly endure to hear him speak for them.[4] It is easy enough to account for her sparing mind. 'Methinks I hear your answer already,' Leicester wrote to Walsingham in January, 'that no man knoweth better than I the difficulty to get money from her Majesty.' [5] But there was more to it than mere inveterate thrift. In the first place, Elizabeth had reason to fear that the Spanish King contemplated a descent by sea upon her own coasts. The reports of English spies in Spain during the early months of the year 1586 indicated that Philip II was

[1] Bruce, p. 144. [2] Ibid., p. 468. [3] Ibid., pp. 68, 87, 137.
[4] Ibid., pp. 152, 175. [5] Ibid., p. 68.

preparing a large naval expedition for parts unknown.[1] The presumption was that after the spring storms were over this armada would be launched against England. Under these circumstances Elizabeth naturally hesitated to send her soldiers and her money out of England. Walsingham tried his best to convince her that her fears from this quarter were groundless.[2] The Spanish preparations', he wrote to Leicester on the 24th of March, 'as they report that came from Lisbon the 10th of this present, will prove nothing this year and I hope less the next.'[3] But there was enough evidence to the contrary to satisfy Elizabeth that the secretary was more optimistic than the facts warranted. Unfortunately at this inopportune moment a Scottish ship happened to pass the palace at Greenwich where the Queen was in residence. It fired a gun in salute, Elizabeth heard the noise, saw the ship, and when she discovered that it had come from Spain directed the master to be summoned before her. She questioned him closely, and he reported that at the time he had left Lisbon he had seen great naval preparations afoot there, and a fleet of 27 galleons making ready for the seas. Some people had told him that this fleet was designed for England. At once Elizabeth turned upon Walsingham in a fury—addressed a few sharp words to him and hurled her slipper at his face, a performance which may be taken to indicate that he had not altogether succeeded in allaying her fears of an attack from Spain.[4]

Under these circumstances Elizabeth's disposition was towards a course which would avoid giving Philip further provocation. Leicester had better be prevented from any aggressive action in the Netherlands. He had proved to be careless of her commands. The surer way was to cut off his supplies. Herein, probably, lies part of the explanation of her parsimony towards him at this juncture. Another part lies in her increased hopes of peace.

Burghley's negotiations with Parma through de Loo and

[1] Bruce, p. 53; *The Spanish War* (Naval Records Society), pp. 52–64; *Cal. Irish*, 1586–8, p. 37.

[2] On Walsingham's attitude, cf. *Cal. Irish*, 1586–8, p. 37.

[3] Bruce, p. 187.

[4] *Cal. Spanish*, 1580–6, p. 573. The Spanish ambassador, in telling the story, remarks that the slipper hurling 'is not a very extraordinary thing for her to do as she is constantly behaving in such a rude manner as this'.

Lanfranchi were making good speed. After de Loo had broached the matter to Burghley in December 1585 and had received an encouraging reply, he had written to Lanfranchi again and Lanfranchi had replied in turn that if the Queen remained steadfast in her desire for peace she should have such terms as pleased her, even to the repayment of the money she had already spent in the Netherlands, provided only that she would not intermeddle in matters of religion.[1] This letter of Lanfranchi's reached England early in March. Elizabeth saw it of course, and it filled her with such good hope of peace that the prospect of advancing more money for the conduct of the war appeared to her less pleasing than ever. Mr. Thomas Vavasour, one of Leicester's gentlemen, who was pleading his master's cause at Court, wrote to him on the 31st of March: 'I thought good to advertise your Excellency, if you know it not already, that I gather by her Majesty that an indifferent peace will not be refused, whereof you are only used for an instrument; for talking with her Majesty of the necessity to put men into field, to the which I found her ears altogether stopped, especially blaming the charges, "and what", quoth she, "if a peace should come in the meantime?"'[2]

Nevertheless Walsingham, with Burghley's and Hatton's assistance, did succeed in inducing Elizabeth to send over to Leicester £24,000 towards the end of March.[3] He wrote to Leicester that he was sorry it was no more, but he saw no hope that it would be increased unless Drake returned with sufficient plunder to restore the depleted treasury. 'If the inconvenience likely to ensue thereby', he wrote again to Leicester, 'cannot be helped through Sir Francis Drake's good success, which is a matter accidental, I fear your Lordship shall receive very scant measure from hence, for you will not believe how the sparing humour doth increase upon us.'[4]

Leicester had asked for men as well as money. But upon this point, although Walsingham argued hard for it, he could not induce the Queen to yield. The most she could allow was that some of her soldiers recently discharged from service in Ireland

[1] Cf. *A Declaration*, &c. in Appendix i; Lanfranchi to de Loo, 27 Feb./9 Mar. 1586, *Cal. Foreign*, 1585-6, pp. 398-400.

[2] Bruce, p. 195. [3] Ibid., p. 180. [4] Ibid., p. 191.

might be conveyed over to Holland, upon condition that it should be done without expense to her. Even this concession, Walsingham told Leicester, was prompted primarily by her fear that she would otherwise be put to the expense of their maintenance in England. 'Nothing', he declared bitterly, 'that can be alleged can draw her Majesty to yield to anything that tendeth to the furtherance of the service there, otherwise than led by mere necessity.' [1]

It is plain from the whole tone of Walsingham's letters at this juncture that he was becoming absolutely desperate. To make matters worse he suspected that his opponents in the Privy Council were seeking to discredit him by intimating to the Queen that his loyalty to Leicester had biased his judgement. This was the last straw. On the 28th of March he wrote to Leicester, 'The opinion of my partiality continueth, nourished by faction, which maketh me weary of the place I serve in and to wish myself amongst the true-hearted Swiss.' [2]

But with the coming in of April the situation took a distinct turn for the better. This may have been due to the encouraging news received of Drake's exploits in the West Indies. 'We hear', Burghley wrote to Leicester on the 31st of March, 'that Sir Francis Drake is a fearful man to the King and that the King could have been content that Sir Francis had taken the last year's fleet so as he had not gone forward to his Indies. We hear that he hath taken seven rich ships on the coast of the Indies. I wish they were safe in the Thames.' [3] On top of this came other news out of Italy that the rumours of Drake's exploits were already seriously affecting Philip's credit with the bankers. 'The enterprise of Sir Francis Drake', Walsingham wrote to Leicester on the 11th of April, 'layeth open the present weakness of the King of Spain, for of late he hath solicited the Pope and the Dukes of Florence and Savoy for a loan of 500,000 crowns but cannot obtain neither the whole nor part of the said sum. The Genoese merchants that were wont to furnish him with money in time of necessity, for that they fear a revolt of the Indians, begin to draw back.' [4]

[1] Ibid., pp. 178–9. [2] Ibid., p. 192.
[3] Ibid., p. 199; cf. *Papers on the Spanish War* (Navy Records Society), p. 66.
[4] Bruce, p. 223.

For these, or for some other reasons not apparent, Elizabeth began to look with greater favour upon Leicester and his projects. Walsingham who had been gloomy enough late in March, wrote to Leicester on the 1st of April, 'I never knew her Majesty better affected to you than she seemeth to be now.'[1] She now consented to allow Leicester to enlist more troops in England. What was even more striking she was induced to reconsider her decision with regard to his title. In February she had sent Sir Thomas Heneage to the Netherlands to command him to resign his new position forthwith. But it will be recalled that Heneage took advantage of a discretionary clause in his instructions to suspend action until he had made his report to the Queen and had received further orders. He dispatched his report on the 10th of March by the hand of Mr. Vavasour, one of Leicester's gentlemen. The dispatch itself is missing, but there can be little doubt as to its purport. In brief, Heneage told his mistress that he found the course she had directed him to follow so dangerous to the welfare of the cause that he had deferred action until he received further instructions.[2] Vavasour was delayed at Flushing by contrary winds and did not reach England until the last week in March.[3] With his arrival at Court Walsingham and Burghley once more took up the cudgels in Leicester's behalf. Elizabeth was disposed at first to insist upon his resignation, but Burghley finally persuaded her to allow Leicester to continue in his office until the Council of State in the Netherlands could devise some way by which his resignation could be accomplished without damage to the cause. 'And for that I presume', Burghley added in writing of the matter to Leicester, 'that they cannot in any way congrue nor, with the good quietness of their state devise any such, I rest satisfied in opinion that the country shall continue in your government, for the most benefit of the country itself.'[4]

Burghley himself was chiefly instrumental in bringing this change to pass. Walsingham co-operated of course, but the 'opinion of his partiality' gave his arguments smaller weight. It was clearly Burghley's opinion that by inducing the Queen to

[1] Bruce, p. 206.
[2] Ibid., Introd., p. xxi.
[3] He arrived there sometime between 24 and 28 March, cf. Bruce, pp. 187, 191.
[4] Ibid., p. 204.

leave the question of his resignation to the Council of State he had succeeded in postponing it indefinitely. Walsingham, however, was not so certain that Elizabeth would be fobbed off in this fashion. He thought that something ought to be done for her satisfaction. On the 1st of April he wrote to Leicester,

'Touching the qualification [of your title] her Majesty so greatly affecteth, I would to God it could be brought to pass accordingly as she desireth, but I fear such a motion at this present may breed in the people's heads some unnecessary jealousy; especially for that it cannot be done without an assembly of the States General. For her Majesty's contentment it shall be well done for the Council of Estate to set down such reasons as may show the inconveniences likely to ensue upon such a motion, and to deliver them to Sir Thomas Heneage at the time of his departure from thence. And I doubt not but your Lordship will in time do your endeavour to bring this to pass which her Majesty desireth, and will by your next letters put her in comfort thereof, if your Lordship shall see any likelihood to perform same.' [1]

Notwithstanding the Queen's more kindly disposition towards Leicester and his cause, the negotiations for peace went steadily forward. Burghley and Crofts kept in touch with Bodenham through Crofts' servant Morris, and Bodenham wrote to Burghley early in April that Parma was well disposed towards peace and would presently send some one to England to discuss the matter with Burghley.[2] At the same time the correspondence between Andrea de Loo in England and Lanfranchi in Antwerp continued. It will be recalled that Lanfranchi had written to de Loo in March that the Queen might have any terms she demanded upon condition that she would not insist upon toleration in religion for the rebels.[3] Burghley was disposed to insist upon this point, but Elizabeth let de Loo understand that she would

[1] Ibid., p. 207; cf. Walsingham to Heneage of the same date: 'Yet could I wish that something were done therein for her Majesty's better satisfaction, but how that will be brought to pass without a general assembly of the States I do not well see, and I find the less hope of the performance thereof for that we have of late made a stay of the sending over both of men and money, and therefore I think some course may hereafter be taken in it' S. P. Holland, vii, f. 180.

[2] S. P. Flanders, i, f. 74.

[3] *Cal. Foreign*, 1585–6, p. 398; cf. also *A Declaration*, &c. printed in Appendix i.

demand no further toleration for the Dutch than Philip could conscientiously concede, which practically meant, of course, that she was willing to waive the question altogether.[1] When this answer was returned through Lanfranchi to Champagny he wrote himself to de Loo in very promising terms. Elizabeth saw his letter in due season expressed her pleasure at the prospect of peace, and intimated that she would be prepared to entertain formal advances so soon as they were made. She declined, however, to make the first move herself.[2] By the time matters had reached this point several of the Privy Councillors were informed of it, notably Lord Cobham, Lord Buckhurst, and Sir Christopher Hatton.[3] Cobham and Buckhurst were two of the three councillors who had been added to the Privy Council after Leicester's departure from England. They were generally regarded as Burghley's partisans, and it is not therefore surprising to discover that they were taken into his confidence. The presence of Hatton among the advocates of peace is not so easy to explain. He was generally regarded as one of Leicester's staunchest friends and advocates. It does not appear that he took any active part in the negotiations. Every effort was made to keep Leicester himself and Walsingham in the dark. So far as Walsingham was concerned these efforts were not altogether successful. Yet even as late as the middle of April he apparently had learned nothing definite about the negotiations. 'We here', he wrote to Leicester on the 11th of April, 'are so greedy of a peace, in respect of the charges of the wars, as in the procuring thereof we neither weigh honour or safety. Somewhat here is

[1] For Burghley's attitude, cf. p. 128, n. 1 above. According to de Loo's account Buckhurst and Crofts informed de Loo that Elizabeth was willing to waive the point of religion (Motley, i. 499, quoting from de Loo's narrative at Simancas).

[2] Cf. Appendix i.

[3] Cf. for Buckhurst, Motley, i. 499. Bodenham told Parma that Burghley, Buckhurst, Lord Cobham, Sir Christopher Hatton, and Sir James Crofts favoured the peace (Motley, i. 493). Motley quotes from Bodenham's account of his mission, which is printed in full in the *Correspondance de Cardinal Granvelle*, xii, appendix, pp. 455 ff. It ought to be pointed out that a comparison between Motley's account of these secret negotiations with the original documents from which he drew them shows that he followed his sources carefully, though he has been led into a few awkward mistakes by misdating some of the documents.

Some further light on the attitude of Sir Christopher Hatton is thrown by the document printed in Appendix i, below.

a dealing underhand, wherein there is great care taken that I should not be made acquainted withal.' [1]

A little later in April, however, Walsingham heard something of the negotiations for peace from Elizabeth's own lips. Some time in April an Italian merchant named Agostino Grafigna, whose residence was in Antwerp, arrived in England. Grafigna came ostensibly on business, but not long after his arrival he sought out Lord Cobham and told him that he had conferred with the Prince of Parma before leaving the Low Countries, that Parma had expressed his strong inclination to come to terms with England, and had intimated his intention to send over commissioners to open negotiations. Grafigna added that Parma had expressed his dissatisfaction at the de Loo-Lanfranchi negotiations, and preferred to open another channel of communication.[2] Cobham, of course, carried Grafigna's message to the Queen, who welcomed it as she welcomed all such advances and probably bade Cobham make what he could out of it. Cobham was thereupon tempted to exploit Grafigna's offer independently, to cut under Burghley's and Crofts' schemes, and to win the glory of the peacemaking himself. Burghley and Crofts were naturally a good deal put out by Grafigna's arrival. Crofts particularly seems to have been very much afraid that his own efforts would all come to naught.[3] Elizabeth herself was apparently quite prepared to follow any path that offered to lead to peace.

So far as Walsingham was concerned the most important

[1] Bruce, p. 223. It is to be noted that Leicester heard that Champagny was talking about peace negotiations afoot and wrote Burghley to that effect. Burghley admitted in a letter to Leicester of 31 March (ibid., p. 200) that some advances had been made by an intimate of Champagny's, but he dismissed the matter rather lightly.

[2] This is the account of the negotiations given by Parma himself (cf. Motley, i. 492, and Parma to Phillip II, 8 July 1586, in *Correspondance de Cardinal Granvelle*, xii, appendix, p. 444), and is substantially what Elizabeth told Walsingham (Bruce, p. 231). It is to be noticed that the story as told in Appendix i, below, makes out that Cobham instigated Grafigna to approach Parma in the first place, but this is probably incorrect. Parma himself made no mention of it, which he almost certainly would have done had it been so, and Grafigna himself denied it (Motley, i. 514). The interest which all these merchants showed in the cause of peace serves to emphasize the importance of the mercantile factors in the whole situation—factors which always weighed heavily with Lord Burghley.

[3] Froude (xii, p. 201 and n. 1) maintains that Crofts was the setter on of Grafigna, a statement which is directly contradicted by the very source of information which Froude quotes; cf. Appendix i.

consequence of Grafigna's visit was to put him in closer touch with the whole negotiations. It may be that Grafigna talked too much. At all events, Walsingham got wind of his dealings at Court and began to ask embarrassing questions. At the same time he succeeded in laying his hands upon some of Sir James Crofts' correspondence which revealed to him the negotiations through Morris and Bodenham, and probably also, those through de Loo and Champagny. Under those circumstances Elizabeth found herself practically forced to reveal to her Secretary the substance of Grafigna's offers as well. After that he seems to have been kept informed of the progress of the various peace projects, though he took no official part in them for some months to come.

On the 21st of April Walsingham, by the Queen's command, sent Leicester an account of the Grafigna mission and added on his own account such information as he had secured in regard to the other negotiations.

> 'To the end', he wrote, 'your Lordship may see what instruments are used in our mediation of peace, I send you the copies of certain letters by good hap come to my hands. I have let her Majesty understand how dangerous and dishonourable it is for her to have such base and ill affected ministers used therein. Morris, the Comptroller's man, is both a notable papist and hath served Monsieur heretofore as a spy. If either your Lordship or myself should use such instruments I know we should bear no small reproach. But it is the good hap of hollow and doubtful men to be best thought of.'

In the same letter Walsingham recommended to Leicester to open up peace negotiations on his own account if any opportunity offered. 'But to return again to the peace,' he wrote, 'seeing her Majesty is so inclined unto it and is found altogether unapt to prosecute the wars, I cannot but wish your Lordship to be a principal dealer therein, as well in respect of your own honour as that I hope it will be performed with both honourable and profitable conditions; whereas I doubt, if it pass to others' hands, it will not be so carefully dealt in.' [1]

It is striking to observe at this juncture how many separate advances for peace were being made to Philip II by Privy

[1] Bruce, p. 231.

Councillors in England. There were at least five—the de Loo-Lanfranchi negotiations, the Bodenham negotiations, the Grafigna negotiations, the Palavicino-Grimaldi-Doria negotiations, and Walsingham's own efforts already described through Dr. Nũnez and Antonio Castilio.

The first two were in Burghley's and Crofts' hands. Lord Cobham seemed to have been the chief exponent of the Grafigna affair. All of these were directed at Parma. Palavicino's efforts to induce Prince Doria of Genoa to mediate a peace were made through a brother who had married a daughter of one Grimaldi, a gentleman close in the councils of the Prince. Burghley was once again behind this move. Walsingham's approach was to Spain directly.

Each separate group of promoters aimed as far as possible to keep their efforts concealed from their colleagues. Walsingham was even guilty of misrepresenting the nature of his to Leicester.[1] They were all stimulated by Elizabeth's well-known desire for peace—and each one apparently wished to reap the glory of bringing peace about. Their failure to co-operate to this end was due in part to the fact that they had already committed themselves to an opposite policy in the Privy Council, partly no doubt to their fear of Leicester's wrath, and partly because they were not all really desirous of peace. Walsingham probably opened his negotiations for the same reason that he had advised Leicester to get his finger into the pie, because he feared 'if it pass to others' hands, it will not be so carefully dealt in'. The effect of these various separate efforts was to weaken the *esprit de corps* of the Privy Council considerably and to prevent their agreement upon any consistent line of policy. There is some reason to believe that Elizabeth herself was responsible for this state of things and that she even fostered it. When Leicester complained to Walsingham that he had never received any instructions from the Privy Council since his arrival in the Low Countries, Walsingham laid the matter before the Council at large. 'They answer,' Walsingham wrote to Leicester on the 25th of April, 'as it is troth, that her Majesty, retaining the whole direction of the causes of that country to herself and such advice as she receiveth underhand, they know not what to write

[1] Bruce, pp. 188, 200.

or to advise. She can by no means, as I have heretofore written unto your Lordship, endure that the causes of that country should be subject to any debate in council, otherwise than as she herself shall direct and therefore men forbear to do that which otherwise they would.' [1] Under these circumstances the Council naturally fell apart on the question into cliques and factions and came to no agreement because they were allowed no debate.

For the moment these dissentions found expression in an effort on Cobham's part to control the peace negotiations through Grafigna and on Crofts' and Burghley's part to control them through de Loo and Champagny. Grafigna left England on the 11th of May and de Loo three days later with directions from Crofts to circumvent Grafigna if he could and to promise Parma that if he followed the course which Crofts and Burghley preferred, he would find the Queen and 'the most and best of her Council' well disposed towards peace, 'except the Secretary [Walsingham] who against so many others should be able to do little hurt.' [2] Parma, however, who disliked Champagny's meddling in the matter, preferred the other course.[3] Early in June he accordingly dispatched Grafigna back again to England with William Bodenham in his company. Grafigna brought with him a letter from Parma himself to Elizabeth.[4] Walsingham on the 24th of June sent an account of their arrival to Leicester. 'The cause of this my dispatch', he wrote, 'is to acquaint your Lordship with the late coming of Agostino Grafigna and Bodenham from the Prince of Parma with some overture of a peace, though but in general terms, having only yet delivered that, if the King of Spain can like to have a peace, the prince, for his part, who hath now received honour enough in that country, will very willingly undertake to become an instrument and dealer in it, for which purpose he meaneth to send over hither some personage of quality if the matter go forward; but to other particularities they descend not. And whether the Prince have any commission or authority from the King to treat appeareth not. Bodenham seemeth to have some further directions and a letter for her Majesty's self, the effect whereof your Lordship shall be made acquainted withal so soon as it is known.' Before Walsingham

[1] Bruce, p. 237.
[2] Cf. Appendix.
[3] Bruce, p. 231.
[4] Motley, i. 511.

sealed this letter he got a view of Parma's letter to the Queen which prompted him to add the following postscript: 'The Prince of Parma, in his letter to her Majesty which I have seen, doth use the matter in such sort as though such as had been dealers in this peace had sought the same at his hands in her Majesty's name, which is taken most offensively against both the Prince and the ministers; for her Highness protesteth that she never gave any such commission, neither generally nor particularly, to deal in the matter, and yet, if her Majesty shall be disposed to have the said peace proceeded in, upon knowledge in what sort she will have the same performed he will be ready to further so good a work. Your Lordship may see what effects are wrought by such weak ministers. They that have been employers of them are ashamed of the matter.' [1]

As Walsingham pointed out to Leicester, although Grafigna and Bodenham had declared that they had no authority to open negotiations for peace, it was suspected that Bodenham had some further instructions. He was cross-questioned closely on this point by Burghley, Crofts, and Cobham, but with no result. He protested frankly that he had no authority to make advances but merely to receive them. The peacemakers were considerably nonplussed at this and Elizabeth herself considerably irritated. She seems somehow to have felt that Burghley and Crofts between them had betrayed her into the undignified position of being a suitor for peace. Probably that was the reason why she ordered Walsingham to be present at the next interview with Bodenham. At any rate when Bodenham and Grafigna came to confer with Burghley again, Sir Francis was immediately sent for. Bodenham told Parma later that he was profoundly astonished at this move since he had been led to believe that Walsingham was to know nothing of the transaction. But Walsingham came and in his presence Grafigna and Bodenham were both closely examined as to how they got mixed up in the business at all. Grafigna admitted that he had acted in the first place on his own initiative, though he had been prompted by Lord Cobham on his previous journey to England to carry the

[1] Bruce, pp. 319–21, but cf. ibid., pp. 327–8, in which Walsingham gives a different version of Parma's letter more complimentary to his peace-hunting colleagues in the Privy Council.

matter farther. Bodenham declared that he had acted throughout at Crofts' instigation and would not be shaken in his story in spite of Crofts' denials. Walsingham merely observed that he saw no reason at all why Parma had sent Bodenham to England, since Parma himself had no commission to treat for peace. Bodenham replied that Parma would quickly get authority as soon as he knew that the Queen was well inclined to treat. To which Walsingham replied dryly that he supposed that might be—but that meanwhile Parma's correspondence seemed to be a mere marking of time and more likely to serve Spain than England.[1]

The outcome of the interview was simply to confirm the fact that the peacemakers had gone rather far in hinting at the Queen's desire for peace without inducing Parma to make any definite advances in return. Walsingham seems to have utilized the situation skilfully and to have stirred up in Elizabeth a considerable amount of wrath at the whole business. Late in July she charged Walsingham to tell Bodenham that she would have nothing to do with informal advances of this nature and to dismiss him forthwith. The letter she wrote to Parma was rather sharp and evidently written at Walsingham's inspiration. She declared that Parma's letter had amazed her; she protested that any assurance which Grafigna or Bodenham or any other had given him in her name had been given without her knowledge and contrary to her disposition. She had already stated her reasons for her action in the Low Countries. For the same reasons she meant to persist in that action. She was determined to remain faithful to her Dutch allies and would entertain no peace except such a one as would leave them in security and liberty.[2]

No doubt Elizabeth's inclination towards peace was a good deal stronger than this letter would indicate. She had been conversant with the efforts of the peacemakers from the first and had approved of them. What provoked her was that they had placed her in an awkward corner without advancing peace at all. It was to be expected that the project would be revived again

[1] Motley, i. 514–17. Motley bases his account on Bodenham's own account printed in *Correspondance de Cardinal Granvelle*, vol. xii, appendix, pp. 455 ff.

[2] Motley, i. 518. The original draft of this letter is in S. P. Flanders, i, dated 8 July 1586.

later. But for the moment Walsingham had succeeded in thwarting the effort of his rivals in the Council. There was little more talk of peace that summer.

Meantime Leicester in the Netherlands was preparing for the summer campaign and imploring his mistress to send him more money and more men. In mid-April she had shown herself graciously disposed towards him, had bade Walsingham acquaint him with the negotiations for peace afoot and instruct him to assure the Dutch councillors that though advances for peace had been made to her 'she meaneth not to proceed therein without their good liking and privity'.[1] Less than a week, however, after these instructions were dispatched, Elizabeth experienced a complete change of heart. She was now insistent that Leicester should resign his post and swore that Walsingham had mistaken her meaning in instructing him to promise that she would make no peace without the assent of the Dutch.[2] Walsingham was at a loss to account for the change.

'How this unlooked-for alteration happeneth at this time,' he wrote to Leicester on the 26th of April, . . . 'I know not, nor can by no means imagine how the same should be wrought. There was only called unto the resolution the Lord Treasurer and I. He moved her to stay the resolution until Sir Thomas Heneage's return ; . . . he protested unto her that if she did go forward with the resolution it would utterly overthrow the cause. She grew so passionate in the matter as she forbade him to argue any more. Surely there is some treachery amongst ourselves, for I cannot think that she would do this of her own head. I conceive also that there are bad offices done from thence by secret letters sent hither, by which they do advertise that the states shall not be able to yield the contributions promised, so as the burden of the wars will light on her Majesty. She is the rather confirmed in this opinion for that your Lordship did signify unto her that the contributions came very slowly in. Now hereupon I gather that her Majesty, doubting that a greater charge will be cast upon her than she shall be able to bear, whereby she shall be forced to abandon the action, she conceiveth it may be done with less dishonour, being an assister, than when her minister shall carry the title of absolute governor. I conjecture also it may grow upon a hope of peace ; for that, as I am secretly informed, there is a safe conduct sent over to Champagny, either for himself or

[1] Bruce, p. 232.

[2] Cf. Elizabeth to Sir Thomas Heneage, 27 April 1586, Bruce, pp. 241 ff.

some other that shall secretly repair unto this realm. Sorry I am that your Lordship should be so ill handled as not to be made acquainted with the proceedings here, having engaged yourself so far as you have done for her Majesty's service. I looked that her Majesty would have written letters of thanks, both unto your Lordship and others there of good desert, . . . but we are more apt to wound than to comfort.' [1]

The result of this sudden change in Elizabeth's course, from whatever causes it sprang, was a letter to Sir Thomas Heneage commanding him to take counsel at once with the Council of State as to how Leicester's title might be changed. Walsingham and Hatton and Burghley all did their best to prevent the dispatch of these instructions, but to no purpose. The instructions were sent on the 27th of April along with a sharp rebuke in Elizabeth's own hand to Heneage. 'Do that you are bidden,' she wrote, 'and leave your considerations for your own affairs; for in some things you had clear commandment which you did not, and in others none and did. . . . I am assured of your dutiful thoughts but I am utterly at squares with this childish dealing.' [2]

After two weeks' labour Walsingham and Burghley together could not induce the Queen to change her resolution. But it is clear from Walsingham's letter to Heneage of the 14th of May that her mood was beginning to soften a little.

'She is now pleased,' he wrote, 'after conference had with the Council of Estate there about the qualification of the title, that you shall return home with their opinion and advice how the same may be executed, and yet the authority remain and continue still in the Lord General, for her meaning is not that his Lordship shall presently give it over, as by his own letters lately unto her she conceiveth his Lordship is disposed to do, for that her Majesty foreseeth in her princely judgement that his giving over of the government upon a sudden, and leaving those countries as it were without a head, cannot but breed a most dangerous alteration there. And therefore her meaning is that the renunciation of the title shall be stayed until such time as there may be some course taken, with the advice of the Council of State there, how the authority may be established in his Lordship agreeable with the treaty passed between her Majesty and the commissioners of those countries.' [3]

[1] Bruce, pp. 239–40. [2] Ibid., p. 243.

[3] Walsingham to Heneage, 14 May 1586, S. P. Holland, viii, f. 48. Heneage protested violently against the Queen's uncertain course in a letter to Walsingham of 17 May 1586 (*Cal. Foreign*, 1585–6, pp. 636–7).

But Walsingham was clearly of the opinion that even with these modifications the course which the Queen insisted upon taking was an extremely dangerous one.

'I had hoped', he wrote to Leicester on the 14th of May, 'that your letters sent by Mr. Atye would have drawn her Majesty to have revoked Sir Thomas Heneage and to have stayed the matter for the qualification of the title, in respect of the alteration that the same is likely to work there. But nothing that can be said can work any stay here, so resolutely is her Majesty bent to have the matter propounded to the Council of State there; who, I do assure myself, will be greatly perplexed with the motion, and, as I take it, they have no authority to treat upon it, but must refer the consideration thereof unto an assembly of the States, which will work such a buss in people's heads and minister to the evil affected there such a plot to work on as, to man's judgement, may peril the whole cause. There hath been as much said touching the danger as might be alleged. And truly, my Lord, I am now persuaded that this strange proceeding groweth from her Majesty's self.' [1]

Another week passed and Elizabeth's mood still held. On the 20th of May she wrote to Leicester censuring him for telling the Council of State of Parma's overtures of peace. 'Herein,' Walsingham observed to Leicester, writing on the same day, 'your Lordship is wronged, for the fault is mine if any were committed. But in very truth she gave me commandment to direct you to acquaint them withal, though now she doth deny it. I have received within these few days many of these hard measures.' Walsingham then went on to say that the Queen had decided to forbid the enlisting of any more English volunteers for Leicester's army. 'This change,' Walsingham wrote, 'as I learn groweth upon a malicious information that the subjects of this realm should murmur greatly at the employment of so many people of this realm in defence of others, to the weakening of the said realm; whereas, contrariwise, all men of judgement, looking into the persons that are employed, being for the most part loose men and having nothing to take to, or into the present dearth, do think her Majesty happy to have so apt an occasion to employ them in so necessary a service. So little love is carried to the continuance of this action as the

[1] Bruce, p. 269.

weakest argument that may be used will suffice to work an hindrance to the cause. I will therefore do my best endeavours to procure your Lordship's revocation.' [1]

At first Walsingham was disposed to blame Burghley for this change in the Queen's attitude, but he became convinced apparently before the end of May that he was mistaken. On the 23rd of May he wrote to Leicester, 'I begin now to put on an opinion that the only thwarts your Lordship receiveth groweth out of her Majesty's own disposition, whom I do find daily more and more unapt to embrace any matter of weight. And whereas I did by Mr. Barker let your Lordship to understand that I thought you were crossed underhand by some great personage, I do now quit him of it and am persuaded that he dealeth honestly in the cause.' [2] Writing to Thomas Randolph in Scotland the next day Walsingham attributed the Queen's attitude to 'the practice and persuasion of such as are addicted to Spain and unfriendly to my Lord of Leicester'.[3] It is not certain to whom he referred, but probably Sir James Crofts was one whom he had in mind.

The situation improved in June. Sir Thomas Heneage arrived in England on the 10th and was graciously received.[4] Elizabeth apparently abandoned her intention of forcing Leicester to resign his title. On the 17th Burghley, Hatton, and Walsingham wrote to him a joint letter to the effect that they found the Queen so well disposed towards him that they could not comply with his request and press for his recall.[5] A few days later Burghley wrote again that Elizabeth was 'very resolute to continue her first purpose for the defence of that action'. Walsingham furnished even better proof of her intentions by announcing that £32,000 was to be sent over for the pay of his troops.[6]

These cheerful messages found Leicester in need of all the encouragement he could get, for things were going badly with

[1] Bruce, pp. 272–3. On 24 May 1586 Walsingham wrote to Randolph in Scotland: 'My Lord [of Leicester] findeth himself so discountenanced, crossed, and disgraced in the service by the practice of ill instruments that he is weary himself of his continuance there and sueth earnestly to be called home again' (S. P. Scotland, xxxix, no. 92).

[2] Bruce, p. 279.

[3] S. P. Scotland, xxxix, no. 92.

[4] Bruce, pp. 295, 307.

[5] S. P. Holland, viii, f. 227.

[6] Cf. 'A general memorial for the Low Countries', in Walsingham's hand, dated 16 June, S. P. Holland, viii, f. 218.

him in the Low Countries. His summer campaigning had started brilliantly enough with the relief of Grave by Count Hohenlo and Sir John Norris, but the prestige which he gained from this initial success was soon lost again in the succession of disasters which followed it. Late in May Parma made a second attack upon Grave and took it. Venloo yielded to him without a struggle in June, Nuys, after a gallant defence, in July. Meantime Leicester did little or nothing. The capture of Axel by Maurice of Nassau and Sir Philip Sidney stood as the single achievement to his credit during the early summer. Possibly if he had taken the field he might have made a better reckoning. He realized that fact clearly enough himself, but he was hampered in so many ways that he did not dare to assume the offensive. The bulk of his forces were shut up in garrison towns. Such troops as he had for active service were underfed, underpaid, and on the verge of mutiny. His finances were in confusion. He was at loggerheads with his best officers.[1] His mistress had estimated his expenses upon the basis of a strictly defensive war and refused to advance him a penny more. It was, indeed, hard enough to get from her what she had agreed upon to give. Under these circumstances Leicester's one hope of support was from the Estates General. But he received little encouragement from that quarter and could hope for less as time went on. They had welcomed him at his coming as the saviour of their country, had conferred on him the most absolute powers, and

[1] His jealousy of Sir John Norris, probably the ablest of the English officers in the Low Countries, was notorious. He discredited Norris in every way he could to the Queen and did his best to have him recalled. But Norris had powerful friends at Court. His mother was one of Elizabeth's favourite ladies-in-waiting. Burghley supported him. Walsingham in his letters to Leicester condemned Norris's conduct and promised to work for his revocation (Bruce, pp. 222, 344, 404), but Norris was his cousin and there is reason to believe that Walsingham's attitude towards him was a good deal more friendly than he made out to Leicester. Wilkes wrote to Norris, 23 September 1586, that he found 'some alteration in her Majesty and Mr. Secretary from the good and solid opinion I left in them of you at my departure', but added that he had set them right so that 'I dare now assure you upon my poor credit that your adversaries shall hardly be able to remove the same' (S. P. Holland, x, f. 56). At all events Norris kept his place in spite of Leicester. In like fashion Leicester fell out with Sir Thomas Cecil, Burghley's son, who had been placed in command of Briel, and even accused Burghley of setting on Cecil against him (Bruce, p. 379). Davison and Thomas Wilkes also suffered from Leicester's wrath. Indeed he antagonized almost all the ablest men, English and Dutch alike, with whom he was associated.

had professed their intention of supporting him to the very limit of their abilities. But since those auspicious days their mood had changed. Elizabeth's wrath at Leicester's acceptance of the governorship, her failure to send him adequate support, the rumours of her secret negotiations for peace which reached their ears, all led them to suspect that Leicester's expedition was merely a blind behind which the English meant to betray them. In consequence their leaders, Barneveldt, Prince Maurice, and Paul Buys, Advocate of Holland, began to watch Leicester jealously and to oppose him at every turn. He complained in his letters home that they were hampering his authority, cutting down his supplies, and doing everything in their power to destroy his prestige. He swore that their government was a many-headed monster; he called them churls, tinkers, bakers and brewers and hired advocates; he denounced Buys in particular as a devil, an atheist, and the only bolsterer of papists and ill men. More than that, he went about to stir up opposition against them among the Dutch themselves. For the most part they belonged to the aristocratic merchant class which had dominated industrial life and monopolized political power in the Netherlands cities for two centuries. They were men of wealth and culture, Calvinists by profession but inclining towards Arminianism in their theology. In all these aspects they stood over against the proletariat in the large cities, made up for the most part of the small craftsmen, who were rigid predestinarians and turbulent democrats and who had long resented the domination of the merchants both in industry and in politics. Leicester saw and seized the opportunity of exploiting this element against his opponents in the States General.[1] He drew around him, in a kind of extraordinary court, three of the popular leaders, Reingoud,

[1] Cf. Blok, *History of People of Netherlands* (trans. by R. Putnam), iii. 214–19; Leicester's attitude is clearly set forth in a letter to Walsingham of 2 October 1586, Bruce, pp. 421 ff. On 27 September 1586, Thomas Wilkes drew up a memorandum of matters to be considered by the Queen and the Privy Council, among which was the following: 'That my Lord [of Leicester] be commanded not to sever from him the good disposition and minds of the States and Council, nor to make any show or meddle in severing the people and the States from their accustomed unity or breed dissension among them, considering how unapt her Majesty is to accept the sovereignty.

'If this last article be not carefully looked to, my Lord's government will grow odious as it beginneth to do and will disjoint all good proceedings.' S. P. Holland, x, f. 77.

Deventer, and Burchgrave. At Reingoud's advice he arranged a chamber of finance, designed to check the innumerable breaches of the restraint of trade and therefore particularly offensive to the merchants as a class. He stirred up a popular revolt in Utrecht, which resulted in the imprisonment of Buys and might have led to his death if Elizabeth had not interfered. He encouraged the orthodox Calvinists in their attack upon the Arminians. He tried to weaken the Province of Holland, which was the stronghold of his opponents, by fostering an independent spirit in the north quarter of the province.[1] In none of these efforts did he succeed, but his attempts had the effect of increasing mightily the opposition to him among the men who actually controlled Dutch affairs.

In the face of all these difficulties Leicester finally came to the conclusion that the only solution of the problem was for Elizabeth to take the sovereignty of the countries to herself and to increase her forces in the Low Countries to such an extent as to warrant an aggressive campaign in the field against Parma. He wrote to her to that effect late in June not long after the fall of Venloo.[2] But Elizabeth took no more kindly to the notion then than she had earlier. Her reaction is revealed in a letter from Walsingham to Leicester of the 9th of July :

'She gathereth,' he wrote, 'upon the view of your Lordship's letter, that the only salve to cure this sore is to make herself proprietary of that country and to put such an army into the same as may be able to make head to the enemy. These two things, being so contrary to her Majesty's disposition, the one for that it breedeth a doubt of a perpetual war, the other, for that it requireth an increase of charges, doth marvellously distract her and make her repent that she ever entered into the action.

'She hath only made the Lord Treasurer and Mr. Vice-Chamberlain acquainted, as they tell me, with part of those letters, and gave them order to consider what were fit to be done upon this alteration. To this conference, by her Majesty's order, I was called. The resolution is not yet taken but hangeth in suspense,

[1] In this particular case Leicester may have cherished ulterior designs. He wrote to Elizabeth, 27 June 1586 : 'I hope not to fail of it, to get into my hands three or four principal places in north Holland, which will be such a strong assurance for your Majesty as you will see you shall both rub these men and make war or peace as you like' S. P. Holland, viii, f. 296.

[2] 26 June 1586, S. P. Holland, viii, f. 287.

for that the Lord Treasurer, being troubled with the gout in his hand, cannot repair unto her. The advice that will be given will fall out to be this: first, that she must prosecute the action without respect of charges; secondarily, that a gentleman of sound judgement be sent over unto your Lordship, to confer with you how both the general and particular discontentment reigning there may be removed, as also to be informed of divers points touching the state of that country; and lastly, that it shall in no sort be fit for her Majesty to take any resolution in the cause until Sir Francis Drake return, at least until the success of his voyage be seen, whereupon in very truth dependeth the life and death of the cause according to man's judgement. She is also advised, in the meantime, to make no show of her dislike, but rather to countenance the cause by all outward means she may which, contrary to her natural disposition, she doth very well perform, forced thereunto by mere necessity, upon the discovery of some matter of importance in the highest degree through my travail and cost, by the which it appeareth to her most plain that unless she had entered into the action, she had been utterly undone, and that, if she do not prosecute the same, she cannot long continue.' [1]

Walsingham alluded at the conclusion of this passage to the Babington Plot which he had already discovered and revealed to the Queen, although he had not yet laid hands upon the conspirators. In his emphasis upon the importance of Drake's success to the cause he revealed once again that the Queen's attitude towards an expensive, aggressive campaign in the Netherlands would be largely determined by the amount of plunder which Drake brought home with him. For the present all that Elizabeth would consent to do was to send a special envoy to the Netherlands, and she was even loath to spend money for that.[2] Thomas Wilkes was the man she chose for the mission. He seems to have been instructed to patch up the differences between Leicester and his officers on the one hand, and Leicester and the Dutch leaders on the other, to assure the States General that their suspicions of her intentions to make peace without them were unfounded, and to observe the state of the country.[3]

Wilkes arrived in the Low Countries early in August. He

[1] Bruce, pp. 340–1. [2] Ibid., p. 343.

[3] Froude, xii. 208; Elizabeth to Leicester, 19 July 1586, S. P. Holland, ix, f. 85.

handled his difficult business there with tact and skill.[1] In consequence Leicester seems to have made his peace with Prince Maurice, and he professed at least to have buried his differences with Norris. Encouraged by the arrival of funds from England and by the grant of other funds from the Estates he decided to muster his forces in August and take the field.[2] The muster took place on the 28th of the month. But after the troops were all assembled the council of war concluded that the force was too weak for a direct attack upon Parma's forces, which were at that time laying siege to the town of Berck. It was consequently determined to attack Duesburg instead, a town which the Spaniards held north of the Waal. The attack was prosecuted with vigour and the city fell on the 2nd of September. Thence Leicester advanced against Zutphen. Parma, alarmed for the safety of his towns in Zeeland, rushed to Zutphen's relief. He succeeded in revictualling the town, in spite of the gallant efforts of a handful of English gentlemen to cut off the convoy of provisions. It was in this encounter that Sir Philip Sidney received his death wound. For the rest of the campaigning season Leicester remained before Zutphen, but he did not take the town that year. Early in October he withdrew into winter quarters.

Meantime Leicester did not cease to urge Elizabeth to take the sovereignty of the country upon her. 'For mine own part,' he wrote to Walsingham on the 4th of September, 'I trust not to leave any dishonour behind me for her Majesty; and except she take the cause princely in hand and call her parliament and accept that her subjects will offer to maintain this charge, it will but consume her treasure and lose the countries. . . . High time it is that her Majesty did resolve one way or the other, for our States grow stately and will be high or low as God shall dispose of this journey.'[3] At the same time Leicester dispatched Wilkes home again.[4]

[1] Leicester wrote to Walsingham, 7 Aug. 1586: 'Wilkes hath exceedingly wisely and well behaved himself. Her Majesty doth not know what a jewel she hath of him' (Bruce, p. 383).

[2] Clark wrote to Burghley, 4 July 1586, that the States had granted Leicester 200,000 florins a month for four months on condition that he would take the field in mid-August (S. P. Holland, ix, f. 9).

[3] Bruce, p. 409.

[4] Wilkes was in London again, 15 Sept.; Bruce, p. 411.

When Wilkes arrived in London he found the councillors so busy with the trial of the Babington conspirators as to have small time for the consideration of the Low Countries affairs.[1] But it was clear enough without debate that the Queen did not intend to follow the course which Leicester had designed for her. For one thing the profits from Drake's enterprise—he returned to England late in July—were distinctly disappointing. His voyage round the world had netted the Queen a profit of 4,700 per cent. on her investment. It is not to be wondered at that she expected an enormous return upon the £20,000 she had advanced in money and ships for his West Indian voyage. The final reckoning revealed a loss so far as the Queen's own investment was concerned of something less than £5,000.[2] The consequences to Leicester followed inevitably. Elizabeth's intention was now rather to cut down her expenses in the Low Countries than to increase them. Wilkes wrote to Norris on the 23rd of September from London: 'Her Majesty and her Council do greatly stagger at the cxcessive charges of those wars under his Excellency's government for the six months past, affirming, as it is true, that the realm of England is not able to supply the moiety of that charge. Notwithstanding, the necessity of the defence of those countries is so conjoined with her Majesty's own safety, as the same is not to be abandoned. But what her Majesty will do further in particular I know not as yet.'[3] Indeed Elizabeth seriously considered calling Leicester home. Wilkes wrote to Norris in the same letter that she meant to do so directly, and he added: 'There is much variety of opinion here whether it be fit to revoke him or not. Such as desire the good of that State do hold that question affirmatively, but such as do not love him, who are the greater number, do maintain the negative.'[4]

Presumably Walsingham was of the number that desired his return. But it is impossible to say anything positively about Walsingham's attitude at this juncture. There are very few of his letters preserved between early July and the date of Leicester's return to England and those few are brief and

[1] Bruce, p. 411.

[2] *Spanish War Papers* (Navy Records Society), p. 94. It is probable that Walsingham had money invested in this enterprise, but there is no proof of it.

[3] S. P. Holland, ix, f. 56.

[4] Ibid.; cf. also *Cal. Spanish*, 1580-6, p. 602.

exceedingly formal in character. It would be interesting to discover how he stood in the quarrel between Leicester and the Dutch leaders, and where his sympathies lay in the issue between the Dutch governing class and the proletariat and between the Arminians and the rigid Calvinists. Some light might then be thrown upon his political principles and his theology. But he either avoided committing himself or else his more significant letters had been destroyed. It would not be safe, under these circumstances, to argue much from his silence. Possibly he was too deeply engaged in unravelling the Babington Plot and weaving his net about the Queen of Scots to give him much leisure for Dutch affairs. Possibly he resented Leicester's treatment of Davison and Norris, two of the oldest and most faithful champions of the Dutch cause, one of whom was Walsingham's cousin, the other an old friend. It may be that he became incensed at Leicester's rather censorious bearing towards him [1] at a time when he was almost the only supporter of the Earl in the Privy Council. At all events, it must not be forgotten that his loyalty to the cause was far deeper than his loyalty to Leicester. To him Leicester was after all merely an instrument. No doubt Walsingham had hoped that he might prove an efficient instrument in the Dutch wars. But the events of the summer had revealed the vanity of that hope. It is consequently very likely that Walsingham came to the conclusion that Leicester could do far more good in the English Council than in the Low Countries.

During the latter part of September the Privy Council were engaged in considering Wilkes's report and in discussing the situation in the Low Countries at large. There is no record of their debates nor of the conclusions they reached, nor of the recommendations which they submitted to the Queen. But the course which Elizabeth elected to follow is clear enough. She decided to send £30,000 to the Low Countries to satisfy the discontented soldiery. She agreed to dispatch a 'wise person' to patch up the broken state of things. Wilkes was the man chosen for the purpose, and he was directed to take Killigrew's place in the Council of State and to give such advice as seemed requisite for the establishment of good order and the furtherance of the service, without fear or dread of any person or persons

[1] Cf., for example, Bruce, pp. 322–6, 393.

whatsoever.'[1] And she admitted the necessity of re-establishing cordial relations between the English governor and the Dutch leaders. To this end she sent Leicester explicit instructions. He was to dismiss Reingoud from the Chamber of Finances; he was to see that Paul Buys had a fair trial; he was to restore to Utrecht the burghers who had been driven out by the popular party and in general to cease exciting the populace against the Estates General. These directions constituted an unequivocal condemnation of Leicester's intrigues in Dutch politics.[2]

With regard to Leicester's recall, Elizabeth apparently gave no explicit instructions, but Burghley, doubtless by royal warrant, intimated to him in a private letter that his presence was desired in England.[3] No conclusion, however, was reached as to what arrangement should be made for the government of the Low Countries in his absence.[4]

Wilkes himself conveyed the Queen's decision over to Leicester in October. He had no sooner arrived in the Low Countries than Leicester began to make his preparations to return to England.[5] It was not, however, until the 15th of November

[1] Wilkes's instructions are given in Bruce, pp. 432 ff.

[2] Cf. Elizabeth to Leicester, 10 Oct. 1586, S. P. Holland, x, f. 140; Leicester enumerates the charges made against his conduct by the Queen and attempts an answer to them in his letter of 11 October 1586; ibid., ff. 146, 146 a. The instructions to Leicester seem to have been based upon the advice of Thomas Wilkes. In a memorial to the Privy Council, dated 27 September 1586, he strongly recommended that Reingoud be removed, Buys be fairly tried, and that Leicester be enjoined to cease from stirring up strife between the people and the Estates (ibid., f. 75). There is no definite evidence that Walsingham endorsed Wilkes's programme, but there is a suggestion to that effect in a letter which Wilkes wrote to Walsingham on 25 October after his return to the Low Countries. 'My arrival is not so grateful here as was expected, albeit for mine own part I am not deceived therein, foreknowing the same. Nevertheless I beseech your honour most humbly, so far forth to defend my poor credit in my absence as in your judgement you shall find me to have deserved, for I do assure myself the same will be oppugned with all violence at the return of his excellency to the court' (ibid., f. 194). It is hardly likely that Wilkes would have invoked Walsingham's aid to his defence against Leicester unless Wilkes had been fairly certain that Walsingham was in sympathy with the course he was taking.

[3] 'And so, my Lord,' Burghley wrote to Leicester on 1 October, 'forbearing until Mr. Wilkes' coming, I take my leave of your good Lordship, whom I wish so to end your journey in the fields as you may return hither without danger to the common cause there, a thing so needful as surely without your presence here I know not how her Majesty will or can resolve upon her manner of proceeding', Bruce, p. 421.

[4] Ibid., p. 450.

[5] Ibid., p. 444.

that he finally took his leave. One of his last acts was to arrange for the government of the country during his absence. Upon this point the Queen had left him uninstructed. Burghley had written to him on the 4th of November :

'For the government there in your Lordship's absence we here cannot give any advice, but, considering your Lordship's great experience there, whatsoever your Lordship shall declare to be meet I shall assent thereto and by my advice to her Majesty, further it as reason is. Some speak of naming the Count Maurice to be governor alone in your absence, and as to have the rule under your Lordship ; some wish that the Count Maurice should be joined with the Lord Gray. The Queen's Majesty would that it were in the States direction again as it was before they committed it to your Lordship, with the direction of Lord Gray as lieutenant of her army. But surely I fear greatly the success hereof, for the general evil opinion conceived, both by the people and the men of war, against the particular persons representing the States, except there might be a new election by the several provinces of new and more upright persons to represent the States.' [1]

By the same post Davison, who had been appointed one of the Principal Secretaries on the 30th of September,[2] wrote to Leicester that the Queen meant to dispatch Gray forthwith and that Leicester was in no wise to depart before his arrival.[3] But Leicester either did not receive these instructions before his departure or else they were subsequently countermanded by other instructions which are missing. At any rate, he made his final arrangements without regard to them, leaving Norris in command of the English forces [4] and the Council of State in general control of the civil and military government. His actual leave-taking was marked by formal expressions of affection and regret on both sides and he received from the States as a parting present a silver-gilt vase as tall as a man ! But the Dutch leaders were not sorry to see him go.

It is hardly necessary to summarize the results of Leicester's first expedition to the Netherlands. His military achievements

[1] Ibid., p. 450. [2] *Acts of Privy Council*, 1586–7, p. 236.

[3] Bruce, p. 452.

[4] Motley, ii. 108. The appointment of Norris is surprising. Wilkes wrote to Walsingham, 25 October 1586, that Leicester preferred Pelham for the position (S. P. Holland, x, f. 194). Possibly Leicester had instructions (which are missing) from the Queen on that point.

there were insignificant and his civil government had the effect of developing internal dissensions among the Dutch themselves which seriously weakened their fighting strength. So far as the goodwill between Elizabeth and the Dutch was concerned, he probably did more to diminish than to increase it. His positive achievement lay in the fact that his expedition definitely committed England to an open war with Spain. And in that fact, to Walsingham and his partisans at least, lay Leicester's justification.

From Walsingham's point of view one of the most serious consequences of the enterprise was its effect upon his relations with Leicester. For ten years the two of them had stood together upon all important matters of public policy and had been generally regarded as the two foremost champions of militant Protestantism in the Privy Council. But a breach began to open between them in the midsummer of 1586 which grew steadily wider as time went on. The reasons for this breach are not easy to define. Leicester seems to have conceived the opinion that Walsingham was not so zealous in his behalf as he had a right to expect. He complained that the Secretary did not promote his private suits [1] and that he was far less active in the defence of his public service than his enemies were against him. 'I see', he wrote Walsingham on the 10th of August, 'all men have friends but myself. I see most false suggestions help other men and my upright, true dealing cannot protect me. Nay, my worldly protector faileth me.' [2] Walsingham on his part, who was doing his level best for Leicester and making himself very unpopular with the Queen in consequence, no doubt resented these charges. He realized indeed that Leicester was not content that a man should be his friend, but wished to make of all men his slaves. He observed the hard measure which the Earl had meted out to Norris and Davison and Wilkes, all stout friends of the cause, and found him prepared to ruin any man who made the least scruple of protest at his conduct. Furthermore, Walsingham was too keen-sighted

[1] Bruce, p. 326; Davison wrote to Walsingham, 10 Dec. 1586: 'My Lord of Leicester doth complain of some unkindness that his leases were not dispatched. I have done the best I can to let him understand the hard terms you stood in almost the whole time of his absence, and thereby yourself unable to do that you would, wherewith he pretendeth to be satisfied.' S. P. Domestic, cxcv, no. 54.

[2] Bruce, p. 395.

not to observe that Leicester in most of his disagreements was generally in the wrong and that he was contriving to do more harm than good to the cause which they both professed to serve. In these facts probably lay the deeper causes of the widening breach between them.

But Walsingham had particular grievances against Leicester as well. It will be recalled that Sir Philip Sidney, who was Leicester's nephew, had married Walsingham's only daughter Frances. So long as Sidney lived, he served as a strong bond of union between his uncle and his father-in-law. Like every one else that came into close touch with his engaging personality, both of them loved him. But Sidney was mortally wounded in one of the closing engagements of the campaign of 1586, and he died shortly before Leicester's return to England. To Walsingham his death, which was a heavy blow in itself, entailed serious consequences. It brought his daughter, Lady Sidney, who had watched out the weary days of uncertainty by her husband's bed while heavy with child, to the very verge of death. Fortunately she recovered, though the child died. Further than that, it appeared probable that Walsingham would have to answer for Sidney's debts, though exactly how this came about is not quite clear.[1] On the 5th of November Walsingham wrote to Leicester: 'Sir Philip hath left a great number of poor creditors. What order he hath taken by his will for their satisfaction I know not. It is true that, immediately after the death of his father, he sent me a letter of attorney for the sale of such lands as might content his creditors, wherein there was nothing done before his death. I have paid and must pay for him above £6,000, which I do assure your Lordship hath brought me into a most hard and desperate state, which I weigh nothing in respect of the loss of the gentleman, who was my chief worldly

[1] Burghley wrote to Walsingham, 2 Nov. 1586: 'I am heartily sorry to imagine how yourself in worldly burden may be now overcharged, for as I did hear, you had good authority to have sold lands for discharge of the debts both of the father, the mother, and the son. But if your authority shall die with him for lack of foresight in making the conveyance for your safety and that you have as the lawyers' term is, assumed upon yourself, you are in very hard case. . . . I shall be sorry if this your hazard, which came of love, shall be a teaching to others to adventure with more surety. You do very well to provide as much comfort as you can for the young lady your daughter, considering that, as I hear, she is with child, which I wish may prove to be a son for some more diminution of all your common grief.' S. P. Domestic, cxcv, no. 1.

comfort.'[1] There is some reason to believe that when all the debts were in they amounted to considerably more than £6,000. Walsingham hoped that Sidney had made some adequate provision for these debts in his will by authorizing the sale of some of his lands, and when the will was read it revealed a conscientious intent on Sidney's part to satisfy his creditors.[2] But the experts to whom Walsingham submitted the will adjudged it insufficient to the purpose.[3] He wrote to Leicester on the 6th of November: 'I have caused Sir Philip Sidney's will to be considered by certain learned in the laws and I find the same imperfect touching the sale of his land for the satisfying of his poor creditors, which I do assure your Lordship doth greatly afflict me, [that] a gentleman that hath lived so unspotted [in] reputation and had so great care to see all men satisfied, should be so [exposed] to the outcry of his creditors. His goods will not suffice to answer a third part of his debts already known. This hard estate of this noble gentleman maketh me to stay to take order for his burial until your Lordship's return. I do not see how the same can be performed with that solemnity that appertaineth without the utter undoing of his creditors, which is to be weighed in conscience.'[4]

The consequence was apparently that Walsingham had to assume the burden of the whole debt. In this predicament he appealed to the Queen for redress. Exactly what form his appeal took does not appear.[5] Burghley urged his case manfully, reminding Elizabeth of Walsingham's diligence in the unravelling of the Babington Plot, but just brought to light, pointing him out, as Davison told Walsingham later, 'as one to whom under God she ought to acknowledge the preservation of her life, which she could not nor might in honour forget, alleging unto her the hard estate you stand in and the dishonour must fall upon herself if such a servant should be suffered to quail, to the great discomfort of himself and his friends and the discouragement of others to take the like course of hazarding their lives and

[1] Bruce, pp. 453–4.
[2] Sidney's will is printed in Collins, *Sidney Papers*, i. 110.
[3] Their opinion is printed in Bruce, pp. 481–2. [4] Ibid., pp. 456–7.
[5] In *Cal. Salisbury MSS.*, iii. 202, there is the draft of a petition from Walsingham for a grant to him and his heirs for ever of £200 a year; whereof £100 was to be taken out of Exchequer lands and the other £100 out of lands whereof the reversion was in the Queen.

fortunes hereafter for the surety of a princess so slow to consider thereof.'[1]

But Burghley made so little speed that Walsingham decided to abandon his suit.

'I humbly beseech your Lordship', he wrote to Burghley on the 16th of December, 'to pardon me in that I did not take my leave of you before my departure from the court. Her Majesty's unkind dealing towards me hath so wounded me as I could take no comfort to stay there. And yet if I saw any hope that my continuance there might either breed any good to the church or furtherance to the service of her Majesty or of the realm, the regard of my particular should not cause me to withdraw myself. But seeing the declining state we are running into, and that men of best desert are least esteemed, I hold them happiest in this government that may be rather lookers on than actors.

'I humbly therefore beseech your Lordship that as I do acknowledge myself infinitely bound unto you for your most honourable and friendly furtherance yielded unto me in my suit (which I will never forget) so you will be pleased to increase my bond towards you by forbearing any further to press her Majesty in the same, which I am fully resolved to give over. I do assure your Lordship, whatsoever conceit her Majesty maketh either of me or of mine I would not spend so long a time as I have done in that place, subject to so infinite toil and discomfort, not to be made Duke of Lancaster.

'My hope is, howsoever I am dealt withal by an earthly Prince, I shall never lack the comfort of the Prince of Princes.'[2]

Burghley did, however, succeed in inducing Walsingham to persist.[3] Whether he finally won his suit or not is not apparent. It may be that the grant to him and his servant Francis Milles of several royal manors to fee-farm in April of the next year was the way the Queen finally took of making up his losses to him.[4]

The bearing of all this upon Walsingham's relations with Leicester appears from a letter which Dr. William Gifford, an English Catholic refugee on the continent, wrote to one of his friends in June 1587. In this letter he told his friend that

[1] Davison to Walsingham, 10 Dec. 1586, S. P. Domestic, cxcv, no. 54.

[2] Ibid., no. 64.

[3] Cf. Walsingham to Burghley, 5 Jan. 1586/7, S. P. Domestic, cxcvii, no. 5.

[4] Patent Rolls, Eliz., memb. 24-34, dated 21 April, 29 Eliz. The grant included a good deal of land which passed to the Crown at the time of the dissolution of the monasteries by Henry VIII and of the chantries by Edward VI.

Walsingham and Leicester were at odds, and gave as one of the causes of their quarrel 'that Sir Philip Sidney, dying indebted to the Flushingers seventeen thousand pounds, for which Walsingham was bound, Leicester refuseth to make payment of one penny out of his land'. It is apparent from other passages in Gifford's letter that he was not very accurately informed as to the state of things in England, but his testimony is probably sufficient to establish the fact that Leicester might have relieved Walsingham of some part of his burden and refused to do so.[1]

Dr. Gifford cites two other matters also which served to increase the breach between the two men. One of these was the marriage of Walsingham's widowed daughter to Leicester's step-son, the young Earl of Essex. It has been generally assumed that this marriage did not take place until after Walsingham's death, the assumption being based upon the fact that the first child of the marriage was not born until April of 1591.[2] But Dr. Gifford's letter is positive evidence to the contrary, and it may be that a marriage was performed in the spring of 1587, but was kept secret from fear of the royal wrath, until the coming of the child made further concealment impossible. If this was indeed the case, it is not unlikely that the marriage did provoke Leicester's hostility since his antipathy to his step-son was notorious.

The other private cause of discord between Walsingham and Leicester which Dr. Gifford mentioned was 'that Leicester preferred Fortesque before him [Walsingham] in the Chancellorship of the Duchy which Sir Ralph Sadler had'. The allusion here is to the Chancellorship of the Duchy of Lancaster which had just been vacated by Sir Ralph Sadler's death.[3] The office was

[1] Lansdowne MSS. xcvi, f. 69. The letter is dated 5 June with the year not given, but from the reference to Sir Ralph Sadler's death, which occurred on 30 May 1587, it may be presumed that the letter belongs to the year 1587. In a letter of an anonymous correspondent to M. de Bellièvre, a French envoy in England, written early in the year 1587, the following passage appears: 'Il y a quelque controverse entre le Conte de Leicestre et le Sieur François pour le testament de son gendre et divers parolles se sont passées' (S. P. Scotland, xlii, no. 8).

[2] It ought to be pointed out that Dr. Gifford's letter is a little obscure on this point. In enumerating the differences between Leicester and Walsingham he wrote: 'Secondly, because Walsingham has married his daughter Lady Sidney to . . . .' The last part of this sentence I have been unable to decipher, but it can hardly refer to any other marriage than that with the Earl of Essex.

[3] Sadler died 30 May 1587. It is not clear as to whether or not he resigned

one of considerable dignity and although the fees and allowances allotted to it were only £142 16*s*., 'with £4 for paper parchment and ink' annually, there were doubtless large perquisites besides.[1] Dr. Gifford was probably mistaken in supposing that Fortesque was Leicester's candidate for the office. Sir Amias Paulet seems to have been his man. Burghley supported Walsingham's suit for the place. 'I am cogitative', he wrote to Walsingham on the 22nd of May, 'of the Duchy matter. I earnestly require you do not neglect it. Your credit is included and my comfort to have so good a neighbour is not the least I mind.'[2] Upon the same topic Sir Edward Stafford, English ambassador at Paris, wrote to Walsingham on the 17th of May:

> 'I am very sorry to hear from some friends of mine that my Lord of Leicester should go about to set forward a man that I have known him not long since not to have esteemed, afore you whom, as the world knoweth, hath esteemed well of him. I have by the last upon the persuasions of some friends of mine that he favoured my mother in her trouble, written to him to offer him my poor service and good will. Truly if I had known this afore I should have done it but with an evil will, for truly I love them that do love my friends and like not of ingratitude of all vices in the world. But truly Sir, pardon me if I write to you as a well wisher to you and am angry in my mind with you that I hear that you will, for lack of earnestness, let slip so good a thing, and if there were nothing but reputation, that they that do deserve nothing should not have that afore you that have deserved so much, I would surely slip in by all means I could.'[3]

Six days later, on the 23rd of May, Walsingham wrote to Burghley: 'Touching the Chancellorship of the Duchy, she [the Queen] told Sir Amias Paulet that in respect of her promise made unto me she could not dispose of it otherwise, but yet hath

his office before his death. Walsingham was certainly trying to get the place before 30 May 1587.

[1] Cf. 'Book of all officers under the Crown, with amounts of Salaries, fees and allowances attached to each.' S. P. Domestic, Eliz., ccxxi. The following entries in this book are of special interest:

- p. 7. The Duchy of Lancaster, Chancellor: Fee and allowance with £4 for paper and parchment and ink, £142 16*s*.
- p. 10. Lord Keeper of the Privy Seal: Fee £365 and his table at Court furnished with two messes of meat.
- p. 11b. Principal Secretaries, 2: Fee each £100 and their table in the court furnished with two messes of meat.

[2] S. P. Domestic, cci, no. 40.

[3] S. P. France, xvii, f. 149.

she no power to deliver the seal unto me, though for that purpose the Attorney is commanded to attend her, whom I suppose will be dismissed hence this day without any resolution.' [1]

Walsingham, however, did finally get the office in June.

One striking circumstance in the affair of the Duchy, as in the earlier affair over Sidney's will, was that Walsingham met and overcame Leicester's opposition largely by virtue of Burghley's co-operation. This circumstance serves to emphasize a fact which is established by other evidence, that as Walsingham drew away from Leicester he drew towards Burghley. In this connexion Stafford's letter cited above is significant. Up to the end of the year 1586 Stafford, who was one of Burghley's most ardent partisans, and Walsingham were at swords' points. It was no mere coincidence that they succeeded at least temporarily in patching up their differences at just about the same time that Walsingham and Leicester began to draw apart.

Walsingham's approach to Burghley was probably the inevitable consequence of his divergence from Leicester, but it was facilitated by a number of other factors. In the first place, most of the points in dispute between Walsingham and Burghley during the preceding decade had one way or the other been disposed of. War with Spain in behalf of the Dutch, which Walsingham had advocated and Burghley opposed, was now assured. The difficult question of the Queen's marriage was finally set at rest by the increasing years of the Queen herself. The Scottish problem was at any rate temporarily solved by the defensive alliance with Scotland which had been signed in the summer of 1586. Mary Stuart was secured from all further mischief-making in her tomb at Peterborough. There can be little doubt that the removal of all these bones of contention had a great deal to do with changing Walsingham's attitude towards his old patron.

It may well be also that increasing years had wrought changes in Walsingham's own temperament which led him to a clearer understanding and a better appreciation of his colleague. The ten years past had brought to him rather more than his fair share of labour and sorrow. For all his diligence and ability in the royal service he had made small progress in the royal favour.

[1] Harleian MSS. 6994, f. 68.

The Queen did little to conceal her dislike of him. What she gave him she gave grudgingly and not overmuch at that. He advanced in power and influence by virtue of sheer ability, but he made no corresponding advance in honour and dignity. In title he was still a mere knight, in office still a mere secretary. Whatever aspirations he may have had for higher rank or more honourable employment were not satisfied and seemed not likely to be, for his bodily infirmities were increasing and he must have realized that his days were numbered. Quite apart from his personal ambitions also, the great cause for which he worked seemed little further advanced than when he first laid hold of it. Protestantism was still fighting for its very existence in the Low Countries and in France. Elizabeth was still as indifferent as she dared to be to the fate of her brethren in the faith. God had not yet vindicated his saints. Redemption seemed still a long way off. All these things bred an increasing pessimism in Walsingham and gnawed at the very heart of his enthusiasm and his faith. He became in consequence more conservative in his temper, less dogmatic in his judgements, and less certain, probably, of his own convictions. It need not be assumed that he ever attained to Burghley's cautious, indecisive frame of mind which sat astride of every fence, or to his conciliatory spirit which was prepared to recognize a camel or a weasel or a whale in every cloud. But Walsingham probably became less aggressive, less pugnacious, and less impatient as he grew older, and in so far as this was so he approximated more nearly to Burghley's own point of view.

Finally, Walsingham must have become convinced, since he could not hope to lead himself, but must follow either Burghley's or Leicester's banner, that Burghley was the safer man to join. If Leicester was more apt for bold courses, he was far less disinterested in his pursuit of them; if he was more enthusiastic, he was less reasonable; if more active in behalf of his friends, far less faithful to them. For ten years Walsingham had served Leicester, and Leicester in the end had abandoned him, while Burghley, whom he had steadily opposed, was ready still to play the friend's part. Walsingham indeed had many reasons and many arguments to prompt him to change his allegiance. As a matter of course the change came gradually and probably more or less undesignedly, but there can be little doubt that during the last three years of Walsingham's life his relations with Burghley were far closer and his relations with Leicester far less close than they had been during the preceding decade.

APPENDIX I

'A Declaration of the manner of treating peace underhand to the Earl of Leicester.'

[There is a copy of this paper in a clerkly hand in the Public Record Office, S. P. Holland, ix, f. 112 b, and another copy in Cotton MSS., Galba C vii, f. 158. No evidence as to who was the author of it appears. The Record Office copy is dated August 1586. It certainly belongs in that year some time in or after the month of May. It may be presumed from the title that it was sent underhand to Leicester. Suspicion falls on Walsingham, who must have been one of the very few men in possession of the facts who was disposed to disclose them to Leicester.]

'Mr. Comptroller hath a kinsman about the Prince of Parma named Bodnam, who by Mr. Comptroller's instigation hath by process of time attempted some communication with the Prince of Parma for some good unity between the King of Spain and the Queen her Majesty, and for this purpose hath Mr. Comptroller a man of his in Calais named Morris by whom intelligence is given to and from Bodnam. The Prince of Parma hath very good liking of Mr. Comptroller and of his good liking towards the peace, and promiseth that the doing and thanks thereof shall not be taken from him, whensoever it shall happen to be dealt in.

'One Carlo Lanfranchi, an Italian merchant in Antwerp, great with M. de Champagny, certain months past wrote here very earnest unto one Andrea de Loo, a Dutch merchant in London, to see if he could move a treaty of peace to some of her Majesty's council great about her Majesty, affected to a peace and fit for the furtherance of it. Andrea de Loo showeth this letter of Lanfranchi unto the Lord Treasurer, who showeth it to her Majesty, who very well liked the motion and wisheth forwardness in the matter.

'This the Lord Treasurer reporteth to Andrea de Loo and willeth him with care and diligence to answer it so to the same effect, but not to name the Lord Treasurer nor by any means to make any more than himself privy to this matter. Andrea de Loo made answer to Lanfranchi according, showing with all the good means he had found of one well affected to the cause and willing and able to further it. The next answer again of Lanfranchi was, that if her Majesty continued that good meaning, that she should have the conditions such as should be to her best liking and contention (amongst other her money repaid her which she hath lent and bestowed in the Low Countries) so far forth as her Majesty would not intermeddle in the matters of religion, that excepted, she should have all other things to content her. This was confidently answered that her Majesty was content not to meddle or deal in any matters of religion. This being understood, M. Champagny himself wrote a very favourable letter to Andrea de Loo, which also as the others before by the Lord Treasurer was showed unto her Majesty, who very well liked and commended it, and answered unto Andrea de Loo by the Lord Treasurer that her Majesty's good will was still as before, which was to have good amity with the King of Spain, but for the peace she looked that the Prince of Parma should first seek it, for she herself would not first begin. For this cause Andrea de Loo was wished and advised to work the same by all means he could, but to have special care her dealings come not to the knowledge of others (and chiefly of all to the Lord of Leicester) for that there were that sought rather war than peace, and whensoever any occasion were offered to her Majesty either by letters or message they should find her willing to further it.

'When things were thus far past, was Mr. Vice-Chamberlain first made acquainted with these doings of Andrea de Loo.

'In the midst of these actions one Agostino Grafigna, an Italian merchant in London, by the means and persuasions of the Lord Cobham, took upon him to go over to the Prince of Parma to treat also about a peace, and coming over had good audience of the Prince, but so handled his matter there as he almost confessed to be sent from hence, his proceedings are known and therefore not material to be told.

'About the beginning of May Mr. Comptroller taketh upon him to treat with Andrea de Loo, having perfect knowledge of all the particulars that were passed before between Andrea de Loo and the Lord Treasurer and beginneth to deal with him as from her Majesty (having made more privy to this matter Mr. Vice-Chamberlain, the Lord Cobham, Sir Walter Mildmay and two more whereof the one is, as it is thought, the Lord of Buckhurst) and with many speeches he persuadeth Andrea de Loo to go over himself and not to stand upon letters, which was but losing of time and occasions, showing among many other persuasions to move him and set him forward, the good liking her Majesty had that he should deal in this action, and the great desire she had to have peace, ascertaining him that upon his treaty she should with all speed call back Drake and stay such other ships as now were of new prepared to go to Sir Francis Drake, besides Sluys, Ostend, Graves, Venlo, and all other towns in her Majesty's power should be rendered to the King. But this much her Majesty would entreat, that all favour and leniency might be showed to her poor subjects of the Low Countries, and that Drake might quietly return.

'Whilst this was doing, her Majesty received a letter in Italian with divers Latin sentences applied, which was delivered to her on Saturday the 7th of May or Sunday following. This letter her Majesty took with good liking and immediately Andrea de Loo, his dispatch over to go was devised and Mr. Champagny's letter and certain of Lanfranchi's letters written to Andrea de Loo, which were in the Lord Treasurer's hands, were redelivered to Andrea de Loo, having each of them notes of the Lord Treasurer's hand upon them which Andrea de Loo with other notes carried with him over.

'Instructions were given to Andrea de Loo and amongst others great charge that by all manner of ways he should foresee that in going or coming he arrived neither in Zeeland or Holland, for that the Lord of Leicester there was, he that sought rather war than peace and might easily by stopping his return hinder the proceedings. Whilst these things were thus a doing and Andrea de Loo was thus solicited to go over, A. Grafigna was won again by the Lord Cobham to go over about this peace and was advised to go before that he might win the spurs.

'Grafigna went from hence Sunday morning the eighth of May, the Wednesday following, being the 11th of May, de Loo with the Lord Treasurer's passport and with many good words from her Majesty, delivered him both by the Lord Treasurer and afterwards by the Comptroller, and with some further instructions and with the Lord Treasurer's commendations to Mr. Champagny, departed.

'And afterwards Mr. Comptroller, having showed unto de Loo her Majesty's great good liking she had in this matter and to see some good fruits come thereof, de Loo departed. Moreover, as for Grafigna's going over, both the Lord Treasurer and he protested to be no doers in it, willing Andrea de Loo not to fear him, for that he thought some had sent him that looked to have the honour and thanks of the matter, but the Prince of Parma had promised him that he would not take it out of his hands, which he held himself sure of and therefore bade de Loo make haste, seeing he went upon a sure ground and so did not Grafigna. And further he warned de Loo from touching Zeeland and Holland, for fear of the Lord of Leicester who had no meaning but to war, and therefore charged him to have great care not to come there.

'And amongst other charges which he gave Andrea de Loo, he greatly charged him to work so as that M. de Champagny might be the man to come over to treat of this peace. First, for that her Majesty had of him best liking, secondly, for that he is known a most fit instrument for this purpose by reason of the help and furtherance he hath and should have by his brother the Cardinal of Granvelle, who is known to bear great rule with the King of Spain. And whensoever he came he should find her Majesty's good disposition and besides the most and best of her Council well inclined in the furthering of it, except the Secretary, who against so many others should be able to do little hurt.'

XIV

SCOTLAND AND FRANCE, 1585–8

The three years which followed the return of Leicester from the Low Countries in 1586 were the last three years of Walsingham's life. During that time he was chiefly concerned with the questions arising out of the war with Spain. No doubt the war increased the burden of his office. To the usual multitude of his tasks at home and abroad it added the exacting business of preparing attacks upon Spain by land and sea and of organizing a defence to meet counter-attacks upon England. In one important respect, however, the war brought him relief. It simplified his problems by defining them. For fifteen years he had been convinced that war with Spain was inevitable, but he had never been able to act upon that conviction because he could not bring his mistress round to his way of thinking. But now, at the close of the year 1586, the case was different. By the dispatch of Drake to the West Indies and of Leicester to the Low Countries Elizabeth had practically committed herself to Walsingham's policy. She had tacitly recognized the hostility of Spain towards her and had gone a long way towards combatting it. War it is true had not been definitely declared by either party. Elizabeth still gathered some comfort from that fact. But she was forced to admit that something so very much like war already existed that she could no longer afford to ignore the ordinary precautions or omit the ordinary provisions which a state of war involved. So Walsingham could hereafter count upon a larger measure of royal attention to his counsels and of royal support to his plans than they had heretofore received. When all these things which he had predicted were coming to pass he found the Queen considerably less disposed to despise him as a mere Puritan and to denounce him as a mere calamity howler.

The war with Spain as Walsingham saw it affected almost every question, domestic and foreign, which Elizabeth had to face.

At home it had its bearing upon the treatment of the English Catholics. The fear that they would rally to the support of Philip II in case he should invade England was no mere phantom. The Ridolfi Plot, the Throgmorton Plot, and the Babington Plot had all revealed a marked disposition on the part of the leading English Catholics to rise in support of any invader who came against Elizabeth in the name of their faith. In that fact lay one of the gravest dangers of the Spanish war. It was a danger which Walsingham above all others in England was expected to guard against. And no small part of his time and energy during the closing years of his life was directed to the hunting down of priests and the careful watching of recusants.

Associated always with this problem was the problem of Mary Stuart. When Leicester returned from the Low Countries in November 1586 the question of Mary's fate was commanding Walsingham's undivided attention. He had already induced Elizabeth to bring her to trial for her complicity in the Babington Plot. She had already been tried and adjudged guilty. And Parliament, summoned for the purpose, had already petitioned for her execution. But Walsingham found his mistress very loath to sign the death warrant. For something like three months he and his colleagues in the Privy Council laboured with her irresolution. In February 1587 they finally achieved their purpose, though they had to resort to a device at the very end which was the ruination of Davison's career and which placed Burghley for a long season under the royal displeasure. Walsingham had an apt attack of his old malady to thank for the fact that he was not a party to the final catastrophe. He therefore escaped the full measure of the royal wrath. But Elizabeth realized too well the large part he had played in Mary's destruction to allow him to escape uncensured. Nearly two months after the tragedy at Fotheringay he wrote to Leicester: 'Our sharp humours continue here still, which doth greatly disquiet her Majesty and discomfort her poor servants. The Lord Treasurer remaineth still in disgrace and behind my back her Majesty giveth out very hard speeches of myself, which I the rather credit for that I find in dealing with her I am nothing gracious, and if her Majesty could be otherwise served I know I should not be used.' [1]

[1] 3 Apr. 1587, Cotton MSS., Galba C xi, f. 288.

With Mary Stuart out of the way the danger of a Catholic uprising in England was appreciably diminished. The next in line for the English throne by any reckoning was her son James of Scotland, and from the point of view of Roman Catholicism there was little to choose between his brand of heresy and Elizabeth's. Consequently the English Catholics had less inducement to contrive Elizabeth's death. It is true that zealous Catholics on the continent like Allen and Parsons were prepared to set James's claim aside and to advance the pretensions of Philip II himself. But this way out of the dilemma did not commend itself to their English brethren at large. Zealous as they were for their faith they were too proud of their Englishry to entertain the thought of a foreign ruler. Had Walsingham been aware of their attitude he might have gathered even greater satisfaction from the fact of Mary's death than he did. As it was, his own impulse to place the interests of his faith first and the interests of his country afterwards led him to the unwarranted assumption that the average English Catholic acknowledged the same order of precedence. His fundamental mistake in this, as in all other questions where the forces of religion and nationality conflicted, was that he overestimated the strength of the one and underestimated the strength of the other. In that respect Elizabeth and Burghley, who were both better Englishmen than he was, were wiser than he.

The Queen of Scots' execution, while it strengthened Elizabeth's position at home, seemed at first likely to damage it abroad. During the interval between Mary's trial and her execution the King of Scotland and the King of France had both intervened vigorously to save her life. Both of them expressed great indignation at her death. So far as Scotland was concerned Elizabeth had been led to believe that James's interest in his mother's safety was largely perfunctory, and that so long as his pension was paid and his title to the English succession unimpaired, he would take no steps to avenge her.[1] But the first

[1] Cf. Gray and Melville to James VI, 21 Jan. 1586–7: 'The greatest hinder which our negotiations have found hitherto is a persuasion they have here that either your Majesty deals superficially in this matter [of Mary Stuart] or that with time you may be moved to digest it' (*Papers relating to the Master of Gray*, p. 134). Courcelles wrote to the King of France from Scotland, 31 Dec. 1586, that the King of Scots had declared he would not attack England

news which reached London from Scotland after Mary's death was known there told a different and a far less pleasant story. Robert Carey, whom Elizabeth had sent north to explain away her action, was stopped at the border. All communication with England was cut off. And every letter from the north bore testimony to the fact that both the King and the Scottish nobility were outraged at Mary's execution and determined to avenge it.[1] Walsingham's private informants told him the same tale. In December he had ordered Maliverny Catlyn, one of his cleverest spies, who had been working among the northern Catholics, to repair to Scotland.[2] Catlyn wrote from Newcastle early in March that he had not ventured to cross the border but that he had been credibly informed that the King was taking 'the death of his mother most heinously' and was making advances to France; that the papists in North England were beginning to stir; that plots were a-brewing against Walsingham's own life.[3] Walsingham of course realized that it was not safe to place too much dependence on reports of this sort, but he was well aware that the party hostile to England in Scotland was strong, that their leaders were negotiating for assistance from the continent,[4] and that Courcelles, the French agent at the Scottish court, was doing his best to induce the King to throw over the English alliance for a French one. Under these circumstances Walsingham viewed the situation in the north with some alarm. Early in March he wrote a letter to John Maitland, the King's secretary and his most influential adviser, in which he undertook to point out the reasons which should deter the King from a breach with England. Undoubtedly he intended that this letter should come before the King himself. It is one of the ablest state papers which survive from Walsingham's pen and

even though Mary were executed, unless Elizabeth attempted to deprive him of his right to the succession in England, and that in consequence the friends of England in Scotland were urging Elizabeth to sign Mary's death warrant (*Courcelles' Dispatches*, Bannatyne Club, p. 25).

[1] *Cal. Border Papers*, i. 247; *Cal. Salisbury MSS.* iii. 228-30; *Cal. Venetian*, 1581-91, p. 266.

[2] Cf. Catlyn to Walsingham, 29 Dec. 1586, Harleian MSS. 286, f. 97.

[3] *Cal. Border Papers*, i. 249-51, where the letter is wrongly attributed to Ballard, who had been executed the previous September. The letter is signed II, which was the mark Catlyn ordinarily used.

[4] Cf. Letters of Thomas Rogers, *alias* Berden, to Walsingham in *Cal. Domestic*, Adda., 1580-1625, *passim*, particularly p. 153.

reveals not only a complete understanding of James's position but also a shrewd insight into his character. On that account, though it is over long, it is quoted at length.[1]

'Sir: Being absent from the court when the late execution of the Queen your sovereign's mother happened, I did forthwith upon my return impart to Mr. Douglas some things concerning the course was conceived here by your said sovereign's best friends fit to be holden in this remediless accident for continuance of peace and amity between the two crowns as a thing for the weal of both nations to be desired. But finding him unwilling to meddle therewith I have thought good to write to the same effect unto yourself. The rather for that I presently understand, by some advertisement out of that country, that the death of the Queen is likely to breed so strange an alienation of his Majesty's mind towards this realm, tending (as is reported) wholly to violence and revenge of that which hath been so necessarily done by the whole body of the same; whereof, as for mine own part I should be right sorry, so it is generally hoped that his Majesty, being of that singular judgement himself, by the good help and advice of such as you are in credit and authority about him, men of wisdom and experience whom he will heed, this mischief will notwithstanding be carefully and prudently prevented, considering how every way, all things being rightly weighed, this course will be found prejudicial as well to your sovereign's estate as to his reputation if he resolve to persist therein.

'For, first, the enterprise will undoubtedly be condemned in the sight of all such as shall not be transported with some particular passion; for that they shall see he takes arms for revenge of an action, besides the necessity wherein it is grounded, full of so honourable and just proceedings, as howsoever the effect was contrary to their liking, the manner thereof by the late Queen's great furtherers could not but be approved and allowed. And as on the one side, the King your sovereign oppugning the course of justice, of so unlawful, unjust and desperate a quarrel cannot be expected any other thing than a most unhappy and miserable issue; so we, being assured that in the defence of justice the assistance of His mighty arm will not fail us whose judgement this was, need not to fear whatsoever attempt man shall attempt to the contrary against this realm.

'But not to stand upon the justness of the quarrel, which every

[1] This letter is printed in Spottiswoode, ii. 365 ff. The original appears to be missing, though there is a contemporary copy of it in Cotton MSS., Caligula D i, f. 133. The letter referred to in *Cal. Spanish*, 1587–1603, p. 29, is probably a French version of it.

man perhaps will not so much regard, it would be considered what means your sovereign shall have to go through with such an enterprise, if he take it in hand. For the forces of his own realm, being so far inferior to those in England, no man is so simple but seeth it were no way safe for his Majesty, trusting only thereto, to make head against the power of this land, neither is it thought that any man will be found so unadvised as to wish him so to do.

'But as it may be that a great number for lack of understanding are carried away with such vain discourse, as some without solid ground imagine of what might be done in this case by the King of Scotland backed and assisted (as they conceive in the air) with the French and Spanish aid; so it is likely enough there shall not want those that, either for satisfaction of their private passions, or supply of their necessities, or better effectuating some other their private designs, would be content to serve themselves of this public occasion and opportunity; who will propound, and promise also, more to his Majesty of such foreign assistance than they know in their consciences can be performed, if he would declare himself enemy to this realm; which that he should (though to his own ruin) the enemies of both realms will do what they can to procure.

'But men of wisdom and understanding, laying before their eyes as well the accustomed delays and, after long solicitation and pursuit, the simple supplies and support commonly found at these foreign potentates' hands; as also how doubtful and uncertain the success of war may prove, England (God be thanked) being so prepared and in case to defend itself, both otherwise and by the conjunction of Holland and Zeeland's forces by sea, in respect whereof this realm need not fear what all the potentates of Europe, being banded together against us, can do for to annoy the same; due consideration, I say, being taken hereof, you will easily judge and find how vain it were for your sovereign, upon so uncertain hopes, to embark himself and estate in an unnecessary war. But much more if you shall consider what a sequel and train of dangers and hazards the war draweth therewith, the consequences whereof reacheth to whatsoever your sovereign possesseth or hopeth for in this life. For, escaping to be slain in field, if he should happen to be taken prisoner or be constrained to retire himself out of the realm (things that have fallen out in experience) and then, having incensed this whole realm against him, he should be disabled from any right in the succession of this crown (as authority is given to do it by the same statute whereby they proceeded against his mother) for attempting the invasion of this land, what extremity should he be reduced unto.

'And truly it could not otherwise be, the ancient enmity between the two nations, now forgotten, being by drawing blood one of another again likely to be in such sort revived, as it would be impossible to make them like of a prince of that nation and especially him who had been, upon so unjust a ground, the author of that unfortunate breach.

'Besides that, the greatest part of the ancient nobility, by whose judgement the late Queen was condemned, and the rest of the principal gentlemen of the realm who confirmed the same in Parliament, should have just cause to adventure anything, even to the marching over their bellies, rather than to yield to his government who, carrying such a vindictive mind, they might doubt would one day call their lives and honours in question.

'And as for the remedy and relief which he might attend (standing in these terms) of foreign princes, there are many examples of the former ages and within fresh memory; as the King of Navarre's grandfather by the mother's side and Christian, King of Denmark, both were allied to Francis the First and Charles the Fifth, two of the mightiest potentates that reigned in long time; and that this present Don Antonio may suffice for example to teach all princes, if they can avoid it, to beware how they fall into that state whereby they shall be enforced to seek their own by other potentates' means. Princes are not so ready in these days to embrace other men's quarrels but where they are extraordinarily interested in their own fortunes.

. . . .

'For it is no safe way for any prince to repose his trust and strength upon their favour and assistance to whose desires and designs his greatness may yield any impeachment and hindrance; so were it clearly against common reason to expect other support and assistance from them than might stand with their own commodities and pretensions, in respect whereof neither of the two aforesaid kings can simply and roundly join with your sovereign to his good.

'First, his religion being odious to them both, and likely to prove most prejudicial to the Catholic cause, he growing so great as he should be made by the union of the two crowns; the consideration whereof caused his mother's affairs to stick a long time, and made her now in the end leave him quite out of reckoning, ordaining the King of Spain her heir, if her son became not Catholic.

'Next it is merely repugnant to the policy of France, were it but in respect of the ancient claim England maketh to that crown, to suffer the uniting of this island under one prince.

'They have been content in former times, when England had a footing in France, to serve themselves of your nation, therewith to annoy this realm by the means of diverting or dividing the forces thereof; and so perhaps the politics of France can be content to wish at this day, by your sovereign's quarrel or any such like, to be eased of the burden and miseries of the present war wherewith they are plagued by transporting the same into this island. But as this realm hath good means to prevent that mischief, if it were intended, so were your sovereign to look, when all were done, but to be made an instrument, as his predecessors have been, of the effusion of much Scottish blood for French quarrels and the desolation of that realm.

'And as things stand presently in France, it is not thought that you should find the King ready to hearken to any enterprise against this land, the said King being most desirous to live in peace with his neighbours abroad and his subjects at home, but that he hath been forced, full sore against his will by the practice of them of the House of Guise, to countenance with his authority the civil war raised in that realm, which maketh him, whatsoever show he maketh to the contrary, to hate them in his heart.

'Neither would it be held sound counsel to be given him by any that depends upon his fortune, to further the advancement of a King of Scots, so nearly allied to that family which he hath discovered and greatly feareth to level at his own crown with an intention to depose him, which by the greatness of a King of Scots they should be so much the sooner and better able to effect.

'The King of Spain's assistance, being now in war with this realm, were more likely to be obtained, but far more dangerous to be used in respect of his insatiable ambition, deep practices and power, accompanied in this case with a colour of right; wherein how far he would seek to prevail, any opportunity or advantage being offered, it may justly be doubted by the experience that sundry states have had, which upon slender grounds of title have been extorted and wrung from the true inheritors and annexed to his own kingdom, as Navarre, Portugal, and all he possesseth in Italy hath been.

'It is believed that the King of Spain, considering his years and unsettled estate every way, would willingly incline to peace if it were offered with reasonable conditions and not over readily at this present embark himself in any new enterprises.

'But otherwise it is well known, that as he had fancied to himself an empire of all this part of Europe, so he had an eye to this realm ever since he was King in right of his wife. The conquest was intended under colour of religion as is discovered by some that were of his own privy council at that time. His pretension to be the heir of the house of Lancaster, and since the late Queen's death, the first Catholic prince of the blood royal of England, as also the donation of this crown made him by the Queen of Scots in her letters, with a promise to confirm it by testament (things blazed abroad by the said King's ambassador at Paris), ought to breed jealousy and suspicion in your sovereign's head and give him to think how he should be used at such an assistant's hand.

'Auxiliary forces have ever been reputed dangerous if they either in number or policy were superior to them that called them in. The assistance therefore of Spain and France, being of this nature, as your sovereign hath need of neither so he shall do well to forbear them both and so shall it be most for his ease.

'It may be some will pretend that by change of his religion your sovereign shall better his condition in regard of these foreign princes, besides a party within this realm that shall be drawn wholly to depend upon his fortune. But the poor distressed estate of Don Antonio, being a Catholic prince despoiled by a Catholic and receiving so little succour at Catholic princes' hands, shall be sufficient bar to all that can be alleged in that behalf.

'As for the Catholic Party in England, it was never so united as they drew all in one line, much less will they be brought suddenly to rely upon him if he should alter his religion (as God defend) which would be his utter discredit and overthrow both with the one and the other party, neither having cause to repose any confidence in him,—the Protestants because he had renounced the religion wherein he was with great care brought up, the Papists because they could not be assured in short space he was truly turned to their faith. Yea, all men should have reason to forsake him who had thus dissembled and forsaken his God.'

It would appear from a letter which Walsingham wrote to Stafford in Paris late in March that the letter to Maitland served to very good purpose. 'There have been divers means used', he wrote, 'to draw the King of Scots to take revenge of his mother's death but he cannot be won to hearken thereunto, finding in his own judgement that his only way to maintain the title he may hereafter pretend to this crown is to continue the good feeling of her Majesty toward him and of the subjects here.' [1] But it must not be forgotten that Walsingham, having good reason to believe that Stafford was playing the traitor in Paris at this time, was more likely to send him false information than the truth. At all events it is quite clear that Walsingham felt the necessity of using stronger arguments than mere words to

[1] S. P. France, xvii, f. 81.

keep James of Scotland faithful to the English alliance. Archibald Douglas, the semi-official representative of the King in London, indicated the way in which this might be accomplished. He proposed that the King's title to the English succession should be cleared from any impediment occasioned through his mother's death by a written assurance from the English judges, sealed with the Great Seal and signed by the Queen herself; and that Elizabeth should confer upon James the Lennox lands in England.[1] Walsingham strongly urged the Queen to make these concessions, but he found her loath to commit herself.[2] 'For Scotland,' he wrote to Leicester on the 3rd of April, 'the Queen's Majesty seemeth to neglect altogether such opportunities as are offered to her, wherewith Mr. Archibald Douglas is greatly discouraged. Such of that realm as stand ill affected to this crown do lose no opportunity that may work a breach.'[3] And again, five days later, 'The ambassador of Scotland received so hard and doubtful answers to certain propositions he made unto her Majesty the other day as he desired (seeing so cold a proceeding towards his master) that without her mislike he might write to his said master for order for his revocation. The gentleman, as I learn by some that have lately seen him, groweth greatly discontented both in respect of his master and of himself. There are many presages of some dangerous alteration in this kingdom, and therefore it will behoove all honest men to provide for a storm; and in the meantime to pray to God to open her eyes to see the evident peril of the course she now holdeth.'[4]

Throughout the next year King James continued to press for some satisfactory establishment of his title to the succession and for the Lennox estates or their equivalent in England,[5] and

[1] Murdin, *Burghley Papers*, pp. 587–8.

[2] Her attitude varied; cf. *Cal. Salisbury MSS.* iii. 243 with S. P. Scotland, xlii, no. 39.

[3] Cotton MSS., Galba C xi, f. 288.

[4] Galba C xi, f. 294. The question of the succession, as Walsingham rightly judged, was what interested James VI most. Gray wrote to Douglas, 10 Nov. 1586: 'Let me feel frankly . . . what your opinion is anent his suit for his title . . . because now the King beginneth to apprehend that matter very far' (*Papers relating to the Master of Gray*, p. 115).

[5] Richard Douglas wrote to A. Douglas in June 1587 that James would be satisfied with nothing less than a public declaration of his right to the English succession failing issue of Elizabeth's own body (*Cal. Salisbury MSS.* iii. 261). On 8 July 1587 James directed A. Douglas to make this demand of the Queen along with a demand for a ducal title with sufficient estates in north

Walsingham on his part continued to urge upon the Queen the expediency of acceding to these demands. It is possible that his zeal in the King's behalf was prompted in some degree by a desire to provide for his own future. The probabilities were that upon Elizabeth's death James would succeed to the English throne, and Elizabeth was not only growing old but she was also constantly exposed to the danger of an untimely death by assassination. Under these circumstances the good favour of James became a matter of considerable moment to English Privy Councillors. Walsingham in particular may well have felt the necessity of changing the bad opinion which the King had formed of him during his mission to Scotland in 1583. It is significant in this connexion to discover that he gave James at this juncture private assurance of support in his pretensions to the English succession.[1] There is no way of proving that the assurance was sincerely meant. Heretofore it had generally been believed that Walsingham favoured the Earl of Huntingdon's claims.[2] But the fact that the assurance was given shows that he not only had James's claims in mind but that they played some part in his calculations.

But quite apart from these considerations, which were hardly likely to carry much weight with Elizabeth, Walsingham had an abundance of excellent arguments for urging her to cultivate the Scottish King's friendship. Everybody in England knew by

England and a right to be consulted before Lady Arabella Stuart's hand was disposed of in marriage (*Cal. Salisbury MSS.* iii. 267–8). James apparently demanded also an increase of his English pension to £5,000 (*Cal. Border Papers*, i, p. 311).

[1] Cf. *English Historical Review*, Jan. 1913, p. 48. R. Douglas wrote to A. Douglas, 22 May 1587: 'He [James] rests gladly contented with Lord Leicester's deliberation and resolution to take his dependence with the rest of his friends upon his Majesty, and is well satisfied with the reasons you wrote that moved him, but especially for the benefit of the professed religion in both the realms' (*Cal. Salisbury MSS.* iii. 256). Again, on 7 June 1587, R. Douglas, in writing to A. Douglas of the King's desire to have his title to the succession established, added: 'His Majesty is sufficiently persuaded of the good will of some of those councillors towards him and the weal of both realms, namely of Lord Leicester and Sir Francis Walsingham, and attributes the fault only to the Queen herself and some of her near favourites' (*Cal. Salisbury MSS.* iii. 261). On the other hand the Spanish ambassador at Paris wrote to Philip II, 7 June 1587: 'I understand that on Walsingham being told that the King of Scotland was showing courage in the matter of his mother's death, he replied that if he boasted much more they would send him the same road as his mother for £1,000' (*Cal. Spanish*, 1587–1603, p. 97).

[2] Cf. *English Historical Review*, Jan. 1913, p. 48, n. 52.

this time that the King of Spain was preparing to descend upon England. It was a nice question to decide whether or not Elizabeth would be able to withstand this attack even from the front where she had her sea walls for bulwarks. The possibility of withstanding it from the rear if James played false and gave the enemy a free foot to land and to organize in Scotland was desperate indeed. Walsingham pointed out that fact in a letter which he wrote to Leicester in November. 'Scotland', he wrote, 'is altogether neglected, whence all our mischief is like to come, where the employment of 2,000 men by the enemy with some portion of treasure may more annoy us than 30,000 men landed in any part of this realm. No one thing more doth prognosticate an alteration of this estate than that a Prince of her Majesty's judgement should neglect, in respect of a little charge, the stopping of so dangerous a gap as that is like to prove.' [1]

No doubt Elizabeth saw the danger but she trusted to James himself to avert it, fancying that his desire to assure himself of the English succession would prevent him from co-operating with England's enemies. In the long run she proved to be right, though in 1587 the facts certainly argued strongly against her view of the case. From every quarter Walsingham received disquieting news of Scotland. Now he heard from France that an agent of the Scottish Catholics was negotiating secretly through the Spanish ambassador in Paris for money and men from Spain. A little later it was reported from Scotland that James was

[1] 12 Nov. 1587, Galba D ii, f. 178. Burghley wrote to Walsingham, 20 Nov. 1587: 'As one sick to another I write uncertainly, understanding that her Majesty is with you and that I am sure she will speak with you of Scottish matters, from which all evil or good is shortly to come. I thought good to send you a copy of a writing that Arch. Douglas gave me four days past. He also declared to me yesternight an accident of a combination of a great part of the nobility for favour of papist religion and Spanish favours. He said that he had declared the same to her Majesty. Many things concur herewith, as your advertisement out of Spain by the way of France, the arrival of Col. Semple at Calais, going to Dunkirk. And we have no concurrence either to prevent or to withstand.

'I send you also a letter from my Lord of Hunsdon, by whose last clause in his letter, written with his own hand, though where he is he has no cause to hope well of the Scottish king, yet I am sure he would be glad to do any office to reclaim him. Absence of conference engendereth stratagems, and so in the end disdain. In this matter is to be considered whether her Majesty may do the King of Scots more harm or he her. Because her Majesty, as I perceive, will come to me from you, I have thought to present you with these lines, of a hand lame.' (S. P. Domestic, ccv, no. 33.)

holding secret counsel with the Catholic leaders there.[1] Throughout the summer the Scots were raiding the English border, and in September came news that Scottish Catholics were planning to seize Berwick. Meanwhile Courcelles, the French agent at the Scottish court, was doing everything in his power to alienate James from the English party.[2] Walsingham felt sure that if Courcelles' papers could be got hold of still more dangerous matter would be brought to light. Through Robert Carville, one of his agents, he got into communication with one Brown, an Englishman in Courcelles' employ. In April 1587 he sent Brown a bunch of skeleton keys to see if he could not open Courcelles' dispatch box and steal his dispatches. The keys failed to fit, and though Brown offered to steal the whole box, Walsingham apparently thought it wiser, at the time, to pursue the matter no further.[3] The episode is significant as showing how anxious Walsingham was about the situation in the north at this time and how far he was prepared to go in order to anticipate the dangers he feared from that quarter.

The news of the plot against Berwick coupled with the border disturbances seems to have aroused in the Queen some sense of the seriousness of the situation. She decided to reinforce her border troopers, and in September she sent Lord Hunsdon, Governor of Berwick, north to strengthen the defences of that city. As soon as Hunsdon reached the border he apparently opened up again some of his old channels of communication with Scotland. The reports which he received through these confirmed what Walsingham's agents had already written of the unfriendly disposition of James towards England. 'Touching the King's good meaning to her Majesty,' Hunsdon wrote to Burghley in October, '. . . surely he hath no good meaning towards her if he had power to his mind, as appears by his dealings in these Border causes, and as bad a company about him! I dare assure your Lordship that he makes full account of some succours to come to him presently either from France or

[1] *Cal. Border Papers*, i. 255. [2] Ibid. i. 270.

[3] Ibid. i. 288. The box was subsequently stolen and the letters secured are probably those now preserved among the State Papers, Scotland, in the Public Record Office. An abstract of the most important dispatches, prepared probably by one of Walsingham's clerks, is printed in *Courcelles' Dispatches*, published by the Bannatyne Club.

Spain.'[1] And a month later, 'I know for certain that the King looks for aid out of Spain before Candlemas.'[2] And again, the following January, 'I dare assure her Majesty that the King means to revenge the death of his mother if ever he be able, and what fair speeches or promises soever is made of him, her Majesty shall find it but plain dissimulation.'[3]

But although Hunsdon agreed that the danger was grave he did not hesitate to say that Walsingham was taking the wrong course to avert it. He insisted that Walsingham placed altogether too much confidence in Archibald Douglas, who had been acting as a sort of unofficial ambassador for Scotland at the English court since July 1586. The King, Hunsdon wrote, distrusted Douglas and disliked him and thought him altogether too intimate with the English secretary.[4] It would be much more profitable, Hunsdon thought, to approach James through some other channel. No doubt this was in part true. James found it expedient not to give Douglas any formal recognition at this juncture and was quite prepared to disavow him altogether if the occasion seemed to demand it. Walsingham knew that well enough, but as the King was willing to make use of Douglas, Walsingham was willing to use him too, especially since Douglas had become a pensioner of the Queen's and was the more likely on that account to further her interests. Furthermore Hunsdon's condemnation of Douglas seems to have been prompted mainly by a desire to get the negotiations with James into his own hands. The failure of his previous by-plot with Arran, though it evidently still rankled in his breast,[5] did not deter him. Rather it stimulated him to try again, with the double purpose apparently of discrediting Walsingham, for whom Hunsdon still cherished a strong resentment, and winning favour for himself. He got into correspondence once more with Cuthbert Armourer, who had formerly served as intermediary between him and Arran, and through Cuthbert opened negotiations with Lord Bothwell, a courtier of considerable influence at the Scottish court at this

[1] *Cal. Border Papers*, i. 282. [2] Ibid. i. 287. [3] Ibid. i. 305.
[4] Ibid. i. 299, 308, 311.
[5] Hunsdon wrote to Burghley in November 1587: 'I pray God her Majesty be not sorry she hearkened no better to me and less to others, who thought they had God by the foot when they were sure of Angus and Mar' (*Cal. Border Papers*, i. 287).

time. It will not be necessary to follow the course of these negotiations.[1] They came to nothing in the end. The Queen evidently disapproved of them.[2] Walsingham, who knew all about them from the beginning, did not take much stock in them though he was disposed to exploit them for what they might be worth. In the long run they probably did more harm than good by revealing to James the differences in the English Privy Council and by giving him a chance to play his game of dalliance with each faction in turn.

It does not appear that Walsingham made any headway with his Scottish policy during the autumn of 1587 or the spring of 1588. He could not persuade his mistress to make any concessions to James's demands either for pension or title or Lennox lands. She did offer to lend him 4,000 troops to defend his kingdom late in December, but James refused the offer indignantly.[4] Since Elizabeth would not commit herself to him, he would not commit himself to her. So it was that during the early months of 1588, when the Spanish Armada was making ready to descend upon England, his attitude towards Elizabeth

[1] Cf. *Border Papers*, i. 268, 293-4, 297, &c. [2] Ibid. i. 320-1.

[3] Walsingham wrote, 23 Jan. 1587-8, apparently to Leicester or to Burghley as follows: 'For myself, as this bearer can show your Lordship, the state of my body is such as may not well endure travail, otherwise I would not have failed, as duty bindeth me, to have given my attendance; though (to be plain with your Lordship) with no great hope to do any good in the cause of Scotland, which groweth every day more and more to be incurable and subject to unnecessary jealousies.

'If Mr. Archibald Douglas had been dispatched hence unto the King his Majesty with some reasonable contentment, there might by his travail and dexterity have been a countermine made to sundry dangerous practices that I fear now will hardly be stayed.

'Seeing Carmichael, who hath acquainted the King his master with Her Majesty's answer to the request propounded by Mr. Archibald, pretendeth by his particular letter to the Lord Chamberlain [Hunsdon] to have charge from his Majesty to deliver unto his Lordship some matter of contentment, it were not amiss in my poor opinion to stay from taking any farther resolution touching that realm until her Majesty shall be informed from my Lord Chamberlain what that matter of contentment is that Carmichael hath charge to deliver unto him. It is likely that it will be pleasible, howsoever the K. . . . standeth affected, for that he is not yet in state to enter into any public action against his Majesty. But if it might have pleased his Majesty to have used Mr. Archibald's service when he offered the same, he was not then without hope to have drawn the said K. . . . to have embarked himself in some public action against . . .' (Cotton MSS., Caligula D i, f. 197. This letter is in Walsingham's hand, but it has been much damaged by fire. The address is missing.)

[4] *Cal. Salisbury MSS.* iii. 300.

remained doubtful, and in appearance at least even dangerous. He held the English at arm's length while he played with the proposals of the Scottish Catholics. It is hardly likely that he ever seriously intended a course hostile to Elizabeth; he had too fine an eye for the main chance. His apparent vacillation between her and her enemies was probably designed to frighten her into some concrete concession. But he did not succeed in winning even a promise from her until the Armada was actually in Scottish waters. He does seem to have succeeded in frightening Walsingham. At any rate he made Walsingham feel that the 'postern gate' was insecure at a time when, in view of the open hostility of Spain, he thought it extremely rash to take any risk in that quarter.

Walsingham might have viewed the situation in Scotland with more equanimity if he had been less doubtful of the attitude of France. A defensive alliance with the French King would have served as a strong bridle against Spanish malice. Even an adequate guarantee of French neutrality would have strengthened Elizabeth's position considerably. But there was no hope of the one and little security for the other. In December 1584 the Guisan Catholic party in France had joined in secret alliance with Philip II of Spain to exterminate heresy both in France and elsewhere. The following July the King of France had been obliged to submit to the policy of the Guises. Under these circumstances it appeared to Walsingham far more likely that France would unite with Spain against Elizabeth than hold a friendly or even a neutral course towards her. And Henry III's bearing towards England in the autumn of 1585 certainly seemed to confirm this view of the matter. In August he recalled Mauvissière, his ambassador at London, whose influence for ten years had been steadily directed to the maintenance of goodwill between France and England,[1] and replaced him with the Baron de Châteauneuf, a strong Guisan partisan.[2] In October he

[1] Mauvissière had been on particularly good terms with Leicester and Walsingham, on rather better terms, one suspects, than was quite compatible with his office; cf. his letters to A. Douglas in *Cal. Salisbury MSS.* iii. 110, 112, 200.

[2] Guillaume de L'Aubespine, baron de Châteauneuf, according to his own statement (accepted by Teulet, *Relations politiques de la France et de 'Espagne avec l'Écosse*, iv. 61, n. 1), arrived in England 7 Aug. 1586 (Teulet, *op. cit.*, iv. 78). The year evidently should be 1585—the day of course is in

dispatched a French agent to Scotland to work against the

the N. S. dating. Henry Talbot wrote to his father that Châteauneuf arrived in London 30 July 1585 (Lodge, *Illustrations*, &c., ii. 269). Sometime later Châteauneuf drew up a *discours* upon the state of affairs in England at the time of his arrival which preserves an interesting record of the Queen and her principal councillors. Of Elizabeth he wrote: 'La dict dame . . . est un princesse fort prudente et accomplie qui a esté fort bien nourrie, jouant de toutes sortes d'instrumentz, parlant plusieurs langues et mesmes la latine fort bien, bon esprit et vif, femme aymant fort la justice, ne exigeant rien sur ses subjectz, qui a esté belle en sa jeunesse; au reste grande mesnagère et quasi avaritieuse, fort colère et soudaine, et surtout grandement jalouse de son estat.

'A son advénement à la couronne elle se servist fort pour ses affaires de M. Guillaume Cecyl . . . que depuis elle fist millord de Burgley et grand trésorier d'Angleterre, qui vivoyt à mon arrivée audict royaume, homme saige, prudent, pacifique, mesnager, d'ung esprit vif et aigu. . . . Sa maistresse s'est toujours fort fiée en luy.

'Elle a eu le milord Robert Dudley, depuis conte de Lecestre, que elle a fort aymé toujours dès sa jeunesse, comme de vray il estoyt fort beau gentilhomme, honneste et courtoys; à mon arrivée il estoyt d'ung cinquante troys ou quattre ans, devenu fort replet. Ces deux-là sont ceux qui ont tout le long de son règne eu plus de puissance près d'elle.'

Again Châteauneuf said of Leicester: 'qui toujours avoyt tenu le premier lieu en ce royaume pour le grand crédict que il avoyt, et avoyt fort avancé tous les siens . . . de sorte que il estoit quasi egal à la royne en auctorité audict royaume et se pouvoit dire chef d'une part et le Grand Tresorier chef de l'autre.

'Il y avoyt le secrétaire d'estat, M. Françoys Vualsingham, fort habille homme et en très grand crédict près sa maistresse lors de mon arrivée, homme capable d'affaires et de très bon esprit, mais au reste si passioné au faict de sa religion que, pour ce seul respect, il se départoyt souvent des conseils les plus sages et tempérés. Le dict Vualsingham estoyt du tout du party dudict conte de Lecestre, tant pour la religion que d'aultant que le dict Vualsingham, n'ayant que une fille unique, il l'avoyt baillée en mariage à Philippe Sydeney, neveu et héritier dudict conte de Leicester.'

Châteauneuf then went on to speak of the question of the succession, naming the Queen of Scots, her son, Arabella Stuart, the Count of Hereford, the Earl of Derby, and the Earl of Huntingdon as candidates.

Of Hereford and Derby he wrote: 'Ils estoyent si foibles que ilz n'avoyent pas grand suport, si n'estoyt du dict Grand Trésorier qui les favorisoyt soubz main. D'aultre part, estant le conte de Lecestre si grand, et craignant si la royne d'Escosse entroyt en la succession que sa ruyne ne s'en ensuyvist pour la religion, l'on suscita le conte de Hungtington, beau-frère dudict de Lecestre . . . que sans doubte la couronne luy appartenoyt. . . . Et de faict le dict Huntington estoyt comme chef des Puritains. Il est de ceux qui vouloyent tenir la religion des Huguenotz de France, mais son principal fondement estoyt la grandeur du conte de Lecestre, de Vualsingham et aultres qui, pour la religion, embrassoyent son party et aigrissoyent journellement la Royne contre les Catholiques, desquelz ilz ruinoyent petit à petit les plus grandz.'

Speaking of Scottish affairs Châteauneuf told of the efforts of the English to overthrow the power of the Earl of Arran by means of Angus, Mar, and the Hamiltons: 'Toutes ces choses fist ladicte Dame audict an 1585 . . . le tout à l'instigation dudict conte de Lecestre et Vualsingham, et au contraire ledict millord Burgley, grand trésorier, luy dissuadant la guerre, comme celuy qui par prudence et mesnage avoyt conservé Sa Majesté en paix si longtemps; comme aussi, estant de son naturel assés espargnante, elle ne prenoyt pas

English interests in the north.[1] Walsingham became convinced that it was far safer to regard Henry III as an enemy than as a friend.[2] He accordingly urged his mistress to resort once more to her time-honoured policy of reinforcing the French Huguenots so that they might keep the King and the Guises engaged in France. An apt occasion for the pursuit of such a policy had been presented to her in the summer of 1585 when Henry of Navarre had appealed to her for assistance in support of his title to the French succession. It will be recalled that Henry's ambassador, Jacques Ségur-Pardailhan, had arrived in England in May of that year and had begged Elizabeth for a loan of 200,000 crowns to enable his master to levy troops in Germany. Walsingham had supported Ségur's request vigorously and the Queen at first had been disposed to accede to it. When the news reached London in July that the French King had gone over to the side of the Catholic league she had offered Ségur half the sum he asked for and had dispatched Thomas Bodley to Germany to invite the German Protestant princes to join with her in support of Navarre's cause. But she had weakened later, and when Ségur finally left England he had carried with him nothing better than her mere promise of 50,000 crowns. It appeared soon after his departure that Elizabeth had no notion of advancing even that paltry sum until she received some definite assurance from Bodley that the German princes would co-operate with her. When Bodley's report proved unfavourable she found herself in a quandary.[3]

grand plaisir à ceste despense de la guerre de Flandre, aussy que je croy que elle ne estoyt pas ayse de veoyr toutes ses forces entre les mains de son subject.' This discourse is printed in full in Teulet, *op. cit.*, iv. 61–88.

[1] This was the Baron d'Esneval, who was simply sent to cloak the intrigues of Courcelles, nominally his secretary, who was a violent partisan of the Guises. Teulet, *op. cit.*, iv, pp. 1 ff.: Courcelles' dispatches were printed in part by the Bannatyne Club in 1828.

[2] Walsingham wrote to Leicester, 21 Sept. 1585: 'The enclosed I received this morning from Mr. Horatio [Palavicino] by the which your Lordship may perceive that in company of the Ambassador's wife there cometh a Florentine who carrieth the note to be a great practicer. It were well done her Majesty were forewarned thereof. In these malicious times there cannot be too great care taken of her Majesty's safety. It were well therefore that the Ambassador's wife had some secret warning given unto her to cause the said party to withdraw himself' (Bodleian Library, Tanner MSS. lxxviii, f. 74).

[3] Bodley's dispatches are for the most part in the Public Record Office, partly among the S. P. German States, 1584–5, partly among the S. P. Denmark, i; cf. particularly his letter to Walsingham of 17 July 1585 (S. P. German States, 1584–5).

It looked very much as though she would either have to assist Navarre herself or else abandon him to his own devices. Neither of these solutions of the problem was to her liking. She agreed with Walsingham that it would never do to let Navarre perish, but in view of the fact that she had just pledged herself to an annual expenditure of some £125,000 in behalf of the Dutch rebels, she was more than ever loath to spend any money in French causes.

In a predicament like this her natural impulse was to avoid the direct issue if she could. Accordingly she spent the closing months of the year 1585 in framing devices for assisting Navarre without loosening her purse strings. In October she decided to make a second appeal to the German princes and she bade Lord Peregrine Willoughby prepare himself for a formal mission to that end.[1] But a fortnight later she had abandoned that project.[2] Bodley's reports were too discouraging. In December she thought seriously of mediating a peace between Navarre and the French King. On the 7th of December Walsingham wrote to the English ambassador at Paris:

> 'Whereas by my late letters I did write unto you that you ought, for the reasons by yourself alleged, forbear to make any motion of peace to the King as you were before directed, wherein I had the opinion and consent of my Lord Treasurer, I find her Majesty since to mislike of that course, thinking the motion of peace very necessary, so that being not disposed, so far as I can perceive, to yield to any contribution for the levy to have been made in Germany, she can be content that any lame peace shall be shuffled up in France rather than to be put to any such charges, and therefore you shall do well now to demand audience of the King and to present the said motion of peace as before you have been directed.'[3]

Walsingham's disapproval of these procrastinating courses is sufficiently obvious from the whole tone of this letter. He held fast to the opinion that the only safe policy for Elizabeth to follow was that of going promptly and effectively to Navarre's assistance, and he urged this policy upon her in season and out

[1] Cf. Walsingham to Willoughby, 14 Oct. 1585, *Cal. Foreign*, 1585–6, p. 86; also Walsingham to Ségur, 13 Oct. 1585, *Archives de la Maison d'Orange-Nassau*, 2nd series, i, p. 18.

[2] Cf. Walsingham to Willoughby, 3 Nov. 1585, *Cal. Foreign*, 1585–6, p. 142.

[3] S. P. France, xiv, f. 223.

of season. No doubt Leicester and his other partisans in the Council seconded his efforts, and even Burghley professed at least to be zealous in his support. Naturally both Navarre himself [1] and his agents in Germany did everything in their power to enforce his arguments. Ségur was incessant in his demands for money. Not content with writing letters he sent de Quitry, one of the members of his train, to England in October to appeal to the Queen in person.[2] Duke John Casimir of the Palatinate, with whom Ségur was negotiating for troops, wrote to Walsingham that the Queen's delay in sending her promised contribution was the only thing which prevented him from entering France at once in Navarre's behalf with an army of German reiters.[3] In the face of all this pressure Elizabeth was finally induced to take one reluctant step forward in the direction which Walsingham pointed.[4] In February 1586 she dispatched Horatio Palavicino to Germany with 50,000 crowns for Casimir's army. But the conditions which she attached to the delivery of the money were altogether out of proportion to its amount. Casimir must pledge himself to lead an army of 8,000 horse and 14,000 foot into France and to keep them there until he had won a good peace.[5] No wonder that Ségur protested that upon such terms the money could not be accepted and begged Walsingham and Leicester both to secure more favourable conditions and a larger sum of money.[6] But he begged in vain. Elizabeth was too heavily engaged with the Dutch to venture more.

[1] *Lettres de Henri IV*, viii. 298.

[2] Ségur to Burghley, 22 Oct. 1585, *Cal. Foreign*, 1585–6, p. 109; cf. also *Lettres de Henri IV*, viii. 297. De Quitry apparently did not reach England until December 1585; cf. Instructions to Palavicino in S. P. German States, 1585–6, dated Jan. 1585–6.

[3] Casimir to Walsingham, 21 Oct. 1585, *Cal. Foreign*, 1585–6, p. 107.

[4] In January 1586 Elizabeth returned de Quitry to Germany apparently with the promise that she would send money immediately. He had demanded 100,000 crowns as definitely pledged and had requested the loan of another 100,000 crowns. How much Elizabeth promised to send is not clear. She sent £15,468 15*s*. by Palavicino the following month (*Cal. Foreign*, 1585–6, p. 378). Walsingham wrote to Ségur on 15 April 1586 that he was sorry the Queen had not accorded to de Quitry as much as Ségur desired and as a wise man could wish, but that he hoped Drake would bring back enough plunder from the Indies to enable the Queen to be more liberal (*Lettres de Henri IV*, viii. 307 n.).

[5] Palavicino's instructions, dated 11 Feb. 1586, are given in *Cal. Foreign*, 1585–6, p. 378; Anquez, *Henri IV et l'Allemagne*, p. 14; Ségur to Leicester, 27 June 1586, in Blok, *Correspondance du Comte de Leicester*, pp. 53–5.

[6] Cf. Ségur's letter to Leicester just cited.

Indeed, she had no sooner dispatched Palavicino than she began to incline once more to the policy of mediating a peace between Navarre and the French King. In March 1586 and again in April she bade her ambassador in France intercede with Henry III in Navarre's behalf, and offered to assist him in opposing the malice of the Guises.[1] She appears to have been of the opinion, which was indeed not without foundation, that Henry III was finding his alliance with the Guises increasingly distasteful and that he was quite prepared to break with them if he could be assured of adequate support. She believed also that the King was of himself kindly disposed towards her and that his manifestations of unfriendliness were altogether due to the compulsion of the Guisan party.[2]

Walsingham for his part remained doubtful of the King's good intentions and still more doubtful of his ability to live up to them. He knew, as every one else knew, that Henry III was clay in his mother's hands, and he believed that Catherine de Médicis had decided to stake her future on the House of Guise.[3] Of course Walsingham did not advocate an open breach with France. In view of the hostility of Spain, he was prepared to admit the desirability of maintaining a show of amity with the French King and even, within limits, of cultivating his goodwill. What he was afraid of was that his mistress would place too much dependence upon the dubious friendship of the weak and vacillating Henry III and would thereby be led to neglect the God-given opportunity to provide against the certain hostility of those who dominated his policy. It might be politic to dally with Henry of Valois, but it was the height of folly to ignore the fact that Henry of Guise was the controlling force behind the French crown and that the real security of England against France lay in the strengthening of Henry of Navarre.

[1] Walsingham to Stafford, 9 Mar. 1585–6, April 1586, S. P. France, xv, ff. 90, 203.

[2] Walsingham to Stafford, 23 May 1586: 'Her Majesty hath many arguments to lead her to think that the King standeth very constantly affected towards her' (S. P. France, xv, f. 271).

[3] Walsingham to Stafford, 9 Mar. 1585–6: 'This I write unto you by her Majesty's commandment, having myself no hope that the same will work any great effect, the king being so weak-minded as he is and betrayed by his mother who, despairing of his life, buildeth her future standing upon the House of Guise' (S. P. France, xv, f. 90). Cf. also Walsingham to Randolph, 2 April 1586, S. P. Scotland, xxxix, no. 41.

During the spring and summer of 1586 Walsingham laboured steadily to impress this fact upon the Queen and to induce her to send Navarre the money he so badly needed. He was assisted in his efforts by Paul Choart, Sieur de Buzanval, whom Henry of Navarre sent to England in January to represent his interests at the English court.[1] Between the two of them they induced Elizabeth to authorize the loan of a second 50,000 crowns for Casimir's levies. Palavicino received his instructions to that effect in June. He was directed at the same time to see to it that the money was applied to the purposes for which it was intended. And he found that job hard enough. Casimir would not begin his preparations until he had adequate funds in hand. Palavicino would not pay over the Queen's money until Casimir had definitely pledged himself. The real difficulty lay in the fact that expected funds from other sources were not forthcoming. Henry of Navarre could not send as much money as he had undertaken to send from France. The German Protestant princes failed to contribute the support which had been counted on from them. Consequently the rest of the year in Germany was given up to haggling over terms. Palavicino proved himself to be a good man of business and he made himself unpopular with Navarre's agents by the tenacity with which he held to his instructions. But the net result of it all was that no troops were

[1] Cf. Henry of Navarre to Walsingham, 23 Jan. 1586, *Lettres de Henri IV*, viii. 304.

[2] On the instructions to Palavicino, cf. 'Memorandum of Directions to Mr. Horatio', dated 1 Mar. 1586–7 in S. P. German States, 1587–9. It must not be forgotten that all the money paid over by Palavicino was simply a loan from Elizabeth to Henry of Navarre which he promised to repay at the end of the war. The best general statement of the difficulties attending Palavicino's negotiations in Germany is given in his own summary dated 28 May 1586 (*Cal. Foreign*, 1585–6, pp. 682 ff.; cf. also his Report to Walsingham, dated 10 Nov. 1586, S. P. German States, iv). La Huguerye in his *Mémoires* gives a confused account of these negotiations (ed. de Ruble, ii. 343, 362–3, 378–9, 390). He was of the opinion that Palavicino was secretly opposed to paying over the money and was doing his best to break up the negotiations (ibid. ii. 363), but this view of the matter receives little or no support from more reliable sources. There is an interesting letter preserved from Palavicino to Sir Edward Stafford, English ambassador to France, written some time in the late autumn of 1586, in which Palavicino complains of the behaviour of Navarre's agents in Germany, but declares that the credit those agents had in England 'with whom you know' made him bear everything (S. P. France, xvi, f. 175). The 'with whom you know' was probably Leicester or Walsingham. A letter from Palavicino to Burghley, dated 2 Apr. 1586 (*Cal. Foreign*, 1585–6, p. 516), makes it clear enough that he deeply distrusted Leicester and his partisans.

levied, the German Protestants being indisposed to fight the battles of the faith except for value received. 'The wine is so weak this year,' Walsingham observed to Leicester laconically, 'as it doth not revive their spirits.'[1]

In February 1586 an occasion was offered to advance some money to Navarre's advantage in France. The suggestion apparently came from Stafford, the English ambassador in Paris. He discovered that Count Soissons and the Duke of Montpensier, two prominent supporters of the league, were prepared to change sides for a consideration. Stafford wrote to Burghley on the 10th of February that he believed £7,000 or £8,000, possibly even £6,000, would do the trick.[2] Walsingham clearly favoured the plan and did his best to induce the Queen to adventure the money, but without success. 'There hath been certain offers made unto her Majesty,' he wrote to Leicester on the 20th of March, 'and by her rejected, and yet of no great charge, that carried great probability to have withstood both God's and her enemies. I pray God the lack of feeling and compassion of others' miseries do not draw upon us His heavy hand.'[3] In April the Queen seemed to be somewhat more kindly disposed towards the plan and Stafford made bold to pay over 6,400 crowns, borrowed with difficulty on his private credit, to Soissons to keep him in train.[4] Elizabeth, however, did not approve of this course and the project seems to have been dropped for a time at least.[5]

[1] 23 May 1586, Bruce, *Leicester Correspondence*, p. 279.

[2] S. P. France, xv, f. 45.

[3] Bruce, *op. cit.*, pp. 179-80. There can be little doubt that Stafford's offer is the one referred to. Stafford wrote to Burghley, 20 Mar. 1585-6, that Walsingham had written to him of the flat refusal of the Soissons offer (*Cal. Foreign*, 1585-6, p. 462).

[4] Stafford to Walsingham, 16 Apr. 1586 (*Cal. Foreign*, 1585-6, p. 554). Stafford says he raised the money by pawning his wife's jewels and his plate.

[5] Further developments of this plan appear as follows: 27 Apr. 1586, Walsingham wrote to Burghley that the Queen wished Stafford to make no further disbursements until 'the parties' had entered into action (S. P. Domestic, clxxxviii, no. 41). Stafford alluded to it occasionally in his correspondence during June and July, but indicated that it was making no headway (S. P. France, xvi, ff. 6, 23, 67). In a letter to Walsingham of 15 July (ibid. f. 67) he said he had told Soissons that he would pay him no money until Montpensier had committed himself, adding that he kept Soissons in a 'quartain ague' that the Queen had sent for the money back again. This would seem to argue that Elizabeth had sent money to France. Judging from Stafford's letter to Walsingham of 24 Apr. 1586 (*Cal. Foreign*, 1585-6, p. 575) money had been sent to Rouen, though Stafford urged that it be transferred to Paris so that he could use it at a moment's notice. It is not

As far as actual concrete results were concerned Walsingham's efforts in the King of Navarre's behalf during the whole of the year 1586 were practically fruitless. Before the summer was out he had begun to fear that Navarre would abandon his religion and his profitless friendship with England and make his peace with the House of Guise.[1]

The discovery of the Babington Plot in August and the trial of Mary Stuart for complicity in it in October contributed new factors to complicate Elizabeth's relations with France. It is quite clear that she was somewhat concerned about the French King's reaction to Mary's trial. Even before her final arraignment Edward Wotton had been dispatched to France with copies of the evidence which was to be adduced against her.[2] The first intimations that Elizabeth got of Henry III's attitude were on the whole encouraging.[3] But later, when Mary had been tried

clear how much money was sent or how much of what was sent was applied to the purposes for which it was intended. The Spanish ambassador at Paris wrote to Philip II, 2 Oct. 1587 (*Cal. Spanish*, 1587–1603, p. 149), that Elizabeth had sent over 100,000 crowns, of which 5,000 crowns at least had been paid to Soissons and 12,000 crowns remained in Stafford's hands which he had spent to meet his private debts. There seems good reason to believe that the Spanish ambassador was right in charging Stafford with the misappropriation of public funds (cf. 'The Fame of Sir E. Stafford', *American Historical Review*, xx, p. 308). On 1 Aug. 1587 Stafford wrote to Walsingham that he did not believe anything could be accomplished by further expenditure (S. P. France, xvii, f. 219), and Walsingham learned independently that Montpensier had accepted a lieutenancy from the French king. In commenting upon this fact to Leicester, Walsingham wrote that he had always considered Montpensier a weak foundation to build on. 'I hope', he added, 'God will bless this action best when they of the religion shall be divided from the Papists and thereby forced to depend upon God. It is hard for such as are divided in religion to concur profitably in any action' (14 Aug. 1587, Cotton MSS., Galba D i, f. 248).

[1] Cf. Burghley to Leicester, 21 July 1586, Bruce, *op. cit.*, pp. 360–1.

[2] Wotton's instructions, dated 29 Sept. 1586, are in S. P. France, xvi, f. 108. Cf. also *Cal. Domestic*, Adda., 1580–1625, p. 188. An account of Wotton's audience with the French king is given in *Cal. Venetian*, 1581–91, p. 219. Stafford wrote to Walsingham from Paris, 19 Sept. 1586, that it was reported in France that Walsingham was to be sent over 'to tell the king the truth about the Queen of Scots' (Harl. MSS. 1582, f. 74).

[3] Stafford wrote, 19 Sept. 1586, that the French king had intended to send an envoy to England in Mary's behalf, but seemed disposed to abandon the plan (Harl. MSS. 1582, f. 74). Early in October, Châteauneuf, the French ambassador at London, came to Court to congratulate Elizabeth on her escape from the Babington conspiracy. He spoke in Mary's behalf, but 'humbly, diffidently, and without touch of menace' (Froude, xii. 294). Châteauneuf complained to one of his correspondents in France that Henry III showed too little concern for Mary's fate (Teulet, *op. cit.* iv. 113). Stafford reported that Châteauneuf was doing his best to arouse Henry's zeal (Harl. MSS. 1582, f. 71).

and found guilty, Henry III protested vigorously, and even sent a special envoy to England to intercede in her behalf.[1] When her sentence of death was proclaimed he wrote to say that he would regard its execution as a personal affront to himself.

It will be recalled that while Mary's fate still hung in the balance, the so-called Stafford plot, which seemed to implicate Châteauneuf, the French ambassador, in a plan to assassinate Elizabeth, was brought to light. This matter has already been discussed at length in another connexion. It is only necessary to recall here that Walsingham later declared the whole affair to have been simply a device on Stafford's part to extort money. Whether by design or not, it served very aptly to the purpose of cutting off Châteauneuf's communication with France during the interval between the signing of Mary's death warrant and her execution. After she was safely disposed of, the plot was dismissed from notice as quickly as it decently might be.

On the 13th of February 1587 Walsingham wrote to Burghley

So apparently was the Spanish ambassador at Paris (*Cal. Spanish*, 1580–6, p. 647). All the evidence at hand goes to show that Henry III was not strongly disposed to intervene forcibly in Mary's behalf.

[1] Bellièvre was the man sent for the purpose. The account of his embassy in England can be followed in Teulet, iv, pp. 115 ff. The Spanish ambassador in Paris believed that Bellièvre had been sent over chiefly to induce Elizabeth to persuade Navarre to make peace and to join in an offensive and defensive alliance with France (*Cal. Spanish*, 1580–6, pp. 660, 667, 689). There is no evidence of this, however, in Bellièvre's dispatches. There is almost nothing on record to indicate the part which Walsingham played in these negotiations. He certainly conferred with Bellièvre more than once (cf. Burghley to Walsingham, 1 Dec. 1586, S. P. Domestic, cxcv, no. 41; Froude, xii. 321, and Teulet, iv. 143). During the latter part of Bellièvre's stay he was absent from Court. Sir Edward Stafford, English ambassador to France, in a letter to Burghley of 10 Jan. 1586–7, throws some interesting light upon Bellièvre's mission. 'The same', he wrote, 'that *your Lordship* writ to *me* in your last letters but one of that that hath been given out of me that I should *favour* the *Queen of Scots* (cf. Burghley to Stafford, 2 Oct. 1586, in Murdin, *op. cit.* 569–70), *Bellièvre told me* the very same tale that Frenchmen in England told it him, and of *your Lordship* too of the Queen of Scots, and that *Leicester* and *Walsingham* were the eggers and givers of it out that *hated* and loved not *your Lordship*, and told *me* also *all the jar between my mother* and *Leicester* and upon what words . . . *Bellièvre* came away with a very good opinion of *your Lordship* and said that if *your Lordship* put not his hand to it there is no good to be hoped for between *England* and *France*, but that he was afraid you were fed with hope of *amity with Spain* but that he knew *your Lordship* so wise that *your Lordship* would easily find that could not be; that he knew nobody of the *Council of England* unpassionate saving only *her Majesty* but *your Lordship*' (S. P. France, xvii, f. 5, passages in italics in cipher). In view of the fact that Stafford was bitterly hostile to Walsingham at this juncture and was eager to curry favour with Burghley his testimony must be received with caution.

recommending that Châteauneuf be received by degrees into favour. 'I know', he added, 'he doth repent his ill manner of proceeding and would be glad to yield any reasonable satisfaction. There hath been some overture made unto me to be an instrument to work his reconciliation. I write not this in regard of the ambassador, but the necessity of the time requireth that her Majesty should hold good friendship with the King.' [1] A little later he joined with Burghley and Leicester in urging Elizabeth to receive Châteauneuf privately. Every letter from France made the necessity for conciliating that country more apparent. The English ambassador at Paris was denied audience. English ships which had been arrested at Rouen the previous autumn as an act of reprisal against the incessant plundering of French traders by English pirates, were not yet released nor seemed likely to be.[2] There were even rumours to the effect that the King of France had actually declared war. Nevertheless Elizabeth rejected the advice of her wisest councillors. She would not receive Châteauneuf. The most she would consent to was that Walsingham should talk with the French ambassador privately and do what he could to smooth things over. On the 15th of March Walsingham with some difficulty induced Châteauneuf to confer with him on neutral ground in a private house by the riverside in London. In the discourse which passed between them it is clear that Walsingham was doing his best to minimize the matters at issue. He exonerated his mistress from responsibility for the death of Mary Stuart, laying the blame upon Davison's shoulders. He apologized for the hard measure which Châteauneuf had received because of his supposed complicity in the Stafford plot. The Queen and the Council were sure of his innocence. She would grant Châteauneuf audience if he would but ask for it. She meant to redress speedily all grievances which the French merchants had against the English. In return she hoped that her merchant ships would be released in France and her ambassador received at the French court. It was no

[1] S. P. Domestic, cxcviii, no. 41.

[2] Walsingham wrote to Wilkes in Holland, 23 Feb. 1586–7: 'The cause of the arrest of our English merchants' goods groweth through the particular suits of private men by reason of great spoils committed on them at the seas by our nation, which in very truth hath been very disorderly and great. We are now in hand to take order for reformation of the same.' S. P. Holland, xiii, no. 62. On this subject, cf. also *Acts of Privy Council*, xiv, pp. 247–8, 252–3, 256, 262, 286; xv, p. 63; *Cal. Spanish*, 1586–1603, p. 18.

time, Walsingham said, for France and England to quarrel. It behoved them rather to combine together to resist the greatness of Spain. And much more to the same effect, with some hint that if France persisted in her unfriendly attitude Elizabeth might come to terms with Spain.

Châteauneuf received these advances without much cordiality. He refused to discuss the question of Mary Stuart, saying that he had no warrant. He was glad that the Queen believed him innocent of conspiring against her life. The English, he protested, were entirely responsible for the interruption of traffic with France. Let them look to it. He rejoiced at the Queen's kindly disposition towards his master, but since he was aware that she was sending money to Germany to assist the King's enemies, he was disposed to question her sincerity. He inquired whether she had instructed Walsingham to bid him request an audience, and when Walsingham was obliged to confess that she had not, Châteauneuf replied that he would not ask for it until he received specific directions from his master.[1] On the whole the interview accomplished very little. Its very fruitlessness probably encouraged the Queen to persist in her perverse course. She still insisted that the best way to keep France in train was by threatening to come to terms with Spain. Walsingham himself condemned this plan as dangerous in the extreme.

'Divers others of best judgement about her', he wrote to Stafford in France on the 22nd of March, 'are of opinion that it will rather do hurt than good, foreseeing that in the state that things do now stand, those of the league may take the advantage thereof to persuade the King to prevent her Majesty by combining first with Spain against her, which happening so, she would then be wholly abandoned and left to herself.'[2] For all that Elizabeth persisted. She even went so far as to write a sharp letter to the King of France. 'Your Lordship may see', Walsingham observed in a letter to Leicester, 'that our courage doth greatly increase for that we make no difficulty to fall out with all the world.'[3]

The fact of the matter appears to be that Elizabeth at this juncture was hoping for great things of Crofts' informal negotia-

[1] For Châteauneuf's account of this interview, cf. Teulet, *op. cit.*, iv. 181–8.
[2] S. P. France, xvii, f. 81.
[3] 8 Apr. 1587, Cotton MSS., Galba C xi, f. 294.

tions for peace with the Prince of Parma and her expectation of coming to terms with Spain made her somewhat careless of her relations with France. 'The hope of peace with Spain', Walsingham wrote to Leicester early in April, 'hath put her in a most dangerous security.'[1] Walsingham for his part during the spring of 1587 worked hard to re-establish a good understanding with the French King. He laboured on the one hand to secure the co-operation of the reluctant Châteauneuf, and on the other to overcome the obduracy of his mistress. And it was largely due to his efforts that the principal matters in dispute between England and France were amicably disposed of. In April the commercial difficulties were adjusted and the goods and shipping detained on both sides the channel released.[2] Early in May Elizabeth received Châteauneuf at Court, when she dismissed the Stafford plot with a jest, promised to give the French King full satisfaction for the death of Mary Stuart, and expressed her hearty desire for a perfect understanding with France.[3] And so, apparently, the danger which threatened England from that quarter was banished.

Walsingham's efforts to cultivate the goodwill of the French King at this time would seem to be quite inconsistent with the opinion which he had expressed again and again, during the previous year, that the friendship of Henry of Valois was too uncertain a commodity to be worth bartering for. The fact of the matter was of course that he placed no more dependence upon Henry than he had in the past. All that he wanted to do was to prevent an open breach with France at a time when England was already at war with Spain and on doubtful terms with Scotland. He still insisted that Elizabeth's best assurance of France was in the Huguenots, and that her wisest policy was

[1] 8 April, 1587, Cotton MSS., Galba C xi, f. 294.

[2] *Acts of Privy Council*, xv, pp. 63, 77; but the matter had not yet been completely settled late in May, cf. Walsingham to Stafford, 24 May 1587, S. P. France, xvii, f. 162.

[3] Cf. Châteauneuf to the King, 13 May 1587, Teulet, iv, pp. 194-202. Unfortunately this is almost the last letter of Châteauneuf's that Teulet has printed. His correspondence after this date has apparently not been preserved, with the exception of a few scattered letters in French archives, copies of which will be found among the French transcripts in the P. R. O. The list of French dispatches, as given in the *Report of the Deputy Keeper of the Public Records*, xxxix, appendix, pp. 573, 826, does not include quite all the dispatches of which copies are preserved in the P. R. O.

to lend vigorous support to Henry of Navarre. He was prepared to maintain that such a course was not inconsistent with a policy of friendship towards the French crown. When the French ambassador complained to him that his mistress was sending money to Germany for the King of Navarre he admitted the fact quite frankly but insisted that Navarre had no intention of waging war upon the French King. Navarre's purposes, he protested, were of the best and altogether directed to the welfare of his sovereign and his country. His preparations in Germany were merely designed to curb the presumption of the King's enemies, the Leaguers. For that reason the Queen considered that in helping him she did her brother of France a service.[1] Naturally Châteauneuf did not accept this interpretation of the situation, but there was just enough ambiguity in the attitude of his master towards the two contending factions in France to give to Walsingham's position some show of justification.

In January of 1587 Horatio Palavicino had finally paid over to Casimir in Germany 100,000 crowns which had so long been promised and so long deferred. But the sum proved to be quite inadequate to the purpose. In February Navarre's agents in Germany were crying out for yet another 100,000 crowns.[2] And in March, John Casimir sent Michel de la Huguerye to England to beg for it in person.[3] La Huguerye arrived in London apparently early in April. In private consultation he told Walsingham that the German princes who had promised to contribute to the support of Casimir's army had failed him and that without further assistance from the Queen the army could not march. Walsingham was able to offer very little encouragement. In writing of La Huguerye to Leicester on the 10th of April he said, 'His errand to her Majesty is so unpleasant as no man here dare present him. I never saw her worse affected to the poor King of Navarre than at this present, and yet doth she

[1] Teulet, iv, p. 187. [2] *Cal. Salisbury MSS.* iii, pp. 219–20.

[3] *Mémoires de la Huguerye*, ii. 393. Unfortunately La Huguerye omitted any account of this embassy in his memoirs. He declared his intention of writing a separate book on the subject dedicated to James I, but the book, if it was ever written, has not been preserved. A few of his letters written in London and addressed to Walsingham are preserved in S. P. German States, 1587–9. He left England about 10 May, as appears from a letter of Burghley to Casimir of that date (S. P. German States, 1587–9) of which La Huguerye was the bearer.

seek in no sort to yield contentment to the French King. If to offend all the world be a good course of government then can we not do amiss.'[1] Again, the next day, Walsingham wrote, 'Unless it shall please God to dispose her Highness' heart otherwise (upon some necessary accident that may happen), so far off is she from any inclination to yield any further supply as she seemeth altogether bent to have the said preparations stayed.'[2]

La Huguerye returned to Germany in May. It seems probable that he did not get the assistance he came for.[3] Nevertheless Casimir went on to muster his forces and by midsummer they were on the march for France. Throughout the summer and autumn Buzanval, Navarre's agent in England, continued to press Elizabeth for money,[4] and Walsingham no doubt seconded his efforts, but probably without success. Meantime Casimir's army had entered France. Early in September Walsingham heard that the Germans were on the verge of mutiny for lack of pay. He was at Barn Elms at the time, laid by the heels by his old malady.

Naturally Navarre's agents invoked his aid in securing further assistance from the Queen, but he was loath to undertake the matter. On the 7th of September he wrote to Burghley. 'Touching the other point, for advice what is to be done for contentment of the reiters, I have let Mr. Wooley understand that my former advices, given in points of like nature, have been subject to so hard censure as I dare not give advice. And yet in general terms I have protested that in case the said army of reiters should quail I do not see how her Majesty can long stand, wherein I have wished that in case her Majesty shall resolve to contribute anything, that neither time might be lost or charges weighed.'[5] Five days later Walsingham urged the matter upon Burghley again. 'There would be some expedition used in taking order for the sending of some present supply unto the King of Navarre. Mr. Horatio [Palavicino] will attend on your Lordship this afternoon to be ready to be employed in case

[1] Cotton MSS., Galba C xi, f. 292. [2] Ibid., f. 317.

[3] Walsingham wrote to Leicester, 14 Aug. 1587, that he greatly feared that Casimir, 'upon the return of Huguerye is so altered upon the cold comfort received from hence as he meaneth not to take upon him the charge of the army.' Ibid., Galba D i, f. 248; cf. also *Mémoires de la Huguerye*, ii. 405.

[4] *Lettres de Henri IV*, ii. 301, 305; viii. 319. *Mémoires de la Huguerye*, ii. 405. [5] Harl. MSS. 6994, f. 90.

her Majesty shall like to use his service. If the Duke of Montpensier shall find her Majesty resolved to back the King of Navarre there is no doubt but that he may be drawn to make himself a party. There is no way so apt to stop the Spanish preparation against this realm as the upholding of the King of Navarre and the keeping under of the house of Guise, whom Spain seeketh to advance. If her Majesty shall lose the opportunity either by long delay in resolving or by not sending such a portion of treasure as may do good, she shall have cause, I fear, to say farewell my days of peace.' [1]

But Elizabeth could not make up her mind. 'For relief of the army of France,' Burghley wrote to Walsingham the next day, 'Mr. Palavicino will report to you how we have gone in and out, but no final conclusion.' [2] One day the Queen ordered Burghley to dispatch Palavicino to France with funds, the next day she revoked the order. 'Sorry I am to find', Walsingham wrote to Burghley on the 18th of September, 'by your Lordship's letter received this evening that her Majesty hath given order unto you for the stay of the delivery of the money unto Mr. Horatio. The whole course of her Majesty's proceedings showeth that she hath no power to do things in season as may work her security and therefore we must prepare ourselves for the cross. Our sins do deserve it, especially our unthankfulness for the great and singular benefits it hath pleased God to bless this land withal.' [3] It seems from a letter which Walsingham wrote to Leicester three days later that Elizabeth did finally decide to send money to France. 'Her Majesty', he wrote, 'hath resolved to yield him [Navarre] support, but the matter is carried with such a vain secrecy as I fear he will be overthrown (through some disorder that will fall out in his army for lack of pay) before he shall be made acquainted with her Majesty's meaning.' [4] As a matter of fact the money was not sent.

It is not surprising that the Queen was loath to lend more

[1] Harl. MSS. 6994, f. 96.

[2] 13 Sept. 1587, S. P. Domestic, cciii, no. 42; cf. also Burghley's letters to Walsingham of 12 and 18 September (ibid. 41, 47).

[3] Harl. MSS. 6994, f. 98.

[4] 21 Sept. 1587, Cotton MSS., Galba D ii, f. 86. Burghley's letters to Walsingham cited in n. 2 above make out that dispatches from Stafford in France were instrumental in deterring Elizabeth from sending the money promptly.

money for Casimir's army. Even if she had been more zealous for the cause than she was she could hardly have hoped for much success from such an array. It was strong enough in point of numbers, but it was badly led and badly organized. After plundering Lorraine it had entered France in September intent to join forces with the King of Navarre south of the Loire.[1] But its march was encumbered by the burden of its spoils and its discipline fatally weakened by the dissensions and incapacity of its commanders. After a month in France it had done nothing but ravage vineyards and arouse the hostility of the peasantry. When the news of Navarre's victory at Coutras on the 20th of October reached it, it was already beginning to fall to pieces, and the stimulating effect of that achievement was not sufficient to save it from its own vices. Even such an insignificant affair as the Guises' night attack at Vimory on the 26th of October served to hasten its dissolution. A month later, surprised a second time at Anneau and despoiled of a good part of its booty, it began its disorderly retreat. The royal army which pursued might have accomplished its total destruction had the King willed it. But Henry III preferred to allow the Germans to withdraw in peace and so they escaped the thrashing they thoroughly deserved and finally got home again. So far as their services to Navarre was concerned, it may perhaps be affirmed that they divided the forces of his enemies, but they by no means justified the time and money spent in securing their assistance. Elizabeth's 100,000 crowns was little better than thrown away.

Even before the disastrous failure of this enterprise was made manifest Henry of Navarre was already planning to levy a second army in Germany. In August 1587 he dispatched envoys both to England and to Germany to raise money for this purpose. The envoy to England, d'Averly, was joined in London by Dr. Junius, an agent of the Duke Casimir, and both together they appealed to the Queen. She did not give them a downright refusal. She even went so far as to intimate that she might advance 40,000 florins to support a second German army, but she declared flatly that she would not send a penny until the army was levied and had crossed the Rhine.[2] Walsingham's opinion of

[1] Anquez, *Henri IV et l'Allemagne*, pp. 18-21.
[2] Ibid., p. 23. On the promise of 40,000 florins for a second levy, cf.

this course of proceeding appears from a letter to Leicester of the 12th of November. 'Monsieur Junius, sent from the Duke Casimir, is now returned with some weak satisfaction such as I fear will breed no great contentment, for we cannot skill here neither of timely nor thorough dealing. The manner of our cold and careless proceeding here in this time of peril and danger maketh me to take no comfort of my recovery of health, for that I see apparently, unless it shall please God in mercy and miraculously to preserve us, we cannot long stand.'[1] Evidently Walsingham was still in favour of lending Navarre vigorous support through the well-worn German channel. Elizabeth, however, had quite lost her taste for German reiters. They had a way of consuming her good money and achieving no results. She was rather disposed to revert once more to her preferred policy of mediation in France.

Already in September, before Casimir's army had entered France, she had instructed Stafford, her ambassador at Paris, to urge the French King to come to terms with Navarre, and had even offered to stay the Germans on the frontier in order to facilitate peace.[2] Henry III did not accept her offer at the time, but he was plainly in a mood for peace. One of his secretaries in conference with Stafford hinted at a league between England and France against Spain. Stafford broached the matter again by the Queen's commands in October and argued strongly in favour of an Anglo-French alliance. Once more the King seemed kindly disposed to both suggestions, but there is no evidence that any progress was made.[3]

Early in the following year the matter was taken up once more and this time the advances appear to have been made by the

Duplessis Mornay to Buzanval, 23 Jan. 1588 (S. P. France, xviii), and Casimir's instructions to his envoy, 19 May 1588 (S. P. German States, 1587–9). According to La Huguerye Elizabeth decided to advance money for a second levy and ordered its payment in Germany but afterwards stopped payment by letter (*Mémoires*, iii. 223). In February 1588, Henry of Navarre sent M. du Fay to England to solicit aid. Du Fay asked Elizabeth to deposit 100,000 crowns in Germany where it might be ready in case of need and where it might serve to encourage contributions from the German princes. He asked her also to send an envoy to Germany to assist him in his negotiations with the German princes. Elizabeth refused to do either. (Du Fay to Burghley, 1 April 1588, S. P. France, xviii.)

1 Cotton MSS., Galba D ii, f. 178.

2 *Cal. Spanish*, 1586–1603, pp. 139, 189.

3 Ibid., pp. 140, 149.

French. In January, Henry's ambassador in England hinted at his master's desire for peace, and one of the King's marshals approached Stafford on the same subject in France.[1] Late in February Henry himself called Stafford to secret conference.[2] At this meeting the King laid bare to the ambassador frankly the difficulties of his position. He confessed that he was tired of the domination of the Guises; he even admitted that he had hoped Casimir's army would have broken their power. But he acknowledged that he was not strong enough by himself to take up the cudgels with them. It was true that he might join forces with Navarre and the Huguenots, but he saw little hope of coming to terms with them except on the basis of toleration for their faith. That concession he dared not make, believing that it would simply have the effect of strengthening the hands of the Guises by rallying to their support the whole of Roman Catholic France. Against such an array King and Huguenots together could not hope to succeed. The only way out of the awkward corner, as the King saw it, was for Navarre to agree to a peace without demanding toleration. If he did this the Guises would lose their only excuse for fighting, the opposition to Navarre's rights of succession, which were based upon his persistence in heresy, would melt away, and the supremacy of the French crown would be restored. To the achievement of this end the King, through Stafford, invoked Elizabeth's assistance. She, if any one, could convince Navarre that his interest lay in abandoning his demand for toleration. He besought her to do so. The inducement he held out was that as soon as peace was restored in France he would join forces with England against their common enemy Spain.

This was in many respects an attractive offer. Nothing could have suited Elizabeth's purposes better at this juncture than an offensive and defensive alliance with a united France against Spain. It would have strengthened her position mightily either for war making or peace making with Philip II. The one great obstacle in the way, however, was the question of religion.

[1] *Cal. Spanish*, 1586–1603, p. 198.

[2] Stafford's account of this interview is quoted in Froude, xii. 410–1, but with several inaccuracies. The original letter is in S. P. France, xviii, f. 47, and is printed in *Hardwicke Papers*, i. 251–69; cf. also Stafford to Burghley, 26 Feb. 1587–8, ibid. 264.

Stafford had told the French King that his mistress could never be induced to persuade Navarre to abandon his faith. Yet in his private letters to Burghley the English ambassador expressed the opinion that such an event was not impossible. He declared that Navarre was not a particularly zealous Protestant, that his insistence upon toleration proceeded chiefly from the fear that if he conceded the point he might be supplanted by Condé or Turenne in the leadership of the Huguenots, and that any decent excuse, a truce or an assembly of the Estates General or even the persuasion of the Queen of England, might induce him to change his religion. 'It is a thing most certain', Stafford wrote to Burghley in January, 'that religion is but a colour and worldly pride and ambition the bottom of their hearts. . . . I can assure you the King [of France] desires nothing more, if the colour of religion were taken away, than to have means of advancing them [of Navarre's party] somewhat, to pull down the League thoroughly. It were well her Majesty should bear a hand in this lest peace come without her means and she be left thankless.' [1]

Stafford was evidently trying to convey the impression that Navarre was likely to concede the point of religion anyway and that it would be well under the circumstances for Elizabeth to set about mediating a peace upon the terms which the French King proposed. His estimate of Navarre's religious zeal is interesting and possibly not altogether inaccurate. Yet Stafford's sincerity in advocating peace is clearly open to question. There can be little doubt that he was a pensioner of the King of Spain at the time and was being secretly prompted by the Spanish ambassador at Paris to prevent an alliance between France and England.[2] It may even be that he was intentionally misrepresenting the facts in order to wreck the negotiations. If so he concealed his purpose with sufficient skill to win for his peace project serious consideration.

Unfortunately there is no record of the discussions in the English Privy Council upon the French question at this time. It may be presumed that Elizabeth, whose inclination towards peace and whose indifference to religious considerations were notorious,

[1] 8 Jan. 1587–8, S. P. France, xviii, f. 5.

[2] *Cal. Spanish*, 1586–1603, p. 223; cf. on Stafford, 'The Fame of Sir Edward Stafford', in *American Hist. Review*, Jan. 1915.

inclined to favour the King's proposals There is some reason to believe that Burghley was of Stafford's way of thinking.[1] Walsingham certainly took the opposite view. To him religion, far from being a mere 'colour', was the fundamental matter at issue and the chief justification for English interference in French affairs. According to his reckoning such a treaty as Stafford proposed would have sacrificed the one point which, above all others, it was necessary for Elizabeth to maintain. It was not only Walsingham's zeal for Protestantism at large which determined his opinion in the matter. He was convinced that the only support which Elizabeth could depend upon in France was that of the Huguenots, bound to her interests by the bonds of a common religion, and he insisted that even if his mistress ignored the ultimate interests of the faith it would be safer for her to cling to them rather than to betray them in exchange for the promises of such a weak and treacherous person as Henry III. He consequently did all he could to dissuade her from following Stafford's advice,[2] and upon the essential point of religion he succeeded. In March she sent instructions to Stafford bidding him tell the King that she could not for many reasons urge Navarre to change his religion.[3]

Elizabeth, however, did not by any means abandon hope of inducing Henry III to make his peace with Navarre by some concessions to the Huguenots and of forming with them both a triple alliance against the Guises and the King of Spain. That was the policy which she pursued steadily in France during the spring of 1588. She met Henry's objections to the granting of toleration by pointing out that since Navarre's strength lay in his Protestant following, his apostasy would strip him bare and make his alliance of small value to the common cause. On the other hand, if some measure of toleration were granted, she promised not only that the King should have the support of the Huguenots, but her own support as well, and so far as her credit would stretch, further assistance out of Germany.[4]

[1] Cf. *English Historical Review*, Jan. 1913, p. 54; cf. also Stafford to Burghley, 26 Feb. 1587–8, in *Hardwicke Papers*, i. 264.

[2] *English Historical Review*, Jan. 1913, p. 53, n. 78.

[3] Her letter to Stafford is missing, but he revealed some part of its contents to the Spanish ambassador (*Cal. Spanish*, 1586–1603, p. 257).

[4] Cf. Stafford to Elizabeth, 30 March 1588, in *Cal. Salisbury MSS.* iii. 314–17. The numbers undeciphered in this letter (77, 74, 30) stand for

Stafford proposed this arrangement to Henry III late in March and found him well disposed towards it, but fearful of the consequences and still insistent upon the danger attending any concession in religion. So little progress was made. Late in April, when the news reached England that the Duke of Guise's cousin, the Duke d'Aumale, was laying siege to Boulogne, the capture of which would bring Elizabeth's most determined enemies to her very threshold, Walsingham bade Stafford to urge the King once more to accept English aid.[1] In May, when the news reached England that Guise was in Paris and that the King, after his humiliation on the Day of Barricades, was a refugee from his own capital,[2] Elizabeth called the French ambassador to her presence and assured him that if the King would join with her and Navarre against the King of Spain and the League she would throw all her strength by land and sea into the struggle.[3] Not content with this she dispatched Sir Thomas Leighton, Governor of Guernsey, to France to urge the King to proclaim Guise a traitor, join with the Huguenots frankly and put down the League by force, and to promise that if he consented to follow this plan she would either send an army to help him from England or else raise troops for him in Germany or Switzerland.[4]

But by the time Leighton reached France, Henry III, prompted by his own fears and by his mother's arguments, had already opened negotiations with the Duke of Guise. He received the English envoy politely but declared that he had need of English assistance. Less than a month later, on the 2nd of July, he signed the Act of Union, by which he delivered himself wholly

Henry III, Catherine de Médicis, and the Duke of Guise, respectively (cf. cipher book in Public Record Office, Burghley–Stafford cipher). It is apparent from this letter that Elizabeth had suggested to Henry III the advisability of seizing the persons of the ' two brothers ', evidently the Dukes of Guise and of Mayenne.

[1] Walsingham to Stafford, 30 Apr. 1588, Harl. MSS. 1582, f. 88.

[2] Stafford's reports of the situation in France at this juncture are not preserved. The story of Guise's offer of protection to him and of his proud rejection of the offer which is related by De Thou and others (cf. *Mémoires de la Ligue*, ii. 350–1, De Thou, *Historia*, x. 264–6) appears to lack confirmation from English sources.

[3] *Cal. Spanish*, 1586–1603, p. 300.

[4] Leighton's instructions are preserved in S. P. France, xviii, f. 206. They do not include any definite offer of aid. Probably he was instructed on that point verbally; cf. Mendoza's account in *Cal. Spanish*, 1586–1603, p. 319. Mendoza got his facts from Stafford.

into the hands of the Leaguers, agreed to renounce his alliance with England and to prosecute the war against Navarre to the utter extermination of the Huguenots.[1] So it was that Elizabeth's policy, fostered by Stafford in France and Burghley in England, of joining forces with France against Spain failed utterly.[2] At the critical moment, when the Spanish Armada was already on the way to England, her neighbour across the Channel was delivered over into the hands of her determined enemies. Had Henry III been a man of firmer fibre the result might have been different and her proposals of alliance more successful. As it was, the event proved that Walsingham had gauged the King's character correctly and that his advice to the Queen to put no trust in the promises of the false and timorous Valois was sound in the main. The situation might have been better and could not have been worse had Elizabeth followed his counsel, yielded to the urgings of Navarre's various envoys, and thrown in her lot frankly with the Huguenots. As it was she had to face the prospect that when the Spanish fleet arrived in the Channel every port on the south from Brittany to the Low Countries would be at its disposal and the armies of Guise free to co-operate with the armies of Parma in an invasion of England.

[1] *Cal. Spanish*, 1586–1603, p. 312.

[2] It cannot be doubted that Stafford's treacherous betrayal of every step in the negotiations with Henry III to the Spanish ambassador had a good deal to do with their failure.

XV

THE COMING OF THE ARMADA

THROUGHOUT the whole of Walsingham's official career he regarded the danger of a Spanish descent upon England in force as the gravest danger which his mistress had to face. It was the strongest argument he could muster to induce the Queen to take active steps against Spain both in the Netherlands and on the high seas. For Elizabeth's favourite policy was a defensive, waiting one. She had little or no sympathy with Walsingham's desire to vindicate the cause of Protestantism. It was the conviction that her own fate and the fortunes of her own realm were inextricably mingled with the fate and fortunes of Dutch Calvinists and French Huguenots that induced her to intervene actively in their behalf. Her aggressive tactics of the year 1585, which found expression in Drake's West Indies voyage and Leicester's expedition to the Low Countries, were from her point of view defensive measures. She was aiming simply to prevent Philip of Spain from attacking her by striking at his fiscal resources in America and by strengthening his opponents in Holland.

It is not at all certain that the danger of invasion from Spain was nearly so great as Walsingham made it out to be. Philip II appears to have been always reluctant to attack England. He had already as many problems on his hands as he could very well handle and he anticipated that a direct attack on England might simply serve to draw England and France together in close alliance against him. For he realized that the French nation, even though the militant Roman Catholic party dominated the Government, could not afford to stand idly by and watch him add England to his domains. With the Turks constantly threatening his flank and the Dutch wars devouring his resources, he recoiled before an Anglo-French combination. If one can trust the dispatches of the Venetian ambassador at Madrid, who was a shrewd observer, Philip's enthusiasm for the cause of Roman Catholicism was not so great as to lead him to adventure against England unless he had been greatly provoked to the business by the English themselves. It is true that Spanish ambassadors in England almost from the beginning of Elizabeth's reign encouraged the English Catholics with large promises of assistance out of Spain. Active Spanish co-operation with English Catholics in revolt was an invariable feature in every plot against his mistress which Walsingham unravelled. But a distinction must clearly be drawn between what Philip said to encourage the English Catholics and what he really intended. At any rate it is pretty clear that the immediate cause of the dispatch of the Armada against England was the aggressive tactics of the English themselves. Leicester's expedition to the Low Countries and more particularly Drake's voyage to the West Indies in 1585 were the impulses which set the sluggish Spanish King in motion.

It is customary to date the beginnings of the Spanish preparations for the Armada from the letters which the Marquis of Santa Cruz wrote to his master in August 1583, just after his easy victory over Strozzi's fleet in the Azores.[1] Santa Cruz urged Philip that now that he was master of Portugal he should assemble his fleets for an attack upon England. Philip was apparently disposed to entertain the suggestion and even issued preliminary orders in accordance with it.[2] But presently his native caution got the better of his resolution, and the project, if it was not altogether dropped, was at any rate indefinitely postponed. The news of Drake's plunderings in the West Indies and of Leicester's disembarkment in the Low Countries quickened it to life again.[3] During the late autumn of 1585 the Venetian ambassador discovered that Philip was making his preparations to attack the English, and even thought of going to Portugal to stimulate them by his presence. In January of 1586 Santa Cruz took advantage of the opportunity to urge on his lagging master and met with a response which was more than usually encouraging.[4] It seems likely that by the end of the year 1585 Philip had definitely made up his mind to attack England directly by sea.

[1] Duro, *La Armada Invencible*, i. 241 ; Corbett, *Drake and the Tudor Navy*, ii. 6.

[2] Duro, *op. cit.* i. 243.

[3] *Cal. Venetian*, 1581–91, pp. 122, 124.

[4] Froude, *The Spanish Story of the Armada* (ed. 1901), p. 14.

His preparations were hardly under way before they were revealed to the English Government. This seems to have been due not to any particular efficiency of Walsingham's secret service but to the fact that no obvious effort was made in Spain to conceal them. It is indeed rather surprising to discover how very few traces there are of anything like a regular system of English espionage in Spain at this juncture. Some time after Walsingham's death it was stated that he employed regular correspondents at Bayonne, Lisbon, Cadiz, San Sebastian, and Madrid, on the Spanish peninsula as well as at Venice, Milan, Florence, and Rome in Italy, for the purpose of keeping himself well supplied with information from those quarters.[1] This may have been the case later, but there is very little indication of any such elaborate system of espionage at the beginning of 1586.[2] At that time Walsingham seems to have depended in the main for his information out of Spain upon the chance observations of such English merchants as still ventured there in spite of the Spanish embargo upon English shipping. To be sure his spies picked up and forwarded to him various rumours of a projected Spanish invasion which they gathered from hopeful English Catholics. Thomas Rogers, who was in France on other business in the autumn of 1585, sent information of this sort in August of that year.[3] But Walsingham must have realized by this time that such rumours were commonly current among the English Catholics and of no particular significance. As a matter of fact the first definite news of the Spanish preparations seems to have been brought from Lisbon by an English merchant who landed at Dartmouth on the 10th of December 1585. He reported that ships were being assembled in Spanish ports from all quarters, that soldiers were being levied in Italy, and that it was generally believed in Spain that these preparations were designed against England.[4] This report was dispatched to the English court at

[1] S. P. Domestic, ccxxxii, no. 12.

[2] There is a trace of such in *Spanish War Papers* (Navy Records Society), i. 58. In March 1586 Walsingham dispatched a certain Antony Pointz to Spain (Bruce, *op. cit.*, p. 208). Pointz posed to Walsingham as a spy upon Spain and to the Spaniards as a spy upon England (*Cal. Spanish*, 1580–6, pp. 570–1). It is not quite clear which he was, or whether, like others of his kind, he sold information to both sides. He does not appear to have done much good or much harm.

[3] *Cal. Domestic*, Adda., 1580–1625, p. 148.

[4] *Spanish War Papers*, i. 52–3.

once. A fortnight later Burghley wrote to Leicester: 'It is here found most necessary that her Majesty shall also make preparation of all the strength that she can make by sea, and for that purpose it is here resolved that her own ships shall be removed to Portsmouth in March next and a great number of her subjects' ships shall also be made ready to come either to Portsmouth or to Plymouth or to other places in the West parts, as by further intelligence of the King of Spain's preparations shall be requisite.'[1]

Walsingham and Leicester were apparently somewhat fearful that the presence of danger from Spain would induce Elizabeth to draw back from her aggressive policy but just launched in the Low Countries. They were accordingly both disposed to underestimate the strength of Spain. Both were easily confident of Elizabeth's ability to cope with it.

'No doubt', Leicester wrote to Burghley from The Hague on the 29th of January 1586, 'the King of Spain's preparation by sea be great for so it standeth him upon. But I know that all that he and his friends can make are not able to match with her Majesty's power by sea, if it please her to use the means that God hath given her. But besides her own, if she need, I will undertake to furnish her from hence, upon two months' warning, a navy for strong and tall ships with their furniture and mariners that the King of Spain and all that he can make shall not be able to encounter them. I think the bruit of his preparations is made the greater to terrify her Majesty and this country people. But thanks be to God her Majesty hath little cause to fear him. And in this country they esteem no more of his power by sea than I do of six fisher boats of Rye.'[2]

These were stout words and Walsingham re-echoed them in writing to Burghley on the same subject on the 15th of January. 'If', he wrote, 'her Majesty might be persuaded to set but a good countenance on the matter she should then have both peace and war in her hands.'[3]

[1] 26 Dec. 1585, Bruce, p. 42; cf. also Burghley's Notes on Public Business, dated 25 Dec. 1585, in *Spanish War Papers*, i. 55: 'For to impeach the provisions of Spain, there must be a consultation to make the Queen's navy ready to be at Portsmouth before the 20th of March. Orders to stay all warlike ships belonging to merchants and to have them ready.' An interesting estimate by John Hawkins of the cost of this naval mobilization at Portsmouth, submitted to Burghley, 28 Dec. 1585, is printed in *Spanish War Papers*, i. 269–80.

[2] S. P. Holland, vi, f. 140.

[3] Harl. MSS. 6993, f. 125.

In any event the Privy Council thought it wise to guard against eventualities, and accordingly decided to dispatch ten ships to the Spanish coast in February with instructions to prevent the mobilization of the Spanish Navy and to spy out the situation. Long before this was done, however, English mariners from Lisbon reported that there was little foundation for the rumours of great naval preparations there. This news was confirmed by other advertisements from Italy to the same effect. Walsingham pronounced the whole matter 'a Spanish bragge'.[1] Accordingly the Queen decided not to dispatch the ten ships, though she ordered the equipment of the fleet to proceed.

During the early months of the year 1586 every favouring wind brought a different story from Spain. Early in February an English merchant confirmed the earlier views of extensive preparations of Spanish shipping, and a little later in the same month similar reports came by way of the Lord Deputy in Ireland.[2] Yet in March Walsingham wrote to Leicester: 'The Spanish preparations, as they report that came from Lisbon the 10th of this present, will prove nothing this year and I hope less the next.'[3]

It may be that Walsingham, in spite of persistent rumours to the contrary, still believed that the danger of a Spanish attack by sea was not immediate. He certainly was convinced that it would be a grave mistake for Elizabeth to allow herself to be distracted by alarms of this sort from her aggressive policy in the Low Countries. Therein, he felt, lay the surest way of preventing Philip's hostile designs. 'I would to God', he wrote to Leicester late in March, 'her Majesty would put on a good countenance for only four months and I doubt not but Spain would seek peace greatly to her Majesty's honour and advantage. But God, for our sins' sake, will not suffer us to do that which might our most good.'[4] He did succeed, as has been pointed out in a previous chapter, in persuading his mistress not to abandon altogether her policy in the Netherlands, but he had the hardest kind of work to secure enough money to keep Leicester's forces alive there. Elizabeth insisted that she must

[1] Harl. MSS. 6993, f. 125. Cf. also Burghley to Leicester, 12 Jan. 1585–6, Bruce, p. 53.

[2] *Spanish War Papers*, i. 61 ff.; *Cal. Irish*, 1586–8, pp. 25, 37.

[3] 24 March 1585–6, Bruce, p. 187.

[4] Bruce, p. 188.

conserve her resources for her own defence. Yet she did comparatively little in this direction.[1] There is nothing to show that she concentrated her naval forces at Portsmouth in March as she had planned to do, and though she charged her commanders along the sea coast and in the Channel Islands to watch the alarm beacons and to lay up stores of powder in the towns, she evidently intended that they should pay for this by a system of local assessments and without any draft upon her treasury.[2]

The Venetian ambassador in Spain remarked later in the year that if the Spaniards were to attack England by sea they must do so either early in May or early in August because of the north winds and the strong tides which prevailed in the late spring and early summer.[3] This statement was probably only very roughly true, but at any rate with the passing of April the news from Spain became much less ominous. Walsingham learned on the 3rd of May that King Philip had only 18 ships ready for the seas, and two weeks later, by dispatches from Biscay, that though the Spanish talked of a fleet of 800 ships for England there was very small trace of it in Spanish harbours.[4] Sometime in June a letter arrived from an Englishman in Seville, apparently a prisoner there. He declared that the Spaniards could not put a hundred ships to the seas without a year's preparation 'It is not here,' he added, 'God be thanked, as it is in England for these provisions, their great gallions are but huge carts and their gallies and galleases are not for our seas, neither have they a good gunner.'[5] Walsingham felt confident that there was little to be feared from Spain that summer. On the 6th of June he wrote to the Earl of Sussex, who was Governor at Portsmouth: 'Your Lordship hath done very considerately in taking so good order for the staying and preventing of any attempt that might happen in that country upon a sudden. Notwithstanding, I see at this

[1] W. R. Scott, *English, Scottish, and Irish Joint Stock Companies*, iii. 522–3, gives some interesting figures on expenditures by the Queen during the years 1583, 1584, 1585, 1586, and 1587. These show that her total expenditures in the Low Countries for the fiscal year March 1585–6 were £61,879 14*s*. 4*d*., for the following year £118,060 15*s*. 1*d*.; her expenditures for victualling the navy during these two years were £8,415 5*s*. 5*d*. and £19,419 19*s*. respectively.

[2] *Acts of Privy Council*, 1586–7, pp. 46–8, 65, 129. Considerable difficulty was experienced in collecting the assessment. Ibid. 114.

[3] *Cal. Venetian*, 1581–91, p. 224.

[4] *Spanish War Papers*, i. 74, 77.

[5] 19–29 May 1586, Harl. MSS. 295, f. 174.

present no great cause to fear any alteration, so long as France and Spain have no power in readiness at sea, yet in these cases it is better to fear too much than too little.' [1]

On this basis apparently and with no immediate expectation of a Spanish invasion the Privy Council in July decided to take certain precautionary measures. These are set forth in a 'Note of Resolutions taken upon the Public Memorial' corrected by Walsingham himself :

'A letter to be written by the Lieutenants [of the counties] to their deputies to cause the foot bands to be viewed, the shot in every band to be trained by the corporals ; to cause good standing watches to be kept in the towns in the night season ; to look to the keeping of the beacons ; to make privy search for seminaries in suspected houses ; to give order to the justices within their several limits to apprehend such as shall spread seditious rumours, to see the contents of the former letters for the furnishing of the markets with corn duly executed, and the justices of the peace to be furnished with petronells at the day limited.' [2]

These were the sort of preparations which betrayed no fear of a sudden attack. The increased activity in the persecution of recusants, and particularly in the hunting down of seminary priests, which characterize the closing months of the year is of the same order. Very likely the discovery of the Babington conspiracy in July, with the possible consequences which it might entail, had as much to do with these measures as the rumours of naval preparations in Spain. The same thing may be said of the 'Catalogue of such men in England as the papistical fugitives make account to be assured if any foreign power should come to invade the realm', a list of six noblemen, seven knights, ninety-two gentlemen, and five yeomen, drawn up late in July evidently by one of Walsingham's agents.[3]

Late in August, however, came a sudden report of the landing

[1] 6 June 1586, Cotton MSS., Vespasian F xii, f. 221. The Venetian ambassador at Madrid reported home in June 1586 that Philip was making preparations for a naval demonstration next year (*Cal. Venetian*, 1581–91, p. 174).

[2] S. P. Domestic, cxci, no. 10, dated 9 July 1586, and evidently a record of the action of the Privy Council on 'A Memorial of Public Matters to be resolved on' drawn up by Walsingham, 6 July 1586 (S. P. Domestic, cxci, no. 5). The letters to the Lord-Lieutenants of the counties were not dispatched until 2 Aug. 1586 (*Acts of Privy Council*, 1586–7, p. 199 ; *Cal. Domestic*, Adda., 1580–1625, p. 183).

[3] S. P. Domestic, cxci, no. 22.

of French forces in Sussex, which set the Privy Council to the task of taking immediate measures for defence. Hurried resolutions were passed at the Council meeting at Windsor on the 30th of August, and were, it appears, handed to Walsingham for immediate execution. His own copy of the resolutions survives and is interesting as throwing light upon the sort of thing which the Council thought most necessary to be done in an emergency. The allusion to the Queen of Scots hints at the fact that the Council regarded this French descent as an attempt to rescue her.

'To send one to Portsmouth to look well to that town.
To remove presently the Scottish Queen.
To write to the Earl of Derby [1] to look well to his charge and to sieze into his hands the chief of the recusants.
To look to the French ambassador.
To warn our friends in Scotland to look to themselves.
To send for the Lord Chancellor and the rest of the Council.[2]
To cause certain ships to be put in a readiness.
To send for the stay of Hawkins.
The sending of forces to the seaside.
The Lord Warden to write to the Deputy Lieutenant in Kent.
9,000 troops to be sent into Sussex.
15,500 troops to attend her Majesty's person.
To write to the Earl of Leicester to arm certain ships.
To send a President to Wales.
To raise 2,300 horse.
To send for Captain Carleill and other captains.
To send powder to the maritime counties.' [3]

This tale of a French invasion proved to be a false alarm. There is no evidence as to how the rumour started. The stir that it made discloses the nervous state of mind into which the revelations of the Babington conspirators had thrown the privy councillors. They were ready to snatch for their swords at the mere motion of their own shadows. A week later they had another scare. The Earl of Sussex, Governor of Portsmouth, wrote to Burghley on the 2nd of September that he had heard of the arrival of a Spanish fleet carrying 10,000 soldiers at Conquette in Brittany.[4] At once the Privy Council dispatched letters to Sussex warning him to be on his guard. To the Lord Deputy of

[1] Lord-Lieutenant of Lancashire, the stronghold of the English Catholics.
[2] Only six councillors were present when these resolutions were taken.
[3] S. P. Domestic, cxcii, no. 62 ; *Acts of Privy Council*, 1586–7, p. 212.
[4] Harl. MSS. 6994, f. 33.

Ireland they sent a similar warning. On the 19th of September they instructed Sussex further to levy pioneers for strengthening the fortifications of Portsmouth, and on the 2nd of October they directed letters to the counties of the Midlands instructing them to prepare a force amounting all told to nearly 20,000 men for the defence of the Queen's person. But it does not appear that the levies were actually made. At any rate, by the end of October the Council evidently felt that the acute stage of the danger had passed, and early in November they began somewhat to relax their vigilance.[1]

It is impossible to distinguish Walsingham's particular part in these measures of defence. Presumably most of the detailed work fell upon his shoulders. Very likely he was not very much in sympathy with purely defensive measures. He had always preferred aggressive tactics, and it seems probable that he exercised his influence at this juncture, as he had exercised it in the past, to induce the Queen to forestall a Spanish attack from the sea by striking a blow at the Spanish naval power. He was doubtless one of the chief promoters of Sir Francis Drake's expedition to the coast of Portugal in the following spring.[2]

[1] *Acts of Privy Council*, 1586–7, pp. 216, 219, 226, 240, 246.

[2] According to Corbett (*Drake and the Tudor Navy*, ii. 61), John Hawkins was sent forth with a fleet in the late summer of 1586 to cruise for the Spanish plate fleets. This statement is based upon Spanish reports. These reports are somewhat confusing, but the essential facts, as deduced from them, seem to be that Hawkins was sent forth to the seas in September with a fleet variously estimated at from twelve to twenty-six ships to watch naval preparations in Normandy. When he reported that these were not of a menacing character he was ordered by Elizabeth, at the instigation of Don Antonio, to make for the Azores for the purpose of intercepting, not the Spanish plate fleet, but the Portuguese spice fleet from the East Indies. According to one account, he learned that the spice fleet had reached Lisbon before he got to the Azores; according to another, he was prevented by storms from going there. At any rate, the Spanish reports agree that he accomplished nothing more than the capture of a few Brazilian traders and that his voyage was a total loss (*Cal. Spanish*, 1580–6, pp. 642, 643, 649, 661, 666). Corbett asserts that there is no mention of Hawkins's cruise in any English authority. He is mistaken. On 6 Aug. 1586 the Privy Council directed Hawkins to repair to the seas with four of her Majesty's ships and two pinnaces (*Acts of Privy Council*, 1586–7, p. 206), and later, 30 Aug., in consequence of a reported French landing in Sussex, Hawkins, 'being upon the seas', was ordered to ply up and down and to prevent the landing of the French (ibid., p. 212). It is not impossible that, as the Spanish reports suggest, this little squadron of Hawkins was subsequently reinforced by a group of merchant adventurers and dispatched to the Azores in the hope of plunder. But it may be that the Spanish agents, knowing that Hawkins was at sea, proceeded to make a mountain out of a mole-hill. There is no evidence that Walsingham

This expedition was long a-hatching. Immediately after Drake's return from the West Indies there was talk in England of sending him forth to the seas again.[1] The purpose of this voyage was variously reported. Spanish agents in London connected it with the ambitions of Don Antonio, the Portuguese pretender. They believed that Drake would sail under the Portuguese flag to assist Don Antonio to his throne, and they found confirmation of their belief in the constant conferences between Drake and the Pretender and in the latter's reiterated boasts that he would be ruler in his own country by Christmas time.[2] On the Continent there were rumours of a larger design. In Rome and in Madrid it was currently believed that Drake's projected expedition was to form part of an enterprise in which the Queen of England, the Sultan of Turkey, and the Portuguese pretender were to combine in a joint attack upon Spain.[3] But this, of course, was largely guess-work. Unfortunately neither Drake nor Walsingham nor any one else who was really acquainted with the plans of the English Government at this juncture has left any record of them. The probabilities are that the Queen herself had no well-defined plan, but was prepared to take advantage of any opportunity for damaging Spain which was not too expensive and not too dangerous. She still provided Don Antonio with a place of refuge at the English court and still with considerable reluctance doled out to him a meagre pension. But she does not seem to have regarded his hopes in Portugal sufficiently promising to be worth exploiting.

Her relations with Turkey at this time are interesting. In the late autumn of 1582 she had dispatched William Harborne to Constantinople to look after the interests of English trade in the Turkish Empire. Harborne's main business during the first three years of his residence at the Turkish court was to maintain the rights of English traders against the intrigues of their Venetian and French rivals. He seems, however, as early as the year 1584, to have turned his hand to general politics. By

had any personal connexion with this enterprise, even if we assume that it took place as the Spaniards reported. Cf. also Monson's *Naval Tracts* (Navy Records Society), i. 134–5.

[1] *Cal. Spanish*, 1580–6, p. 602.

[2] Ibid., pp. 602, 612, 632.

[3] *Cal. Venetian*, 1581–91, pp. 170, 183, 200. Don Antonio was said to be making approaches to the Sultan in his own behalf (ibid. 58, 61, 90, 129). Cf. also Pears, in *English Historical Review*, viii. 443 ff.

his own account the Sultan's councillors had sworn to him even then that if Elizabeth would attack Spain on the Atlantic, Turkey would at the same time attack on the Mediterranean. But there is no evidence that the English Government seriously contemplated any such arrangement with the Turk until the next year. In the spring of 1585 Harborne received verbal instructions from Walsingham to incite the Turk to attack Spain. Walsingham elaborated on these instructions in a letter which he dispatched to Harborne on the 8th of October 1585:

'As by *instructions given to Jacobo Manuci* for to impart to you about VI months since, I did advise you *of a course to be taken* there for procuring the *Grand Seigneur*, if it were possible, to convert some part of his *forces bent*, as it should seem by your advertisements, from time to time wholly *against the Persians*, rather against *Spain*, thereby *to divert the dangerous attempt and designs of* the said *King from* these parts of Christendom. So am I at this present, *her Majesty* being, upon the *success of the said King of Spain's affairs in the Low Countries*, now fully resolved to *oppose herself* against his proceedings *in defence of that distressed nation*, whereof it is not otherwise likely but *hot wars between him* and us, *wills me* again to require you effectually to use all your endeavour and industry in that behalf, the rather for that it is most evident that if *the said king* might be kept thoroughly occupied, either by *some incursion from the coast of Africa in itself* or by the *galleys of the Grand Seigneur* in his dominions of *Italy* or otherwise, as may be best considered of you in those parts, *with the order taken to annoy him* from this side of Europe, *his power* should be so *weakened and divided* as it would be no small advantage to *her Majesty* presently, *but to all Christendom* hereafter; the *limbs of the devil* being thus *set one against another*, by means thereof the true Church and doctrine of the gospel may, during their contention, have leisure to grow to such strength as shall be requisite for *suppression of them both.*

'And therefore, for the better effectuating hereof, you shall do well to *practise all apt m[ea]ns with the Vizier* and such others as bear credit in that country. Make them find a taste in this *course*, laying before them how much more the *greatness of Spain* is to be regarded and *doubted* at this season than that of *Persia*, who professeth the *same religion* that *themselves* and hath no such difference with *Persia* for *dominion* but may be easily compounded *with both their honours and safeties*, and shall never be of that power but that *the Grand Seigneur* shall be as able as he is presently always to *deal with him; whereas the King of*

Spain, under colour of subduing the rest of the *princes of Christendom which differ* from him *in faith*, and by other quarrels daily picked to *his neighbours*, as he hath this summer made a party against *the King of France of his own subjects* with his money even in his own realm and hath sought to do the like against *her Majesty*, whose dominion of *Ireland* not long since *he invaded*, is *rising to that greatness*, with the accession of some of their *realms and territories*, as cannot but give just cause of jealousy to that *empire* which he and his pretendeth to *invade*, having obtained their purpose in *these parts*. And you may *show* how that he is already *the greatest monarch of Christendom*, possessing the whole country of *Spain*, the *realm of Portugal with the riches* thereof being lately fallen into *his* hands, the richest provinces in *Italy and Germany*, *the whole Indias* both *east and west* whence he draweth infinite treasures, the sinews of war; that the Emperor is but *his vassal in effect*, depending upon *his* directions and executing his will where *he hath to do*; the Pope, *his creature*, applying all his ecclesiastical or spiritual jurisdiction and power over the consciences of men to the advancement of *the King of Spain's* greatness. The pretence of his favours is that it is necessary to *draw all Christendom under him* to the end by his means *the Sultan his empire may be broken*; that sundry *old prophesies* are caused to *fly about Europe*, signifying the time to be at hand when *it shall be brought to pass*. In the meanwhile there is a bruit lately given out by the favourers and subjects of the King of Spain in these parts that a most royal present should be sent to the said King from the Grand Seigneur with letters, the copies whereof are dispersed in all places and one of them herewith sent to you, wherein he is *made to fawn upon him* for his friendship as if *already he stood in fear* and were *forced to beg his* peace. Whereby you shall let *them* understand, that as *the King of Spain's credit* is greatly *increased in Europe*, so *the Sultan's* reputation, with the most part that believe it and *know him not, is much impaired*. All these points, *amplifying them to the uttermost*, you shall do well to *lay before them*. And for to *draw them* the rather *on*, let them understand that there could never be . . . *better occasion than at this time* that he is entered into a quarrel with *her Majesty*, who shall have means to give him *such annoyance on this side of Europe* that if *the Sultan* will embrace the opportunity of *assailing him on the other side*, there is no question but he shall *sink under the burden of so heavy a burden*, and so *the Sultan* not only gratify *a princess* able and ready to show him all friendly offices, but also work the *assurance of his own estate* with less charge and trouble than if he attend to be assailed by the *King of Spain*, come to the *full pitch of his might and strength*.

'If you shall see that *the Sultan* cannot be brought altogether *to give ear to this advice* you shall, after you have done your best to gain this first point, procure *at least that*, by making *show of arming to the sea* for *the King of Spain's dominions, hold the King of Spain in suspense*, by means whereof he shall be the less bold to *send forth his best forces* into these parts, which may serve to good purpose if you fail of the first.

'Herein *her Majesty* maketh great account of the service *you* shall be able to do *her by means of your* experience and acquaintance in that court *rather than by any other*, a stranger and raw therein to be sent from *hence*, which is the only cause that, whereas you *hav[e been] suitor* diverse times to *return, your time of continu[ing]* in these parts agreed upon being *expired, her Majesty* is loath as yet to yield to *your* desire in that behalf, thinking it necessary that you *stay one year longer* at least for *compassing a matter of* such importance, which I am sure you for your part, as well for satisfaction of her Majesty, to whom we owe every of us the services of our best powers, as also for the service of Christendom and your own credit, which by your dexterity in managing this matter shall be greatly augmented, will not refuse. And so praying God to bless your travails with good success I bid you heartily farewell. London this 8th of October, 1585.

Your assured loving friend,
FRA. WALSINGHAM.'

For the next three years Harborne left no stone unturned to accomplish this purpose, now exploiting commercial interests, now religious differences. He begged the Turk, if he would not put forth his whole power against Spain, to send forth sixty or eighty galleys to harry the Spanish possessions in Italy. He met with some encouragement at the Porte, but unfortunately the Sultan was so much interested in the prosecution of the war against Persia that he lacked either the will or the resources to participate in western enterprises. So Harborne in the end accomplished little or nothing to the purpose. It does not appear that Elizabeth ever entertained any large hopes that he would.

It is not unlikely that Walsingham regarded the possibility of effective co-operation both with Don Antonio and with the Turk a good deal more hopefully than did his mistress. He had always been disposed to befriend the Portuguese pretender and had done what he could to interest the Queen in his cause.

There is no direct evidence to prove that he was co-operating in any plan to dispatch Drake in Don Antonio's behalf at this juncture, but the probabilities are that if such a scheme was afoot the Secretary was behind it. It need not be supposed that he had any great confidence in Don Antonio's ability to make good his pretensions. More likely Walsingham saw in the Portuguese question simply another opportunity to embroil England in a war with Spain which was the end and aim of his policy at this time.

With regard to the Turkish alliance, there is once again no direct evidence of Walsingham's part in it. In a paper from his pen dated 1580 he urged the desirability upon commercial grounds of sending an English agent to Constantinople.[1] From this it may perhaps be argued that he was responsible for Harborne's dispatch. Probably he saw no objection on religious grounds to an alliance which was hideous in the eyes of the Roman Catholic Powers. He would hardly have agreed with that Turkish Pasha who declared that the only thing wanting to make an English Protestant a good Mohammedan was a formal confession of faith.[2] Yet as between Murad of Turkey and Philip of Spain he probably regarded the latter as the greater idolater. That he favoured an alliance with the Turk is clear from the tenor of his correspondence both with Harborne and with his successor.[3] It would be going too far, however, in view

[1] S. P. Domestic, cxliv, no. 70; in a letter to Walsingham, dated 27 Jan. 1583/4 at Constantinople, Harborne tells Walsingham that it was by his means that he (Harborne) became one of the Queen's servants. (*Cal. Foreign*, 1583–4, p. 329.)

[2] Cited by Pears, *English Historical Review*, viii. 439.

[3] Most of Harborne's extant correspondence is in the P. R. O. among the Turkey papers. Unfortunately, however, his letters for the significant years 1586–7 are lacking there. There is none of his correspondence in the P. R. O. between the dates 7 Sept. 1585 and 9 Feb. 1588. His statement that the Turk had offered to co-operate with England against Spain in 1584 appears in his letter to the Sultan dated 9 Feb. 1587/8 in S. P. Turkey, i, f. 47. The letter from Walsingham of 8 Oct. 1585 is preserved in the Bodleian Library, Tanner MSS., lxxviii, f. 66. It is written largely in cipher, but the code is the same as that in the correspondence with Barton, his successor, the key to which is preserved in the P. R. O., Cipher Books, Eliz. i, f. 34. There is another letter from Walsingham to Harborne, written in June 1587, in the Tanner MSS., and there is an abstract of a letter from Harborne to Walsingham among the Harleian MSS. in the British Museum. These are printed in full in the Appendix to this Chapter.

The best account of Harborne's mission will be found in the *Cal. Venetian*, 1581–91, Introduction, pp. xxix–xlvi; cf. also von Hammer,

of the paucity of the evidence to ascribe to Walsingham the whole project of a Turkish alliance.

At all events, Walsingham certainly had no notion of postponing aggressive measures against Spain until the Porte was prepared to co-operate. He favoured the dispatch of Drake forthwith. Drake was certainly eager to go. According to Spanish reports, he was making ready his ships early in October. Yet it was not until the following spring that he got away. The reason for this long delay cannot be stated with certainty, but it should probably be assigned to the inveterate procrastination of the Queen, encouraged perhaps by Burghley and his partisans in the Privy Council. The Spanish ambassador in Paris was informed that the chief difficulty was lack of funds. According to his account, Elizabeth refused to bear the whole burden of financing the expedition and Drake found private investors less eager to co-operate because of their losses in his West Indies voyage.[1] This explains why Drake went over to the Low Countries in October to solicit the assistance of the Dutch. He found the Dutch Government indisposed to take part officially but perfectly willing to assist him in securing the co-operation of private Dutch investors.[2] Upon his return to England early in December he applied at once to the Privy Council for licence to equip his fleet. Official permission was refused him, but Walsingham told him to go ahead with his preparations nevertheless and promised to help him to his licence. According to Spanish reports, some of the other members of the Council were not so sure that the Queen's consent could be obtained.[3] This sounds like a reference to the reluctant Burghley whom the Spaniards thought was using his influence at this juncture on the side of peace.[4]

Leicester's return to England from the Low Countries early in December brought Drake another strong supporter, but both Walsingham and Leicester were too much engaged with the question of Mary Stuart during the early winter of 1586–7 to devote much time to anything else.[5] Yet it is clear that they did

Geschichte des osmanischen Reiches, iv. 157; *Hakluyt's Voyages* (ed. Maclehose), v, *passim*; and Pears's article already cited in *English Historical Review,* viii.

[1] *Cal. Spanish,* 1580–6, p. 650.

[2] Motley, *History of United Netherlands,* ii. 103, n. 3.

[3] *Cal. Spanish,* 1580–6, p. 672.

[4] Ibid. 674.

[5] Corbett (*Drake and the Tudor Navy,* ii. 65) asserts that it was decided on

not abandon their efforts. In January Don Antonio heard from Portugal that there was good promise of a rebellion there in his favour if he could bring a fleet to the coasts. Leicester and Walsingham, joined this time by Lord Admiral Howard, promptly seized upon the occasion to urge Elizabeth once more to dispatch Drake in Don Antonio's behalf. According to Sir Edward Stafford, the English ambassador in Paris, the Queen was induced to advance Don Antonio considerable sums of money together with several ships of her own and several from the Low Countries, and to solicit in his behalf further naval assistance from the French Huguenots.[1] But later, as was to be expected, Elizabeth seems to have wavered in her resolution. Up to the last moment there was apparently some doubt as to whether she would consent to Drake's departure or, even if she did, whether she would allow him any ships from the royal navy.[2] When the expedition finally did sail, half of its strength was made up of ships supplied by private investors in London.[3]

Exactly when Elizabeth finally consented to let Drake go is not clear, but it was probably early in March 1587.[4] He got away on the 2nd of April.[5] In a last letter to Walsingham, which

25 Dec. 1586 to mobilize the whole English fleet at Plymouth, citing as authority a document which indubitably belongs to the previous year. Cf. *Spanish War Papers* (Navy Records Society), p. 53.

[1] Stafford betrayed these plans to the Spanish ambassador in Paris, which betrayal marks perhaps the beginnings of his treachery. (*Cal. Spanish*, 1587–1603, p. 8; cf. 'The Fame of Sir Edward Stafford', in *American Historical Review*, Jan. 1915.)

[2] *Cal. Spanish*, 1587–1603, pp. 18, 47–8.

[3] Corbett (*Drake and the Tudor Navy*, ii. 66, n. 3) seems to think that these investors were members of the Merchant Adventurers Company. They are spoken of on one occasion as Merchant Adventurers (*Camden Miscellany*, v. 45), but the probabilities are that the term was not used in its specific sense. Mr. Corbett is well aware that any group of merchants combining in any maritime enterprise were customarily spoken of in the sixteenth century as Merchant Adventurers. The French Huguenots took no part in the expedition. The Dutch ships which came over to join with it were, according to the Spanish ambassador at Paris, detained to guard the English Channel (*Cal. Spanish*, 1587–1603, p. 88). Don Antonio did not join in the expedition, perhaps for the reasons given later by the Spanish ambassador at Paris (ibid., p. 99).

[4] At the last moment he was embarrassed by a wholesale desertion of his mariners. He wrote to Walsingham that every one believed the deserters had been prompted by letters from those opposed to the enterprise (*Spanish War Papers*, i. 103). It does not appear whom he had in mind. The Spanish ambassador in Paris declared that Sir Walter Raleigh 'is very cold about these naval preparations and is secretly trying to dissuade the Queen from them' (*Cal. Spanish*, 1587–1603, p. 24).

[5] The final preparations were kept very secret. Mendoza in Paris said later

he dispatched when his sails were already bending to the wind, he commended himself to the Secretary's goodwill. 'Let me beseech your honour to hold a good opinion not of myself only, but of all these servitors in this action, as we stand nothing doubtful of your honour. . . . The wind commands me away. Our ship is under sail. . . . Let me beseech your honour to pray unto God for us that He will direct us the right way, then we shall not doubt our enemies for they are the sons of men. Haste! From aboard her Majesty's good ship, the *Elizabeth Bonaventure*, . . . by him that will always be commanded by you and never leave to pray to God for you and all yours.' [1]

This was no lip service. Drake's devotion to the Secretary was as sincere as it was strong. It sprang from the conviction that Walsingham was not only his surest friend at court, but was also the greatest exponent among Elizabeth's statesmen of his own fighting gospel. It is hardly too much to say that taken together they stand forth as the great protagonists of militant English protestantism.

Up until the very last the object of Drake's enterprise was kept secret. Three weeks after his departure Walsingham briefly summarized them in a letter to Stafford, the English ambassador at Paris: 'Sir Francis Drake, as I doubt not but you have heard, is gone forth to the seas with four of her Majesty's ships and two pinnaces and between twenty and thirty merchant ships. His commission is to impeach the joining together of the King of Spain's fleet out of their several ports, to keep victuals from them, to follow them in case they should be come forward towards England or Ireland and to cut off as many of them as he could and impeach their landing, as also to set upon such as should either come out of the West or East Indies unto Spain or go out of Spain thither.' [2]

It was well for Drake that he got off in haste. He had scarcely

that he had done everything in his power to get precise news of Drake's departure, but that the English ports had been closed to prevent any intelligence of it from getting abroad, adding that Walsingham had even refrained from sending dispatches to Paris, lest the messenger might betray something (*Cal. Spanish*, 1587–1603, p. 97).

[1] *Spanish War Papers*, i. 103–4.

[2] 21 Apr. 1587, S. P. France, xvii, f. 126, printed in *Spanish War Papers*, i. 106–7. Stafford evidently showed this letter to the Spanish ambassador at Paris (*Cal. Spanish*, 1587–1603, p. 87).

left before the Queen decided to amend his instructions. She had heard from Spain that Philip had abandoned his naval preparations, and in consequence she sent a messenger post-haste to Plymouth to order Drake on no account to enter Spanish harbours or to make any land attack.[1] 'This resolution', Walsingham wrote to Leicester on the 11th of April, 'proceedeth altogether upon a hope of peace which I fear will draw a dangerous war upon her Majesty by the alienation of the hearts of the well-affected people in the Low Countries.'[2] But Drake was too quick for his procrastinating mistress. When her message reached Plymouth he was clear away, and the pinnace which was dispatched to overtake him encountered convenient gales which thwarted its purpose. Walsingham wrote to Leicester a few days later that he had heard rumours that the Queen meant to recall Drake altogether,[3] but this policy, if it was contemplated, was not followed, and Drake was left unhampered by further instructions to set about the singeing of King Philip's beard.

At the time of Drake's departure the season was at hand for the renewal of military operations in the Low Countries and the question as to what Elizabeth intended to do further for the Dutch rebels became increasingly pressing. Her connexion with their cause was at this juncture a curiously ambiguous one. Leicester, the Lieutenant-General of the forces in the Low Countries, was still their Governor-General, but he had returned to England the previous December, after delegating his civil power to the Council of State and his military command to Sir John Norris. The Dutch presumed that he would return; a large party of them even hoped that he would be instrumental in persuading his mistress to assume complete sovereignty over the United Provinces. For the time being, however, the connexion of Elizabeth with their cause was represented merely by a few thousand half-starved English troops under Sir John Norris and by Thomas Wilkes and Bartholomew Clark, the two English members of the Council of State.

When Leicester got back to England he was plunged at once into the business of disposing of Mary Stuart and for the time being all other matters had to attend upon that one. 'Touching

[1] *Spanish War Papers*, i. 100.
[2] Cotton MSS., Galba C xi, f. 317.
[3] Ibid., f. 300.

the Low Country causes,' he wrote to Wilkes on the 4th of December, 'very little is done yet, by reason of the continued business we have had about the Queen of Scots' matters. All the speeches I have had with her Majesty hitherto touching those causes have been but private.'[1] For the next two months little or nothing was done.

Leicester seems to have been more concerned about the ill treatment he had received at the hands of the Dutch in the past than about their future welfare. His hatred of Barneveldt, Buys, and the other leaders of the States General increased as he brooded over the fancied wrongs which they had done him. From his home in England he still continued to lend secret encouragement to the popular turmoils which his adherents in Utrecht, Friesland, and North Holland were inciting against their governors. As a matter of course, he denounced Barneveldt and his coadjutors in unmeasured terms to his mistress. Sir John Norris, commander of the English forces in the Netherlands during his absence, remained his *bête noire*. At the time of his departure he had done his best secretly to vitiate Norris's authority by appointing commanders to the important towns of Zutphen and Deventer independent of his control. It was hardly to be expected that Leicester would do much to further the interests of the English army overseas so long as Norris had charge of it. Finally, Leicester had begun to cultivate a violent hatred of Thomas Wilkes for the simple reason apparently that Wilkes was too honest to juggle accounts and too wise to endorse Leicester's hostile courses against the States General. So it appears that Leicester's 'private' speeches to the Queen about Low Country causes were largely confined to wholesale denunciation of the conduct of Barneveldt and his crowd and Norris and Wilkes. In all these matters Leicester seems to have won his royal mistress to his own point of view. But the remedies which he proposed were little to her taste.

During the previous summer he had more than once expressed the opinion that the wisest policy for her to pursue was to take the sovereignty of the Low Countries into her own hands and establish her power there by means of an adequate military force. He cast for himself the part of viceroy and was quite

[1] S. P. Holland, xi, f. 146, cited by Motley, ii. 190.

prepared, if he were given sufficient authority and adequate resources, to make short work of that many-headed monster the States General, to say nothing of Norris and Wilkes. But he found Elizabeth less than ever disposed to an aggressive policy. She had already begun to make her reckoning of the cost of her year's campaigning in the Netherlands, and she was astounded at the figures. Something like £140,000 had been spent and there was precious little to show for it. Nor did there seem to be any end to her outlay. Every letter from Wilkes and Norris brought with it reiterated demands for more money to pay her troops. To make matters worse, she began to discover that a large part of the money already spent had been wasted. Lord Burghley, in his capacity of Lord High Treasurer, had been going over Leicester's accounts and he reported to his mistress that they were 'obscure, confused, and without credit'.[1] This revelation naturally did not increase Leicester's love for Burghley, nor did it dispose the Queen more favourably to her favourite's ambitious projects. She stormed at him, she stormed at Burghley, and she turned a deaf ear to the requests of Norris and Wilkes. No doubt her attitude is to be explained in part by her inveterate parsimony. It is to be explained in part also by her hope of peace. Although Walsingham had succeeded in quashing the negotiations of Bodenham and Grafigna for peace with Parma the previous summer, the other negotiations through Burghley and de Loo persisted, and in the early winter of 1587 seemed to the Queen at any rate to give some promise of success. Added to all these factors was her alarm at the naval preparations in Spain and her fear that Mary Stuart's execution, which she had almost decided was inevitable, would bring down upon her head the wrath of all the Catholic Powers.

So far as can be gathered from the rather scant evidence on the subject, the Privy Council at large supported Leicester in his position that the Dutch cause must be vigorously followed. Burghley, at any rate, protested as much to Leicester and added bitterly that he had got well scolded for his pains.[2] Walsingham's attitude may be taken for granted. He regarded the Queen's hopes of peace, as he had always regarded them, as a mere

[1] Motley, ii. 192, n. 3; cf. Cotton MSS., Galba C xi, f. 227.
[2] For Burghley's attitude cf. Motley, ii. 193 n.

delusion.[1] His feelings towards Leicester at this juncture were probably not very cordial for reasons which have been pointed out already. It is pretty clear that he did not share Leicester's opinion of Wilkes and Norris. But he was convinced that the Dutch rebels must be effectively supported, and he was well aware that no one in England was so likely to succeed in winning the Queen's consent to such a policy as the royal favourite. Yet his attempts to influence his mistress in that direction met with dismal failure. In December 1586 everything seemed to be conspiring together against him. His friend and son-in-law, Sir Philip Sidney, had but just died; his one daughter was dangerously ill; his finances were seriously embarrassed, his old malady was troubling him; the Queen turned a cold shoulder to his private necessities and his public counsel. On the 16th of the month he wrote to Burghley that he had decided to leave the Court. 'Her Majesty's unkind dealing towards me', he wrote, 'hath so wounded me as I could take no comfort to stay there. And yet if I saw any hope that my continuance there might either breed any good to the church or furtherance to the service of her Majesty or of the realm, the regard of my particular should not cause me to withdraw myself. But seeing the declining state we are running into, and that men of best desert are least esteemed, I hold them happiest in this government that may be rather lookers on than actors.' [2]

For something like two months Walsingham played the spectator's part and during that period nothing at all seems to have been done by the Queen in behalf of the Dutch.[3] In February 1587 a delegation of five envoys arrived from the Low

[1] Walsingham to Wilkes, 23 Feb. 1586/7. 'Touching our treaty with Spain, there is small hope of profit to grow thereby, for that the fruits thereof being rightly considered, it is found rather to be a means to increase danger and hurt than a way to yield security or commodity to us' (S. P. Holland, xiii, no. 62). The French ambassador in London wrote to his master in March 1587: 'Le Sieur de V [Walsingham] m'a dist que le Roy Catholique traictoyt avec la Royne et que elle ne se vouloyt plus mesler des Pays-Bas; qui sont tous comptes à plaisir, estant le milord Boucours en Holland et cherchant, tant que il peult, de traicter avec le Prince [de Parme] sans que cependant la Royne laisse de bien fournir les villes que elle tient et contribuer aux frays de la guerre aultant que l'an passé, et Drac [est] en mer vers la coste de Hespaigne' (Teulet, *Relations politiques de la France et de l'Espagne avec l'Écosse*, iv. 188).

[2] S. P. Domestic, cxcv, no. 64.

[3] She apparently consented to the dispatch of £5,000 to her troops in the Netherlands in February 1587; cf. Privy Council to Norris, 21 Feb. 1586/7, S. P. Holland, xiii, no. 50.

Countries to solicit aid from her. The sum and substance of their request was that the Queen should increase her forces in the Low Countries to 10,000 foot and 2,000 horse and should lend them £60,000.[1] To this request Elizabeth's first reply was a strong speech of denunciation of the Dutch and all their ways. She berated them for their ingratitude to her, for their cruel treatment of her soldiers, for their misuse of Leicester, for their usurpations of power, for everything indeed that came to her mind in her passion. Of future aid and comfort she said little or nothing. Later the matter was discussed more temperately with the envoys by some members of the Queen's council, among whom were Burghley, Hatton, and Leicester himself.[2] Walsingham does not appear to have taken any part in the negotiations. Presumably he was still in retirement. After some days' debate the Dutch envoys seem to have gathered hope that something might be done for them after all, when suddenly dispatches arrived from the Low Countries which changed the whole complexion of affairs. These dispatches brought news that the two Dutch towns of Zutphen and Deventer, commanded by English captains appointed by Leicester himself, had been treacherously sold to the enemy. With this intelligence came a letter from Barneveldt to Leicester which contained in unvarnished terms a detailed condemnation of his conduct in office and which placed squarely upon his shoulders the responsibility for the surrender of the two towns.

This letter, a copy of which was sent to the Queen, put her in a fine rage. Once more she stormed at the Dutch envoys and once more denounced their masters for their shameless ingratitude towards Leicester. She swore that he should never set foot in the Netherlands again.[3] In spite of which tirade the discussion of the matter was not altogether abandoned. Walsingham throws some light upon the course of affairs at this juncture in a letter which he wrote to Wilkes on the 10th of February. After relating that the Queen had refused with angry words the Dutch request for men and money, Walsingham added:

'The Commissioners have earnestly solicited the return of the Earl [of Leicester] as a thing desired both by the States and the people, and therefore the advertisement sent, as you know, that

[1] Motley, ii. 197. [2] Ibid. 202. [3] Ibid. 206 ff.

he would not be welcome unto the States, appeareth not to be true, for that I have seen that both in their public and particular letters written hither they do earnestly desire the same. The Earl doth refuse to go unless the commissioners may be returned with better satisfaction. It is thought that her Majesty would have assented to have yielded a greater support, but that by some secret advertisement from thence she is advised to the contrary, being informed that the contribution already yielded will suffice, . . . and therefore, if through the means of those underhand counsellors, there fall out a revolt of those countries, the burden thereof must lie upon their shoulders.' [1]

In a private letter to Wilkes some days later Walsingham added illuminating details :

'*Leicester*', he wrote, 'beginneth now to calm towards you. Captain Williams hath done good offices between you. The dislike between him [Leicester] and *Sir John Norris* is irreconcilable, who shall find the *Queen* stand but weakly to him. For the worthiness of the gentleman I could wish he had taken another course. I will employ my best skill in removing the dislike between them. A man of his value would not be shaken off, our necessity and use of such men being so great and the number so few. His advice given to the *Queen* not to increase the contribution (though it were a pleasing counsel) is like to overthrow the cause and put her Majesty and state in peril. The deputies in respect of the denial of their requests, which groweth out of his advice, depart hence ill satisfied, which cannot but increase the discontentment there.' [2]

The outcome of the whole business was that Elizabeth decided early in March to send Lord Buckhurst to the Low Countries on what Wilkes called a mission of expostulation. He was instructed to protest against the changes which had been made by the Dutch in their government, to demand a prompt payment of the money granted for the pay of the troops, to inquire into the causes of discontent in the provinces and to do his best to remove them.[3] But he took with him no money and no men,

[1] S. P. Holland, xiii, no. 17.

[2] 23 Feb. 1586/7, S. P. Holland, xiii, no. 62*a*, passages in italics in cipher.

[3] Motley, ii. 214. A draft of Buckhurst's instructions corrected by Burghley and Walsingham is in Harleian MSS. 285, f. 285, dated in a later hand 3 Mar. 1586/7 ; cf. also 'Heads of Lord Buckhurst's instructions', dated 13, 14 Mar. 1586/7 in S. P. Holland, xiii, no. 109, and 'A Memorial for Lord Buckhurst', same date, in ibid., xiii, no. 110. Buckhurst's letters from the Low Countries are printed in part in *Cabala, sive Scrinia Sacra* (ed. 1691), Part 2.

nor even any definite promise of them,—nothing more indeed than a vague intimation that if all their abuses were reformed the Queen would show her goodwill towards them.[1]

Buckhurst's very first letters from the Netherlands indicated that two things were above all necessary to set right the disordered state of things among the Dutch, the one was money to pay the Queen's soldiers, the other was the presence of the Earl of Leicester. 'I find', he wrote to Leicester himself on the 26th of March, 'that as your Lordship's absence hath been one of the chief causes of this alteration, so will your presence restore all to his former state again.'[2] Wilkes's reports were in the same vein.[3] This advice fitted well into Walsingham's own view of the situation, and he exerted his best efforts during the spring of 1587 to persuade the Queen of the necessity of Leicester's dispatch and to induce her to send money for her starving soldiers. But he made little headway. On the 3rd of April he wrote to Leicester: 'It appeareth by late letters out of the Low Countries that the foot bands and horse bands in her Majesty's pay there are greatly decayed, insomuch as there remain not of the five thousand footmen above three thousand and of the one thousand horse but five hundred. I have acquainted her Majesty herewith and moved her for a supply, but I find her not disposed to resolve therein, and yet is she given to understand in what readiness the enemy is to march. Her Majesty doth wholly bend herself to devise some further means to disgrace her poor Council that subscribed [to the death warrant of the Queen of Scots], and in respect thereof she neglecteth all other causes.'[4] Again, three days later, he advised Leicester that he had urged upon the Queen the necessity of his return to the Netherlands, 'and yet', he continued, 'do I not see her moved to hasten the same, which I find proceedeth only of her unwillingness to enable you, but would rather hazard the increase of confusion there, which may put the whole country in peril, than supply your Lordship's want. The like course her

[1] Cf. 'A Copy of a Writing devised to be notified at the arrival in the Low Countries of Lord Buckhurst' in Burghley's hand, dated 11 March 1586/7, S. P. Holland, xiii, no. 96.

[2] *Cabala*, ii. 6; cf. also Buckhurst to Walsingham, same date, S. P. Holland, xiii, no. 135.

[3] *Cabala*, ii. 9.

[4] Cotton MSS., Galba C xi, f. 288, printed in Wright, *Queen Elizabeth and her Times*, ii. 336.

Majesty holdeth in the rest of her causes, which maketh me to wish myself from the helm.'[1] Again on the 8th of April he wrote:

'I have often pressed her Majesty, since the receipt of the late letters out of the Low Countries, by the which she might perceive how greatly your Lordship's return unto these countries is desired, to grow to some speedy resolution therein; but I find her very slow and cold therein, which proceedeth chiefly for that your Lordship standeth upon a loan of £10,000. I have urged her Majesty also for the sending over of money, for that by the 12th of this month there will be due to the bands serving there four months' pay. But I can prevail nothing therein. When I lay before her the perils she scorneth at it. The hope of peace with Spain hath put her in a most dangerous security. I have seen what hath passed between her Majesty and the Duke of Parma as also between the Comptroller and Champagny which I assure your Lordship giveth rather cause of despair than hope. . . . I am sorry that her Majesty sticketh with your Lordship for the £10,000, for I see without your return both the cause and many an honest man that have showed them most constantly affected unto your Lordship will go to ruin. I wish you there and though it were but for two months. I see this summer the enemy is not like to attempt any great matter in respect of his wants. But I am most sorry to see so great an advantage as her Majesty might have had [lost] in case she had been induced to have contributed towards the putting of any army into the field.'[2]

Leicester himself was willing enough to go if he could get the loan of £10,000 from the Queen to meet heavy mortgages on his estates, but the Queen still resisted all importunities.

'I would God', Walsingham wrote to Leicester again on the 10th of April, 'I could find as good a resolution in her Majesty to proceed in a princely course in relieving the United Provinces as I find an honourable disposition in your Lordship to employ yourself in that service, if it might please her Majesty to enable you thereunto, and to embrace the cause in such an effectual sort as might carry likelihood to work good effect. I never found her Majesty less disposed to take a course of prevention of the approaching mischiefs towards this realm than at this present. And to be plain with your Lordship there is none here that hath

[1] 6 Apr. 1587, Cotton MSS., Galba C xi, f. 296.

[2] Ibid., f. 294. The last leaf of this letter will be found in Galba C xi, f. 304, where it has been misplaced in binding.

either credit or courage to deal effectually with her in any of her great causes. Mr. Vice Chamberlain [Hatton] who returned to this court on Saturday last hath dealt very plainly and dutifully with her, which hath been accepted in so evil part as he is resolved to retire for a time. I assure your Lordship I find every man weary of attendance here.'[1]

Four days later Walsingham wrote to Leicester again that the Queen was willing to lend him the £10,000 provided he would repay it within a year. But this hard-wrung concession served to little purpose since Leicester swore that on such terms he would never set foot in the Netherlands.[2]

It is rather striking to discover that not only Walsingham and Hatton, but Burghley also, were zealous in their efforts to secure Leicester's prompt dispatch to the Low Countries.[3] None of them can have laboured under the delusion that he was likely to accomplish very much by the expedition. All of them were aware that the strongest men in the Netherlands were opposed to his coming and likely to hamper him in every possible way. The explanation of their attitude lies probably in their relations to Leicester himself. Burghley in particular, and to a lesser degree Hatton and Walsingham as well, all rested under the Queen's displeasure on account of their share in Mary Stuart's execution. Leicester alone among the more influential councillors remained in the royal good graces. It may very well be that he was exploiting his favourable position to their disadvantage, and it is not impossible that they wished first of all to get him overseas in order the better to recover the Queen's favour and in order perhaps to diminish his own credit. Walsingham no doubt felt as well that, though Leicester was far from being the best instrument to use in behalf of the Dutch, he was likely, by reason of his influence over the Queen, to accomplish more than

[1] Cotton MSS., Galba C xi, f. 292; Walsingham wrote to Wilkes to very much the same effect on 13 Apr. 1587, S. P. Holland, xiv, 31. Burghley expressed the same opinion in a letter to Leicester of 16 Apr. 1587, Galba C xi, f. 306. In a letter to Hatton, 12 May 1587, Burghley dwelt upon the necessity of peace in order to restore the English cloth industry, but maintained that the best way to win Parma to reasonable conditions was to cut off his supplies and to strengthen the hands of the Dutch. S. P. Domestic, cci, no. 15, printed in Nicolas, *Life of Hatton*, p. 470.

[2] Galba C xi, f. 299; Motley, ii. 213, n. 2.

[3] Cf. n. 1 above and also Burghley to Walsingham, 22 May 1587, S. P. Domestic, cci, no. 40. 'Generally I perceive that my Lord of Leicester's return is both desired and is necessary.'

any other man.[1] At all events he was assured that Leicester was eager to go and realized that if he were thwarted in his desire he would probably do more harm to the cause by way of revenge than he could do by returning to his old charge. Burghley, who favoured peace, felt sure, as he wrote to Hatton a little later, that a better peace could be secured sword in hand than any other way. He believed a demonstration in force under Leicester was the quickest way to bring Parma to reasonable terms.

Meanwhile overseas Buckhurst and Wilkes together were doing their utmost to quiet the discontent and to pave the way for Leicester's return. Though it is not at all certain that either of them was quite sincere about the matter,[2] both of them continued

[1] It is evident, however, that Walsingham did consider the possibility of an alternative, *Cabala*, ii. 20. Sir Francis Knollys wrote to Leicester, 9 Sept. 1587: 'It may please your excellency to remember that Mr. Secretary Walsingham did first give occasion to my Lord of Buckhurst to advertise his opinion how such a new government might be established [in the Netherlands] in the absence of your excellency, as though there were doubts whether your excellency should have returned to your government there or not.' Cotton MSS., Galba D ii, f. 121. Buckhurst's project of government is printed in *Cabala*, ii. 22–3. Leicester later accused Buckhurst of drawing up this plan in order to supplant him in the Netherlands. On this subject Buckhurst wrote to Walsingham, 13 July 1587: 'As I was advertised by you so also Leicester has written hither that the project sent was but to bring unto myself the government here wherein he might think me base and foolish, if I would have affected that poor authority and not rather the place which he hath, which if I might have a kingdom I would never accept.' Cotton MSS., Galba D i, f. 93.

[2] Buckhurst's letters to Walsingham at this time are unusually interesting. He wrote, 18 June 1587: 'I have sent her Majesty another letter from de Loo where it seemeth that now very lately her Majesty hath given him to understand that she will not insist upon that matter of religion further than shall be with the king's honour and conscience, whereupon de Loo taketh no small hold, and if she keep that course all will go to ruin as I have written to her Majesty.

'The *States* are in wonderful fear of *Leicester*, for by the *spreading* of these *letters* they doubt the alienation and tumult of the *people* upon *them*, and I assure you as the course is kept it is greatly to be feared; the end whereof no man knoweth whereto it will tend but like enough to endanger *Leicester himself* and to bring all to the enemy. *Leicester*, by divers letters and bruits of *his followers*, hath given out to the *people* that the only cause why the *Queen's Majesty* hath not better holpen them hath been for that *the States* wrote that letter unto him and sent the *copy* to the *Queen*, and that if they had not done so *her Majesty* had done great things and our *parliament* had also granted the aid of £20,000. This is a most dangerous course and maketh the *States* greatly to fear the end, for if *Leicester* come with a mind to *revenge*, the cause will come to subversion.' (S. P. Holland, xv, passages in italics in cipher.)

Again Buckhurst wrote, 22 June, 'The States said that if *her Majesty* knew what great hindrance their cause is like to sustain by the departure of *Norris* that *she* would not *revoke him*. There will be I fear great difference found betwixt *him* and *he* that *succeeds him*. It had been better bestowed upon

to write that his early dispatch was absolutely essential.[1] They both insisted also that for the success of the cause Elizabeth should without delay reinforce her own troops with some 1,000 or 2,000 men, and in order to assist the Estates in their summer campaigning should yield to their request for a loan of £50,000.[2] None of these suggestions was pleasing to Elizabeth. Walsingham in a private letter to Wilkes explained the situation to him with great bitterness of spirit.

'We are displeased', he wrote, 'with two points of your negotiations; the one for your acceptation of so slender satisfaction for so great indignities done her Majesty, the other for your earnest recommendation of a request thought so unreasonable by us here as the loan of £50,000. This request doth much trouble us. If we deny it we fear some change there and to grant it is a matter that goeth against our heart to disburse so great a treasure. And although it hath been oft times alleged that the only way to make a peace (which is the thing her Majesty doth chiefly affect, and to say the truth is most fit both for her and the realm) is to put on a good countenance by being strongest in the field, for that always the strongest giveth law unto the weakest, yet no reason that breedeth charges can in any sort be digested. Touching the Earl of Leicester's repair over, it resteth yet doubtful and therefore I do forbear to move her Majesty for your revocation according to your desire until his return shall be determined upon. . . . The *Earl of Leicester* is greatly incensed against you by some information given unto him . . . that you were privy to the offensive letter written by *the States* against him. But the chief ground of his mislike is in respect of the good will he conceiveth you bear to *Sir John Norris*. You are greatly beholding to Cleantes [?] who in my hearing did very friendly with *her Majesty* for you, who was greatly incensed against you by *Leicester's* informations, who now doth greatly possess *her* favour. I would we were both well established in Basel. *Il mal mi prene e mi spaventa il peggio.*'[3]

a meaner man of more *skill*. . . . I beseech you Sir, for the love of God, to get me hence, for when *Leicester* comes it will be worse than before.' (S. P. Holland, xv, passages in italics in cipher.)

In Cotton MSS., Galba C xi, f. 149, is a paper endorsed: 'To his Excellency touching Wilkes' in which the writer reports to Leicester that Wilkes had adversely criticized Leicester's government to the Queen. In the same letter the writer reports that Elizabeth herself had told the French ambassador that Leicester had once cherished the idea of marrying Lady Arabella Stuart to his son, and after the son's death to his bastard son.

[1] *Cabala*, ii. 33, 34.
[2] Ibid., ii. 11–13, 14–16.
[3] S. P. Holland, xiv, 80*a*; words in italics in cipher. Cleantes is a cipher

Notwithstanding Walsingham's desperation Elizabeth was evidently prepared to make some concessions. She instructed Buckhurst at a pinch to offer the States a loan of £15,000, and she promised to dispatch over the Earl of Leicester if they would agree to pay into the hands of a Treasurer to be named by him the sum of £100,000 for the expenses of the campaigning. Further than that she would not go. Walsingham wrote to Leicester on the 19th of May that nothing could 'draw her to take any full resolution in this cause until she receive answer of her last dispatch from the Lord of Buckhurst '.[1] Four days later he wrote again to Burghley : 'Yesterday at the earnest request of the Earl of Leicester I did press her Majesty to grow to some present resolution touching his employment, letting her understand that the same could abide no delay, the harvest approaching so fast as it doth. But after long argument I could draw no conclusion from her. I found some disposition in her rather to use my cousin Norris than the Earl. I did humbly pray her, the matter importing her as it doth, it might be considered of by certain of her choice councillors, which motion was also rejected.'[2] The matter was, however, discussed by some of the Council informally, and they reached the conclusion that the Queen ought to make substantial loans to the Dutch. But when Walsingham submitted this recommendation to Elizabeth he found her opposed as usual. 'According as I was directed,' he wrote to Burghley on the 26th of May, 'I acquainted her Majesty with our proceeding at the late conference. She doth nothing like of the resolution. I find she hath some secret advertisement from Holland which maketh her to stand upon the £15,000. I advised her therefore to commit the direction of the wars there to the author of that counsel, seeing the Earl of Leicester will not undertake it. She hath commanded me to send for him and sayeth he shall go with those forces that she thinketh fit. I wish your Lordship here, so as it might stand with your health, to

and probably stands for Burghley. The Italian quotation is from Petrarch, *Canzoniere*, no. 244 (Sonnet 206, 1st line). Apropos of Leicester's hostility to Wilkes, Walsingham wrote to him later, 'I doubt not but that you will carry yourself so wisely and warily there as no advantage may be taken against you' (27 May 1587, S. P. Holland, xiv, 124).

[1] Cotton MSS., Galba D i, f. 11.

[2] Harleian MSS. 6994, f. 68 ; printed in Wright, *Queen Elizabeth and her Times*, ii. 339.

the end there might be some resolution taken in the great causes.'[1]

The end of all this labour and sorrow was that early in June Elizabeth finally decided upon Leicester's dispatch. She agreed to lend Leicester £6,000, which was a little more than half of what she had promised him.[2] She also furnished him with £30,000 for campaigning purposes and she supplied him with some 5,000 fresh troops.[3] According to his instructions, which were drafted on the 20th of June, he was directed to demand full authority from the States to administer their war funds, to command their forces and, by advice of the Council of State, to issue ordinances. If the States did not concede such a large measure of authority he was to appeal from them to the separate provinces and towns. Failing this, he was to declare that his mistress meant 'to leave them to their own counsel and defence and to withdraw the support that she had yielded to them; seeing plainly that the continuance of the confused government now reigning among them could not but work their ruin'.[4]

Finally Leicester was instructed 'to incline the hearts of the people to hearken to a peace' both by direct dealing with the States General and privately with the popular leaders. He was to indicate to them that if they were unwilling to partake in a motion for peace his mistress would be compelled to withdraw her aid and treat separately with Spain, 'having nothing left that may not be easily accorded betwixt us and the King but only that shall concern their safety.'

These instructions were evidently drafted by Burghley and Walsingham in concert. It is rather striking to observe that

1 Harleian MSS. 6994, f. 70; printed in Wright, *op. cit.*, ii. 339–40.

2 In return for this loan Leicester pledged to the Queen his lease of the customs on sweet wines and of the fines and alienations office. (*Cal. Salisbury MSS.* iii. 265; Ellis, *Original Letters*, 3rd Series, iv. 75.)

3 Motley, ii. 267, says 3,000. It seems that Elizabeth's original purpose was to send over 6,000 men; cf. Walsingham to Buckhurst, 15 June 1587 (S. P. Holland, xv), 'Her Majesty is resolved to send over 6,000 men.'

There is a good deal of difference of opinion among the authorities as to the precise numbers sent over. Leicester, in a letter to Burghley of 30 Sept. 1587 (*Hardwicke Papers*, i. 342), says 5,000. In a list of Principal Officers and Captains that serve and have served in the Low Countries (S. P. Holland, xxix) there is the following entry: 'Extraordinary foot bands of 311 companies, being 4,650 men, sent for the relief of Sluys.'

4 S. P. Holland, xv, draft of Instructions corrected in Burghley's and Walsingham's handwriting.

both of them were here expressing concurrence in Leicester's old bad device of playing the people against the States General. Some time later Walsingham declared himself in a letter to Leicester more precisely upon this point. 'Sorry I am', he wrote, 'to see the States, or at least some of them, to deal so lewd and maliciously both towards her Majesty and your Lordship. The wrong done by Barneveldt, the advocate of Holland, ought not to escape without severe punishment. If Paul Buys had the last year been dealt with according to his deserts this se.... error of Barneveldt's would not have ensued.'[1] In view of the fact that both Buckhurst and Wilkes, who undoubtedly commanded Walsingham's confidence at this time, were strongly urging that any attempt to play the people against the States was certain to bring disaster upon the common cause, Walsingham's approval of such a course seems strange. The probabilities are that he and Burghley both were simply acquiescing in Leicester's own view of the situation because they saw the futility of opposing him and believed that more might be gained with his co-operation than any other way. At all events it is evident that Leicester practically dictated his own instructions. He left England on the 26th of June. With him went two councillors who were to supersede Clark and Wilkes on the Dutch Council of State. One of these was Henry Killigrew, the other Robert Beale. Killigrew, besides being related by marriage to Burghley, was one of Walsingham's oldest friends. Beale was his brother-in-law. Killigrew was a diplomatist of ripe experience, Beale, a distinguished civilian. Both were ardent Protestants. Their hardest job was to be that of keeping a watchful eye upon Leicester's doings without incurring his disfavour.

Besides these two Leicester took with him for secretary, Francis Needham, one of Walsingham's most trusted servants. Here Walsingham's hand is plainly apparent, and the private correspondence which he maintained with Needham after his arrival in the Low Countries makes it evident that Walsingham had placed him in Leicester's service in order to spy upon him.[2]

[1] Walsingham to Leicester, 15 Sept. 1587, Cotton MSS., Galba C vii, f. 329. This letter is damaged by fire along the edges and some words are burned away. It is dated 1584, but it evidently belongs to 1587.

[2] That Needham was acting as Leicester's secretary appears from the

Even before Leicester left England he revealed his intention to resume his machinations with the so-called popular party in the Provinces. On the 10th of June he wrote to Junius, one of his instruments in the Netherlands, commanding him to go through the good towns ' and comfort the ' well-affected ' with the news of his coming. Junius was further to tell ' those who have the care of the people ' that Leicester looked to them to see to it that his authority should not be questioned and countermanded by the States as in times past.[1] Unfortunately a copy of this letter came into Barneveldt's hands along with a copy of Leicester's instructions.[2] So that the States were made aware of his purposes even before his arrival and were consequently in no very friendly mood towards him when he came.[3]

It is scarcely necessary to follow in any detail the course of Leicester's second expedition into the Low Countries. The fact which perhaps more than any other had hastened his dispatch was the siege of Sluys which the Prince of Parma had begun early in June. The danger to England if the Spaniards should gain possession of a seaport was so obvious that even Elizabeth appears to have appreciated it. Nevertheless, as Leicester discovered after his arrival in the Low Countries, the States were

following: 17 Sept. 1587, Leicester wrote to Walsingham: ' I thank you Mr. Secretary again and again for this honest, able, young man [the bearer of the letter]. He hath lost much time, for since my last coming over I have not had much to do for my secretaries ' (S. P. Holland, xviii). That Needham was the man referred to in this letter is evident from a letter of 18 Sept. from Ed. Burnham to Walsingham. ' By the bearer, my fellow Needham, . . . I find by him that upon my arrival his Excellency [Leicester] was minded to dispatch him ' (S. P. Holland, xviii). It is evident from Needham's private correspondence with Walsingham that Walsingham had secured him a position beside Leicester in order to keep close watch on Leicester's doings; cf., for example, Needham to Walsingham, 12 Aug. 1587, ' I complain of the weariness of this place, where I would never endure one day were it not that your honour hath commanded me, not for any travail I take, for I am idle all the day and almost every day, but of the fashion here, for hardly can I endure to be made an instrument to expostulate matters *which himself* [*Leicester*] *for shame will not*.' (S. P. Holland, xvii, passages in italics in cipher.)

[1] Motley, ii. 255, n. 1, dates this letter 15 June; a copy, endorsed by Burghley in the Cotton MSS. (Galba D ii, f. 25), is dated 10 June.

[2] Motley, ii. 258–9.

[3] Buckhurst wrote to Walsingham, 22 June, that the States even hesitated about going to the coast to extend to Leicester a formal welcome: ' *The States* have held a council whether they shall go to *Leicester* into *Zeeland* and are yet resolved not to go though I have earnestly persuaded *Count Hollock* to go. They seem afraid of *Buys*' example.' (S. P. Holland, xv, words in italics in cipher.)

not prepared to co-operate vigorously with him for the relief of the town. This was due in part, as Wilkes pointed out in a letter to the Queen, to the fact that the deputies of Holland and Zeeland who dominated the States General thought it wiser to concentrate their efforts upon their own defence.[1] In part it was due also to their distrust of Leicester. At any rate it prevented effective action.[2] On the 26th of July Sluys fell. During the interval which followed Leicester was chiefly occupied in laying responsibility for its surrender upon other people's shoulders. He laid it first of all and with some justice upon the States. But he proceeded from them to charge all his enemies indiscriminately. He did not hesitate to say that Buckhurst[3] and Wilkes and Norris were in part to blame. Indeed he even ventured to call in question the courage of Captain Roger Williams, a soldier of well-known gallantry and one of the most valiant of Sluys' defenders.[4]

Elizabeth was much provoked when she heard of the loss of this city. She blamed the Dutch most of all but Leicester did not escape her censure. Walsingham wrote to him on the 7th of August:

> 'The loss of Sluys has wrought in her Majesty some alteration of her favour towards your Lordship and also towards the cause itself, in such sort as she seemed bent and resolved to abandon those countries and to have revoked your Lordship. . . . The Lord Admiral stood very friendly for you to her Majesty, being very well backed by the Lord Chancellor and my Lord Treasurer, who did let her Majesty very roundly and plainly understand how greatly this hard course would not only discourage you but all others that should be employed in public service, to be charged in that sort your Lordship is with other men's errors, and further

[1] 13 July 1587, S. P. Holland, xvi.

[2] Walsingham wrote to Burghley, 20 July: 'I send your Lordship such letters as I received yesternight late from the Earl of Leicester. I am sorry to find by them so much backwardness in the States. I fear the division between the said Earl and them will be the loss of Sluys or rather the loss of the whole country.' (Harleian MSS. 6994, f. 84, printed in Wright, ii. 341.)

[3] Buckhurst wrote to Walsingham on 17 August: 'For myself I account his [Leicester's] accusation of the loss of Sluys to be so ridiculous as except he will also charge me with taking the Tower of London I mean not to answer it' (S. P. Domestic, cciii, no. 14). Cf. also Walsingham to Leicester, 1 Aug. 1587, Cotton MSS., Galba D i, f. 232.

[4] Motley, ii. 276 n. It may be noted at this point that Leicester even got to loggerheads with his valiant supporter Lord Willoughby over the question of the ransoms of prisoners, *Cal. Ancaster MSS.*, pp. 53 ff.

that if the States learn of it all would go upside down and make you unfit to deal either for war or peace. She promised that she would forbear to give out any speeches of dislike, denying that she had delivered any but to one or two of her Council, though the Court be full of it and therefore hard to be kept from the States.'[1]

Walsingham for his part believed that the chief reason for the fall of Sluys was the lack of co-operation between Leicester and the States and he came to the conclusion, prompted no doubt by what he heard from Wilkes and Buckhurst and by what Francis Needham wrote him, that unless something were done to reconcile these differences still more disastrous consequences might follow. To Beale and Killigrew he wrote on the 31st of July: 'Sorry I am besides the loss of Sluys to see so great a disunion between the Lord General and the States. I am devising some way to remedy. It is a matter of no small difficulty and therefore you have the wolf by the ears. God direct you to advise and resolve well.'[2]

Walsingham even went so far at this juncture as to warn Leicester himself of the gravity of the situation. Nothing, he wrote to Leicester, would encourage the Spaniard more than the present disunion reigning in the United Provinces.

'Those wishing well to both the cause and to your Lordship's self do most earnestly desire that, as by evil instruments the disunion is grown, so by some good instruments the former good union might be restored. To take a violent course of revenge cannot but breed an irreparable breach, the enemy being as strong as he is. . . . Though the people stand well affected yet is it a very weak foundation to ground on, being naturally uncertain and inconstant, and will be easily carried away with false bruits. Her Majesty is very sharply bent both against the States and the two Earls who have shown themselves most ungrateful to her. She would like them to be persecuted with all extremity. Yet if anything should fall out otherwise than

[1] Cotton MSS., Galba D i, f. 244. Walsingham wrote to Leicester, 2 Aug., to instruct him by the Queen's orders to attempt the recovery of Sluys provided that Parma had withdrawn with his army before the breaches in the walls were repaired. 'Her Majesty', he added, 'doth greatly desire to have somewhat done for the reparation of her honour which she thinketh greatly touched through the loss of Sluys.' (Galba C vii, f. 258, where it is wrongly placed among the papers of the year 1582.)

[2] B.M. Egerton MSS. 1694, f. 163. In a postscript Walsingham added: 'Commend me to my good friend Sir Roger [Williams].'

well it is doubtful (for that the well or ill liking of Princes in matters of State standeth greatly upon the issue of things) how your doings would be taken. The ill success of Sluys, though your Lordship hath done your uttermost for the relief thereof, hath wrought some alteration in her Majesty's favour towards you. . . . Sir Thomas Shirley and the Lord Treasurer stood most faithfully and friendly in justification of your Lordship's doings. I find that there is some dealing underhand against your Lordship, which proceedeth from the younger sort of our courtiers that take upon them to censure the greatest causes and persons that are treated in council or serve her Majesty, a disease that I do not look to see cured in my time.' [1]

There is no reason to believe that Leicester paid any heed to his timely warning. Walsingham indeed had deviated from his usual policy at this time in uttering it. Generally speaking, he found it more expedient to keep on good terms with Leicester by seeming agreement than to try to mend his ways by crossing them. There can be very little doubt indeed that Walsingham was playing a double game with Leicester during the summer of 1587. This is immediately apparent in the correspondence of Francis Needham, Walsingham's trusted servant, who was acting at this time as Leicester's secretary. It is hardly likely that Needham would have written in the terms he did had he not been confident that Walsingham was essentially in sympathy with his own point of view. The following passage, from Needham's letter to Walsingham of the 29th of July, will serve to illustrate this point: *I do now utterly despair to hope for any good success in this action for that the world doth plainly see that the Earl of Leicester seeketh only to serve his turn of all men without any hearty respect to any.*[2] Further evidence of Walsingham's

[1] 2 Aug. 1587, Cotton MSS., Galba D i, f. 230. It is not unlikely that Walsingham's last sentence has reference to Sir Walter Raleigh who, according to the Spanish ambassador in Paris, had opposed Leicester's plans earlier in the year (*Cal. Spanish*, 1587–1603, p. 24). Raleigh had been under suspicion of opposing Leicester the previous year (Bruce, *Leicester Correspondence*, pp. 193, 207). Wm. Herle wrote to Leicester, 21 Sept. 1587: 'Sir Walter Raleigh, either of his ill-nature or of emulation to the Earl of Essex, for that he doth good offices with her Majesty for your Excellency, favours Norris all that he may, labouring most earnestly for him' (Galba D ii, f. 27). Cf. also *Cal. Rutland Papers*, i. 234. 'Even Sir Walter Raleigh did not escape suspicion of ill done to the Earl [of Leicester], from which cause grew his sudden departure to the west country the day before the Earl came to court.'

[2] Harleian MSS. 287, f. 41; the entire passage cited is in cipher in the

duplicity is to be found in his attitude towards Buckhurst, Wilkes, and Norris, the three Englishmen above all others who were the devoted victims of Leicester's wrath in the summer of 1587. It is clear from Walsingham's correspondence to Leicester that he was pretending to share Leicester's antipathy towards these men.[1] He did it is true make some feeble attempt to

original; cf. also the following from Needham's letter of 12 Aug. 1587: 'The Prince of Parma has tried by all possible means *to gain Sir Roger Williams but could not in any wise prevail although he thought the kind usage* he had *received at his hands* would be an occasion to make him to *quit the Earl's party* if he were not *used upon his* return *as he deserved. Leicester* hath hereupon conceived *great jealousy of Williams* and hath not spared to give warning to *Sir Wm. Russell* to beware of him as one who would be his undoing and it seemeth reported as much to Lord North and Sir William Pelham . . . who have cast out some speeches to the gent's disadvantage, as he repenteth himself to have forsaken the favours of *so many good friends here*, both the *States, Count Maurice and Hollock*, who wished him well, and to fall out with *Norris* whom he had followed in wars these seven years. . . . The gentleman is wonderfully perplexed. . . . He knoweth *the nature of Leicester* to be such as will leave no means unsought to *overthrow his credit* and *ruin him. . . . Lord North* hath bestowed his credit here not to so good purpose as he might, but rather *to feed the dislikes between Leicester, the States and the Earls* and, which is more dangerous, hath been the cause that he hath of late *fallen out with his best soldiers* and *men of war* even so far as *Sir William Russell* himself hath not been spared.' (S. P. Holland, xvii, passages in italics in cipher.)

[1] Cf. for example a paper in Walsingham's hand, not dated but probably belonging to late July 1587, which is headed: 'A Memorial for Needham' (Harleian MSS. 1582, f. 53). Apparently this paper contained brief memoranda of verbal messages to be delivered by Needham to various personages in the Netherlands:

'E. Leicester

'That the Lord Treasurer hitherto dealeth most friendly towards him; that his L. shall do well to write him letters of thanks; that he [Burghley] does not greatly favour B [Buckhurst ?].

That I do not find but the whole council also well bent towards him in outward show, though underhand there may be some foul play.

That I suppose N [Norris ?] had some secret conference with B [Buckhurst ?].

That the continuance of her Majesty's favourable countenance towards his L. holdeth them all in.

That his L. shall do as much as shall lie in him to avoid charges, which will most offend and consequently give greatest advantage to his enemies.

That I suspect that R [Raleigh ?] is made an instrument for B [Buckhurst ?] by Nor[ris] persuasions and the mislike of E [Essex ?] brought in as he supposeth by L [Leicester ?].

That the L. Chancellor was absent at the time that Nor[ris] and Wil[kes] were charged; that he doth greatly condemn B [Buckhurst ?] for his dealings towards his Lordship though otherwise he do love him, and that he standeth constantly affected towards his Lordship.

. . . .

'Burgrave

That the Earl's enemies hope that his Lordship's seeking to take revenge of C. Hollock and the States will take some disgrace.

That he should do well to persuade him to continue the temperate course

reconcile the differences between Leicester and Norris earlier in the spring, but his suggestion met with such an unfavourable reception that he did not follow it further.[1] On the other hand his correspondence with Wilkes and Buckhurst at any rate (there are no letters at this time between him and Norris preserved) reveal the fact that both of them regarded him as their friend and reckoned on his support. Buckhurst for example wrote to him in August: 'Although you have of me a friend of small power yet have you and shall have of me a friend faithful and constant. . . . I hear you are not free from mislike for your good favour towards some of us; by such dealing towards yourself you may the better judge of that proceeding towards us.'[2] Leicester indeed did get wind that Walsingham was not altogether sincere in his professed hostility to Buckhurst and the others. Francis Needham wrote home to his master on the 25th of July that Leicester had heard that when Wilkes was committed to prison Walsingham had sent a private letter to the Warden of the fleet, 'that he should be *well used* for that he was *not to be a close prisoner* but was only *done for* and upon a *slight* displeasure conceived by her Majesty.' Leicester had told Needham that his enemies in the Low Countries would know how to make their profit of such doings, especially as they proceeded from Walsingham, 'one whom the world accounted and he esteemed *his dearest friend* . . .; and with an oath pro-

that he hath begun and to seek by all means he may to recover the C. and the States.'

There are brief messages as well to Sir William Russell and Col. Morgan but not of any great moment. The extensions of the initials in brackets are purely conjectural based upon the context.

[1] Cf. Walsingham to Leicester, 14 Apr. 1587, in which Walsingham wrote that the Queen was very anxious to effect a reconciliation between Leicester and Norris, though she did not wish her own hand to appear in the business. 'I think', Walsingham added, 'if Norris might be sure of your Lordship's good favour, he would never again lose you' (Cotton MSS., Galba C xi, f. 299). Leicester's reply is printed in Motley, ii. 213, n. 2, in which he swore that he would never serve again with Norris, not for £100,000.

It is evident also that Walsingham laboured to heal the breach between Leicester and Buckhurst, though he refused to be a dealer in the matter himself, cf. his brief notes for a letter to Sir Thos. Shirley in June 1587: 'Sorry for the dislike between the Earl and the L. of Buckhurst, that I wish by his [Shirley's] travail might be removed' (S. P. Holland, xv, 2–13, June 1587). In a letter to Wilkes of 1 Jan. 1588 Walsingham advised him by all means to seek a reconciliation with Leicester (S. P. Domestic, ccviii, no. 1).

[2] S. P. Domestic, cciii, no. 14; many papers on the Leicester-Buckhurst-Wilkes-Norris quarrels are printed in *Cabala*, ii. 55–82.

tested that if his *nearest kinsman* in the world had done the like to any of their Lordships [of the Council] *he would never speak for him.*'[1] Four days later Needham wrote to Walsingham again: 'He [Leicester] is in *jealousy that your honour favours the three more than he thinks them to deserve.*'[2] Walsingham thought it expedient to write to Leicester at once and to explain away his seeming consideration of Wilkes. Common humanity had prompted him, he said, to commend the man who was 'suffering from a grievous infirmity' to his jailor. 'Thus', he concluded, 'your Lordship seeth upon what ground these favours proceeded and therefore I do hope that you will rest satisfied with this report of my proceeding herein.'[3] It does not appear whether the explanation was satisfactory to Leicester or not.

As time went on the expediency of maintaining Leicester in the Netherlands became more and more doubtful even to Walsingham. It was clear that the breach between the Earl and the States instead of diminishing, as Walsingham hoped and tried his best to effect, kept on increasing. At Leyden, at Utrecht, in North Holland, and even in Amsterdam Leicester's intrigues with the popular party developed only to be defeated by the superior astuteness of Barneveldt and his colleagues.[4] To one as interested in the cause of the Dutch as Walsingham was it was abundantly clear that Leicester's presence was serving rather to weaken their powers of resistance by sowing dissensions among them than to strengthen them. The Secretary had hoped that in spite of all these things Leicester's influence with the Queen might induce her to lend such effective military aid in the compaigns against Parma as would more than counterbalance Leicester's personal unpopularity. But this proved not to be the case. In spite of his constant efforts, which seem to have been vigorously seconded by Burghley and Hatton, Elizabeth was not willing to send over the money which was so urgently needed to keep her troops in fighting trim. The fact was that her hopes of coming to terms with Spain made her blind to all other considerations and deaf even to Burghley's

[1] Harleian MSS. 287, f. 37, passages in italics in cipher.
[2] Ibid., f. 41, 29 July 1587, passages in italics in cipher.
[3] Cotton MSS., Galba D i, f. 139, 29 July 1587.
[4] Blok (trans. Putnam), iii. 231.

arguments that the best way to secure an honourable peace was by waging a vigorous and effective war. £44,000 was due to her soldiers on the 1st of July. When the Council pressed her to sign a warrant for the sum she swore that she would send no more than £20,000 and she bade Leicester collect from the Estates the £30,000 she had sent last.[1] 'I would to God', Walsingham wrote to Leicester on the 29th of July, 'her Highness were as warm therein as she is in the matter of peace and then your Lordship should not lack treasure. . . . Unless her Majesty shall be better resolved to maintain the cause than I find her disposed to do, I wish your Lordship rid of that charge and the government of those countries in their own hands whose ingratitude (I mean the States) is unsupportable. Her Majesty may keep the two cautionary towns and the towns in Flanders and Brabant according to your Lordship's opinion.'[2]

This was the note upon which Walsingham continued to harp during the remainder of the summer. He left Court early in September to undergo further treatment for his old malady, but even in retirement he bent his efforts to bring Leicester back. 'I shall not need', he wrote to Leicester on the 21st of September, 'to write unto your Lordship what is done in our court for that this bearer Mr. Atye can yield you a better account than I that am absent from thence. I have acquainted him with my opinion what way were best to be taken to quit yourself of that unfortunate service where, instead of honour, your Lordship shall receive discredit, besides the overthrow of your estate.'[3] He wrote again to Leicester on the 12th of November:

'Although it hath pleased God to quit me of my fever yet is not my body restored to that state of strength as that either my hand or my head can endure the weight of my pen and therefore I am humbly to pray your Lordship to excuse me in that I write not with mine own hand. Touching the resolution taken, both for your Lordship's return and the causes of those countries, . . . I can say nothing. I pray God they may fall out to your Lordship's contentment, who hath received as hard measure as ever nobleman, or other meaner minister that hath at any time been employed in foreign service. I fear there is

[1] Cf. Walsingham to Leicester, 14 Aug. 1587, Cotton MSS., Galba D i, f. 248.
[2] Ibid., f. 139.
[3] Ibid., Galba D ii, f. 86.

not that care taken in the manner of your Lordship's revocation both of her Majesty's honour and your Lordship's as appertaineth. But, good my Lord, let nothing stay you there (unless some extraordinary cause fall out as your return may breed such a change there as may endanger this estate) for your continuance will but work you increase of dishonour and disgrace.'[1]

Leicester on his part was urgently demanding his recall. Indeed it seems hardly likely that Walsingham would have besought him to come home had he not found that the Earl's wishes ran in that direction. The Queen at first was reluctant to recall him. She told Essex, his step-son, in August that she feared his sudden departure might be construed into an intention on her part to abandon the Dutch cause.[2] More probably her real reason lay in the hope she cherished that Leicester might succeed in inducing the Dutch to think well of her projects of peace.[3] Walsingham hinted in his letter to Leicester of the 12th of November that some of the Queen's advisers were not over-zealous for his return and William Herle, one of Leicester's clients, said the same thing in even stronger terms. But the evidence on the point is too scant to gather much from it. Herle went no farther than to accuse Sir Walter Raleigh of favouring Norris and of charging Hatton with indifference.[4] Everything that Burghley and Walsingham said on the subject would seem to indicate their desire to have Leicester in England again. Nothing further can be stated positively, though it may be suspected that no one of the Privy Councillors was very eager for the return of the favourite. At all events Elizabeth finally decided to recall Leicester in November.[5] He wasted little time with his leave-taking and got away early in December. It is characteristic of him that towards the end of his sojourn in the Netherlands, when he was altogether sick of the business, he should have sought to lay the blame for his failure on Walsingham's shoulders. 'I will you say', he wrote to Walsingham on the 10th of October, 'what labyrinths you have brought me

[1] Ibid., Galba D ii, f. 178, printed, with some verbal inaccuracies, in *Hardwicke Papers*, i. 359.

[2] Essex to Leicester, 1 Sept. 1587, Galba D ii, f. 139.

[3] Cf. Leicester to Burghley, 30 Sept. 1587, *Hardwicke Papers*, i. 340.

[4] Cf. p. 250, n. 1 above.

[5] *Cal. Salisbury MSS.* iii. 297.

into and no man will I blame so much as yourself that so hastened me hither where I am now in worse case than ever I was.' [1]

No doubt Leicester's temperamental defects were largely responsible for his failure to accomplish more in the Low Countries than he did. Yet it is doubtful whether an archangel could have done much with the backing which Leicester received from his mistress. He found the English regiments ragged and mutinous when he arrived among them and he could get no money, or at any rate not enough money either from the Queen or the States to convert them into an effective fighting force. The consequence was that he never was strong enough to undertake aggressive tactics against Parma, who according to all reports was very much embarrassed for want of munitions and might have been decisively defeated had a vigorous blow been struck in season.[2]

The fact was of course that Elizabeth was so eager for peace at this time that she saw no virtue in any aggressive policy. It is easy to condemn her attitude, yet it ought to be observed that a great deal of pressure was being brought to bear upon her by mercantile interests in England to terminate the war. There can be no matter of doubt that the English cloth trade overseas was suffering very greatly from the continuance of hostilities. The Spanish and the Portuguese and the Flemish markets were closed to the English. Parma's control of the middle Rhine blocked the ordinary channel of trade into western and southern Germany and Spanish intrigues joined with the efforts of the Hanseatic League had all but barred the gates of Hamburg, the great outlet for English cloth in north Germany.

[1] S. P. Holland, xviii. In the same letter Leicester wrote: 'I only send you salutations at this time, having directed my letters as you willed me. I am sorry for the cause of your absence and yet more sorry for my abode here, because it toucheth myself, else your care is as dear to me as any friend I have living.'

[2] Cf. Burghley to Walsingham, 22 May 1587 (S. P. Domestic, cci, no. 40): Walsingham to Leicester, 8 Apr. 1587 (Cotton MSS., Galba C xi, f. 294); and particularly Walsingham to Wilkes, 13 Apr. 1587: 'I have received secret advertisement that the Prince will not be able to make any great attempt this year for want of victuals, so that if her Majesty would be moved to make her profit of so fit an opportunity by yielding to an increase of her charges, with care had that the same were well and duly employed, it were not to be doubted but she should recover a great part of those countries that hath been lost, whereby she should be the better able to attain to peace, which is the thing she chiefly desireth' (S. P. Holland, xiv).

Burghley wrote to Sir Christopher Hatton in May: 'This great matter of the lack of vent, not only of cloths, which presently is the greatest, but of all other English commodities . . . cannot but in process of time work a great and dangerous issue to the people of this realm, who heretofore in time of outward peace, lived thereby, and without it must either perish for want or fall into violence to feed and fill their lewd appetites with open spoil of others.' And Burghley held that the cause of all this trouble was the quarrel between Spain and England and that the sovereign remedy lay in the restoration of peace and of trade on the basis of the old treaties: 'Seeing', he added, 'there is a signification notified of the good inclination of both the places and a great necessity to press them both thereto for the soulagement of their people, it were a pity any course should be taken either to hinder this or not to hasten it.' So far Burghley's ideas probably coincided with those of his mistress. He insisted, however, that the best way to gain a speedy peace was by waging a vigorous war, and there Elizabeth would not, in practice at any rate, follow him.[1]

The pinch of the restraint of trade upon the cloth industry became so sharp in the late autumn of 1586 that the Privy Council was forced to take cognizance of it.[2] Naturally the weavers were the ones to suffer first. The Merchant Adventurers, who found that they could not market cloth overseas, ceased to buy from the clothiers, or middle men, and they in turn, finding no sale for cloth in London, ceased to buy it of the weavers and so the looms stopped working and the weavers began to starve. It was only a question of time before their idleness in turn would begin to affect the wool growers on the one hand and the cloth finishers on the other. When one considers how large a part the cloth industry in its various ramifications played in the industrial life of England at this time, one can realize how great the pressure for peace might have been. This is a concrete fact to be set over against the zeal of men like Walsingham in the cause of Protestantism. Protestantism with all its virtues after all buttered no bread. And it may well be questioned whether Elizabeth's yearning

[1] Burghley to Hatton, 12 May 1587, S. P. Domestic, cci, no. 15, printed in Nicolas, *Life of Hatton*, p. 470.

[2] *Acts of Privy Council*, 1586-7, p 273.

for peace at this time did not come nearer to representing the wishes of the average Englishman than did the sentiments of soldiers like Norris, sailors like Drake, and zealous Puritans like Walsingham. Anyway, it was clear in the spring of 1587 that something would have to be done to give the weavers employment. The temptation as always was to place the blame on the large corporations of traders, particularly upon the Merchant Adventurers, who handled the bulk of the overseas trade in cloth, and most of the remedies proposed were aimed at their monopoly. At first an effort was made, following good sixteenth-century precedent, to force them to buy cloth whether they wanted it or not, under penalty of depriving them of their monopoly if they refused to do so. This was the remedy proposed by the Privy Council in December 1586.[1] But this threat evidently failed to accomplish its purpose.[2] Conditions were not better, were indeed worse, the following May when Burghley wrote the letter already cited to Hatton. In that same letter Burghley proposed various remedies of the old pattern. He suggested that the old privilege be restored to the Merchants of the Steelyard —that is to say, the Hansa Merchants, who had been in the past the chief competitors of the Merchant Adventurers for the German trade and who had lost their privileges largely at the instigation of these same merchants. He proposed that other foreign merchants be allowed a reduction of duty to the amount of 2*s.* the piece upon all 'white coarse cloth' which they exported, and that these same merchants be either permitted to buy cloth freely at Blackwell Hall, the London cloth market, or else that a special market be erected for their benefit in the city of Westminster. From a letter of Walsingham, written two days later,

[1] *Acts of Privy Council*, 1586–7, pp. 273–4.

[2] Leicester wrote to Walsingham from Bath, 6 Apr. 1587, a letter describing the great decay of the cloth trade in west England: 'The cause of this we have been informed of but will not believe it, but at my coming up you shall hear more and that concerns yourself and her Majesty deeply. The next is the extreme cry and complaint of the poor for lack of work, such as have been set on work heretofore by clothiers and by their decay are forced to turn them off. The cause you have heard heretofore, as the clothier doth alledge that he cannot have reasonable price nor utterance for his clothes at London whatsoever is informed to us. Some of the clothiers here deserve great favour for keeping the poor at work to their great loss. They offer to be bound to increase their workmen so they may have good usage at the merchants' hands.' (S. P. Domestic, cc, no. 5, abstracted, not quoted verbatim.)

it appears that Burghley was also considering another course of action.[1] The Merchant Adventurers, who naturally recoiled before the loss of their monopoly, had evidently proposed to the Queen that if she would lend them enough money to tide them over the evil times they would see to it that the clothiers did not lack a market, nor the weavers employment. This proposal evidently appealed to Burghley, but it did not commend itself to the parsimonious Elizabeth. She was, however, attracted by Burghley's suggestions in his letter to Hatton and she made up her mind with surprising alacrity to establish them by proclamation.[2] Walsingham wrote to Burghley to that effect on the 14th of May. He was, however, more than doubtful about the efficacy of such a course. 'I could have wished', he wrote, 'that her Majesty for the benefit of the merchant strangers might have been moved to have abated more than *2s.* upon a cloth for I cannot think, in this dead time for vent, that the abatement of the *2s.* will yield that encouragement that is looked for. It is also to be feared that the Merchant Adventurers, having so many cloths beyond the seas in their hands, will supply the foreign wants in such a plentiful sort as the stranger that followeth him will find but a cold market, which the said stranger foreseeing will not easily enter into the trade. The more I wade into this matter the more doubtful and dangerous I find it, concluding with myself therefore that the only way were to furnish the Merchant Adventurers with a convenient sum of money.'[3]

The outcome of the matter was that at a meeting of the Privy Council at Lord Burghley's house the following day it was resolved: first, that the Hansa merchants should be

[1] S. P. Domestic, cci, no. 17.

[2] Cf. Steele, *Tudor and Stuart Proclamations*, i. 86. Proclamation dated 23 May 1587, summarized by Steele as follows: 'Clothiers are used to sell only at Blackwell Hall where none but the Merchant Adventurers did buy and none but the freemen of the city may bargain. The Merchants of the Steelyard and all other merchants foreign or native may buy any cloth unwrought, unbarbed or unshorn and learn at the Custom House what dues they have to pay. Merchants that have not the liberty to buy at Blackwell Hall may buy cloths at The George, in King's Street, Westminster.'

Burghley had told Hatton in the letter already cited that he supposed the Londoners would rather throw open Blackwell Hall to outsiders than see a cloth market established at Westminster. It appears, however, from a letter of Hatton to Walsingham of 27 May 1587 (Nicolas, *Hatton*, p. 472) that such was not the case.

[3] Cf. n. 1 above.

allowed their old privileges of exporting cloth upon condition that the old liberties of English traders at Hamburg be restored; second, that other foreign merchants were to be allowed an abatement of two shillings duty on every piece of cloth exported; third, that all English merchants not members of the Merchant Adventurers should be allowed to transport cloth to all parts of Germany except to the city of Emden, which was reserved to the Adventurers, and to the Baltic ports in which the Eastland Merchants were to retain their monopoly.[1]

These measures were taken but apparently without much benefit to the cloth worker.[2] They were all based upon the assumption that the monopoly of the Merchant Adventurers was responsible for the decay of the cloth trade, whereas, in fact, the causes lay far deeper. For the most part, they probably arose out of the disordered state of things on the continent in general, though Burghley was doubtless quite right in saying what Walsingham would hardly have cared to confess, that the war between England and Spain was a factor of some importance. Elizabeth at any rate was pleased to account it so and her natural inclination towards peace was greatly strengthened, if it was not prompted, by the consciousness that peace would serve the material welfare of her people.

So she pressed the matter for all it was worth. In the late autumn of 1586 Andrea de Loo had gone over from England to the Netherlands with a tentative proposition of the terms upon which Elizabeth would be willing to treat. The Dutch must be restored to their ancient liberties, Spanish troops and foreign governors must be removed, Elizabeth's expenses must be paid, English merchants in Spain must be freed from the persecutions of the Inquisition. Finally it was very desirable, though Elizabeth does not seem to have been very emphatic upon the point, that toleration should be granted to the Dutch in their religion.[3] Upon the point of toleration Parma made strong objection on the grounds that Elizabeth could not fairly exact from the subjects of the King of Spain what she had

[1] 'Notes of resolutions taken at the L. Treasurer's house for facilitating the export of cloths,' corrected in Walsingham's hand, 15 May 1587, S. P Domestic, cci, no. 19; cf. also *Acts o 'Privy Council*, 1588, pp. 77–87.

[2] Scott, *Joint Stock Companies*, i. 97.

[3] Burghley to de Loo, 7 Mar. 1586–7, S. P. Flanders i.

refused to allow to her own subjects.[1] But he did not choose at this time to press the matter and when Andrea de Loo returned to England in April 1587 with Parma's reply the prospect of peace appeared to the Queen more than fair. Walsingham wrote to Leicester on the 6th of April that Parma's letter 'putteth her Majesty in great security'. He added, 'I find not [Parma's reply] to be such as ought to make her so secure as she is. He only acknowledgeth to have sufficient authority to treat and conclude a peace so as the conditions be reasonable. Who shall be the judge in that case resteth the difficulty. The treaty may greatly serve the Prince's turn in winning of time this summer, being altogether unprovided to attempt anything in the field, as also to breed a dislike and jealousy in the States of the United Provinces, being nothing inclined to any treaty of peace, as a thing full of peril and danger and that cannot be performed with surety.'[2] But Elizabeth was of a different mind. She was indeed so eager for peace at this juncture that she even gave Parma to understand that she was not disposed to press the question of toleration for the Dutch any farther than was agreeable to the honour and conscience of the King his master.[3]

Upon these terms Parma was eager enough to open negotiations and according to de Loo wished the Queen to send over commissioners to treat as soon as might be.[4] Naturally even Elizabeth was not prepared to appear quite so openly as a suitor for peace. But an opportunity soon offered by which she could save her face and still attain her object. Early in June she received a letter from the King of Denmark in which he tendered his good offices as mediator between her and Parma. The king said that he proposed to send commissioners for that purpose to Emden in August and invited both Elizabeth and Parma to dispatch commissioners there as well. Elizabeth leaped at the offer. She bade Burghley and Crofts to write at once to

[1] Motley, ii. 293, n. 1. [2] Cotton MSS., Galba C xi, f. 296.

[3] Buckhurst to Walsingham, 18 June 1587: 'I have sent her Majesty another letter from de Loo wherein it seemeth that now very lately her Majesty hath given him to understand that she will not insist upon that matter of religion further than shall be with the King's honour and conscience; whereupon de Loo taketh no small hold, and if she keep that course all will go to ruin as I have written to her Majesty.' (S. P. Holland, xv.)

[4] Buckhurst to Elizabeth, 27 May 1587, *Cabala*, ii. 39.

de Loo instructing him to inquire how Parma felt about the Danish proposal and directing him, if he found the Prince well disposed, to indicate to him Elizabeth's readiness to send commissioners to Emden, or better still to some more convenient place. De Loo was at the same time to demand a cessation of arms until the effect of the negotiations could be seen.[1] De Loo's reply to this letter was to the effect that Parma was ready and willing to appoint commissioners to treat for peace, but he was not prepared to agree to a cessation of arms until the commissioners were actually convened. His letter had hardly arrived, however, before Morris, one of Sir James Crofts' servants, came post haste from the Low Countries with the news by word of mouth that Parma was prepared to arrange an armistice with Leicester even before the commissioners arrived. Of these two contradictory messages Elizabeth preferred to believe that one which Morris brought. She accordingly directed Burghley to write to de Loo that she would send the commissioners without fail if Parma would arrange an armistice with Leicester. When Burghley suggested that she had better wait until she had got Leicester's opinion on the subject she replied that Leicester would obey orders. Burghley remonstrated that the orders were the very matter in question but was answered peremptorily that so it should be. 'She will', Burghley wrote to Walsingham in recounting the interview, 'that I shall send back for Needham your servant to receive letters to my Lord of Leicester for the purpose and so I pray you return him hither with speed for so her Majesty earnestly commandeth. I am unfit to be an executor of these sudden directions, especially when the effects are so large and dangerous, but lords and ladies command and servants obey.'[2]

But for some reason or other the armistice was not arranged after all. Parma pressed the siege of Sluys with vigour and eventually, as has been observed already, he took the city late in July. The immediate effect of its fall was to dampen Elizabeth's ardour for peace, but it was soon kindled again. Walsingham wrote to Leicester on the 7th of August:

[1] Burghley and Crofts to de Loo, 14 June 1587 (S. P. Flanders, i, no. 239); Walsingham to Buckhurst, 13 June 1587 (S. P. Holland, xv).

[2] Burghley to Walsingham, 16 July 1587 (S. P. Domestic, ccii, no. 56).

'The loss of Sluys has wrought in her Majesty some alteration of her favour towards your Lordship and also towards the cause itself, in such sort as she seemed bent and resolved to abandon those countries and to have revoked your Lordship presently. But now this overture of peace, whereof before she seemed (upon the loss of Sluys) to be in despair, hath calmed those sharp humours, being thoroughly persuaded that the Duke meaneth sincerely and that a peace will fall out accompanied with both honour and safety. Others fear that the overtures of the peace, considering in what terms things stand in those countries, will breed some dangerous schisms there, being the only cause, as some conjecture, why the Duke is so forward in the matter. So as a peace may be made with surety there is nothing more to be desired. I never saw her Majesty's disposition so unfit for the wars as at this present. And as for the States, carrying themselves so unthankfully both towards her Majesty and your Lordship's self as they do, it is most dangerous (considering the condition of that government, which threateneth nothing but ruin) for her Majesty to join her fortune with theirs. There would, notwithstanding, great consideration be had in the disjoining of herself from them. It is not a thing to be done upon a sudden, neither do I see well how it can be done at all with safety, for that it is apparent that without the continuance of her Majesty's support they shall not be able long to hold out, the King of Spain being resolved to prosecute the wars there more effectually than at any time before. Now, when he shall be possessed of those countries, we are to look for a war at our own home; a matter fearful to think of, considering the corruption of this estate, the doubtful terms we stand in with Scotland and how unfurnished we are of martial men to make head to the enemy in case we should be assailed sundry ways (a thing greatly to be feared). I would to God therefore that your Lordship could dispose the hearts of that people to give ear to a peace, seeing both they and we are so unapt for a war.' [1]

Without much doubt the chief obstacle to a peace at this time lay in the attitude of the Dutch themselves. Elizabeth, for all her eagerness, was not quite prepared to ignore their wishes altogether. She had charged Leicester upon his departure for the Low Countries to induce them to consent to a peace. But Leicester had accomplished little or nothing in that direction and until he did so Elizabeth did not feel like beginning formal negotiations. She bade Burghley write to that effect to de Loo in September in reply to a letter in which he had written that

[1] Cotton MSS., Galba D i, f. 244.

Parma was getting impatient at her delay in sending commissioners.[1] Nevertheless she was irritated at the Dutch and particularly irritated at Leicester because of his failure to win them from their unaccommodating attitude.

'I hear', Walsingham wrote to Leicester on the 15th of September, 'as well by others as by Mr. Atye that she disliketh that the overture of the peace hath been so long delayed, wherewith in my opinion her Majesty ought to rest satisfied, considering the weightiness of the reasons that moved your Lordship thereunto; but her Highness is greatly transported with the desire of peace as nothing without that can content her. . . . The Prince of Parma's earnest solicitation for the commissioners coming over, pretending, in respect of the delay therein used, some doubt of her Majesty's sincere and good meaning touching the proceeding in the said treaty, doth greatly provoke her Majesty to hasten the matter and therefore it will be very hard (as your Lordship adviseth) to put over the matter for any long time, considering how earnestly her Majesty is bent therein.'[2]

No doubt Walsingham, even though he was absent from Court at this juncture, was doing everything he could to delay matters. 'To think', he wrote to Leicester on the 21st of September, 'that the King of Spain, having his treasure now come home in greater quantity than ever he had, his forces doubled in those countries when the levies made in Italy and Germany shall be arrived and the Pope ready to back him with three millions of crowns and all against England, will make a peace but with such conditions as will work the overthrow both of her Majesty and of those countries, is but a mere vanity, for always the strongest giveth law to the weaker.'[3]

Even Burghley, apostle of peace though he was, professed at any rate to believe that the Queen was altogether too urgent in the matter. He told Elizabeth frankly that he considered it dangerous 'to run a contrary course in sight of the enemy'. 'I think', he observed to Walsingham, 'my short writing will offend, but I am indeed so chaffed that I cannot hold my peace.'[4]

[1] *Hardwicke Papers*, i. 339–40, undated but probably written about 15 Sept.

[2] Cotton MSS., Galba C vii, f. 329, 15 Sept. 1587, misdated, in the original, 1584.

[3] Ibid., Galba D ii, f. 86.

[4] 5 Sept. 1587, S. P. Domestic, cciii, no. 34. Hume (*The Great Lord Burghley*, pp. 427–8) is of the opinion that Burghley was one of the foremost advocates of peace at this time, basing his opinion apparently on the reports of

But Burghley also was absent from Court and Sir James Crofts, the most ardent of the Spanish partisans, held the field. So that Leicester was commanded sharply to get about his business and honey-sweet letters were sent off to de Loo desiring him to bid Parma be patient for a little.[1] More than that, the English commissioners were actually named and instructed to make ready.[2]

It is interesting to observe that Walsingham had some hopes of disentangling all the difficulties in the Low Countries by cutting the knot straight across. His idea was nothing less than that of tempting the Prince of Parma to sever his allegiance to Spain and to establish himself as an independent prince in the Netherlands. On the 18th of September 1587 one of Walsingham's secretaries drafted a letter to one of Walsingham's agents in Antwerp from which the following is extracted :

'His honour willed me to tell you that he would be glad to hear from you of that he commanded me to write to you about so long since, which was about an overture or motion he wished

Spanish agents in London (*Cal. Spanish*, 1587–1603, p. 166) and on what would seem a priori probable from Burghley's previous attitude. But everything on the subject from Burghley's pen at this time points to the conclusion that though he thought peace desirable he did not believe it expedient to sue for peace at this time. Cf. 'Arguments upon matter of the offer to treat for Peace', 27 Dec. 1587, in Burghley's hand (S. P. Holland, xix). Cf. also Burghley's memorandum to Derby, 27 Nov. 1587 (S. P. Spain, i), quoted by Froude, xii. 408.

[1] *Hardwicke Papers*, i. 340, 344. On 20 Sept. 1587 instructions were drafted for Daniel Rogers to go to the King of Denmark. Rogers was directed to deal with the King about the treaty of peace and to let him understand that the chief obstacle would be religion. He was to urge the King to instruct his commissioners to urge Parma to assent to some toleration for the Dutch Protestants, and to urge the King also to persuade the German princes to join in demanding the same (S. P. Denmark, i).

[2] *Hardwicke Papers*, i. 334, cf. *Cal. Spanish*, 1587–1603, p. 141. It was apparently intended at this time to use Robert Beale, Walsingham's brother-in-law, as one of the commissioners, and Walsingham wrote to Beale to that effect, 2 Sept. (*Cabala*, ii. 49). Apparently Walsingham wrote to Leicester at the same time desiring him to send Beale home. According to Motley (*op. cit.*, ii. 327) Leicester strongly recommended Beale for the job. It appears, however, from Leicester's letter to Walsingham of 17 Sept. 1587 (S. P. Holland, xviii) that such was not the case. 'Albeit,' Leicester wrote, 'you profit him to have him a commissioner (as you say her Majesty would) I must say that you look more to your brother Beale than to the common service for the Church of God, for if you will appoint weak friends to deal with strong adversaries you must look for the success accordingly. And the more I think of that great and weighty cause, the treaty of peace, I mean, the more do I think you be all bound in duty and conscience that be present about her Majesty to persuade her to appoint her wisest, her learnedest and soundest in religion to be in commission for her.'

you to make to the P. there to this effect; that her Majesty here could wish him to provide for himself in taking the possession of those countries, considering the hard measure that both his father and himself had always received at the King of Spain's hands. And her Majesty could far better endure him as Duke of Burgundy and her neighbour there than a King of Spain, in which kind of treaty he should find her Majesty so well disposed as he could wish touching any reasonable conditions he might propound.' [1]

There is evidence that almost a year before this time this same secret agent was making approaches to Parma on the same subject.[2] No doubt Elizabeth herself was aware that these efforts were being made. Some rumours of them even came to the ears of the Spanish ambassador in Paris.[3] They were, it appears, quite abortive. From the point of view of Walsingham's history they are chiefly interesting as throwing light upon his methods.[4] Whatever the Queen's hopes from them may have

[1] A paper endorsed M. to B., 18 Sept. 1587; not dated or addressed, probably from one of Walsingham's secretaries to a spy; reference is made in the letter to the elevation of Allen to the cardinalate, and to the fact that B. is now free to write again (S. P. Holland, xviii).

[2] Cf. a letter from B., dated 29 Oct. 1586 (S. P. Flanders, i), cited by Froude, xii. 201, n. 3. 'That his honour [Walsingham] may make this foundation for sure, that the Prince of Parma for certain is not Spanish, but hath a secret pretension in great colour for Portugal. Somewhat I have felt him. The words which were spoken between us would greatly satisfy him, but time doth not permit. About the offer which your honour did present him touching Holland and Zeeland for him I find him marvellous well disposed.'

[3] *Cal. Spanish*, 1580–1603, p. 140. Mendoza says that Stafford told him that Herbert was instructed to broach this matter to Parma. This, however, seems doubtful, though Walsingham may have said as much to Stafford, knowing he would repeat it to Mendoza and hoping through that channel to sow distrust between Philip II and Parma.

[4] Who the secret agent in the Low Countries was is not quite clear. He usually did not sign his letters, but they are all of them endorsed 'from B.' One such letter endorsed 'from B. in Antwerp' is signed Alessandro de la Torre; it is dated 10 Sept. 1587, and is evidently from some agent who was working to stir up dissension among the English Catholics overseas. Another letter in Italian, dated 24 Oct. 1587, is also signed Alessandro de la Torre and endorsed 'from B. at Antwerp' (S. P. Flanders, i): still another similarly endorsed, dated 2 Dec. 1587 (Harleian MSS. 287, f. 51), refers to factions friendly to Elizabeth at Rome, and begs favour for Aldred's suit.

The probabilities are that de la Torre was an assumed name. Suspicion points to Thomas Barnes, to whom reference has been made in chap. xii, Appendix. After the execution of Mary, Queen of Scots, Barnes was employed by Walsingham among the English Catholics abroad. It is significant to observe that Barnes was engaged later, in 1591, in a project to marry the son of the Prince of Parma to Lady Arabella Stuart (Lechat, *Les Réfugiés anglais aux Pays-Bas*, pp. 168–9). Evidently he knew Italian or he would hardly have been employed in such business. Gilbert Gifford on one occasion

been she held fast to her purpose to push the regular negotiations with Parma as hard as she could. In mid-October, since Leicester seemed unable to win the States to approve of a peace, she determined to send special envoys to them.

'I know', Walsingham wrote to Leicester on the 9th of October, 'you are informed how offensively it is taken that the matter of the peace goeth so slowly forward there.[1] It is reported that both Mr. Herbert and Mr. Ortell shall presently repair over to deal effectually with the States for the advancement of the said peace. And it is also said that our commissioners shall put themselves presently in a readiness to depart into those countries, to the end that when the States have given their assent to yield to the treaty there may be no time lost. There is the more haste made in this matter for that Andrea de Loo doth write that the Prince of Parma doth think he is but mocked and dallied withal and that he doubteth greatly that if the commissioners shall not presently be sent over the said Duke will break off and not proceed to the treaty; which we do believe here to be most true and will by no means be persuaded that the King of Spain and the said Duke do but dally with us, so strong a conceit are we grown to have of both their sincerities, contrary to the opinion of all men of judgement, seeing the great preparations made both by sea and land.

'Sir Edward Stafford hath advertised hither that the French King hath especially sent unto his agent in Spain to learn there whether the King of Spain meant soundly to proceed in this treaty of peace with the Queen, from whom he hath received undoubted answer that the King doth it only to win time and to abuse the Queen of England. This, notwithstanding that Mr. Stafford hath gotten it from one of good account about the King, is offensively taken here, so much do we mislike anything that may hinder the said treaty of peace.'[2]

So Sir John Herbert was dispatched to the Low Countries on the 12th of October to persuade the States to join in treaty with the Queen. He was to promise them that Elizabeth would have as great care for their welfare as for her own if they would

wrote to Thomas Phelippes that Barnes was known to Morgan by the name Pietro Mariani (Morris, *Sir A. Paulet*, p. 381), which suggests Italian connexions. Of course the fact that his letters are endorsed 'From B.' strengthens the case.

[1] Leicester's defence of his tardiness in this particular is given in his letter to Burghley of 30 Sept. 1587 (*Hardwicke Papers*, i. 340); cf. also ibid., i. 351.

[2] Cotton MSS., Galba D ii, f. 146, 9 Oct. 1587, printed in *Hardwicke Papers*, i. 357 ff.

join and to intimate that she would conclude with Spain without them if they would not.[1] Even so it was doubtful whether Elizabeth would wait until she had received his answer. With Walsingham away from Court sick and Crofts in command of the Queen's ear, it was hard to restrain her passion for peace even within reasonable grounds. Herbert wrote to Walsingham from Flushing in November: 'I perceived at my departure from your honour that for a time you would withdraw yourself from dealing in the affairs of State. . . . Your determination in respect of your private health all such as know you must and do approve, yet must they that be of judgement lament that God hath laid his hand upon you at so unseasonable a time.'[2]

It appears indeed that Walsingham's illness was the one thing which saved him from being himself appointed one of the commissioners to treat for the peace. He wrote to Leicester on the 12th of November:

> 'A letter from the Prince of Parma to her Majesty hath bred in her such a dangerous security as all advertisements of perils and dangers are neglected and great expedition is used in dispatching of the commissioners, Sir Am[ias Paulet] being now appointed to supply Mr. John Herbert's [place, where]unto I hear, that if my sickness had not been the im[pediment], I had been preferred, which would have drawn her [Majesty's] displeasure upon me, being fully resolved in no sor[t to have] accepted thereof; for that I would be loath to be em[ployed in] a service that all men of judgement may see appa[rently, in] respect of the handling of the matter, cannot but work [her] Majesty's ruin. I pray God I and others of my opinion may prove in this false prophets.'[3]

[1] An anonymous correspondent wrote to the Earl of Shrewsbury, 11 Oct. 1587: 'Mr. Secretary hath been ill and at home in his house this good while, troubled with his old disease, the tympany and carnosity. It will be this month yet before he be able to go to the court, good gentleman, the more the pity, for he is very unquiet in mind; for this course [for peace] if it hold, goeth against his opinion' (Lodge, *Illustrations of British History*, ii. 318). Herbert's instructions, dated 12 Oct. 1587, are in S. P. Holland, xviii.

[2] 15 Nov. 1587, S. P. Holland, xix.

[3] Cotton MSS., Galba D ii, f. 178. This letter is printed in full in *Hardwicke Papers*, i. 359, but with many inaccuracies. The Hardwicke version gives Sir Jas. Crofts instead of Sir Amias Paulet. In the original, which is damaged by fire, only 'Sir Am' of the name remains, but Paulet seems the more probable emendation since he was one of the commissioners and was more likely a substitute candidate than Crofts, who must have been chosen among the first. Cf. also *Cal. Spanish*, 1587–1603, p. 174.

However, the commissioners did not go and Elizabeth seems to have wavered somewhat in November about the desirability of sending them. According to a Spanish agent in London 'on the 17th instant she was in a tremendous rage with Walsingham, the Treasurer and the Controller upon whom she heaped a thousand insults, saying that it was through them that she was induced to negotiate for peace with the Prince of Parma, who had drawn her on with fair words, so that while she was listening to them she might cease her preparations and so be caught unawares.'[1] On the face of it this report seems hardly credible so far as it refers to Walsingham at any rate, for it may be presumed that even so irrational a creature as Elizabeth would have realized the absurdity of laying the blame for her treaty making upon Walsingham's shoulders. Yet it is undoubted that both Burghley and Walsingham were objects of her censure at this time, and evidently for the reason that they had neglected to provide against the dangers which beset her. This is apparent from the fact that Walsingham felt obliged early in December to draw up a 'Memorial of Things executed at home and advices given for foreign matters abroad by A. B. [Lord Burghley] and C. D. [Sir Francis Walsingham] tending to the Defence and Preservation of her Majesty and her Estate'. In this paper Walsingham began at first with a description of what he and his colleague had done for home defence. He pointed out that chiefly through their efforts 26,000 footmen and —— horse had been organized, trained and supplied with powder and match for the defence of the sea coasts, 'a thing never before put in execution in any of her Majesty's predecessor's times'; and that 24,000 foot and —— horse had also been levied and trained for a bodyguard to the Queen. At the same time, he protested, both he and Burghley had done everything in their power to remove all causes of discontentment among the Queen's subjects and to set right all legitimate grievances of foreigners. In proof of this he appealed for the former to the 'censure and opinion' of all Englishmen and for the latter to the testimony of resident foreign ambassadors.

With regard to foreign affairs Walsingham bade the Queen recall how importunately both he and Burghley had urged her

[1] 23 Nov. 1587, *Cal. Spanish*, 1587–1603, p. 166.

to assure herself of Scotland, how they had laboured with her in behalf of the King of Navarre and how they had pressed her to advance enough money to the Dutch that they might have taken the field in force, saved Sluys, cut off Parma's reinforcements and enabled the Queen to make peace on honourable terms.

'Lastly', Walsingham concluded, 'her Majesty doth also know how, immediately upon Sir Francis Drake's arrival into this realm, after the taking of the carrack, she was advised both by A. B. and C. D. to have returned him again to the sea with an increase of forces, which if it had been performed, there was great likelihood to man's judgement that the West India fleet should have been intercepted, whereby the present storms that now lay over this realm might have been both cleared and prevented.'[1]

After six months of enforced silence upon all matters opposed to peace Walsingham must have rejoiced at the opportunity to prove his zeal for more aggressive measures. But if he cherished any delusion that Elizabeth really meant to leave her peace talks and love days and grasp her sword firmly he was soon disabused. Before December was out the Queen was once again calling for peace at any price. She ordered Burghley and Walsingham to press forward the negotiations, and when Walsingham inquired what she meant to do about the knotty point of religion she announced angrily that she would agree about religion and everything else.[2] For all that it seems not unlikely that Leicester's return from the Low Countries had the effect of strengthening considerably the position of those in the Privy Council opposed to a hasty peace.[3]

At any rate he and Walsingham together succeeded in preventing any positive action until the following February.[4]

[1] 2 Dec. 1587 (S. P. Domestic, ccvi, no. 2); blanks are left in the original for horsemen levied. This paper is endorsed in Burghley's hand, 'From Mr. Secretary by Mr. Robert Beale.' There can be no doubt that Walsingham was the author of it, and internal evidence points strongly to the belief that A. B. and C. D. are meant to stand for Burghley and Walsingham. It is doubtful whether Burghley was in favour of sending Drake forth again in the summer of 1587 (*Cal. Spanish*, 1587–1603, p. 126), but no doubt Walsingham was, and since he was making out a joint case for himself and his colleague, he naturally included Burghley in this as well.

[2] 27 Dec. 1587, *Cal. Spanish*, 1587–1603, p. 184.

[3] Ibid., p. 175. Leicester, upon his return, is reported to have been in highest favour with the Queen, *Rutland MSS.* i. 234.

[4] *Cal. Spanish*, 1587–1603, pp. 184, 191.

Probably they did not hope to do any more than drag the matter along until Philip was forced to show his hand. Walsingham had long ago reached the conclusion that the Spaniards were merely using the negotiations as a screen to hide their military and naval preparations, and a glance at the correspondence between Philip and Parma at this juncture proves that Walsingham was entirely right.[1] Leicester was of the same opinion. Lord Burghley, however, who had a provoking way of seeing the other side of the case when resolution was most essential, began to find reasons for believing that Philip might be sincerely anxious for peace after all.[2] Yet it is not at all certain that they had not all of them decided to humour the Queen's whim and to let her play at treaty making while they pushed forward the military and naval preparations with vigour. They no doubt realized that Elizabeth's inveterate habits of procrastination could be depended upon to defeat even her own purposes of peace in the long run. Burghley's position was probably that of one who sincerely prayed for peace but believed in being fully prepared for war. 'Surely, Sir', he wrote to Walsingham in April, 'as God will be best pleased with peace, so in nothing can her Majesty content her realm better than in procuring of peace, which if it cannot be had yet is she excused before God and the world.'[3] Walsingham for his part accepted the peace playing with as much fortitude as he could master. But his God was the God of battles and his prayers were offered not for the tedious diplomatists about to take ship for Ostend, but for Howard off Queensborough and Drake's squadron tugging at its cables in Plymouth harbour.

On the 1st of February Elizabeth ordered Herbert, who had been in the Low Countries since October, seeking to interest the Dutch in the peace project, to come home. At the same time she bade him tell the Dutch leaders that she had waited for their co-operation as long as she intended to. It was now her intention to dispatch her commissioners overseas. If they wished to take part in the negotiations they had better appoint

[1] Motley, ii. 303 ff.

[2] 10 Jan. 1587/8, 'Considerations for and against a Treaty with Spain', in Burghley's hand, Cotton MSS., Galba C xi, f. 81.

[3] 10 Apr. 1588, S. P. Domestic, ccix, no. 83.

their commissioners forthwith. Otherwise she would go ahead without them. And she proceeded at once to act upon this statement. In mid-February she sent away her commissioners to Ostend. Their instructions seem to have given them a great deal of latitude upon most of the points at issue. They were first of all to arrange if possible for a peace between the King and the Dutch; and they were to urge very strongly the need of toleration for Dutch protestants, but neither of these points apparently was to be pushed to the breaking point. Similarly they were to avoid committing the Queen in precise terms to the abandonment of Don Antonio; they were to urge her right of free trade in the Indies and they were to protest against the persecution of English merchants by the Spanish Inquisition. But these points again were not insisted upon. It was characteristically Elizabethan that the one clause in the instructions from which the Queen admitted no deviation was that the money she had spent in the Low Countries should be repaid and that she should be permitted to retain the cautionary towns until it was repaid. In a word, if she could get her money back, she was apparently prepared at a pinch to let all other matters at issue between her and Spain go by the board.[1]

There were five commissioners altogether, the Earl of Derby, Lord Cobham, Sir James Crofts, Valentino Dale, and Dr. John Rogers. Dale and Rogers were trained civilians and Dale had had considerable diplomatic experience both at Vienna and at Paris. Derby and Cobham and Crofts were Privy Councillors. It had originally been intended to send Sir Amias Paulet as well, who more than any one else in the group represented the views of Leicester and Walsingham.[2] Unfortunately his failing health prevented him from going. Lord Cobham, however, in spite of the fact that he was usually regarded as a partisan of the anti-

[1] Cf. 'Project for instructions for the Queen's Commissioners sent to the Low Countries' (S. P. Flanders, i). The full instructions are preserved in S. P. Flanders, ii, 7.

[2] *Cal. Spanish*, 1587–1603, pp. 175, 191. According to Mendoza, Paulet was originally charged with a private commission to try and lure Parma to abandon Spain and to seize the Low Countries for himself (ibid. 189) but subsequently this commission was revoked (ibid. 214). It is interesting to observe in this connexion that Cobham wrote to Walsingham, 16 Apr. 1588, that he thought the occasion now opportune, Parma being loved by all save the Spaniards, that he might be sounded 'to continue and become master of all'. (Harleian MSS. 287, f. 77.)

Leicesterians, shared Walsingham's views as to the futility of the peace and seems in some sort to have served his purpose in blocking it.[1]

It is not necessary to trace in detail the abortive negotiations which followed. Parma's commissioners appeared to be bent on killing time and the English commissioners as a whole were not disinclined to humour them. Sir James Crofts, who was the one real enthusiast for the peace, did his best to expedite matters. When he found his colleagues disposed to stand on terms he undertook to negotiate with Parma without reference to them. Crofts' attitude came out well in a letter which he wrote to his mistress on the 22nd of February: 'Those', he wrote, 'that recommend war recommend it for sundry respects; some for war's sake, as I should do perhaps if I were young and a soldier; others for religion; others for spoil and robbery, whereof your Majesty feeleth too much. They are all inclined to their peculiar interests, caring nothing for the Prince's treasure, the impoverishing of the subject and the overthrow of trade. It is my duty to remind your Majesty that if you do not stand fast in what is best for the whole estate and commonwealth, many practices will be used to persuade yourself against yourself.'[2]

All this was true enough and no doubt it fitted well to the Queen's fancy. But Crofts was to discover, as Leicester had discovered, that his arguments lost weight with her when they came by post from overseas. It is not unlikely indeed that Walsingham had realized that fact and had felt that Crofts could do far less damage at Ostend than he could at Court with his whisperings in the royal ear. At any rate Crofts was to learn that his private dealings with Parma found small favour with his mistress. When first she heard of them she bade Derby and Cobham rebuke Crofts sharply and command him to act no more hereafter without his colleagues. His manner of dealing, she protested was such 'as might give just cause to

[1] Cobham wrote to Walsingham, 20 Mar. 1588, that he observed from Walsingham's letters that he was still opposed to the peace making. 'Oppose yourself still', Cobham added, 'against such resolutions for, for mine own part, I would think myself most unhappy to be a means to so conclude an irreligious peace.' (Harleian MSS. 287, f. 71.)

[2] Quoted in Froude, xii. 435, n. 4.

the world to give ear to such jealous conceits as have been given out of his unsound affection towards us.' [1]

It is clear enough that Walsingham stood beside the royal shoulder when Elizabeth penned these words. Crofts himself must have been as much surprised as he was grieved to hear them, for he was probably right in believing that his own eager efforts for peace came nearer to coinciding with the wishes of his mistress than did the dilatory tactics of his colleagues. Very likely he ascribed the letter to the temporary influence of his opponents and felt justified in going ahead with his particular course in spite of it. This at any rate was what he decided to do. Walsingham perhaps perceived this and knowing the imperious temper of his mistress realized that Crofts was courting disaster. It was, however, no part of Walsingham's plan to avert such a catastrophe. Quite the contrary, from his point of view nothing was more desirable than a breach between Crofts and the Queen. It is therefore not surprising to discover that instead of warning Crofts off he lured him on. The private letter which Walsingham wrote to him just after Elizabeth had berated him for his frowardness is a masterpiece in its way. It is circumspect, cautious, not so effusive as to lead Crofts to question the writer's sincerity, yet distinctly encouraging.

'I am very glad', Walsingham wrote, 'to find by your late letters your faith strengthened touching the hope you have always had of the good success of the present treaty. It is notwithstanding greatly doubted here that when you shall resort to the body of the matter, being as yet but entered into the bark, there will fall out some difficulties of very hard digestion, especially for that the States cannot be drawn to join with her Majesty in the treaty, without whose concurrency men of best judgement here do think it hard to make a sound peace, such as shall carry surety withal. It may be that you there may draw some more light from the other side to work in you satisfaction in that behalf than yet we can perceive here; for yourself, all men here conceive that you carry a very good and honourable meaning in the prosecution of this cause, a thing most necessary for her Majesty and the realm. Only it is doubted you may be overreached by some Spanish cautels whereof I doubt not, according to the long experience you have had in matters of state, you will have a watchful eye.' [2]

[1] 17 Apr. 1588, S. P. Flanders, iii, f. 146.
[2] 22 Apr. 1588, S. P. Flanders, iii, f. 175.

Crofts might well have scented danger in these friendly words from an inveterate enemy, but he was, as Parma himself remarked, 'a weak old man of seventy with very little sagacity '[1] and more likely saw in Walsingham's letter a grudging approval of his conduct than a practice to beguile him. At all events he held his course. In May, once more impatient at the procrastination of his colleagues, he set forth to Ghent on a private visit to Parma and there on his own responsibility made an offer of terms which he told Parma the Queen would accept if he negotiated with her directly. The gist of his offer was that if Philip would withdraw his foreign troops from the Netherlands and restore the old administration there and allow so much toleration to the Dutch in religion as he might do in conscience and honour, the Queen would make her peace with him, withdraw her troops and hand over to Spain the towns she held in pawn.[2]

Crofts was probably right in thinking that the terms which he proposed approximated closely to Elizabeth's own view of the matter, or at any rate to a view which she had been disposed to entertain favourably in the past. But when his report of his interview reached the Queen Walsingham and Leicester had her ear, her fleet was on the seas and her soldiers flocking to arms. England at large had girded up its loins for heroic enterprises and was in no mood for the betrayal of old allies by humiliating treaties of peace. Elizabeth might have resisted her Council but she had not the courage to resist her people. So Crofts, poor fool, confidently expecting her approbation, had poured upon his 'white head witless' the vials of her wrath. She rebuked him for his temerity, indignantly disavowed his offers of peace, and bade him come home and answer for his disobedience.[3]

Meanwhile the formal negotiations dragged their slow length along. After three months of unprofitable wrangling over credentials and meeting-places the English and the Spanish commissioners finally came together at the end of May.[4] Then

[1] Motley, ii. 386. [2] Strype, *Annals*, iii, pt. 2, p. 5.

[3] Elizabeth to Peace Commissioners, 21 May 1588, S. P. Flanders, iii, f. 357. Later, when Crofts pleaded sickness, she excused him from coming home, but she threw him into prison when he finally did return in August (Strype, *Annals*, iii, pt. 2, p. 124). [4] Motley, ii. 393.

they spent another month trying to agree about a cessation of arms. While they wrangled back and forth twelve thousand copies of 'a roaring hellish papal bull' excommunicating Elizabeth were being struck off by the presses at Antwerp [1] and Parma himself was supervising the translation of Cardinal Allen's pamphlet denouncing Elizabeth and invoking Catholic England to rise up and depose her.[2] It ought to have been perfectly obvious that the time had passed for peace making, yet even as late as the middle of July Burghley advocated that the negotiations be continued [3] and Elizabeth refrained from denouncing Parma's conduct 'lest it might breed a present breach'.[4] So it came about that at the very moment that Howard and Drake were pouring their broadsides into the Spanish Armada in the Channel, Derby and his colleagues were solemnly discussing terms on the Belgian shore and Crofts was writing home to Burghley that he felt convinced of Philip's sincere desire for peace.[5]

It is rather curious to discover that at just about the same time that the peace commissioners were beginning their *pourparlers* in the Low Countries Walsingham was once more endeavouring to open negotiations for peace direct with Spain. There is very little evidence about this matter but enough to substantiate it. Sometime in April 1588 Walsingham wrote a letter to some one going from Florence into Spain in which Walsingham urged his correspondent to do his best to further good amity between England and Spain. 'And although', he added, 'I know that I am reputed a principal nourisher of the discord between their Majesties yet I pray you assure yourself, whatsoever you hear to the contrary, that no councillor the Queen my mistress hath doth more desire a peace than myself, so far forth as may stand with her Majesty's honour and safety.' [6]

[1] Burghley to Walsingham, 24 June 1588, S. P. Domestic, ccxi, no. 56.

[2] Motley, ii. 406.

[3] Burghley to Walsingham, 18 July 1588, S. P. Domestic, ccxii, no. 63; Burghley even advocated sending a special envoy to Parma (Laughton, *Armada Papers*, i. 268).

[4] Walsingham to Burghley, 18 July 1588, Harleian MSS. 6994, f. 126.

[5] Motley, ii. 407. The English commissioners returned to England 8 Aug. 1588. Walsingham to Burghley, 8 Aug. 1588: 'The commissioners landed this morning at Dover. They write nothing touching the Prince of Parma's proceedings' (Harl. MSS. 6994, f. 136).

[6] Apr. 1588, S. P. Spain, iii, 'Minute of a letter to A. B. sent from Florence into Spain.'

The person to whom this letter was addressed can only be guessed at, but the probabilities are that he was Giovanni Figliazzi, who had been the ambassador of the Grand Duke of Tuscany at the Court of Madrid,[1] and who had been dispatched by the King of Spain to Florence sometime in the winter of 1587–8 with a view to arranging a marriage between Ferdinand, the new Grand Duke of Tuscany,[2] and some princess affiliated with the Spanish royal house. Now Figliazzi was an old acquaintance of one of Walsingham's agents in Florence, a man who called himself Pompeo Pellegrini. Pellegrini in a letter to Walsingham in February had commended Figliazzi as a staunch friend of England's and had recommended that Walsingham write to him.[3] It seems probable therefore that Walsingham wrote the letter already quoted to Figliazzi shortly after his return to Spain in the spring, sending it by way of Italy under cover to Pellegrini who was himself in Spain at the same time. The effect of the letter is described in a letter from Pellegrini to Walsingham of the 7th of June.[4] As soon as Figliazzi received

[1] *Cal. Venetian*, 1581–91, pp. 317, 318.

[2] Ferdinand succeeded his brother Francis, who died 19 Oct. 1587, *Cambridge Mod. Hist.* iii. 396.

[3] P. Pellegrini to Walsingham, 1/11 Feb. 1587/8: 'The *Duke of Florence* hath begun speech with the *Archduke Charles* for his daughter which is here holded will take effect, the rather to content the *King of Spain*, from whom is come hither *Gian Figliazzi, a Knight of Malta*, my great friend and well known to Mr. *Waad* at his being in Spain. This gentleman is very discreet and passing courteous and of nature inclined to do good and none of these *boutefeus* and to you in particular much affectionate. . . . He hath divers times dealt with the *King of Spain* about our matters so commanded by him, in which reasonings he hath often debated with the *King of Spain* and alleged just reasons why her *Majesty* was to be offended with that manner of dealing, and especially about the affront used to *her Majesty's messenger* when he was there, whose counsel, if *Mr. Waad* had followed, things had no doubt fallen out better. The *King of Spain* liketh so well of this gentleman as he offered him large *stipend* to stay with him, and here he is much in grace, to our matters, I know not how it falleth out, greatly affectionate and to your person, as I say in particular, much addicted, whereof I thought good to touch, that if you will write him a letter of thanks, inferring that you have understood his good will to *her Majesty* and to that *crown*, as to yourself also, I think it to very good purpose, he having good means out of *Spain*, and, writing this letter, make me the deliverer.' (Harl. MSS. 286, f. 122, words in italics in cipher.)

[4] This letter is calendared in *Cal. Salisbury MSS.* iii. 327. Neither the writer nor the person to whom it was addressed is indicated, but circumstantial evidence points to the conclusion that it was from Pellegrini to Walsingham. This must be the letter to which Walsingham refers in a letter of 18 July 1588 to Burghley, in which he begs Burghley not to let any one else see the letter in cipher, since he does not wish to put Cavalier Figliazzi in danger. (Harl. MSS. 6994, f. 128.)

it he went to court and conferred with Idiaquez, one of the King of Spain's secretaries. The proposal was not very cordially received at the Spanish court. They said it was 'an ordinary meal of Secretary Walsingham's corn', and that heretofore Walsingham had been tampering in a like manner with others and that all was but abuse and craft. They complained that the letter was too general and therefore they refused to have anything more to do with the matter. So Walsingham's efforts seem to have come to nothing. Figliazzi told Pellegrini to tell Walsingham that if the matter had been broached to him earlier he might have accomplished more, but that now that the Armada was ready for the seas and the Duke of Guise triumphant in France, he thought the Spanish would hardly come to terms but rather try their fortune.

It would be idle to conjecture exactly what Walsingham's motives were in this separate bid for peace. On the face of it, it looks like another attempt on his part to direct the *pourparlers* into channels which he might more easily control. Possibly he wanted to get a more direct line on Philip of Spain's intentions than it was possible to get from the tedious negotiations in the Low Countries. There is little likelihood that he either desired or expected that his efforts would result in peace, notwithstanding his protestations. Probably the Spaniards were right in denouncing the whole matter as 'abusions and craft'. At all events Walsingham ascertained that there was small indication of a sentiment favourable to peace in Spain and no doubt he turned Pellegrini's report to some purpose by using it as an argument to dissipate Elizabeth's own hopes of peace.

There is a letter from Burghley to Figliazzi written shortly after Walsingham's death among the Lansdowne MSS. (ciii, f. 68), which throws some further light upon this matter. In it Burghley told Figliazzi of Walsingham's death and informed him that the Queen had commended to Burghley the consideration of such things as passed between Walsingham and Figliazzi. Burghley expressed Elizabeth's goodwill towards the Duke of Tuscany and her thanks for the efforts he had made to mediate a peace between England and Spain and indicated the Queen's wish 'that the intelligence begun betwixt you and Mr. Secretary should not be let fall or broken off by his death but continued by the interposition of me, being . . . of inward acquaintance with the said Mr. Secretary in all his public actions since he came first to public service'. This letter proves that Figliazzi was in regular correspondence with Walsingham for some time before his death in 1590, and proves also that the Florentine had been involved in efforts to arrange a peace between England and Spain.

One of the most complicated factors in the whole business was the increasing estrangement between Elizabeth and her Dutch allies. The seeds of this estrangement, as has been pointed out already, were sown during Leicester's régime. In Leicester's conflict with the Dutch leaders in the States General and particularly with Barneveldt and Maurice of Nassau, he had not scrupled to join forces with democratic, ultra-Calvinistic factions in some of the large towns. In consequence he taught all those elements in the United Provinces who were opposed to the control of the States General to look for support to England. This was true as well during Leicester's second expedition to the Low Countries as during his first one. It was notably true after his final departure thence in November 1587. He did not at that time relinquish his authority, but placed his Council of State in general charge and Lord Willoughby in command of the English forces. Willoughby discovered as soon as he took command that he was called upon to father all sorts of popular discontents. Colonel Sonoy, who had been placed by Leicester in charge of Medemblik in North Holland, had ambitions to emancipate himself from the control of the Provincial Estates of Holland. He therefore refused to submit to the government of Count Maurice, pleaded his oath to Leicester, and called upon Elizabeth to back him. Provinincq, the successful leader of the popular uprising in Utrecht against its old governors, leaned heavily on English support. The garrisons at Gertruidenberg, at Vere, at Arnemuyden, and at some other places, whose antagonism to the States General rose from the fact that they were not paid their wages, appealed to the English also. Poor Willoughby had his hands full in trying to compose all these differences. He seems himself to have had an honest desire to restore peace and goodwill[1] but he was considerably handicapped during the first five months of his service by the ambiguity of his position. Leicester had decided to resign his position as governor-general in December 1587, but his resignation was not formally presented to the States until the following March.[2] Meanwhile Willoughby found himself forced to play

[1] *Cal. Ancaster MSS.*, p. xvi.

[2] Killigrew to Burghley, 18 Apr. 1588: 'Since my L. of Leicester's resignation (which being sent to me enclosed in a letter from your Lordship and Mr. Secretary dated 22 February I received at Dortrecht the 14th of March,

the part of deputy general and to give some countenance to the acts of Leicester's partisans even when he did not approve them. After Leicester resigned Willoughby's task became easier, but he was still of course subject to the Queen's orders and Leicester had the royal ear. The difficulty with regard to Sonoy was finally settled early in April—the Dutch in fact bought him off with a fat sum of money, but the mutinous garrisons remained to breed trouble.[1] Sir William Russell, English commander at Flushing, strongly advised that Elizabeth take the Captains of Vere and Arnemuyden into her own pay if only to safeguard her forces at Flushing. Walsingham's reply to Russell, dated the 8th of April, reveals his position in the matter:

'I do not find her Majesty disposed to make any increase of charges either by the entertaining of the garrisons now in Vere and Arnemuyden or by reinforcing of the said garrisons and the levying of new companies to be placed at the Hake within that island by the said captains required. I did at the first not greatly like to enter into any dealing with the said captains, not for that I did not think it a thing most necessary and profitable for her Majesty to be assured of the said towns, but because I did see no disposition in her Majesty to take a thorough course with the matter, a manner of proceeding we hold in all our actions, both at home and abroad, which breedeth both danger and dishonour.

'I have moved her Majesty that some consultation might be had what answer were fit to be given to the said captains, as a matter that importeth greatly the conservation of the town whereof you are governor, for that it is greatly to be doubted that, if the said captains may not receive contentment from her Majesty, being fallen into a mortal hatred of the States, they will rather fall to the enemy than ever yield to be reconciled to them.'[2]

Two days later Walsingham wrote to Willoughby with reference to Gertruidenberg in Holland: 'It is greatly feared here that the town of Gertruidenberg will fall to the enemy, which

and at my return from thence delivered it to the States General the 21st of the same, not without suspicion and speech also bruited abroad that I had kept it a long time, because the date thereof was in December) but since the delivery of the same a great change and alteration is fallen out, and good hope of reconcilement.' (S. P. Holland, xxiii, f. 100.)

[1] *Cal. Ancaster MSS.*, pp. 121–6.

[2] 8 Apr. 1588, S. P. Holland, xxiii, f. 58.

will lay open a dangerous gap into Holland. I fear your Lordship's travail to work a reconcilement by way of mediation will take no great effect. Surely in my poor conceit, having embarked ourselves so far with that country as we have and the issue of the peace being so doubtful as it is, such a town would not have been lost. For no one thing would more have hastened the peace than if her Majesty might have gotten the possession of those towns which of late offered themselves to be at her devotion. But regard of charges hindereth or rather overthroweth all good actions.'[1]

Even more illuminating is Walsingham's letter of the 28th of April to Captain Christopher Blunt, one of the most active Leicesterians in the Low Countries, with reference to certain suggestions of his as to 'how her Majesty might make profit of the present division there betwixt the States and the soldiers and the people'. 'That course', Walsingham wrote, 'might be embraced if her Majesty had a disposition to hold fast that which she may lay hold on, but the matter having been considered of here, it is thought generally that unless her Highness have another intention in the action than she hath, which is only to assist, it were over dangerous a course to nourish the said division and therefore better to compound things and to unite and to enable them to bear the burden of the wars, seeing we ourselves mean not to do it.'[2]

It is not difficult from these extracts to discover how Walsingham felt about this matter of dealing with the mutinous garrisons. At first he strongly favoured supporting them in their position, partly because he feared they might otherwise go over to the enemy, partly, one may suspect, because he hoped they might serve as stepping stones to lead his reluctant mistress farther and farther into Dutch affairs. But later, as he came to see that Elizabeth had gone as far as she meant to go, he concluded the cause would be better served by composing these internal disorders than by aggravating them.

He accordingly addressed himself to that task. 'I desire to tell you', he wrote on the 30th of April to Provinincq, the leader

[1] 10 Apr. 1588, S. P. Holland, xxiii, f. 60.

[2] 28 Apr. 1588, *Cal. Ancaster MSS.*, p. 131; cf. also Walsingham to Deventer, 30 Apr. 1588, ibid.

of the Utrecht insurgents, 'that since this way of reconciliation removes all suspicion and jealousy of ill-treatment from those who may have been doubtful, there is no longer cause for any to hold aloof, and I trust to your prudence and wisdom (amongst others) to give all the help that in you lies, so that the state, being strengthened by mutual concord and good understanding, may the better, by the help of her Majesty, (which is very great considering the other great difficulties in which she is at present embroiled) make head against the common enemy.'[1]

Walsingham's letter to Lord Willoughby of the 21st of May advocated the same policy, and late in June he bade Captain Blunt do the best he could to reconcile the warring factions in Utrecht. 'Touching the state of Utrecht', he wrote to Blunt, 'I am likewise of the same opinion with you that, considering the doubtfulness of these times, there can be no better remedy used than to hold on in persuading earnestly with them that, for the present strengthening of those countries, they would grow to some good and sound union amongst themselves.' In a postscript to this letter Walsingham added in his own hand, 'It is a common mishap in these days to be subject to misreports. The greatest are not free from that mishap. A man that is armed with sincerity contemneth those blasts. And therefore, good Sir Christopher, let not the envy and malice of detractors trouble you. Assure yourself I will not fail to defend you, when your credit shall be called in question.'[2] Here perhaps Walsingham anticipated Blunt's fear of Leicester's hostility in the pursuit of a course opposed to his policy. Indeed the memory of what had happened to Wilkes and Norris and even Lord Buckhurst may well have daunted 'good Sir Christopher'. But Leicester was apparently too busy with other things to pick more quarrels with old friends in the Netherlands and so the policy of reconciliation proceeded with such success that, when the Armada actually did appear, dissensions among the Dutch had been perceptibly lessened if not altogether banished.

There was, however, one further demonstration on the part of the ultra-Calvinists in the Provinces at the beginning of July

[1] *Cal. Ancaster MSS.*, p. 132, from a French original.
[2] 21 June 1588, ibid., p. 154.

which is of some interest because of Walsingham's part in it. This took the form of a deputation from the Dutch churches, who came over to England to implore the Queen to accept the sovereignty of the Low Countries, to break off her negotiations with Spain, and to provide henceforth that the reformed religion might be freely exercised in the Provinces to the exclusion of any others. Although this deputation came with permission of Count Maurice and the States General it is obvious that it represented the Leicesterian faction. It was not from any agreement with their purposes, but probably because he realized the futility of their mission, that Maurice had permitted them to depart. They held their first interviews with Walsingham and submitted to his consideration long and tedious discourses, 'filled with astounding parallels between their own position and that of the Hebrews, Assyrians and other distinguished nations of antiquity.' Walsingham commended their sentiments but advised brevity. The Queen, he said, could not be induced to read papers more than a page long. He warned them moreover that his mistress was not so zealous in matters religious as she might be. Political considerations were apt to bear greater weight with her. However, he assured them that, so far as the peace negotiations were concerned, they were about to be terminated and not likely, after the infamous libels which Spain had launched against the Queen, to be soon renewed. With regard to the practice of religion in the Low Countries, Walsingham said he thought that Elizabeth was disposed to demand toleration for a short period; after which the matter was to be settled by the States General. The deputies protested that the majority of the States were popish. Even so, Walsingham replied, they will hardly adventure another war on that issue. His comments on the demand for the exclusion of all the worship from the Provinces save that of the reformed religion is particularly interesting because it throws light upon his own position on the question of toleration. 'Her Majesty', he said, 'is well disposed to permit some exercise of their religion to the Papists. So far as regards my own feelings, if we were now in the beginning of the reformation and the Papacy were still entire, I should willingly concede such exercise; but now that the Papacy has been overthrown I think it would not be safe to give such permission. When we were disputing at the time of the pacification of Ghent whether the Popish religion should be partially permitted, the Prince of Orange was of the affirmative opinion, but I who was then in Antwerp entertained the contrary conviction.' It is evident that Walsingham's toleration was of a parcel with that of most men of his time, he favoured toleration when his faith was likely to suffer from the lack of it and opposed toleration when his faith had the upper hand. In this respect he stands in rather sorry contrast to the broader view of the Prince of Orange. Yet it may be questioned whether the tolerant spirit of Orange, like that of Elizabeth and Henry of Navarre, did not spring from the fact that religious considerations were subordinated by him to political considerations. His toleration like theirs was rather one of compromise than of conviction, a necessary expedient to keep the peace rather than an ideal to be fought for. Walsingham's bigotry, like that of Philip of Spain, had at least the virtue of being not only sincere but vigorous and militant. It was a matter for which he was prepared to fight hard and sacrifice much and it has a heroic quality pretty generally lacking in the religious attitudes of his more tolerant contemporaries as a whole.

Anyway, Walsingham while expressing his own position took care to impress upon the Dutch deputies the fact that his mistress was of another mind. And when they were received by her a few days later they found that he had interpreted her point of view accurately enough. The upshot of the matter and the only positive result from their mission was that the Queen promised to support the Dutch and to demand for them free exercise of their religion in any agreement which she might make with Spain. She would not consider their offer of sovereignty and she refused to support their demand for a monopoly of religion.[1]

It seems strange, looking backwards, to discover Dutch envoys in England anxious lest Elizabeth should sell them out to Spain scarcely a fortnight before the Armada sailed up the Channel. Yet so it was, and certain it is that their fears were not without foundation. Though grim war was at Elizabeth's very threshold peace was still the thought nearest her heart

[1] Cf. Motley (quoting from Bor), ii. 438–44.

and there can be little doubt that until the very moment when Howard and Medina Sidonia exchanged the first broadsides off Plymouth harbour she did not accept war as inevitable. This is not altogether surprising. For thirty years her councillors had been urging her to prepare for war with Spain, and for thirty years war had not come. Small wonder if she began to regard herself as immune from war and looked sceptical when Walsingham and Burghley solemnly warned her of the impending danger. The consequence of her attitude was that such preparations as were made to meet the Spanish attack were made more or less in spite of her.

In the making of these preparations no one in England, with the possible exception of Lord Burghley, was more active than Francis Walsingham. His task was a twofold one. Not only did he have to make England ready to meet the blow when it fell, but he also had to discover when and with what force the blow was to fall.

It is not easy to trace the various ramifications of Walsingham's secret service for obtaining information about Spanish designs. Dr. James Welwood, writing a hundred years after the event, tells an ingenious story of the way in which Walsingham discovered Philip's intentions against England. According to Welwood Walsingham heard from Spain that Philip had dispatched a letter to the Pope acquainting him with the true design of his preparations. This letter the King wrote in his own hand and did not reveal the contents of it even to his most intimate councillors. But Walsingham no sooner heard of the dispatch than he sent orders to one of his spies in Rome to procure a copy of it. The spy thereupon induced a gentleman of the Pope's bed-chamber to extract the letter out of the Pope's cabinet. This the gentleman succeeded in doing by stealing the Pope's keys out of his pocket while he slept. So Walsingham in due course got sight of the letter and all the doings of the Spanish King were made plain to him.[1]

[1] Welwood goes on to say that Walsingham found a way to retard the Spanish invasion for a whole year by getting the Spanish bills protested at Genoa, which would have supplied them with money to carry on their preparations (Welwood, *Memoirs* (ed. 1820), pp. 8–9). There was a tradition at the Charterhouse School that Thomas Sutton, founder of the school and a rich merchant of Elizabethan times, was largely instrumental in having the Spanish bills of

Unfortunately this story, which has been repeated more than once, is absolutely unsupported by contemporary evidence. On the face of it, it seems hardly probable. Even as early as the year 1586 the fact of Philip's naval preparations were patent even to casual observers and almost every tavern gossip in Spain knew that these preparations were designed against England. There was little need for Walsingham's spies to risk damnation by picking the pocket of Christ's vicar, when every merchant trader coming from Spanish ports was full of the news. And it was from such traders that Walsingham seems to have got his first information of Spanish designs.[1] Obviously these reports were vague and general in character, but they were sufficient to put Walsingham on his guard and sufficient also, it appears, to induce the Queen to consent to Drake's voyage to the Spanish coast.

In the spring of 1587, shortly after Drake's departure, Walsingham apparently began to make more careful provision for espionage in Spain. It must have been about this time that he drew up his 'Plot for Intelligence out of Spain' which is preserved in the State Paper Office. The paper is worth quoting at length because of the light it throws upon the arrangement of his secret service:

'A Plot for Intelligence out of Spain.

1. Sir Edward Stafford [English ambassador in France] to draw what he can from the Venetian ambassador.

2. To procure some correspondence with the French King's ambassador in Spain.

3. To take order with some at Rouen to have frequent advertisements from such as arrive out of Spain at Nantes, Newhaven [Havre] and Dieppe.

4. To make choice of two especial persons French, Flemings or Italians to go along the coast to see what preparations are a making there. To furnish them with letters of credit.

exchange protested (cf. Life of Sutton, in *Biographia Britannia*, vi, p. 3852). There is no reliable evidence to substantiate this story, and though Spanish credit was certainly not strong among the Genoese bankers at this time it appears more likely that Drake's expedition along the Spanish coast in 1587 was the principal factor in delaying the Armada.

[1] *Spanish War Papers* (Navy Records Society), i, pp. 192–7; S. P. Spain, ii, Feb. 1586–7, 'Advertisements touching the preparation in Spain' from one Richard Gibbes, &c.

5. To have intelligence at the Court of Spain, one of Finale, one of Genoa.'

6. To have intelligence at Brussels, Leyden, Bar. (*sic.*)

7. To employ the Lord of Dunsany.'[1]

It is impossible to discover how completely Walsingham carried out this programme. Facts about political espionage are by their very nature obscure. It is interesting to observe, however, that between March 1587 and June 1588 he received from the Queen £3,300 for secret service, a larger allowance apparently than he ever got before or after during the same length of time.[2] It is probable also, as all of his earlier biographies agree, that he added to this sum considerably from his private purse.[3] If he had only made an accounting of the expenditure of it, it might be possible to discover with some precision how it was that he kept himself informed of the plans and preparations of Philip of Spain during the next eighteen months. As it is, one must be content with such a fragmentary picture of his activity in this regard as the surviving reports of his secret agents afford.

It appears that his favourite approach to the secrets of Spain was through Italy. This was probably due in part to the fact that Walsingham had a wide acquaintance in Italy which he lacked in Spain. It was due also in part to the naturally closer connexion between Italy and England. Few Englishmen went to Spain except for trade and now that trade was cut off an Englishman in Spain was a marked man. For that very reason, when Walsingham wished to get reports from the Spanish coast towns he was disposed to use either Frenchmen or Flemings or Italians for the job. In Italy, on the other hand, Englishmen were familiar figures. It was the fashion in the sixteenth century for young Englishmen to complete their education by an *italianische Reise.* So spies could pose as innocent tourists and pass unnoticed. Italy moreover was an excellent place to get information about Spain because the connexion of the two countries was a very close one. From his Neopolitan possessions

[1] S. P. Domestic, ccii, no. 41, in Walsingham's hand, undated.

[2] Dec. 1587, S. P. Domestic, ccxxix, no. 49.

[3] Camden, *Annales* (Eng. trans. 1635), p. 394; Lloyd's *Worthies*, p. 514. It was Walsingham's first maxim, Lloyd remarked, that 'knowledge is never too dear'.

Philip drew a large part of his naval resources. Through Milan he dispatched his reinforcements to the Low Countries. In Genoa, now that Antwerp was ruined, he negotiated most of his loans and in Rome naturally he concerted his plans for crusades against heretics like Elizabeth. Tuscany, Savoy, and most of the small states of central and northern Italy were connected with his house by marriage. So little of importance passed in Spain that was not presently known in Italy. To Italy accordingly Walsingham turned in the spring of 1587 when he began to seek out diligently the plans and preparations of Philip of Spain.

He seems to have regarded Rome, Venice, and Florence as the best places for news gathering. There is some evidence that he had a correspondent in Milan late in the year 1587, but it is of a rather fragmentary sort.[1] About his connexions at Rome very little is ascertainable, though it is certain that he had spies there and it seems probable that he exploited the dissensions between the English Jesuits and seculars at the English college in Rome for the purpose of securing information. In Venice there had probably been an English agent for some years[2] and Sir Richard Shelley, Knight of St. John, had supplied some information from that town ever since he took up his residence there in 1569.[3] But Walsingham decided to send another agent to Venice in the spring of 1587. Stephen Paule was the man sent and for over a year he continued to send Walsingham the gossip he picked up on the Rialto about Spanish preparations.[4] But the most serviceable of Walsingham's

[1] Cf. letters of one Giovanni Sovico in Cotton MSS., Nero B vi, ff. 259, 261, 440.

[2] *Cal. Foreign*, 1583, p. 663.

[3] Cf. Art. 'Shelley', *D. N. B.* Some of Shelley's letters to Walsingham are given in *Cal. Foreign*, 1583–4 and 1584–5, *passim*. Stephen Paule wrote to Walsingham, 24 July 1587, 'Sir R. Shelley, Lord Prior, having had some conflict in reasoning with certain Jesuits about their justifying of the English traitors executed in England this last summer, grew extremely sick thereof and died about three days after, which was the 15th of July' (Bodleian Library, Tanner MSS. cccix, f. 73). The *D. N. B.* conjectures that he died in 1589, which is evidently wrong.

[4] Paule wrote to Walsingham from Frankfort-on-Main, 8 Apr. 1587: 'But wheresoever I remain your Honour shall be informed every three weeks of the occurrents by me: and though I adventure never so many dangers I will by the favour of God to go to Venice to take order that the weekly advices be sent me. And if any other intelligences may be procured by my industry I will acquaint your Honour therewith likewise' (Tanner MSS. cccix, f. 67). Other letters of Paule will be found among the Tanner MSS. and in the Public Record

Italian agents was located at Florence. This man generally signed himself Pompeo Pellegrini, but he was none other than Antony Standen, an English Catholic refugee who had left England twenty years before and had sometime later entered the service of the Grand Duke of Tuscany.[1] Walsingham was in touch with Standen as early as the year 1582,[2] but there is no evidence of any regular correspondence between them until the spring of 1587. At that time Standen was definitely in the Secretary's service and sometime afterwards was granted a pension of £100 a year by the Queen.[3] A letter which Standen

Office, S. P. Venice, i. Walsingham received regular news-letters also from J. Wroth in Venice (S. P. Venice, i, *passim*). The nature of Paule's reports appears from the following:

'It is given out only of report as a matter of great secrecy, that because the year will be spent before their preparations now making can be in readiness for the enterprise of England, that the King of Spain mindeth to use these men leagued in Naples, Romagna, Tuscany, Genoa, and Urbino for the kingdom of Algiers' (24 July 1587, dated at Venice, Tanner MSS. cccix, f. 73).

1 There were two Antony Standens, both of whom had gone to Scotland in the train of Lord Darnley in 1565. They were both rather dissolute young English Catholics, whose escapades did not a little to injure Darnley's good name. The one in question apparently went to France in 1565 in Darnley's service (Lang, *Mystery of Mary Stuart*, p. 75). He seems to have remained there. It is not easy to follow his wandering career in Europe or to say just when he entered the service of Tuscany, though it was probably before the year 1582. He interested himself in the cause of Mary Stuart and corresponded with her representative in Paris, the Archbishop of Glasgow (*Cal. Foreign*, 1583, p. 591: ibid. 1583–4, p. 5), and with Thomas Morgan (*Cal. Scottish*, 1585–6, p. 15). Some interesting letters written from Florence in March and June 1583 show his connexion with the Scottish Catholics and also with the Duke of Tuscany (*Cal. Scottish*, 1581–3, pp. 339, 341, 509). In one of these (ibid. 509) he gave an interesting account of the important part Florence played in international finance. Circumstantial evidence goes far to identify Standen with the mysterious Pompeo Pellegrini, but there is more direct testimony to the same effect, to wit:

(1) A letter among the Harleian MSS. (296, f. 46) written 28 August 1587, apparently in the same hand as those signed Pompeo Pellegrini, is signed B. C., addressed to Jacopo Manucci, but endorsed 'from Mr. Standen'.

(2) Another letter (Harl. MSS. 286, f. 122) dated 11 Feb. 1587/8 in this same hand, is also signed B. C., and also addressed to Manucci, but endorsed 'From Pellegrini'.

(3) In a letter dated 7 May 1587 (S. P. Spain, ii), Pellegrini speaks of himself as a 'poor Englishman'.

2 *Cal. Foreign*, 1583, p. 644. Walsingham wrote to Beale, 30 Sept. 1583, that he had just received a letter from Standen out of Italy, but that he suspected the man's honesty (*Cal. Scottish*, 1581–3, p. 625).

3 On the pension, cf. Standen's letter to A. Bacon, dated 8 Apr. 1591, B.M. Additional MSS. 4110, f. 1. This volume of the Additional MSS. with those immediately following contain Thos. Birch's transcripts of letters from the Lambeth Palace library, evidently made for the purpose of writing his *Memoirs of Queen Elizabeth*. Many of the papers are printed in that volume. Birch, *op. cit.*, i, pp. 66–504, gives the best account of Standen's life, but fails to identify him with Pompeo Pellegrini.

wrote to Jacopo Manucci, one of Walsingham's servants, on the 7th of May 1587, will serve to indicate his methods of work. He reported that he had heard little from Spain recently, that official dispatches were only sent thence to Italy once a month, and that unless a galley came out of the usual course from Spain to Genoa he was dependent for news upon merchant carriers. He added, however, that the Duke of Tuscany's ambassador in Spain was a great friend of his and kept him steadily advised of what was happening at the Spanish court. In the same letter he told Walsingham that four galleys of the Genoese fleet had gone to Spain and that he had heard from Naples of four more about to be dispatched thither. But the closing passages in the letter are the most significant. 'Since your last', he wrote, 'in which you desire diligence in intelligence of *Spanish matters*, I have borrowed one hundred crowns and dispatched *to Lisbon* a *Fleming* who hath there a *brother in service* with the *Marquis of Santa Cruz*, and of his chamber. I have given him address for his letters to me at the ambassador's house in Madrid who straight will send them to me. He is a proper fellow and writeth well and I sent him away with these last four gallies.' [1] Here then was evidently a spy of unusual value whose close acquaintance with Giovanni Figliazzi, the Tuscan ambassador at Madrid, opened a convenient door for news from the Spanish court and whose agent, connected with the household of the Grand Admiral of the Spanish fleet, furnished an admirable opportunity to keep in touch with the details of Spanish naval preparations. It seems likely that the most accurate information Walsingham received of Spanish naval preparations came through this channel. Probably he had Pellegrini to thank for the copy of Santa Cruz's detailed report of his ships, forces, and stores which the Spanish admiral sent to his master in March 1587, and which came into Walsingham's hands sometime later.[2]

Standen's communications from Florence came to Walsingham

[1] 7 May 1587, S. P. Spain, ii, passages in italics in cipher.

[2] Cf. 'The Copy of the General and Particular Relation which the Marquis of Santa Cruz and the Secretary Barnaby de Pedrosa have sent to his Majesty, being dispatched this Saturday, 22 Mar. 1586/7 (S. P. Spain, ii). This relation contains a list of ships in various places, of sailors, of soldiers, of stores, of wages, and other expenses.

pretty regularly during the summer and autumn of 1587.[1] Most of the news he sent related to the military and naval preparations in the Spanish parts of Italy. In June 1587 he expressed his conviction that the Spaniards would do nothing against England that year. This was evidently the letter which Walsingham forwarded to Burghley with the comment: 'Your Lordship by the enclosed from Florence may perceive how some stay is made of the foreign preparations'; and in a postscript Walsingham added: 'I humbly pray your Lordship that Pompey's letter may be reserved to yourself. I would be loathe the gentleman should have any harm through my default.'[2] It is apparent from this that he attached considerable importance to Standen's correspondence.

Early in the year 1588 Standen reported the arrival in Florence of Giovanni Figliazzi, Tuscan ambassador to Spain. 'Here', Standen added, 'he [Figliazzi] is much in grace, to our matters, I know not how it falls out, greatly affectionate and to your person as I say in particular much addicted, whereof I thought good to touch, that if you will write to him a letter of thanks, inferring that you have understood his goodwill to her Majesty and to the crown as to yourself, I think it to very good purpose, he having good means out of Spain.'[3] It has already appeared that Walsingham followed this advice and so opened a correspondence with Figliazzi which continued for some years. Still later in the spring of 1588 Standen went himself to Spain and advised Walsingham of the Spanish movements direct from Madrid.[4]

[1] I have found letters from him of 5 June 1587 (Harl. MSS. 295, f. 183), 18 June 1587 (*Cal. Salisbury MSS.* iii. 262), 3 July 1587 (Camden Soc., *Miscellany*, v. 47), 30 July 1587 (Harl. MSS. 286, f. 118), 28 Aug. 1587 (Harl. MSS. 296, f. 46). [2] Harl. MSS. 6994, f. 76. [3] Harl. MSS. 286, f. 122.

[4] Cf. his letters of 30 Apr. 1588 (Harl. MSS. 295, f. 84) and of 28 May 1588 (Harl. MSS. 295, f. 190), also *Cal. Salisbury MSS.* iii, p. 327. The later history of Standen is well set forth by Birch, *op. cit.* In 1593 he finally returned to England and there remained during the rest of Elizabeth's reign; he was to a minor degree mixed up in the Essex intrigues. Early in the reign of James I he was sent to Italy on a diplomatic mission, but his eagerness to effect a reconciliation between England and the Roman Church led him to exceed his instructions. He was in consequence imprisoned in the Tower after his return home (S. R. Gardiner, *History of England* (ed. 1900), i, pp. 141–3). While in the Tower he wrote what A. Lang called a Romantic Memoir, a copy of which s preserved at Hatfield House (A. Lang, *Mystery of Mary Stuart*, p. 75).

A letter which Standen wrote to Burghley, 7 June 1591, from Bordeaux, contains an interesting passage regarding his service for Walsingham. It is printed in Birch, *op. cit.*, i. 67. 'Touching my endeavour heretofore, I may

Standen was one and perhaps the most important one of many sources of information about Spanish preparations which Walsingham had at his command during the spring and summer of 1587. He gathered something also from the reports of the traders. Indeed there is some reason to believe that a certain amount of trade with Spain was licensed by the Queen for the express purpose of keeping open a direct channel of communication.[1] Walsingham also utilized the Portuguese connexions of such eminent Portuguese in England as Dr. Hector Nũnez.[2] He gathered in, through the English governor of Guernsey, the gossip which the Breton ships picked up in Spanish ports, and from an agent at Rouen the talk of the Spanish merchants there.[3] And he learned much through Irish channels.[4] How many agents he employed in Spain itself it is impossible to say. One of them, Nicholas Ousley, was at Malaga. The Spanish ambassador at Paris in July 1587 wrote of his presence there to Philip II and reported that Walsingham had said that Ousley was one of the cleverest men he knew and that the Queen was much indebted to him for his regular and trustworthy information.[5] Yet Ousley seems to have eluded capture and was making reports to Walsingham of Spanish preparations in April 1588.[6] Certainly Walsingham was well supplied with efficient agents in Spain. The detailed and accurate reports which he received in

not doubt how her Majesty hath been duly informed of them, for so Sir F. Walsingham by his letters did assure me, as also of my reintegration to her Highness favour concerning my youthful forfeit, assuring me fully thereof and for a sufficient token told me of an hundred pounds pension it had liked her Majesty to have assigned yearly for my maintenance, of which, at my coming back from Spain to Florence in the year 1588, I found the effect by the receipt of a year's pay, and now this last year another towards my voyages which hath not sufficed for my expenses in travelling to and fro; and especially this last time, being forced to remain for passage at Genoa five months. The year 88 which was the time that huge Armada went and perished I was by his order at the Court at Lisbon, where I had the view of all and by the way of Italy gave advice of the whole manner of their designs, which by his letters I found in Florence seemed most grateful to her Majesty. Thence proceeded the persuasion he used with me to procure this last time my return again to Spain which accordingly I did put in execution.'

[1] Cf. 8 June 1588 (Harl. MSS. 295, f. 197); *Cal. Spanish*, 1587–1603, p. 221.

[2] Ibid., pp. 221, 326.

[3] Wright, *Queen Elizabeth and her Times*, ii. 342, 353; *Armada Papers* (Navy Records Soc.), i. 169.

[4] *Cal. Irish*, 1586–8, pp. 485, 489.

[5] *Cal. Spanish*, 1587–1603, p. 123.

[6] Cf. Ousley to Walsingham, 17 Apr. 1588, Harleian MSS. 295, f. 76; for further information on Ousley, cf. *Armada Papers*, i. 301, and note.

May of the Spanish fleet, its force and tonnage, its munitions, its soldiers, sailors, and galley slaves, friars, provisions, and the rest, bear ample testimony to that fact.[1] More than this he kept spies engaged in the camp of the Prince of Parma and learned from them of Parma's preparations to throw a force across to England in flatboats when the Spanish fleet should have cleared the Channel.[2] The coming of the Armada was therefore no surprise party to the English, thanks to Walsingham's efficient espionage. Elizabeth knew for years beforehand that Philip was preparing to attack her, and she was informed month by month of the completeness of his preparations. When the Armada was off the Scilly Islands she could have read from Walsingham's reports almost as accurate an account of its equipment and of its plans as the Spanish Admiral himself could have furnished.

But it was one thing to advise Elizabeth of the dangers which threatened her and quite another thing to induce her to face them. This was the most serious business he had to face from the time of Drake's return to England after his voyage to the Spanish coast in the midsummer of 1587 to the time when the Spanish Armada was put to flight. No doubt Drake had done great damage to the Spanish shipping. Probably if it had not been for his enterprise the Armada would have got away in 1587. Walsingham was of the opinion that Drake should be dispatched again to the Spanish coast forthwith, or rather to the Azores to intercept the fleet from the Indies. He had heard from Standen in Florence that the King could not borrow any money from the Genoese bankers and that in consequence he was entirely dependent upon his India bullion for his naval preparations.[3] Walsingham therefore argued that the best way 'to bridle their malice is the interrupting of the Indian fleets'. And so he wrote on the 16th of July to Burghley.[4] Other members of the Privy Council were also of his opinion, but Elizabeth did not apparently favour the idea and Drake in consequence was not dispatched.[5]

[1] May 1588, S. P. Spain, iii.

[2] Cf. Burnham to Walsingham, 30 Sept. 1587, S. P. Holland, xviii (on Burnham's earlier career as a secret agent cf. Birch, *Memoirs of Queen Elizabeth*, i, pp. 14 ff.); Trent to Walsingham, 6 Oct. 1587, S. P. Holland, xviii.

[3] *Cal. Salisbury MSS.* iii. 263.

[4] Harleian MSS. 6994, f. 76, printed in Wright, ii. 340.

[5] Stafford, the English ambassador in France, told the Spanish ambassador that Howard, Hunsdon, Cobham, and Walsingham were in favour of dispatch-

Walsingham was of the opinion in July 1587 that the Spanish Armada would not arrive for another year, and his opinion was generally shared not only in England but also abroad.[1] Consequently there was very little done in England during the summer in the way of warlike preparations. Drake's fleet lay at Plymouth and a small blockading squadron under Sir Henry Palmer was set to watch the Flemish coast, but the main English fleet lay out of commission at its moorings in Gillingham Reach.[2]

Meanwhile in Italy and in Spain things were happening which increased very considerably the danger of a Spanish attack upon England. In the first place Philip's ambassador at Rome, Count Olivarez, succeeded, after much negotiating, in persuading Pope Sixtus V to sign a treaty with Spain for a crusade against England by which the Pope agreed to contribute 1,000,000 ducats in gold to the enterprise.[3] In the second place the Plate fleet from the West Indies, which Walsingham had been so anxious to intercept, got safe home late in August, with a cargo of some 16,000,000 ducats in gold, of which 4,000,000 was consigned to

ing Drake again, but that Burghley opposed the project (*Cal. Spanish*, 1587–1603, p. 126). Walsingham on the other hand, in his memorial to the Queen of December 1587, already cited, maintained that he and Burghley had both advocated the dispatch of Drake to the seas again in order to intercept the West India fleet. Walsingham at the time was trying to prove to the Queen that he and Burghley had long advocated an aggressive policy. Stafford's tale sounds more like Burghley, though he in turn was always trying to prove that Burghley opposed war with Spain.

[1] Cf. his letter of 16 July 1587 : 'It seemeth that next year the King of Spain and his confederates are resolved to set up their rest' (Harl. MSS. 6994, f. 76). The Venetian ambassador at Madrid was of the same opinion, *Cal. Venetian*, 1581–91, p. 300 ; cf. also Burghley to Walsingham, 13 Sept. 1587, S. P. Domestic, cciii, no. 42.

[2] Corbett, *Drake*, ii, p. 111. The main fleet was temporarily out of commission, but was under the care of Sir John Hawkins, Treasurer of the Navy, who was bound by contract to keep it ready for the seas. Burghley wrote to Walsingham, 13 Sept. 1587 : 'I am sorry to hear every day that her Majesty's ships are in such decay as they will not be fit to serve except great charges be spent on them' (S. P. Domestic, cciii, no. 42). This statement was probably based upon the charges of Hawkins's detractors and was almost certainly untrue (cf. Oppenheim, *Administration of the Royal Navy*, pp. 392 ff. ; and *Spanish War Papers* (Navy Records Soc.), pp. 207 ff. Lord Howard made a very favourable report on the condition of the royal fleet in Feb. 1588 (*Armada Papers* (Navy R. S.), i. 79).

[3] One half of this sum was to be paid when the Spaniards landed in England and the other half in bi-monthly instalments to follow. The text of the treaty is given in Meyer, *England und die katholische Kirche unter Elisabeth*, i. 454 ; Olivarez' comments on the negotiation are given in *Cal. Spanish*, 1587–1603, p. 127.

the King alone.[1] In a word, Philip's resources for warlike enterprises were enormously increased during the summer of 1587.

Walsingham certainly knew of the arrival of the Plate fleet and he had heard of the Pope's willingness to co-operate in the Spanish attack on England. 'To think', he wrote to Leicester on the 21st of September, with reference to the Queen's desire for peace, 'that the King of Spain, having his treasure now come home in greater quantity than ever he had, his forces doubled in those countries [the Netherlands] when the levies made in Italy and Germany shall be arrived and the Pope ready to back him with three (*sic*) millions of crowns, and all against England, will make a peace but with such conditions as will work the overthrow both of her Majesty and of those countries, is but a mere vanity, for always the strongest giveth law to the weaker.'[2] In Madrid the Venetian ambassador, who had previously been of the opinion that the Armada would not sail until the following year, announced to his masters that Philip was determined to dispatch his fleet at once.[3] Walsingham's spies in Spain very likely sent similar reports. At any rate the English Privy Council early in October became alive to the sense of immediate danger, and at a meeting on the ninth of the month Burghley laid before it a long proposal of active measures for defence—a pinnace should be dispatched to reconnoitre the Spanish coast; the Lord Admiral should be commanded to put the whole of the royal fleet in readiness; all English ships should be detained and all owners of ships fitting for the navy should be commanded to repair to their ships forthwith and hold themselves ready to serve; letters should be dispatched to the Lord-Lieutenants of the counties to make ready their military forces; letters should be written to Leicester in the Low Countries to procure men-of-war from the Dutch; the Lord Deputy of Ireland should be put on his guard; and orders should be taken that the Catholic recusants within the country should be rendered innocuous.[4]

Some part of these suggestions the Privy Council endorsed at

[1] *Cal. Venetian*, 1581–91, pp. 308–9.
[2] 21 Sept. 1587, Cotton MSS., Galba D ii, f. 86.
[3] *Cal. Venetian*, 1581–91, pp. 315 ff.
[4] *Spanish War Papers*, pp. 197–200. This paper is dated 3 Oct., but it appears from *Acts of Privy Council*, 1587–8, p. 252, that the Privy Council acted upon these suggestions, 9 Oct.

once. The Lord-Lieutenants were instructed to have their trained men ready for service at an hour's notice. Leicester was warned in the Low Countries [1] and the Lord Deputy of Ireland put on his guard. Merchant shipping was stayed and held in readiness for service.[2] But the recommendation of Burghley which seemed to be the most pressing one of all, namely, the mobilization of the whole royal fleet, was not adopted. Presumably the Queen balked at this. The other measures proposed were cheap enough, but the placing of her ships on a war footing involved expense and she was not yet sufficiently aroused to the danger which threatened her to loose her purse strings. She had indeed great hopes of peace at this juncture, in spite of Walsingham's warnings and her Council's pleadings and 'the opinion of all men of judgement'.[3] The most she would consent to apparently was the addition of two ships to Sir Henry Palmer's small fleet in the Channel, and those only for six weeks' service.[4]

Walsingham for his part was brought absolutely to despair by the Queen's slackness at such a dangerous time. 'We cannot skill here,' he wrote to Leicester on the 12th of November, 'neither of timely nor thorough doing. The manner of our cold and careless proceeding here in this time of peril and danger maketh me to take no comfort of my recovery of health, for that I see apparently, unless it shall please God in mercy and miraculously to preserve us, we cannot long stand.' [5]

And yet something had been done. England at any rate had staunch ships for the seas, thanks to Hawkins's care in the administration of the navy, and her land forces, poor as they always were, were far better than they had been. Early in December Walsingham felt called upon to point out to his mistress that through his labour and Burghley's 26,000 footmen and . . . horsemen had been reduced into bands and trained for the defence of the coasts, 'a thing never put in execution in any of her Majesty's predecessors' times', and 24,000 footmen and . . . horse had been levied and trained for a guard to the Queen's

[1] Cf. Memorial for Mr. Herbert, 12 Oct. 1587, S. P. Holland, xviii.
[2] *Acts of Privy Council*, 1587–8, pp. 252–4.
[3] Cf. Walsingham to Leicester, 9 Oct. 1587, *Hardwicke Papers*, i. 357.
[4] *Acts of Privy Council*, 1587–8, p. 267.
[5] Galba D ii, f. 178, printed in *Hardwicke Papers*, i. 359.

person.[1] England at least had an army, some kind of an army, though one wonders how these trained bands, the target of the London wits, would have stood up against Spanish pikemen had Parma ever got across the Channel.

During November Walsingham and his colleagues still looked for the coming of the Spaniards. On the 27th of the month a Council of War, which included Lord Grey, Sir Walter Raleigh, Sir John Norris, Sir Francis Drake, and some others, met to consider where the Spaniard might be expected to land and how the English forces should be disposed to resist him.[2] Two days later a false rumour of the presence of the Spanish Armada off the Irish coast sent messengers scurrying from the Privy Council to the military commanders in the western counties.[3] Early in December the gossips about Court were saying that Lord Howard was to put to sea with the main fleet and that Drake, with twenty or thirty vessels, was to be dispatched to the Spanish coasts again.[4] And this in fact proved to be true. On the 15th of December Howard received his instructions, on the 21st his commission as commander-in-chief was signed, and the next day he announced that in two or three days the whole of the ships would be ready for the seas. Two days later Drake received a commission for the command of an independent fleet of thirty sail, including seven of the Queen's ships. His instructions were to proceed to the coast of Spain and to attack the Spanish shipping in port as he had done before. If he discovered that the Spanish were already at sea he was to report home at once and himself dog the enemy's course, doing what damage he could.[5]

There is unfortunately no indication in the sources as to how Elizabeth, whose hopes were certainly running strong for peace at this juncture, was persuaded to take so vigorous and bellicose a course. It cannot have been a mere coincidence that her decision followed hard upon Walsingham's return to the Court and Leicester's return from the Low Countries. Walsingham was in better trim physically than he had been for months [6] and

[1] S. P. Domestic, ccvi, no. 2.
[2] *Monson's Naval Tracts* (Navy Records Soc.), ii. 267 ff.
[3] *Acts of Privy Council*, 1587–8, p. 288.
[4] *Cal. Rutland MSS.*, i. 232.
[5] Corbett, *Drake*, ii. 113, 119.
[6] Wm. Stubbes to Mr. Darell, 22 Dec. 1587, 'My master, thanks be to God,

Leicester was in the highest favour with his mistress, and probably between the two of them lay the responsibility for this surprising manifestation of royal resolution.

During December and the early part of January England was in a bustle of warlike preparations by land and sea, in which Walsingham undoubtedly played his part both as royal secretary and privy councillor, though apart from the ordinary functions attached to these offices it is not possible for lack of evidence to define his part very accurately. He probably was the chief instrument employed for executing the orders of the Privy Council. As such, early in December, he dispatched trained officers, most of them veterans of the Low Countries' wars, to the maritime counties to inspect the local levies there.[1] As such he conveyed to the Lord-Lieutenants of the several counties the general order, issued early in January, for the restraint of all Catholic recusants,[2] a measure which Burghley had recommended the previous October and which Walsingham must certainly have favoured, though it may well be doubted whether the general fear of an uprising among the English Catholics in favour of the Spanish invader was justified. Walsingham also kept in touch with Lord Admiral Howard, who was busy at Chatham completing the mobilization of the main fleet, and with Drake, who had sped west to Plymouth shortly after the New Year to prepare for his descent upon the Spanish coast.

It will be observed that these naval preparations had both a defensive and an offensive purpose in view. According to Howard himself the Queen's intention was to use the main fleet

is better since he was at the Court, than when he was at home' (S. P. Domestic, Supplementary xv).

[1] *Acts of Privy Council*, 1587–8, pp. 295–6, 310–11. It is evident that some such inspection as this was contemplated in October, but that Elizabeth vetoed the plan because of the expense entailed. Burghley wrote to Walsingham, 24 Oct. 1587: 'When her Majesty was informed from me by Mr. Wooley of the names of such as should have been sent to the Lieutenants of the maritime counties she changed her mind, resting upon answer from the lieutenants, as I think misliking the charge which would not have been above 200 marks' (Murdin, *Burghley Papers*, p, 590).

[2] Cf. Wright, *Queen Elizabeth and her Times*, ii. 358–9, where the order sent to the Lord-Lieutenant of Sussex is printed; cf. also Harl. MSS. 703, f. 52, and S. P. Domestic, ccviii, *passim*. Some interesting facts about the execution of the order in Derbyshire are printed in Lodge, *op. cit.*, ii. 338–44. Curiously enough there is no mention of this important order in *Acts of Privy Council*, which is one more proof of their incompleteness.

to prevent the landing of the Prince of Parma either in England or in Scotland.[1] Drake, on the other hand, was to wage aggressive warfare against the Spanish fleet in Spanish harbours after the manner of his attack the previous summer. It may safely be presumed that Drake himself was largely responsible for this plan of campaign, and there can be little doubt that Walsingham lent it his vigorous support and did everything in his power to hasten its execution. His main problem at Court was unquestionably that of keeping his mistress true to her course at least until Drake got clear away. Here he had to face the open opposition of the peace party led by Sir James Crofts,[2] and possibly the covert antagonism of Burghley himself. Leicester, and probably Hatton, were his strongest allies. Unfortunately Drake's departure was delayed, and before the month of January was well advanced Elizabeth was already wavering. Early in the month she ordered that the crews of the main fleet be reduced to half their war strength. This may have been due in part to information which Walsingham received from Spain that the Armada would not sail until April.[3] It was probably due in the main to the Queen's inveterate parsimony,[4] joined to her hope of peace. Howard for his part protested that with half crews her fleet was as little good as the ' hoys which lie at Lyon Quay ', and he begged Walsingham to labour with the Queen in the matter, ' knowing that you are so well bent to spend her Majesty's purse rather than to hazard her honour,' but all to no purpose.

The reduction was carried through. This step in itself embodied little damage to the plan of campaign, indeed it may be reckoned as a wise conservation of resources while the danger of attack seemed still remote. More serious was Sir Francis Drake's delay at Plymouth. The reinforcements promised him from the main fleet were slow in coming, and while he waited the inevitable epidemic played sad havoc with his crews. But more disastrous still were the machinations against him at Court.

[1] *Armada Papers*, i. 57.

[2] On Crofts' attitude cf. Corbett, *Drake*, ii. 122.

[3] *Armada Papers*, i. 57.

[4] Corbett, *Drake*, ii. 114. Corbett has justified this reduction in numbers of the crews in part by a memorandum of Lord Burghley which is undated, but which is assigned (*Armada Papers*, i. 55) to January 1588. A comparison of this paper with one printed in *Spanish War Papers*, p. 53, leaves little doubt that these two papers belong together and that both should be assigned to December 1585.

Sir James Crofts not only opposed his dispatch but even argued in favour of forcing him to restore his Spanish plunder in order to facilitate peace-making. And Burghley himself seems to have sought to persuade the Queen that Drake's expedition was likely to be of more profit to himself than to England.[1] The result was that January passed and February and March, and Drake was still kept at Plymouth, fretting to be off and so impatient at the Queen's delay that he even contemplated slipping away without her consent, hoping perhaps that a successful campaign might serve to mitigate her wrath.[2]

Towards the end of February the Queen definitely abandoned her original plan of campaign. This fact is evident from the programme submitted to her by a group of her most confidential advisers on the 25th of the month. It was now proposed to abandon aggressive tactics by sea or at any rate to subordinate them to an arrangement which was in the main purely defensive. The fleet was to be divided in two, one part to be eastward in the narrow seas and the other westward south of Ireland, the intention being apparently to guard the English coast against Parma on the one hand and the Irish coast against a direct attack from Spain on the other, with the further purpose of catching the Spanish fleet between the two divisions if it should seek to come against England up the Channel. It is true that at the same time it was proposed that an expedition should be prepared for Portugal in favour of Don Antonio, and another expedition for the Azores to intercept the India treasure fleet, but these proposals were obviously regarded as incidental to the main plan which was purely defensive.[3] Burghley, Leicester, Hatton, and Walsingham were all present at the drafting of this programme, though obviously enough it represents in the main Burghley's cautious counsels. Walsingham would plainly have preferred Drake's bolder project of attacking the main Spanish fleet at its point of departure. The reason why Burghley's ideas prevailed at this juncture is very likely to be found in the

[1] This at any rate was the story which Stafford, the English ambassador at Paris, told the Spanish ambassador there (*Cal. Spanish*, 1587–1603, p. 213). In itself this evidence is not very convincing, but there are other grounds for the belief that Burghley was opposed to Drake; cf. Corbett, *Drake*, ii. 116.

[2] Corbett, *Drake*, ii. 123.

[3] *American Historical Review*, ii. 93–8; cf. Corbett, *Drake*, ii. 130–1.

dispatch of the English commissioners to treat of peace with Parma a day or so before. Elizabeth was now strongly bent to settle her differences with Spain by diplomacy, and was therefore averse from any further singeing of King Philip's beard or from anything else calculated to aggravate the ill feeling between him and her.

Yet in spite of Elizabeth's pacific purposes she could not ignore the fact that every dispatch from Spain brought fresh proof of hostile purposes against England. Howard wrote to Walsingham on the 10th of March, ' All that cometh out of Spain must concur in one to lie or else we shall be stirred very shortly with heave and ho.' Scout ships which Drake dispatched to the coast of Spain confirmed this view of the matter.[1] With this fresh evidence at hand both Walsingham and Leicester laboured with the Queen once more to take the bolder course. They urged her in fact to dispatch Drake at once. Had Sir James Crofts been present with Spanish poison for the royal ear he might have thwarted their purpose. But Crofts was now busy with his peace-making in Flanders. Burghley, it is true, counselled delay, but according to Stafford, the English ambassador at Paris, Walsingham and Leicester chose a moment to push their argument home when Burghley was temporarily absent from Court.[2] So the Queen yielded. Drake was instructed once more on the 15th of March to reorganize his squadron for a vigorous offensive.[3] Unfortunately, however, he needed reinforcements and supplies, and long before these were furnished timid counsels prevailed again.

Nevertheless from the middle of March onward the preparations to meet the Spaniards both by land and sea proceeded much more vigorously than they had during the winter. On the 29th of March Walsingham wrote by the Queen's command to Lord Willoughby in the Low Countries directing him to request the Dutch to make ready the ships they had promised her in case of need.[4] A little later she applied to them for sailors. ' I nothing doubt ', Walsingham wrote to Willoughby on the 10th of April, ' if mariners be got out of that country, but that her Majesty will be so strong by sea (so willing are the good subjects of this realm to assist in this action) as we shall not need to fear the

[1] *Armada Papers*, i. 90, 103, 107.
[2] *Cal. Spanish*, 1587–1603, p. 257.
[3] Corbett, *Drake*, ii. 129, n. 2.
[4] S. P. Holland, xxii.

great preparations in Spain of which all the world speaketh.'[1] In England meanwhile a general embargo was laid upon the shipping and the port towns were called upon to furnish men-of-war to supplement the royal fleets. On the same day orders were sent to the Lord-Lieutenants of the several counties directing them to review their troops and muster them afresh. On the 5th of April Sir John Norris was dispatched to the south coast to inspect the defences, on the 12th the arms and armour of the Catholic recusants were ordered to be seized and sold for the 'arming of her Majesty's true and well-affected subjects'.[2] Five days after that Lord Admiral Howard was commanded to convey his fleet from the Thames mouth and to join forces with Drake's squadron in the west.[3] All these preparations betrayed the Queen's reluctant conviction that she would have to fight.

Walsingham had certain information out of Spain that the Armada would leave Lisbon about the middle of May.[4] On St. George's Eve he wrote to his cousin Edward Norris: 'My good cousin, I thank you for your letters. This bearer can tell you that here we do nothing but honour St. George, of whom the Spanish army seemeth to be afraid for that, as we hear, they will not be ready to set forward before the midst of May, but I trust it will be May come twelve month. The King of Spain is too old and too sickly to fall to conquer kingdoms. If he be well counselled his best course will be to settle his own kingdoms in his own time. And so, in haste, I commit you to God.'[5]

This brief note reveals a man who was busy but confident. When one considers the unpreparedness of England for an encounter with the greatest power in Europe it is amazing how confident he was. Drake and his sea dogs knew that the Spaniard could be beaten because they had beaten him on the seven seas. But Walsingham knew it no less surely, though he hardly had strength in his sickly little body to bear the weight of armour. He knew it because of the faith that was in him—the Puritan faith that the Lord of Hosts was fighting on his side.

During April and May Walsingham was chiefly engaged in

[1] S. P. Holland, xxiii.

[2] *Acts of Privy Council*, 1588, pp. 7, 9, 16, 20, 39; *Cal. Rutland MSS.* i. 246.

[3] Corbett, *Drake*, ii. 136; cf. *Armada Papers*, i. 159.

[4] His information was surprisingly accurate; the Armada left Lisbon, May 18–20 (Corbett, ii. 164).

[5] 22 Apr. 1588, S. P. Holland, xxiii.

herding in the Recusants, gathering together the ships levied upon the maritime towns, and getting England ready for defence. It must have been about this time that he drafted 'A Consideration What Were Fit to be Done When the Realm shall be Assailed'. The paper is interesting as illustrating the multifarious duties that fell to his lot:

'The defence to be made by sea and land.
The defence by sea committed to the Lord Admiral.
Defence by land—
To be considered
What number of men are put in readiness throughout the realm, horse and foot.
How they are directed to assist upon any invasion.
Who be the lieutenants of the shires and captains of the men both trained and untrained.
What pioneers appointed for every band and what carriages.
What powder appointed for every band.
What field pieces and munition is placed in certain of the maritime counties.
These being done
(*a*) Where is it likely that the enemy will attempt anything against this realm.
(*b*) How may he best be withstood—whether by offering a fight when he has landed or in avoiding a fight (which it is likely the enemy will affect) and to make head against him with the use of the pioneers and withdrawing of victuals.
What men of sufficiency meet to be sent to those places where the descent is likely to be made.
What engineers there are in this realm meet to be used for the direction of the pioneers.
What forces were meetest to be about her Majesty's person both horsemen and footmen.
If anything should be attempted against the city of London which way it would be attempted and how it may be best withstood.' [1]

It is apparent from this paper that Walsingham not only had upon his hands the organization and supply of the land forces, but was even forced to consider broad questions of strategy. His correspondence at this juncture reveals the fact that every kind of question was referred to him, or rather to the Privy Council through him. The trained bands had to be provided with

[1] S. P. Domestic, ccix, no. 47, in Walsingham's hand, given here in abstract.

weapons, towns along the coast had to be supplied with artillery, gunpowder had to be purchased abroad or manufactured in London or rooted out of private stores, supplies had to be sent to the fleet, maritime towns had to be prodded to hasten the equipment of the ships requisitioned upon them, a thousand excuses had to be weighed and ten thousand petty quarrels adjusted.[1] All this business passed through Walsingham's hands and received his attention at the time when his main energies were focused upon the problem of keeping Scotland in line and winning France to some kind of an alliance against Spain. His burden would have been heavy enough if he could have acted according to his own judgement, but here again as everywhere his difficulties were made ten times more difficult because of the uncertain and inconstant temper of his mistress, whose cheese-paring policy forced a reduction in every estimate of expenses and whose natural tergiversation blocked every straightforward course. Of all those whose efforts saved England in the crisis of 1588 Walsingham certainly had the most distasteful work to do. The plumed troop and the armed war and all the stimulating gallantry of the open field were not for him. His portion lay in court intrigue and backstairs influences, in tedious and ineffectual arguments with the Queen, in slippery dealings with treacherous diplomats, in the devising of plans which other men were to execute and in the sharpening of swords for other men to wield. And yet no man perhaps, not even Drake himself, was more indispensable to the final issue.

Meanwhile Drake at Plymouth was still urging the Queen to follow her original plan and attack the Spanish Armada upon its own coasts. In a letter dated the 28th of April he presented his case with so much force[2] that Elizabeth once more decided to lay the question before the Privy Council. On the 10th of May they discussed it and concluded that since Lord Admiral Howard with the main fleet had already been ordered to join Drake in the west, the question be referred to him for his decision.[3] The conservative members of the Council and the Queen herself may have felt

[1] *Acts of Privy Council*, 1588, Introduction, *passim*.

[2] *Armada Papers*, i. 166.

[3] Ibid., 170. This decision was apparently ratified by the Queen, for Howard himself spoke later in terms which suggest that he had been given a free rein (*Armada Papers*, i. 204).

quite secure in leaving the matter to Howard because he had previously opposed an aggressive course of action.[1] At all events so it was. Howard apparently had full power to act, and he had no sooner joined Drake late in May than he summoned a Council of War to discuss the plan of campaign. The result of the discussion was that Drake with the support of Hawkins and Frobisher converted Howard to his own views. It consequently was decided that the whole fleet should set forth for the Spanish coast as soon as they got a favouring wind and the necessary provisions. Unhappily the wind held steady from the south-west and not only bottled them up in Plymouth harbour but prevented their supply ships from reaching them. Howard would have sailed without his supplies, and when the wind shifted to the eastward on the 30th he set forth,[2] but he had hardly got clear of the harbour before the wind veered round again to westward. In fact the same ill luck attended his aggressive purposes as had attended those of Drake late in March. The worst of it was that every day spent in harbour gave the Queen twenty-four hours more in which to weaken in her resolution. Walsingham must have watched the weather-vanes in London as anxiously as Drake did at Plymouth and prayed long prayers to the God of the winds. But all in vain. Howard's letters to Court betrayed his purpose but did not announce his departure. So it was that, as every one must have expected, Elizabeth got frightened at the thought of leaving her coasts denuded of her fleet and bade Walsingham instruct Howard to abandon his aggressive tactics and 'to ply up and down in some indifferent place between the coast of Spain and this realm, so as you may be able to answer any attempt that the said fleet shall make either against this realm, Ireland or Scotland'.[3] Walsingham must have written the letter with a very heavy heart and he picked out the slowest of all his messengers to bear it to Plymouth,[4] hoping still that Howard might get away before the dispatch reached him. But the adverse winds held fast and the orders eventually found Howard still nursing his impatience in Plymouth harbour.

Meantime news had reached the English coast of the departure

[1] *Armada Papers*, i. 205.
[2] Strype, *Annals*, iii, pt. 2, p. 544.
[3] *Armada Papers*, i. 192.
[4] Corbett, *Drake*, ii. 162.

of the Spanish fleet from Lisbon on the 20th of May, and gave a great stimulus to the preparations for defence. On the 18th of June the Queen called upon the English gentry to rally to her defence with their retainers, and ten days later the Privy Council sent special messengers to the Lord-Lieutenants of the counties to hold the county levies ready to march at a moment's notice.[1] Elizabeth even contemplated the recall of English troops from the Low Countries.[2] It was decided, too, at the eleventh hour to dispatch a messenger to the King of Scotland, 'but I do not look', Walsingham wrote to Burghley, 'that he shall carry with him . . . sufficient matter as shall make a strong gap.'[3] Walsingham, indeed, found the Queen at this critical juncture curiously careless. 'I am sorry', he wrote to Burghley on the 19th of June, 'to see so great danger hanging over this realm so slightly regarded and so carelessly provided for. I would to God the enemy were no more careful to assail than we are to defend and then were there less cause for fear. Seeing we have neither recourse to pray nor to such effectual preparations as the danger importeth, I cannot but conclude (according to man's judgement) '*Salus ipsa non servare hanc rempublicam*'.[4] Three days later he wrote to Archibald Douglas, 'I would to God Dr. Michaeli would speed well in the matter you wot of [the search for the philosophers' stone] and that we were all three at Basel to pray for princes.'[5]

There was this ray of hope in the situation, however, that on the 17th of June Walsingham and his partisans succeeded in inducing the Queen to leave the strategy of the naval campaign to Howard and his Council of War.[6] As soon as Howard learned

[1] *Acts of Privy Council*, 1588, p. 138.
[2] *Cal. Ancaster MSS.*, p. 154.
[3] 19 June 1588, S. P. Domestic, ccxi, no. 36.
[4] Ibid. Burghley also complained of the waste of time at this juncture. He wrote to Walsingham, 24 June 1588: 'I can be content to be at the court on Wednesday, but if you knew what sudden determination hath been by my Lord Chancellor and all the Lords in the Star Chamber to be there [at the Star Chamber at Westminster] on Thursday and I think on Wednesday also, surely, besides yourself, there will be no Councillor absent from Westminster. If you ask any there you will so understand it. But in very truth I think the cases at the Court, as the time is, ought to have place, but yet I see many times that we that do employ ourselves both forenoons and afternoons at Westminster, when we are called to the court, in manner of alarm, many times the greater part of our time at the court is not spent in serious causes. Yet I hope that time will amend these courtly errors' (S. P. Domestic, ccxi, no. 56).
[5] *Cal. Salisbury MSS.* iii. 332.
[6] *Armada Papers*, i. 217.

that his freedom of action had been restored he declared his intention to seek out the Spanish fleet at once. Unfortunately, however, the adverse winds persisted and the provision ships did not arrive. Again and again Howard, like all the other naval commanders, complained of the pernicious system of victualling the ships which was ordinarily done for a month at a time. The consequence of the system was that about one week out of every four was spent by the fleet in picking up their supply ships and transferring their stores, and, what was worse, that their range of free action was limited to about three weeks, at the end of which they must return to their base to revictual.[1] The system was an inheritance from earlier times, but in spite of all protests Elizabeth persisted in it, chiefly because she intended to demobilize her fleet at the earliest possible moment and did not wish to have an excess of stores on hand at that time which she must sell at a loss. Her thriftiness in such matters became at times quite grotesque. As it happened, adverse winds prevented Howard from cruising abroad even if his larders had been full, but the Queen is not to be excused because Providence saw fit to cover her shortcomings.

While Howard was praying for a fair wind and fresh supplies Lord Harry Seymour with a fleet of fifteen ships was cruising up and down the Narrow Seas, guarding against a possible descent by Parma upon the English coasts. It was currently reported that Parma had ready 30,000 trained soldiers to throw across the Channel and a great fleet of flat-bottomed boats assembled for their transport.[2] Yet Seymour was of the opinion that the Prince would not attempt the crossing. He came to the conclusion in fact that Parma's design was against the Island of Walcheren.[3] The Dutch Estates-General were of the same opinion and they wrote in haste to request that Seymour's fleet be sent to prevent him.[4] But the Queen wisely decided against such a course, and Walsingham for once shared her opinion. 'It seemeth', he wrote to Sir Edward Norris on the 13th of July, 'by letters from Sir William Russell that the States have

[1] Ibid. i. 220.

[2] Ibid. i. 231; Killigrew to Burghley, 30 June 1588, S. P. Holland, xxiv.

[3] *Armada Papers*, i. 231; Winter was of the same opinion, ibid. i. 212, 253.

[4] Cf. Sir W. Russell to Walsingham; 6 July 1588, S. P. Holland, xxv.

advertisement that the Prince's [Parma's] intention against this realm is altered, finding many things to fail that were to accompany his purpose, whereupon they doubt his meaning against some of their islands and desire that both their own ships and her Majesty's may be appointed to guard their coasts, which for my part I do not like of, for that by such a colour our ships should be drawn that way and in the meantime the Prince put over hither, it might prove over dangerous. And for the danger that impendeth to any place of their dominion or to that town [of Flushing], so long as we continue strongest by sea as hitherto we are, we shall be able at all times to rescue them and to send assistance of men and victuals.' [1] Walsingham revealed here a grasp of the importance of sea power which was remarkable in a sixteenth-century landsman.

So Seymour kept to his station in the Channel while Howard lay at Plymouth waiting his chance to put forth to the Spanish coast. On the 21st of June the wind came in from the east, and on the 22nd at midnight his supply ships arrived.[2] The next day he received news that a portion of the Spanish fleet had been sighted off the Scilly Islands. The fact was undoubted. When the Armada sailed from Lisbon in May it was ordered to proceed at once to a place of rendezvous off the Scilly Islands. But the stormy winds which had kept Howard locked in Plymouth scattered the Spanish galleons. Most of them, badly damaged, put back into Corunna harbour. Some score of them did, however, reach the mouth of the English Channel and lay there the better part of a week for their fellows to join them.[3] It was this squadron which Howard's scout ships had sighted. When he heard the news his preparations for putting to sea were redoubled. All day and all night his men worked getting in the stores. He wrote to the Queen that he expected to get out after the Spaniards on the 24th. 'I hope in God,' he added, 'we shall meet with some of them, we will not stay for anything.' [4]

But a third time the wind played him false. He had not yet got clear of the Channel before it set in again south-south-west and made further progress towards Spain impossible. Still, in the hope of catching the stray Spanish squadron, he dispatched

[1] 13 July 1588, S. P. Holland, xxv.
[2] *Armada Papers*, i. 218, 226.
[3] Corbett, *Drake*, i. 165.
[4] *Armada Papers*, i. 225.

Drake with ten ships to the French coast, but no Spaniard was found. And then Howard found himself in a quandary. He could not sail to the west because of adverse winds. Some portion of the Spanish fleet was at hand; with the wind fair from Spain the chances were that the main Armada was close behind them. Howard therefore decided to take up a position across the Channel mouth, scattering his ships in three squadrons from Ushant on the Breton coast to the Scilly Islands. This position he took up on the 5th of July, but on the 7th the wind once more set in from the northward, and since no Spanish ships had been sighted in the Channel the fact seemed to be established that the stray squadron had returned to Spain, and so it was decided once more to resume the offensive and attack the Spaniards on their own coasts.[1] For two days before a north wind the English fleet sped southward until it came almost within sight of the Spanish coast. Then the fickle wind once more swung around south-south-west. Had Howard been

[1] Corbett (*Drake*, ii. 167) censures Howard for abandoning offensive tactics between the time when the wind turned against him on 24 June and the time when he resumed offensive tactics on 6 July, and Corbett maintains that Drake and Howard were sharply at variance as to the plan of campaign at this juncture. This view of the matter is not borne out by the evidence. Howard himself says that they set sail with a fair wind on the evening of 23 June, but that sixteen hours later the wind turned SSW., so that he had to beat back and forth in the Channel but could make no progress westward. Then it was that he decided to dispatch Drake with ten ships into the 'Trade' (the passage between Brest and Ushant). Drake must have been two days at least on this adventure. The next record we have from the fleet is a paper dated 4 July, in which Drake advised that offensive tactics be assumed against Spain on the grounds that the stray Spanish squadron had undoubtedly returned to Spain and there was no pressing need for guarding the south coasts. Corbett argues from this that Howard was opposed to such a course. But according to Howard's letter to Walsingham of 6 July the wind had been steady from the SW. since 29 June, which would have made offensive operations against the Spanish coast during that interval practically impossible (*Armada Papers*, i. 247). It appears that on 5 July Howard ranged his fleet in three squadrons across the Channel mouth, the wind being still from the SW. (ibid.), so that Drake's advice of the 4th could not have been followed. As soon as the wind swung round to the north Howard and his Council agreed to resume aggressive tactics (ibid., i. 240). There is nothing in this story to support the view that Howard was favourable to a defensive course while Drake was fuming to be off. There is nothing indeed to prove that Drake's paper of advice, dated 4 July, was intended for Howard at all. A similar paper by Fenner, dated 14 July (ibid., i. 238), was pretty clearly for Burghley's perusal, and it may well be that Drake drew up his paper not to convince Howard, but to support him against the opposition of cautious councillors like Burghley. This view of the matter finds some slight support in the fact that Drake's paper is filed among the State Papers.

adequately provisioned he might have hung on in the teeth of the weather until the wind shifted again. As it was he had no choice but to return to England and revictual. On the 12th of July he was back again in Plymouth. So it was that Drake's bold plan of campaign failed again partly because of the weather, but largely also because of the Queen's hand-to-mouth administration.[1]

Meantime the reports that reached the Court of the progress of the Spanish fleet had been various. The news of its departure from Lisbon on the 18–20th of May had stirred up the Queen to considerable activity in preparations for defence. The later news from Drake of the presence of the stray Spanish squadron off the mouth of the Channel had further stimulated this activity. Then it was that the English gentry were called upon to rally to the Queen's defence with their retainers and that the Lord-Lieutenants of the counties were advised to have the county levies ready to march at a moment's notice.[2] But presently the Queen learned that the stray Spanish squadron had returned to Spain and that Medina Sidonia's main fleet had been dispersed by storms and had taken refuge in Corunna and other harbours thereabouts, where it lay disordered, weather-beaten, and distressed.[3] Elizabeth, always over-credulous of reports which promised a postponement of the inevitable, at once became convinced that the Spanish fleet was not to be looked for that year, and she instructed Walsingham to write Howard to dismiss four of his largest ships.[4] There is even some evidence to support the belief that Walsingham himself took Elizabeth's view of the matter. On the 9th of July he wrote to Sir Edward Norris: 'For the navy of Spain we have lately received advertisements that by reason of their great wants, as well of mariners as of necessary provisions, but especially through the infection fallen among their men, they are forced to return and have dispersed themselves.'[5] This passage, however, hardly justifies Motley's statement, which is based upon it, that 'Walsingham believed

[1] Corbett, ii. 169–72; *Armada Papers*, i. 238–43.

[2] About the same time Lord Willoughby in the Low Countries was instructed to prepare to send back to England 2,000 English troops from the Netherlands; *Cal. Ancaster MSS.*, pp. 159–60, cf. also ibid. 169, 174–5.

[3] *Cal. Venetian*, 1581–91, p. 366.

[4] Camden, *Annales* (Eng. trans. 1635), p. 366; Corbett (*Drake*, ii. 175) says three ships, which is wrong.

[5] Motley, ii. 435, n. 1.

just ten days before the famous fleet was to appear off Plymouth, that it had dispersed and returned to Spain never to reappear'. Walsingham simply told Norris what he had heard, which after all approximated pretty closely to the truth, not what he believed. There can be little doubt that the news of the Spanish fleet's dispersal was welcome news to him, for he was convinced that England was in every way unready for the coming struggle. But he certainly did not share the Queen's opinion that the time had come to begin to demobilize.

It appears that Howard was given some discretion in the matter of discharging the four ships. At any rate he decided that the situation was too dangerous to let them go. Two Dutch flyboats which his scouts picked up in the Channel reported that the Armada was assembled at Corunna and making ready to put to the seas again.[1] The week following his return to Plymouth he spent in refurnishing and revictualling his fleet. He was anxious to put to sea again as soon as possible, realizing that the same wind which would carry the Armada up the Channel would practically bottle him up in Plymouth Harbour.

While Howard was refitting at Plymouth the Queen and her Council seem to have been chiefly concerned with the defence of the capital. Reports came from the Low Countries that Parma had resolved to attack London either by land or sea and Elizabeth feared that with her main fleet windbound in Plymouth Parma might seize an occasion when the Channel was clear of English men-of-war and make the passage.[2] Special measures were accordingly taken for the defence of the Thames,[3] and Elizabeth decided to post 5,000 foot and 1,000 horse in Essex in the places most exposed to danger.[4] This step was a significant one, for it appears to have been the first mobilization of troops at the Queen's charge. The county levies, to be sure, had been mustered and were being trained, but so long as the Queen did not actually order them to march the expenses both of equipment and of training were borne by themselves or by the county to

[1] *Armada Papers*, i. 272–3.

[2] Wright, ii. 378.

[3] *Acts of Privy Council*, 1588, p. 168; *Cal. Domestic*, 1581–90, p. 503; Wright, ii. 378.

[4] Cf. Walsingham to Burghley, 18 July 1588. Harl. MSS. 6994, f. 126; Walsingham to Leicester, 22 July 1588, Cotton MSS. Titus B vii, f. 26; Leicester to Walsingham, 22 July 1588, *Armada Papers*, i. 298.

which they belonged. The same thing was true of the bands of retainers furnished by the gentry. Accordingly, when the Queen decided to station men in Essex, her decision involved at once a considerable increase in her expenses. In regard to this Walsingham wrote to Burghley on the 18th of July: 'For the defraying of the charges [of these forces] her Majesty's pleasure is your Lordship shall consider what course may be held for the taking up of a convenient sum of money. Her Majesty named £40,000 or £50,000. I had some speech with Mr. Horatio [Palavicino] about the matter who can give best advice therein. He thinketh that upon the Merchant Adventurers' bonds there will be money found. There be divers rich Flemings residing in Cologne, Hamburg, and Frankfort that can furnish great sums.' [1]

It is evident from this passage that the Queen's treasury was so depleted of ready money that even so meagre a sum as £50,000 had to be sought for abroad. This question of financing the English preparations for war is one which belongs rather to a life of Burghley than to one of Walsingham.[2] It can only be touched on here, but should not be altogether ignored because it was undoubtedly a large factor in determining the reluctance both of the Queen and the Lord Treasurer.

There can be no manner of doubt that during the spring of 1588 Elizabeth was hard pushed for money. The subsidy granted by the Parliament of 1586–7 was coming in very slowly.[3] The customs revenues had fallen off with the stoppage of trade.[4] The Low Countries wars, in spite of all her thrift, consumed nearly half of her ordinary annual revenues.[5] She had to borrow freely during the winter and spring. In January 1588 she extorted, under the decent name of Privy Seals, a forced loan from her richer subjects, which brought in some £75,000.[6] In March she had been forced to negotiate a loan for £30,000 with the City of London at 10 per cent. interest.[7] And now that the navy was on a war footing the demands for victuals and wages were such

[1] Harl. MSS. 6994, f. 126.

[2] Some data on this subject will be found in Scott, *Joint Stock Companies*, i. 91–2.

[3] Scott, *op. cit.* i. 92.

[4] Ibid. iii. 519.

[5] Scott (*op. cit.* iii. 519) reckons the Queen's revenues of the fiscal year 1587–8, without taking account of loans, at £261,185 9*s.* 1½*d.* The expenses of the wars in the Low Countries for one year were £125,389 13*s.* 4*d.* (*Cal. Domestic*, Addenda, 1580–1625, p. 243).

[6] *Victoria County Hist.*, *Dorset*, ii. 144.

[7] Scott, *op. cit.* i. 92.

that Burghley saw no way to meet them.[1] It might have been urged that Parliament be called and additional money raised by taxes. But the fact was that between ship-money and the mustering of the county levies the country was already bearing as great a burden as it could well stand. Burghley himself remarked that the people were grumbling already at the unsupportable charge of the musters, that some of the towns were paying the equivalent of four subsidies in ship-money and that in consequence he thought it extremely unwise to increase ill feeling by the levy of new taxes.[2] The only expedient which occurred to him was that one which Walsingham had suggested, namely, that money be raised by loans abroad. But the fatal objection to that course was that it would take time and the demand was immediate. 'A man would wish,' he wrote to Walsingham on the 19th of July, 'if peace cannot be had, that the enemy would not longer delay but prove as I trust his evil fortune, for as these expeditions do consume us, so I would hope by God's goodness upon their defeat we might have one half year's time to provide for money.'[3]

While Howard was refitting his ships at Plymouth and Burghley was scratching his head in London for ways and means and Walsingham, desperate, was wishing himself in Basel, news suddenly reached Howard of the arrival of the Spanish fleet at the Lizard. Still weather-bound in Plymouth he managed to work his vessel out into the Channel and with great difficulty won a position to windward of the enemy. On the 21st he sent a brief letter announcing the fact to Walsingham. 'Sir,' he added in a postscript, 'the southerly wind that brought us back from the coast of Spain brought them out. God blessed us with turning us back. Sir, for the love of God and our country let us have with some speed some great shot sent us of all bigness, for this service will continue long, and some powder with it.'[4]

This news reached the Court at Richmond on the 23rd, and for the next ten days Walsingham and his colleagues of the Privy Council were in almost continuous session taking measures which seemed appropriate to meet the emergency. It appears

[1] *Armada Papers*, i. 284–5. Later Burghley estimated the charges of the fleet for one month for wages and victuals at £16,800 (*Armada Papers*, ii. 109).

[2] Burghley to Walsingham, 18 July 1588, S. P. Domestic, ccxii, no. 63.

[3] *Armada Papers*, i. 285.

[4] Ibid. i. 288.

that Elizabeth handed over the whole direction of affairs during this crisis to her Council,[1] and Walsingham's activity at this juncture was rather that of a Privy Councillor than of the Queen's Secretary. Nevertheless as the normal intermediary between the Queen and the Council he still had to do much of the work of both. All reports from the fleet, from the armed forces in camp and throughout the counties, from agents and ambassadors abroad, came to his hands. All requisitions for supplies were made through him, and the probabilities are that most of the business which the Council put through in these fateful times was prepared for it by Walsingham himself.

The problems which the Privy Council had to face during the fortnight when the Spanish Armada threatened the coasts of England were largely those imposed by the hand-to-mouth policy of the Queen. England, as Walsingham remarked the very day before the Armada was sighted, was every way unfit for war. There was little ready money in the treasury, there was a shortage both of weapons and of powder, the county levies, ill trained and very imperfectly equipped, were practically the only land forces upon which the Queen could draw, and the fleet was under-supplied with every necessity for a protracted struggle. The first thing to be done was to get an army together in order that some sort of resistance might be offered to the Spaniards in case they succeeded in affecting a landing. Steps were taken in this direction at once. Letters from the Council to the nobility called upon them to march to Court with their retainers. Other letters to the Lord-Lieutenants of the counties directed them to send up their forces to London. On the 23rd of July over 20,000 men were set in motion,[2] but it was perhaps well for Elizabeth that her throne did not depend upon their prompt mobilization.

The concentration of the English army was attended with the thousand and one details which such an operation involves, particularly in a country like England where the absence of a standing force denoted the absence of adequate machinery or officials to organize and maintain such a force when it was

[1] She apparently did, however, on at least one occasion contravene Council's orders (*Acts of Privy Council*, 1588, p. 189).

[2] Ibid., pp. 169–71. On the number of troops available and those summoned for service cf. Murdin, *Burghley Papers*, pp. 594–613.

suddenly collected. All this business the Privy Council had to assume, and in its relation to the army at this juncture it seems to have busied itself with everything from the question of disposing the troops to meet the enemy to the question of supplying them with small beer.[1] The most serious problem perhaps was that of equipping the half-armed county levies. The troops in this array were expected to provide their own equipment and in consequence they were for the most part very ill provided. Even the retainers of the gentry lacked complete equipment both of arms and armour. These deficiencies were made up in part from the arsenals at the Tower and at Windsor Castle and some muskets were imported out of Germany.[2] Yet it is doubtful whether the supply from these sources was sufficient to meet the demand. One of Walsingham's agents in the Low Countries was directed to ascertain what the possibilities were of purchasing arms and armour in that quarter, but it does not appear that any supply was secured from there.[3] Here again the Queen's lack of foresight is abundantly apparent. Her raw levies at best were a sorry company, without weapons they were little better than a mere mob. The royal arsenals at least should have been adequately supplied for their equipment. It was no time to be pricing muskets and breastplates in Amsterdam when the Spanish Armada was in sight of the English coast.

It is curious to remark that Elizabeth was even dilatory about availing herself of such trained soldiers as she had at her disposal. In the Low Countries there were some five or six thousand Englishmen who knew how to push a pike and let off an arquebus. With these as a nucleus a respectable fighting force might have been created for defensive purposes. There was talk of recalling English troops from the Low Countries as early as June, and early in July Lord Willoughby announced to the States General that the Queen would probably be forced to recall 2,000 of her English troops.[4] Yet no positive orders to this effect appear to have been dispatched to Willoughby until the 26th of July, and then only 1,000 men were recalled for the purpose of reinforcing

[1] *Acts of Privy Council*, 1588, p. 202.

[2] Ibid., pp. 197–8, 203, 205, 207, 220. It should be observed that these muskets were sold to the soldiers, not freely distributed; prices are noted in *Acts of Privy Council*, 1588, p. 288.

[3] *Armada Papers*, i. 312.

[4] *Cal. Ancaster MSS.*, pp. 154, 159.

Howard's fighting forces in the fleet.[1] Even those did not arrive in England until the need for them had passed.[2] It is true that the Dutch objected to the reduction of their forces and reminded the Queen that she was bound by treaty to maintain 5,000 men for their support. Yet they were prepared to acquiesce if Elizabeth would allow them the pay of the troops she meant to withdraw in order that others might be provided in their place.[3] Here was probably where the shoe pinched, Elizabeth preferring to do without her soldiers rather than to increase her expenses.

In connexion with the preparations of armed forces for defence by land it is interesting to observe that Walsingham's personal contribution to the Queen's army was larger than that of any member of the nobility or of the Council with the exception of Hatton's and Essex's. He agreed in fact to supply 50 lances, 10 petronels, and 200 foot soldiers for the defence of Elizabeth's person.[4] He may have hoped to get into the fight himself if fight there should be. At any rate he ordered a new suit of armour.[5]

The raising and equipping of an army for defence, though very important as a precautionary measure, was far less important than that of sustaining the fleet grappling with the Armada in the Channel. For the Privy Council knew, Walsingham best of all, that, if the fleet failed, the army was a broken reed to lean upon. So the main energy of the Councillors during the critical

[1] *Armada Papers*, i. 328 ; *Cal. Ancaster MSS.*, p. 175.

[2] Walsingham wrote to Burghley, 9 Aug. 1588 : 'To-day at noon her Majesty had news from Sir Thos. Morgan who has arrived at Margate with his 1,000 shot' (Harl. MSS. 6994, f. 142).

[3] *Cal. Ancaster MSS.*, pp. 159–60.

[4] *Cal. Foljambe MSS.*, p. 40. It is hardly to be presumed that Walsingham could recruit so large a force as this from his personal retainers. A letter which he wrote to the deputy-lieutenant of Wiltshire throws some light upon the way he recruited them. He wrote that being desirous to erect a cornett of horse to attend upon her Majesty and being at this present not so well furnished therewith as he could wish, he had made choice, among other gentlemen, of Mr. William Darell of Wiltshire to serve him personally with as many horses as he conveniently may. Walsingham desired the deputy-lieutenant not to throw any obstacles in Darell's way (S. P. Domestic, Supplementary, xv, undated). Further correspondence between Walsingham and Darell on this subject will also be found in S. P. Domestic, Supplementary, xv. On Darell, cf. Hall, *English Society in the Elizabethan Age*, passim.

[5] Burnham to Walsingham, 15 July 1588 : 'Adrian the armourer is gone to Utrecht and Amsterdam to get your honour's armour done, in the which there shall be no want of diligence used that your honour may be served speedily' (S. P. Holland, xxv).

period which followed the discovery of the Spanish Armada in the mouth of the Channel on the 19th of July was directed to the supply and the reinforcement of the fleet. The most pressing need was for powder and shot. Every letter from Howard brought new demands for these indispensable commodities, and the Council did its best to satisfy him. Two lasts[1] of powder were sent him on the 23rd, five on the 24th to Portsmouth, ten more on the 25th to the Downs, and thirty more via Dover on the 26th.[2] How much of that which the Council ordered to be sent Howard actually received it is difficult to say. According to Sir Thomas Heneage the Lord Admiral never got a single corn of it.[3] This statement was certainly an exaggeration,[4] yet Howard himself bore it out in part. On the 7th of August he wrote to Walsingham thanking him for his zeal in attending to the wants of the fleet. 'I would', he added, 'some were of your mind. If we had had that which had been sent, England and Her Majesty had had the most honour that ever any nation had.'[5] There is a hint here that every one was not so eager as Walsingham to see the fleet adequately supplied. The probabilities are, however, that it was not lack of zeal but lack of powder which was chiefly responsible for the shortage. Quite evidently the store on hand was very low, so low that the Privy Council had to take all sorts of measures to replenish it. Some powder was imported from Germany, some requisitioned from private stores, and some manufactured.[6] An attempt was even made to fetch some over from Flushing, but the speed with which captured Spanish ships were plundered of their ammunition to furnish Howard's navy shows how serious the deficit was.[7]

After Gravelines, when the Armada was fleeing northward with Drake hot on its trail, it was shortage of powder and shot which prevented the English from striking a last decisive blow. To be sure the consumption of ammunition in the Channel

[1] The last of powder was 24 barrels of 100 lb. each.

[2] *Acts of Privy Council*, 1588, pp. 171, 176–81, 187; cf. also Walsingham to Burghley, *Armada Papers*, i. 327.

[3] Ibid. ii. 95.

[4] Cf. ibid., i. 363, and ii. 63, for evidence to show that some of the ammunition sent actually did reach the fleet.

[5] Ibid., ii. 55.

[6] *Acts of Privy Council*, 1588, pp. 30, 191, 193.

[7] *Armada Papers*, i. 303, 326, 334, 338, 357; *Acts of Privy Council*, 1588, pp. 189–90, 192.

engagements far exceeded all precedent. Spanish veterans confessed that even Lepanto was child's play beside Gravelines.[1] Under these circumstances the Privy Council's handling of the emergency was highly commendable. The fault lay with the Queen, whose thrifty economy in the past had prevented the accumulation of adequate supplies.

Even more than from lack of ammunition the fleet suffered from lack of victuals. Here again the Privy Council sought to meet the demand by accumulating stores of provision along the South and East coasts, so that Howard might pick them up as he passed.[2] Yet once again the supply proved inadequate to the demand and Howard had to abandon his pursuit of the Spaniards for lack of meat. According to Sir Thomas Heneage the supply on the flagship ran so low at the last 'that my Lord Admiral was driven to eat beans, and some to drink their own water'.[3] No doubt this was an exaggeration, though it is certain that shortage of victuals, like shortage of ammunition, seriously hampered the effectiveness of the English fleet. 'I am sorry', Walsingham wrote to Hatton on the 8th of August, 'the Lord Admiral was forced to leave the prosecution of the enemy through the wants he sustained. Our half-doings doth breed dishonour and leaveth the disease uncured.'[4]

After the actual fighting began both the Queen and her Council left the management of the main fleet to Lord Howard and his captains. The only attempt apparently which was made to influence his tactics from the Court was a suggestion that he should reinforce his crews to such an extent that he could risk grappling with the enemy and boarding their ships.[5] In the opening engagements Howard had wisely preferred to fight at long range in order to take full advantage of the superior mobility of his ships and of his superior gunnery. But these tactics brought in few prizes and were too new to naval warfare to appeal to the more conservative Councillors reared in an older school. Howard was not only advised to fight at close quarters but musketeers were provided for him in Kent and troops were brought from the Low Countries under Sir Thomas Morgan to

[1] Corbett, *Drake*, ii. 271; *Armada Papers*, ii. 60.
[2] *Acts of Privy Council*, 1588, pp. 183, 211, 213.
[3] *Armada Papers*, ii. 95. [4] Ibid. ii. 69.
[5] *Acts of Privy Council*, 1588, p. 185; cf. also *Armada Papers*, i. 317.

reinforce his crews. Howard, however, does not seem to have acted on the suggestion, and in consequence the Queen was disposed to call him to question.[1] His defence is not on record, but Sir Walter Raleigh wrote a brilliant justification of his tactics somewhat later.[2]

With Seymour's fleet in the Narrow Seas both the Queen and her Council were a good deal more meddlesome. After the opening engagements between Howard and the Armada Elizabeth seems to have wavered between the policy of keeping Seymour still to watch Parma and sending him westward to reinforce the main fleet. On the 25th of July the Privy Council ordered him to join Howard; but later on the same day the Queen instructed Walsingham to write and stay him.[3] Three days later these instructions were changed again and Seymour was ordered once more to the westward. By that time, however, he had already taken the bull by the horns, and pleading urgent appeals from Howard set off to join the main fleet on the 27th.[4] So he was present at the affair of the fire-ships off Calais on the 28th and played a valiant part in the action off Gravelines on the 29th. Meantime the Privy Council had undertaken to strengthen the Narrow Seas by the dispatch of eight ships from London under Gorges on the 26th and of ten more furnished by the Merchant Adventurers under Edward Billingham on the 1st of August.[5] None of these, however, arrived until the Armada had been driven into the North Sea, and during the most critical period, when the Spanish fleet was still intact off Calais, the Narrow Seas seem to have been almost stripped bare of English men-of-war. The Dutch fleet, however, was closely watching Parma's obvious ports of egress, Nieupoort and Dunkirk,[6] and in any case it was safe to presume that Parma would not put to sea in his flatboats with the main English fleet still undefeated to windward. It was the soundest sort of strategy, as Drake and the old sea dogs knew, to concentrate all the available forces of England upon Medina Sidonia at Calais. If Sidonia could keep his place and guard the

[1] *Armada Papers*, i. 355.
[2] Ibid. i, p. lxvi.
[3] *Acts of Privy Council*, 1588, pp. 180, 189; cf. *Armada Papers*, i. 330.
[4] *Armada Papers*, i. 335; ii. 57.
[5] Ibid. i. 311, 315; *Acts of Privy Council*, 1588, pp. 181, 210; cf. *Armada Papers*, i. 339; ii. 42, 48. Men had to be impressed for service in Gorges' fleet.
[6] *Armada Papers*, ii. 49–50.

passage for Parma's crossing England was in real danger of invasion, but if Sidonia was driven to leeward and prevented from recovering his position, Parma might gaze across the Channel as he would, but he was powerless to follow his glance. Had Elizabeth grasped this fact she might have been less concerned about guarding the Straits of Dover than she was. Fortunately Seymour did not receive her various commands and counter-commands or ventured to ignore them if he did. He was certainly, through no fault of his mistress, in the place where he was most needed in the critical action of the 29th July.

Of Walsingham's attitude towards the naval strategy in the Channel fighting there is unhappily no trace or record. The presumption is that being of Drake's school of thought he preferred aggressive tactics throughout. He was evidently one of the most zealous of all the Councillors in his efforts to keep the fleet adequately supplied. In this connexion it is interesting to observe that some days before Howard drove the Armada from the Calais roads by the use of fire-ships Walsingham had dispatched seventy-two barrels of pitch to Dover and had ordered the preparation of fire-ships there. It cannot of course be argued that Walsingham anticipated exactly the situation at Calais, but he no doubt realized that Medina Sidonia, in order to assist Parma's projected invasion, would have to come to anchor somewhere near the Channel passage, and he made his provision accordingly. It is not impossible that Giambelli, the Mantuan engineer who had blown up Parma's bridge at Antwerp in 1585 and who was in England at the time, may have suggested the idea to Walsingham,[1] although it was one which would naturally occur to anybody acquainted with the tactics of sixteenth-century naval warfare. Walsingham's fire-ships were certainly very simple affairs, mere boats filled with faggots and pitch, none of your elaborate, mechanical, Giambelli 'hell burners'.[2] Howard sent in to Dover for these fire-ships on Sunday night but decided later not to wait for their

[1] Giambelli went over to England in August 1585 with a note from Sir John Norris commending him to Walsingham as follows: 'Frederick Jembell, an Italian born, a man very famous for his knowledge and skill in fireworks and the only inventor which framed the late fireworks sent out against the bridge from Antwerp' (23 Aug. 1585, S. P. Holland, iii). On 21 June 1590, Giambelli was granted a life pension of £100 a year by Elizabeth (*Cal. S. P. Domestic*, 1581–90, p. 672).

[2] *Armada Papers*, i. 362–3.

arrival.[1] The fire-ships which dislodged the Spaniards from their anchorage off Calais were not of Walsingham's provision, but improvised ones made up from small vessels in the fleet itself.

It is not necessary to repeat here the story of the naval battles in the Channel. Off Plymouth and again off St. Alban's Head and again at the Isle of Wight, the two opposed fleets engaged but without decisive consequences. Sidonia meanwhile was moving steadily up the Channel. When he reached Calais he cast anchor in order to establish connexion with Parma on shore and to arrange for joint action. There it was that the English fleet found him and thence on Sunday night, the 28th, dislodged him with their fire-ships. The battle of Gravelines which followed the next day was the greatest single engagement of the whole conflict, and though Howard did not decisively defeat the Spaniards even then, he drove them out of the Channel and to leeward of Parma's position. Indeed, he very nearly drove them on to the Zeeland shoals, but a fortunate shift of the wind saved them from that disaster and allowed them to shape their course northward through the German Ocean. Gravelines practically ended the struggle between the English and the Spanish fleets. They never engaged again though Drake and Howard followed close upon Sidonia's heels and hoped to finish the work they had begun. 'We have the army of Spain before us,' Drake wrote to Walsingham on the 31st of July, 'and mind with the grace of God to wrestle a pull with him. There was never anything pleased me better than the seeing the enemy flying with a southerly wind to the northward. God grant you have a good eye to the Duke of Parma, for with the grace of God, if we live, I doubt it not but ere it be long so to handle the matter with the Duke of Sidonia as he shall wish himself at St. Mary Port among his orange trees.'[2]

With the departure of the Spanish fleet from the Channel the question which most troubled the Queen and her Council was as to where they were going and whether they would come back. The greatest fear was of Scotland where the attitude of the King was uncertain if not actually hostile, and where, as Walsingham remarked, a few months before, 'the employment of 2,000 men

[1] Ibid. ii. 8–9.
[2] Ibid. i. 364.

by the enemy with some portion of treasure may more annoy us than 30,000 men landed in any part of this realm.' [1] To face this danger the Earl of Huntingdon had for months been mustering and training the county levies in North England, but it was generally agreed that the best way to secure the 'postern gate' was by securing the goodwill of the Scottish King. In June Walsingham had strongly urged that an ambassador be dispatched to James with 'such sufficient matter as shall make a strong gap',[2] but nothing was done until July, when a certain Mr. Asheby was sent north early in the month.[3] Exactly what Asheby's instructions were does not appear, but judging from his conduct it may be presumed that he was directed to entertain the King with words and general fair promises. Probably Walsingham whispered in his ear before he left that if occasion seemed to warrant it he had better not scruple to exceed his instructions.[4] Asheby had audience with James on the 24th of July and spoke many words and made many fair promises,[5] but the King was evidently not satisfied and seemed disposed to hunt with the Spanish party. By that time news of the approaching Armada had reached Scotland and Asheby decided that he had better follow another course. 'The necessity of the time', he wrote to Burghley on the 6th of August, 'and the imminent danger of a revolt in this country by the approaching of the Spaniard into the Narrow Seas, has made me make such offers as follow to satisfy his Majesty for the time and to qualify the minds of the nobility to keep all in quiet whilst her Majesty and her Council resolve what is to be done.' [6] The offers which Asheby made were an English Duchy with appropriate revenues, a pension of £5,000, a royal guard of 50 gentlemen to be maintained about his person at the Queen's charge, and a force of 100 foot and 100 horse to be maintained at the border. The offer served its purpose. On the 5th of August James definitely

[1] 12 Nov. 1587, Cotton MSS., Galba D ii, f. 178.

[2] 19 June 1588, S. P. Domestic, ccxi, no. 36.

[3] His dispatch had been decided on sometime before 9 July (*Cal. Salisbury MSS.* iii. 337). He was in Edinburgh on 20 July (*Cal. Scottish*, 1586–8, p. 582).

[4] Cf. Camden, *Annales* (Eng. trans. 1635), p. 371. In referring to the large offers which Asheby a little later made to the King, Camden wrote: 'Whether [Asheby made these offers] out of his own head or by commandment of others I cannot well say nor do I list to be curious in searching.'

[5] *Cal. Salisbury MSS.* iii. 342.

[6] S. P. Scotland, xlii, no. 108.

proclaimed his hostility to Spain and ordered out the country to repel invasion.[1] So the Scottish danger was ended for the time. Late in August, when the Spanish fleet had passed beyond recall, Walsingham wrote a sharp letter to Asheby reproving him for making offers to the King which Elizabeth had not authorized,[2] though £3,000 was sent to James to alleviate his disappointment.[3]

Besides the Scottish danger the Privy Council foresaw the possibility that Medina Sidonia might put into some German or Danish port or into the Baltic Sea to refit, and thence when the winds favoured sally forth once more against England.[4] Howard and Drake, even after they had returned from their pursuit of the Armada as far north as the Firth of Forth, were both of this opinion.[5] Indeed, as late as the 1st of September, the Privy Council sent a letter to Lord Willoughby in the Low Countries informing him that they had reason to believe that the Spanish Armada was about to descend from the north of Scotland into the Narrow Seas and charging him to urge the Dutch to keep their fleet at sea.[6]

It was generally feared also that Parma in desperation, notwithstanding the failure of the Armada, would attempt a sudden descent upon England if he found the English fleet off its guard.[7] Walsingham himself gave voice to this fear when he wrote to Burghley on the 9th of August: 'The Flushingers were forced to retire from Dunkirk the last storm and the gap left open being not as yet retrieved. But I hope that through the Lord Admiral's care they will be stopped in their passage.' [8]

Nevertheless, in spite of the pretty general feeling that the danger had not yet passed, Elizabeth set about at once to disarm. On the 3rd of August Walsingham wrote to William Darell: 'Order is given to the counties abroad here for the stay of the forces now coming out of the same hitherwards, because (God be thanked) the success of her Majesty's services at the sea is such that we are in good hope to stand in no need of land service. Howbeit the stay of these forces is such that they may be in readiness upon any sudden or short warning again to be given

[1] *Cal. Salisbury MSS.* iii. 343.
[2] Walsingham to Asheby, 22 Aug. 1588, Cotton MSS., Caligula D i, f. 326.
[3] *Cal. Border Papers*, i. 332.
[4] *Acts of Privy Council*, 1588, p. 225.
[5] *Armada Papers*, ii. 59, 68.
[6] *Acts of Privy Council*, 1588, p. 257.
[7] Ibid., p. 213.
[8] *Armada Papers*, ii. 83.

them.'[1] Two days later Leicester was directed to dismiss two-thirds of his force at Tilbury if he saw no cause to the contrary, though the precaution was to be taken of discharging first those who came from counties near adjoining so that they might be recalled upon short notice.[2] It is not certain whether or not Leicester carried out this suggestion. At any rate nine days later the Privy Council left him no discretion in the matter but commanded him to reduce his forces to 6,000 footmen forthwith.[3] Three days after that he was ordered to dismiss even this residue and to dissolve his camp.[4]

The fleet was kept in full strength somewhat longer, but late in August Drake and Hawkins began to reduce it by the discharge of many of the armed merchantmen,[5] and this reduction continued at such a rate that by the 4th of September, out of 197 ships with crews aggregating 15,925 men which had gone to make up the naval strength of England when the Armada was in the Channel, only 34 ships with crews aggregating 4,453 men remained at the Queen's charge.[6] The problem of discharging the others, which involved paying them off, fell for the most part upon Sir John Hawkins's shoulders as Treasurer of the Royal Navy, and between the demands of the sailors and the parsimony of the Queen he had a bitterly hard time of it. 'God I trust will deliver me of it ere it be long,' he wrote to Walsingham on the 5th of September, 'for there is no other hell.'[7] Early in September the men-of-war which had formed the nucleus of Howard's main fleet were laid up at Chatham and Seymour's squadron in the Narrow Seas was reduced to some half a dozen ships under Sir Henry Palmer.[8] Late in September, when news reached London of the arrival of the Spanish fleet on the west coast of Ireland, it was proposed to dispatch a squadron to Ireland under Sir Richard Grenville, loaded with soldiers under the command of Sir Walter Raleigh. But as it became apparent that the Spaniards there were in no mood for fighting, the project was

[1] S. P. Domestic, Supplementary, xv; cf. *Acts of Privy Council*, 1588, p. 215.

[2] *Acts of Privy Council*, 1588, pp. 222–3.

[3] Ibid., p. 234.

[4] Ibid., p. 239, but apparently Leicester was directed to retain 400 men, who were ordered to be paid off on 2 September (ibid., p. 261).

[5] *Armada Papers*, ii. 146, 163.

[6] Ibid. 212, 331.

[7] Ibid. 214.

[8] Ibid. 212; *Acts of Privy Council*, 1588, p. 265; *Cal. Spanish*, 1586–1603, p. 431.

abandoned. The last of all the measures for retrenchment of charges by the Queen was the discharge of the beacon watches along the coast early in October.[1]

After the Armada had passed beyond the Channel it was Walsingham's principal care to prevent the Queen from disarming herself too quickly. 'It were not wisdom,' he wrote to Burghley on the 9th of August, 'until we see what will become of the Spanish fleet to disarm too fast, seeing her Majesty is to fight for a kingdom.' Howard and Drake were both of his opinion, but Burghley, even as early as the 9th of August, seems to have held that there was no further danger to be apprehended from the Spanish fleet and to have advocated a reduction of forces.[2] Like the Queen his thoughts ran to the necessity of speedy retrenchment. Fortunately his sanguine expectations were justified and the sudden return of England to a peace footing proved to be a safe course.

Enough has been said already to indicate the part which Walsingham played in the defence of England in 1588. He was without doubt mainly instrumental in inducing the Queen to make such preparations as she did make to withstand the Spanish attack. He was above all others the man who provided her with accurate reports of the plans and purposes of the Spanish fleet and of its fighting strength. It was largely due to his diligence that the English navy was kept supplied with enough victuals and munitions to maintain the week's fighting in the Channel. The glory of the achievement has been given to Howard, and above all to Drake, but Walsingham deserves a larger share of it than has ordinarily been accorded to him. Without him Burghley's too timid counsels coupled with Elizabeth's inveterate parsimony and procrastination might have exposed England altogether unready to the blow which Philip of Spain aimed at her. Sir Francis Drake was keenly conscious of that fact and Lord Henry Seymour had the grace to bear testimony to it. 'I will not flatter you,' he wrote to Walsingham on the 18th of August, 'but you have fought more with your pen than many have in our English navy fought with their enemies, and but that your place and most necessary attendance about

[1] *Acts of Privy Council*, 1588, pp. 277–8, 297, 302, 331.

[2] *Armada Papers*, ii. 59, 62, 68, 84, 85.

her Majesty cannot be spared, your valour and deserts in such places opposite to the enemy had showed itself.'[1] Even Elizabeth, who was never prodigal of words of praise for her secretary, did not let his services pass altogether without recognition. Thomas Windebank, Clerk of the Signet, wrote to Walsingham on the 14th of September:

'After her Majesty had read these letters the first thing she said was to know how you did, whereunto I answered that you had begun your physic yesterday because you would lose no time. Hereupon her Majesty continued her speech and willed me so to write to you, that such as having power to seek and take remedy in time for any their griefs were like to find remedy and so she hoped you should do. Whereupon I said that among other things wherein God had lately showed His goodness this was one to be accounted, that He had given you health and strength in these late occasions of troubles to attend to the service and spared you from sickness hitherto. Her Majesty confirmed my saying with many gracious and comfortable words towards you.'[2]

With this poor reward for all his travail, the only reward his mistress vouchsafed him, Walsingham, now that the danger to England had passed, crept back into retirement once more to renew his losing battle with his mortal disease.

APPENDIX TO CHAPTER XV

Correspondence of Wm. Harborne

1. William Harborne to Sir Francis Walsingham, [9th of March, 1586/7?].

The following document is preserved in the B.M. Harleian MSS. 295, ff. 176 ff. It is apparently in the hand of Thomas Phelippes, Walsingham's secretary. It is undated, but from the references to its contents made in document 2 below, it appears to have been written in the spring of 1587. Probably it is an abstract of Harborne's letter of 9 March 1587. On the margin in a later hand is written 'An extract of a letter showing the King of Spain's earnest labouring to get a truce with the Turk that so he might convert all his forces against Q. Eliz.' There is no external indication as to the sender or the recipient of this letter, but there can be little doubt from its contents that it was from Harborne to Walsingham.

'One John Stephano, a Milanese, being secretly arrived at Constantinople in February, has by the means of the Viceroy

[1] *Armada Papers*, ii. 126.

[2] Harleian MSS. 286, f. 149.

and Ebrahim Pasha and the Beglerbey of Grecia, upon a promise of 60,000 Ducats &c., obtained a truce for the K. of Spain, the Pope, the Florentine and the Genoese for three years, although it were given out that the same was deferred till the coming thither of Mavillano, for whom he pretendeth to abuse the English and French Ambassador that he came to fetch a passport to come and conclude the same.

The words of the Spanish agent's expostulation to the Viceroy was to this effect. For so much as the truce passed between their masters had been royally accomplished &c. his Mr. required that the same might be renewed and perfectly observed for the said K. his Mr., the Pope, &c. for three years, whereby the Grand Signor should have the better means to subdue the Persian, whom his Mr. would by no means assist, as also his said Mr. might prevail against her Majesty, against whom he had in readiness great forces by land and a navy of 400 ships by sea, to revenge certain manifest injuries her Majesty had of late done to him, but in special in taking a great treasure in a ship of his subjects coming from the Indies, which notwithstanding if she would peaceably return, he would in no sort molest.

The Viceroy, mere Spanish, doth by all means travail to weary him and ceaseth not to offer him all sort of injuries.

The Beglerbey of Grecia, the Grand Signor's mignon, has taken upon him to draw the Grand Signor from consenting to the said truce, but, being won with Spanish presents, he findeth him secretly to join with the rest.

He therefore addressed himself to the Grand Signor's Schoolmaster, of great reputation in that Court, as it were the Pope among papists, [*passage underlined crossed out*] by whose hands he presented a supplication to the Grand Signor, discovering the malice of his adversaries and showing it not to be for the Grand Signor's honour and commodity to yield the K. of Spain's request, whereof he received 2 answers in one day, viz.—That he should send her Majesty one flying in post to certify her that the K. of Spain their common enemy's request for truce should neither now nor hereafter be granted. And therefore that she should courageously persecute her quarrel and that he, being from time to time advertised of the success, would assist those proceedings in all good offices.

The second, that his Schoolmaster, in his conference with the Viceroy of the Span. proceedings, should not be known of that which had passed between the Grand Signor and him, to whom the promise made in her Majesty's behalf should be faithfully accomplished, and that he should send a Courier to the end her Majesty might be first certified of that which was passed, for that he would stay his answer therefore to the Spaniard.

He, being destitute of friends otherwise and daring not trust anybody to be sent purposely of his own with the Viceroy's passport, which were necessary, was fain to attend this Venetian courier.

In the meantime, to give the Spanish agent a more open foil, he hath presented a second petition, replying to the Grand Signor's answer, with an addition penned by the Grand Signor's Schoolmaster, whereof he hath sent copies, and expecting answer according to his liking, he desireth to have particular advice by the bearer what he shall say in that matter on her Majesty's behalf, which would be necessary, for he undertakes the Q. shall keep the K. of Spain occupied during the Persian wars.

One of the occasions why the K. of Spain demandeth this truce is, as he is informed, for that being desirous to use the forces which certain Barons of Apulia, Calabria, Naples, Cicilia, Sardinia &c. do by their tenures and oaths maintain against invasion of the Turks, they refuse to suffer them to be employed any other way, without assurance by truce or league with the Turk that it shall be no way to their prejudice in that behalf.

He hath been credibly informed, by one that heard it of the Venetian Baglio his own mouth, that in secret he hath uttered that the Signoria had certain advice from their ambassador in Spain that all the forces the K. of Spain could possibly make this year by sea and land was against her Majesty, which he doubted not but should proceed forthwith upon assurance of this truce by Stephano.

The French Ambassador Lancino hath dealt with him earnestly by interposed persons to join for the common welfare of their sovereigns against the Sp. K. proceedings, and desired personal conference, excusing his former incivility. But, because their credit decays greatly in Turkey and the conference with any papist might give occasion of slander to his proceedings in that Court, he hath forborne to treat with him, only satisfied him with good words and assurance that he will perform all good endeavours on his part, though he mean not to acquaint him with his secret proceedings. And yet and truth he findeth that the said F. Ambassador exposeth himself seriously against Stephano, the Spanish Agent.

He wrote before (I remember) that he might deliver some good words in her Majesty's name to one don Alvaro a Portuguese there who hath The Viceroy [*words underlined crossed out*];

The Admiral with much ado hath restored nine English captives which, upon the Grand Signor's commandment reiterated, he durst no longer detain, but yet for spite would not give them to himself but to one Don Alvaro a Portuguese, who after he had paid their charges presented them to the Ambassador gratis in demonstration of his affection to her Majesty's service, which he doth in all things advance without any benefit to himself whatsoever he is able by his credit in those parts, being very great in regard of his experience, wisdom and wealth. If it were thought convenient he could crave her Majesty's grateful letter to him for a mean to continue and encourage him in like endeavours.

He desireth to be advised how to proceed in defence of Paulo Mariane, constituted Consul of the English nation at Cairo, whereof he wrote 24 October, as also with the Admiral, whereof he wrote in his letters in June last.'

Endorsed: 'Extract of Mr. Harborne's letter.'

2. Sir Francis Walsingham to Wm. Harborne, 24th of June 1587.

[This is the original letter signed in Walsingham's own hand written, largely in cipher undeciphered. It is preserved in the Bodleian Library, Tanner MSS. lxxix, ff. 125 ff. This letter is written in the code later used with Barton, Harborne's successor, the key to which is preserved in P. R. O. Cipher Book, Eliz. i, f. 3. The passages in italics are in cipher in the original. In Tanner MSS. lxxix, ff. 127 ff., there is a contemporary copy of this letter also in cipher, but with the passages put into cipher selected a little differently. It also shows some slight verbal changes in the text. It is endorsed 'Copy of the letter sent 7th of June', though the original is plainly dated 24 June. Possibly, because of the difficulties attending the conveyance of letters to Constantinople, two copies of this letter were sent by different routes at different dates.

There are four other letters from Walsingham to Harborne among the Tanner MSS. Two are dated 23 May 1585, and commend a bearer, named in one of the letters as Mr. Jerome, to Harborne's good offices (Tanner MSS. lxxviii, ff. 76, 108); one is dated 8 October 1586, and commends a certain Captain Ellis to Harborne (ibid., f. 68); one is dated 18 June 1586, and recommends the cause of an English merchant captured by the Algerian pirates (ibid., f. 154). None of these is in cipher. There is also a copy of a letter from Harborne to Walsingham undated, but probably written in the spring of 1587 (ibid., f. 40). None of these is of first-rate importance.]

'I have received your letters of the 9th of March brought hither from Venice by an express messenger about the end of the last month whereby, as also by sundry others of yours, I find how carefully and discreetly you have proceeded in your negotiations *with the Sultan and his Counsellors upon points committed to you in charge*, wherewith, having also acquainted her Majesty, she resteth very well satisfied, being right glad that you have received *so direct an address to the Sultan* as you write by *his Schoolmaster*, *whose friendship* for that purpose *she wisheth you by all good means* to nourish and maintain. And for answer of that you write, her pleasure is that you let the Grand Signor understand that she most thankfully taketh this *his stay*, by you signified, *of renewing the truce desired by the King of Spain* which you shall in her name not only persuade him to continue but also show unto him how *necessary it is for him to attempt* somewhat *presently for* the impeachment of the said *Spaniard's greatness*, much more in truth to be doubted than of *Persia*, against whom his forces seem to be altogether bent, and may be performed by *setting such princes as are in Barbary at his devotion upon the King of Spain*, furnishing them for the purpose with some number of galleys, which with *small cost shall give him great annoyance*, whereunto *her Majesty's* hand will not be wanting. And you may tell him that if her Majesty already had not impeached the *King of Spain both by sh—pe* [illeg.] *sent to them and by forces sent into Flanders under the conduct of the Earl of Leicester, he had been possessed of* 99 *and other* such *places in Africa as would have been not a little prejudicial to the said Sultan ere this.* And for further proof hereof you may affirm that he beareth the princes of this part of the world in hand that *so soon as he hath ended his wars with her Majesty he will then join with them against the Sultan.* Howbeit the said K. of Spain hath sundry ways made *her Majesty* great offers of *peace, which have been by her hitherto refused* and would be *still if other princes,* who ought to *oppose themselves to his greatness, would concur with her against him.* And for the present you may signify unto the Grand Signor that her Majesty hath *lying upon the coast of Spain a fleet of very strong*, well furnished ships under the conduct of Sir Francis Drake which the last year spoiled and burned Carthagena and other places in the West Indies, who hath already entered divers ports of Spain and Portugal and within the Bay of Cales and other places, destroyed and taken a great part of the shipping and provisions of war and victuals provided for England and impeacheth all traffic by sea, wherein, although *her Majesty needeth no assistance of other princes* yet shall it be a great encouragement *and contentation to her Majesty as a more terror to the King of Spain*, they having like interest, *use like endeavour for to abate his power.* All which, as well to satisfy and stir up the Grand Signor as also to *disgrace your adversaries in that court and country*, I leave to yourself to be published, urged and enlarged as you shall see cause.

The letters nor the copies of the 14th of June which you mention in your letters of the 23rd of August containing the *lewd speeches used* by the *Admiral* against *her Majesty* &c. never came to my hands, so as nothing can directly be answered in that behalf. But where in respect of the said *Admiral's malice, so* [*un*]*willing* to reconcile himself unto you, and *the Viceroy's* partiality, being *corrupted by the King of Spain* and *the Venetian ambassador*, you seem to affect *your present return* and in a manner advise *a surcease of the trade*; considering the means you have now found by the *schoolmaster* both for speedier *remedy in causes concerning traffic* and for more *credit in your negotiation*, as it is everyway best for her Majesty's service and the benefit of the realm that the trade should continue, so I think for your own part your mind is *altered touching this point* and *therefore will hear thereof from you.* I have thought good to *forbear to deal with her Majesty therein.* Besides that by this time the Grand Signor I trust hath understood the great grace shown to his nation by our merchants, in causing all those which Sir Francis Drake the last year delivered out of the Spanish servitude, being slaves in their galleys, to be sent to Algiers free, which in all reason must move both the said Grand Signor, the Admiral and all that Court, if any be otherwise ill-affected, to favour the causes of our nation and be an occasion that hereafter none of them receive such hard measure as in times past.

You must excuse *her Majesty's seldom writing in regard of her sex*, the custom of our country and with such other arguments as your own discretion will readily afford; and principally by the effects of *her as it the most manifestly* and beneficially for that State appearing, both in *free traffic with the Sultan's subjects and prosecuting of his greatest and dreadful enemy the King of Spain*, which they that *write most can be content to let grow to the prejudice of* their allies. Besides you may allege the difficulty of *passage during* the Civil wars of France, which indeed is very true.

Her Majesty hath satisfied Ebrahim Pasha his request touching *Don Alvaro de Mendes to whom Don Antonio hath directed* a packet going herewith. I have also recommended his case as you require to Sir Edward Stafford and written a few lines in Latin unto himself to the effect you wished, which you may *accompany with all circumstance convenient.* And withal, to the end he may think his kindness towards our nation the better bestowed, you may make him acquainted how *by order from her Majesty Sir Francis Drake in this his present exploit upon Spain doth set free all Portugals with money in their purses* which come into their hands, where he *selleth the Spaniard to the Moors.*

And as it were well to seek by all fair means to win the *Admiral's favour*, if directly you cannot do it without dishonour to her Majesty, the said *Don Alvaro* might prove a good instrument to work a reconcilement underhand, having such credit with him as it seems, upon such instructions as yourself may devise for the purpose.

It is thought great reason you should maintain Paul Mariane, whom you write of, to the utmost of your power, being sworn to her Majesty's service, and therefore you are to employ your credit every way that he be not inquired to her Majesty's dishonour. Although her Majesty wisheth that L[ancino] be used with all ordinary and outward courtesy in respect of the good amity between his Mr. and her Majesty, and yet she liketh well that you *open not yourself nor your proceedings in* the *negotiations with the Sultan against the King of Spain.*

And so I commit you to the Almighty. From the Court at Greenwich the 24th of June 1587.

Your very loving friend,

FRA. WALSYNGHAM.

Since the writing hereof I received your letters of the iiij and xxth of April which require no other answer than is contained in the above written. Only I am to let you understand that her Majesty is well pleased, as well for your own satisfaction in that you have *a desire to be eased of that service*, as also for the reasons by you alleged that you should *return, leaving* your *secretary* in the place according to the *custom, whom the merchants* are content to *maintain*, whereof I thought good to advertise you to the end you may *prepare yourself* accordingly. And you shall between this and then receive such letters as you require to Viceroy, &c. And in the meanwhile you may, in pursuing the present *negotiations, make overture of your resolution* unto *the Sultan* and the rest in that Court, pretending that your meaning is by *personal journey* to effect and conclude such things as shall fall out there to be *projected* and *concluded.*

You may suffer *the French Ambassador to challenge* the *glory* of *chasing away the King of Spain again* for we can be content the *bruit in Christendom should* be that it was *his work*, which will be an occasion to *keep the King of Spain and his master joined.*'

Addressed to

The right honorable Mr. William Harborne, Esquire, Ambassador Resident for her Majesty at Constantinople.

XVI

THE YEAR AFTER THE ARMADA

THE defeat of the Armada did not of course, as the old books used to say, crush the power of Spain or establish the power of England. But it put the two combatants upon a different footing. England had now proved herself and from an insignificant island Power had become in the eyes of Europe a force to be reckoned with. Pope Sixtus V did not conceal his admiration for Drake's exploits and he swore that if Elizabeth were only a Catholic she would be his best beloved.[1] Philip of Spain found himself suddenly on the defensive and for the rest of his life, in spite of many projects to attack England again, he remained on the defensive. The story of the direct war between him and Elizabeth during the next ten years is a story of various English expeditions to the Spanish coast.

There can be little doubt that the result of the Armada infused a new spirit into the English or rather diffused through England at large the spirit and confidence of Drake and his sea dogs. England could fight—she had fought. The Spaniard could be thrashed—he had been thrashed. Even Walsingham, confirmed pessimist as he had come to be, felt the change, and though he railed still against the Queen's 'irresolutions and lacks' he did not prophesy the same dire calamities in consequence as he had prophesied in the past. His problem was now to induce the Queen to secure the fruits of victory rather than to ward off impending disaster.

It is not unlikely that Elizabeth herself began to take somewhat more kindly to the role of the militant virgin. There was after all something splendid about the plumed troop and the great wars which appealed to her love of splendour. Though the story of her speech at Tilbury is probably apocryphal she

[1] *Cal. Venetian*, 1581–91, p. 379. Gregorio Leti in his life of Elizabeth tells a ridiculous story of a plan to arrange a marriage between Elizabeth and the Pope.

was certainly present at the camp and rather more careless of her royal person than seemed quite safe to her counsellors. Something of her father's spirit was mingled in her with the thrifty bourgeois instinct of her grandfather and came out at times. Yet to the end of her days she never spent a penny cheerfully and her wars were waged in the same cheese-paring spirit that had characterized her days of peace.

For the moment, while England was ringing its bells and lighting its bonfires to celebrate victory, she was nursing a private grief. Leicester died early in September. It would perhaps be going too far to say that she loved the man. She lacked the power either to bestow or to command personal affection, but he certainly occupied a unique place in her regard and her grief at the loss of him reveals more of the woman in her than any other event in her whole career. According to Camden she had designed to make him Lieutenant of her whole kingdom under her, had not Burghley and Hatton prevented it. Yet she did not scruple at his demise to put his goods to sale in order to collect the debts he owed her.[1]

No man ever quite replaced Leicester in Elizabeth's affections and none ever combined as he had so much personal favour with so much political influence. The favourites who came after him, men like Raleigh and Essex, were courtiers rather than counsellors. Elizabeth, indeed, during her declining years, distinguished much more sharply between her statesmen and her playthings than she had in her youth. During the brief interval between Leicester's death and Walsingham's (a matter of less than two years) Elizabeth's affairs of state were handled in the main by Burghley, Hatton, and Walsingham.

Walsingham's active part in public business was appreciably diminished by his failing health. He was frequently away from Court either taking physic or recovering from the effects of it. Yet he virtually died in harness. Within a fortnight of his demise he was in his seat at the Council chamber.[2] His relations with his royal mistress seem to have been more kindly and cordial during this period than at any other time in his official

[1] Camden, *Annales* (Engl. trans. 1635), p. 373; Ellis, *Original Letters*, 3rd series, iv, p. 75.

[2] An Agenda paper in his hand, of business for the Privy Council, dated 23 Mar. 1589/90, is in S. P. Domestic, ccxxxi, no. 40.

Sir Francis Walsingham
from the original in the National Portrait Gallery

Emery Walker ph. sc.

career. This was perhaps the inevitable consequence of the crises through which they had passed together. After the Babington Plot and the Armada Elizabeth must have realized more completely than ever before the full value of Walsingham's services. She must have realized too, when she observed on his face the ravages of disease, that his days were numbered and that sobering fact may have induced in her a kind of consideration which was ordinarily foreign to her nature.

In Walsingham himself years and suffering had wrought manifest changes both in his temper and his purposes. If he did not altogether forgo the ambition of his earlier years to lead England forth as the champion of the Faith, he had probably come to the conclusion that such a glorious consummation was not to be expected in his lifetime. The difficulties in the way were too enormous to be overcome in the brief span of days which were allotted to him. Indeed the thoughts of his latter end must have bred in him a conviction of the futility of all human effort. He seems to have accepted the vacillations and caprices of his mistress with increased fortitude and to have adjusted himself as best he might to her hazy and fluctuating purposes, hoping for nothing perhaps so much as rest from his labours.

Besides these temperamental adjustments the course of events in itself had much to do with composing the relations between the Queen and her secretary. Much of their wrangling in the past had developed out of their differences of opinion over the problem of disposing of Mary Stuart, even more over the problem of peace or war with Spain. By the end of August 1588 both of these problems had been solved. Mary had been executed, England was at war with Spain. And so the two largest bones of contention between Walsingham and Elizabeth were disposed of. The fact that the disposition in each case accorded with Walsingham's advice served inevitably to increase his credit with his mistress.

Walsingham's relations to his colleagues in the Privy Council during the year and a half following the Armada are not easy to define with certainty. Leicester's death robbed his party of its most powerful advocate, though it may safely be presumed that Walsingham saw him go without much regret. He probably had done more harm than good to the cause during the years which followed his first expedition to the Low Countries. If he had any successor to his place in the Queen's affections it was Sir Christopher Hatton, now Lord Chancellor. In some measure also Hatton replaced Leicester as court champion of the Puritan party in the Council though he was too much the courtier to be a very ardent partisan. He and Walsingham stood together upon most questions of public policy as they had in the past.[1] Burghley's position as one of the chief pillars of the state and his relations to Walsingham remained unchanged. They were together the two men in whose wisdom the Queen chiefly relied and upon whose shoulders the chief burden of her mistakes inevitably fell.[2] The differences between them, which have been remarked on many times, tended to become less pronounced as time went on and particularly as the differences between Walsingham and Leicester developed. During the closing months of Walsingham's life he and Burghley worked together and even played together with cordial good feeling. As for the younger generation at Court the most conspicuous among them were Sir Walter Raleigh and the Earl of Essex. Neither of these had seats in the Privy Council while Walsingham lived, but their influence with the Queen was sufficiently great to be reckoned with. Of the two Walsingham seems to have distrusted and opposed Raleigh and to have favoured Essex.[3] Essex in fact became Walsingham's son-in-law, but the political connexion between them was at most slight. The star of Essex had hardly emerged from the horizon before Walsingham's star had set.

During the two years following the defeat of the Armada the matter of chief interest in English policy was of course the war with Spain. So far as the direct conflict between the two countries was concerned they developed into a series of raids, the more important of them under royal auspices, the less

[1] *Cal. Spanish*, 1587–1603, p. 431.

[2] Burghley to Walsingham, Nov. 1588: 'All irresolutions and lacks are thrown upon us two in all her speeches to everybody. The wrong is intolerable.' (S. P. Domestic, ccxviii, no. 50.)

[3] As early as July 1587 the relations between Walsingham and Essex were particularly intimate. On 21 July 1587, Essex wrote to his friend Dier an account of his quarrel with the Queen about Raleigh. In a postscript he added: 'If you show my letter to anybody let it be to my mother and Mr. Secretary.' (Devereux, *Lives of the Earls of Essex*, i. 189.)

important purely private ventures, upon the Spanish coast and the Spanish colonies. But in its larger aspects the Anglo-Spanish war involved also the rebellion in the Netherlands and even the civil wars in France. Walsingham had long insisted, and Elizabeth at last had come to believe, that the sand dunes of Holland and Zeeland were her chief bulwarks against Spain and that the cause of the Dutch rebels, much as she hated to admit it, was essentially the cause of England. She had discovered too, thanks again to Walsingham's reiterated arguments, that the Catholic league in France was little better than the tool of the Spanish King and that her own fortunes were very intimately involved in those of Henry of Navarre and his Huguenot following. Indeed she found herself surrounded by a ring of neighbours, in each one of which a struggle was in progress between a Roman Catholic party, whose plans and purposes were directed by her arch enemy, and a Protestant party which she was bound to regard as her first line of defence.

Scotland was the single exception. In Scotland the King was or seemed to be a good Calvinist and the reins of government were in the hands of the Calvinistic Protestant party. But the political complexion of the Scottish court had a quick way of changing overnight. There was a strong Catholic party in the country whose leaders were closely in touch with Spain and ready to promise that if sufficient money were furnished them Philip might have the kingdom at his command. The worst of it was that, as Elizabeth very well knew, these Catholic leaders were hardly over-stating the case. No argument was more potent with the impecunious Scottish noblemen than that of hard cash. Even his Calvinism had been known to succumb to it. And James VI was still little more than a plaything in the hands of the Scottish nobility.[1]

So it was that while Elizabeth was engaging Spain on the high seas and in the Netherlands and in France, she had to keep her eye ever open to the danger that her enemy might gain a footing at her 'postern gate'. No one in England was more alive to this danger than Walsingham himself and none had done more to avert it. Throughout the year 1587 he had tried hard to induce the Queen to secure the friendship of her Scottish brother

[1] Cf. Lang's Jocko story, *History of Scotland*, ii. 345.

by substantial concessions. He could not even persuade her to pay over to James the £4,000 pension which she was bound by treaty to send him. The consequence was that the Spanish Catholic party in Scotland, particularly its leader, the turbulent Earl of Huntly, increased steadily in favour at the Scottish court, so that at the very moment when the Spanish Armada was approaching the coast of England neither Walsingham nor his mistress was at all certain that the ports of Scotland might not be thrown wide open to receive it. At the eleventh hour hasty measures were taken to prevent such a calamity. £2,000 was dispatched to James early in July 1588 and later in the same month William Asheby was hurried off to Edinburgh to beguile the King with vague promises of larger favours. Some mention has been made of Asheby's mission already. He found the situation in Scotland so uncertain that he thought it expedient to venture beyond the strict limits of his official instructions and to make the King an offer of a large pension, an English dukedom, and a bodyguard. Probably Walsingham had prompted him to do as much at a pinch.

As a matter of course Elizabeth repudiated Asheby's offers so soon as the immediate danger from the Armada had passed.[1] James tried to force her hand by threatening to take advantage of Spanish offers, but without success.[2] The most she would yield him was £3,000 in cash, which was sent north early in September.[3]

'It is hoped here', Walsingham wrote to Sir Robert Sidney, 'that upon the delivery of the £5,000, whereof it seemeth they have more need than titles, they will not stand so peremptory upon Mr. Asheby's offers, which will not be assented unto whatsoever show they make of running foreign courses. . . . He [the King] is ill counselled if any cause draw him out with England, for if he should lose the possibility that he pretendeth to have to this crown after her Majesty's decease by serving Spain or France his turn by growing to a pike with us, there is neither of

[1] Walsingham to Asheby, 22 Aug. 1588, Cotton MSS., Caligula D i, f. 326.

[2] *Cal. Salisbury MSS.* iii. 350; cf. *Bardon Papers* (Camden Soc.), pp. 103 ff.

[3] *Cal. Border Papers*, i. 332; £2,000 had been sent to him in July (ibid. 550; Cotton MSS., Caligula D i, f. 163); £4,000 was due to James on his pension, or rather £8,000, since his pension of the previous year had not been paid. Elizabeth was really £3,000 in arrears to James even with her two payments aggregating £5,000.

them both that either can or will bestow the like kingdom upon him.' [1]

No doubt the strongest card Elizabeth had to play in her game with her Scottish brother was the prospect of the English throne. It was of course true that the presumptive title to the succession was already his by inheritance, but there can be little doubt that if Elizabeth had thrown the weight of her influence in favour of some other candidate her parliament would have been quite as ready to establish a new rule of succession as they had been in her father's time. No one realized this fact better than the Queen herself and she exploited it for all it was worth. She was careful not to commit herself in favour of James's claim, and yet at the same time to let him understand that she would offer no impediment to it if he showed himself friendly to her interests and to the interests of Protestant England. It would seem on the face of it that James had no choice but to follow her lead.

Yet there were other factors in the situation. It was not impossible that if he made terms with her enemies he might utilize the strength of Spain and Catholic France and of the large Catholic element in England itself to dethrone her and take her place without waiting for her to die. The shining example of his own mother's career taught James to look askance at any such alternative; still it was not without its merits from the point of view of diplomatic relations with England. He gave Elizabeth to understand that he might resort to it if she used him too badly, and Elizabeth recognized that such a course, even though it brought no profit to James, might bring disaster to herself. She could not therefore afford to be too dictatorial.

Another factor in the Scottish problem upon which the Queen always had to reckon was the effect of James's title to the succession upon her own councillors and courtiers. In spite of her desire to keep the matter in suspense it is pretty certain that by the year 1588, and probably even earlier, the most influential men at the English court were convinced that in the natural course of events James would be the next king in England.

[1] Walsingham to Sidney, 7 Sept. 1588, Cotton MSS., Caligula D i, f. 333. This letter is badly damaged by fire. One passage, and probably a significant one, is omitted in the extract quoted because the telling words are destroyed in the manuscript.

This conviction inevitably affected their attitude towards him, particularly as the Queen grew older. No statesman or courtier that hoped to survive his mistress was likely to do anything calculated to antagonize his future master. Walsingham observed as early as 1584 that men were beginning to look to the rising sun. Even before that Lord Hunsdon on the one hand and Leicester on the other had been making private bids for James's favour. How much intrigue of this sort was afoot in 1588 is difficult to say, but it is curious to observe that in June Elizabeth evidently intended to dispatch Sir Robert Carey—Hunsdon's son—to James, but later decided to send instead Sir Robert Sidney, Leicester's nephew.[1] There may be more in this than meets the eye. Certain it is that at the time of Leicester's death in September the King regarded him as the all-important factor in his relations with England.[2]

Walsingham's own attitude towards the succession during the brief residue of his life is not easy to discover from the rather scant surviving evidence. At the beginning of his official career he had been a strong advocate of the Earl of Huntingdon's claims. In 1586, however, he seems to have given James some sort of promise of support. This probably accounts for the changed attitude of the Scottish King towards him. The same James who in 1583 could not say enough hard things of Walsingham claimed him in 1588 as one of his staunchest friends and wisest counsellors.[3] Yet Walsingham is less open than most of his colleagues to the charge of seeking to feather his own nest. He was too near death himself to be troubled about his own position after the Queen's demise, and since he had no sons he had no family interests to serve like Hunsdon and Burghley. It is true that his son-in-law, the Earl of Essex, was making private bids for James's favour in the autumn of 1589 through the medium of John Hotman, one of Leicester's old servants, but there is no evidence that Walsingham was involved in the intrigue.[4]

[1] *Cal. Salisbury MSS.* iii. 329.
[2] Ibid. 359.
[3] *Cal. Scottish*, 1586–8, p. 650.
[4] *Cal. Salisbury MSS.* iii. 435–6, 438. Lady Penelope Rich and her admirer the poet Constable were also involved in this intrigue. A letter of hers to Hotman in which she mentioned Constable is printed in Blok, *Correspondance inédite de Robert Dudley, Comte de Leicester, et François et Jean Hotman*, p. 178. The curious letter in *Cal. Salisbury MSS.* iii. 441 probably has something to do with this Essex intrigue.

To Walsingham as to his mistress the matter of most concern in Scottish affairs during the eighteen months following the Armada was the extraordinary leniency which James showed to the leaders of the Roman Catholic party, particularly to the Earl of Huntly. There was no manner of doubt that Huntly and his associates were intriguing with the Prince of Parma for money and men to re-establish Roman Catholicism first in Scotland and then in England. Elizabeth demonstrated that fact to James by sending him in February 1589 a bundle of their letters intercepted on the way to the Low Countries.[1] She urged him to make short work of the traitors, but James saw the matter differently. In deference to the clamour of the Protestant ministers he warded Huntly in Edinburgh Castle but went to dine with him there the next day and not long afterwards released him. It was currently reported at the Scottish court that the incriminating letters had been forged in England.[2]

The King's attitude was naturally regarded by the English partisans in Scotland as nothing short of alarming. Some of them were for a *coup d'état* of the good old Scottish variety, always provided that Elizabeth would furnish the funds.[3] One impecunious rascal offered Walsingham 'the death of those traitors now in Scotland' for a mere matter of £200.[4] Asheby, the English ambassador in Scotland, advocated a different course. He thought the King's intentions were good and attributed his failure to prosecute Huntly and his followers to lack of means. He accordingly recommended that James be conciliated and reinforced.

This was the course which Elizabeth elected to follow. In

[1] Calderwood, v, pp. 6–35. [2] Thorpe, *Scottish Calendar*, i, p. 555.

[3] T. Fowler to Walsingham, 1 Mar. 1588/9. After describing the King's great affection for Huntly, Fowler added in cipher: 'And all this the King is cause of by his fond dealing, which not any can alter. Yet he saith he will do much, but they of the best and wisest sort doubt him greatly and are determined that if he dissemble, if they may have the Queen's support, they will not leave one of the Spanish faction in Scotland, and yet will they serve their king the better, and they desire to know shortly and secretly what her Majesty will do if need be' (S. P. Scotland, xliii, no. 16).

[4] Wm. Fownde to Walsingham, 23 Apr. 1589: 'Whereas I offered to your honour the de: of those traitors now in Scotland, I still find such encouragement in the aforesaid Scotchman that I think me able to perform my duty herein. He demands for himself and Scotch consort £200, one to be paid before, the other after the thing is performed' (S. P. Scotland, lxiii, no. 65). The significant word 'death' is not written out in the original, but presumably the abbreviated 'de' is meant to stand for it.

May 1589 she sent £3,000 to Scotland to enable James to arm himself against the rebels.[1] About the same time the Master of Gray, who had long been in exile, returned to the Scottish court at her instigation. Gray's presence there was evidently expected to increase the strength of the English party and to serve as a counterpoise against the personal charms of Huntly. Yet none of these measures seems to have changed the situation in the north very materially. Before the money arrived James had already taken arms against Huntly and had met and subdued him at the Brig o' Dee. But his trial which followed was a mere garden party, and those of his associates who were imprisoned were released before the summer was out.[2] James in fact was determined not to throw away his strongest card in his little game with Elizabeth. The best she could hope for was that he would at least contrive to maintain the balance between her enemies and her friends. So matters stood in the north at the time of Walsingham's death.

Elizabeth seems to have entrusted the management of Scottish affairs at this time to Walsingham in preference to any other councillor.[3] Possibly she realized that he was one of a very few who could be depended upon to take a disinterested attitude towards the heir-presumptive. He evidently promoted the scheme to re-establish the Master of Gray in King James's good graces.[4] It may be gathered also, from a letter which he wrote to Burghley late in April 1589, that he was largely instrumental in persuading his mistress to send James the £3,000 which went to him over the border in May. 'If', he wrote to Burghley in April, 'the King shall for lack of assistance give over the prosecution of Huntly and his confederates they will draw some foreign forces into that realm for the strengthening of their party. I pray

[1] Asheby to Walsingham, 2 May 1589, S. P. Scotland, xliv, no. 2; cf. also *Cal. Domestic*, Adda., 1580–1625, p. 352.

[2] A. Lang, *History of Scotland*, ii. 347.

[3] Cf. A. Douglas to Walsingham, 20 Apr. 1589: 'I caused speak (*sic*) my Lord Chancellor [Hatton] according to the proscribed order. He said he could have been contented with the offer if her Majesty had not within these three days said to him that she would have none to meddle in that matter but Sir Fra: Walsingham, whom she would have to bring that matter to a final point' (S. P. Scotland, xliii, no. 62). The meaning of this passage is obscure, but it evidently relates to some Scottish matter and seems to support the qualified statement in the text. Cf. also *Cal. Scottish*, 1586–8, p. 621.

[4] Thorpe, *Scottish Calendar*, i. 560.

God her Majesty's delay in this cause of Scotland do not breed both charge and danger greater than hath befallen to her since her coming to the crown.'[1] The closing sentence in the letter reveals the fact that Walsingham as usual had to wrestle with the Queen's inveterate procrastination and thrift. It may be taken for granted that if Elizabeth finally agreed to send £3,000 Walsingham had asked for £5,000 at least, and that if she sent it in May he had urged it in January.

Walsingham apparently believed that the King's half-hearted prosecution of Huntly proceeded from lack of means. Indeed he attributed most of the evils to which Scotland was heir to the weakness of the royal power. Upon this subject he wrote an illuminating letter to the Scottish court in December 1588. The letter was addressed to Thomas Fowler, but it was pretty evidently intended for the King's perusal. It is worth citing at length, not only because of the light which it throws upon Walsingham's views of Scotland, but also because of its broader revelations of his opinions about government at large.

'Yours of the 14th of this present I have received, which I do assure you hath given me more light of the true state of that realm than any letter I received from thence since I supplied the place I now hold of secretary. God send that young prince (being of himself as I understand both by you and others every way well inclined) good, wise and faithful counsellors that may carry him in a constant course for the upholding of religion and the establishing of justice in that realm, the lack whereof doth greatly weaken the royal authority, for that every great personage in that realm pretendeth to be a king and thereby taketh liberty to commit strange and great insolencies and oppressions on the weaker sort. The use of a Star Chamber might work great redress therein. It is almost impossible for any prince to be in surety in a realm or kingdom where the royal authority is not merely derived from the King. The only way to work true redress of that diseased state is for the King to bend himself altogether for a time to matters of government, calling about him such as are not limed with faction but inclined to justice. Hard it will be to bring to pass a thorough redress without a parliament compounded of persons that prefer the public before their particular, by whose travail and votes the extraordinary regalities the nobility of that realm do challenge, either by usurpation or otherwise, may be kept within such limits as

[1] 27 Apr. 1589, Harleian MSS. 6994, f. 172.

the law may have her just and due course without respect of persons.

'It is likely that the barons and burgesses of the borough towns within that realm will be forward enough in this action and so many of the noblemen as are wise and truly religious. The opposition then is likely to grow only from them that are fit to be bridled. Surely the King, by bringing such a matter to pass, besides he should work to himself surety where now run like hazard as the Kings his predecessors have done, he should do an act worthy of a Christian prince to his perpetual fame and renown forever. Thus, sir, you see how I am transported with a desire of the good of that King and country to show myself *curiosus in aliena respublica.*' [1]

It was commonplace enough to tell Scottish kings to strengthen their position and suppress their tumultuous nobility. For some centuries they had been endeavouring to do just that thing. The only matter for surprise is that such counsels should have emanated from an English statesman. England had generally found it best for her fishing to muddy the political waters in the north, preferring the customary turmoil to a well-established kingship. For Scottish kings had generally leaned to the side of England's enemies. It was the protestantism of James VI, joined with his presumptive title to the English throne, that wrought the change both in his own attitude and in the attitude of his southern neighbour towards him. Yet from the English point of view Scottish affairs were still, as they always had been, chiefly of moment because of the danger of a conjunction between Scotland and greater enemies overseas. If Walsingham wished James to strengthen his position it was because Walsingham believed that the King could be trusted to exert his strength in England's behalf and that Spain might make her profit out of his weakness.

The war with Spain was indeed the determining factor in all of Walsingham's calculations. In the actual conduct of the war he inevitably played a very large part both because of his position as leader of the war party in the Privy Council and also because of his intimate relations with the warriors in the field. He remained, as in the past, the chief advocate of men like Sir John Norris and Sir Francis Drake. No doubt as long as he lived he was the moving spirit behind the English enterprises

[1] 22 Dec. 1588, S. P. Scotland, xlii, no. 129, draft in Walsingham's hand.

in the Low Countries, in France and on the Spanish coast. The strategy of the earlier years of war plainly reveals his handiwork just as the cheese-paring spirit in which this strategy was put in practice reveals that of the Queen.

After the defeat of the Spanish Armada the natural course for the Queen to follow was to press her victory home by striking at Philip before he had a chance to recover. This was the course which her Allies overseas urged her to pursue,[1] and the one which she herself in the stimulating glow of victory was disposed to favour. Even before August was out, and while the Armada was still in English waters, she was considering the possibility of dispatching a fleet forthwith to intercept Philip's treasure galleys from the Indies. This was Walsingham's project, and it seems not unlikely that he suggested the idea to her. Howard and Drake, however, were both of the opinion that no such expedition was to be thought of until the navy was overhauled, and so nothing came of it for the time being at least.

Yet Drake was eager to follow up the Armada victory as soon as might be. So, for that matter, was Sir John Norris who had been Leicester's chief of staff and was the foremost of English soldiers. Between the two of them they concocted a plan which they submitted for the Queen's approval in September. They proposed in fact that a joint-stock company should be formed with a total capital of £60,000 for the purpose of organizing an expedition against King Philip. They requested the Queen to subscribe to one-third of the stock, to lend six ships of the royal navy and to permit the levying of troops. The rest of the capital they agreed to raise from private adventurers. Their purpose seems to have been threefold: first, to set Don Antonio on the throne of Portugal; second, to destroy the shipping in Spanish harbours; and third, to intercept the Spanish treasure fleet. By the accomplishment of all these things they hoped at once to strike a shrewd blow at King Philip's power and to line their pockets well with the gold and silver of Mexico and Peru.

Elizabeth gave her official assent to these plans early in October, but it is nevertheless important to remember that the enterprise was projected and executed as a private adventure.

[1] Cheyney, *History of England*, 1588–1603, i, p. 154.

It is true of course that the interests of the nation were deeply engaged, but Elizabeth did not commit herself except to the extent of her investment in ships and money. She is therefore not to be held entirely responsible for the lack of proper provisions which hampered Drake and Norris from start to finish.[1]

Don Antonio's interest in the enterprise was of course very great. He had in fact everything to gain and nothing to lose. Apparently he had no money to invest, but he was profuse in promises. He went so far as to agree to repay the whole cost of the expedition as soon as he had landed in Portugal.[2] There was a story afloat in Spain later that he had made much more extravagant offers, but it seems likely that these were fabricated by his enemies to discredit him among his countrymen.[3] Don Antonio laboured under the delusion that if once he landed in Portugal with a small force behind him, the whole country would rise to his support, and he seems to have convinced Drake that there was something in his view of the matter. At any rate the Pretender's value as an asset to the expedition clearly lay, if it lay anywhere, in his ability to stir up rebellion against Philip in Portugal. As for the private investors who were the third party to the adventure, £15,000 was raised without much difficulty among London merchants. Drake contributed £2,000 and raised £6,000 more among his friends. For the balance it is difficult to account.[4] A good deal of it was subscribed by courtiers,[5] probably some part by Walsingham himself. Years afterwards the Earl of Essex claimed that it was due to his influence among his friends that the deficit was finally made up.[6] It may be presumed that all these private adventurers were induced to engage their capital by fair hopes of large profits. Drake's prowess in the past had proved to be a perfect gold mine for speculators. The single East Indiaman which he had picked up almost by chance in his adventure of 1585 had been

[1] By far the best account of this expedition is in Cheyney, *op. cit.*, pp. 154 ff. Interesting details are supplied by Corbett, *Drake*, ii, *passim*, and by Oppenheim in his notes to *Monson's Naval Tracts* (ed. Navy Records Soc. i. 182 ff. M. A. S. Hume's account (*The Year after the Armada*) is in many respects untrustworthy.

[2] Cheyney, *op. cit.*, i, p. 159.

[3] Hume, *op. cit.*, pp. 19 ff.; Corbett, *op. cit.*, ii. 308 n.

[4] Cheyney, i. 158–9.

[5] Many of these defaulted later, Hakluyt (ed. Maclehose), vi. 474.

[6] *Monson's Naval Tracts*, i. 190.

worth nearly £100,000. His earlier voyage round the world had yielded the fabulous profit of 4,700 per cent.

There is little reason to doubt that Walsingham was one of the foremost advocates of this enterprise among the statesmen as Essex was among the courtiers. Lord Admiral Howard on the other hand opposed it, so did Sir Walter Raleigh;—Howard, because he thought he should have been put in command; Raleigh, perhaps, because his rival Essex favoured it.[1] According to a Spanish spy in England both Burghley and Hatton lent it their support, but Burghley's attitude was doubtful, to say the least. When troops were summoned home from the Low Countries to reinforce the army he was heard to mutter that a bird in the hand was worth two in the bush, or some such wise saw. Incidentally he managed to increase the financial difficulties in the way. The prevalent sentiment both at the Court and in the Council was, however, clearly in favour of the expedition.[2]

It was apparently intended from the very start that the nucleus of the army which was to go with the expedition should be formed from English veterans drawn out of the Low Countries. In order to secure them the assent of the Dutch was of course essential, and Elizabeth dispatched Norris himself to the Netherlands early in October to explain her plans to the States General.[3] He succeeded after many delays in securing their assent to the transport of about 2,000 English and 1,500 Dutch footmen with 600 English horse, though probably less than one half of these were ever actually sent.[4]

While Norris was in the Low Countries Drake was busy in England making preparations for the victualling of the fleet and the equipment and transportation of the army. In all these matters he was assisted by government officials acting under instructions from the Privy Council, but he apparently remained in general control and assumed the final responsibility. This

[1] Corbett, ii. 296; *Cal. Spanish*, 1587–1603, p. 525. [2] Cheyney, i. 158.

[3] The letter which Elizabeth sent to Willoughby by Norris is dated 9 October (*Cal. Ancaster MSS.*, p. 197). According to Cheyney Elizabeth did not issue her formal commission to Drake and Norris until 11 October (*op. cit.*, i, p. 158). Norris arrived in the Low Countries on or before 23 October (*Cal. Ancaster MSS.*, p. 214). The Earl of Northumberland and Sir Roger Williams accompanied him.

[4] Corbett, ii. 298; *Monson's Tracts*, i. 190; Cheyney, i. 160.

must have been so if the enterprise was to retain its character of a private adventure. By the end of December all the preliminary preparations had been completed and Walsingham wrote to Stafford in France that the expedition would get away in January.[1] The last step was the assembling of the troops. On the 30th of December the Privy Council sent out writs to the lord-lieutenants in the southern counties for the levy of the inland forces,[2] and early in January directed Willoughby to make ready the forces which were to be drawn out of the Low Countries.[3] And then came the inevitable delays. The soldiers from the Low Countries were not sent at the time appointed;[4] the county levies proved to be so slenderly equipped that a great deal of time and money had to be spent on them. Some of the adventurers withdrew their subscriptions at the last moment and others had to be found to take their place. Elizabeth, with characteristic vacillation, delayed to pass the final instructions under the Great Seal.[5] So it was that the rendezvous which had been appointed for the 20th of January had to be postponed until February, and then until March. It was not until the 20th of March that Drake finally assembled his forces at Plymouth[6] and announced himself ready to sail. Even then he lacked nearly £12,000 of the money due to him from private adventurers, and was so short of ships for transport that upon a rather flimsy pretext he seized some sixty Dutch flyboats in the Channel.[7]

The next four weeks Drake spent in Plymouth harbour whistling for a fair wind and consuming ship supplies already overscant. He got away finally on the 12th of April, with instructions first of all to destroy Spanish shipping in Spanish harbours, then, if Portuguese sentiment seemed to warrant the

[1] 20 Dec. 1588, Cotton MSS., Galba E vi, f. 396; Walsingham told Stafford that Drake would sail with some 15,000 men and about 120 ships. Cf. also *Cal. Spanish*, 1587–1603, p. 482.

[2] *Acts of Privy Council*, 1588, p. 418.

[3] *Cal. Ancaster MSS.*, p. 246.

[4] Later, when the Dutch complained that their soldiers employed in Portugal were not returned at the time promised, Walsingham retorted that this was due to the fact that they had not been sent at the time promised to Norris, 'whereby his voyage was greatly hindered and had not met with the success it should have had if the King of Spain had been taken unprepared as he would have been' (Walsingham to Bodley, 4 July 1589, Cotton MSS., Galba D v, f. 6).

[5] *Cal. Salisbury MSS.* iii, p. 233; misdated, February, 1587.

[6] *Monson's Tracts*, i. 192.

[7] Ibid.

attempt, to attack Lisbon in Don Antonio's behalf, and finally to cruise against the Azores.[1]

In Drake's exploits overseas Walsingham of course had no share, and there is no single letter of his surviving to indicate that he sought in any way to direct or even to influence the campaign after it got under way.[2] His business was at home with the Queen, and his service to the enterprise was mainly perhaps that of preventing her from recalling it before it had accomplished or at least attempted what it set out to do. In this business his work was considerably complicated by the escapade of his son-in-law, the Earl of Essex, who had joined the fleet in spite of the Queen's commands to the contrary and had got safe away with Sir Roger Williams in the *Swiftsure* notwithstanding her angry efforts to recall him. Elizabeth was disposed to attribute Essex's escape to the connivance of Drake and Norris, and her wrath at the disobedience of her favourite was consequently visited upon the expedition as a whole. Early in May she dictated a letter to the commanders full of the sharpest censure for their share in the business. Williams, she protested, was worthy of death and should be placed at once under arrest.[3] Walsingham did what he could to mitigate the royal temper. He was away for the time nursing his malady at Barn Elms, but his efforts appear in his letter to Windebank, who as Clerk of the Signet seems to have been acting as the Queen's confidential secretary. Walsingham wrote: 'Where affection carrieth sway it is hard to set down any reasons to temper the same. The draft of the letter is in as mild terms as may be, considering how her Majesty standeth affected. The two generals are wise and men of courage. They will venture rather to hazard her Majesty's dislike than to overthrow the action. You may let fall unto her Majesty at the time you shall offer the letter to be signed that it is greatly to be doubted, considering

[1] Ibid. 195–6.

[2] One small service is indicated in a letter from Walsingham to Burghley of 13 May 1589 (Harl. MSS. 6994, f. 177), in which Walsingham wrote that certain merchants had been instructed by Drake before he left to send after him provisions and powder as soon as they should hear of any descent of the English on Spain or Portugal. Walsingham requested Burghley, now 'that there is powder in good store in the kingdom', to give orders for the dispatch of some to Drake.

[3] Corbett, ii. 327, n. 2. The letter is printed in full in Devereux, *Lives of the Earls of Essex*.

how greatly Sir Roger Williams is beloved of both captains and soldiers, that the proceeding against him may breed a mutiny and division in the army, with the overthrow of the whole action to her Majesty's infinite dishonour. I would be glad to know to whom the carrying of this letter is committed.'[1] It does not appear that Walsingham's counsels of moderation carried any weight with the angry Queen. No doubt he sent private letters to Drake and Norris by the same messenger that bore her dispatch, and they may have been acting upon his advice when they sent Essex home but spared Sir Roger.

In any event Walsingham's advocacy of the cause was not so fervid as to provoke the royal wrath upon his own head. He seems indeed to have stood very high in the Queen's good graces during the spring of 1589. In May she paid him a visit at Barn Elms.[2]

Late in June Drake and Norris got back to England. The sum and substance of their achievement had been the destruction of a few ships in Corunna harbour, the temporary occupation of three small towns and an unsuccessful attack upon Lisbon. Don Antonio's hopes of a general rising in Portugal had proved quite illusory. The Azores had not even been attempted. Champions of the expedition pointed out that enormous prestige had been gained by actually carrying the war into the enemy's country, but most men agreed that it was a sorry failure. As an investment it certainly was. The only large plunder secured was some 'eighty Hansa hulks' laden with grain which Drake intercepted off Lisbon harbour and seized on the ground that their cargo was contraband.[3] There was, however, considerable doubt as to whether these could be reckoned lawful prize. The Aldermen of the Steelyard, representatives of the Hansa towns in England, of course protested;[4] and the Privy Council, after debating the matter at length and hearing the opinion of the civil lawyers, finally resolved: first, that 'such ships as are not ships of war or provided for Spain should be restored; second,

[1] 2 May 1589, S. P. Domestic, ccxxiv, no. 12.

[2] Cf. Sir T. Heneage to Walsingham, 16 May 1589, S. P. Domestic, ccxxiv, no. 48. Heneage wrote that the Queen would visit Walsingham on Thursday or Friday next. He added: 'She is very well satisfied with your dealing.'

[3] On this contraband question, cf. Cheyney's excellent chapter xxii, particularly pp. 492 ff.

[4] *Acts of Privy Council*, 1588–9, p. 380.

that all merchandise not reputed by civil law to be munitions of war or victuals should be restored '.[1] This ruling, as it proved, involved the restoration of all the ships,[2] though according to the Council's definition of contraband it probably condemned most of their cargoes. In any event it cut down the possible returns of the enterprise from something over £100,000 to a small fraction of that sum. Under these circumstances it is not surprising to discover that Elizabeth did not take very kindly to the decision of the Council. Walsingham wrote to Burghley on the 15th of July 1589:

'I find her Majesty most backward in following the advice given touching the restoring of the Easterlings to their ships and such goods as are not comprehended within the title of munitions. The only reason that moveth her to be so stiff therein is profit, which I showed her that I feared the same would be purchased at too dear a price, and that it was the general opinion of all her Council and therefore besought her that she would be pleased that the matter might be debated before her, whereunto I could, by no argument I could use, draw her to assent. It is of so great weight as it will behoove us all, for our own discharge, to press her effectually therein. In the meantime it shall be convenient that the commission and the instructions be put in readiness for Dr. Ford, whereof I will have care. I hope her Majesty, upon the debating of the matter, will be drawn to relent.'[3]

This passage reveals not only Elizabeth's attitude in the matter but Walsingham's as well. It was characteristic of the Queen that she was prepared to risk dangerous foreign complications for the sake of a few thousand pounds in plunder. She was, however, induced to accept the advice of her Council,

[1] There is a copy of these resolutions in Walsingham's hand in S. P. Domestic, ccxxv, no. 25.

[2] Cheyney, i. 495.

[3] 15 July 1589, Harleian MSS. 6994, f. 187. Walsingham went on to say: 'Touching the declaration your Lordship desireth to be done with speed, I have committed the same to my brother Beale and have advised him to acquaint Mr. Dr. Ford and Mr. Dr. Hammond withal and to use their advice therein.' This is evidently a reference to the printed pamphlet entitled: *A Declaration of the Causes which moved the chief commanders of the Navy of her most excellent Majesty, the Queen of England, in their expedition for Portugal, to take and arrest in the mouth of the River of Lisbon certain ships of corn and other provisions of war bound for the said cities,* in which Elizabeth undertook to justify her course to the rulers of Europe. Cheyney has surmised (i. 495) that Burghley was the author of this pamphlet, but this letter of Walsingham's makes it clear that his brother-in-law, Robert Beale, a trained civilian, composed it.

and upon that basis the ships of the Easterlings were eventually released. The sale of their contraband cargoes[1], with that of some 150 brass cannon fetched from the Spanish forts, represented practically the total assets of the enterprise. Over against that pittance and whatever prestige the voyage conferred the Queen had to set the loss of some of her best captains and about 10,000 fighting men.[2]

Perhaps the most unfortunate consequence of Drake's failure was to discredit the aggressive policy of which he was the great exponent. If he had performed any service for the cause it was by revealing the weakness of the Spanish position at home. And that service might have justified its cost had Elizabeth been alert to take prompt advantage of it. She seemed at first disposed to do so,[3] but later she reverted to her earlier tactics of commerce destroying which was at once more lucrative and less hazardous, though of course quite inadequate to the purpose of destroying the fighting power of Spain.

Walsingham has unfortunately left no evidence of his own reaction on the failure of the Portugal expedition although he must have felt it bitterly. He more than any one else in the Council, now that Leicester was dead, had championed an aggressive policy against Spain, and he could hardly deny that Elizabeth by consenting to the dispatch of Norris and Drake had given his policy a fair trial. The men in charge were experts, the best undoubtedly for the business in all England; the moment of attack was not inopportune. Though the expedition had not got away as soon as it was intended, there can be little doubt that Philip was utterly unprepared to receive it. Supplies of course had been inadequate; but supplies always were inadequate, and Drake captured enough provisions at Corunna to make good that deficiency. The weather was no more unfavourable than the old Plymouth sea dogs had reason to expect.

[1] According to Corbett (ii. 331) the Hanseatic prizes, plus the brass cannon, sold for £30,000. Of course the Hansa ships were not sold. Corbett cites no reference for his statement. Oppenheim (in *Monson's Naval Tracts*, i. 216) says that the Hansa ships and cargoes were valued at £100,000 and that two-thirds of their cargoes were stolen or spoiled at sea by the soldiers and sailors, and that one-third of the remainder disappeared at Plymouth. By this reckoning the Hansa cargoes must have netted precious little.

[2] For various estimates as to the losses on this expedition, cf. Corbett, ii. 331; *Monson's Naval Tracts*, i. 216; Cheyney, i. 183.

[3] *Acts of Privy Council*, 1588–9, p. 360.

With all these circumstances in mind, Walsingham must have been hard put to it to vindicate his policy in the face of the more cautious counsels of Burghley and his conservative colleagues. Probably he was too wise to try, and counted himself fortunate that with Drake and Norris both in disgrace he managed to escape the royal displeasure.

It will be observed that the issue between Walsingham and the conservatives by this time had ceased to be one between peace and war, and had become one on the method of conducting the war, Walsingham favouring a direct attack upon Spain, Burghley and his colleagues preferring what had been Walsingham's earlier policy of effective co-operation with Dutch Protestants and French Huguenots.[1] Drake's enterprise marked the temporary triumph of the more aggressive policy; his failure marked its abandonment. For the rest of Walsingham's life the course of the war with Spain followed the well-worn channels. Most of the fighting was on land and the scenes of action were in the Low Countries and in Northern France.

During the spring and summer of 1588 there was little fighting in the Netherlands. The Prince of Parma was busy with his preparations for co-operation in the attack against England and the Dutch were either unwilling or unable to carry the warfare against him. With the failure of the Armada, however, Parma was quick to see the futility of undertaking an invasion of England in the face of the victorious English fleet and he turned at once to resume operations against the Dutch. Early in September he sat down before Bergen-op-Zoom, an important outpost of the Dutch in North Brabant which commanded the water passages to the islands of Zeeland. The town was held by a mixed garrison of Dutch and English troops under Sir Thomas Morgan, but Lord Willoughby, general in command of the English forces in the Low Countries, wrote to Elizabeth early in September that it was too weak to stand a siege.[2] The reluctance of the Dutch to strengthen it made it apparent that unless Elizabeth sent prompt reinforcements the town would fall. The Queen, for once in her lifetime, acted promptly. On the 23rd of September her Privy Council wrote to Willoughby

[1] Cf. Pollard, *Hist. of England*, 1547-1603, pp. 411-12.
[2] *Cal. Ancaster MSS.*, p. 181.

that she had ordered five companies to be sent to Bergen from her garrisons in Flushing, Briel and Ostend, and that she meant forthwith to send 1,500 English footmen and 500 Walloons for its defence.[1] These troops were, in fact, dispatched under the charge of Sir John Norris on the 9th of October; [2] though they did not apparently arrive in time to assist in the defence of the town.[3] Parma was, however, repulsed, and so the campaign of 1588 in the Low Countries terminated favourably.[4]

Unfortunately, however, all was not well between the Dutch and their English allies. They were, in fact, at odds upon so many points that it is rather amazing to discover that they were able to co-operate at all. Many of these differences had their root in the rather ambiguous position of the English in the Low Countries. They were supposed to have a share in shaping the public policy of the Dutch, and two English councillors—George Gilpin and Thomas Bodley—still sat upon the Council of State. But this body, created in Leicester's time, had been shorn of most of its powers and the control of the government was actually in the hands of the States General dominated by the deputies of the province of Holland—notably by John of Barneveldt. Here was a situation rich in opportunities for disagreement. The English councillors protested again and again that important questions of public policy were determined without any reference to them, and that the official relations between the Dutch and the English Governments were conducted over their heads. But they protested to no purpose. The fact of the matter was that Barneveldt and his colleagues in the States General had had more than enough of English meddling in their affairs. The large power they had conferred upon Leicester he

[1] *Acts of Privy Council*, 1588, pp. 288–9. Walsingham wrote to Sir E. Stafford 30 Sept. 1588: 'Upon advertisement received that the Duke of Parma hath brought his forces upon Bergen-op-Zoom and drawn the cannon thither, intending to employ his whole power against that place, her Majesty, meaning not to give over the honour she hath already gotten, hath given order for the sending thither of 1,500 men from hence of her own subjects and 500 Waloons of the strange churches which, together with the strength that is already in the town, we hope shall be able to hold the place and to repulse the Duke' (Cotton MSS.; Galba E vi, f. 384; printed in *Hardwicke Papers*, i. 364).

[2] *Cal. Ancaster MSS.*, p. 197.

[3] Norris arrived at Bergen 30 October (ibid., p. 214). The siege was raised 3 November.

[4] Cf. Willoughby's own account of the siege of Bergen in ibid., p. 201, with that of Motley, particularly with reference to Grimston's Plot.

had exploited for the purpose of organizing a democratic party in the cities, designed to strike at what Barneveldt regarded as the very fundamentals of the Dutch constitution. He knew that Leicester's policy had been merely scotched, and his efforts to reduce the power of the Council of State were pretty certainly dictated by a desire to prevent the English from doing any further harm of a similar sort.

The representatives of England on their part were convinced that Barneveldt was altogether opposed to the English alliance and therefore used such influence as they could command against him. Lord Willoughby was even for reviving Leicester's old schemes and urged the Queen to join forces with the people, seize the principal towns in Holland and Zeeland, and force Barneveldt and his 'lewd' colleagues to their knees.[1]

This mutual distrust naturally aggravated many of the older points at issue, such as those over the financing of the war and the restraint of trade with Spain. Regarding the distribution of military expenses, the English and the Dutch were each constantly complaining that the other was not bearing a fair share of the burden. The difficulties over restraint of trade increased with Elizabeth's increased efforts to cut off the Spanish supply of food-stuffs in which the Dutch still drove a lucrative commerce.[2] All of these matters taken together constituted a very formidable obstacle to the smooth running of the Anglo-Dutch alliance.

It is clear that Elizabeth was quite out of patience with the Dutch and Walsingham hardly less so. He had instructed Bodley when he went over to the Low Countries in November 1588 to win over Barneveldt if possible to the English cause, but Bodley had to confess that his efforts had been altogether futile. 'Your honour may remember', he wrote to Walsingham in the spring of 1589, 'how I came hither prepared with your letter of recommendation and other special means to Barneveldt to win him to her Majesty, but in truth I could never find in him but a rude and untractable nature, delighting continuously to oppose himself against the English government, for so it pleaseth him and some others to term her Majesty's directions.'[3]

[1] *Cal. Ancaster MSS.*, p. 239.
[2] Ibid., pp. 268–70.
[3] 15 April 1589, Galba D iv, f. 160.

Failing in these methods, Walsingham turned to threats. Late in March 1589 he addressed a remonstrance to the States General on the subject of their general attitude towards the Queen. His mistress, he said, was very indignant at their contemptuous treatment of her officers and the scant attention they paid to her wishes. He supposed they thought her so much attached to their cause that she could not for her own safety's sake abandon them, or else that they fancied themselves so strong that they could defy the whole world. He therefore bade them take care lest the Queen take advantage of the many opportunities offered to her to make her own peace with Spain, and not to presume too much on their own strength at a time when their state was shot through with internal dissensions.[1]

But Barneveldt seemed to be impervious alike to blandishments and threats. To make matters worse, the town of Gertruidenberg, which was commanded by Sir John Wingfield, Lord Willoughby's own brother-in-law, was betrayed to the Spaniards in March. It is quite probable that Wingfield was not to blame for the treachery. Indeed the Dutch seem to have brought it on themselves by their failure to pay the garrison what was justly due them. Nevertheless the States General published a placard denouncing the fact and its perpetrators in a sweeping statement which included not only Wingfield but even Sir Francis Vere and which touched the honour and good fame of Lord Willoughby himself.

Willoughby naturally was furious, so for that matter was the Queen. Walsingham's reaction on the situation is revealed in a letter to Bodley of the 27th of April.

'I like very well', he wrote, 'that the placard should rather be answered by Lord Willoughby than by her Majesty—but to have it not answered at all were best, so as the States would have it suppressed. . . . Their ingratitude is great, but yet, seeing we cannot sever ourselves from them without infinite danger, their errors are to be winked at for a time. . . . It may be that the disgrace inflicted on them through the loss of Gertruidenberg will somewhat humble them, for seeing Barneveldt, the principal ringleader amongst them, beginneth to strike sail, I think the rest will stoop. But when I look into their strange course in publishing their placard, after the loss of the town thereby to hazard the

[1] 2 March 1589, Galba D iv, f. 84.

loss also of her Majesty's favour, I know not what to think of them, but must conclude that with the loss of the town they have also lost their wits.'[1]

Before the news of the fall of Gertruidenberg became known in England, Elizabeth contemplated sending either Lord Buckhurst or Sir Thomas Wilford to arrange some settlement of outstanding differences. She asked Walsingham which of the two men he thought better fitted for the business. Walsingham pronounced in favour of Buckhurst, and recommended that Thomas Wilkes also be sent in the humble position of dispatch bearer.[2] The significance of this recommendation becomes apparent when it is recollected that Buckhurst had been one of the most resolute opponents of Leicester's policy in the Low Countries and that Thomas Wilkes had stood forth in the past as a champion of the States General against the democratic ideas of the Leicesterians. Walsingham evidently still favoured a policy of conciliation towards Barneveldt and his partisans.

But Buckhurst's mission was postponed.[3] Walsingham wrote to Burghley early in May that he had learned of the intention of the States General to send over commissioners to England and judged that in consequence it would be unnecessary for Buckhurst to go.[4] The Dutch commissioners did, in fact, arrive early in June.[5] It was evidently the Queen's intention to take up with them the broader points at issue in her relations with the Dutch and to negotiate a new agreement which should amend the defects of her contract with them.[6] But when the Privy Council broached these matters they soon discovered that the Dutch commissioners had no authority to deal with them. Bodley was accordingly instructed to procure from the States General an enlargement of their instructions and was

[1] Galba D iv, f. 175, quoted by Motley, ii. 548 n., with some verbal inaccuracies.

[2] *Cal. S. P. Domestic*, 1581–90, p. 592.

[3] In the life of Buckhurst in *D. N. B.* it is said that he went over to the Low Countries in November 1589, but it is evident from the *Acts of Privy Council* that Buckhurst was in regular attendance at Council meetings during the autumn of 1589 and the spring of 1590. Wilkes went over in May 1590 (Murdin, *Burghley Papers*, p. 793).

[4] 3 May 1589, Harl. MSS. 6994, f. 175.

[5] *Acts of Privy Council*, 1588–9, p. 287; they left the Low Countries 12 May (*Cal. Ancaster MSS.*, p. 280).

[6] *Acts of Privy Council*, 1588–9, p. 288; these defects, as the English saw them, are set forth in *Cal. Salisbury MSS.* iv. 10.

particularly informed of the points which the English wished to have considered.[1] This last precaution was doubtless taken to obviate if possible the diplomatic delays in which the Dutch had proved themselves to be past masters. Meantime, while waiting for the new instructions, the Dutch commissioners were harangued at length by the English councillors. Upon the question of the Gertruidenberg placard they assumed, as Walsingham told Bodley later, a very lofty attitude, which Walsingham interpreted as an indication either that they were expecting assistance from France or contemplating peace with Spain.[2] The deputies were also obliged to listen to some pretty sharp criticism of Barneveldt's behaviour, which of course reached Barneveldt's ears and had the effect of aggravating his Anglophobia. Walsingham thought it not unlikely that some of the deputies who were opposed to Barneveldt had repeated to him the remarks of his English critics with the malicious intent of stirring up his wrath to such a pitch as to make him intolerable. 'And if I be not deceived by some other private advice which I have from hence,' Walsingham remarked to Bodley, 'it will so fall out in the end, for I learn that his [Barneveldt's] doings are very much misliked there and that he is likely to wear himself out before it be long if he change not the course of his humours.' [3]

Barneveldt, however, was to hold his place for many long years to come and for the time being he seemed no wise disposed to change the 'course of his humours'. In spite of Elizabeth's requests that the Dutch deputies in England be empowered to negotiate an amendment of the Anglo-Dutch treaty, no such authorization was sent them. Early in August, after two months in England spent in doing practically nothing at all, they requested leave to depart. Walsingham protested that they had altogether ignored the Queen's request, but to no purpose. 'They grow very proud,' he wrote to Bodley, 'which maketh us to suspect some wrong measure at their hands. . . . I wish that our fortune and theirs were not so straitly tied as it is, so as we cannot well untie without great hazard, and then there would be easily found some way to free us from them without peril.' [4]

[1] 16 June 1589, Cotton MSS., Galba D iv, f. 287.
[2] 23 June 1589, ibid., f. 307.
[3] 28 July 1589, ibid., v, f. 52.
[4] 2 Aug. 1589, ibid., f. 65.

The deputies of the States left England late in September, leaving the fundamental points at issue between Elizabeth and the Dutch still unsettled. It was evidently the Queen's intention to dispatch Lord Buckhurst to the Low Countries to bring these matters to a treaty, but the plan was not followed and nothing further was done in this regard during Walsingham's lifetime.[1]

In the autumn of 1589 opportunity was offered the Queen to revert to Leicester's favoured policy of joining forces with the Dutch factions opposed to Barneveldt's control. Bodley informed Walsingham in September that the town of Groningen and some other towns were prepared to surrender themselves to Elizabeth. Walsingham even heard that the province of Friesland was anxious to acknowledge her sovereignty.[2] But Elizabeth was not prepared to entertain any such suggestions. In spite of Barneveldt's evil ways, she thought it the sounder policy to discourage dissensions among the Dutch in order to keep them strong against the common enemy. It does not appear how Walsingham regarded this proposition at this time, but he was certainly convinced that it would be futile for the Queen to dally with individual towns or even individual provinces unless she were prepared to assume the sovereignty of the whole Low Countries.[3]

One fact which did much to mitigate the ill feeling between the Dutch and the English at this time was the departure of Lord Willoughby. Since Leicester's return from the Low Countries in the autumn of 1587 Willoughby had been in command of the English forces there. He was a man far less arrogant and far more conciliatory than Leicester had been, but he shared Leicester's views of the 'bakers and brewers' who controlled the States General and favoured Leicester's policy of intrigue with the democratic elements in the towns against Barneveldt and his partisans. Consequently Willoughby's presence served to aggravate rather than to assuage the distrust and dissension between the allies. In the early spring of 1589 he got leave to return to England, and in March he departed, leaving his sergeant-major, Sir Francis Vere, in command of the

[1] Walsingham to Bodley, 25 Sept. 1589, Cotton MSS., Galba D v, f. 125; 28 Nov. 1589, ibid., f. 199.

[2] Same to same, 25 Sept. 1589, ibid., f. 125.

[3] Same to same, 28 Nov. 1589, ibid., f. 199.

English troops. Vere's position was intended to be merely temporary, but Willoughby's resignation in May led to Vere's definite appointment in August. He retained his old rank of sergeant-major, the position of general and lieutenant-general being left vacant. Vere therefore could claim none of the state or the prerogatives of a generalissimo, and this fact in itself did much to prevent conflicts of the old sort between him and the States General. He was besides a man of far greater discretion than either Leicester or Willoughby and his heart was too much wrapped up in the profession of arms to leave him much time or ambition for affairs of state. Thomas Bodley wrote of him to Burghley in September 1589: 'I may not omit to advise your Lordship that Sir Francis Vere by means of his valour and good government hath won great reputation not only with the Count [Maurice] and the other governors and statesmen here, but with the common captains and soldiers of both nations. And whether in process of time it be not likely to prove that conductors here of meaner calling, than such as heretofore have been sent from her Majesty, will better fit with the humour of this people, I leave to be considered by your Lordship.' [1]

With Vere's appointment, in fact, the position of the English in the Low Countries was put upon a basis which made effective co-operation with the Dutch really practicable. It proved to be a long step forward in the right direction, the only forward step perhaps in the year of contentions between the allies which followed the defeat of the Armada. It is therefore gratifying to discover that Walsingham was largely instrumental in securing Vere's appointment and that Vere regarded Walsingham as one of his best friends at the English court.[2]

It will not be necessary to follow the career of Vere in the Netherlands. Elizabeth in spite of her wrangles with the Dutch seemed more disposed to support him than she had been to support his predecessors, and Vere's cordial relations with Maurice of Nassau made it possible for them to co-operate in a way which redounded to the military prestige of them both. Undoubtedly, however, they had a rather easier problem to face

[1] *Cal. Bath MSS.* ii. 32.

[2] Vere admitted that himself (Markham, *Fighting Veres*, p. 134 n.), although of course the fact that Lord Willoughby had married Vere's first cousin no doubt prepossessed Willoughby in his favour.

than had confronted the allies during the preceding years. During most of the summer of 1589 Parma's health was so bad that he could hardly undertake aggressive campaigning, and when the spring of 1590 broke, affairs in France claimed his attention and diverted his forces from their main object.

This diversion was brought about by the course of the French civil wars. It will be recalled that not long after the death of the Duke of Alençon in 1584 a league had been formed in France under the leadership of the Duke of Guise, the main purpose of which was to debar Henry of Navarre, the Protestant heir-presumptive, from the French succession. Spain was secretly a party to this league, Philip II being of the opinion that the accession of a Protestant king to the throne of France was absolutely incompatible with his own interests and with the larger interests of his faith.

Henry III, the ruling king in France, who had no mind to become the plaything of Guise and his Spanish accomplices, favoured the succession of Navarre and would have formed an alliance with him had Navarre been prepared to sacrifice his religion in the interests of his royal prospects. But Navarre, though he was far from being a zealous Protestant, doubted the wisdom of divorcing from himself the strength of his Protestant following for the sake of the friendship of the weak and vacillating King. He therefore rejected Henry III's suggestions and in consequence forced the King into the hands of the League. By the treaty of Namours in July 1585, Henry III definitely committed himself to the Guisan programme and for the next three years stood officially by their side in their efforts to annihilate Navarre and his Protestant following. It is quite evident, however, that the King's heart was not in the business and that he would have welcomed any promising opportunity to change sides, or at any rate to assert his independence of his Guisan masters.

The interests of England were identical with those of Henry of Navarre for very much the same reason that the interests of Spain were at one with those of the League. Indeed, it became apparent to Elizabeth or at least to wise heads about her, like Walsingham, that the civil war in France was merely another phase of her world-wide struggle with Spain. Her obvious policy therefore was to strengthen Navarre against his enemies. This was the course which Walsingham urged upon her and this was the one which during the years 1585–8 she pretended to follow. Her efforts in this direction have already been described at length. She tried to enlist in Navarre's behalf the support of Protestant Germany, she loaned him very grudgingly some small sums to levy soldiers, and she laboured to win over the French King to his side. Her money was what Navarre wanted most and what she was most loath to give. Her intercessions in Germany proved fruitless. The policy of alienating the French King from the League was on the whole the course of action which Elizabeth preferred, mainly because it was an inexpensive one. Walsingham thought she was mistaken in trying to build up her French policy on such an unstable basis as Henry of Valois, but agreed that the support of the King was worth getting if it could be got. During the months immediately preceding the advent of the Spanish Armada in English waters, Elizabeth's activity in France was chiefly directed to the formation of a triple alliance between herself, Henry of Valois and Henry of Navarre. In the early spring Valois seemed about to agree to such a combination, but when in May the Duke of Guise forced his hand at Paris in the famous Day of Barricades the King had practically no choice but to submit once more to the demands of the League.

It looked indeed in the midsummer of 1588 as though the Spanish party was to have its way in France. The Queen Mother, Catherine de Médicis, had gone over to their side;[1] the King, her son, seemed too weak to resist them. In fact, the only obstacle in the way of their complete success was Henry of Navarre, whose resources were hardly great enough to make him very formidable. Such was the situation in France when the Spanish Armada sailed up the English Channel. During the actual combat France showed herself on the whole more friendly to the Spanish than to the English, but it can hardly be doubted that Henry III rejoiced at the Armada's defeat. It was a shrewd blow at the Spaniard's prestige which was bound to have its effect upon their position in France. At the same time it

[1] *Séances et Travaux de l'Académie des Sciences moraux et politiques*, clix. 697.

increased the prestige of England and of English partisans in France. After the fight was over, Elizabeth was disposed to protest to Henry III against the friendliness he had shown to the ships of her enemies on his coasts and so she instructed Walsingham to write to Stafford, the English ambassador in France. But Walsingham while conveying her directions added a note of caution on his own behalf. 'This', he wrote Stafford, 'do I write by her Majesty's commandment and yet can I not but advise you, if you see the delivery thereof unto the King in such sort as the same is set down will do any harm, to use your discretion; for it is hard here to prescribe what is fit to be done there. It behooveth her Majesty greatly to continue amity with that Crown and therefore it is not convenient that any breach should grow between us upon light quarrels.'[1] Obviously the affair of the Barricades and the submission of Henry III to the Guisan programme which followed it had not convinced Walsingham that the French King ought to be accounted as an enemy. Walsingham still thought it possible that Henry might assert his independence of Guisan control, but distrusted the King's weakness. 'If there were true magnanimity in the French King,' he remarked to Stafford, 'I should hope well, but when I look into his weakness I rather despair than hope.'[2]

Walsingham's diagnosis of the situation in France proved in the main to be the correct one. Henry III was evidently determined to shake himself free of Guisan control if he could. His dismissal of several ministers who favoured the policy of the League was obviously a step in that direction.[3] His conciliatory attitude toward England was another. In December he acceded to Elizabeth's request that the exportation of food-stuffs from France to Spain should be restrained, an act which evidently ran directly counter to the pro-Spanish sympathies of the Guises.[4] All these measures were naturally welcomed in England, and Walsingham was of the opinion that if Henry III came boldly forward as the champion of the French nation he might dispose of the Guisan domination for good. In Walsingham's opinion the assembly of the French Estates General at Blois in September gave the King his great opportunity.

[1] *Hardwicke Papers*, i. 362.
[2] Ibid. i. 363.
[3] Lavisse, *Hist. de France*, vi, pt. 1, 280–1.
[4] *Hardwicke Papers*, i. 370.

'There was never a more apt occasion offered unto him', he wrote to Stafford in December, 'to have been revenged of the heads of the League than in the present assembly of the States, to have laid before them the miserable and dangerous state that France is cast into through their ambitious pretexts and designs under the visor of religion; and although perhaps there be many of the present assembly there that stand affected towards them, yet no doubt of it the generality, through the natural affection they bear to the preservaton of their country, would easily be drawn to take revenge if they might find in the King a princely resolution to go through with the matter. The present diseases of France will not be cured with that temporizing course that he now holdeth. For while he seeketh to recover a few towns that are in the hands of those of the League, he will hazard his whole kingdom. But I fear there hangeth a fatal destiny over that realm which will not be avoided.'[1]

It is gravely to be doubted whether Henry III, even if he had been a far more magnetic personality than in fact he was, could have won such a pronouncedly Guisan assembly as the Estates General of 1588 to an anti-Guisan policy. At any rate he preferred another course, which seemed to him to offer an easy way out of all his difficulties, though it proved fatal to him in the end. Three days after Walsingham had dispatched the letter just cited to Stafford, the Duke of Guise was assassinated by the King's orders at Blois.

Henry III believed that with the murder of the Duke he had put a final end to the Holy League and all its intrigues. It remained to be seen whether this was in fact the case. At any rate it was clear that the King had not only abandoned his policy of conciliation and concession, but had burned his bridges behind him. Either the partisans of Guise would submit or they would fight to the death. There was no longer any question of half-way measures. It was therefore singularly appropriate that at this juncture the great exponent of such devices should have left the scene for good. Just two weeks after the murder of the Duke of Guise, Catherine de Médicis died.

In England both deaths were regarded as distinctly favourable to the English cause in France. Walsingham wrote to Stafford that Elizabeth rejoiced at the news and that she intended to send an envoy to the French King at once to encourage him

[1] *Hardwicke Papers*, i. 371.

'to proceed to a correction of his corrupt subjects at home and his enemies abroad'. Walsingham himself felt that the time had come for a close alliance between England and France against Spain, and told Stafford that if the French King were as well disposed towards such a course as the English were 'then is it a match'. He even contemplated inviting the concurrence of the Venetians and other Italian princes.[1]

Henry III was not, however, quite prepared to join forces openly with England. He had but just shaken himself free from the control of the Guisan Spanish party and he was not yet disposed to commit himself to the policy of their opponents. He did not yet realize that the murder of the Duke of Guise had made such a course inevitable, but fancied himself for a season superior to all factions, King of France indeed.

The reorganization of the League at Paris in February under the Duke of Mayenne, brother of the murdered Duke, finally convinced the King of his error. In April he came to terms with Henry of Navarre. Probably about the same time he made advances to England. Stafford, the English ambassador at Paris, who left for England in March, seems to have carried with him requests from the King for Elizabeth's assistance in levying troops in Germany.[2] Lord Burghley remarked in a letter to the Earl of Shrewsbury late in May: 'The state of the world is marvellously changed when we true Englishmen have cause for our own quietness to wish good success to a French king and a King of Scots, and yet they both differ one from the other in profession of religion; but seeing both are enemies to our enemies we have cause to join with them in their actions against our enemies.'[3]

Elizabeth was not, however, any prompter than usual in lending the French King the assistance he asked for. Consequently, in May Henry sent over an ambassador of his own, M. de Buhy, to

[1] Cotton MSS., Galba E vi, f. 397.

[2] Mendoza wrote to Philip II, 21 June 1589: 'The King and Bearn [Navarre] are very friendly, but they have no forces to help the Queen of England in the invasion of Spain. This King wishes the English troops in the fleet [Drake's counter-armada] should come hither and help him, and Stafford went to England about this. The Queen would not consent.' (*Cal. Spanish*, 1587–1603, p. 545.)

The Venetian ambassador in France wrote in March 1589: 'The English ambassador has left. The object of his journey is to persuade the Queen to interest herself in favour of a large levy of troops in Germany.' (*Cal. Venetian*, 1581–91, p. 431.)

[3] Lodge, *Illustrations*, &c., ii. 373.

repeat his request.[1] The purpose of his mission, its progress, and Walsingham's attitude towards it may all be gathered from Walsingham's letter to Burghley of the 15th of July:

> 'Her Majesty', he wrote, 'stayeth to resolve touching de Buhy's dispatch until Mr. Horatio [Palavicino's] return. By that which passed between us she showeth herself inclined to perform her promise touching the £20,000. I did, without urging her in any particular sort touching that point, lay before her in what danger she stood in, having so many and so puissant enemies abroad and so weak means at home to make head against them, and therefore did humbly pray her to be well advised before she neglected so good an opportunity to strengthen herself as was offered her by the request of the French King. I did also show her the enclosed letter from Florence which threateneth some great matter to be attempted the next year by Spain against this crown. I acquainted her Majesty with the letter sent from Denmark and did also let her understand in how doubtful terms things stood in Scotland. These things, I observed, wrought some impression in her, so as I hope Mr. Horatio shall find the soil seasonable to receive seed.' [2]

Evidently de Buhy was seeking money for the levy of troops in Germany. Elizabeth had about committed herself to a loan of £20,000, and Palavicino, whom she had employed before on a similar mission, was making ready to depart for Germany.[3] Walsingham and Burghley, it seems, had combined to urge this course of action upon the Queen and it must have been largely due to their efforts that she was induced to assent to it.

Palavicino was just about to start for Germany when news came from France which upset all calculations. On the 21st of July [O.S.] the King was stabbed by Jacques Clement and died the next day.

The effect of this catastrophe was tremendous. On his death-bed Henry III had pointed to the King of Navarre as his successor, but France was in two minds about the matter. The Roman Catholics could not stomach the idea of a Protestant King. Henry of Navarre undertook to conciliate them by a promise to support the Roman Catholic religion and by a broad hint at his own readiness to be converted. Even so he found that the nation as a whole was not prepared to rally to his

[1] *Lettres de Henri IV*, ii. 481; de Buhy was an older brother of Duplessis Mornay, the famous Huguenot publicist.

[2] Harleian MSS. 6994, f. 187.

[3] *Cal. Spanish*, 1586–1603, p. 559.

support. The principal towns and many of the greater nobles adhered to the League and preferred the claims of his rival, Charles of Bourbon. Henry, in fact, discovered that if he would have a kingdom, he must conquer it.

Naturally he turned at once for assistance to England. Less than a month after the death of his predecessor he dispatched Beauvoir la Nocle to Elizabeth with an appeal for help in men, money, and supplies, and he wrote friendly letters both to Burghley and to Walsingham soliciting their co-operation.[1] Elizabeth responded with extraordinary alacrity. She agreed at once to lend Henry £20,000, to send him powder and other munitions and to reinforce him with 4,000 troops. The money and the supplies were shipped early in September [2] to Dieppe under the care of Sir Edward Stafford, who returned to France as Elizabeth's ambassador to the new King. Preparations were made forthwith for the raising of troops and Lord Willoughby was appointed to command them. It was intended that they should be shipped to France on the 20th of September.[3] As an example of prompt action in an emergency these measures stand almost unparalleled in the reign of Elizabeth. One wonders how Walsingham and Burghley managed to impress upon their mistress such an immediate sense of the danger of delay. It is not surprising to discover that after the money was gone, but before troops were sent, the Queen began to weaken a little. Walsingham wrote to Stafford about the middle of the month that she was now resolved not to send the troops until she was reassured of their immediate necessity. Walsingham advised Stafford that he would do well under the circumstances not to put the King in 'greater hope than may stand with the weakness of our resolutions, which are subject to many changes when they are accompanied with matters of charge'.[4] However, the troops did get away by the end of the month and the last of them landed in Normandy on the 1st of October.[5] A good deal of the detailed labour involved in preparing them and providing for their transportation, victualling and pay fell upon

[1] *Lettres de Henri IV*, iii. 25–6 ; Cheyney, i. 215.

[2] Henry's envoys signed an obligation to repay £22,350. The £22,350 may represent the cost of supplies (S. P. France, xx, f. 19).

[3] *Acts of Privy Council*, 1589–90, p. 87.

[4] S. P. France, xx, f. 45.

[5] Cheyney, i. 221.

Walsingham's shoulders.[1] Navarre himself was quick to recognize and quick to acknowledge that Walsingham had been chiefly instrumental in securing the Queen's prompt action in his behalf. 'I can assure you', he wrote to Walsingham on the 20th of October, 'that if my friendship can ever be fruitful to you, you will discover what a goodly share of it you have and will never regret what you have done to win it.'[2]

The death of Henry III, by the elimination of one very uncertain factor in the French situation, greatly simplified the French problem from the English point of view. Thereafter the issue was clearly joined in France between a party inevitably committed to an English alliance and a party inevitably opposed to it. There was no longer a *tertium quid* to be reckoned with and speculated about nor any longer an opportunity for Elizabeth to play her favourite game of oscillation between alternate policies. She had either to support Navarre or to abandon him. By the dispatch of Willoughby to France she definitely committed herself to the policy of supporting him and from that policy she did not waver, though she laboured as always to reduce her support to the absolute minimum.

So far as Walsingham was concerned, the dispatch of the expeditionary force to France in 1589 with the loans of money and supplies which accompanied it may be taken to mark the final triumph of his French policy. Throughout his whole official career he had laboured to persuade the Queen that the safest course for her to pursue in France was to throw in her lot with the Huguenot party and to strengthen and support them with all the means at her disposal. Now at last his mistress was forced to accept his view of the matter. The only problem he still had to face was that of making sure that her support to her French ally was timely and sufficient. No doubt he was instrumental in securing for Henry a further loan of £15,000 from the Queen in October and a similar amount from London merchants about the same time.[3] He certainly played a large

[1] The draft of Willoughby's instructions in S. P. France, xx, f. 56, is in Walsingham's hand. It contains some interesting data on the evils prevalent in Elizabethan armies. 'A Memorial for the Expedition of 4,000 men for France' (S. P. Domestic, ccxxvi, no. 36), also in Walsingham's hand, shows how he busied himself with the details of preparations.

[2] *Lettres de Henri IV*, iii. 61, translated.

[3] Cheyney, i. 217.

part in inducing the Queen to allow Willoughby to remain in France somewhat longer than she had originally intended.[1] Scarcely a month before his death he was still vigorously championing Navarre's cause.[2]

Here then it will be appropriate to conclude a very long and tedious examination of Walsingham's foreign policy. When he left the scene in 1590 the most of all that he had planned for and worked for had been brought to pass. Elizabeth was at war with Spain, and fighting side by side with her against the same enemy were the Dutch Protestants and the French Huguenots. In fact, if not in theory, Walsingham's dream of a grand Protestant alliance against the forces of Rome in Europe had almost been realized. Of all the resources of Protestantism the German princes alone were wanting, while on the other side were ranged Spain, ultra-Catholic France and the Catholic provinces of the Low Countries. The issue was clearly joined. Christ and Belial, as Walsingham would have put it, stood at last face to face. Though the outcome of the conflict was still a long way off, to one of Walsingham's faith the eventual victory of the righteous side could not be doubted. To the modern observer it will appear that the forces which organized the combatants were not altogether, perhaps not even primarily, religious forces. But Walsingham saw things differently. And now that the chief followers of the Cross had been drawn together and were fighting under one banner, though on many battle-fields, his work was in the main done. The time had come for soldiers and sailors, the time of Norris and Drake, to carry forward the work he had planned. He could now, without great jeopardy to the common cause, give up his long fight with the malady which had been wrestling twenty years with his indomitable spirit for the possession of his frail body, and close the book and sit him down and die.

[1] *Cal. Ancaster MSS.*, p. 299.

[2] Cf. Windebank to Walsingham, 24 Feb. 1589/90: 'The danger that her Majesty considereth may fall out to herself and realm, in case there be no assistance rendered to the French King, as your honour hath by your letter remembered and I have declared unto her, hath now caused her to yield and like of the speedy going of Sir Horatio [Palavicino] and Mr. du Fresur, so that there shall be now no need of propounding that matter to my lords of the Council' (S. P. Domestic, ccxxx, no. 84). Cf. also *Cal. Spanish*, 1586–1603, p. 575, 5 March 1590: 'Horatio Palavicino left here on the 6th [O. S.] to raise troops for the Queen'; cf. also Anquez, *Henri IV et l'Allemagne*, *passim*.

XVII

ENGLISH MARITIME ENTERPRISE

So far Sir Francis Walsingham has been considered almost entirely in connexion with the business of the state. He was indeed primarily a statesman. But there are other sides to his career which deserve attention. Next to Burghley, no one of Elizabeth's advisers was more interested than he in the development of English trade, and in maritime exploration and discovery he was far more zealous than Burghley. In this particular field his active interest may well challenge comparison with that of Sir Walter Raleigh himself.

Walsingham's connexion with English trade overseas began apparently with his membership in the Muscovy Company. Exactly how and exactly when he established this connexion is not definitely demonstrable. Probably it was one of the consequences of his first marriage.[1] His first wife, Anna Carleill, was the daughter of Sir George Barnes, one of the two Consuls of the Russia Company as it was incorporated in 1555.[2] Her first husband, Alexander Carleill, was one of the original charter members.[3] Her son-in-law, Christopher Hoddesdon, was one of the earliest and most active agents of the company in Russia.[4] It may be presumed that when Alexander Carleill died his stock in the company passed with his other effects to his widow, and through her in turn to Walsingham. If this was the case, Walsingham's connexion with the company began early in the year 1562. The first definite mention of him as a member occurs, however, six years later, in 1568.[5] The next year he

[1] It should be observed also that Blaise Saunders, Walsingham's cousin (*Cal. Domestic*, 1581–90, p. 273), was one of the assistants of the company as incorporated under Queen Mary. Blaise was probably Walsingham's second cousin. Walsingham's first cousin, Alice, daughter of Sir Edmund Walsingham, married Thos. Saunders (cf. Walsingham pedigree in Harleian MSS. 1174, no. 53). Blaise may have been the son, or possibly the brother, of this Thomas. Blaise was evidently one of the governors of the Muscovy Company in 1561 (Hakluyt, *Voyages*, ed. Maclehose, iii. 14).

[2] Hakluyt, *op. cit.*, ii. 306.

[3] Cheyney, *Studies in Tudor Commerce*, p. 117.

[4] Cf. Life of Hoddesdon in *D. N. B.* supplementary volumes.

[5] 12 Aug. 1568, cf. S. P. Foreign, Elizabeth, ci.

was one of the assistants of the company, or as we should now term it, one of its directors. It is impossible to say how much money Walsingham had invested in this enterprise. The original capital stock was £6,000 divided into shares of £25 apiece.[1] Probably Alexander Carleill did not own more than one share.[2] It is not improbable, however, indeed it is quite likely, that Walsingham acquired other shares besides. The fact that he was made one of the assistants of the company establishes a fair presumption that his interest was rather larger than the average. At the most, however, it cannot have exceeded a few hundreds of pounds. Assessments levied upon the stock before 1565 amounted to £175 per share,[3] which of course had the effect of multiplying Walsingham's original investment eightfold. It is probable that during the earlier years of his connexion with the company it constituted a constant drain upon his resources. After 1566, however, the investment seems to have begun to yield a profit and for the next fifteen years probably more than compensated Walsingham for his earlier losses. After 1581 again the company began to lose money and in 1586 was reorganized.[4] What part, if any, Walsingham played in this reorganization does not appear. Indeed there is practically no evidence of his connexion with the company after 1569.[5] Sometime after 1580 he is said to have been involved in a scheme promoted by Sir Jerome Horsey to undertake private trading in Russia in contravention of the company's monopoly, but the evidence on the point is rather too scanty to substantiate it.[6]

Leaving out of account for the moment Walsingham's connexion with enterprises to discover the North-West Passage, which probably developed out of his connexion with the Muscovy Company, the next trading company with which he appears to have been associated was that entitled 'The President,

[1] Scott, *Joint-Stock Companies*, ii. 39, n. 2.
[2] 205 members are listed as of the original company (Cheyney, *op. cit.*, p. 116).
[3] Scott, *op. cit.*, ii. 40.
[4] Ibid. 44–8.
[5] He concerned himself with the affairs of the company later than this, but it is not clear whether he did so as a member of the company or in his governmental capacity. (*Cal. Domestic*, 1581–90, pp. 75, 91, 135, 138.)
[6] Cf. *Horsey's Travels* (Hakluyt Soc.), p. lxxxix. Horsey was befriended by Walsingham later (ibid., p. 216) and dedicated his account of his travels to Walsingham (ibid., p. 155).

Assistants, and Fellowship of Merchants of Spain and Portugal'. This company was incorporated on the 5th of June 1577.[1] It developed out of an earlier group of English merchants trading in Andalusia who had received a grant of privileges from Henry VIII in 1530.[2] Walsingham's name appears after those of the Earl of Leicester and Sir James Crofts in the list of grantees named in the charter, but it seems likely that in his case, as in the case of Leicester, he was included in the company because the merchants wished to gain his favour and protection. Walsingham certainly can have had little real interest in Spanish trade. Indeed, his policy of war with Spain made him one of the most dangerous enemies to the prosperity of the company in England.[3]

Of the other trading companies organized during Walsingham's time, the only one with which he seems to have been very intimately associated was the Levant Company. This company developed out of the private efforts of two prominent London merchants, Sir Edward Osborne and Richard Staper, to exploit the Levant trade.[4] About 1575 these two merchants, on their own initiative apparently, dispatched two agents to Constantinople to procure from the Sultan a safe-conduct for a factor of Osborne's, by name Wm. Harborne. The agents were successful in this and in July 1578 Harborne proceeded to Constantinople overland. There he was able to procure from the Sultan a concession for English traders to buy and sell in Turkey upon the same terms

[1] The charter of this company is printed in an abbreviated form in Shillington and Chapman, *Commercial Relations of England and Portugal*, pp. 313–26.

[2] This grant is printed in *Select Charters of Trading Companies* (Selden Soc., vol. xxviii), pp. 1 ff. For an account of this early organization cf. Williamson, *Maritime Enterprise, 1485–1558*, pp. 216–25. Some account of the company organized in 1577 will be found in Shillington and Chapman, *op. cit.*, pp. 153–61.

[3] Cf. *Cal. Spanish*, 1580–6, pp. 130, 208–9. On one occasion, according to the Spanish ambassador in London, the Spanish merchants tried to induce Walsingham to abandon his hostility to Spain by offering him a bribe of 10,000 marks (ibid., p. 130). Naturally the outbreak of hostilities with Spain practically broke up the company. Later, in the reign of James I, when the question came up as to the renewal of the charter of 1577, it was stated that the company had not even elected a president for some eighteen years (i. e. since 1587) although the charter called for an annual election. Cf. Thomas Fleming, Ed. Coke *et al.* to Privy Council, 7 Feb. 1604/5 (S. P. Domestic, James I, xii, no. 59).

[4] Epstein, *Early History of the Levant Company*, pp. 8 ff. Both of these men were assistants of the Spanish Company (Shillington and Chapman, pp. 316–17).

as those already accorded to the French and the Venetians. It was upon the receipt of this commission that Osborne and his colleague made ready to open up a trade with the Levant and very probably in that connexion that Walsingham drew up a paper entitled 'A Consideration of Trade with Turkey'.[1]

This paper is illuminating and deserves to be considered in some detail. It was designed to set forth the advantages to be gained from such trade and the difficulties in the way of it. Like a good mercantilist, Walsingham first of all sought to justify the adventure from the point of view of the national welfare. 'You shall set a great number of your greatest ships in work, whereby your navy shall be maintained which otherwise were like to decay.' He then proceeded to enumerate the more direct advantages. Referring to the fact that English commodities sold in Turkey had heretofore been handled by foreign merchants, he pointed out that the English merchants by trading directly with Turkey might eliminate this foreign middleman and pocket his profits themselves. In like manner and with like advantage they might exploit the trade in Turkish commodities. He did not ignore the fact, however, that there were formidable obstacles in the way of direct trade between England and the Turk. The foreign traders who monopolized the trade were hardly likely to admit English competition in their business without resistance. Of these foreign traders, Walsingham enumerated three, the Venetians, the Ragusans, and French traders of Marseilles. The King of Spain also, he thought, might oppose the English traffic as likely to benefit his inveterate enemy the Turk. Walsingham therefore warned the English merchants that they might expect opposition from these quarters both 'by finesse and by force'. By finesse he meant diplomatic intrigue. Both the French and the Venetians, he thought, through their resident ambassadors at Constantinople, would do what they could to discountenance English traders. By force he meant direct attack upon English ships

[1] This document is in S. P. Domestic, cxliv, no. 70. It is endorsed 'A Consideration of Trade into Turkey, 1580. By Mr. Secty. Walsingham.' The document is printed in full by Epstein, *op. cit.*, pp. 245 ff. In one instance Epstein, by modernizing the spelling, distorts the sense. In the original is the word 'fines'. Epstein renders this 'fines'. It plainly should be finesse.

in the Mediterranean, which he anticipated might be expected from the Italians and the French, while Spain might be tempted to intercept the English merchantmen at the Straits of Gibraltar. To meet these difficulties Walsingham recommended that in the first place an ' apt man ' be sent to reside at Constantinople whose business should be to undermine the intrigues of rival states, and he advised that such a man should be sent secretly so that he might not be discredited before his arrival. For defence against direct attack Walsingham suggested that the English should choose good ships, well manned, and should organize them in a fleet of at least twenty sail. Furthermore, he urged that this fleet should go and come in the winter season so that it might have good wind for manœuvring and not fall a prey to the attacks of rowed galleys in summer calms. He does not seem to have been altogether certain that a fleet of twenty ships would be sufficiently strong to repel attacks even under the most favourable conditions. And yet he questioned whether cargo could be found to load twenty ships, and if so whether there was sufficient demand for English commodities in Turkey to furnish a market for such a cargo without depressing prices and profits. In order to prevent the latter calamity, he suggested that ' it were very good a calculation were made what kersies have been transported yearly by the Italians and Ragousers out of this realm, whereof the greatest part hath been sent into Turkey, as also what kersies are sold yearly by our merchants that trade with France to those of Marseilles '. To meet the difficulties which might arise from insufficient cargo out of England, he suggested that commodities marketable in Turkey which were produced in neighbouring countries might also be carried. Even so he thought it doubtful whether the cost of carriage, in view of the expense of equipping the ships for defence, might not eat up the profits of the trade. He feared also that the wars between Turkey and Persia might affect the Turkish market unfavourably. Some other questions he discussed as well, but enough has been said to indicate the character of his ' Considerations '. It will be apparent that he was keenly interested in the success of the new adventure and that he had a firm grasp of the initial problems which faced it. It is likely that he assisted the adventurers to secure a charter from the

Queen the next year.[1] There is, however, no evidence whatever to show that he was financially engaged in their enterprise,[2] nor need this be assumed to explain his friendly attitude towards it. The opening up of trade relations with Turkey had its political as well as commercial aspects, and Walsingham may have already had in mind the possibility of securing the co-operation of Turkey in a joint enterprise against Spain—an idea which he certainly attempted to exploit later.

With the other important aspect of English trade in the Mediterranean, namely, that with Venice and its dependencies, Walsingham's connexion was, apparently, rather less creditable. This trade, in spite of the long tariff war between Venice and England, had by the reign of Elizabeth assumed considerable proportions.[3] It was chiefly an import trade in sweet wines, olive oil and currants. In 1575, at the instance of the Earl of Leicester, Elizabeth granted a monopoly of this import trade to Acerbo Velutelli, a native of Lucca resident in London and rather prominent in London banking circles. Velutelli presently revealed his intention to exploit his grant not by engaging in the trade himself but by levying a tribute upon the regular traders. This course of action naturally aroused a storm of protest both from the Venetian and the English merchants engaged in the trade. They appealed to the Queen through her Privy Council to cancel Velutelli's patent and found Lord Burghley at least disposed to support their plea. Leicester, however, was strong enough to thwart them. Of Walsingham's position in the matter there is only one indication, which occurs in the letter of a Venetian merchant to the Venetian ambassador at Paris.[4] From this letter, however, it appears that Walsingham

[1] Cheyney, *History of England from the Defeat of the Armada to the Death of Elizabeth*, i. 377. Cheyney also cites evidence to indicate Burghley's interest in the business.

[2] The Spanish ambassador in London wrote on 6 Jan. 1583: 'They are trying to raise a large capital to sustain this Levant negotiation, and not only have the richest merchants and companies contributed largely, but the councillors and the Queen herself. £80,000 has already been got together' (*Cal. Spanish*, 1580–6, p. 432). From this some possibility of an investment by Walsingham may be gathered. Mendoza's figures are clearly preposterous, though Scott (*op. cit.*, i. 70) accepts them without question. Cheyney has pointed out (*op. cit.*, i. 384) that after the company had been under way for three years £45,000 had been invested altogether.

[3] There is an admirable account of this whole business in Cheyney, *op. cit.* i. 386 ff.

[4] 6 Feb. 1576, *Cal. Venetian*, 1558–80, p. 545.

supported Leicester's side of the case. The evidence is too slight to give any insight into his motives in the matter, but the presumption is that he was prompted either by expectations of private gain or by a desire to curry favour with his powerful patron. Possibly there were extenuating circumstances of which there is no record. The facts as they stand certainly reveal Walsingham in a rather unpleasant light.[1] The matter was eventually compromised and in 1582 the merchants bought out Velutelli's licence, which still had three years to run, for £1,000.[2] In the spring of the following year the same group of merchants themselves secured a monopoly of the import trade in currants. They were later, in 1592, amalgamated with the Turkey Company. It does not appear, however, that Walsingham took any particular interest in their fortunes after Velutelli's claims had been disposed of.

Even if it be conceded that Walsingham's position with regard to the Venetian trade was antagonistic to the interests of the English merchants engaged in it, it must be admitted that, generally speaking, he was, like Burghley, a vigorous champion of the rights of English merchants in foreign commerce. This appears very clearly in his connexion with the dispute, which reached its climax in his time, between the German merchants of the Hansa League and the various groups of English merchants who were seeking to develop English trade with northern Europe. Before the beginning of the sixteenth century this trade had been almost entirely in the hands of the Germans. Indeed it seems likely that as late as the death of Henry VIII they still carried the bulk of it. Even at that time they continued to enjoy special privileges in the payment of customs which enabled them to import and export their commodities at a lower rate than English traders themselves enjoyed. Against this state of things the English merchants had been protesting for centuries, but their protests availed them little until the reign of Edward VI when the Hansa, for the time being at least, lost their favoured position. Under Mary they secured for a season a restoration of some part of their old

[1] That Velutelli regarded Walsingham as his particular friend is evident from his appeal to Walsingham in 1583. *Cal. Foreign*, 1583–4, p. 291.

[2] Cheyney, *op. cit.* i. 388; a reservation of a payment of 20*s.* a butt on wines was made in favour of Leicester.

privileges, but Elizabeth was not disposed to concede so much. In the privileges which she granted to the Hansa in 1560 she reduced them to an equal footing with English traders in the payment of customs.[1] Even so she displayed more liberality towards them than her chief adviser, Sir William Cecil, was disposed to favour. Of course the Germans complained that they got too little. The English merchants were equally positive that their rivals had got too much. Upon these grounds the issue was joined and fought over during most of Elizabeth's reign.[2]

The English mercantile interests in the quarrel were represented in the main by the Merchant Adventurers, who had long enjoyed by royal patent the monopoly of the trade in English bottoms with the ports of northern Europe which lay between the mouth of the Somme and the Cattegat. The Muscovy Company was also in part concerned by reason of their trade with Narva (in the Baltic), and a little later the Eastland Company, which received from the Queen in 1579 a patent of monopoly for trade in the Baltic.

It will not be necessary to trace the course of this struggle in detail; it is sufficient here to identify Walsingham's position with regard to it. From what little evidence there is available it appears that he steadily opposed the pretensions of the Hansa and steadily favoured those of the English. He does not seem to have been identified with the Merchant Adventurers, in fact there is some evidence to indicate that on one occasion at any rate he favoured English interlopers who were infringing upon the company's monopoly.[3] But as between the Merchant Adventurers and the German merchants he was at one with Burghley in supporting the native trader. This fact appears from his own writings on two separate occasions. In 1584 the Queen arrested some ships of the Merchant Adventurers by reason, apparently, of the fact that they had infringed upon certain rights of Sir Walter Raleigh in the matter of the export of cloth.[4] Walsingham wrote to Burghley on the 17th of June 1584 that he had urged the Queen to release the ships, but that

[1] Cf. Walsingham's statement in *Cal. Foreign*, 1583, pp. 593–4.

[2] On this whole subject cf. Ehrenberg, *Hamburg und England im Zeitalter der Königin Elisabeth.*

[3] Ehrenberg, *op. cit.* 153.

[4] Stebbing, *Sir W. Raleigh*, p. 37.

she had refused to do so. 'When I showed her', he added, 'the great inconveniences like to ensue thereby, her Majesty did in a sort charge me as an encourager of the Merchants to stand in the matter, whereof I sought, as I had just cause, to clear myself and therein did greatly offend her. I find by her she is determined to overthrow that company and to raise up the Staplers as also to restore them of the Steelyard to their former liberties. I am sorry to think of the dangerous inconveniences likely to ensue by these strange courses, but I see no hope of redress. God direct her Majesty's heart to take another way of counsel.'[1] As a matter of fact, Elizabeth did not do what Walsingham feared she would. What she did do does not appear. But one point at any rate is clear, namely, that Walsingham in 1584 stood forth as a champion of the Merchant Adventurers against their English rivals of the Staple on the one hand and their German rivals of the Steelyard on the other.

Again in 1587 he took much the same position. Attention has already been called to the crisis in the English cloth trade of that year. An explanation of this crisis has been offered elsewhere. The situation was so grave that the Queen and her Council were obliged to consider remedies for its relief. Elizabeth's inclination was to place the blame for the crisis upon the shoulders of the Merchant Adventurers and she favoured a policy of coercing them by restoring the privileges of the German merchants and by reducing the export duties on cloth in the case of other foreign merchants. The effect of such a course would have been to rob the Merchant Adventurers of their monopoly. Walsingham and Burghley both opposed the plan and proposed instead that the Queen should advance enough money to the Merchant Adventurers to enable them to maintain the cloth industry in England until the crisis passed. Elizabeth rejected this alternative, but the fact that Walsingham favoured it reveals clearly enough his attitude towards the Merchant Adventurers.[2]

Walsingham's favourable disposition to English competitors of the Hansa traders appears again in connexion with the negotiations of the Eastland Company for trade privileges at

[1] S. P. Domestic, clxxi, no. 35.
[2] Cf. above, Chap. xv, pp. 258–60.

Elbing. This company had been incorporated in 1579 and had been granted a monopoly of the English carrying trade in almost the whole Baltic. Of course it encountered at once the opposition of the German league, particularly of Danzig. To thwart this opposition the English merchants made a strong bid for the friendship of Danzig's two great opponents in the Baltic region, namely, the town of Elbing and the King of Poland. After some years of arduous negotiating the English finally secured trading concessions from Elbing, which the Polish King was willing at any rate to consent to. The result was of course that English carriers got a foothold in the very heart of the region which had heretofore been regarded as the stronghold of the Hansa monopoly. The significance of this fact in the decline of the Hansa and the expansion of the English carrying trade is apparent.[1] Walsingham's connexion with the whole affair is not easy to define with certainty, for it is hard to determine how much of all he wrote on the subject represents his own personal attitude and how far he merely spoke as the official mouthpiece of the English Government. Nevertheless the evidence at hand points to the conclusion that he was decidedly friendly to the purposes of the Eastland merchants and that he furthered their efforts to the extent of his power.[2] Once again he revealed himself as the champion of the English trader against his foreign rival.

Besides Walsingham's interest, direct and indirect, in the fortunes of the various Elizabethan trading companies he had himself an individual interest in English trade, which grew out of certain particular trading privileges conferred upon him at various times by his mistress. It was Elizabeth's favourite practice to reward her servants and courtiers by granting them special privileges in industry or in trade. Sometimes these privileges took the well-known form of patents of monopoly. At other times they consisted of licences to export or to import commodities in which the trade was prohibited by statute. Now and then they conferred permission to carry on a certain

[1] Cf. Szelagowski and Gras, in *Trans. Royal Hist. Soc.*, 3rd series, vi, pp. 163–84, and Deardorff, in Cheyney, *Studies in English Commerce*, pp. 286–325.

[2] *Cal. Foreign*, 1581–2, p. 657; ibid. 1583, pp. 531, 578, 667; Deardorff, in Cheyney's *Studies*, pp. 307, 319–22.

amount of foreign commerce in a specified commodity without paying the usual customs duties. These special dispensations were of course prejudicial to the interests of the trading classes at large and towards the end of Elizabeth's reign they provoked a considerable amount of protest. But this particular form of bounty appealed strongly to the Queen. It always seemed to be so much easier and so much more economical to sign a draft of this sort upon the wealth of trade and industry than it did to confer titles or make gifts of money or gifts of land. She was ever penny wise and pound foolish.

It does not appear that Walsingham ever enjoyed a patent of monopoly in the strict sense of the term. He was, however, one of the most favoured of the Queen's beneficiaries in the matter of trade privileges. Her concessions to him in this regard usually took the form of licences to export what were currently called 'whites', that is to say, unfinished broad-cloths. English law forbade the export of these cloths unfinished with a view to encouraging the development of the English finishing trades.[1] But the practice of granting dispensations from the operation of this law was common even before Elizabeth, and Elizabeth herself conferred many dispensations of this sort. The cloth trade of the Hansa merchants, like that of the Merchant Adventurers, was largely in 'whites' and depended for its continuance upon royal dispensation.[2] The Merchant Adventurers seem regularly to have enjoyed a licence to export 30,000 'whites' a year.[3] But besides these professional traders many noblemen and courtiers received licences to export. In December 1598 one of the customs' searchers at London wrote to Secretary Cecil advising him to sue for such a licence, 'being a thing', he added, 'profitable in respect it is in her Majesty's gift out of the customs paid by strangers and not hurtful to any manner of persons. These licences are customarily granted to such noblemen as have deserved well of the service as appears hereunto: Lord Huntingdon had one for 8,000 long cloths, Bedford the like, the late Lord Burghley for 12,000 short cloths,

[1] Cf. Statutes of the Realm, 3 Henry VIII, c. 7; 5 Henry VIII, c. 3; 27 Henry VIII, c. 13; 33 Henry VIII, c. 19; 8 Eliz., c. 6.

[2] *Cal. Domestic*, 1547–80, p. 193; *Cal. Salisbury MSS.* ii. 80, 134, 182, 232.

[3] *Cal. Domestic*, Adda., 1547–65, p. 542; ibid., Adda., 1580–1625, pp. 402–3.

Lord Sussex for 20,000 long cloths, Mr. Secretary [Walsingham] for 8,000 short cloths, Sir Walter Raleigh for 8,000 long cloths, Lord Hunsdon for 20,000 long cloths.'[1] This letter makes plain how common and how extensive such licences were. Walsingham's licences exceeded in amount that of all the rest. Indeed, most of the bounty which he received from his parsimonious mistress appears to have come to him in this form. Perhaps he preferred it so. His position as Secretary placed him in an exceptionally favourable position to reap the full advantage of trade concessions.

The Patent Rolls reveal a number of licences to him to export unfinished cloth. On the 6th of September 1574 he received a licence to buy and export within the next four years 8,000 broad cloths or kersies (accounting three kersies to the broad cloth). Elizabeth bound herself in this patent to confer no other licence of a similar sort for four years and gave Walsingham permission to see to it that the general statutory prohibition to export such cloths was enforced, granting him one-half the profits from fines and confiscations arising out of breaches of the law.[2]

Less than three years later, on the 15th of April 1577, he received a further licence to export 30,000 pieces of cloth of the prohibited variety. The grant, however, conferred no monopoly like the previous one and no special permission to see to the enforcement of the law.[3] Again, some two years later, on the 7th of September 1579, Walsingham received further licence of the same sort to export 70,000 pieces of cloth.[4] And finally, three years after that, on the 2nd of July 1582, he received still another licence to export 100,000 pieces.[5] These are all the licences which appear to have been granted to him, but they aggregate over a period of something less than eight years 208,000 pieces. It was estimated in 1563 that the annual export of these prohibited cloths amounted to some 50,000 or 60,000 pieces a year.[6] At this rate the concessions to

[1] *Cal. Salisbury MSS.* viii. 475; numerous small licences also appear in the Patent Rolls, Eliz., *passim.*

[2] Patent Rolls, Eliz. 1116, memb. 1.

[3] Ibid. Eliz. 1159, memb. 28–9.

[4] Ibid. 1182, memb. 21–2.

[5] Ibid. 1222, memb. 24.

[6] *Cal. Domestic,* Adda., 1547–65, p. 536; but another document estimates

Walsingham alone amounted to nearly fifty per cent. of the whole export. Probably this is an exaggerated estimate, but it is near enough to the truth to establish the fact that Walsingham controlled for some eight years a very considerable proportion of the export trade in the unfinished cloths of the finer grades.

It is not of course to be presumed that he himself exported these goods. He probably made his profit out of the business by selling his rights to professional traders. It is not unlikely that the Merchant Adventurers purchased some part of them, since their exports of unfinished cloths far exceeded the 30,000 pieces which they were licensed to ship. Possibly this fact accounts in part for Walsingham's friendly disposition to that company. But he seems to have had no compunction at all about selling his licences to groups of English interlopers who were trying to compete with the Merchant Adventurers in the German cloth trade. According to a German agent in London, Walsingham disposed of the right to export 30,000 pieces to such a group of interlopers in 1579.[1] There are unfortunately no figures extant to show how much Walsingham made out of these transactions. According to one statement, the Merchant Adventurers netted a profit of some four shillings a cloth on the goods they exported.[2] If Walsingham made anything like that amount, his returns must have been very considerable. At any rate they were probably sufficient to clear Elizabeth of the charge that she gave no particular recognition to his long and painful services.[3]

the annual export of these cloths by the Merchant Adventurers alone at 60,000 pieces (*Cal. Domestic*, Adda., 1547–65, p. 542).

[1] Ehrenberg, *op. cit.*, p. 153, citing a letter of M. Zimmerman to Dr. Sudermann, dated 10 Oct. 1579. It will be recalled that in September of the same year Walsingham received from the Queen a licence to export 70,000 pieces.

[2] *Cal. Domestic*, Adda., 1547–65, p. 536.

[3] A charge frequently made, cf. Froude, xii. 336. Walsingham also received a licence from the Queen, dated 21 May 1572, to buy and sell 1,000 sarplars of wool (reckoning 3 sacks to the sarplar) with right to ship the same upon payment of the customs (Patent Rolls, Eliz. 1089, memb. 35). This grant was made for seven years, but according to a note on the margin of the Patent Rolls it was surrendered by Walsingham, 12 Jan. 1575/6. The letter patent is also crossed out on the rolls. Nevertheless a note drawn up by one of Walsingham's servants, probably after his death, recites the fact that Walsingham received on several occasions an extension of time on this licence and that several years later the full amount of the wool allowed had not been exported (Harleian MSS. 167, f. 149). It appears from the same document that the regular custom of 40*s*. the sack was to be paid on this wool, so the

One of the most interesting of Walsingham's adventures indirectly connected with English trade was his farm of the customs. In August 1585 he secured from the Queen for six years a lease of the customs of all the important ports of western and northern England in return for an annual rent of £11,263 0*s.* 7*d.*

The practice of farming the customs had been reverted to early in Elizabeth's reign. In 1567 two Londoners had bought the right to collect the export duties on woollen cloth and the import duties on wines for a period of six years. The next year their lease was suspended, apparently without compensation. Shortly afterwards the farm of the wine duties was leased to the Earl of Leicester. Two years after that the farm of all the customs excepting the wine duties at the port of London and adjacent ports was leased to Thomas Smythe, an opulent London merchant. His original lease was for four years, but by repeated renewals it was continued to 1589. He paid a regular rent semi-annually and met all the major expenses of collection. He was, of course, obligated to collect no more nor any less than the rates of duty prescribed by law, and he had to keep his account books open to inspection by the officers of the Queen's Exchequer. Although the rent Smythe paid was considerably in excess of the average collections from the ports of his farm when they were made by the Government directly, there can be little doubt that he made a handsome profit out of his rental. This was due in a large measure to the rapid expansion of trade under Elizabeth, but it was due also, no doubt, to the greater efficiency of his administration.[1]

At all events Smythe paid more to the Queen than she ever

value of the licence probably resided in the fact that it constituted an infringement upon the monopoly of the Staplers. Walsingham apparently sold the wool to dealers. His profit on the transaction is not recorded.

Walsingham also received, 31 Dec. 1584, a licence to export 3,000 tuns of double beer duty free (Patent Rolls, Eliz. 1260, memb. 11). It appears that he sold this (*Cal. Domestic*, 1598–1601, p. 87) and that he reaped his profit by collecting a customs duty of 16*s.* the tun, which would have yielded him a return of £2,400.

[1] The best account of the farming of the customs under Elizabeth is that by A. P. Newton, 'The Establishment of the Great Farm of the English Customs', *Trans. Royal Hist. Soc.*, 4th series, i, pp. 129–55. On Walsingham's farm Professor Newton is very brief. He is probably mistaken in his assumption that Walsingham lost money on his lease.

had got from her own collections. She, therefore, was well disposed towards the arrangement and in a frame of mind to consider favourably its application to the other English ports, commonly known as the out-ports. At the moment the out-ports were, generally speaking, farmed out individually either to the royal collectors or to the burgesses of the town. This form of administration was not a satisfactory one. It led to a good deal of corruption and the net returns to the Queen were distressingly small. The situation in the out-ports was, in a word, ripe for a change and the nature of the change was indicated by the success of the London farm.

It is certain that Walsingham was interesting himself in the matters of the customs as early as 1576, though exactly what form this earlier interest took is not quite clear.[1] He had begun to petition for a farm of the customs at least as early as January 1585 and he apparently encountered some opposition from Lord Burghley in his pursuit of it.[2] The lease was finally granted to him on the 17th of August 1585. It conferred upon him the right to collect import and export duties on all commodities except wine entering and clearing from the ports of Plymouth, Exeter, Poole, Bridgwater, Bristol, Gloucester, Milford, Cardiff, Chester, Berwick, Newcastle, Hull, Boston, Lynn and Yarmouth. In

[1] Walsingham's letter to Burghley of 12 Sept. 1576 shows that he was interesting himself in some matters connected with the customs as early as 1576. 'The Earl of Leicester acquainted me with so much of your Lordship's letters as concerned the custom, who telleth me that her Majesty maketh stay in resolving therein until she receive from your Lordship the several rates to the end she may choose the highest. And as her Majesty is very careful to choose the highest, so am I very fearful to deal with the lowest in respect of the doubtfulness of the time, unapt for traffic. Howsoever the matter take place, I think myself greatly bound unto your Lordship for your honourable dealing therein towards me. I am fully persuaded that unless I shall find her Majesty persuaded that I deal withal rather in respect of her service than of any profit to grow unto myself, I will not meddle therein' (S. P. Domestic, cix, no. 6).

[2] A letter from Walsingham to Burghley, dated 30 January 1584/5 (S. P. Domestic, clxxvi, no. 19), throws some interesting light on Burghley's connexion with Walsingham's lease. 'But touching my late conceits had of your opposition in my suit for the farming of the customs. . . . I saw so many reasons, confirmed so many ways, to lead me so to think as did not only induce me to believe that to be true, but did in a sort work in me a confirmation of the truth of former reports of your Lordship's mislike of me.' This passage reveals the fact that Walsingham had begun his suit for the farm of the customs at least seven months before he secured it. It also reveals the fact that Walsingham regarded Burghley's attitude to his suit as a hostile one and felt so sure of his ground that he did not hesitate to charge Burghley with it.

return for this he was to pay the Queen annually £11,263 0s. 7d. in two instalments. He received authority to publish all necessary orders for the administration of the customs, to board ships and to search cellars and storehouses for smuggled goods. He undertook to pay all officers of the customs in these ports and to reserve to Lord Burghley certain rights of appoint ment to these offices which he had hitherto enjoyed.[1] In case the outbreak of war seriously diminished the bulk of trade he was to be allowed a reasonable abatement of the annual price of his farm. He agreed, however, to make no reduction in the current rates of duty for the purpose of attracting trade from other ports.[2]

This farm of the customs seems to have been an individual enterprise which Walsingham undertook on his own resources. An agent of the Hansa League in London at the time intimated that he was acting as the agent of the Merchant Adventurers,[3] but this was clearly mere surmise and all the evidence available about the matter contradicts it. It is evident that Elizabeth submitted the terms of the agreement to Lord Burghley before she ratified it. A memorandum of 'Notes on the Articles of the Lease' endorsed in Burghley's own hand survives, which shows that Burghley carefully reviewed the various terms of the agreement and suggested some amendments. He seems to have been particularly anxious to guard against any abatement of the customs. This was evidently no uncommon practice among farmers of the customs, their purpose being of course to attract more trade to the ports of their farm by offering lower rates of duty. It may have been at Burghley's suggestion that the clause prohibiting this practice was inserted in Walsingham's agreement.[4]

It is not clear by what process the price which Walsingham was to pay for the customs was reached. A statement of the net

[1] This concession afterwards caused complications and led one of Walsingham's agents to suggest that he purchase from Burghley these rights of appointment for £1,000 a year (cf. Laurence Tomson to Walsingham, 17 June 1586, S. P. Domestic, cxc, no. 39). This suggestion indicates that Burghley's rights of appointment were worth a considerable sum in hard cash.

[2] An abstract of the terms of Walsingham's lease will be found in S. P. Domestic, clxxxi, no. 50, another in S. P. Domestic, Supplementary, bundle 9, and another in Harleian MSS. 306, f. 142.

[3] Ehrenberg, *op. cit.*, p. 174.

[4] Harleian MSS. 167, f. 159.

returns from the customs of the ports of Walsingham's farm for five years from November 1577 to November 1582 reveals the fact that the average annual return from these ports in customs duties amounted to a little less than £7,000.[1] If these figures be accurate, it will be evident that Walsingham's offer of £11,000 and odd for his farm was a profitable bargain from the Queen's point of view.

There is little or no evidence available upon which to base a detailed account of Walsingham's administration of the customs leased to him.[2] It is clear that from the first he did not live up to his agreement. An examination of his accounts with the Queen during the first three years of his administration reveals the fact that he paid into the Royal Exchequer £21,050, instead of the £33,789 1*s.* 9*d.* which he had agreed to pay.[3] This left him in debt to the Queen £12,739 1*s.* 9*d.* In the spring of 1589 he petitioned the Queen to be excused from this debt on the grounds that the frequent restraints of trade, the troubles in France and the 'fear of war' with Spain had reduced the customs revenues at his ports to such an extent as to justify a reduction of his rent.[4] In August of the same year Elizabeth consented to grant his petition and forgave him his debt. She

[1] Cf. Collection of Customs at several ports for six years from 20th to 25th Eliz., certified 17 Nov. 1584 (Harleian MSS. 106, f. 41). This document gives the customs returns from the various ports of Walsingham's farm exclusive of the two Welsh ports of Cardiff and Milford. The totals of these returns for each of the six years are as follows: £6,645 6*s.* 7¾*d.*; £7,294 14*s.* 11¼*d.*; £6,184 1*s.* 8¼*d.*; £7,544 5*s.* 6¾*d.*; £6,973 0*s.* 9¼*d.*; £6,809 3*s.* 9¼*d.* The figures for the first four years do not include any return from Gloucester; but since Gloucester only returned £34 8*s.* and £59 5*s.* 4*d.* for the last two years given, it may be presumed that for the earlier years Gloucester returned little or nothing. The omission of the Welsh ports is probably to be accounted for in the same way. Under Walsingham's administration of the customs the Welsh ports altogether never yielded a gross return of more than £61 per annum (Harleian MSS. 167, f. 151). In 1595 the port of Milford yielded £75 0*s.* 4½*d.* and that of Cardiff £38 1*s.* 1*d.* (*Cal. Salisbury MSS.* v. 393). It is not stated whether the returns as indicated above were gross or net, but the presumption is that they were net, since otherwise Walsingham's offer would have been unbelievably magnanimous. A note in Burghley's hand at the end of the document makes it clear that these figures passed under Burghley's eye. Quite probably they were compiled for him.

[2] 'The orders to be observed in the ports whereof the customs are devised to Sir F. W.' are preserved in S. P. Domestic, clxxxi, no. 51. A brief mention of an incident arising in the course of his administration is also made in a letter from Walsingham to Burghley, 28 Aug. 1589, Harleian MSS. 6994, f. 191.

[3] A detailed account of his payments, signed by Thomas Moryson, deputy to the clerk of the Pipe, is preserved in Harleian MSS. 306, f. 39.

[4] Walsingham to Burghley, 23 Apr. 1589, Harleian MSS. 167, f. 157.

even went farther than that and agreed to accept £7,000 a year in satisfaction of his lease during the remaining three years it had to run, or at least so long as the restraint of trade or the fear of war continued.[1] This lower rate seems to have been the one charged to Walsingham so long as the lease remained in his hands or in those of his heirs. His death in April 1590 naturally terminated his own personal connexion with the affair.

Some six months after Walsingham's death an investigation was made of his administration of the customs. It does not appear that this investigation was provoked by any particular distrust of Walsingham's administration. The three men appointed on the investigating committee were Thomas Middleton, William Bland and Lisle Cave. Cave had been Walsingham's secretary, Bland and Middleton the most prominent of his customs officials.[2] Their letter of instructions directed them 'to survey the said ports and all the books and writings belonging to the same, to find out and reform abuses, to minister an oath and to take bonds to her Majesty's use of such officers as they shall think meet . . . and also to do and execute all things as the assigns of Sir Francis Walsingham were warranted to do'.[3] This letter suggests that Cave and his colleagues were acting primarily in the interest of Walsingham's estate.[4] At any rate their investigations made many important revelations.

¹ Patent Rolls, Eliz. 1330, memb. 34–5, dated 6 August, 31 Elizabeth.

² On Bland cf. Walsingham to Burghley, 23 Apr. 1589, Harleian MSS. 167, f. 157; on Middleton cf. his life in *D. N. B.*

³ Harleian MSS. 167, f. 145.

⁴ At Walsingham's death the Queen apparently took over the remainder of his lease to her own use, though she applied £6,000 from the profits to the payment of Walsingham's debts. It need not be assumed, however, as Professor Newton assumes, that this £6,000 represented unpaid balances due on his lease. Among the Harleian MSS. in the British Museum (167, f. 157B) is a document entitled 'A brief note of the accounts of the ports farmed out to Sir F. W. and hath been kept for her Majesty's use one year and a half ending Michelmas, 1591'. From this note it appears that the total receipt from the ports for the eighteen months in question was £22,822 12*s.* 8*d.*, which was assigned as follows:

	£	*s.*	*d.*
Sir F. W.'s rent for 1½ years	10,500	0	0
Set apart for his debts	6,000	0	0
All charges for 1½ years	3,822	12	8
Profit	2,500	0	0

From this it appears probable that Elizabeth administered these ports for eighteen months at least after Walsingham's death, assigned a portion of the profits to the payment of his debts (possibly secured by his lease of the customs), and pocketed the remainder.

In the first place, Bland prepared a detailed account of Walsingham's receipts from the customs for the four and a half years between the 1st of October 1585 and the 1st of March 1590. The totals for each year are as follows: 1585–6, £17,193 15*s.* 8½*d.*; 1586–7, £17,633 4*s.* 4½*d.*; 1587–8, £21,292 12*s.* 7*d.*; 1588–9, £16,801 16*s.* 8*d.*; Oct. 1589–Mar. 1590, £10,008 5*s.* 10½*d.*[1] These figures represent of course the gross receipts. Of the expenses of Walsingham's administration there are several estimates, no two of which exactly concur. John Daws,[2] another one of Walsingham's deputies, estimated, on the assumption that Walsingham paid £11,263 0*s.* 7*d.* annually for the farm of his customs, that his net profits were as follows: 1585–6, £893 12*s.* 6½*d.*; 1586–7, £741 0*s.* 1½*d.*; 1587–8, £2,833 0*s.* 4½*d.*; 1588–9, £1,072 8*s.* 7*d.* (loss); Oct. 1589–Mar. 1590, £2,859 0*s.* 5½*d.*

These figure are, however, invalidated by the fact that Walsingham did not pay £11,263 0*s.* 7*d.* for his farm but only £7,000. In order to get therefore his actual profits it will be necessary to add to the year's net returns in every case £4,263 0*s.* 7*d.* This will give the annual profit as follows: 1585–6, £5,156 13*s.* 1½*d.*; 1586–7, £5,004 0*s.* 8½*d.*; 1587–8,

[1] Harleian MSS. 167, f. 151. Bland gives the return from each port for each year. The figures are independently interesting as showing that with the exception of the year following the Armada Walsingham's receipts steadily increased. It is striking to observe that even the war with Spain seems to have caused a relatively slight reduction of the customs. An account of the customs of these ports for the eighteen months following 1 March 1590 does reveal some falling off in the returns. For the year ending 1 March 1591 the total receipts are given as £16,047 1*s.* 8½*d.*, and for the ensuing six months £6,775 10*s.* 11½*d.* (Harleian MSS. 167, f. 157B).

It ought to be pointed out that another report of Walsingham's annual receipts was submitted in July 1590 by John Daws, another one of Walsingham's deputies. Daws's estimates, a trifle lower than those of Bland, follow:

	£	*s.*	*d.*
1585–6	16,893	19	5½
1586–7	17,342	1	11½
1587–8	21,180	8	8
1588–9	16,765	19	4
October 1589—November 1590	9,994	9	11

The details of Daws's report will be found in Harleian MSS. 167, f. 156. In some cases his individual figures for individual ports agree with Bland's.

Bland heads his own report as follows: 'A declaration of the receipts grown due in the several ports demised to Sir Fra. Walsingham, which is in some particulars to be justified by an account exhibited to your honour by one John Daws, and in the rest by the books audited and given up yearly to the said Sir Francis and others interested in the farm of the customs.'

[2] Harl. MSS. 167, f. 142. In 1594 Daws is referred to as 'surveyor for customs causes in the out ports' (*Cal. Salisbury MSS.* iv. 479).

£7,096 0*s.* 11½*d.*; 1588–9, £3,190 12*s.*; Oct. 1589–Mar. 1590, £4,990 15*s.* 4*d.* By this reckoning it appears that Walsingham's annual profits averaged considerably over 50 per cent. and on two occasions over 100 per cent. His claim, therefore, that he could not afford to pay the full contract price for the farm of the customs is by this reckoning unjustified. Another series of estimates based on Bland's figures is given by Burghley himself as follows: [1]

Profits for	1585–6 . . .	£2,053	14	1
,, ,,	1586–7 . . .	£3,852	19	3½
,, ,,	1587–8 . . .	£6,965	7	6
,, ,,	1588–9 . . .	£1,765	14	3½
,, ,,	Oct. 1589–Mar. 1590	£2,976	15	7

It does not appear whether these profits are based upon the supposition that Walsingham paid the full price originally agreed upon for the customs or the £7,000 which Elizabeth subsequently accepted. The presumption is, however, since Burghley himself has used the figures, that the actual price paid for the customs was the basis of the reckoning. If this presumption be accepted, then the figures just cited probably represent Walsingham's actual profit from the customs. Reckoned in approximate percentages this would mean that his profits on his investment year by year were as follows: 27, 55, 99, 25, and 85 per cent., which gives an average yearly yield of over 58 per cent. This was of course a handsome profit even for Elizabeth's days. Still, according to this reckoning, Walsingham was justified in petitioning the Queen for a reduction of the rent agreed upon, since it appears that if he had paid the full price the customs would have yielded him a profit during but one year of the four and a half which he had them in farm.

In connexion with the report on Walsingham's administration of the customs Bland and Cave drew up a paper in which they pointed out that the cost of Walsingham's administration had in some respects been greater than they need have been. They found that the fees which he paid the officers and certain other charges incident to his administration were excessive, and they expressed the opinion that out of the total of annual costs, which amounted under his administration to some £2,362, about

[1] Harleian MSS. 167, f. 143.

£830 might have been saved. They said further that Walsingham had lost money by the malpractices of some of his officers, and had given away much in order to entice merchants to his ports; and they estimated that if the Queen relaxed somewhat her restrictions on the grain trade she might reap a profit of almost double what Walsingham had actually paid her.[1] An account of the administration of the customs of these ports by the Queen during the year and a half from Lady Day 1590 to Michaelmas 1591 goes far to justify this view of the case. The gross receipts of the ports for this period were £22,822 12*s.* 8*d.*, the charges for administration during the same period amounting to £3,822 12*s.* 8*d.* This revealed the fact that Elizabeth's net profits from the ports was £19,000 or £8,500 more than she would have received had the farm remained in Walsingham's hands

[1] 'A Difference in the Fees and charges paid by Sir Francis Walsingham to his deputies in the time of his farm and those that are now allowable by her Majesty', signed by Bland and Cave, 10 August 1590 (Harl. MSS. 167, f. 138). Some idea may be gathered of the various expenses incurred by Walsingham in his farm of the customs by consulting Daws's account of Walsingham's receipts and expenses, though Daws's figures are to be taken with caution (Harl. MSS. 167, f. 142). His account of expenses follows:

	1585–6	1586–7	1587–8	1588–9	Oct. 1589–Mar. 1590
	£ *s.* *d.*	£ *s.* *d.*	£ *s.* *d.*	£ *s.* *d.*	£ *s.* *d.*
1. To the Queen's officers in fees	894 2 6	659 11 5	597 0 0	678 16 8	444 2 11
2. For yearly annuities	89 2 6	77 1 11	69 2 6	129 2 6	54 11 9
3. To officers of the exchequer	26 0 4	159 9 4	128 16 0	128 16 0	50 0 0
4. To his honour's officers in fees	2,249 14 5	817 18 11	1,362 11 7½	1,379 2 4	724 10 0
5. Abatements to Merchants	169 9 2				
6. Rent of customs houses and rewards to officers with all other charges	683 6 0	803 2 11	[illeg.]	1,438 12 11	220 9 11
7. Doubtful and desperate debts yet unpaid	624 11 5	624 11 5	624 11 5	624 11 5	
8. Yearly rent	11,263 0 7	11,263 0 7	11,263 0 7	11,263 0 7	5,631 10 3½

Another document (Harl. MSS. 167, f. 144) gives in detail the fees and annuities yearly paid out of the customs at the ports under Walsingham's farm, though it does not appear whether these sums were paid out during Walsingham's administration or at some other time. In this document fees to customers total £800 9*s.* 4*d.*; exchequer fees, £140 4*s.*; annuities, £124 8*s.* 9*d.*

and had he paid £7,000 per year for it.[1] Yet it ought to be recalled that when Walsingham took the customs in hand they were apparently yielding to the Queen something less than £7,000 a year. The enormous increase in the net return from these ports between the years 1584 and 1590 was no doubt largely due to a very considerable expansion of trade in spite of wars and rumours of wars. It may have been due also in part to the fact that Walsingham, in spite of some mistakes, instituted reforms in the administration which effected large economies in the cost of collection. At all events it seems that he made a considerable profit out of the adventure.

It has been pointed out already that Walsingham was directly connected with the Spanish Company and the Russia Company and that he revealed an active interest in the affairs of the Venetian Merchants, the Turkey Merchants, the Eastland Merchants, and the more venerable company of Merchant Adventurers. Indeed, it is fair to say that there was no branch of English trade in which he was not interested. Yet he was clearly not of that sober and sedate type of business man who is content to place his capital in safe investments and watch it grow by degrees. There was in him, as in so many others at the court of Queen Elizabeth, a decided taste for speculation which preferred to take long chances for exorbitant profits. On this account the more problematical enterprises of his time which undertook to discover gold mines, or short cuts to the wealth of the East, or unguarded Spanish treasure galleons, attracted him far more than the slower courses of the European trade. Adventurous spirits like Humphrey Gilbert and Martin Frobisher and Francis Drake and John Davis found in him a man after their own heart. He was, in fact, and remained as long as he lived, their readiest advocate at Court.

His first recorded connexion with Elizabethan voyages of discovery was with Frobisher's first expedition in search of the North-West Passage in 1576. Walsingham does not seem to have had anything to do with the inception of this adventure. Frobisher probably received his initial stimulus from Sir Humphrey Gilbert, who had projected such a voyage ten years

[1] Harleian MSS. 167, f. 157.

before [1] and had written a plausible pamphlet supporting his belief in the existence of the Passage in 1574 or thereabouts.[2] Neither can Walsingham be accounted one of Frobisher's active promoters. The Earl of Warwick, brother of the Earl of Leicester, was Frobisher's chief patron [3] and was probably the man most instrumental in securing for him the goodwill of the Queen and the modest capital of £875 which was raised, chiefly among the courtiers, to finance the expedition. Walsingham appears simply among the contributors to the joint stock. His contribution amounted to £25 and was more likely made in order to gratify Warwick than from any strong interest in the adventure itself.[4]

Frobisher's first voyage, which set forth in June 1576 and got back in October, accomplished little more in the direct line of its purpose than to encourage the hopes of its commander in the eventual discovery of the North-West Passage. Its principal result indeed was to draw a red herring across the main trail. A piece of black pyrites which a member of Frobisher's company had picked up on one of the northern islands was handed over to Baptista Agnello, an Italian alchemist, for analysis. Agnello reported it to contain gold in paying quantities. This discovery was brought to Walsingham's attention. He was disposed to regard it 'but as an alchemist matter such as divers others before had been brought to her Majesty', but consented finally to submit some specimens of the ore to the goldsmiths for further analysis. They reported that they found no gold. This ought to have ended the matter, but Agnello was so positive about his findings that Walsingham submitted the ore a second time to the goldsmiths. Once again they reported nothing.[5] It will be obvious that Walsingham, for all his enter-

[1] Slafter, *Sir Humphrey Gilbert*, pp. 182–6. Frobisher, however, was considering plans for a voyage to the North-West in 1569. Cf. *The Three Voyages of Martin Frobisher* (Hakluyt Society), p. 70.

[2] Printed in Hakluyt's *Voyages* (ed. Maclehose), viii. 158. The date of this pamphlet is uncertain. Professor Raleigh in his introduction to the Maclehose edition of Hakluyt's *Voyages* places it at 1574 (Hakluyt, xii. 26). Coote, in the article on Frobisher in the *Dictionary of National Biography*, says 1566, but internal evidence proves that it must have been later than 1568.

[3] *The Three Voyages of Martin Frobisher* (Hakluyt Society), pp. 70–1. Almost all of the available sources on the Frobisher voyages are printed in full in this volume.

[4] Ibid. 108. Burghley subscribed £50; Sussex, Warwick, and Leicester, each £50.

[5] Ibid. 94–7.

prising spirit, took the cautious and careful attitude and was not one of those to rush madly forth into the unknown after ship-loads of fool's gold.

But Frobisher himself felt differently about the matter and was all on fire to set out at once in search for more of the precious metal. He succeeded with the help of his friends in persuading the Queen that the adventure was at least worth the risk and secured her permission to set sail. She even consented to the incorporation of a company with exclusive rights to exploit the North-West Passage.[1] Frobisher proceeded at once to invite contributions to a second expedition and the promise of gold seems to have provoked an immediate response. Elizabeth herself put in £1,000, Burghley £100,[2] and curiously enough even Walsingham, in spite of his well-grounded scepticism, adventured something over £200.[3] He was indeed one of the largest single investors. Presumably his better judgement had been undermined by the contagion of the gold fever which swept the Court.

Frobisher departed on his second voyage late in May 1577 and got back again in September with some 200 tons of the ore under his hatches.[4] The voyage was regarded for the moment as a complete success and the precious cargo was carefully locked away, some of it in Bristol Castle, the rest in the Tower of London.[5] Elaborate preparations were made for its reduction, but before they were completed spring had come again and with it the fair weather for another voyage if one was to be undertaken. It might have been expected that the adventurers would have hesitated to advance more capital until they were better assured of the returns from their earlier investment, but one or two preliminary assays of Frobisher's cargo yielded promising results[6] and stimulated his promoters to greater

[1] Scott, *Constitution and Finance of English . . . Joint-Stock Companies, to 1720*, ii. 78.

[2] *Frobisher's Voyages*, p. 107.

[3] It is not easy to say exactly how much Walsingham put in. One list (*Frobisher's Voyages*, p. 107) puts him down for £200 ; another (ibid. 108) for £50 ; and a third (ibid. 164) for £400 for himself and others, with a later assessment for wages at the end of the second voyage of £80. Two later assessments seem in fact to have been imposed, one of 20 per cent. for wages (ibid. 163), and one of 20 per cent. for working the ore (ibid. 172).

[4] Ibid. 175.

[5] Article on Frobisher in the *Dictionary of National Biography*.

[6] *Cal. Colonial, East Indies*, i, nos. 82–6.

efforts than ever. In May 1578 they dispatched him once again with a fleet of fifteen vessels. The money for his equipment was apparently raised, in part at least, by a *pro rata* assessment upon the stockholders in the previous voyage.[1] The total amount which was to be raised amounted to something over £6,500,[2] but only a portion of it had been collected before Frobisher's departure. Walsingham paid in at the outset £182 7*s*.[3] He was obliged to pay in more when Frobisher returned in the autumn with an expense account in wages and freightage which came to nearly £6,000.[4] Altogether Walsingham is on record as having contributed to the third adventure £475 which, in addition to his contributions to the previous voyages, brought his total investment to at least £825. He probably lost every penny of it, for the ore proved in the end to be hardly worth the expense of reducing it.[5] So Walsingham's first adventure in voyages of discovery was not exactly encouraging. The amazing feature of it is that a man of his discretion should have flown in the face of the sober London goldsmiths and followed the glittering hopes held out by an Italian alchemist fellow.

Yet there was better metal in the western world than iron pyrites and there was a shorter way to it than by laborious digging. Sir Francis Drake had demonstrated that fact by his lucrative expedition to the Spanish Main a few years before, and, while Frobisher was carting back to England his ship-loads of pyrites, was already at sea determined to make further demonstration. The expedition which set forth under his command in 1577 hardly belongs to a discussion of exploration and trading ventures because it was frankly designed to plunder the Spaniards in the Pacific. However, it deserves some mention here because of its consequences, which reached far beyond its original purposes. Drake himself first conceived of the enterprise among the peaks of Darien in 1573.[6] It was not, however, until 1575 that he got a chance to present it at Court. In that

[1] Scott, *op. cit.* ii. 81.

[2] *Frobisher's Voyages*, pp. 325, 358.

[3] *Cal. Colonial, East Indies*, i, no. 94.

[4] *Frobisher's Voyages*, pp. 320, 358; *Cal. Colonial, East Indies*, i, no. 105.

[5] Michael Lok offered later to give £5 a ton for the ore (*Frobisher's Voyages*, 356), but there is no indication that his offer was accepted.

[6] Corbett, *Drake and the Tudor Navy*, i. 178–9.

year he came to London with a letter of introduction to Walsingham, who was even then, though he had been a member of the Queen's Council for less than two years, recognized as one of the chief exponents at Court of a policy hostile to Spain.[1] What passed between Drake and Walsingham in their first interview together is not recorded, but it is certain that Walsingham approved Drake's plan and presented it in flattering terms to the Queen. The tedious business of winning Elizabeth's assent to it must have fallen largely to Walsingham's lot, though both the Earl of Leicester and Sir Christopher Hatton threw the whole weight of their influence in support of it. Somehow or other, in spite of the powerful opposition of Burghley and the more conservative members of the Privy Council, the Queen was brought to acquiesce. With this point gained, Drake set about raising the necessary capital for the equipment of a small fleet by seeking subscriptions to a joint stock after the manner employed by Frobisher. The necessity for keeping the matter secret naturally limited the possible investors to a very few. On the other hand, it is probable that Drake required altogether not more than £5,000.[2] Very likely the amount was made up by Drake himself and the few courtiers who had been taken into his confidence. There is some reason to believe that Elizabeth herself subscribed 1,000 crowns.[3] Leicester, Hatton, and Walsingham seem to have been the other important members of the syndicate.[4] How much Walsingham subscribed there is no means of knowing. It would be a mistake to assume that his interest in it was merely commercial. His lifelong conviction that Spain was the chief menace both to his faith and to his country always prompted him to favour blows struck at the Spaniard in any quarter. If money was to be made as well, so much the better. In Drake's plan he detected an opportunity to serve at once God and mammon.

After nearly two years' delay Drake finally got away from England in November 1577. The story of his voyage is too well known to need further repetition. So far as his connexion with England was concerned, he was for three years a dead man.

[1] Ibid. 205. [2] Scott, *op. cit.* i. 78. [3] Ibid. 80.

[4] There is no positive proof of this, but all the attending circumstances tend to confirm the Spanish ambassador's statement that they were the principal 'owners' of the adventure. *Cal. Spanish, Eliz.*, 1580–6, 55.

But the Spaniards along the western coast of America found him very far from dead. The amount of plunder he secured at their expense was enormous and by taking the bold course of returning to England by way of the Cape of Good Hope he brought the bulk of it home with him. Exactly how much he secured cannot be stated with any certainty; probably it was not far short of £500,000. Of this amount something less than half was divided among the promoters, who are said to have received back 4,700 per cent. on their investment. Most of the rest of the plunder probably found its way into the royal treasury.[1]

In view of the enormous profits from this enterprise it is not surprising to discover that Drake had scarcely got his treasure ashore before various projects were on foot to send him forth again. The most ambitious of these is associated with the claims of Don Antonio to the throne of Portugal. In the dispute over the Portuguese succession which followed upon the death of the childless Portuguese King in 1580, Philip of Spain had easily made good his claim to the Portuguese mainland. But the Azores held out for Don Antonio and Walsingham and his partisans thought they might be used as a base for an attack upon Spanish commerce. It was accordingly proposed to send Drake with a strong squadron to establish himself under Don Antonio's flag in the Azores and there to lie in wait for the Spanish plate fleets from the West Indies.[2] Walsingham calculated in this way to cut off Philip's chief financial resource and to divert it into the English treasury. But the Queen, although she was sorely tempted by the prospect of plunder, finally rejected the plan as too dangerous in its possible consequences.

An alternative proposition had already been suggested, probably by Drake himself. On his previous voyage he had touched at the Portuguese spice islands, had discovered that the native chiefs were disposed to trade and had loaded up his ships with all the spices he could find room for. This episode in his famous voyage has ordinarily been neglected by historians though it was regarded in his own day as one of his great achievements.[3] Probably it lay at the foundations of a plan which was under consideration before the end of the year 1580 to exploit

[1] Scott, i. 81–2. [2] Corbett, *op. cit.* i. 326. [3] Ibid. 298–300.

the East India trade by sending Drake back to the spice islands with a fleet of merchantmen. Bernardino de Mendoza, the Spanish ambassador at London, fathered this project upon Leicester,[1] but there is very good reason to believe that Walsingham was one of its principal promoters. It must have been in this connexion that he drafted a plan for an English East India Company which anticipated by twenty years the formal inauguration of English trade with the Far East. Mendoza was disposed to regard this plan as a mere pretext for plunder, but it gives evidence on the face of it of having been seriously meant. From Walsingham's rough draft it appears that he had in mind a joint-stock company of the usual English pattern under Drake's presidency. He spoke also of a *casa de contratación* and evidently intended the concentration of the East India trade at designated ports in accordance with the Spanish practice.[2] But he had hardly got beyond the bare outlines of his plans for trade before his interest was diverted to the more bellicose scheme of sending Drake to the Azores. The trading project was not, however, altogether abandoned and, when the Azores enterprise was finally vetoed by the Queen, was revived again in a somewhat different form.[3] In the autumn of 1581 it was finally decided, chiefly it appears through Leicester's efforts, that a trading expedition should be sent to the East with Frobisher in command. A little later, in consequence of some dissensions between Frobisher and his patrons, Edward Fenton was put in his place.[4] Fenton finally got away from England in May of 1582.[5]

[1] *Cal. Spanish*, 1580–6, pp. 70, 75.

[2] S. P. Domestic, cxliv, no. 44: 'A Project for a Corporation of such as shall adventure unto such dominions and countries situate beyond the equinoctial line.' This paper is written in Walsingham's hand. It is printed in full in *New Light on Drake* (Hakluyt Society, 2nd series, vol. xxxiv), p. 430.

[3] *Cal. Spanish*, 1580–6, pp. 95, 101.

[4] Corbett, i. 334.

[5] Scott (*op. cit.* ii. 81–2) associates this enterprise of 1582 with the three earlier voyages of Frobisher to the North-West as the last of four adventures attempted by the Cathay Company. There seems, however, to be no further evidence of a connexion than in the fact that Frobisher was originally designated for the command and that several of those who were financially interested in his voyages to the North-West were interested also in Fenton's voyage. This in itself is hardly conclusive evidence, since very much the same group of men supported every one of the Elizabethan voyages of discovery.

The account of Fenton's voyage as given in the life of Fenton in the *Dictionary of National Biography* is inaccurate in many particulars. It is said there that the two largest ships were furnished by the Queen, although there is no proof that Elizabeth took any share in the enterprise. Certainly the

In view of the fact that Walsingham had been one of the chief promoters of the project to send Drake to the East Indies, it is rather surprising to discover that he apparently took little interest in Fenton's voyage. It is pretty clear that the preparations for the voyage were well under way before Walsingham's contribution was even solicited,[1] and the £200 which he did contribute was a small investment when compared with those of the other adventurers—no more in fact than the cautious Burghley was willing to hazard.[2] Apparently, as soon as it was decided that Drake should not command the expedition, Walsingham's interest in it began to flag. Possibly he saw small chance of profit in a purely trading adventure. Possibly he distrusted Frobisher whose three abortive expeditions to the North-West had certainly not established his ability as a money-maker. Possibly, even, Walsingham foresaw in the dissensions over the command the fiasco which was to ensue. Altogether too little is ascertainable about the court intrigues in which the enterprise early became involved to permit of a precise definition of Walsingham's position in the matter. At any rate he had good reason to rejoice that he had adventured no more than he did, for the enterprise from every point of view was a miserable failure.

Thus far Walsingham's interests in the voyages of discovery were associated either directly or indirectly with attempts to exploit the trade of the Far East. He was hardly less active in the efforts to win for the English a share in the new world of the West. In this field of enterprise his first adventure was with the voyage of Sir Humphrey Gilbert in 1578. It may be that Walsingham had interested himself in Gilbert's earlier schemes for discovering the North-West Passage or with the proposal to attack Spanish shipping in the West which he had laid before the Queen in 1577,[3] but there is no evidence to prove

largest ship in Fenton's fleet (the galleon *Ughtrede, Leicester* or *Bear* as it was variously called) was not contributed by her (*Cal. Colonial, East Indies*, i, no. 180). It does not appear either that the expedition was even 'nominally' directed to the discovery of the North-West Passage, though Fenton was instructed to pick up in the Far East any information on the subject that he could, without time lost in extensive exploring. It is also wrong to say that Walsingham's step-son, Christopher Carleill, went with Fenton, though up until the last moment it was intended that he should go (Hakluyt, xi. 171).

[1] *Cal. Colonial, East Indies*, i, no. 156.

[2] Ibid., no. 183.

[3] Slafter, *Sir Humphrey Gilbert*, p. 237. The petition of 'Certain gentlemen

that this was the case. There can be no doubt, however, that Walsingham did take an active interest in securing from the Queen for Gilbert the charter granted him in 1578 to discover and colonize 'remote heathen and barbarous lands not actually possessed of any christian prince'.[1] Gilbert himself bore ample testimony to that fact. On the 23rd of September 1578 he addressed Walsingham as 'his principal patron as well in furthering and procuring him her Majesty's favour and licence for performance of his sea voyage as also many other ways'.[2] Again in November Gilbert wrote to him: 'My principal care is to satisfy you above all others because your Honour was the only means of my licence,'[3] and again: 'As you have been always the pillar unto whom I leant so I hope you will always remain.'[4] There is no evidence to show that Walsingham invested any money in Gilbert's first enterprise, but it is clear enough that he did much otherwise to make it possible.[5]

Of the voyage itself practically nothing is known except that it was fruitless. Gilbert was not discouraged; but since he could not for the moment raise sufficient funds to equip another expedition, he hit upon the plan of making assignments from his grant to others who were disposed to undertake the establishment of colonies 'in the north parts of America'. In this

of west England to discover unknown lands', dated 22 March 1573/4, cannot certainly be connected with Gilbert though it usually has been. His name appears in the endorsement of the petition, but in such a form as to make it uncertain whether the endorsement is intended to apply specifically to the petition or to a whole bundle of papers relating to voyages of discovery of which the petition in question simply formed the cover. Cf. *Cal. Colonial*, Addenda, 1574–1674, no. 1.

[1] Hakluyt's *Voyages*, viii. 17 ff.

[2] *Cal. Colonial*, Addenda, 1574–1674, no. 4

[3] Slafter, *op. cit.*, p. 249.

[4] *Cal. Colonial*, Addenda, 1574–1674, no. 5.

[5] It is noted that one Simon Ferdinando, 'Secretary Walsingham's man', sailed to the coast of America and back in three months in 1579 (*Cal. Colonial*, i, p. 2). Now we know that in Gilbert's first voyage of 1578 Walter Raleigh, who commanded a small frigate (the *Falcon*) in Gilbert's fleet, did not return with Gilbert, but undertook a voyage to the West Indies on his own account (Holinshed, *Chronicles* (ed. 1587), iii. 1369). According to Holinshed, Raleigh never got beyond the Azores. It is also recorded that Simon Ferdinando was master of the *Falcon* when Raleigh was captain (*Cal. Colonial*, Addenda, 1574–1674, no. 8). So Ferdinando's voyage alluded to above may be none other than this cruise of Raleigh, and Holinshed may be wrong in his statement that he got no farther than the Azores; or, more probably, Walsingham may have dispatched Ferdinando, after Raleigh's return, on a quick journey to the coast of America. Cf. also on Ferdinando, *Cal. Spanish*, 1568–79, p. 591; ibid. 1580–6, p. 330.

wise he hoped to retain the monopoly conferred upon him, which, by the provision of his charter, he must forfeit if he did not succeed in planting a colony within seven years.[1]

The first definite evidence of such an assignment appeared in a signed agreement between Sir Humphrey Gilbert on the one part and Sir George Peckham and Sir Thomas Gerrard on the other, dated the 6th of June 1582. This agreement, in brief, recited that Gilbert, in consideration of the fact that Peckham, Gerrard, and their associates had advanced divers sums of money towards an intended voyage to America, conveyed to them the right to occupy and settle 1,500,000 acres of land between Florida and Cape Breton upon condition of making certain annual payments to Gilbert. A significant clause in the agreement provided that Gilbert should do his best to procure the Queen's assent to the migration of all those whom Peckham and Gerrard should set down 'in a register book kept for the purpose'.[2] This clause is probably explained by a petition which Peckham and Gerrard presented to Walsingham a little later.[3] The substance of this petition was to secure a licence for 'all such persons whose names shall be set down in a book intended for that purpose' to travel into heathen lands. It is evident from the terms of this petition that those whose names were to be set down were Roman Catholic recusants. In a word, it appears that Gerrard, who was a notorious Papist, and Peckham, who was without doubt a Roman Catholic sympathizer, were undertaking a scheme for the establishment of a Roman Catholic colony in America.[4] Their object, of course, was practically the same as that which

[1] Cf. Edward Hay's account of Gilbert's second voyage in Hakluyt, viii. 40–1.

[2] *Cal. Colonial*, Addenda, 1574–1674, no. 14. Peckham had been one of the adventurers in Gilbert's voyage of 1578 (ibid. no. 19).

[3] This petition is printed in full in Shea, *History of the Catholic Church in the United States*, i. 20–2. It is undated in the original. Professor Merriman (*American Historical Review*, xiii. 495) fixes the date in the spring of 1582. It is evident from the introductory sentence of the petition that it belongs in point of time after the grant of 6 June 1582 just cited. 'That where Sir Humphrey Gilbert, Knight, hath granted and assigned to the said Sir Thomas and Sir George, authority . . . to discover and possess, etc., certain heathen lands, etc.'

[4] This matter is developed more fully by Professor R. B. Merriman in an article entitled 'Some Notes on the Treatment of the English Catholic in the Reign of Elizabeth' (*American Historical Review*, xiii. 480–500).

drew the Puritans overseas a few decades later, namely, to secure a place under the flag of England where they might worship God as they pleased.

One of Walsingham's spies among the Catholics had already informed him of this design in April,[1] but he probably had known of it from the beginning. It is hardly likely that Gilbert would have opened negotiations with the Catholics without Walsingham's assent and approval. Indeed, the Spanish ambassador declared that Walsingham himself was the first to approach Peckham and Gerrard with this proposition. According to Mendoza, Walsingham had 'intimated to them that if they would help Humphrey Gilbert in the voyage their lives and liberties might be saved and the Queen in consideration of their service might be asked to allow them to settle there [Florida] in the enjoyment of freedom of conscience and of their property in England'.[2] There is no reason to question Mendoza's statement in this matter, and if it be true it marks Walsingham as one of the most far-sighted men of his time. The idea of peopling a colony with religious dissenters from the mother country establishes his right to a position among those whose religious views were far more tolerant than the average of their generation. Generally speaking, the colonizers of the sixteenth century were even more zealous to maintain the true religion, however they might define it, overseas than they were at home. Both Spain and Portugal rigidly excluded religious dissenters from their colonies. France, after a hint at better things in Coligny's ill-fated attempts in Florida, reverted to the same policy. Even in England the plan of utilizing religious discontent for colonial purposes was not formally exploited by the Government for nearly a century to come. Anglican bigotry would not suffer it. Yet, from the point of view of English colonial expansion, no suggestion made during Elizabeth's reign was more fruitful in its consequences. At the same time, of course, Walsingham's proposal gave promise of an easy solution of one of the most difficult problems which Elizabeth had to face. If the Catholics could be induced to migrate, they might be converted from potential rebels in England to loyal subjects in English colonies. The possibilities of the proposal from this point of view were

[1] S. P. Domestic, cxlvi, no. 40. [2] *Cal. Spanish*, 1580–6, pp. 384–5.

well appreciated by the Spanish ambassador and it is no wonder that he did what he could to thwart it.

The suggestion had been made that Walsingham's motive in urging the Catholics to take advantage of Gilbert's patent were not altogether disinterested. It has been pointed out that Walsingham at this juncture was endeavouring to arrange a marriage between his daughter and Sir Philip Sidney, and the opinion has been expressed that Walsingham felt Sidney's poverty to be an insuperable obstacle to the match. Now Sidney received from Gilbert in July 1582 a grant of three million acres of land in the New World, and this grant he conveyed about a year later to Sir George Peckham. It has been intimated that Peckham purchased this land from Sidney at Walsingham's suggestion, so that Sidney might have sufficient money to get married on.[1] This is an ingenious interpretation of the facts, hardly creditable to Walsingham, which is worth considering. There is no doubt that Walsingham at this time was interested in arranging a marriage between his daughter and Sidney, although there is no proof whatever that Walsingham regarded Sidney's poverty as an obstacle to the match. The obstacle of poverty, so far as it was considered at all, seems to have been urged by Sir Philip's own father.[2] It is true that Sidney received a grant of three million acres from Gilbert in July 1582,[3] but it will be recalled that Peckham had also received a grant from Gilbert a month previously of more land (one million five hundred thousand acres) than he could possibly exploit. There would seem to have been no point in his purchase of rights to three million more acres from Sidney. Nor is there any proof that he made any such purchase. Undoubtedly Sidney conveyed his grant to Peckham in July 1583, but there is no mention in the articles of conveyance of any payment of money on Peckham's part.[4] It seems more likely that Sidney had secured the grant of land with the hope of making some

[1] This view of the matter is set forth in Professor Merriman's article cited above.

[2] Cf. Life of Sir Philip Sidney in *Dictionary of National Biography*. Sir Henry Sidney, Philip's father, discussed the match at some length in a letter to Walsingham dated 1 March 1582/3 (S. P. Domestic, clix, no. 1).

[3] An abstract of this grant is given in *Cal. Colonial*, Addenda, 1574–1674, no. 28. On the question of its date cf. Merriman, *op. cit.*, p. 497, n. 46.

[4] *Cal. Colonial*, Addenda, 1574–1674, no. 29.

money by exploiting it, but that the arrangement of his marriage provided him with another means of livelihood and induced him to abandon colonizing. Upon what terms he disposed of his patent to Peckham does not appear, but it can hardly be imagined that Peckham paid much for it when Gilbert was quite prepared to grant away land in America by the millions of acres to any one who would undertake to develop the grant. At any rate the suggestion that Walsingham's interest in Peckham's scheme grew out of a desire to assist Sidney's fortunes, if tenable, is hardly demonstrable.

It is not possible to say exactly how far Peckham's efforts to enlist the support of the Catholic recusants in his enterprise were successful. According to the Spanish ambassador's report, the accuracy of which there is no means of testing, the Catholics did supply sufficient funds to equip two small ships, which Gilbert determined to dispatch at once on a reconnoitring expedition, intending to cross the seas himself with a larger fleet the following year.[1] Upon the same authority it appears that two ships actually sailed.[2] This, however, is hard to believe in view of the fact that none of the other sources makes any mention of any such preliminary expedition. In any event it is clear that the effort to exploit Roman Catholic discontent was only one of many plans to which Gilbert and his friends resorted for the purpose of raising funds. They appealed with some success to the town of Southampton, offering as a particular inducement to investors there to make Southampton the sole staple town for all commodities imported from the New World. By this device they succeeded in collecting from sundry merchants, brewers, bakers, tailors, and yeomen, to say nothing of one lone widow, of that place some £500. To this sum Walsingham himself added £50, making about £550 all told. With so much ready money as a working basis Gilbert evidently intended to form a chartered trading company, in which Walsingham was cast to play a large role.[3] It does not appear that the company was actually formed. Nevertheless, during the spring following, Walsingham was doing what he could to interest others in the venture. He appealed to the merchants of the

[1] *Cal. Spanish*, 1580–6, p. 392. [2] Ibid. 452.

[3] *Cal. Colonial*, Addenda, 1574–1674, no. 18.

Muscovy Company at Bristol and dispatched Richard Hakluyt himself to present the case to them.[1] The Bristol merchants responded with a promise to contribute 1,000 marks to the enterprise and, if that were not enough, to furnish and equip two vessels besides.[2] Walsingham apparently appealed to others as well, though with what results is not known.[3] His step-son, Christopher Carleill, seems to have succeeded also in interesting the Muscovy Merchants of London in the enterprise.[4] One way or another, enough money was raised by the early summer of 1583 to equip a fleet of five small vessels which set sail on the 11th of June 1583.

The history of this ill-fated enterprise is well known. It was the one, of course, in which Gilbert lost his life. His death did not divert his associates from their intention to exploit the possibilities of the western continent. Even while his fate was still uncertain, Sir George Peckham brought out a pamphlet intended to stimulate further interest in the enterprise.[5] Walsingham himself was particularly active about the matter in the early spring of 1584. His first intention seems to have been to combine Gilbert's scheme of colonization and settlement with a further attempt to open up the North-West Passage. Before Sir Humphrey set forth on his fatal voyage Walsingham had been discussing the possibilities of the North-West Passage with Adrian Gilbert, Sir Humphrey's brother, John Davis and the astrologist, John Dee.[6] Some time later Walsingham drafted

[1] Hakluyt, viii. 132, 148.

[2] Ibid. viii. 133–4. They seem to have increased their offer a little later to £1,000 (ibid. 148).

[3] Cf. Merriman, *op. cit.*, pp. 496–7. It is interesting to compare the draft letter of appeal printed by Merriman with that sent to the merchants of Bristol. They are enough alike in phraseology to make it probable that they were prepared at the same time. The Antony Brigham mentioned in the Merriman letter is probably the same as the Antony Bridham (*sic*) mentioned (*Cal. Colonial*, Addenda, 1574–1674, no. 19, p. 17) in connexion with adventurers of Totnes and Dartmouth, and though Merriman infers that the letter he cites was sent out to English Catholics, it seems quite as probable that it was intended for Devonshire merchants, irrespective of their creed.

[4] Hakluyt, viii. 133. Carleill wrote a discourse upon the advantages of the American enterprise which is printed in Hakluyt, viii. 134. The effect of this discourse appears in the appointment of a committee by the Muscovy Company to consider the whole matter. The recommendations of this committee are printed in Hakluyt, viii. 147. Cf. also *Cal. Colonial*, i. 1, and *Cal. Colonial*, Addenda, 1574–1674, no. 24.

[5] Printed in Hakluyt, viii. 89 ff.

[6] Brown, *Genesis of the United States*, i. 12.

proposals for the formation of a company to attempt once more the discovery of the Passage. He suggested that a patent be granted to Adrian Gilbert by the Queen conferring similar privileges to those accorded to his brother; that the Russia Company, which claimed a monopoly of the trade routes north-west, be urged to grant him liberty to explore the Passage with the sole right to the trade that way for twenty years; that such adventurers be solicited 'as shall venture their money and not their names'; that ships be chosen and that staple ports be erected at London and Dartmouth.[1] Walsingham's desire to get adventurers who would contribute something more substantial than their names reveals a current difficulty in company organizing. His proposal to erect staple towns recalls his earlier project for an East India company. But his suggestions as a whole contain very little that is remarkable besides the general evidence they bear to his keen interest in the enterprise.

In February 1584, doubtless largely through Walsingham's influence, Adrian Gilbert received a patent from the Queen which conferred upon him ample rights not only for the discovery of a passage by the 'North-West and North-Eastward or Northward' to the East, but also to trade and settle in any country encountered by the way.[2] In accordance with Walsingham's suggestion, staple towns were, by the terms of the patent, established at London and Dartmouth, with a third also at Plymouth. This new company was called 'The Colleagues of the Fellowship for the Discovery of the North-West Passage'. Adrian Gilbert, John Davis, Dr. Dee and Walter Raleigh were pretty certainly among its members, as was Walsingham of course. A little later it appears that certain merchants, both in London and in Devonshire, were financially interested in the project,[3] but whether this mercantile element was associated with Adrian Gilbert from the first or whether its co-operation was secured after the patent had been granted is not certain.

Before the preparations for operating under this patent were more than begun the interest of one of its principal promoters was diverted to another project. In March 1584, Walter Raleigh

[1] *Cal. Colonial, East Indies*, i, no. 234, undated.
[2] Hakluyt, viii. 375–7.
[3] *Voyages of John Davis* (Hakluyt Society), pp. xii, xvii.

secured from Elizabeth a re-grant in his own favour of the patent which his step-brother, Sir Humphrey Gilbert, had received six years before.[1] It is not certain, thought it is probable, that this new grant was the signal for Raleigh's withdrawal from the Fellowship of the North-West Passage.[2] Possibly it indicates a definite breach between Raleigh and his former associates.[3] In any event, Raleigh's interest in exploration thereafter was directed to the exploitation of his own patent by the establishment of settlements on the coast of North America. Of the various expeditions which he dispatched to this end it is not necessary to treat here. There is sufficient evidence to prove that Raleigh's Virginia voyages, like those of Sir Humphrey Gilbert's before him, were not purely individual ventures, but were financed in part at least on the joint-stock plan.[4] There is,

[1] A comparison of Raleigh's patent (Hakluyt, viii. 289) with Sir Humphrey Gilbert's (ibid. viii. 17) reveals the fact that the two are substantially, almost verbally, identical. This is true of the clauses which, in Gilbert's patent, were evidently held to limit his monopoly to six years (Hakluyt, viii. 41). In view of this fact Professor Channing's statement (*History of the United States*, i. 124) that Elizabeth granted Raleigh 'a charter which confirmed to him, *without limit of time*, the powers that Gilbert had had', seems open to question.

It may be noted in this connexion that when the bill designed to confirm Raleigh's patent by Act of Parliament was brought before the House of Commons, it was referred to a committee of which Walsingham was a member (D'Ewes, *Journals*, p. 339). The bill passed the Commons but probably failed to pass the Lords (Channing, i. 124, n. 2).

[2] It is pretty clear, however, that Raleigh did not altogether abandon the pursuit of the North-West Passage. In his last book, on the West Indies, he expressed the opinion that the North-West Passage might be sought for 'as well by river and overland as by sea' (*Cal. Colonial, East Indies*, i, no. 237). It is not unlikely that he contemplated combining a search for the North-West Passage with his plans for exploiting Virginia.

[3] Walsingham and Raleigh never seem to have been on particularly good terms. They appear on opposite sides upon most of the questions which divided the Queen's councillors. In 1583, for instance, Walsingham believed that Raleigh was supporting a policy opposed to his in Scotland. 'I hear', Walsingham wrote to Leicester on 22 Sept. 1583, 'there is a by course in hand with Arran and the Colonel [Stuart] wherein Mr. Rawley is used for an instrument. I hope he is too wise to be used in any such indirect dealing' (Cotton MSS., Caligula C ix, f. 95). Again, in 1586 Walsingham intimated in a letter to Leicester that Raleigh was opposing their policy in the Low Countries (Bruce, *Leicester Correspondence* (Camden Society), p. 207). According to the Spanish ambassador in Paris, Raleigh opposed the policy which Walsingham favoured of sending Drake to the Spanish coast to 'singe the king of Spain's beard' in 1587 (*Cal. Spanish*, 1587–1603, p. 24). In the same year Walsingham appears as one of the supporters of the Earl of Essex in his famous quarrel with Raleigh (Devereux, *Lives of the Earls of Essex*, i. 189). Raleigh's biographers have hardly paid enough attention to the position he occupied among the factions at Court in the years preceding the Armada.

[4] Scott, ii. 244; *Davis Voyages*, p. xvii.

however, little or nothing to indicate that Walsingham was financially interested in them, though he seems to have been regarded by their promoters as favourably disposed towards them.[1]

Walsingham was probably far more interested in Adrian Gilbert's projected voyage to the North-West. No doubt Raleigh's diversion from this project was a severe blow to its supporters, but not so severe as to induce them to abandon their plans. Throughout the summer and autumn of 1584 Walsingham was actively engaged in seeking support for Gilbert among the merchants of London.[2] He succeeded in inducing them to advance some capital. The rest that was necessary was subscribed by merchants in the west of England [3] and by individual investors at the Court and elsewhere.[4] How much was subscribed altogether is not ascertainable, but judging from the size of the expedition when it set sail, the total capital raised could hardly have exceeded £1,500.[5] It may safely be presumed that Walsingham was one of the subscribers, though the amount of his subscription is not recorded. The expedition, consisting

[1] It is true that Walsingham received letters from both Ralph Lane and Sir Richard Grenville, the two leaders of Raleigh's second expedition of 1585 (*Cal. Colonial*, i. 2–4), but these in themselves hardly indicate more than that Lane and Grenville realized the importance of interesting Walsingham in their enterprise if only because he was so near to the ear of the Queen. One passage in one of Lane's letters seems to suggest that Walsingham was more directly interested. As summarized in the *Colonial Calendar* (p. 3) the passage runs as follows: '[Lane] has undertaken with a good company to remain there [in Virginia], resolute rather to lose their lives than to defer possession of so noble a kingdom to the Queen, their country and their noble patron, Sir Walter Raleigh, through whom and his Honour's [Walsingham's] most worthy endeavour and infinite charge an honourable entry is made to the conquest of.' This may be construed to read that Walsingham had assisted the enterprise with 'most worthy endeavour and infinite charge', in the precise sense of the terms, or it may mean nothing more than that Walsingham had simply befriended the adventure in his official capacity. I have found no other evidence which even hints that Walsingham was directly interested financially in any of the Raleigh voyages.

[2] *Davis Voyages*, p. 232.

[3] Hakluyt, vii. 381; *Davis Voyages*, p. xvii.

[4] It is not impossible that the names of some of the other adventurers are revealed in the names which Davis bestowed, during his first voyage, upon the various places of his discovery. Upon this presumption Gilbert, Raleigh, Walsingham, and Edward Dyer, with merchants of Exeter and Totnes, were among the number (*Davis Voyages*, pp. 9–10).

[5] Frobisher's first expedition, which consisted of two small vessels and a pinnace, cost altogether £1,613 19*s.* 3*d.* (*Frobisher's Voyages*, p. 116). Davis's first expedition consisted of two small barks (Hakluyt, vii. 381) and was gone for about the same length of time as Frobisher's.

of two small barks, did not get away until the early summer of 1585 and then, curiously enough, it was not Adrian Gilbert but Captain John Davis who was in command. Davis returned home in September confident that he had discovered the entrance to the North-West Passage. 'I am hereby, according to my duty, to signify unto your Honour,' he wrote, upon his arrival in England, to Walsingham, 'that the North-West Passage is a matter nothing doubtful but at any time almost to be passed, the sea navigable, void of ice, the air tolerable and the waters very deep.'[1]

It appears that Davis succeeded in conveying to Walsingham and the other adventurers some measure of his own confidence. They decided, after they had heard his report, to dispatch him forth again the following year. Subscriptions were invited to this second adventure and seem to have come in even more readily than for the first one. Devonshire merchants responded unusually well.[2] By the end of April 1586 Davis had raised from mercantile sources alone nearly £1,200. It does not appear whether Walsingham contributed to his second expedition or not, but enough money was secured to equip three small ships and a pinnace for a six months' voyage.[3] With these Davis set sail once again early in May 1586.

His achievement upon his second voyage was distinctly disappointing. Yet he was resolute to try his fortunes once more. 'Surely,' he wrote to his friend William Sanderson, 'it shall cost me all my hope of welfare and my fortunes of Sandridge but I will, by God's mercy, see an end of these businesses.'[4] He evidently cherished the hope that he could make a further voyage pay for itself. He had discovered that the waters of Davis Strait were fairly alive with fish and it appeared to him that by combining fishing and exploring he might make the former pay for the latter. Davis talked this plan over with Walsingham, who not only approved it himself but saw in it an opportunity to interest Lord Burghley in the venture. As Davis tells the tale, Walsingham advised him to present to Burghley some of the fish caught in Davis Strait.

[1] Dated 3 Oct. 1585; reproduced in facsimile in *Davis Voyages*, frontispiece.
[2] Hakluyt, vii. 442; *Davis Voyages*, p. xx. [3] Hakluyt, vii. 442.
[4] *Davis Voyages*, p. 32.

The point obviously was to appeal to Burghley's notorious zeal in the promotion of the English fisheries. Yet it is to be hoped that Walsingham was not so unconscious of the humour of the transaction as Davis evidently was. One catches in it a sly thrust at Burghley's fish days and a whimsical allusion to his staunch refusal to share in the plunder of previous western enterprises. If Burghley did not smile when he accepted the fish he deserves to be branded as a Polonius indeed. Anyway, he approved Davis's plan. But when it came to the practical problem of raising money for a third voyage, Davis discovered that the merchants were indifferent fishermen. Those in Devonshire refused to advance further funds and most of those in London took the same stand.[1] Nevertheless, Davis was able to secure from other sources sufficient money to equip two ships and a pinnace the following spring. It seems not unlikely that the court element was larger and the city element smaller in this third adventure than in the previous ones.[2] If so, it may safely be presumed that Walsingham had been active in Davis's behalf among the courtiers. How much else Walsingham did, either financially or otherwise, to promote this third voyage is unknown. It set forth in May 1587 and returned in September of the same year. Davis himself seems to have been encouraged by what he found. 'The Passage', he wrote to Sanderson when he got back home, 'is most probable, the execution easy.'[3] He would have gone forth again, but when the season for sailing arrived the next year, every English ship was needed at home to guard against the threatened descent of the Spanish Armada. After that the project was not revived. Davis himself attributed this fact on more than one occasion to Walsingham's untimely death in the spring of 1590.[4] This in itself is sufficient proof of the large part he played in Davis's ventures. He was, in fact, by Davis's own testimony, an essential factor.

With the last of the Davis voyages Walsingham's activity in the exploring and colonizing enterprises of the Elizabethan

[1] Hakluyt, vii. 443.

[2] It will be observed that the names which Davis bestowed upon places of his discovery on his third voyage were mainly those of eminent persons at court, for instance, Warwick's Foreland, Cumberland's Isles, Lumley's Inlet, Darcie Islands.

[3] *Davis Voyages*, p. 59.

[4] Hakluyt, vii. 445; *Davis Voyages*, 232.

period terminated. It will appear that in all the adventures in which he shared his interest was mainly directed either to the plundering of the Spaniards or to the opening up of a trade-way to the East Indies. With colonizing as such he had little connexion, though he must not be forgotten as one of the earliest promoters of the plan, so fruitful in its consequences, of exploiting colonization as a means of dealing with religious discontent. Of any imperial purpose in him, there is hardly a trace. He does not seem to have cherished any dreams of a British empire overseas. He was, however, as eager as any of his contemporaries that England should have its share with Spain in the wealth of the West Indies and with Portugal in the trade of the East. In this respect, as in so many others which concerned maritime affairs, his views were at one with those of Sir Francis Drake. It is quite possible that Drake prompted and in some measure guided his interest in maritime enterprise. But wherever Walsingham got his inspiration, the fact remains that he was, without doubt, during the last fifteen years of his life, a very zealous promoter of English exploration and discovery.

XVIII

PRIVATE AFFAIRS

It has seemed expedient to follow the course of Walsingham's life not so much from the point of view of his individual development as from the point of view of the development of public affairs in which he played a part. This method of treatment has been imposed in part by the nature of the subject, but in large part also by the nature of the surviving testimony regarding it. Historically speaking, Walsingham has scarcely any existence outside his public setting. He has, it might almost be said, scarcely any existence outside the larger problems which presented themselves to his sovereign Queen during the course of his official career. And yet there are here and there among the surviving records occasional revelations of the man in other capacities which cannot be neglected, though they must perforce be gathered together in what can be little better than a heap of fragments. It is a great pity that he had no son to guard his private papers and to hand them down to posterity. As it was, they were scattered to the four winds of heaven after his death and only those of public importance escaped destruction. Walsingham and Leicester both suffered sorely in this regard. One wonders how much the fame of Burghley is due to the pious care with which his sturdy descendants preserved the Cecil archives.

So much the most important part of Walsingham's public life was spent in his capacity of Principal Secretary and Privy Councillor that the other official positions which he held can be dismissed with a brief mention. Attention has already been called to the fact that he served in the House of Commons as member for Lyme Regis in Elizabeth's second Parliament, which assembled in January 1563 and after many adjournments and postponements was finally dissolved in January 1567. There is nothing to indicate that he took any conspicuous part in the business of that Parliament. He does not seem to have been elected to Elizabeth's third Parliament (2 April—29 May 1571) obviously because he was absent from England as ambassador to France at that time. In the fourth Parliament, which assembled in May 1572, he was not one of the original members. It happened, however, that in January 1573 Charles Howard, one of the members for Surrey, was called by the death of his father to the House of Lords as Lord Howard of Effingham.[1] To the seat which he vacated Walsingham was elected shortly after he became Principal Secretary in 1573. This seat he retained during the rest of his life, being re-elected in 1584, 1586, and 1588.[2] Of course from the point of view of parliamentary prestige the county seat marked a step in advance beyond the borough seat which he had previously occupied. Yet Walsingham's actual part in the business of the House does not appear to have increased in significance, and though he was appointed a member of more than one committee, it seems not unlikely that he owed the appointment rather to his position as Privy Councillor and Principal Secretary than to any more personal interest in parliamentary affairs.[3] There can be no doubt that Elizabeth used her Privy Councillors who were members of the House of Commons for the purpose of conveying informally her own will to that House, and that they did exercise considerable influence in keeping the debates as well as the legislation in accord with the royal pleasure. But it was Sir Christopher Hatton and not Walsingham who was her chief instrument for that purpose.[4]

[1] Cf. Life of Howard in *D. N. B.*, *Members of Parliaments*, 1213–1874 (Parl. Papers, 1878), i. 414.

[2] Ibid. i. 415, 420, 425. The Earl of Lincoln and Lord Howard of Effingham wrote to Sir William More and other gentlemen in Surrey, 26 Oct. 1584, recommending Sir Francis Walsingham and Mr. Howard as fit persons to represent Surrey in the next Parliament (*Hist. MSS. Comm. VIIth Report*, Appendix, p. 640.)

[3] D'Ewes, *Journal*, pp. 262, 279, 301, 309, 332. In 1575 he served with Knollys, Mildmay, Hatton, and others, to confer upon a bill ' touching wharves and quays ' (D'Ewes, p. 262) ; in 1580 he was appointed with Knollys, Crofts, and Mildmay to join with a committee of the Lords to present a petition to the Queen (ibid. 279) ; again in the same year he was appointed together with Sir Thomas Wilson, Hatton, and Mildmay to carry a message to the House of Lords (ibid. 301) ; again in the same year he was joined with five other privy councillors to deal with the misdemeanours of one Arthur Hall (ibid. 309). In every case Walsingham appears on committees which were evidently for one reason or another composed largely or solely of privy councillors.

[4] Cf. D'Ewes, *Journal, passim* ; *Bardon Papers*, pp. xiii, xiv. A letter from Burghley to Walsingham, dated 1 March 1584/5 (*Cal. Domestic*, 1581–90, p. 229), may perhaps be taken to indicate that Walsingham was more active in furthering the Queen's affairs in the Commons than appears on the surface. Burghley wrote to the effect that the Queen desired the Commons to hasten

It is unfortunate that Walsingham did not leave behind him any expression of opinion upon the large issue between the crown and parliament which was to occupy so large a part of the attention of English statesmen for centuries to come. His close affiliations with the Elizabethan Puritans might lead one to suppose him to have been in some sort of sympathy with their more democratic views about the government of church and state. But there is no trace of it in his writings. Quite the contrary, he preached to his ardent Puritan brethren prayer and patience as the only proper remedy for the grievances they endured, and on one of the few occasions upon which he expressed an opinion as to the relative positions of crown and parliament in the state, he evidently favoured the view that the proper position of parliament was to serve the interests of the crown.

with the Subsidy Bill and that they should choose another Speaker in place of the one then sick. This may perhaps be construed to read that Elizabeth wished Walsingham to expedite these matters.

There is evidence also that Walsingham had some connexion or other with the preparation of projected legislation for the Parliament. In his memorandum book (Harl. MSS. 6035) which covers the period 25 March 1583 to 3 December 1584 the following entries appear:

f. 45 b (undated, but immediately before January 1584). To consider what laws are fit to be repealed.

f. 97 (undated, but immediately before 20 October 1584).

New Statutes for Parliament.

A Statute to disable any successor that shall seek to trouble her Majesty in her lifetime.

A Statute against the harbouring of Jesuits or Seminaries.

A Statute against the bringing in of seditious books, tending to the defaming of her Majesty's person or government.

f. 98 b, 25 October 1584. To set down the causes why a subsidy should be yielded.

f. 102 (not dated, but between 25 October and 20 November 1584). To draw a preamble for the book of subsidy.

f. 105 b (not dated, but between 20 November and 3 December 1584). To finish the preamble for the subsidy.

These memoranda are so brief that it is difficult to judge exactly what they mean. It will be recalled that parliament reassembled after an interval of over a year on 23 November 1584. Walsingham's memoranda were made just before parliament reassembled. They may represent matters he laid before Privy Council, they may record decisions reached in Privy Council, they may be directions for his subordinates, or they may simply be reminders for himself. Other memoranda in the same book indicate that these rough notes were used in all of these ways. This much, however, is clear, that Walsingham and his colleagues had under consideration the statutes which were subsequently passed in parliament regarding conspiracies against the Queen's person (27th Eliz. c. 1) and the harbouring of Jesuits (27th Eliz. c. 2). It further appears that Walsingham himself or at any rate the secretary's office prepared the books of the subsidy for parliament. These facts point to the conclusion that legislation desired by the Queen was prepared for presentation to parliament in Walsingham's office.

His letter to King James of Scotland on that subject has already been quoted at length elsewhere.[1] It will be recalled that Walsingham in that letter denounced any division of the royal authority and advocated the calling of parliament, not at all with a view to giving the people a share in the government, but because he thought the burgesses might strengthen the King's hand against the rebellious nobility. Those in parliament who remained obstinate in their opposition were to be bridled. This view of the matter came near to expressing the political philosophy of James himself, and one might almost say that Walsingham had prompted him to the very course of action which later got him into trouble with the Commons of England. Of course it may well be that Walsingham was concocting his medicine in this particular instance with a view to the tastes of his royal patient, and it would be going too far to argue from what he said in this connexion that his theory of the state was at one with that of Laud and Strafford. Still the fact can hardly be gainsaid that his whole bearing in the course of his public career was that of a good royalist and a bad parliamentarian.

There is one other aspect of Walsingham's connexion with parliamentary affairs which deserves some mention, and that is his interest in the elections for parliament. Queen Elizabeth was no better than her father in her exploitation of the royal prerogative to secure the election of members to the House of Commons who could be counted upon to support her policies. In the course of her reign she created thirty-one boroughs returning sixty-two members, most of them rotten boroughs in every bad sense of the term. More than that, she occasionally undertook through her ministers to instruct the electors both in the counties and the towns as to whom they should vote for.[2] In borough elections Lord Burghley, and after him his son, Secretary Cecil, more than once intervened directly, although not always with success.[3] Walsingham's activity in borough elections appears in two instances. On the 27th of September 1586 he wrote to the Sheriff of Surrey in the name of the Privy

[1] Cf. Chapter XVI, pp. 343–4.

[2] Porritt, *The Unreformed House of Commons*, i. 375–7.

[3] Ibid. 376–7; on the younger Cecil's activity in this behalf (which Porritt has omitted to mention) cf. *Cal. Salisbury MSS.*, vii, pp. 385, 415, 429, 432.

Council directing them to deprive Mrs. Copley, 'for that she is known to be evil affected', of her right to name the two members for the borough of Gatton and to instruct the burgesses to return instead Wm. Waad, one of the clerks of the Privy Council, and Nicholas Fuller, 'whom', he added, 'if they [the burgesses] shall not be willing to make choice of for their burghers, at the least you must see that care be had there may discreet persons be chosen and well affected.'[1] In this same connexion the following extract, dated 26 Elizabeth (1583-4), from the Assembly Book of the Borough of Colchester is also significant. 'At this Assembly it is fully agreed and consented by the bailiffs, aldermen and common council that Sir Francis Walsingham shall have the nomination of both the burgesses of this town for the Parliament for to come according to his Honour's letter to the bailiffs, aldermen, &c., directed.'[2] This right of nomination seems to have been made appendant to Walsingham's position as Recorder of Colchester to which he was probably appointed at the same time. There can be no doubt that he exercised his right of nomination in 1585 and again in 1588.[3] Yet it would be unjust to argue either from the Gatton or the Colchester case that Walsingham was an active and wilful perverter of the representative principle in parliamentary government. The Gatton letter he evidently wrote by instruction from the Privy Council, and the effect of it would obviously have been no more than the substitution of royal appointees to the seats of that borough in place of the appointees of Mrs. Copley. No violence to the representative principle could be done here, for the representative principle was clearly non-existent. Very much the same thing can be said in regard to Walsingham's position at Colchester. The right to nominate its members was evidently conferred upon him freely by the town government—no doubt for the purpose of enjoying his patronage at Court. In both cases the worst that can be said of him, as can be said of Lord Bacon in another connexion later, is that he conformed to

[1] Porritt quotes this letter in an abstracted form. The letter is printed in full in Kempe, *Loseley MSS.* p. 242 n.

[2] Cromwell, *History of Colchester*, 277.

[3] Ibid.; *Biographica Britannica*, art. Walsingham, note Q, prints in full several letters of Walsingham to the Corporation of Colchester on these and other matters.

a vicious practice. It is obvious of course that he had no convictions about the virtues of the representative principle in the English government sufficiently strong to provoke his opposition to a condition of affairs which was common in his time.

Walsingham's connexion with parliament in general appears rather to have been incidental to his office as privy councillor and principal secretary than to have had any independent significance in his career. The various other offices which he held at one time or another added somewhat to his dignity and a little perhaps to his income, but were otherwise of no great moment.[1] Two of the most significant of them he owed to the Queen's favour. These were the chancellorship of the Duchy of Lancaster and the chancellorship of the Order of the Garter. To the first of these he was appointed in June of 1587 after some contest for this honour with Sir Amias Paulet.[2] In this capacity he presided over the court of the Duchy which exercised equity jurisdiction over all the tenants of the Duchy lands and had general charge of the royal interests involved there.[3] He received from the Queen a regular allowance of £142 16*s*., 'besides £4 for paper, parchment and ink', for his services in this office,[4] and no doubt something in the way of perquisites besides. Of his administration as chancellor almost nothing is known. There is, however, a letter preserved from an unknown correspondent to Sir Thomas Heneage written five years after Walsingham's death which throws some light upon the matter.[5] The writer began with the statement that he had been requested by Walsingham to write down a history of the Duchy of Lancaster and to suggest reforms in its administration. He continued: 'I made no great haste therein, the cause was for that I perceived followers of Sir Francis Walsingham to take upon them authorities, the which in my simple understanding were contrary to law, the usage

[1] It may be appropriate in this place to call attention to the fact that Walsingham was named in 1581 Governor of the Mines Royal (cf. Life of R. Beale in *D. N. B.*). But beyond the bare fact nothing is known about his activity in this connexion, though there are slight indications here and there of his interest in mining (*Cal. Dom.* 1581–90, pp. 68, 692; *Cal. Irish*, 1574–85, pp. 435, 457).

[2] Harland, *Lancashire Lieutenancy under the Tudors*, p. 186, n. 2.

[3] *Lancashire and Cheshire Record Soc.*, xxxii, Pleadings and Depositions, County Court of Lancaster, Intro.

[4] Cf. Book of all Offices under the Crown (S. P. Domestic, ccxxi), p. 7.

[5] Dated 16 May 1595, in Bodleian Library, Ashmole MSS. 1157, no. 87.

of the dukedom . . . and for that cause, seeing those matters so far past and so far out of all course that I saw no manner of reformation was likely to take place, I did therefore cast all my notes into the dungeon of silence for that I would be deemed to be a busy body or else a Golypragmion. But this briefly : in my conscience that honourable gentleman was abused by such in whom he put his trust who are right worthy (being well able to make condign recompense) to be called to answer for such . . . disorders as have been by them committed.' From this it appears that in one man's opinion at any rate Walsingham's administration of the Duchy was something less than perfect—though not much can be concluded from the vague testimony of a single anonymous correspondent.

To the chancellorship of the Garter Walsingham appears to have been appointed in succession to Sir Thomas Smith on the 22nd of April 1578. He held the office for nine years, being succeeded by Sir Amias Paulet in April 1587. It will be recalled that Paulet was a candidate for the office of chancellor of the Duchy of Lancaster at about the same time. It is possible that when this office was accorded to Walsingham he resigned the office of chancellor of the Garter in Paulet's favour.[1] According to the constitution of the Order of the Garter, the office of chancellor was a 'very noble and honourable one, of great trust and care, requiring a person of much honour and reputation'. The constitution provided that no one should be appointed to the office unless he should be, in the case of an ecclesiastic, an archbishop or a bishop, in the case of a layman, a knight of known family, skilful, learned, and of good fame. The Chancellor received a pension of £100 a year, and was provided with a habitation in Windsor Castle—with allowance of diet and livery, paper, wax and wafers at the royal charge. The office apparently offered nothing further in the way of perquisites and was probably

[1] Burghley's Diary (Murdin, *Burghley Papers*, 787) gives the date of Walsingham's appointment as chancellor of the Garter as February 1587/8. In Walsingham's life in *D. N. B.* it is given as 22 April 1578. Paulet was appointed 23 April 1587 (art. Paulet, *D. N. B.*), but he died 26 September 1588. Sir John Wooley, whom Ashmole (*Order of the Garter*, p. 719) names as Paulet's successor, was not appointed until 23 April 1589 (art. Wooley, *D. N. B.*). There is no indication as to who held the office between September 1588 and April 1589.

esteemed chiefly by reason of the honour and dignity which it conferred.[1]

The bestowal of these offices upon Walsingham should probably be regarded as evidences of the Queen's desire to do him honour. She was on the whole rather chary in her disposal of favours of this sort upon him. The only positive increase of rank which he received at her hands was that of knighthood which she conferred upon him at Windsor, 1st December 1577.[2] He certainly merited a peerage and there was some talk at Court early in the year 1589 that he was to receive one, but it came to nothing.[3] Elizabeth was very parsimonious of peerages. William Cecil was practically the only commoner among her Privy Councillors whom she honoured in this fashion, and even among her favourite courtiers she only distributed very few It will be recalled that neither Hatton nor Raleigh, near as they both were to her heart, were ever raised above the rank of knights. She preferred to favour them in other ways. There is no evidence indeed that Walsingham ever coveted a peerage. The fact that he had no son to perpetuate a title possibly made him careless about it. He had something to say about the matter in a short essay on fortitude which he wrote not long before his death :

'As for titles, which at first were the marks of power and the rewards of virtue, they are now according to their name but like the titles of books, which for the most part the more glorious things they promise, let a man narrowly peruse them over, the less substance he shall find in them. And the wooden lord is like the log that Jupiter gave the frogs to be their king. It makes a great noise ; it prepares an expectation of great matters ; but when they once perceived it inactive and senselessly lying still, the wiser sort of frogs began to despise it, and in fine every young frogling presumed to leap up and down upon it.

[1] For the Constitution of the order cf. Ashmole, *Order of the Garter*, Appendix ; cf. also pp. 237 ff. In the Bodleian Library, Ashmole MSS. 786, there is a small book of unknown authorship containing designs and descriptions of coats of arms dedicated to Walsingham as Chancellor of the Garter.

[2] Art. Walsingham, *D. N. B.* In a memorial for the raising of a loan by 'privy seals' belonging to the year 1589 Walsingham is spoken of as Keeper of the Privy Seal (*Cal. Domestic*, 1581–90, p. 606). There is no evidence that he actually enjoyed the title of Lord Privy Seal, though he probably did have custody of the Privy Seal. Davison wrote to him, 10 December 1586 : 'If you return not to-morrow it may please you to send me the signet and privy seal' (S. P. Domestic, cxcv, no. 54).

[3] *Cal. Spanish*, 1587–1603, p. 515.

'Some few there are, who lest the species of our ancient worthy lords should be lost, do preserve in themselves the will and desire, since they want the means, to do brave and worthy acts. And therefore I say, let a man by doing worthy acts deserve honour, and though he do not attain it, yet he is much a happier man than he that gets it without desert. For such a man is beforehand with reputation, and the world still owes him that honour which his deserts cry for, and it hath not paid. Whereas that man that hath a great reputation without deserving it, is behind-hand with the world; and his honour is but lent, not paid. And when the world comes to take account of its applause, and finds his title of merit, by which he pretends to it, weak and broken, it will recall its approbation, and leave him by so much the more a notorious bankrupt in his good name, by how much the estimation of his wealth that way was the greater.' [1]

Notwithstanding all of which one cannot resist the feeling that mingled with his fortitude there was a tincture of hopes disappointed as well.

There is, however, something less than justice to Elizabeth in the statement commonly made that she withheld from Walsingham any adequate recompense for his long and faithful services. The patent rolls of her reign tell a different story, and though it is not possible to reckon the exact measure of her bounty to him, there can be little doubt that it was considerable.[2] Attention has already been called to his farm of the customs and to the large licences for the export of cloth and wool which she at various times bestowed upon him. He also received from her many grants of crown lands upon terms which were probably very

[1] *Cottoni Posthuma*, ed. Howell, pp. 337–8; fuller reference is made to this essay later in the chapter.

[2] In the Signet Book and in the Exchequer of Receipts warrants there is record of innumerable sums of money paid out to Walsingham, the purpose of which is almost never precisely stated. Probably almost all of it was for public service. There is one warrant, however, dated 24 July 1582 (Exchequer of Receipts, Warrants, cxxiv), to pay to Walsingham £750 a year in quarterly instalments 'as for very special considerations we have agreed, determined and granted', for which Walsingham was required to make no further accounting than the mere acknowledgement of its receipt. 'To be accounted as given by our mere liberality.' It is possible that this was a definite pension assigned to Walsingham, though by no means certain. Four years later, 14 December 1586, Walsingham petitioned for a grant to him and to his heirs for ever of £200 a year (*Cal. Salisbury MSS.* iii. 202). There is no indication, however, that he got it. His regular allowance as Secretary was £100 a year and 'his table in the court furnished with two messes of meat' (Book of all the Offices of the Crown, S. P. Domestic, ccxxi, p. 11 b).

favourable to him, some of which, like the manors of Barnes and Odiham, he retained for his personal use, but most of which formed the basis of extensive land speculations in which he seems to have engaged.[1] Here again, as in the case of the farm of the customs and of the licences to trade, Elizabeth's bounty to Walsingham took the form most popular with her of giving him opportunities for making money by exploiting the resources of the crown. It appears, in fact, that Walsingham was what would be called in modern American parlance one of the 'arch-grafters' of his times.

Besides his official position in the national government Walsingham held at one time or another in his career various local offices. He was Custos Rotulorum of Hampshire,[2] Chief

[1] The following grants of land from the Queen to Walsingham are recorded :

1. 8 March 1570/1. The Priory of Carisbroke in the Isle of Wight, lease for 31 years from the expiration of the existing lease at £165 8*s.* 2½*d.* annual rental and a fine of £100. (Book of Royal Leases, S. P. Domestic, clxvi, p. 58). Cf. in general on this property *V. C. H. Hampshire*, v. 229, 232–3. The lease passed to Walsingham's daughter in 1590; his widow petitioned for a reversion of it in 1602 (*Cal. Salisbury MSS.* xii. 152).

2. 23 February 1578/9. The manor of Barnes in Surrey with all appurtenances in Barnes, Mortlake, and Putney at an annual rental of £40 0*s.* 10*d.* (Patent Rolls, Eliz. 1182, memb. 10). This manor had been leased to Sir Henry Wyatt for 96 years in 1504 at an annual rental of £16 6*s.* 8*d.* Walsingham bought the remainder of this lease in 1579, and in the same year secured from Elizabeth a lease to the manor which she had bought to begin in 1600 (*V. C. H. Surrey*, iv. 5 ff.). This was of course Barn Elms.

3. 23 August 1585. The manor of Odiham in Hampshire at a yearly rental of £46 9*s.* (Signet Book, Elizabeth, i, under date). This became one of Walsingham's country houses and the Queen visited him here on one occasion.

4. 21 April 1587. A grant in fee farm of manors in Devon, Oxford, York, Durham, Worcester, Northampton, Nottingham, Wilts, Middlesex, Huntingdon, Gloucester, Somerset, Dorset, Stafford, Leicester, Bucks, Norfolk, Suffolk, Essex, Kent, and Lincoln, and all lands of monasteries, priories, and chantries, dissolved by Henry VIII and Edward VI, with certain exceptions specifically stated, to the use of Walsingham and Francis Milles (Patent Rolls, Eliz. 1289, memb. 24–34). The precise significance of this grant is hard to determine. Presumably Walsingham and Milles received a lease for 21 years (the usual term of a crown lease) on all that was left of the monastic and chantry lands confiscated earlier in the century. Upon what terms Walsingham received these lands does not appear. He was licensed to dispose of several of the leases secured at this time in the course of the years following (Patent Rolls, Eliz., *passim*). The whole affair rather looks like a real estate speculation on a large scale.

5. 8 August 1587. The manor of Little Park of Otford in Kent for 21 years, terms not stated (Patent Rolls, 29 Eliz., part vii, under date).

6. 22 March 1588. Conveyance of manors in Durham and York which Elizabeth had acquired from the Bishop of Durham in return for certain rents to Walsingham upon the same terms as those upon which she had acquired them (Patent Rolls, 30 Eliz., part viii, under date).

[2] Life of Walsingham in *D. N. B.*

Steward of Salisbury,[1] High Steward of Ipswich, of Kingston-on-Hull,[2] and of Winchester,[3] and Recorder of Colchester.[4] All of these positions were positions of great dignity and some influence but with practically no duties or emoluments. They were almost always held by gentlemen of high position, and no doubt Walsingham was chosen in every case in order that he might protect the interests of the towns at Court.[5] Incidentally the position gave him no little influence in the town affairs which he sometimes exercised. In Colchester, for instance, he appointed the borough representatives in Parliament, in Ipswich on one occasion he intervened to place a preacher in one of the town churches.[6] It is rather surprising to discover that he was never apparently directly connected with the government of London, although he spent most of his life there. He did, however, on several occasions exert his influence for the purpose of securing offices in the gift of the City for his friends and dependants.[7] He even intervened on occasions in local affairs elsewhere in behalf of particular individuals. In January of 1588, for instance, he wrote to the Corporation of the city of Lincoln requesting that a certain Laythorpe might be re-elected to the position of alderman of which he had been deprived. It is interesting to observe that the Corporation refused to re-elect the man.[8]

Of Walsingham's private life there are unfortunately very few traces. As has been observed already, he first married when he was about thirty years of age Anna Carleill, a widow of some substance with a half-grown son, Christopher. She died about two years after Walsingham had married her and bore him no children. Of their wedded life together there is absolutely no trace. One is tempted to conclude that the marriage was rather

[1] *Hist. MSS. Comm. Various Collections*, iv. 229. This office conferred an annuity of £6 8*s*. 4*d*. After Walsingham's death Hatton secured it.

[2] Cooper, *Athenae Cantabrig.*, p. 545; cf. for Ipswich, *Hist. MSS. Comm. IXth Report*, Appendix, p. 255.

[3] Life of Walsingham in *D. N. B.* Walsingham was instrumental in securing a new charter for Winchester from the Queen in January 1587/8 (*V. C. H. Hampshire*, v. 25).

[4] Life of Walsingham in *Biog. Britannica*, note Q.

[5] On the office of Steward and Recorder cf. S. and B. Webb, *English Local Government, The Manor and Borough*, part i, pp. 321–3.

[6] *Hist. MSS. Comm. IXth Report*, Appendix, p. 253.

[7] Cf. his letters to the Lord Mayor in London Guildhall MSS. Remembrancia, i, nos. 280, 282, 334, 361, 389, 443, 501, 521, 528, ranging in date from 11 October 1581 to 22 July 1583.

[8] *Cal. Lincoln MSS.*, p. 72.

one of convenience than of love. At any rate Anne had scarcely been dead two years before he took another bride—once more a widow, Ursula Worseley, whose year of mourning for her first husband was hardly complete at the time of her second nuptials. Ursula was also a woman of means, though her estate was somewhat entangled with that of her two sons by her first marriage, and Walsingham had to invoke the assistance of the crown in securing part of it. Ursula's portrait painted in early middle age reveals a woman of well-poised practical temper,[1] a serviceable rather than a stimulating help-meet. Perhaps it was these very qualifications, coupled with her comfortable jointure, which attracted Walsingham to her at the first. He evidently preferred widows, possibly because widows are proverbially easier to court.

There is so very little of anything like romantic passion in all that we know of Walsingham that he must have been an indifferent lover if indeed he ever assumed the role at all. At all events, Ursula, however she was wooed and for whatever motive, commanded the confidence of her husband throughout his life.[2] She survived him twelve years. There are unfortunately no letters surviving of the many which must have passed between Walsingham and his wife, nor does he often allude to her in his correspondence with others. In writing to his friend William More, the 18th of January 1574, he concluded with these remarks: 'Bear, Sir, with my earnestness in recommending my wife's causes. You are yourself a married man. You know therefore of what force Mrs. More's commandments are to you.'[3] Again, in a letter to Thomas Heneage from Paris, dated the 1st of June (1571), Walsingham, in speaking of the personal attributes of the Duke of Anjou and his qualifications as a husband for the Queen, added, 'Though he be choleric yet lacketh he not reason to govern and bridle the same. And you know that these natures are the best

[1] In the National Portrait Gallery in London; reproduced in vol. i facing p. 258.

[2] It will be recalled that she played a careful part in the affair of the Don Antonio diamond. She was also one of the executors of her husband's will.

[3] Cited by Stählin, p. 194, n. 4. In Walsingham's memorandum book (Harl. MSS. 6035) the following entries relating to his wife appear:

f. 27. 2nd of August 1583. To give order for my wife's repair to London (preliminary to Walsingham's departure for Scotland).

f. 27 b. To write to my wife.

f. 51 b. 9th of January 1583/4. To send to the Lady Walsingham.

natures and commonly prove the best husbands. Or else should not you and I be in the highest degree in such perfection as we are.'[1] Without laying too much stress upon a pleasantry of this sort it suggests that Walsingham's domestic life had its tempestuous intervals.

Ursula bore her husband two children, both of them daughters. The elder, Frances, was probably born in 1567.[2] As to her relations with her father there is little surviving testimony. The probabilities are that she was a young girl of unusual charm, for she was married three times, and her first two matches were among the most brilliant of her time. Her father probably was responsible for her match with Sir Philip Sidney, which took place on the 20th of September 1583, when she was scarcely sixteen years of age. Sir Philip's father was evidently not enthusiastic for the match in spite of his protestations to the contrary,[3] and Sir Philip himself was probably more interested at the time in Lady Penelope Rich, the Stella of his sonnets, than in the secretary's daughter. Possibly the marriage had its political significance and may have been intended in part to cement the political alliance between Walsingham and the Earl of Leicester, who was Sir Philip's uncle. The Queen vehemently opposed the match at first, but finally yielded to its consummation.[4] There is no reason to believe that the marriage was otherwise than a happy one. During most of his married life Sidney and

[1] *Cal. of A. G. Finch MSS.* (*Hist. MSS. Comm.*), i, p. 18.

[2] Stählin (p. 95) says 1568, but a letter from John Worseley to Wm. More, dated 18 July 1567, describes his sister Walsingham as being near her confinement (*Hist. MSS. Comm. VIIth Report*, Appendix, p. 620). In the life of Philip Sidney in *D. N. B.* Frances is made out to have been fourteen years of age when she married Sidney in September 1583. More probably she was nearly sixteen. Frances is spoken of as being over twenty-four years of age, 27 September 1592, when the 'Inquisitio post mortem' was taken of her father's estates (Webb, *Chislehurst*, p. 362). This makes it likely that she was born after 27 September 1567, but not long after, if Worseley's statement cited above is accurate.

[3] Cf. Sir Henry Sidney to Walsingham, 1 March 1582/3, S. P. Domestic, clix, no. i.

[4] In July 1584 Walsingham conveyed a large part of his landed property, including all the manor of Bradford and the hundred of Bradford and the messuages, lands, &c., in the villages of Bradford, Atworth, Troile, Stoke, Leigh, Wraxall, Holt, and Windesley in Wiltshire, and of 17 tenements in Bradford, and of all his messuages, lands, closes, &c., in Barnes, Putney, and Mortlake, to William Brunkhard and Thomas Fleming to the use of himself and his wife during their lifetime and after their decease to the use of Philip Sidney and Lady Frances his wife (Webb, *Chislehurst*, pp. 361–2).

his wife made their home with Walsingham, who was certainly very much attached to his amiable young son-in-law.

In this connexion Sir Fulk Greville, Sidney's friend and biographer, pays a graceful tribute to Walsingham's generosity of spirit.

'That wise and active secretary', Greville wrote, . . . 'hath often confessed to myself that his Philip did so far overshoot him in his own bow, as those friends which at first were Sir Philip's for this secretary's sake, within a short while became so fully owned and possessed by Sir Philip as now he held them at the second hand by his son-in-law's courtesy. This is that true remission of mind whereof I would gladly have the world take notice from these dead men's ashes, to the end that he might once again see that ingenuity amongst men which by liberal bearing witness to the merits of others, show they have some true worth of their own and are not merely lovers of themselves without rivals.'[1]

Walsingham deeply lamented Sidney's untimely death in the autumn of 1586, and it left his young bride quite prostrate. 'Your sorrowful daughter and mine', Leicester wrote to Walsingham in announcing Sidney's heroic ending, 'is here with me at Utrecht till she may recover some strength, for she is wonderfully overthrown through her long care since the beginning of her husband's hurt, and I am the more careful that she should be in some strength ere she take her journey into England, for that she is with child, which I pray God send to be a son if it be His will; but whether son or daughter they shall be my children too. She is most earnest to be gone out of this country and so I could wish her, seeing it so against her mind, but for her weakness yet, her case considered.'[2] A little later, Lady Frances returned to England, where her father and mother nursed her back to health. Walsingham wrote to Leicester on the 24th of December 1586: 'I thank my God for it I am now in good hope of the recovery of both my daughter and her child.'[3] But the child died. In the long run, as has been pointed out elsewhere, the Walsingham alliance with Sidney proved an expensive luxury, for Sir Philip left behind him at his death an estate badly

[1] Greville, *Life of Sidney* (Clarendon Press reprint, 1907), p. 30.
[2] Bruce, *Leicester Correspondence*, p. 446.
[3] Cotton MSS., Titus B vii, no. 24.

entangled and a number of large debts contracted upon his father-in-law's security, most of which Walsingham had to pay. Some time later, Lady Frances married again, to no less a person than Robert, Earl of Essex, whose charm was to captivate the old Queen and whose inordinate ambition was finally to lead him to a traitor's death. Exactly when Essex married Lady Frances is uncertain, though there is some reason to believe that the match took place in 1587 and not in 1590 as has usually been stated.[1] After the death of Essex Lady Frances married a third husband, Richard Burgh, Earl of Clanricard, but that was long after her father had been laid in his grave.[2]

Walsingham had one other child, also a daughter, named Mary. She was born early in the year 1573,[3] but she died seven years later and she was the last of Walsingham's children.[4]

Though Walsingham's immediate family was small, his relatives were numerous and his family connexions through them unusually large. He had five sisters, all of whom married distinguished public men. Elizabeth, the eldest of his generation, married first Geoffrey Gates, whose brother John was one of the most ardent supporters of the Duke of Northumberland in his efforts to place Lady Jane Grey on the English throne. After Geoffrey's death Elizabeth married Peter Wentworth, perhaps the most vigorous exponent of parliamentary freedom as against the royal prerogative in Elizabeth's reign. Walsingham's second sister, Barbara, married Thomas Sidney, who, by a curious coincidence, was lord of the manor of Little Walsingham in Norfolk, and was related to Sir Henry Sidney, the son-in-

[1] Cf. Dr. Wm. Gifford to Dr. Ely, 5 June (1587), Lansdowne MSS. xcvi, f. 69.

[2] Lady Frances had many children. She bore Sidney a daughter (31 Jan. 1583/4), who subsequently married Roger Manners, Earl of Rutland, but died without issue (*D. N. B.* art. Philip Sidney, p. 228). To Essex she bore three sons and two daughters, of whom the most conspicuous was Robert Devereux, 3rd Earl of Essex, the parliamentary general of the seventeenth-century civil wars. To Clanricard she bore one son, of whom there is a sketch in *D. N. B.* art. Ulick de Burgh.

[3] Cf. Sir Thomas Smith to Burghley, 7 Jan. 1572/3, in which he relates his efforts to persuade Elizabeth to recall Walsingham from France. 'I said . . . that the poor gentleman [Walsingham] there was undone, having been at so great charge, all things waxing so dear, and his wife being here and great with child' (Harl. MSS. 6991, no. 9). This letter was probably written very shortly before the birth of Walsingham's second daughter.

[4] A letter of condolence to Walsingham upon her death from Sir A. Paulet, dated 16 July 1580, is preserved in Cotton MSS., Titus B ii, f. 345.

law of the Duke of Northumberland and the father of Sir Philip Sidney. Through both of these sisters Walsingham was more or less directly connected with the fortunes of the house of Dudley, and it is not impossible that his later relations with the Earl of Leicester grew out of these earlier connexions.

With his turbulent brother-in-law, Peter Wentworth, there is no evidence that he had any transactions whatever. It is hardly likely that Walsingham sympathized with Wentworth's political opinions and there is no evidence that he ever sought to interpose himself between Wentworth and the royal wrath. Yet Wentworth's religious views accorded with Walsingham's own, and it is just possible, though there is no proof of the matter whatever, that Walsingham may have secretly provoked some of Wentworth's outbursts in Parliament against the Anglican bishops. At any rate the family connexion was there and with it the opportunity for family co-operation. Of Walsingham's three remaining sisters, Eleanor married Sir Wm. Sherington, one of the coadjutors of Admiral Seymour in his project to wed Princess Elizabeth in Edward's reign; Christiana married first John Tamworth, a member of the Queen's household, and after his death in 1569, Wm. Dodington, an officer of the royal mint; and Mary married Sir Walter Mildmay, Elizabeth's Chancellor of the Exchequer and one of the most ardent and vigorous supporters of Walsingham's policies in the Privy Council.[1]

On Walsingham's wider family connexions it is hardly necessary to dwell at length. His relations with the Careys and through them with Lord Hunsdon, and more remotely with the Queen herself, have already been pointed out in connexion with his step-father, Sir John Carey.[2] It did not apparently serve to reconcile the differences between Hunsdon and Walsingham upon most matters of public policy, nor does it seem to have softened the Queen's normal asperity towards her secretary. Of his mother's family, the Dennys, if they played any part in Walsingham's career at all it must have been in the days of his boyhood. Apart from the fact that Henry Denny, his cousin, spent a few weeks with Walsingham in 1571, when he was

[1] Stählin, pp. 89, 121.

[2] There is a letter given in the *Cal. Scottish*, 1574–81, p. 84, from Edward Carey to Walsingham, addressed: 'To the right honourable, my very loving brother.' This Carey must have been Walsingham's half-brother.

ambassador at Paris,[1] there is no positive evidence of any association with them. With his wife's family he had at least one close bond. Robert Beale, who married his sister-in-law, Edith St. Barbe, was perhaps Walsingham's most trusted counsellor in public affairs, serving him while ambassador in France as secretary, and taking his place as secretary when he was absent on various diplomatic missions later in life. During part of his life Beale lived at Barnes in Surrey within easy range of Walsingham's favourite residence, Barn Elms. With the remoter branches of his father's family Walsingham's relations were of the slightest. His first cousin, Sir Thomas Walsingham, was the father of a numerous progeny, but none of them was particularly noteworthy unless it be Anna, who married Thomas Randolph, one of the most conspicuous diplomatists in Elizabeth's service. His various missions to Scotland and France have already been alluded to elsewhere. He was a somewhat older man than Walsingham, but they were in close agreement upon most matters of public policy. Both of them had been refugees abroad during Mary's reign and both leaned strongly towards Puritanism in their religious views. It is evident from the letters which passed between them that they were intimate friends. Indeed Walsingham sometimes injected into his letters to Randolph a touch of humour which is wofully lacking in most of his correspondence. For instance, Walsingham began a letter written to Randolph from Paris in April 1572: 'My good Uncle, you know that great personages do not commonly write letters with their own hands, unto means of state, but do own therein the help of their secretaries and therefore you must be contented (considering the diversity of our calling) to accept these lines, though not written with mine own hand, in good part.'[2] Again, he wrote to Randolph from the Low Countries in July 1578: 'My wife, your niece, telleth me that I am greatly beholden unto you for your friendly dealing towards me in my absence and hath given me express charge to be thankful for the same. What credit she hath with me you and Captain Cockburne know, and therefore I dare do no other but thank you howsoever you have deserved the same. It is given out both there and here that we shall be hanged at our return, so ill have we behaved

[1] Stählin, pp. 50–1. [2] 19 Apr. 1572, B.M. Additional MSS. 33531, f. 107.

ourselves. The worst is I hope we shall enjoy our ordinary trial, my Lord [Cobham] to be tried by his peers and myself by a jury of Middlesex.' [1] Randolph of course was not Walsingham's uncle, but his second cousin by marriage. Walsingham apparently used the term uncle in the familiar affectionate sense in which it was often applied in his day. Yet it should be observed that Randolph, like Beale, had established his place in the public service before Walsingham's official career began. He did not give either of them their start, nor did he do much to advance their fortunes after he had attained an influential position in the Government. He appears, in fact, to have been little disposed at any time in his career to exploit his office for the benefit of his relatives. To a lesser degree than most public men of his time did he lay himself open to the charge of nepotism.

Of Walsingham's private friendships there is little record. His relations with Leicester at times bordered on the familiar, as for instance in the late autumn of 1578 when he wrote Leicester that he hoped to entertain him with a Friday drinking 'after the ancient Catholic order'.[2] But Leicester's general attitude towards Walsingham was far too condescending to admit of any real intimacy. They were at best never more than political allies and even that connexion appears to have been strained after Sir Philip Sidney's death. With Burghley, Walsingham's relations were formal though in the main not unfriendly. They were probably more intimate during the earlier years of Walsingham's official service than later when the differences between them on matters of public policy grew more acute. After Walsingham's break with Leicester he and Burghley drew together again. One small indication of the nature of their social relations appears in a letter from Burghley to the effect that he found Walsingham's trees too hard to hew.[3] From this one gathers that Burghley, like Gladstone long after him, made of wood-chopping a pastime and occasionally visited Walsingham, axe in hand, to levy a friendly tribute upon his woodlands. Yet even this can hardly be taken to argue any familiarity between the two men. Burghley was some fifteen years older

[1] S. P. Holland and Flanders, vii, f. 85.

[2] *Cal. of C. Cottrell Dormer MSS.* (*Hist. MSS. Comm. IInd Report*, Appendix), p. 82.

[3] 12 Oct. 1584, S. P. Domestic, clxxiii, no. 72.

than his colleague and their difference in age was accentuated by a marked difference in temper. That they maintained a formal friendship in spite of sharp differences of opinion upon matters political and religious was probably due rather to Burghley's good-humoured tolerance than to any real sympathy between them.

With his other colleagues in the Council Walsingham's personal relations seem to have been largely determined by his political affiliations. Sir Walter Mildmay, Chancellor of the Exchequer, was his friend and staunch political ally as well as his brother-in-law. Dr. Thomas Wilson, who was associated with him as Principal Secretary after Sir Thomas Smith's death, appointed him executor of his will.[1] He and Sir Christopher Hatton were certainly on friendly terms if they were not intimates and the unfortunate William Davison was one of his closest political associates. Indeed the whole radical element in the privy council appears to have been bound together not only by their agreement upon public questions but also by close personal ties.

Of Walsingham's friends outside the circle of his political associates so little evidence survives that a word or two will serve to dispose of them. Mr. Brockett, of Brockett Hall, was evidently among them. Walsingham wrote to him from Paris on the 10th of August 1572: 'The bearer shall inform you how we do and how we are here and how much we desire to return home and to spend a month or two at Brockett Hall to refresh our spirits, for since my repair to this country I have had no great pleasure nor playing time.' [2] Another was pretty certainly Sir Henry Wallop, Vice-Treasurer of Ireland, who expressed on one occasion the intention to give Walsingham the charge of his son in case of his death, and on another occasion borrowed £40 of him.[3] To him Walsingham wrote on the 29th of July 1579: 'Because I hope to have some fruition of your company, being now become your neighbour, I grow more zealous of your well doing. It is not the least cause to make me digest my hard pennyworth of odium to think that I am neighbour to Sir Henry

[1] *Cal. Salisbury MSS.* ii. 391. Wilson was a contemporary of Walsingham's at King's College, Cambridge (Stählin, p. 71 n.).

[2] Cotton MSS., Vespasian F vi, no. 122.

[3] *Cal. Irish*, 1574–85, pp. 223, 225.

Wallop. Therefore I pray you look well to that gentleman that he may be long my neighbour.' [1]

Another one of Walsingham's intimates was certainly Sir Thomas Heneage, Treasurer of the Queen's Chamber and later Vice-Chamberlain. During Walsingham's first embassy to Paris he corresponded regularly with Heneage, and some of the letters which survive show clearly upon what familiar terms they were. But these few surviving fragments from Walsingham's more familiar correspondence give a meagre enough impression of the group of intimates with whom he loved to share his leisure.[2] It is apparent at any rate that such a group was not wanting.

Walsingham's private life was evidently that of the gentry class to which he belonged. His official position of course obliged him to spend a large part of his time at Court, but such brief leisure as the arduous duties of his office allowed him he preferred to spend in the country. Up until 1563 his country seat was at Footscray in Kent on the manor which he had inherited from his father.[3] In that year he rented the manor of Parkbury in Hertfordshire, and probably transferred his household there at the same time. After he had acquired the manor of Barnes in Surrey in 1579, Barn Elms (now the club house of the Ranelagh Club) became his usual country residence. During the last ten years of his life he spent much of his time there. Its position on the Thames gave him easy access to Westminster and enabled him to come and go from Court more frequently than would otherwise have been possible. After 1585 when the Queen conveyed to him the manor of Odiham in Hampshire he occasionally resided there and he entertained the Queen there on one occasion. He also kept

[1] S. P. Domestic, xlv, p. 30.

[2] Among these must certainly be included Sir Henry Killigrew, who was Burghley's brother-in-law. Killigrew was a staunch Puritan who had been in exile during Mary's reign. Possibly Walsingham had met him at that time. Killigrew was one of Walsingham's most regular correspondents during his first embassy to France (cf. Walsingham's *Diary*, pp. 49, 54).

It is unfortunate that Walsingham in his diary did not long continue the practice he began of keeping a careful record of his correspondents. During the first few months of 1571 his record seems to be fairly complete, but it is very imperfect after that. Among the private persons with whom he corresponded most regularly during the early months of 1571 were his wife, Edward Dyer the courtier and poet, and Drue Drury the courtier; but none of these letters survives. His familiar letters to Heneage have been quoted in previous chapters.

[3] Stählin, pp. 124–5.

a residence in London. Probably his town house during the earlier years of his married life was in the parish of St. Giles outside Cripplegate,[1] but in 1568 he purchased a rather pretentious dwelling facing London Wall just to the east of St. Mary Axe, which was familiarly known as the Papey, by reason of the fact that it had formerly been a hospital for poor priests, converted into a dwelling-house after the suppression of that institution by Edward VI. It was commodious and boasted of a courtyard and a garden. It was, moreover, as fashions ran in London of that day, in a rather distinguished neighbourhood. Sir Thomas Gresham lived near by and Crosby Place was within a stone's throw. Thomas Heneage lived just across the street. Some time later Walsingham moved his London establishment eastward towards the Tower and settled on Seething Lane, a street of 'divers fair and large houses', where he lived in the company of such distinguished neighbours as the Earl of Essex.[2]

There can be little doubt from the attention which that observant tailor John Stow bestowed upon them that Walsingham's town houses were pretentious mansions and that they represented a degree of luxury even among affluent London burghers. Yet Walsingham, like most English gentlemen of his time, evidently preferred to spend his leisure on his country estates. Barn Elms was his favourite abiding-place during the last ten years of his life. It was far less magnificent than Burghley's great country seat at Theobalds, but an ample dwelling nevertheless and equal to the problem of entertaining the Queen and her whole court on occasions. Of the size and character of his household establishment there is little or no indication. Burghley, in the days of his affluence, maintained eighty servants in livery, and we are told that the best gentlemen in England competed to enter his service.[3] Walsingham's household can hardly have rivalled this splendour,[4] though it must have been

[1] Ibid., p. 126.

[2] *Stow's London* (ed. Kingsford), i. 146; Stählin, p. 199. The purchase of the Papey is recorded in Guildhall MSS., Husting Rolls, cclv, 49, under date 5 March 1567/8. In August 1582 and again in June 1583 Walsingham received letters dated 'at your house in Paris' (*Cal. Domestic*, Adda. 1580–1625, pp. 71, 122), but it is hardly likely that this means any more than a reference to the house at which he stopped when he was in Paris in 1581 on diplomatic business.

[3] Hume, *Great Lord Burghley*, p. 47.

[4] At least one person petitioned Walsingham to be allowed to wear his livery, *Cal. Domestic*, 1581–90, p. 59.

large if one may judge from his stables. At Barn Elms alone he kept sixty-eight horses and half as many more in various other places.[1]

It must be admitted that Walsingham in his recreations was a ' bookish person ', who took his pleasures soberly and preferred his library and the conversation of his learned friends before the more vigorous pastimes of the out-of-doors. His health at best was never good and he must have been physically rather frail. It is not recorded that he ever played tennis, a very popular sport among his contemporaries, or ever rode to hounds. It may be presumed from the numerous presents of falcons which he received that he hawked on occasions. According to the fashion of his times, he was interested in his garden, but there is nothing in his correspondence which reveals anything like the enthusiasm in such matters that, for example, his colleague Sir Thomas Smith displayed.[2] It appears from the presents that Walsingham now and then received in the form of rare plants that he shared the current taste for exotics and was probably among those who fell for that reason under the jovial Harrison's strictures. ' For hereby ', Harrison wrote in his

[1] Cf. Account of Thomas Underwood of all the horses entrusted to his keeping since entering his Honour's service :

Sum total of all such horses as your honour hath of your own and also of others feeding at your charge :

At Barn Elms . . .	68	Of these 91 are your own.
At Haneworth . . .	9	5 Lady Sidney's.
At Fulham . . .	10	2 Mr. Southwick's.
At Court	11	3 Digby's.
At Mr. Cary's . . .	21	1 Thomas Underwood.
With your servants to be returned	9	
At Bagshaws . . .	1	
At Greenwich . . .	3	
Sum Total	102 (sic)	(S. P. Domestic, ccxxiv, no. 80.)

[2] Cf. Sir Thomas Smith's delightful letters to his wife on this subject which are buried in *Cal. Foreign*, 1583, Addenda. Smith wrote these letters when he was in France with Walsingham in 1572–3.

Some brief entries in Walsingham's memorandum book (Harl. MSS. 6035) attesting to his interest in gardens :

f. 73b. 15th of April 1584. Arthur to seek out a gardener.

f. 96 (not dated, but some time in October 1584). To talk gardener, set between the trees hawthorne.

To remove trees.

To provide trees.

To renew the elms.

These jottings appear in Walsingham's own hand scattered among memoranda on political affairs.

chapter on gardens, 'we have neglected our own good gifts of God, growing here at home, as vile and of no value, and had every toy and trifle in admiration that is brought hither from far countries, ascribing I wot not what great forces and solemn estimation unto them, until they also have waxen old, after which they have been so little regarded, if not more despised, amongst us than our own.' [1]

But Walsingham was probably a man of outlandish notions in more ways than one. The year or two which he spent in Italy in his youth evidently made a great impression upon his tastes and temperament, and if he did not return as Asham would have it a devil incarnate, he was nevertheless in many respects that monstrous type of Englishman which Asham and Harrison along with many of their contemporaries combined to brand as *italianate.* Of course he was far too sane and sober a man to affect the more fantastic attributes of the type, but he possessed to a remarkable degree its cosmopolitan spirit and its breadth of interest. Like Burghley he was thoroughly in sympathy with the classical renaissance but he had an acquaintance with and a sympathy for the contemporaneous culture of France and Italy which Burghley never possessed if he did not actually despise. Walsingham's earliest biographer declares him to have been the best linguist of his times, and David Lloyd said of him: 'He could as well fit King James his humour with sayings out of Xenophon, Thucydides, Plutarch or Tacitus, as he could King Henry's with Rabelais' conceits and the Hollander with mechanic discourses.' [2] Probably no Englishman of his times had so wide an acquaintance abroad, not merely among statesmen and political agents but also among men of letters.

Edmund Spenser in one of his introductory sonnets to the *Faerie Queen* proclaims Walsingham

> the great Maecenas of this age
> As well to all that civil arts profess,
> As those that are inspired with martial rage.[3]

He was indeed a bountiful patron to men of talent in almost every walk of life. The substantial encouragement which he

[1] Cf. Harrison's *Description of England* (ed. Withington), pp. 24–5.
[2] Lloyd's *Worthies* (ed. 1670), p. 517.
[3] Spenser's *Works* (Globe ed.), p. 9.

gave to adventurers and navigators has already been remarked upon. He encouraged Hakluyt to make his famous collection of voyages,[1] and Hakluyt dedicated the first edition of his work to Walsingham in these terms: 'Whereas I have always noted your wisdom to have had a special care of the honour of her Majesty, the good reputation of our country and the advancing of navigation, the very walls of this our island . . . and whereas I acknowledge in all dutiful sort how honourably both by your letter and speech I have been animated in this and other of my travails, I see myself bound to make presentment of this work to yourself as the fruits of your own encouragements.'[2] It was to Walsingham also that Hakluyt turned for support in a plan which he had very much at heart of establishing a lectureship in navigation at the University of Oxford.[3] Nor was Hakluyt the only student of navigation who acknowledged Walsingham's patronage. Thomas Nicholas dedicated to him *The Pleasant Historie of the Conquest of the West India*,[4] and Sir George Peckham his *True Report . . . of the Newfoundlands*,[5] and Sir Jerome Horsey the account of his Russian travels.[6] It is, apparent, too, that Walsingham befriended that famous mathematician, astronomer and charlatan, Dr. John Dee. It was at Dee's house that he discoursed with Adrian Gilbert about the North-west Passage, and it was partly by Dee's assistance that the charts for Davis's famous adventure were prepared in Walsingham's own study.[7] Whether Walsingham was interested in Dee's alchemy and his crystal gazing does not appear. It might be conjectured that the Secretary was too sane a man to be allured by such will-o'-the-wisps, but delusions about such matters are by no means the monopoly of the simple. Elizabeth herself called upon Dee on one occasion to save her from the impending mischief which she feared because of a waxen figure of herself transfixed with a pin which had been found in Lincoln's

[1] Hakluyt's *Voyages* (ed. Maclehose), viii. 131.

[2] Ibid. i, p. xxii.

[3] Ibid. xii. 80.

[4] Brown, *Genesis of the United States*, i. 1041; a translation of Gomara's *La Conquista de Mexico*, first published in 1578; Purchas includes it in his *Pilgrimes*.

[5] Published in November 1583, reprinted by Hakluyt, viii. 89, with the dedication to Walsingham omitted.

[6] Horsey's *Travels* (ed. Hakluyt Soc.), Dedication.

[7] Dr. Dee's *Diary*, p. 18.

Inn Fields. It may perhaps be taken as an ill omen of Walsingham's credulity that he appeared to Dee on one occasion in a dream. Yet such evidence as there is at hand upon the matter indicates that on the whole Walsingham's interest in Dee was based upon his sounder attainments in mathematics and the art of navigation.[1] At any rate he almost certainly assisted the needs of that curiously infatuated, learned man.

Walsingham's patronage was very catholic in its scope, ranging from the makers of Latin dictionaries to the makers of court jests. John Rider in 1589 dedicated his *Bibliotheca Scholastica* ('A Double Dictionary penned for all those that would have within a short space the use of the latin tongue either to speak, read or write') to Walsingham as the 'highest patron of good letters', and Richard Tarlton, the Queen's poor fool, wrote from his death-bed to Walsingham to pray him to protect the interest of his young child.[2] Obscure poets like Christopher Ockland and Paul Melissus sought and probably found his favour.[3] Robert Adams the architect dedicated to him as

[1] It will be recalled that very shortly after the publication of the *Gregorian Calendar* in 1582 Dee was called upon by the English Government to make calculations for the adoption of the new calendar in England. Dee submitted his results in the form of a book in which he pointed out that an omission of eleven days would be more accurate than the omission of ten as Pope Gregory proposed (Life of Dee in *D. N. B.*), but for the sake of uniformity Dee was prepared to endorse the Gregorian arrangement. Upon the basis of this report the Government decided to consult Archbishop Grindal and other prominent Anglicans in order to get their opinion on the proposed change. It fell to Walsingham's task to lay the matter formally before the ecclesiastics. They were slow in making their report and he had to prod them up a little before he finally received their answer. In this answer they opposed the change for the following reasons :

(*a*) On religious grounds, as likely to breed offence to the reformed churches abroad, and to appear to proceed from fear of the threatened papal excommunication.

(*b*) On grounds of policy, since the English calendar already differed a quarter of a year from that abroad without inconvenience, and since the proposed change if made would simply establish a difference with those who did not change.

The bishops admitted that the change would be convenient to those who engaged in commerce, but considered this insufficient compensation for the trouble which the change would occasion within the kingdom by confusing all the almanacs and ready ways of reckoning. In the face of their objection the proposed reform was dropped. Walsingham's opinion about it is not on record, but his correspondence on the subject with the bishops will be found in B.M. Additional MSS. 32092, ff. 28, 29.

[2] S. P. Domestic, ccxv, no. 90. Undated.

[3] *Cal. Domestic*, 1581–90, p. 307. On Ockland, cf. *D. N. B.*

Maecenati suo optimo a map of Flushing.[1] In connexion with the more distinguished literary figures of his time one hears of Walsingham but little. He preferred perhaps to assist the obscurer aspirants to fame. Edmund Spenser he doubtless knew through his close connexion with Sir Philip Sidney, and Spenser, it will be recalled, addressed to him one of the prefatory sonnets in the *Faerie Queen.* But so many of the prominent men at Court were marked by the same measure of the poet's notice that his verses to Walsingham can hardly be taken to signify much. Sidney himself of course enjoyed much at Walsingham's hands, but this should probably rather be explained by their family connexion than by any literary interest on Walsingham's part in Sidney's various productions. Sir Fulk Greville, Sidney's biographer, enjoyed Walsingham's friendship for the same reason,[2] and so probably also did Angel Day, who dedicated to Walsingham a life of Sidney which he published in 1586.[3] Indeed it is highly probable that Sidney was responsible for drawing Walsingham and incidentally his purse into touch with a large group of literateurs who gathered about the gentle Astrophel at Barn Elms. Not the least noteworthy of these was the poet Thomas Watson, who published shortly after Walsingham's death in 1590 an Eclogue upon that mournful subject, first in Latin, under the title *Meliboeus*, and a little later in an English translation.[4] Watson's dedication of the English version to Walsingham's daughter spoke of him as 'a sound pillar of our commonwealth and chief patron of virtue, learning and chivalry'. The poem itself is unfortunately so vague in its lamentations that it contains nothing at all informing upon Walsingham's life or works. Outside the circle of Sidney's close associates almost the only secular writer who enjoyed Walsingham's patronage was Sir John Harington, the Elizabethan wit and epigrammist, whose licentious propensities of speech provoked the wrath of the Queen on one noteworthy occasion. Walsingham's connexion with Harington dates from the time when he was a student at King's College, Cambridge. In a letter from King's, dated the 2nd of November 1580, Harington, then a mere boy of nineteen, thanked Walsingham for his patronage.

[1] *Hist. MSS. Comm. VIIth Report,* p. 193, on Adams, cf. *D. N. B.*
[2] *Cal. Domestic,* 1581–90, p. 369. [3] Cf. Life of Walsingham in *D. N. B.*
[4] *Poems of Thomas Watson* (ed. Arbor), pp. 140 ff.

At that time Harington had established no claim to a literary reputation, and it seems probable that Walsingham's favourable notice of him was chiefly due to the fact that the Queen herself was young Harington's godmother.[1]

With the Elizabethan dramatists Walsingham had apparently little or nothing to do. It may be that he shared the Puritan's dislike of stage plays although there is plenty of reason for believing that Walsingham was very far from sharing the dour Puritan attitude towards pleasures of a similar character. He was in any event clearly no patron of the drama and to all appearance was quite indifferent to the fact that a group of obscure young men in the Mermaid Tavern and elsewhere were about to produce the greatest monuments of the English language.[2]

It is not surprising to discover, when one considers Walsingham's pronounced religious interests, that his patronage was extended liberally to students, writers and preachers of divinity, and particularly, of course, to those of Puritan tendencies. Among his beneficiaries in this field of labour were William Harrison, a fellow of King's and later Vice-Provost of Eton. In December 1585 Harrison offered to Walsingham, as his Maecenas, a copy of verses addressed to 'that anti-Christ at Rome'.[3] Another was his namesake, Francis Walsingham, who owed his education to the Secretary's patronage though he had the ill grace later to turn Jesuit.[4] Of his more conspicuous clients among the Puritans mention has been made already in the discussion of his religious views. It is worth observing that on one occasion at least a foreign divine tasted of his bounty. John Sturm of Strasburg, the prominent German schoolmaster and theologian, dedicated a book to him and gratefully acknowledged his liberality.[5] We should probably discover, if the evidence were at hand, that Walsingham ministered also to the needs of French and Dutch and Scottish ministers on occasion,

[1] *Cal. Domestic*, 1547–80, p. 685; cf. also life of Harington in *D. N. B.*

[2] He appears, however, to have been instrumental in the organization of the court company of players known as 'Queen Elizabeth's Men', Chambers, *The Elizabethan Stage*, ii. 104.

[3] *Cal. Domestic*, 1581–90, p. 292; Cooper, *Athenae Cantabrig.* (ed. 1913), iii. 49.

[4] Cf. *A Search into Matters of Religion*, by Francis Walsingham (ed. 1609), The Preface to the Reader. There is a brief life of this Francis in *D. N. B.*

[5] Cf. *Cal. Foreign*, 1583–4, pp. 61, 131; *Zurich Letters* (Parker Soc.), 2nd series, pp. 285–7, 303.

for certainly he was hardly less interested in their labours than in those of his own countrymen. His religious zeal never acknowledged national limitations.

Walsingham's broad sympathy with the advancement of learning led him to take an active interest in the affairs of the English Universities. Though he was a Cambridge man himself, the Oxford colleges enjoyed their fair share of his attention and his support. In December 1582 the Master and Fellows of Queen's College, Oxford, wrote to thank him for the care he had taken of their welfare.[1] In May 1583 the Fellows of Exeter College, Oxford, expressed their gratitude to him for his favours.[2] In January 1589 the Master and Fellows of Balliol desired him to assist them in maintaining the liberties conferred upon them by charter.[3] He supported All Souls College in its efforts to prevent Lady Stafford, one of the Queen's favourite ladies-in-waiting, from securing part of their property and was no doubt largely responsible for their success.[4] He befriended John Reynolds, a Fellow of Corpus Christi College, who was later to distinguish himself on the Puritan side in the famous Hampden Court Conference, and was largely instrumental in patching up a quarrel between Reynolds and the powerful Earl of Warwick.[5] He intervened in behalf of a number of Fellows in Magdalen College who had been expelled by the president, Dr. Humphreys.[6] But Walsingham's interest in Oxford revealed itself in larger ways than by interference in the petty difficulties of the various colleges. He was, for instance, largely instrumental in bringing about a revival of interest in the study of the Civil Law there. For this revival Alberico Gentile, the notable Italian civilian who was appointed Regius Professor of the Civil Law at Oxford in 1589, was directly responsible, but Gentile himself acknowledged that he owed his appointment mainly to Walsingham's influence.[7]

[1] *Cal. Domestic*, 1581–90, p. 80. [2] Ibid., p. 110. [3] Ibid., p. 574.

[4] *Collectanea* (ed. Fletcher, Oxford Hist. Soc.), i. 181 ff. One wonders how far Walsingham's antagonism to Lady Stafford's son, Sir Edward, influenced his position in this matter.

[5] Fowler, *Hist. of Corpus Christi* (Oxford Hist. Soc.), pp. 137–40.

[6] Cf. Walsingham to Bishop of Winchester, 11 July 1575, S. P. Domestic, cv, no. 16; *Cal. Domestic*, 1547–80, pp. 499, 501, 597.

[7] Holland, *Studies in International Law*, p. 11. It is impossible to say how Gentile established his connexion with Walsingham in the first place. Gentile was a D.C.L. of Perugia and was apparently forced to leave Italy because of

Probably Walsingham's interest in Gentile was quickened by his studies in the field of international law. The Italian had been consulted by the English Government as to the proper course to be pursued with the Spanish ambassador after his share in the Throgmorton Plot had been discovered. The problem which this case presented directed Gentile's attention to the whole question of the status of ambassadors and called forth his book on Ambassadors (*De legationibus*) which he published in 1584. By his development of this subject he established himself as an authority in the department of public affairs to which Walsingham had devoted most of his attention. It is not unlikely that Walsingham secured his appointment at Oxford as much for the purpose of allowing him to pursue further his researches in international law as for that of developing the study of Roman jurisprudence at large. Certainly that was the most important consequence of the increased leisure and increased income which the position afforded him. During the year following his appointment he brought out his treatise on the Laws of War (*De Jure Belli*), which goes far to establish his claim to the title of Father of International Law. If the title be conceded Walsingham has an equal claim to that of its godfather, or at least it must be admitted that he was one of the most sympathetic and one of the most helpful of the wise men who attended at the cradle of the modern law of nations.[1]

In addition to all these evidences of interest in the welfare of Oxford University, Walsingham in 1586 established a divinity lecture there. According to Antony à Wood, Walsingham's motive in making this foundation was to widen the breach and

his Protestant religion. He came to England in 1580 and seems to have made one of the group of learned men who surrounded Sir Philip Sidney. As an Italian, a Protestant, and a friend of Walsingham's son-in-law, he had a claim upon Walsingham's interest. It was apparently through Leicester's influence that he was incorporated at Oxford in 1581 (Wood, *Fasti*, ed. Bliss, ii. 117). In 1587 he dedicated a volume of Disputations to Walsingham (Holland, *op. cit.*, p. 11, n. 6). Holland maintains that Gentile 'had some claim to dispute with Grotius himself the title of the father of international law'.

In a letter from H. Palavicino to Walsingham dated at Frankfort, Germany, 22 May 1586, Palavicino wrote that he 'shall use the aid of Dr. Gentile in the Latin tongue according to your Lordship's remembrance' (*Cal. Foreign*, 1585–6, p. 652). Palavicino was at the time acting as envoy for the Queen to Duke Casimir. It seems not unlikely that the Dr. Gentile he refers to was Alberico and that he formed part of Palavicino's train.

[1] Holland, *op. cit.*, pp. 1 ff.; life of Gentile in *D. N. B.*

inflame the differences between the churches of Rome and of England.[1] Apparently Walsingham indicated his desire that John Reynolds, Fellow of Corpus Christi, should be appointed to the lectureship.[2] Of Walsingham's earlier friendliness to Reynolds mention has already been made, and attention has also been called to Reynolds's pronounced Puritan bias. It is not unlikely that Walsingham chose this means of increasing Puritan sentiment among the rising generation of Oxford students. According to Wood the lectures were very popular and were held by the Puritans to have done great good. Wood also declared that some people at the time maliciously censured the foundation as a colour to 'convey the sacrilege of the founder out of sight under a pretence of propagating the true religion'. The basis of this charge seems to lie in the fact that the £20 a year with which Walsingham endowed the lectureship was derived from lands formerly belonging to the bishopric of Oxford which Elizabeth had granted to Walsingham. It has been justly observed, however, that Walsingham was under no obligation to devote the revenue from those lands to that purpose and that 'if he founded a lecture in divinity out of them when knowledge of that kind was extremely scarce he showed a generosity which he was not obliged to from any other motive than the propriety of it'.

On the whole Oxford fared better at Walsingham's hands than did his own alma mater Cambridge. But Cambridge was not forgotten. To Emmanuel College, founded by his brother-in-law Sir Walter Mildmay, he gave the advowson of Thurcaster in Leicestershire.[3] But his own college, King's, naturally enjoyed the largest measure of his favour. On several occasions he seems to have given pecuniary assistance to indigent students at King's,[4] and according to David Lloyd he provided the college with a library of his own books which was the best of its time for matters of public policy.[5]

[1] *Biographia Britannica*, art. Walsingham.

[2] Fowler, *Corpus Christi*, p. 160.

[3] *D. N. B.* art. Walsingham.

[4] *Cal. Domestic*, 1581–90, pp. 278, 292.

[5] Lloyd's *Worthies*, art. Walsingham. Through the kindness of A. R. Benton, Esq., Assistant Librarian at King's College, I am informed as follows: 'The only books in the College Library presented by Sir Francis Walsingham are:

'1. *Biblia Montani*, septem voluminibus.

'2. *Lexicon Hebriacum Pagnini*.

All these facts, strung out at what probably has proved wearisome length, go far to justify Spenser's designation of Walsingham as the great Maecenas of his age. In a man so obviously interested in the advancement of learning and letters one should perhaps expect to find some evidences of a personal literary effort. But there is very little surviving from Walsingham's pen outside of his official correspondence. Once or twice he wrote political pamphlets, like the one denouncing the projected marriage between Mary Stuart and the Duke of Norfolk and the one setting forth Elizabeth's reasons for going to the assistance of the Dutch, but these, although eloquent enough, are hardly to be distinguished from formal state papers. He wrote also on one occasion a short paper, the title of which explains its character: *An Order for the Ready and Easy Training of Shot and the avoiding of Great Expense and Waste of Powder.*[1] It displays no particular knowledge of military science. Now and then he suggested plans for the better administration of the laws regarding religion as in his *Plot for the Creating of an Exercise of Catechizing in London*,[2] but none of these ever found their way to print and none of them takes the form of a literary exercise. The only evidence of literary activity in the man entirely distinct from his statescraft is revealed in three short essays printed two generations later by James Howell among *Divers choice Pieces of that Renowned Antiquary Sir Robert Cotton.*[3] Howell

'According to the College account £1 1*s.* was paid (1580–1) for covering with white calfes skinnes and for chains to the great bible.

'In 1583–4, 3*s.* was paid to Hobson (of Hobson's choice fame) for the carriage of it to the college.'

There is an interesting list in the Ashmole MSS. at the Bodleian Library (836, f. 76), entitled 'A Note of such Special books of Mr. Somersett as were sold to Mr. Secretary'. The incidental mention of Lady Walsingham's name in this list makes it probable that Walsingham was the Mr. Secretary referred to. The books being all genealogical in character it is probable that the Mr. Somersett in question was the Somerset Herald.

1 Printed in full in Kempe, *Loseley MSS.*, p. 296 n. It may be to this that Walsingham refers in his memorandum book (Harl. MSS. 6035, f. 36b) when he wrote some time in November 1583, 'To finish the order for the training of soldiers.'

2 S. P. Domestic, ccxxiii, no. 112.

3 Howell dedicated this volume, entitled *Cottoni Posthuma*, to Sir Robert Pye in a dedicatory notice dated April 1651. According to *D. N. B.* (art. Howell and Cotton) the first edition of this book appeared in 1657. It was subsequently published in 1672 and again in 1677. I have not been able to find any other proof that Walsingham wrote the Essays attributed to him in this volume, but there appears to be no good reason for questioning his authorship.

groups these three essays under the joint title *Sir Francis Walsingham's Anatomizing of Honesty, Ambition and Fortitude.* According to Howell, Walsingham wrote them during the last months of his life.[1] Probably the consciousness of his approaching end itself provoked the philosophic mind in him. He was in his vigorous moments too much the man of action to find the time or the mood for such leisurely pastimes as the anatomizing of either ambition or fortitude. The spirit of resignation which pervades all three essays can hardly be accepted as Walsingham's normal reaction upon the vicissitudes of life. Yet they are interesting and illuminating if only in their revelation of the thoughts which passed through his mind as he considered the life that lay behind him and made ready to take his final leave of it.

It is commonly believed that Walsingham's last days were embittered by the pinch of poverty. Camden declared that he weakened his estate by his large expenditures for secret service and died surcharged with debt.[2] And this view of the matter is supported by Walsingham's own statement in his will which he drew up less than a year before his death. 'And I will that my body, in hope of a joyful resurrection, be buried without any such extraordinary ceremonies as usually appertain to a man serving in my place, in respect of the greatness of my debts and the mean state I shall leave my wife and heirs in.'[3] The fact may therefore be accepted though it is difficult to determine just what the condition of his affairs was at his demise. In July 1584 he had agreed to effect a conveyance of a large part of his landed property in such a way as to leave to himself and his wife a life interest in it with remainder to his daughter Lady Frances and her heirs. All this land was valued in an 'Inquisitio Post Mortem' taken two years after his death at £70 1*s.* 10*d.* yearly rental. Presumably it was not liable for his debts.

Shortly before his death he also possessed the manors of Axford and Chilton in Wiltshire, the first of which was valued at £44 yearly rental and the second at £13 6*s.* 8*d.* yearly rental. Both of these, however, he sold three days before his death. He also possessed at the time of his death a few other tenements in Wiltshire, the value of which is not stated. All these facts are

[1] They are dated by Howell, 1590.

[2] Camden, *Annals* (Eng. trans. 1635), p. 394.

[3] The will is printed in full in Webb, *Hist. of Chislehurst*, p. 383.

derived from the 'Inquisitio Post Mortem' of his real property taken two years after his death.[1] But of course this makes no reckoning of his leaseholds or of his chattels or of any other forms of wealth which he left behind him. For these the impulse is at once to turn to his will, which had fortunately been preserved but which is, for any precise index of his estate, singularly disappointing. Its provisions so far as they refer to his property are as follows: he left an annuity of £100 to his daughter (in addition to one of £200 already deeded to her) and he left some £30 worth of plate to the overseers of his will. The residue of his estate he bequeathed to his wife, but without any indication as to its value. It certainly included his leasehold to the Priory of Carisbroke in the Isle of Wight which Lady Walsingham still held as late as 1602.[2] It certainly included money due to Walsingham from the Low Countries, probably some part of the £5,000 which he and Cobham had secured for the Dutch in 1578.[3] It seems to have included also a debt of £1,948 10*s.* 6*d.* due from the Queen as part of a debt which she owed to the banker Palavicino.[4] How much more it included there is no means of telling, but we have Walsingham's own testimony that it was very little. Perhaps Camden is right in saying that Walsingham spent most of his estate in perfecting the secret service. Certainly a good deal of money slipped through his fingers in the course of his official life. At one time he must have been a man of considerable wealth, if we may judge from the large grants of lucrative privileges which he received at one time or another from the Queen.

As to his debts at his decease, there are two pieces of evidence upon them, though neither is very enlightening. Shortly after his death Burghley drew up a brief statement of Walsingham's debts which follows:

Due to the Queen:	£
For the custom of wools	3,016
For the farm of the customs	7,000
For money out of the Duchy, &c.	2,000
	£12,016

[1] Webb, *Chislehurst*, pp. 361 ff.
[2] *Cal. Salisbury MSS.* xii. 152.
[3] Cf. Chap. VII above; *Cal. Salisbury MSS.* viii. 444.
[4] *Cal. Domestic*, 1595–7, pp. 187–8.

Due to Subjects :

	£
Alderman Spencer	1,066
Sir Thomas Shirley	1,000
Customer Smith	800
The account for the Span (?)	1,400
Sir Thomas Shirley	11,042
	£15,308
	12,016
This would make his total debts	£27,324[1]

But Burghley's notes are too obscure to make it certain that they even justify this reckoning.

From an investigation of Walsingham's estate which for some reason or other was made in 1611 it appears that in May 1590 Robert Beale, his brother-in-law, filed the following statement of his account with the Queen :

	£	s.	d.
Debit :			
By Privy Seals	24,169	16	11
For the licence of beer	1,333	6	6
Debts owing by him to the Queen	17,678	4	5½
	£43,181	7	10½
Credit :			
Disbursed for the Queen's service	£38,089	6	11
Disbursed by his servants to the Queen's use	10,438	3	6
Which left Walsingham a favourable balance of	£5,346	2	6½

But Sir Julius Caesar who made the reckoning in 1611 questioned whether the accounts as submitted by Beale should be accepted at their face value. At all events he thought the matter should be settled by a general acquittal given by the crown to Walsingham's heirs of all moneys due to the crown and a like acquittal given by the heirs to the crown of all moneys due from it.[2] In a word he was for disposing of the matter without payment by either party. All of which is not very illuminating but makes it likely that Walsingham's indebtedness

[1] S. P. Domestic, ccxxxi, no. 82, dated 15 April 1590. In Burghley's hand on the margin is written 'Mr. Secretary's Estate '.

[2] B.M. Lansdowne MSS. clxvii, f. 294.

to the crown, however much it was, was never acknowledged by his executors and was finally excused. Of his debts to private individuals, which amounted, according to Burghley's statement, to £15,308, nothing more can be said. From the terms of Walsingham's will he evidently had calculated that his estate would be adequate to meet his debts and leave some small residue to his wife. In any case if he died solvent he probably died poor.

From the very beginning of his official career Walsingham was a constant sufferer from ill health. At the time of his first embassy to France in 1571 he wrote to Burghley: 'Touching my own private estate, my disease groweth so dangerously upon me as I most humbly desire her Majesty to take some speedy order for some to supply my place. I hope my life shall stand her Majesty in more stead than my death, and upon these extreme points standeth the deferring of my cure.' [1] In answer to this stirring appeal Elizabeth sent Henry Killigrew to France in October and ordered Walsingham to place himself at once in the hands of his physicians.[2] In December of the same year Walsingham was still in retirement. 'I find', he wrote to Burghley on the 2nd of December, 'it will be the latter end of the next month before I shall return to my charge, for that I am diseased by three sundry carnosities which will require the longer time in the cure.' [3] It was not until towards the end of the following February that he was in condition to resume his duties again.[4] For something like two years after this he appears to have enjoyed ordinary health, but in February 1574, after he had been serving in the office of principal secretary for about a year, he fell sick again and had to leave Court for a fortnight.[5] In January 1575 the French ambassador in London reported that Walsingham had been obliged to retire from Court for a month to take treatment for *son accoustumée difficulté d'urine*.[6] It appears in fact that he was ill during most of the winter and spring of 1575. In April he wrote to the Regent of Scotland, 'As yet I remain at mine own house under the hands of the physicians of whom I hope shortly to be rid, being in very good

[1] 16 Sept. 1571, Digges, *Compleat Ambassador*, p. 136. [2] Ibid., p. 145.
[3] Ibid., p. 151. [4] Ibid., p. 166. [5] Walsingham's *Diary*, p. 18.
[6] *Correspondance de la Mothe Fénélon*, vi. 358.

way of thorough cure.' [1] Yet in spite of his optimism he was once again incapacitated in November ' because of an indisposition of my body '.[2] An ambassador from the Low Countries found him once more absent from Court because of his illness in February 1576.[3] During the next two years there is no mention of his health, but on the 23rd of January 1578 his colleague, Thomas Wilson, wrote to Burghley, ' Mr. Secretary Walsingham lyeth sick upon his bed, being pained both in his head and stomach.' [4] This spell, however, seems to have been of relatively short duration. He was back at Court again early in February,[5] and appears to have pursued his work without interruption for the next year and a half. In August of 1579 he was once more ill and remained so during the rest of the autumn.[6]

For nearly four years following this time he made no complaints about his health. But the midsummer of 1583 found him once more confined to his chamber.[7] On the 2nd of July 1583 he wrote to Burghley: 'The same night that your Lordship departed from hence I was taken with an extreme fit of the colic which held me until next day at noon, and since that time till now I have been so greatly troubled with a pain in my back and head as I am not able to write, wherefore your Lordship is to pardon me that I use not now mine own hand.' [8] How long this spell of sickness lasted does not appear, but in February of 1584 he wrote to the English ambassador in Paris, ' I have been driven to my house of late by the indisposition of my body.' [9] He had recovered early in March.[10] In the autumn of the next year he was once more forced to retire from Court and was very sick during the following winter but pulled up again in February 1586.[11] Once more, in the spring of 1587, he was driven by his infirmities from Court (fortunately for him at the time when Mary Stuart's execution was in question) and in the summer he

[1] B.M. Additional MSS. 33531, f. 151.

[2] Walsingham to Burghley, 21 November 1575, Harl. MSS. 6992, no. 13.

[3] K. de Lettenhove, *Relations politiques*, &c., viii. 177.

[4] S. P. Domestic, cxxii, 15.

[5] *Diary*, p. 34.

[6] *Cal. Irish*, 1574–85, pp. 181, 201.

[7] 4 July 1583, *Cal. of A. G. Finch MSS.* i. 35.

[8] Harl. MSS. 6993, f. 50.

[9] 8 Feb. 1583–4, at Barn Elms, S. P. France, x, f. 46.

[10] *Cal. Rutland MSS.* i. 162.

[11] S. P. Domestic, clxxxiii, no. 56; *Cal. Irish*, 1586–8, p. 27; *Cal. Rutland MSS.* i. 190.

had a sudden seizure during a visit to London on official business. For a day or so, as he wrote to Leicester, he despaired of his life, but he grew better rapidly.[1] In September he once more placed himself in the hands of his physicians for a course of treatment,[2] and he seems to have been ill during most of the autumn of 1587 and the early spring of 1588, but he was fortunately in good health when he was called upon to face the crisis of the Armada.

The following spring, however, he was once more away from Court attending to his cure[3] and in August was laid again by the heels. On the 27th of that month he wrote to Burghley, 'I have caused these enclosed, sent me by your Lordship to be read to me, being advised by my physicians to keep my bed, waiting whether I shall be visited with another fit of my fever, whereof I am in doubt for that I have this night taken no good rest.'[4] Burghley was sympathetic but expressed the fear that Walsingham's fever was due to extraordinary pains provoked by the hot applications he was using to effect a cure.[5] At any rate he was able to resume his seat in the Council soon afterwards and continued to attend pretty regularly until late in March 1590. On the 2nd of April 1590 Thomas Windebank wrote to him from Court, 'I told her Majesty of your last night's fit which I heard by Mr. Lake and

[1] Walsingham to Leicester, 14 Aug. 1587, Cotton MSS., Galba D i, f. 248. He was 'taken with a stoppage of his water' and tried various remedies without relief.

[2] Burghley to Walsingham, 5 Sept. 1587: 'I wish you good success in your intended labour and pain with your physicians' (S. P. Domestic, cciii, no. 34).

[3] Burghley to Bodley, 28 March 1589, Cotton MSS., Galba D iv, f. 121.

[4] Harl. MSS. 6994, f. 189.

[5] S. P. Domestic, cciii, no. 53. In March 1581 Walsingham wrote an interesting letter to Antony Bacon which throws light upon his tendency to resort to the immoderate use of physic in the earlier days of his illness. In this letter he took occasion to rebuke Bacon for his disposition to resort to medicines, 'a thing,' he added, 'which as I have by experience found hurtful in myself when I was of your years so you shall find in time many incommodities if you do not in time break it off. Your years will better wear out any little indisposition by good order of exercise and abstinence with some other little moderation in diet, than abide to be corrected by physic, the use whereof altereth nature much, yea maketh a new nature if it be without great cause used in younger years. And therefore if it be so that you do take any such order with yourself you shall do well to leave it and by charging nature with her own offices rather choose to make her strong than to weaken her, which undoubtedly you shall if you hold on any such course' (Birch, *Memoirs of Queen Elizabeth*, i. 14). At the time this letter was written Bacon was 23 years of age. We may presume from it that Walsingham had been dosing himself with drugs even as a young man, long before he entered official life.

thereupon took occasion to move her for speedy easing of your Honour, whereunto she answered that shortly she would call another to the place, so that I hope when a full presence of councillors shall be here the effect of her resolving will take place.'[1] Evidently Walsingham was so ill that he desired the Queen to appoint some one else to his place, though he seems even then to have been able to consider affairs of state. Four days later he was dead.[2] On the following night, according to his own expressed wish, he was quietly buried in St. Paul's.

Burghley wrote some time later to one of Walsingham's friends in Florence:

'I cannot otherwise think but you have afore this time heard, or else I am sure you shall hear, before this letter can come to your hands, of the death of Mr. Secretary Walsingham, who left this world the 6th of April as we account by ancient custom; whereby, though he hath gained a better state, as I am fully persuaded, for his soul in heaven, yet the Queen's Majesty and her realm and I and others his particular friends have had a great loss, both for the public use of his good and painful long services and for the private comfort I had by his mutual friendship.'[3]

A Spanish agent in London wrote to Philip of Spain on the 8/18th of April, 'Secretary Walsingham has just expired, at which there is much sorrow.' When the letter came under the King's eye he scribbled on the margin, 'There, yes! But it is good news here.'[4] In such wise, among the grievings of his colleagues and the rejoicings of his enemies, the great secretary left the scene.

[1] S. P. Domestic, ccxxxi, no. 62.

[2] *Diary of John Dee*, p. 33. 6/16 April 1590. 'Good Sir Francis Walsingham died at night, hora undecima.' According to Camden (p. 394) Walsingham died of a fleshy growth within the membrane (*tunicas*) of the testicles, or rather through the violence of medicines. From the scant evidence as to his malady incorporated in the text Dr. Joseph L. Miller of Chicago hazards the diagnosis that he was afflicted with a stone in the kidneys.

[3] Burghley to Count Figliazzi, undated, Lansdowne MSS., ciii, f. 68.

[4] *Cal. Spanish*, 1587–1603, p. 578.

BIBLIOGRAPHICAL NOTE

BIOGRAPHIES

The oldest extant biographical sketch of Francis Walsingham was written by Sir Robert Naunton, Secretary of State under James I. It is in *Fragmenta Regalia*, which was probably written about 1630, but not published until 1641, six years after Naunton's death. (Reprinted by Edward Arber in *English Reprints*, 1895, from the edition of 1653.) The sketch of Walsingham is less than two pages long. It is written in the seventeenth-century manner, and is rather a character study than a biography. Naunton was born in 1563. In 1589 he accompanied his uncle, Wm. Asheby, on a mission to Scotland. He may well have known Walsingham personally. Nevertheless his book, as has been well said, is an old man's recollection of his early life, and serves rather to preserve a contemporary impression of Walsingham than any very definite facts about him.

About twenty-five years after the appearance of Naunton's book, David Lloyd published another character sketch of Walsingham in his *Statesmen and Favourites of England since the Reformation* (published in London, 1665, reprinted under the title of *Lloyd's Worthies*, 1766). This is nothing more than an elaboration of Naunton's sketch and is of no independent value.

The next serious attempt at a biography of Walsingham was printed in the *Biographia Britannica*, which was published in 1766. The article on Walsingham there, though it is brief and very incomplete, contains some valuable data drawn from local English archives.

The best complete life of Walsingham, written by Sir Sidney Lee, appears in the *Dictionary of National Biography*. It is excellent so far as it goes and furnishes the obvious point of departure for any more ambitious study. Its bibliographical references and its discussion of Walsingham's portraits are particularly useful, though necessarily incomplete.

About twenty-five years ago (1899), E. A. Webb, G. W. Miller, and J. Beckwith published an elaborate history of Chislehurst. The association of the Walsingham family with this charming old Kentish town led the authors to an investigation of the history of Walsingham's ancestors. They did the work very carefully and well. Drawing their information chiefly from the Hustings Rolls of the City of London they succeeded in tracing back the authentic history of the Walsinghams to the fourteenth century. They also recovered Walsingham's will, and the *Inquisitio post mortem* of his estate, both of which they have printed in full, together with many other family documents. Dr. Karl Stählin worked through the material which Mr. Webb and his colleagues had used, and I myself worked through it independently, but neither Dr. Stählin nor myself has been able to add any facts of moment to the history of Walsingham's ancestors as set forth in this history of Chislehurst. I must take this occasion to express my gratitude to Mr. Webb for his kindly assistance to me many years ago at the beginning of my researches.

Not long after this work appeared Dr. Karl Stählin began extensive researches in England with a view to writing a complete life of Walsingham. The firstfruits of his labour appeared in 1902 under the title of *Der Kampf um Schottland und die Gesandtschaftsreise Sir Francis Walsinghams im Jahre 1583* (Leipziger Studien aus dem Gebiet der Geschichte, ix. 1). It was a very scholarly work, and although it covered no more than a few months of Walsingham's public career it revealed the fact that an adequate biography of Walsingham was actually under way. Three years later Dr. Stählin published a pamphlet entitled *Die Walsinghams bis zur Mitte des 16. Jahrhunderts*, in which he traced the history of the Walsingham family down to the birth of Sir Francis. This pamphlet, which runs to about eighty pages, presents, with one or two exceptions, all the data available on the family of Walsingham. It contains a short bibliography of printed and unprinted sources on the subject. Once more in the preface of this pamphlet Dr. Stählin gave promise of a complete life of Walsingham. In 1908 the first volume of this life appeared at Heidelberg under the title *Sir Francis Walsingham und seine Zeit*. The first chapter of this work is little more than a reprint of the pamphlet printed three years before. The last chapter carries Walsingham's life down to the end of his career as Resident Ambassador in France in the spring of 1573. It ends just before Walsingham assumed his duties as Principal Secretary to Queen Elizabeth and began the really significant period of his public career. It constitutes, therefore, in its 636 pages little more than an elaborate introduction to Walsingham's public life. So far as it goes it is admirable. I had completed my researches into this earlier phase of Walsingham's life before Dr. Stählin's book appeared, but I have learned much from him and gladly acknowledge the debt. It was certainly Dr. Stählin's intention to carry the life of Walsingham farther in subsequent volumes, but after the lapse of seventeen years nothing more on this subject has appeared from his pen.

Since Dr. Stählin has printed an adequate bibliography on the sources of Walsingham's family history in his pamphlet cited above, there is no need to repeat the performance. On Walsingham's early life there is little available. All the existing information regarding his college career at King's College, Cambridge, is to be drawn from the records of the College. I have to thank Mr. F. L. Clarke, the Bursar's clerk at King's, for his kindness in making a transcription of the pertinent data for me. Walsingham's connexion with Gray's Inn is established by an entry of his name in the record of admissions to the Inn. There is nothing else. Of his early travels on the continent there is or was a record on his tomb in St. Paul's, but it is merely a phrase and probably no more trustworthy than tombstone phrases generally are. The archives of the University of Padua make brief mention of Walsingham's career there (compare C. F. Andrich, *De Natione Anglica et Scota Juristarum Universitatis Patavinae,* p. 31). But all the available sources of information about his career before he entered public life would, if set forth *in extenso,* hardly fill a page of ordinary type.

First to last, the records of Walsingham's private life, as distinct from his public life, are meagre in the extreme. Of family archives he has left nothing, a fact which is not so surprising when we recall that he had no male children. There are probably not half a dozen letters in existence either from him or to him which can be considered as private and personal letters. Most of these are preserved in a letter-book which is in the Public Record Office (State Papers, Domestic, Elizabeth, xlv). One or two of his private letters are in the Finch MSS., and will be found in the *Calendar of Finch MSS.* prepared by the Historical MSS. Commission. There are also a few among the Loseley MSS. which are calendared in the *Report of the Historical MSS. Commission,* vii, Appendix, pp. 596 ff. (A. J. Kempe's *Loseley MSS.*, 1836, does not include most of Walsingham's letters in this collection).

Among the few surviving papers of a private nature from Walsingham's pen is one entitled *Instructions which Sir Francis Walsingham gave his nephew when he sent him into foreign parts to travel.* This is printed in full in the text. The original, not in Walsingham's hand, was formerly in the Finch collection at Burley-on-the-Hill. It was unfortunately destroyed by fire a few years ago. Dr. Stählin was kind enough to lend me his copy which had been made for him by Miss P. Finch. Some fifty years ago a *Journal of Sir Francis Walsingham* was in the possession of Col. Carew of Crowcombe Court. It was edited in 1870 for the Camden Society and appears in *Camden Miscellany*, vi. It runs from December 1570 to April 1583, but there are four breaks in the entries, the longest being between June 1578 and March 1580. The original is in the hand of one of Walsingham's secretaries. It is little more than a brief itinerary of Walsingham's movements and a brief record of his correspondence, but even on these topics it is far from complete. Another diary, or memorandum book, similar in character, is preserved in the British Museum (Harl. MSS. 6035); possibly it followed the journal just mentioned. It runs from April 1583 until December 1584 with no entries for August and September 1583. It is partly in Walsingham's own hand, partly in the hand of one or another of his secretaries. It contains here and there brief references to private affairs, although it is mostly a memorandum of public business (compare also on this subject the book entitled *Walsingham's Table Book* in British Museum, Stowe MSS. 162, which is an inventory of official records compiled doubtless for Walsingham's use).

Walsingham was evidently a man of some ability as a pamphleteer. His *Discourse touching the pretended match between the Duke of Norfolk and the Queen of Scots*, which is printed in full in the Appendix to Chapter I, was published in at least two editions before 1570. Later he was employed by the Queen to write at least a part of her public explanation for going openly to the assistance of the Dutch rebels in 1585 (cf. Murdin, *Burghley Papers*, p. 295). A paper from his pen on military drill, evidently prepared for use at the musters, is also preserved (cf. Lodge, *Illustrations*, ii. 284). But all of these three should, perhaps, be regarded as in the line of service. Of literary work unconnected with politics only three essays of uncertain authenticity survive. These were published by James Howell in a little volume entitled *Cottoni Posthuma; Divers Choice Pieces of that renowned antiquary Sir Robert Cotton*, which appeared in London, 1657 (second edition, 1672). The essays in question are given the title *Sir Francis Walsingham's Anatomizing of Honesty, Ambition and Fortitude.* They are said to have been written in the year 1590. No manuscript of them appears to have survived, although it may have been destroyed in the fire in Cotton's library in 1731. There is no other evidence, except Howell's statement, that these essays were written by Walsingham, but there is on the other hand no valid reason for questioning their authenticity, apart from the fact that they are unique surviving examples of this kind of writing from Walsingham's pen.

GENERAL HISTORIES

Walsingham's public life is so indissolubly connected with the history of his times that it would be futile in a bibliographical note to try to distinguish between them. The history of his public life is the history of the twenty years of Elizabeth's reign which runs between 1570 and 1590.

The best general survey of this period down to the year 1588 still remains that of James Anthony Froude (references in the text are to Scribner's ed., 1899). It is easy to criticize Froude, but hard to improve upon him. His manner of presentation is inimitable. As to his matter, it is open to a good deal of criticism in details. On the whole he paid too little attention to French and Dutch sources. He made too much of Burghley, and too little of Elizabeth. He underrated the part which Leicester played, particularly in alliance with the Puritans, and he failed altogether to identify Walsingham's position as distinct from Burghley's. In treating of the French, and particularly of the Dutch wars, he exaggerated the religious elements in the struggle, and paid too little attention to national rivalries. He failed to perceive how largely Elizabeth's policy towards the Dutch was influenced by her fear of French ambitions in that quarter. He is too much disposed to condemn the Queen's parsimoniousness without taking into account such prosaic matters as the annual balance sheet. Nevertheless, his six volumes on Elizabeth remain the most brilliant exposition in print of her policy. Outside of his account the only general account of the reign which needs to be considered is that of Prof. A. F. Pollard in vol. vi of the *Political History of England,* edited by Wm. Hunt and Reginald L. Poole. Prof. Pollard's work is disappointingly brief for the last fifteen years of Elizabeth's reign, but for that portion of it in which Walsingham played his part it is admirable, though necessarily brief, and based almost entirely upon material available in print. It contains an excellent bibliography. Of the other general histories of the period Lingard should be mentioned if only because he presents a Roman Catholic viewpoint as opposed to Froude's too ardent Protestantism. But Lingard needs correction upon so many points that he is an unsafe guide. The student will get a much more scholarly presentation of the Roman Catholic position on controverted points in the studies of Arnold Oscar Meyer and of Father John Hungerford Pollen which will be considered below.

Under the general heading of books on the period as a whole, it will perhaps be appropriate to consider the outstanding political biographies. Of the lives of Elizabeth those of Bishop Creighton and of E. S. Beesley are slight estimates based upon secondary material. The earlier works of Lucy Aikin and Agnes Strickland are of no great value. Nichols's *Progresses of Queen Elizabeth* (1823) deals with the pageantry of court life. It is a valuable book, but not in connexion with Walsingham's career. Frederick Chamberlin's *Private Character of Queen Elizabeth* (London, 1922) is only worth mentioning because it contains a useful compilation of the facts available about Elizabeth's personal health. The conclusions drawn from these facts need to be scrutinized carefully. There is no first-class biography of Burghley. Nare's ponderous tomes hardly touch upon Burghley's connexion with foreign affairs. M. A. S. Hume's *Great Lord Burghley* (London, 1898) cannot be regarded as much more than a by-product of the late Major Hume's rather faulty edition of the Spanish State Papers. There is no life of Leicester worth considering at all except that in the *Dictionary of National Biography*. Strype's biographies, particularly that of Sir Thomas Smith, are well documented so far as they go, but Strype's eye was fixed on ecclesiastical matters. He hardly glanced at the Foreign Office papers. Sir H. Nicholas's *Life of Davison* (1823), and particularly his *Life of Hatton* (1847) are invaluable. The life of Hatton is little more than a reprint of Hatton's Letter-Book now preserved in the British Museum, Additional MSS. 15891. For the biographies of others of Walsingham's contemporaries the best source of information is the *Dictionary of National Biography* with references there given.

CHRONICLERS

Modern historians are too much disposed to underrate the value of the contemporary Elizabethan chroniclers, particularly of John Stow and Wm. Camden. The best of Stow's work appears in the chapters on the reign of Elizabeth which Stow wrote for Holinshed's *Chronicles*. The second edition of Holinshed, published in

1587, and reprinted in 1808, should be consulted in this connexion. It will be quite evident to the careful student that Stow drew upon sources very close to the Government for some particulars of his story. It might even be asserted that the Government made use of his various *Chronicles* in something like the way in which modern governments make use of the press to influence public opinion. This is particularly observable in his accounts of the plots against Elizabeth's life. There is a good account of Stow's historical writings in Kingsford's edition of *Stow's London*, Introduction, pp. lxxxii ff. Kingsford, however, fails to point out in his bibliography Stow's connexion with Holinshed. Evidently the numerous editions of his *Chronicles*, *Annals*, *Summaries*, and *Abridgements* must have served contemporary Englishmen in something like the way they are served to-day by almanacs and annual registers.

Wm. Camden, we know, was closely in touch with Elizabeth's court, and with some outstanding men there, particularly Lord Burghley. His *Annales*, though not brilliantly written, contain information not available elsewhere, which recent research proves to be worthy of very serious consideration. This is notably true of his account of the Babington plot. The best edition of his *Annales* is that of Thomas Hearne (3 vols., 1717).

DOCUMENTARY MATERIAL

It is not intended to consider here all the documentary sources for the history of Elizabeth's reign, but only those serviceable in establishing Walsingham's relations to Elizabeth's policy. It will be most convenient to consider these under the general headings of Foreign Relations, Scottish Affairs, Mary Stuart, and Ecclesiastical Affairs. But there are certain very valuable sources of information which do not readily classify themselves under these heads.

The Acts of Privy Council (32 vols., ed. Sir J. R. Dasent). These are brief records of the meetings of Privy Council. So far as they have been discovered they have been printed complete for Elizabeth's reign. There is one serious gap in them between June 1582 and February 1587. They very evidently do not contain a complete record of the business of Privy Council. But even so, they are invaluable.

The Manuscript Collections at the British Museum. For Elizabethan history the most valuable collections in the British Museum are the Cotton MSS., the Harleian MSS., the Lansdowne MSS., the Stowe MSS., and the Additional MSS. The Cotton MSS.

represent what survives from the notorious pilferings of the public records by Sir Robert Cotton. Some part of his collection was destroyed by fire in 1731. The best catalogue of them is that compiled by Joseph Planta in 1802. It is not absolutely trustworthy. A great many of Walsingham's letters will be found in this great collection. Students should not neglect the fifty-odd volumes of Cotton MSS., Appendix, which are very imperfectly catalogued, and which probably represent unclassified documents gathered up after the fire.

The Harleian MSS. are also extremely valuable. A catalogue of them in four volumes was printed in London, 1808–12. It also is not absolutely trustworthy. The Lansdowne MSS. (Catalogue, London, 1819) are for the most part papers which formerly belonged to Lord Burghley. They ought to be considered in connexion with the Salisbury MSS. preserved at Hatfield House.

THE MANUSCRIPT COLLECTIONS AT LAMBETH HOUSE. These collections (Catalogue, ed. Todd, London, 1812) are chiefly valuable for ecclesiastical history though they contain important papers of Anthony Bacon, brother of Sir Francis Bacon, several letters of Nicholas Faunt, one of Walsingham's secretaries, and several letters of Antony Standen, perhaps the cleverest of his spies in Spain. Dr. Thomas Birch published a large number of extracts from these papers in 1754 under the title of *Memoirs of the Reign of Queen Elizabeth*, &c. Birch's transcripts of the originals are preserved in the British Museum (Additional MSS. 4109–4124).

THE MANUSCRIPT COLLECTIONS AT THE BODLEIAN LIBRARY, OXFORD. Of these the most valuable are the Tanner MSS., the Rawlinson MSS., and the Ashmole MSS. (*Catalogus Codicum MSS. Bibliothecae Bodleianae*, Oxford, 1845–1909). The Tanner MSS. contain very important letters in cipher from Walsingham to William Harborne, English agent at Constantinople. They also include several letter-books of Sir Amias Paulet, containing much of his correspondence when he was ambassador to France, and part of his correspondence when he was keeper of the captive Mary Stuart. The first of these letter-books, covering the period from May 1577 to January 1578, was edited in 1866 for the Roxburghe Club by O. Ogle. The fragmentary third letter-book containing the correspondence of Paulet, as Mary's keeper, was printed by Father John Morris in *The Letter-Books of Sir Amias Poulet*, 1874.

THE HATFIELD HOUSE COLLECTION OF SALISBURY MSS. From the point of view of Elizabethan history the most important of all the private manuscript collections in England, or elsewhere, are those belonging to the Marquis of Salisbury at Hatfield House. In this collection are preserved many of the papers of Lord Burghley. Some of these were printed *in extenso* in Haynes's *Collection of State Papers . . . left by Lord Burghley* (1740), covering the period from 1541 to 1570, and some in Murdin, *Ibid.* (1759), covering the period from 1570 to 1596. A much more complete analysis of the collection has been printed by the Historical MSS. Commission in fourteen volumes under the title *Calendar of MSS. of . . . Marquis of Salisbury, preserved at Hatfield House.* This Calendar is of very unequal value. Some of the documents are printed *in extenso,* some are merely analysed. The last volumes are much fuller, and better done than the earlier ones. Unfortunately the first four, which cover the period of Walsingham's public life, are the poorest of the lot. They abound in misprints, and in cases where documents lack a date they have generally been wofully misplaced. This is notably true of the very valuable letters which passed between Queen Elizabeth and her French suitor Francis, Duke of Alençon, most of which are to be found in this collection. Many of Burghley's private papers, preserved at Hatfield House, are not included in this Calendar.

Other Private Collections of MSS. Most of the private collections of manuscripts in England have been calendared by the Historical MSS. Commission. Attention has already been called to the Molyneux MSS. at Loseley Park, and the Finch MSS. which contain valuable material on Walsingham's private life. Next to the Salisbury MSS. perhaps the most valuable collection of private papers relative to the policy of Queen Elizabeth is the so-called Yelverton MSS. now in the possession of Lady Calthorpe at Grosvenor Square, London. This collection consists in large measure of papers of Robert Beale, Walsingham's brother-in-law. Beale was one of the most distinguished civilians of his time, as well as one of the foremost champions of Puritanism. He was consulted by the Queen upon many questions involving international law, and his papers contain much of value on foreign relations. They contain also exceedingly important papers connected with the trial of Mary Stuart, and with the Earl of Leicester's expedition to the Low Countries. Strype evidently had access to this collection and printed some documents from it in his *Annals of the Reformation* (Oxford, 1824). Some notice of the contents of this collection is given in E. Bernard's *Catalogi librorum et manuscriptorum Angliae et Hiberniae,* published at Oxford in 1697. It was briefly reviewed also by the Historical MSS. Commission in its *Second Report,* Appendix, pp. 39–46. An adequate edition of Beale's papers in this collection, or even an adequate calendar of them, is much to be desired.

The Talbot Papers contain much of the correspondence of George Talbot, Earl of Shrewsbury, the keeper of Mary Stuart, and many of the gossipy letters of his son, Gilbert. They are preserved at the King's College of Arms to which they were presented by Henry Howard, 6th Duke of Norfolk. Many of them are printed *in extenso* in Lodge, *Illustrations of British History* (London, 1838).

The Sidney Papers are preserved at Penshurst, Kent, and are reviewed in the *Historical MSS. Commission, Third Report,* pp. 227 ff. Many of them are printed *in extenso* in Collins, *Letters . . . of State . . . written by . . . Sir Henry Sidney . . . Sir Philip Sidney, &c.* (London, 1746). Considering the fact that Sir Philip Sidney was Walsingham's son-in-law, this collection is distinctly disappointing though not to be neglected.

The Hardwicke Papers, now in the British Museum (Additional MSS. 35834–6, 35841) contain valuable material on Mary Stuart, and also much of Sir Edward Stafford's correspondence when ambassador to France.

Other private collections are of value on particular phases of the subject. They will be considered below.

FOREIGN POLICY

General. Outside the general books already mentioned, there is no good account of the foreign policy of Queen Elizabeth during the twenty years of Walsingham's public service with the possible exception of Sir John Seeley's *The Growth of British Policy* (Cambridge, 1895). Most of the first volume of this book deals with Elizabeth. The introduction to the various volumes of the Foreign Calendars, particularly those edited by the late A. J. Butler, and by Mrs. Sophie C. Lomas, are valuable, though confining their attention in the main to the material in the Public Record Office.

By far the most important sources for the history of Elizabeth's foreign policy are the foreign papers preserved at the Public Record Office in London. These are arranged under countries. They consist, for the most part, of dispatches from ambassadors and other agents abroad, and of the minutes of dispatches sent to them. There are, besides, many treaty papers among the Foreign Office papers in the Public Record Office, and some miscellaneous diplomatic documents, preserved in the Treasury of the Receipt of the Exchequer (P. R. O.). Many of the treaties, and some other diplomatic documents, are printed *in extenso* in Rymer's *Foedera*. The Foreign Office papers in general have been printed in calendar form in the *Calendars of State Papers, Foreign, Elizabeth,* down to the year 1586. Further volumes are in preparation. This series of calendars gets steadily better as it proceeds. The volumes edited by A. J. Butler and by Mrs. Lomas (1577–86) are very scholarly pieces of work. Unfortunately the editors have been obliged to limit their attention to the papers in the Public Record Office, though it is well enough known that the extremely valuable papers on foreign affairs in the Cotton MSS., in the British Museum, originally formed part of the State Archives. In a few instances important papers on foreign affairs have got classified among the State Papers Domestic in the Public Record Office, and have escaped the attention of the editors of the Foreign Calendars. But generally speaking, students who are not in a position to consult the originals will find in the Foreign Calendars, as edited by Mr. Butler and Mrs. Lomas, trustworthy *résumés* of their contents.

ANGLO-FRENCH RELATIONS. For the relations between England and France, 1570–90, the State Papers, France, in the Public Record Office are the most valuable collection of sources, supplemented as they must be by the papers in the Harleian and Cotton MSS. in the British Museum, and the Salisbury Papers at Hatfield House.

Beside the Foreign Calendars the following printed collections of French dispatches are important :

The Compleat Ambassador (London, 1655) covers the dispatches to and from Walsingham when he was ambassador to France, 1570–3, and again when he was on mission to France in 1581. The book is very badly printed, but it contains some documents the originals of which are now missing. Most of the letters printed are in the Public Record Office and the British Museum.

Miscellaneous State Papers, 1501–1726 (*The Hardwicke Papers*) (London, 1778). This book contains many of the dispatches from Sir Edward Stafford when he was ambassador to France (1583–8).

Cabala, sive Scrinia Sacra, 2nd edition, London, 1691. It contains many dispatches from Cecil to Norris, English ambassador to France, 1568–70.

Hector de la Ferrière-Percy, *Le XVIe Siècle et les Valois*, Paris, 1879, discusses Anglo-French relations 1558–74, and prints many documents from the Public Record Office and the British Museum relative to Elizabeth's intrigues with Alençon and the French Huguenots after St. Bartholomew's.

Some years ago the Deputy Keeper of the Public Records employed M. Baschet to examine the French archives, to report upon the papers relative to English affairs preserved in France, and to make transcripts of them. The results of Baschet's preliminary investigations are printed in the *Reports of the Deputy Keeper of the Public Records*. Of these the most important are a list of the French ambassadors in England (Report 37, Appendix 1, pp. 188 ff.), and a list of dispatches of French ambassadors in England, Henry VIII to George I, preserved in French Archives (Report 39, Appendix 1, pp. 573 ff.). Baschet made transcripts from all the dispatches found from Henry VIII to the end of Elizabeth. These transcripts are preserved in the Public Record Office. There are thirty-five bundles in all, of which the last twelve cover the reign of Elizabeth. The transcripts made include many dispatches not listed in Report 39. (Cf. corrected list in Round Room, Public Record Office.) Baschet made an extremely careful survey of the public archives, but unfortunately he did not investigate the French private archives. He did not include in his transcripts the dispatches of La Mothe Fénélon, ambassador to England between 1568 and 1575, whose dispatches are printed in full in Teulet, *Correspondance diplomatique de . . . La Mothe Fénélon* (Paris and London, 1838–40). Nor did he include those dispatches of La Mothe Fénélon's successor, Michel de Castelnau de la Mauvissière, which are printed in Le Laboureur's edition of the *Mémoires of Castelnau* (3 vols., Paris, 1731). Other dispatches of Castelnau's omitted in the transcripts are to be found in the archives of the family of Esneval and have been partly printed in Teulet's *Relations politiques de la France et de l'Espagne avec l'Écosse* (Paris, 1862). These have also been utilized by G. Hubault in *Ambassade de Castelnau en Angleterre* (St. Cloud, 1856–7). Baschet's transcripts are chiefly valuable for Castelnau's dispatches. He was able to find very few dispatches of Castelnau's successor, Châteauneuf (1585–9). Perhaps the most important surviving papers from Châteauneuf are his discourse on the state of affairs in England upon his arrival (Teulet, *op. cit.* iv, pp. 61 ff.) and his discourse on the Babington Conspiracy (Labanoff, *Lettres &c. de Marie Stuart*, vi, pp. 275 ff.). In *Les Mémoires de M. le Duc de Nevers* (ed. de Gomberville, Paris, 1665) are printed many documents relative to Elizabeth's French courtships.

A great many documents of importance on Anglo-French relations are included in *Lettres de Catherine de Médicis* (ed. H. de la Ferrière-Percy and B. de la Puchesse. Paris, 1880–1909), and in *Lettres missives d'Henri IV* (ed. B. de Xivrey and Grondet. Paris, 1843–76). The dispatches of M. de Forquevaux, French ambassador in Spain 1565–72 (ed. Douais, 1900), and of Mondoucet, French agent in the Low Countries (ed. Didier, 1892), are also of some value, as are Canastrini et Desjardins, *Négociations de la France avec la Toscane* (Paris, 1865–75), and Charrière, *Négociations de la France dans le Levant* (Paris, 1884). Most of the extant correspondence of Admiral Coligny is printed in Delaborde, *Coligny* (Paris, 1882). The correspondence of Jeanne d'Albret (ed. Rochambeau, Paris, 1897) is less important and distinctly disappointing on Anglo-French affairs.

Among contemporary French memoirs there is relatively little of importance on Anglo-French affairs. The *Mémoires* of Duplessis-Mornay (Paris, 1868–9), written by his wife, are very brief on his missions to England. The *Mémoires* of Michel de la Huguerye (ed. de Ruble, Paris, 1877–80) contain much on English affairs. La Huguerye was sent on more than one mission to England by the Prince of Condé. He wrote, however, many years after the event and is so obviously inaccurate upon those matters where it is possible to check his narrative, that it is unsafe to put much dependence upon his unsupported statements. The *Mémoires* of Marguerite of Valois (ed. Guescard, Paris, 1842) supply some facts regarding the intrigues centring about the Duke of Alençon and the Netherlands.

In the works of the two great contemporary French historians, D'Aubigné and de Thou, there is very little of value on Anglo-French relations. The same thing can be said of Davila's great work on the French civil wars and of La Popelinière's *Histoire de la France* (Paris, 1581).

Space does not serve to discuss the secondary material on French affairs. The bibliography of H. Hauser in Molinier, *Les sources de l'histoire de France*, and those in Lavisse, *Histoire de France*, vi, pt. 1, are adequate enough. Particular mention should perhaps be made, however, of the work of Count Hector de la Ferrière-Percy, who has probably done more than any other Frenchman to illuminate Anglo-French relations in Walsingham's time. His scholarly introductions to the various volumes of the *Lettres de C. de Médicis* and his articles in the *Revue des Questions Historiques* (cited in the text) are particularly noteworthy. Atkinson, *The Cardinal of Châtillon in England, 1568–71* (London, 1890), prints in full most of the documents relating to the genesis of the Anglo-French *rapprochement* of 1570–2. Kervyn de Lettenhove's brilliant, though untrustworthy *Les Huguenots et les Gueux* (Bruges, 1883–5) remains, for all its faults, the best general account of the tangled intrigues between France, the Dutch rebels, and England during the years 1560–85. M. A. S. Hume's *The Courtships of Queen Elizabeth* (2nd ed., London, 1904) and La Ferrière-Percy's *Les Projets de Mariage de la Reine Élisabeth* (Paris, 1882) are more concerned with the picturesque side of Elizabeth's French love affairs than with their diplomatic significance. Hume's book is based chiefly on Spanish sources, La Ferrière-Percy's on French. No student of the times can afford to neglect Mariéjol's brilliant biography of Catherine de Médicis (Paris, 1920) which has appeared since the standard French bibliographies of the period were published.

England and the Low Countries. Here again the most valuable sources of information are in the Public Record Office in the State Papers, Holland and Flanders, supplemented by those in the British Museum, and at Hatfield House. There is not much of value in private collections in England except in the Ancaster MSS. (Historical MSS. Commission, 1907) which contain much of the correspondence of Peregrine Lord Willoughby, who in 1587 succeeded Leicester in charge of the English forces in the Low Countries. Extracts from Willoughby's letters are printed in Lady Bertie's *Five Generations of a Loyal House* (1845). The Yelverton MSS. contain many of Lord Buckhurst's letters from the Low Countries.

Of printed sources by far the most important collection is Kervyn de Lettenhove and Gilliodts van Severen, *Relations politiques des Pays-Bas et de l'Angleterre sous le Règne de Philippe II* (Brussels, 1882–1900). This prints *verbatim et literatim* practically all the documents available on Anglo-Dutch affairs from the beginning of Elizabeth's reign down to the end of the year 1579. It represents a diligent search not only of English, but also of Dutch, Spanish, and Imperial archives. Unfortunately it was never finished. Attention ought to be called to the fact that letters from English archives are often not given entire but only those parts which relate to Dutch affairs. Omissions of irrelevant matter are unfortunately not indicated in the text.

The Foreign Calendars, so far as they have been printed, give adequate abstracts of papers relating to Dutch affairs in the Public Record Office. Much of the correspondence relative to Leicester's first expedition to the Low Countries in 1585–6 is printed in *The Correspondence of Robert Dudley, &c.*, edited by John Bruce for the Camden Society in 1844. Bruce, however, has omitted many important dispatches preserved in the Public Record Office. In Part II of the 2nd edition of *Cabala* (*vide supra*) are printed many important dispatches to and from Lord Buckhurst relative to Leicester's government in the Low Countries.

The royal archives at The Hague, at Brussels, and at Vienna, the Spanish archives at Simancas and the papers formerly at Simancas which are now in Paris contain valuable material on the relations between England and the Low Countries. A useful inventory of the documents at Simancas relative to the Low Countries is given in Gachard, *Correspondance de Philippe II*, i, pp. 89 ff. In the same place, i, pp. 23 ff., will be found an account of the papers removed from Simancas by Napoleon and now preserved in the Bibliothèque Nationale at Paris. There is no satisfactory index of these papers at Paris in print, but a manuscript inventory is available at the Bibliothèque Nationale.

Most of the important papers in the Low Countries which appertain to the relations between England and the Dutch rebels are at The Hague. The dispatches to and from Dutch envoys to England are in the main preserved there, though, strangely enough, those for the critical year 1586 are missing. Some dispatches of importance have been printed by Bor, *Oorspronck, begin ende aenvang der Nederlandscher oorlogen* (Amsterdam, 1679). Many of the dispatches of Joachim Ortell in 1585, for instance, are printed in Bor, xx, ff. 59 ff. Some are also printed in *Kronijk van het Historisch Genootschap*, vols. xvi ff., notably (xxii, pp. 215–77) the long report of the Dutch envoys sent to England in 1585.

The official resolutions of the Estates-General of the Dutch Republic for the years 1576–89 are printed in N. Japiske, *Resolutiën der Staten Generaal van 1576 tot 1609* (Rijksgeschiedkundige Publicatiën, vols. 26, 33, 41, 43, 47, 51. The Hague, 1915–22). Gachard's

Actes des États Généraux, 1576–85 (Brussels, 1861–6), should also be consulted.

The most important printed collections of sources on the relations of the Dutch with England are Gachard, *Correspondance de Guillaume le Taciturne* (Brussels, 1847–57), and Groen van Prinsterer, *Archives ou correspondance inédite de la Maison d'Orange-Nassau,* 1st Series, 2nd Series (Leyden, Utrecht, 1835–62). L. V. Deventer, *Gedenkstukken van Johan v. Oldenbarneveldt* (The Hague, 1860–5) yields little for the period of Walsingham's public service. P. J. Blok, *Correspondentie van . . . Lodewijk de Nassau* (Utrecht, 1887), adds disappointingly little to our information about the early intrigues of Walsingham with Louis of Nassau. Some letters of importance on the intrigues of Leicester with the popular faction in the Netherlands are printed in Blok, *Correspondance inédite de . . . Leicester et de François et Jean Hotman* (Haarlem, 1911), and some others are scattered through the *Kronijk* (*vide supra*), particularly in volume xxii.

The documentary material relative to the Duke of Alençon and the Low Countries has been gathered from French, Dutch, and Belgian archives with great diligence and set forth with great erudition by P. L. Muller and A. Diegerick under the title *Documents concernant les relations entre le Duc d'Anjou et les Pays-Bas* (1889–99, printed in *Werken van het Historisch Genootschap,* Utrecht, nos. 51, 55, 57, 60, 61).

English Relations with the Spanish Government in the Low Countries. In addition to the sources already noticed Gachard's *Correspondance de Philippe II sur les affaires des Pays-Bas* (Brussels, 1848–79) is indispensable so far as it goes. It does not go beyond the year 1577. Gachard's *Correspondance d'Alexandre Farnese . . . avec Philippe II, 1578–81* (Brussels, 1853), is also incomplete but very valuable for the years it covers. Some of Parma's subsequent correspondence is given in the appendices to Poullet et Piot, *Correspondance du Cardinal Granvelle* (Brussels, 1878–97). In the same place (vol. xii, Appendix) will be found many pertinent documents bearing upon Elizabeth's secret efforts to come to terms with Parma in 1586–7. Free translations of many of these will be found in the text of Motley, *History of the United Netherlands.* The *Coleccion de documentos ineditos para la historia de España* (Madrid, 1842–95) contains many important documents from the archives of Simancas. An analysis of this great collection from the point of view of its bearing upon the history of the Low Countries is given by Bussemaker in *Bijdragen voor vaderlandsche geschiedenis*, &c., 3rd Series, ix, pp. 352–458.

There is no adequate secondary account of the relations between England and the Low Countries before 1584. Froude's is the most complete but Froude has failed to recognize the full importance of the French factor. After 1584 Motley's account in his *History of the United Netherlands* is in the main excellent. In his earlier work on the *Rise of the Dutch Republic*, Motley paid scant attention to Anglo-Dutch relations. He went into them at great length in his *United Netherlands*, making extensive use both of English and of Spanish sources. Motley saw what Froude missed, the fundamental difference between Walsingham's position and Burghley's on Dutch policy. Motley failed, however, to show how much the Dutch themselves were to blame for the dilatory tactics of Elizabeth in 1584 and 1585.

On special topics, Blok, *De Watergeusen in England, 1568–72* (The Hague, 1896) is good on the relations of England to the beginnings of the Dutch revolt. Stirling-Maxwell's *Don John of Austria* (London, 1883) covers the period 1577–8. Markham, *The Fighting Veres* (London, 1888), is useful for the military side of the story, particularly from 1587 onwards. A careful study of Leicester's expedition to the Low Countries in the light of all the available evidence and with reference not only to the factions in England, but also to the factions in the Netherlands is much to be desired. Neither H. Beijerman's *Oldenbarneveld: de Staten van Holland en Leycester* (Deventer, 1847) nor R. Broersma, *Het Tusschenbestuur in het Leycestersche Tijdvak* (Goes, 1899) is adequate.

ANGLO-SPANISH RELATIONS. During the period under consideration Spain maintained a resident ambassador in England up to 1572 and again from 1578 to 1584. During the intervening times up to 1590 there were semi-official Spanish agents in England who sent reports to Madrid on English affairs. The dispatches to and from these ambassadors and agents are given for the most part in the *Calendar of State Papers, Spanish, Elizabeth*, not always accurately translated, as will appear by a comparison with the originals, many of which are printed in *Documentos Ineditos* (*v. s.*), vols. lxxxvii, lxxxix–xcii. There were no English ambassadors regularly resident in Spain during the period of Walsingham's public service. Dispatches from English envoys and agents in Spain are preserved for the most part in the Public Record Office, State Papers, Spain, and are calendared in the foreign calendars. A good deal of information relative to English relations with Spain will be found in the dispatches of the Spanish ambassadors in France, the originals of which are in the Bibliothèque Nationale at Paris. Some of these are given in the Spanish calendars, but by no means all. Teulet's *Relations politiques de la France et de l'Espagne avec l'Écosse* (Paris, 1862) contains (vol. v) many Spanish dispatches relative to Anglo-Scottish affairs. Much pertinent Spanish material is also given in the appendices to Poullet et Piot, *Correspondance du Cardinal Granvelle* (*v. s.*).

On the naval war with Spain there is an abundance of material in the State Papers, Domestic, in the Public Record Office, and in the Cotton, Lansdowne, and Harleian MSS. in the British Museum. Much of the material available in English archives on the unofficial war before 1585 is printed in Hakluyt's *Voyages* (ed. Maclehose, 1903) and in the publications of the Hakluyt Society. Most of the documentary material in the State Papers, Domestic, bearing on the naval war from 1585 to 1588 is printed in full in Corbett, *Papers relating to the Navy during the Spanish War, 1585–7* (Navy Records Society, xi) and in Laughton, *State Papers relating to the Defeat of the Spanish Armada* (Navy Records Society, i, ii). For the Spanish side of the story the important sources are printed in Duro, *La Armada Invencible* (Madrid, 1884–5). Duro's *Armada Española* (Madrid, 1895–1903) should also be consulted, particularly for its appendices and its bibliography. A good deal of information about the Armada is to be found in the *Calendar of State Papers, Venetian, 1581–91*. An analysis of this material was published by E. Armstrong in E. H. R. xii. 659–78.

On the preparations in England to meet the Armada, the *Acts of Privy Council* (*v. s.*) are of first-rate importance. There is also a great deal of documentary material scattered through the Harleian MSS., the Lansdowne MSS., and the Stow MSS. in the British Museum. Among private collections, the *Foljambe Papers* (Historical MSS. Commission, 1897) are valuable. Pertinent material on this subject was collected and printed by John Bruce in 1798 under the title *Report on the Arrangements which were made for the internal defense of these Kingdoms when Spain projected the Invasion and Conquest of England*, &c. A copy of this rare book, of which only twenty-five copies were printed, is in the British Museum (977 b. 32). There is a useful discussion of the sources on the military musters under Elizabeth in G. S. Thomson, *Lords Lieutenants in the Sixteenth Century* (London, 1923), pp. vii ff.

On Walsingham's secret service in Spain at the time of the Armada the letters of Pompeo Pellegrini (*alias* Antony Standen) are the most importance source. Most of these letters are in the British Museum. Some of Standen's letters are also preserved among the Bacon papers at Lambeth Palace and are printed by Birch in his *Memoirs of Queen Elizabeth* (*v. s.*).

The printed accounts of the defeat of the Armada are very numerous. Many of those put out by the English Government immediately after the event are reprinted in *Harleian Miscellany*, ii. For a more complete bibliography of this contemporary propagandist literature cf. British Museum Catalogue, Spain, Navy. One of the earliest accounts was written by Sir William Monson and is printed in the first book of his *Naval Tracts* (Navy Records Society, xxi). The best modern accounts are by Tilton, *Die Katastrophe der Spanischen Armada* (Freiburg, 1894), and by Corbett, *Drake and the Tudor Navy* (London, 1898). There is no first-rate secondary account of the military preparations in England to meet a Spanish invasion. Grose, *Military Antiquities* (London, 1801), and Fortescue, *History of the English Army* (London, 1899 ff.), should be consulted; cf. also Thomson, *Lords Lieutenants in the Sixteenth Century* (*v. s.*), chap. iv, and *The Victoria County History*, *passim*.

In her war against Spain, Elizabeth attempted to stir up the Turks to strike at Philip II in the Mediterranean. A discussion of this phase of the subject is given in Pears, *The Spanish Armada and the Ottoman Porte* (E. H. R. viii. 439–66). Pears, however, failed to locate any of the important dispatches of Wm. Harborne, who was the English agent at Constantinople, most active in these intrigues. Some of his dispatches are preserved among the Tanner MSS. in the Bodleian Library at Oxford. The most important of them are printed in the Appendix to Chapter XV, above. There is a good deal of data on this subject in the *Calendar of State Papers, Venetian, 1581–91*. The Introduction to this volume is valuable.

Anglo-German Relations. The relations between England and Germany during the period of Walsingham's public service were confined in the main to trade controversies with the Hansa League and to the levy of German mercenaries in the Palatinate for the benefit of Dutch and Huguenot rebels. With the trade controversies Walsingham had very little to do. This phase of the subject is adequately treated in Ehrenberg, *Hamburg und England im Zeitalter der Konigin Elisabeth* (Jena, 1896), based partly upon English material and partly upon material in German municipal archives, notably those of Köln, Lübeck, Bremen, Emden, and Lüneburg. The archives of Hamburg and Stade were unfortunately largely destroyed by fire. Some material, not utilized by Ehrenberg, is to be found in the Public Record Office, State Papers, Hanse Towns, and in the Yelverton MSS. Cf. also, for English trade relations with Emden, B. Hagedorn, *Ostfrieslands Handel u. Schiffahrt im 16. Jahrhundert* (Berlin, 1912).

For the relations of England with the Palatinate, the most significant German material has been printed in Kluckhohn, *Briefe Friedrich des Frommen* (Brunswick, 1868–72), and in Bezold, *Briefe des Pfalzgrafen Johann Casimir* (Munich, 1882–4). For the years 1585–90 some additional information is to be found in the Vatican archives in the dispatches from the Papal Nuncios in Germany. These are printed in *Nuntiaturberichte aus Deutschland, 1585–90* (Görres-Gesellschaft, Paderborn, 1895–1905). The correspondence of Philip II of Spain with the German princes is of some slight value for English affairs (*Documentos Ineditos*, iv). *Venetianische Depeschen vom Kaiserhofe* (ed. Turba, 1876) covers the period 1554–76 and contains many papers of importance upon English relations with Germany not included in the Venetian calendars.

Of secondary accounts, Heppe, *Geschichte des deutschen Protestantismus, 1555–81* (Marburg, 1852–9), gives a fairly full account, based chiefly upon German sources, of Elizabeth's efforts to found a league with the German protestant princes. This needs to be supplemented by material in the Public Record Office, State Papers, German States, and by other material among Robert Beale's papers in the Yelverton MSS. Waddington, *La France et les Protestants allemands sous Charles IX et Henri III* (Revue Historique, xlii. 2, 1890), surveys the relations between the French Huguenots and the German Protestant princes. Platzhoff, *Frankreich und die deutschen Protestanten in den Jahren 1570–73*, gives a more detailed account of these relations for a brief period. E. Bekker, *Beiträge zur englischen Geschichte im Zeitalter Elisabeths*, pt. 2: *Königin Elisabeth und der deutsche Söldnermarkt* (Giessen, 1887), is useful but does not exhaust the possibilities of the English archives.

ANGLO-ITALIAN RELATIONS. *Venice.* The dispatches of Venetian ambassadors, which are of great value for earlier reigns, are of relatively little value for the reign of Elizabeth, since there was no Venetian ambassador resident at her Court. The dispatches of Venetian ambassadors in France and elsewhere, however, often contain comments of importance on English affairs. The relevant material in Venetian archives is given for the most part in the *Calendars of State Papers, Venetian,* but Alberi, *Le Relazioni degli Ambasciatori Veneti,* contains some additional material.

Milan. The archives in Milan have been searched for material bearing upon England and the results of this search have been published in *Calendar of State Papers, Milan,* which covers the period to 1618. The only documents of importance found for the reign of Elizabeth are a number of letters relating to English Catholics preserved in the Ambrosian Library.

Tuscany. The Tuscan archives in Florence have not been systematically examined for Elizabethan material. It is not unlikely that some incidental facts of value might be gathered from them although there were no direct diplomatic relations between England and Tuscany during Walsingham's term of service. The dispatches of Tuscan ambassadors to France during the second half of the sixteenth century have been printed in Canestrini and Desjardins (*v. s.*). These contain material of value on Anglo-French relations.

It will be recalled that it was through the connexion of Antony Standen with the court at Florence that Walsingham was able to get precise information about the preparations of the Armada in Spain. Standen's correspondence has been referred to elsewhere. There are a few documents of no great importance illustrating the casual contacts of the English Government with Tuscany in the Public Record Office, State Papers, Tuscany.

Rome. Perhaps the most important archives in Italy for Elizabethan affairs are in Rome, notably in the Vatican Archives, the Vatican Library, and the Archives of the English College. Transcripts have been made of most of the documents which deal with English affairs in these repositories. These transcripts are in the Public Record Office. Down to the year 1571 they have been calendared in the *Calendar of State Papers, Rome.* Further volumes are in preparation.

One of the most valuable sources of information in the Vatican Archives is the reports of Papal nuncios. Although there were no formal relations between England and the Papacy during Walsingham's term of service, the reports of nuncios in Spain and France and Germany often contain information of value on English affairs. The reports of the German nuncios have been published (*v.* Anglo-German relations). Extracts from the reports of nuncios in Spain and in France are included in the Roman Transcripts in the Public Record Office.

The Vatican Library and the Archives of the English College are chiefly valuable for the light they shed upon the history of the English Catholics. They have been exploited by A. O. Meyer, and particularly by Father John H. Pollen (*v.* The English Roman Catholics).

ANGLO-SCOTTISH RELATIONS. Easily the most important sources of information on Scottish affairs are the State Papers, Scotland, in the Public Record Office, supplemented by those in the British Museum and at Hatfield House. Those covering Walsingham's term of service have been twice calendared. The first calendar, in two volumes, edited by M. J. Thorpe (1858), is little more than an index to the documents, and contains no adequate survey of their contents. A much fuller calendar, edited up to 1569 by J. Bain, has been continued by W. K. Boyd and is still in progress. The last volume published (1923) goes to March 1589. This calendar undertakes to include documents in the Public Record Office, the British Museum, and elsewhere in England. It contains practically all the Scottish papers in the Public Record Office and many of those in the British Museum, but except on its title-page it hardly pretends to include pertinent material in private collections.

Generally speaking, Mr. Boyd's calendar publishes very full *résumés* of the original documents though too often the editor has omitted highly important material. Indeed, it is a very misleading kind of work, full enough to justify the assumption that it is quite complete, yet revealing often, by comparison with the original documents, very serious omissions. Detailed criticism illustrative of this defect appears in the foot-notes in the text.

A good deal of important material on Scottish affairs is to be found also in the *Border Papers*, preserved at the Public Record Office, which have been adequately calendared by J. Bain (Edinburgh, 1894). Vol. i of his calendar covers the period from 1560 to 1594. The Hamilton Papers, formerly in the possession of the Duke of Hamilton, and now in the British Museum, are extremely important for Scottish affairs, particularly for the decade between 1580 and 1590. These have been printed for the most part in full in *The Hamilton Papers*, edited by J. Bain (Edinburgh, 1892). Vol. ii covers the period from 1543 to 1590. There is also material of value on Anglo-Scottish relations in the *Register of the Privy Council of Scotland*, ed. J. H. Burton, vols. ii–iv (Edinburgh, 1878–81), in *Rotuli Scaccarii Regum Scotorum*, ed. G. P. McNeil, vols. xx–xxii (Edinburgh, 1899–1903), and in the *Register of the Great Seal of Scotland*, ed. J. M. Thompson, vols. iv–v (Edinburgh, 1886–8).

Outside the Salisbury MSS. and the Yelverton MSS. there is little of importance for Anglo-Scottish relations during this period in private English archives.

The pertinent material in French and Spanish archives has already been discussed, but mention should be made again of Teulet, *Relations politiques de la France et de l'Espagne avec l'Écosse au XVIe Siècle* (1862), and of the *Extracts from the Dispatches of the Marquis de Courcelles* (Bannatyne Club, 1828). Courcelles was French ambassador to Scotland in 1586–7.

Some important source material has been printed in full. *The Correspondence of Sir Robert Bowes* (Surtees Society, 1842) is highly important for Anglo-Scottish relations between 1577 and 1583. Many of the letters printed are in the British Museum, but many also are from a letter-book of Bowes preserved at Streatlam Castle in Durham. *The Letters and Papers relating to Patrick, Master of Gray, 1584–89* (Bannatyne Club, 1835) are invaluable for Gray's missions to England. *The Letters of John Colville*, 1582–1603 (Bannatyne Club, 1858), are also of value. Many important documents relative to Walsingham's embassy to Scotland in 1583 are printed in the appendices to K. Stählin, *Der Kampf um Schottland* (Leipzig, 1902). Other documents of importance are incorporated in the text of David Calderwood, *History of the Kirk of Scotland* (Woodrow Society, 1842–9), and in J. Spottiswoode, *History of the Church and State of Scotland* (Spottiswoode Society, 1847).

Of private memoirs, the only ones of importance on Anglo-Scottish relations during Walsingham's public service are those of Sir James Melville (Bannatyne Club, 1827).

Of modern writers P. F. Tytler, *History of Scotland* (London, 1876), and J. H. Burton, *History of Scotland* (Edinburgh, 1893), are the best of the older writers. P. Hume Brown, *History of Scotland* (Cambridge, 1899 ff.), and A. Lang, *A History of Scotland* (Edinburgh, 1902 ff.), are the best of the more recent ones. Lang is fuller but not so dispassionate as Brown. W. L. Mathieson, *Politics and Religion in Scotland* (Glasgow, 1902), is a brilliant essay on the subject announced in the title. R. S. Rait, *Scottish Parliaments* (London, 1901), should be consulted on the relations of the Scottish kings to their parliaments; P. Hume Brown, *Scotland in the Time of Queen Mary* (London, 1904), on social and economic conditions in Scotland. Stählin, *Der Kampf um Schottland*, is excellent on conditions in Scotland and on Anglo-Scottish relations in 1583.

MARY STUART

Volumes have been and may be written on the literature concerning Mary Stuart. With her career in France and in Scotland, including the thorny questions of her relations with Bothwell and her complicity in the murder of Darnley, this book is not concerned. Walsingham's connexion with Mary began after her arrival in England.

For her life as an English prisoner by far the most important collection of sources is in the Public Record Office, State Papers, Scotland, and State Papers, Mary Queen of Scots, to be supplemented always by the collections in the British Museum. Almost all the important documents in these great collections have now been calendared by W. K. Boyd in his Scottish Calendars mentioned above. Mr. Boyd has missed, however, important letters bearing on the Babington conspiracy in British Museum, Cotton MSS. Appendix L, and in the British Museum, Additional MSS., among the Egerton MSS., the Hardwicke Papers, and the Sadler Papers. Egerton MSS. 2124, the so-called *Bardon Papers* which contain material of importance on the trial of Mary, have been edited by Conyers Read for the Royal Historical Society (Camden Soc., 3rd Series, xvii). Some of the pertinent material from the Hardwicke Papers was published in *Miscellaneous State Papers, 1501–1726* (London, 1778). *The Sadler Papers* were edited by A. Clifford (Edinburgh, 1809).

In private collections the most important material is in the Salisbury MSS. and in the Yelverton MSS. In the latter collection are preserved many valuable papers relative to the Babington conspiracy, notably Babington's various confessions which are missing from the Public Record Office. There is some material also in the Talbot Papers in the Heralds' College, much of which is printed in Lodge, *Illustrations of British History* (*v. s.*). Mary's own correspondence is printed for the most part in Labanoff, *Lettres, Instructions et Mémoires de Marie Stuart* (Paris, 1844), though some important correspondence of hers with the French ambassador at London in 1572–4 is omitted by Labanoff. These letters are, or were, in the private collection of Mr. John Murray, who has kindly let me examine them. Mary's correspondence with Babington is printed by B. Sepp, *Maria Stuarts Briefwechsel mit Antony Babington* (Munich, 1886). Practically all the pertinent material concerning Mary's connexion with the Babington Plot has been collected and edited with an admirable introduction by Father John Hungerford Pollen, in *Mary Stuart and the Babington Plot* (Scottish History Soc. 1922). The Letter-Books of Sir Amias Paulet preserved at the Bodleian Library at Oxford contain much of value on the later stages of Mary's imprisonment. The pertinent material from this source together with many other important documents have been published by J. Morris in *The Letter-Books of Sir Amias Poulet* (London, 1874). Reference should also be made, of course, to the French, Spanish, and Italian sources mentioned above, and once again to Teulet's printed collection of French and Spanish material relating to Scotland.

The contemporary or nearly contemporary literature on Mary Stuart should not be neglected. A full account of this will be found in J. Scott, *Bibliography of Works relating to Mary, Queen of Scots, 1544–1700* (Edinburgh Bibliographical Soc. 1896). J. Anderson's *Collections relating to the History of Mary, Queen of Scots* (Edinburgh, 1727–8) and S. Jebb, *De Vita et Rebus Gestis Mariae*, &c. (London, 1725), contain the most important contemporary pamphlets. Camden's *Annales* (*v. s.*) should be consulted, particularly for the Babington conspiracy, also Holinshed (*v. s.*) who incorporated in his text the official accounts of the Throgmorton and the Parry plots.

The extensive modern literature on Mary is for the most part concerned with her career in Scotland. The following biographies may be noted for special reasons: Chantelauze, *Marie Stuart* (Paris, 1876), prints the Journal of Bourgoing, Mary's physician. Mignet, *Histoire de Marie Stuart* (Paris, 1851), was the first biography of her to utilize the relevant material in Spanish archives and remains one of the most scholarly biographies of her. Kervyn de Lettenhove, *Marie Stuart* (Paris, 1889), contains the best statement of the efforts of the French and the Scottish kings to save Mary after she had been found guilty of high treason. Leader, *Mary Queen of Scots in Captivity* (Sheffield, 1880), supplies a useful detailed account of her imprisonment in England. Henderson, *Mary Queen of Scots* (London, 1905), is perhaps the best recent biography though it is inadequate on the last phase of her life. Pollen's introduction to his documents on Mary Stuart and the Babington Plot (*v. s.*) is easily the best critical examination of her connexion with Babington and his plans.

The various plots against Elizabeth and the various projected invasions of England with which Mary Stuart was more or less directly associated are dealt with in considerable detail, but not always with strict impartiality by Froude. A much more dispassionate account is given in J. Kretzschmar, *Die Invasionsprojekte der katholischen Mächte gegen England zur Zeit Elisabeths* (Leipzig, 1892). Cf. on this subject the references given in the section following.

THE ENGLISH ROMAN CATHOLICS

The policy of Elizabeth's government towards the Roman Catholics in England furnishes the necessary background for any study of Walsingham's attitude towards them. This is set forth in the penal laws (cf. Statutes of the Realm), in the royal proclamations (collected in large part by Humphrey Dyson and preserved in the Grenville Library in the British Museum, a calendar of Tudor and Stuart proclamations has been edited by R. Steele in the *Bibliotheca Lindseiana*, 1910–11), and in the *Acts of Privy Council* (ed. Dasent). The execution of this policy can be followed best in the State Papers, Domestic, and the State Papers, Domestic, Addenda. (The *Calendar of State Papers, Domestic*, for the years 1547–90 is very brief and inadequate, the *Calendar of State Papers, Domestic, Addenda* is much fuller, but the original documents should be consulted.) There are also a few papers of interest in the State Papers, Domestic, Supplementary which have not been calendared. A good deal of the official correspondence concerning the Catholics is scattered through the various collections in the British Museum, at Lambeth Palace and at Hatfield House. Some of this correspondence has been printed by J. H. Pollen in *Unpublished Documents relating to the English Martyrs* (Catholic Record Soc. v). Strype also prints some of it in his *Annals of the Reformation* (Oxford, 1824).

There is a good deal of information regarding Elizabeth's treatment of the Roman Catholics in the correspondence of the Spanish and French ambassadors in England, particularly that of Bernardino de Mendoza, La Mothe Fénélon, and Castelnau de la Mauvissière, which has been discussed more at length above.

The records of the Catholics themselves are scattered. Among the manuscript collections in England, outside the public repositories, the most valuable are those preserved at Stonyhurst College and those among the Petyt MSS, in the Inner Temple Library at London. The Stonyhurst MSS. contain much material relating to Parsons, the Jesuit, including his Memoirs, which have been edited by J. H. Pollen for the Catholic Record Society (vols. ii, iv). The archives of the Roman Catholic Archbishop of Westminster contain little for the period before 1590. *The Letters and Papers of Cardinal William Allen* (ed. T. F. Knox, London, 1882) and *The First and Second Douay Diaries* (ed. ibid. 1878) are indispensable, particularly for Catholic plots aganist the English crown. There is a good deal of material also in the Vatican Archives, the Vatican Library, and the English College at Rome, which has been discussed under the heading Anglo-Italian relations. Cf. further on this subject *Calendar of State Papers, Rome,* Introduction, and A. O. Meyer, *England und die Katholische Kirche unter Elisabeth,* i, Introduction and Appendices.

The attitude of contemporary Roman Catholics towards Elizabeth and her government must be sought out, for the most part, from the contemporary Catholic writings. Of these the ones of first-class importance are the writings of Robert Parsons, S.J., and of Cardinal William Allen. A list of their writings will be found in the biographies of them in the *Dictionary of National Biography.* The writings of Southwell, Verstegen, Stapleton, and Creswell should also be consulted. John Bridgwater's *Concertatio Ecclesiae Catholicae in Anglia* is the fullest of the contemporary martyrologies, of which the second edition (Treves, 1594) is the more complete. The best of the modern martyrologies are those of Bede Camm and of Pollen and Burton (London, 1904, 1914). Challoner's *Memoirs of Missionary Priests* (ed. Pollen, 1923), Foley's *Records of the English Province of the Society of Jesus* (London, 1877–84), and J. Morris, *The Troubles of our Catholic Forefathers* (London, 1872–7), contain many illustrative documents, as does Dodd-Tierney, *Church History of England* (1839).

On the dissensions in the ranks of the English Catholics, Parson's Memoirs, cited above, are of first-class importance for the earlier phase. For the later phase, which falls rather outside the scope of this book, cf. T. G. Law, *Jesuits and Seculars in the Reign of Elizabeth* (London, 1889), and Ibid., *The Archpriest Controversy* (Camden Soc. New Series, vols. 56, 58).

On the Catholic refugees on the continent the letters of Thomas Morgan, of Charles Paget, and of Thomas Rogers (*alias* Nicholas Berden) in the State Papers, Mary Queen of Scots, and State Papers, Domestic, at the Public Record Office are valuable as is also the correspondence of Sir Henry Cobbam and of Sir Edward Stafford, English ambassadors to France, in the State Papers, France. Some light is also thrown upon this subject by the *Letters of Sir Thomas Copley . . . to Queen Elizabeth and her Ministers* (Roxburghe Club,

London, 1897). Documents illustrative of the intrigue between Walsingham and Dr. William Gifford are printed in Butler and Pollen, *Dr. Gifford in 1586* (The Month, March and April 1904). A curious contemporary pamphlet on this subject, *The Estate of the English Fugitives under the King of Spain and his Ministers*, was printed in London in 1595. For modern accounts consult R. Lechat, *Les Réfugiés anglais dans les Pays-Bas* (Louvain, 1914), P. Guilday, *English Catholic Refugees on the Continent* (London, 1914), and J. H. Pollen, *The Politics of English Catholics during the Reign of Elizabeth* (The Month, February–August 1902).

Easily the best modern accounts of the Roman Catholics under Elizabeth are those of A. O. Meyer, *England und die Katholische Kirche unter Elisabeth* (Rome, 1911), (An English translation of this book, supervised by the author, was published by J. R. McKee in London in 1916); and of J. H. Pollen, *The English Catholics in the Reign of Queen Elizabeth* (London, 1920). Unfortunately, Father Pollen has so far only carried his story to the year 1580. It is to be noted that both of these books bear the imprimatur of the Roman Church. Father Pollen, of the Society of Jesus, has brought more solid scholarship and diligent research to bear upon the subject than any other modern writer, though his judgement of Walsingham seems to me to be more severe than the facts warrant. Probably the best account from the Protestant standpoint is in W. H. Frere, *A History of the English Church . . . 1558–1625* (London, 1904). Neither Froude nor Lingard is to be relied upon in these matters. A valuable discussion of Elizabeth's policy towards the Roman Catholics with particular attention to a plan to establish a Roman Catholic colony in America is given in R. B. Merriman, *Some Notes on the Treatment of the English Catholics in the Reign of Elizabeth* (Am. Hist. Review, xiii, pp. 480 ff.). The late Prof. F. W. Maitland's essay on the Elizabethan Religious Settlement in the *Cambridge Modern History*, vol. ii, and his *Elizabethan Gleanings* (E. H. R. xviii) are noteworthy. E. L. Taunton's *History of the Jesuits in England* is not altogether trustworthy.

THE PURITANS

The bibliographical material for Walsingham's connexion with the Puritans and with Elizabeth's policy towards them is so far scattered that an orthodox bibliography of Puritanism under Elizabeth would contribute little. The student is referred to the foot-notes in the text.

CONSTITUTIONAL HISTORY

The best general account of the administrative system under Elizabeth is in E. P. Cheyney, *History of England from the Defeat of the Spanish Armada to the Death of Elizabeth*, i, Part I. There is no adequate modern account of the English Parliament under Elizabeth. D'Ewes, *Journals*, supplies what is known of Walsingham's activities in the House of Commons. On the office of Principal Secretary the best and indeed the only adequate account is in E. M. G. Evans, *The Principal Secretary of State* (Manchester, 1923). A shorter statement on the subject will be found in Sir H. Nicolas, *Proceedings of the Privy Council*, vi, Introduction, pp. xcvii–cxl, and in Tanner, *Constitutional Documents* (Cambridge, 1922), pp. 202 ff. There are four useful contemporary statements about the office, to wit: Nicholas Faunt, *Discourse on the Secretary's office* (E. H. R. xx, pp. 499 ff.); Sir Robert Cecil, *State and Dignity of a Secretary of State's Place* (*Harleian Miscellany*, ii. 265 ff.); Dr. John Herbert, *Duties of a Secretary* (Prothero, *Select Documents*, pp. 165 ff.); Robert Beale, *A Treatise of the Office of a Councellor and Principall Secretarie*, 1592 (Yelverton MSS. clxii, ff. 1–11, printed in full above, vol. i, Appendix).

The literature on the Privy Council is more extensive. The obvious source is the *Acts of Privy Council* (ed. Dasent) cited above, which are, however, far from being a complete account of the activities of the Privy Council. A pretty exhaustive survey of the whole official correspondence of the period under consideration is necessary to supplement the official register adequately. Steele's *Bibliography of Tudor and Stuart Proclamations* (*v. s.*) should also be consulted. Of secondary accounts, in addition to the well-known account of A. V. Dicey, Lord Eustace Percy's *The Privy Council under the Tudors* (Oxford, 1907) and Dorothy M. Gladish, *The Tudor Privy Council* (Retford, 1915), deserve mention. The latter book is full of inaccuracies but contains many useful details. An unpublished Ph.D. thesis on the same subject by J. Viles in the Harvard University Library is also of value, as are Dasent's Introductions to the various volumes of the *Acts of Privy Council*. Tanner, *op. cit.*, pp. 216 ff., gives a brief statement. A discussion of the factions in the Privy Council during Walsingham's term of service by Conyers Read appears in *Annual Report of the American Historical Association*, 1911, pp. 109–19. Another article by the same author, *Walsingham and Burghley in Queen Elizabeth's Privy Council* (E. H. R. xxviii, pp. 34 ff.), deals with the same subject.

ACKNOWLEDGEMENTS

IT is easier to estimate the value of pertinent books and manuscripts for the preparation of a book of this sort than it is to acknowledge adequately the advice and assistance of friendly coadjutors. First of all I owe a large debt of gratitude to my old teacher and friend, Prof. Roger B. Merriman of Harvard University, at whose prompting this book was begun and who has ministered to it at every stage of its growth. I acknowledge, also, debts to the late Prof. York-Powell, and to Sir Charles Firth, his late successor as Regius Professor of History at Oxford ; to my friend and tutor the late Mr. A. L. Smith, Master of Balliol; to Mr. H. W. C. Davis, now Regius Professor of Modern History at Oxford ; to the Master of King's College, Cambridge ; to Mr. E. A. Webb of Chislehurst ; to Dr. Karl Stählin of Heidelberg ; to Mr. Hubert Hall, the late Mr. A. J. Butler, and Mrs. Sophie C. Lomas of the English Public Record Office ; to the Officials of the Reading Room and the Manuscript Room of the British Museum ; to the Officials of the Bibliothèque Nationale at Paris, and of the Bodleian Library at Oxford ; to the late Sir George W. Prothero, to Father John Hungerford Pollen, S.J. ; to my colleagues at the University of Chicago and at the University of Pennsylvania ; to Lady Calthorpe and to Mr. John Murray for permission to examine their private collections of manuscripts ; to Mr. James D. Milner of the National Portrait Gallery for valuable assistance in locating Walsingham's portraits, and to Lady Beatrice Thynn for permission to reproduce the portrait of Walsingham in her private collection ; and finally to Mr. Kenneth Sisam and Mr. D. Nichol Smith, and particularly to Mr. J. de M. Johnson of the Clarendon Press for many different kinds of services.

INDEX

DATE DUE

DE 2 '85			

GAYLORD

PRINTED IN U.S.A.